CW00921893

דברי הימים

CHRONICLES

SONCINO BOOKS OF THE BIBLE

EDITOR: REV. DR. A. COHEN, M.A., Ph.D., D.H.L.

Chronicles

HEBREW TEXT & ENGLISH TRANSLATION
WITH AN INTRODUCTION
AND COMMENTARY

by

THE REV. DR. I. W. SLOTKI, M.A., LITT.D.

O give thanks unto the LORD, call upon His name;
Make known His doings among the peoples.

I CHRONICLES XVI. 8

THE SONCINO PRESS

LONDON . JERUSALEM . NEW YORK

FIRST EDITION 1952
SECOND IMPRESSION 1962
THIRD IMPRESSION 1965
FOURTH IMPRESSION 1969
FIFTH IMPRESSION 1971
SIXTH IMPRESSION 1975
SEVENTH IMPRESSION 1978

PUBLISHERS' NOTE
Thanks are due to the
Jewish Publication Society of America
for permission to use their very beautiful
English text of the Scriptures

PRINTED IN GREAT BRITAIN AT
THE SPOTTISWOODE BALLANTYNE PRESS
BY WILLIAM CLOWES & SONS LIMITED,
LONDON, COLCHESTER AND BECCLES

FOREWORD BY THE GENERAL EDITOR

WITH this volume the work of producing THE SONCINO BOOKS OF THE BIBLE, begun nearly ten years ago, is completed. For the first time a Commentary in English on the whole of the Hebrew Scriptures, written by Jews, has been issued. I express my gratitude to the band of scholars who assisted me, and to Mr. J. Davidson, Founder and Governing Director of the Soncino Press, for his unfailing interest and painstaking care in the technical side of the publication. A special word of thanks is due to Mr. E. Cashdan, M.A., who helped me with the correction of the Hebrew proofs and made many valuable suggestions.

The series is distinctive in the following respects:

(i) Each volume contains the Hebrew text and English translation together with the commentary. (ii) The exposition is designed primarily for the ordinary reader of the Bible rather than for the student, and aims at providing this class of reader with requisite direction for the understanding and appreciation of the Biblical Book. (iii) The commentary is invariably based upon the received Hebrew text. When this presents difficulties, the most probable translation and interpretation are suggested, without resort to textual emendation. (iv) It offers a *Jewish* commentary. Without neglecting the valuable work of Christian expositors, it takes into account the exegesis of the Talmudical Rabbis as well as of the leading Jewish commentators.

All Biblical references are cited according to chapter and verse as in the Hebrew Bible. It is unfortunate that, unlike the American-Jewish translation, the English Authorized and Revised Versions, although made direct from the Hebrew text, did not conform to its chapter divisions. An undesirable complication was thereby introduced into Bible study. In the Hebrew the longer headings of the Psalms are counted as a separate verse; consequently Ps. xxxiv. 12, e.g., corresponds to verse 11 in A.V. and R.V. It is also necessary to take into account a marginal note like that found against 1 Kings iv. 21, 'ch. v. 1 in Heb.', so that the Hebrew 1 Kings v. 14 tallies with iv. 34 in the English.

It is hoped that this commentary, though more particularly planned for the needs of Jews, will prove helpful to all who desire a fuller knowledge of the Bible, irrespective of their creed.

A. COHEN

DEDICATED WITH AFFECTION AND REVERENCE

TO THE MEMORY OF

MORRIS AND ANNA PROPP

ר׳ משה ב׳ר אפרים ז׳ל

ומרת הינדא בת ר׳ אריה הכהן ז׳ל

THE BELOVED PARENTS OF

MORTIMER J., SEYMOUR AND EPHRAIM

שלום שלום לך

Peace, peace be unto thee

I Chronicles xii. 18

CONTENTS

CHRONOLOGICAL TABLE

OF THE

KINGS OF JUDAH AND ISRAEL

The kings	Length of reign in years		Year of accession in contemporary reign of		B.C.E.
	JUDAH	ISRAEL	JUDAH	ISRAEL	
Rehoboam	17	—	—	—	932
Jeroboam	—	22	—	—	932
Abijam	3	—	—	18th	916
Asa	41	—	—	20th	914
Nadab	—	2	2nd	—	912
Baasa	—	24	3rd	—	911
Elah	—	2	26th	—	888
Zimri	—	7 days	27th	—	887
Omri	—	12*	31st	—	887
Ahab	—	22	38th	—	876
Jehoshaphat	25	—	—	4th	874
Ahaziah	—	2	17th	—	855
Jehoram	—	12	18th	—	854
Joram (Jehoram)	8	—	—	5th	850
Ahaziah	1	—	—	12th	843
Athaliah	6	—	—	—	843
Jehu	—	28	—	—	843
Jehoash (Joash)	40	—	—	7th	837
Jehoahaz	—	17	23rd	—	816
Jehoash	—	16	37th	—	800
Amaziah	29	—	—	2nd	798
Jeroboam II	—	41	15th	—	785
Azariah (Uzziah)	52	—	—	27th	790
Zechariah	—	6 months	38th	—	745
Shallum	—	1 month	39th	—	745
Menahem	—	10	39th	—	745
Pekahiah	—	2	50th	—	736
Pekah	—	20	52nd	—	735
Jotham	16	—	—	2nd	739
Ahaz	16	—	—	17th	735
Hoshea	—	9	12th	—	732
Hezekiah	29	—	—	3rd	720
Manasseh	55	—	—	—	692
Amon	2	—	—	—	638
Josiah	31	—	—	—	637
Jehoahaz	3 months	—	—	—	607
Jehoiakim	11	—	—	—	607
Jehoiachin	3 months	—	—	—	597
Zedekiah	11	—	—	—	597

* This includes the duration of the war against Tibni.

INTRODUCTION

NAME AND DIVISION

THE Books of Chronicles derive their name from the Latin, *Liber Chronicorum*, the title adopted by Jerome in the Vulgate. The Hebrew title is *Dibrë Hayyamim*, 'the words of the days,' or more freely, 'the events of the times.' The division of the history into two parts, 1 and 2 Chronicles, may be traced to the Greek Version of the Books which is regarded by some as part of the Septuagint. In the Hebrew MSS. of the Scriptures *Chronicles* forms one Book.

Some authorities maintain that *Chronicles*, *Ezra* and *Nehemiah* formed originally one continuous work, while others hold that only *Ezra* and *Nehemiah* constituted one Book.

POSITION IN THE CANON

In A.V., R.V. and other English versions, the place of *Chronicles* is immediately after *Kings*, an arrangement which is due to the influence of the Greek through the Vulgate. To the authors of the Greek Version the Books of Chronicles were 'the things omitted' from the Books of Kings 'concerning the kings of Judah.' As 'supplementary' history, the position of the Books in close proximity after the principal records of the Books of Kings was the natural order.

Some MSS. place them at the beginning of the 'Writings' or Hagiographa (the third and last section of the Hebrew Scriptures). In the majority of Hebrew MSS., however, and in all printed editions of the Hebrew Bible, *Dibrë Hayyamim* is the last Book and this is also the Talmudical tradition.

DATE AND AUTHORSHIP

From the fact that 2 *Chronicles* concludes with the proclamation of Cyrus, which was issued in the first year of his reign (537 B.C.E.), the Book could not have been written before that year. But the enumeration in 1 Chron. iii. 19-24 of six or more generations after Zerubbabel (who lived in the middle of the sixth century), reckoning 20-30 years for a generation, must lead to the conclusion that the Book could not have been written earlier than 350. Some authorities limit the date of the compilation to the period between 300 and 250 B.C.E.

No author's name appears in the Books, but a perusal of their contents shows that he was a priest or Levite, if not actually a member of the Temple choirs or orchestra. He was undoubtedly a student of history, a statistician and, above all, a pious man steeped in religious belief and practice. According to Rabbinic tradition, *Chronicles* was begun by Ezra, who also wrote the Book which bears his name, and was concluded by Nehemiah.

CHARACTER AND AIM

The dominant feature of *Chronicles* is a presentation of the historical events from a religious angle. All historical successes or failures are the direct results of Divine reward for piety and good deeds or punishment for apostasy and sin. The Chronicler is concerned mainly with the history of the Kingdom of Judah; but he introduces it with a brief summary of the generations that preceded it since the Creation, with fuller details of the reigns of David and Solomon, the founders of the Judean dynasty. Special attention is paid to the Temple services and ritual and the religious institutions prescribed in the Mosaic law. The organization of the priestly and Levitical courses, the singers and doorkeepers; the religious reforms and the celebration of the statutory feasts, such as the Passover in the reigns of Hezekiah and Josiah, receive full and detailed treatment. The honour and dignity of David, the anointed of the Lord, and of his Divinely chosen dynasty, are scrupulously upheld, and all reference to events derogatory to either is studiously avoided.

RELIGIOUS OUTLOOK

The Chronicler is an earnest believer in the Divine rule of the universe and in the manifestation of Providence in all human affairs. He writes with a sense of reverence even when narrating social, military or political events. He neglects no opportunity of preaching implicit obedience to the will of God and a devotion to, and love for, His service and worship. God does not desire the destruction of the sinner whom He offers opportunities of returning to Him and resultant salvation. Invariably he points to the blessings that follow the performance of good deeds and the retribution that results from backsliding and wickedness. His moral and religious lessons are systematically illustrated by the description of the success and prosperity that were the reward of righteous rulers and the disaster and tribulation that befell the godless.

HISTORICAL VALUE

Having been written mainly with a religious and moral aim, the Books of Chronicles have rather the form of a Midrash, an homiletical or didactic work, than of an objective historical record. This, in fact, is the view of the Rabbis which coincides with that of modern commentators. The Rabbis also doubted the reliability of a number of passages which present a contradiction with parallels in *Samuel* and *Kings*, and held that their meaning was not to be taken literally but expounded homiletically. All this, however, does not alter the fact that *Chronicles* contains also valuable historical material which expands, supplements or clarifies the records in the earlier historical Books.

LANGUAGE

The Hebrew text of *Chronicles* presents many linguistic peculiarities and difficulties. The style is forced and the syntax involved. The language has much in common with that of *Ezra* and *Nehemiah*; it is late Hebrew which has many affinities with Aramaic which, at the time of the Chronicler, must have been forcing its way into Judea and exercising powerful influence on the vocabulary, phraseology and syntax of the earlier speech. It is further characterized by an influx of rare and altogether new words as well as by the use of old terms with new meanings. Its general standard is in every way below that of the other historical Books of the Bible.

THE SOURCES

The Chronicler quotes a number of works as the sources upon which he based his history and as documents for fuller details of various sections of his narrative. These sources may be roughly classified as (i) historical and (ii) prophetic.

The historical works named are *the commentary* (Midrash) *of the book of the kings* (2 Chron. xxiv. 27); *the book of the kings of Israel* (1 Chron. ix. 1; 2 Chron. xx. 34); *the book of the kings of Judah and Israel* (2 Chron. xvi. 11, etc.); *the book of the kings of Israel and Judah* (2 Chron. xxvii. 7, etc.).

The prophetic sources, so called on account of their authorship, are *the words of Samuel the seer*, *the words of Nathan the prophet* and *the words of Gad the seer* (1 Chron. xxix. 29); *the words of Nathan the prophet*, *the prophecy of Ahijah the Shilonite* and *the visions of Jedo the seer* (2 Chron. ix. 29); *the histories of Shemaiah the prophet and of Iddo the seer* (2 Chron. xii. 15); *the commentary* (Midrash) *of the prophet Iddo* (2 Chron. xiii. 22); *the words of Jehu the son of Hanani* (2 Chron. xx. 34); 'the history of the acts of Uzziah which the prophet Isaiah wrote' (cf. 2 Chron. xxvi. 22); *the vision of Isaiah the prophet* (2 Chron. xxxii. 32) and *the history of the seers* (2 Chron. xxxiii. 19).

Whether all these titles represent separate works or parts of the same work, and whether the Isaiah mentioned refers to a book now lost or to our Isaiah xxxvi-xxxix, are much debated questions. According to one outstanding authority, the two original books were a 'history of the kings of Israel' and 'a history of the kings of Judah' which served as sources for *the book of the kings of Israel and Judah* and for the canonical Books of Kings, both of which were ultimately the sources of *Chronicles*.

HISTORICAL OUTLINE

The contents fall into four sections:

I (1 Chron. i-x) deals mainly with the genealogy from Adam to Saul, various statistics, and the organization of the Temple service.

II (1 Chron. xi-xxix) describes the reign of David. It gives prominence to matters concerning the priests and Levites, the building of the Temple and its administration, the history corresponding with that of *Samuel* and *Kings* with considerable variations.

III (2 Chron. i-ix) is concerned with the reign of Solomon, its magnificence and wealth, with special emphasis on the building and furnishing of the Temple and the organization of its services and personnel.

IV (2 Chron. x-xxxvi) narrates the history of the Kingdom of Judah from Rehoboam to the captivity.

(i) 1 CHRON. I-X

The genealogies from Adam to Noah and his sons (i. 1-4), the races descended from Japheth, Ham and Shem (i. 5-23), the ten generations from Noah to Abraham (i. 24-27), Abraham's first two sons (i. 28), the tribes of Ishmael (i. 29-31), the Arabian and Edomite descendants of Abraham and the clans of Seir (i. 32-42), the first kings and chiefs of Edom (i. 43-54), the sons of Israel (ii. 1f.), the genealogies of the tribe of Judah (ii. 3-55), the house of David (iii. 1-24), supplementary genealogy of the Judahite tribes (iv. 1-23), the Simeonite families and territories, their migrations and exploits (iv. 24-43), the families of Reuben, Gad and half Manasseh and their exile to Assyria (v. 1-26), the High Priest, the Levitical and priestly families and the Temple choirs (v. 27-vi. 38), the priestly and Levitical cities (vi. 39-66), genealogies of Issachar, Benjamin, Naphtali, Manasseh, Ephraim and Asher (vii. 1-viii. 32), the genealogy of the house of Saul (viii. 33-40), the families that settled in Jerusalem and the Temple doorkeepers (ix. 1-44), Saul's death and burial (x. 1-14).

(ii) CHRON. XI-XXIX

David's coronation, capture of Jebus (Jerusalem) and the exploits of his mighty men (xi. 1-47), David's followers in exile who secured for him the throne of Judah (xii. 1-40), removal of the ark of God from Kiriath-jearim (xiii. 1-14), Hiram's friendship, some of David's sons, successful repulse of Philistine attacks (xiv. 1-17), transfer and installation of the ark of God in the City of David, the blessing, the psalms and praise, introduction of the daily service and sacrifice (xv. 1-xvi. 43), David's plan for building a Temple to God postponed by Divine direction to the reign of his son, the king's thanks and prayer (xvii. 1-27), David's wars with the Philistines, Moabites, Arameans, Edomites, Ammonites and Amalekites, the gifts of Tou and the spoils of David's enemies (xviii. 1-xx. 8), the census and the plague (xxi. 1-27), selection of the Temple site (xxi. 28-xxii. 1), David's collection of materials for the building of the Temple and his charge to Solomon (xxii. 2-19), census and organization of the Levites in courses, the organization and census of the Aaronites and a supplementary list of Levites (xxiii. 1-xxiv. 31), the Temple musicians, the order of precedence of the courses, the doorkeepers and the officers over the treasuries (xxv. 1-xxvi. 32), the superintendents of the courses, military organization and civil administration (xxvii. 1-34), David's exhortation to the people and instructions to his son and successor (xxviii. 1-21), his appeal for offerings and the leaders' response, his benediction, thanks, prayer and the people's sacrifices and rejoicing, and the coronation of Solomon (xxix. 1-30).

(iii) 2 CHRON. I-IX

Solomon's vision, prayer and Divine assurance, his fabulous wealth (i. 1-18), preparations for the building of the Temple, treaty with the king of Tyre (ii. 1-17), the construction of the Temple, its decorations, furnishings and smaller vessels (iii. 1-iv. 22), transfer of the ark from the City of David to the Holy of Holies, Solomon's blessing and prayer, the descent of fire from heaven, the festivities, his second vision (v. 1-vii. 22), his building enterprises, conscription of foreign labour, organization of the Temple personnel, the expedition to Ophir for gold (viii. 1-18), the queen of Sheba's visit, Solomon's magnificence, wealth and power, his death (ix. 1-31).

(iv) 2 CHRON. X-XXXVI

The revolt and division of the kingdom (x. 1-xi. 4), the reign of Rehoboam, his fortifications, family and character, the invasion of Shishak (xi. 5-xii. 16), the reign of Abijah (xiii. 1-23), Asa (xiv. 1-xvi. 14), Jehoshaphat (xvii. 1-xx. 37), Jehoram (xxi. 1-20), Ahaziah (xxii. 1-9), Athaliah (xxii. 10-xxiii. 21), Joash (xxiv. 1-27), Amaziah (xxv. 1-28), Uzziah or Azariah (xxvi. 1-23), Jotham (xxvii. 1-9), Ahaz (xxviii. 1-27), Hezekiah (xxix. 1-xxxii. 33), Manasseh (xxxiii. 1-20), Amon (xxxiii. 21-25), Josiah (xxxiv. 1-xxxv. 27), Jehoahaz (xxxvi. 1-4), Jehoiakim (xxxvi. 5-8), Jehoiachin (xxxvi. 9f.), Zedekiah, the captivity (xxxvi. 11-21), the proclamation of Cyrus (xxxvi. 22f.).

THE COMMENTARY

Taking account of the latest results of Biblical criticism and modern scholarship while remaining loyal to Jewish tradition was the principle adopted in the preparation of the commentary on *Chronicles*, and all views were carefully balanced and tested before any conclusion was arrived at.

The writer is under a deep debt of obligation to all who preceded him in this field of study but, as he stated in his Introduction to *Kings* and *Isaiah* in this series, several scholars may arrive independently at the same opinion and it is often difficult, if not impossible, to ascertain the first source. References are, therefore, only occasionally given; and the student desirous of obtaining fuller information on any particular problem or passage is referred to the list of 'Authorities Quoted or Consulted.' For all comments and opinions which occur in no previous work the present writer must assume responsibility.

The commentary is mainly intended for the layman. All forms of speculation, conjecture and emendation were, therefore, avoided and attention was concentrated on the explanation and elucidation of the text which is, both linguistically and historically, one of the most difficult in the entire field of Biblical literature.

דברי הימים
CHRONICLES

FIRST CHRONICLES

1 CHAPTER I א

1. Adam, Seth, Enosh; 2. Kenan,
Mahalalel, Jared; 3. Enoch, Methu-
selah, Lamech; 4. Noah, Shem,
Ham, and Japheth.

5. The sons of Japheth: Gomer,
and Magog, and Madai, and Javan,
and Tubal, and Meshech, and

1 2 אָדָם שֵׁת אֱנוֹשׁ׃ קֵינָן
3 מַהֲלַלְאֵל יֶרֶד׃ חֲנוֹךְ
4 מְתוּשֶׁלַח לָמֶךְ׃ נֹחַ שֵׁם חָם
וָיָפֶת׃
5 בְּנֵי יֶפֶת גֹּמֶר וּמָגוֹג וּמָדַי וְיָוָן
6 וְתֻבָל וּמֶשֶׁךְ וְתִירָס׃ וּבְנֵי

v. 1. א׳ רבתי

CHAPTER I

THE GENEALOGIES FROM ADAM TO ABRAHAM AND HIS SONS

Before recounting the history of his people, which begins with chapter x, the Chronicler traces, in the most concise form, its origin from Adam through Noah, Abraham and Isaac, mentioning also in the briefest terms the genealogies of the other peoples who descended from the sons of Noah. These are recorded in fuller detail in Gen. v-xxxvi.

1-4. Genealogies from Adam to Noah's three sons (cf. Gen. v).

1. *Adam*, etc. Seth was the son of Adam and Enosh the son of Seth. In this and the following two verses, the first of each pair of names is that of the father, the second that of the son. The other sons of Adam, e.g. Cain and Abel, are not mentioned since their birth was of no consequence to the history of Israel to which the genealogy is the introduction.

3. *Enoch*. In verse 33 the same Hebrew name is transcribed as *Hanoch*.

4. *Noah*, etc. Shem, Ham and Japheth were his sons. Being the ancestors of the peoples enumerated below, all three sons are named.

5-7. The fourteen peoples descended from Japheth (cf. Gen. x. 2-5).

5. *the sons of Japheth*. As Japheth was the last name in the preceding verse, his descendants are enumerated first. They are followed by the descendants of Ham who immediately preceded him in the verse and finally, in fuller detail, by those of Shem with whom the Chronicler is particularly concerned.

Gomer. Cf. Ezek. xxxviii. 6. This people is identified with the *Gimirrai* and the *Kimmerioi*. The former are mentioned in the Assyrian inscriptions and inhabited Cappadocia (as it was called later) in the seventh century B.C.E. The latter are referred to by Greek historians as having migrated to Asia Minor from South Russia.

Magog. Cf. Ezek. xxxviii. 2; perhaps the Scythians.

Madai. Presumed to be the Medes of Azerbaijan and Irak Ajemi in the north-west of modern Iran. The Madai are mentioned in an Assyrian inscription of king Rimmon-nirari III, 812-782 B.C.E.

Javan. The Ionians who inhabited the west coast of Asia Minor.

Tubal. This name, together with *Meshech*, occurs several times in *Ezekiel* and is identified with *Tabali* of the Assyrian monuments. Both Tubal and Meshech lived in the territory north-east of Cilicia in the days of the later Assyrian empire. Subsequently the former settled in Pontus and the latter farther east.

Tiras. 6. And the sons of Gomer: Ashkenaz, and Diphath, and Togarmah. 7. And the sons of Javan: Elishah, and Tarshish, Kittim, and Rodanim.

8. The sons of Ham: Cush, and Mizraim, Put, and Canaan. 9. And the sons of Cush: Seba, and Havilah, and Sabta, and Raama, and Sabteca.

גֹּמֶר אַשְׁכְּנַז וְדִיפַת וְתוֹגַרְמָה׃
7 וּבְנֵי יָוָן אֱלִישָׁה וְתַרְשִׁישָׁה
כִּתִּים וְרוֹדָנִים׃
8 בְּנֵי חָם כּוּשׁ וּמִצְרַיִם פּוּט
9 וּכְנָעַן׃ וּבְנֵי כוּשׁ סְבָא וַחֲוִילָה
וְסַבְתָּא וְרַעְמָא וְסַבְתְּכָא וּבְנֵי

Meshech. Muski of the Assyrian monuments. Another *Meshech*, a descendant of Shem, is named in verse 17.

Tiras. The identification of this name is uncertain. Josephus (*Antiquities* I. vi. 1) wrongly equated them with the Thracians.

6. *Ashkenaz.* Cf. Jer. li. 27; probably the people that lived on the east or north of Cappadocia, the country of Gomer their ancestor.

Diphath. The reading in Gen. x. 3, which some Hebrew MSS. have here, is *Riphath*; the identity is unknown.

Togarmah. Cf. Ezek. xxvii. 14, xxxviii. 6; presumed to have been a neighbour of Gomer, Tubal and Meshech, but its location is not identified.

7. *Elishah.* Ezek. xxvii. 7 speaks of *the isles of Elishah* as distinguished by the use of blue and purple. According to some authorities it is to be identified with Cyprus. Others think of islands in the neighbourhood of the North African coast.

Tarshish. Usually presumed to be the Tarsus which was the capital of Cilicia as early as the end of the fifth century B.C.E. The *Tarshish* of Ezek. xxvii. 12 is Tartessus, a town in the south of Spain.

Kittim. The inhabitants of Cyprus, so called perhaps after Citium, one of the oldest towns on the island.

Rodanim. In Gen. x. 4 *Dodanim*; probably the Rhodians whose island was renowned as far back as the time of Homer.

8-16. The twenty-five races descended from Ham (cf. Gen. x. 6-20).

8. *the sons of Ham.* After the enumeration of the descendants of Japheth who was mentioned last in verse 4, the Chronicler proceeds to describe those of Ham, the next in reverse order.

Cush. Usually rendered 'Ethiopia.' In the inscriptions of Assur-bani-pal, *Ku-u-su* or *Ku-su* (Ethiopia) is frequently mentioned in association with *Mu-sur* (*Mitsraim* or Egypt) as in this verse. The Cushites, like the present-day Soudanese, were a brown race. The Negroes are of different origin.

Mizraim. i.e. Egypt. The ending of the noun (*aïm*) is the dual form denoting the two Egypts, the Upper and Lower.

Put. It may possibly be the same as *Punt* of the Egyptian monuments, which includes the Somali and parts of the adjacent Arabian coast.

Canaan. The whole country on the western side of the Jordan was so named; but originally it perhaps designated only Philistia and Phoenicia on the coast which was Egypt's highway to the countries of the East. Hence the close association in the text between Egypt and Canaan.

9. The first five peoples in the verse were, according to one opinion, inhabitants of Arabia; but according to others the first two (*Seba* and *Havilah*) inhabited the western coast of the Red See and the Gulf of Aden, while the last three (*Sabta, Raama* and *Sabteca*) lived in Arabia.

And the sons of Raamah: Sheba,
and Dedan. 10. And Cush begot
Nimrod; he began to be a mighty
one in the earth. 11. And Mizraim
begot Ludim, and Anamim, and
Lehabim, and Naphtuhim, 12. and
Pathrusim, and Casluhim — from
whence came the Philistines—and
Caphtorim. 13. And Canaan begot
Zidon his first-born, and Heth;
14. and the Jebusite, and the
Amorite, and the Girgashite; 15. and
the Hivite, and the Arkite, and the

10 רַעְמָא שְׁבָא וּדְדָן׃ וְכוּשׁ יָלַד
אֶת־נִמְרוֹד הוּא הֵחֵל לִהְיוֹת
11 גִּבּוֹר בָּאָרֶץ׃ וּמִצְרַיִם יָלַד
אֶת־לוּדִיִּים וְאֶת־עֲנָמִים
וְאֶת־לְהָבִים וְאֶת־נַפְתֻּחִים׃
12 וְאֶת־פַּתְרֻסִים וְאֶת־
כַּסְלֻחִים אֲשֶׁר יָצְאוּ מִשָּׁם
פְּלִשְׁתִּים וְאֶת־כַּפְתֹּרִים׃
13 וּכְנַעַן יָלַד אֶת־צִידוֹן בְּכֹרוֹ
14 וְאֶת־חֵת׃ וְאֶת־הַיְבוּסִי
וְאֶת־הָאֱמֹרִי וְאֵת הַגִּרְגָּשִׁי׃
15 וְאֶת־הַחִוִּי וְאֶת־הָעַרְקִי

v. 11. יתיר י׳

Sheba, and Dedan. The same two names occur in verse 32 as the sons of *Jokshan* who was of the descendants of Shem. The former was a wealthy land (cf. 2 Chron. ix. 1ff.); the latter is mentioned with *Sheba* and *Tarshish* in Ezek. xxxviii. 13.

10. *Nimrod.* Fuller details of his life and warlike activities are given in Gen. x. 8ff.

11. *Ludim.* Probably the Lydians. They served at certain periods of history in the armies of Egypt and helped Psammetichus to gain the independence of Egypt.

Anamim, etc. Nothing is known of these.

12. *Pathrusim.* They inhabited Pathros in Upper Egypt.

from whence came the Philistines. The intermarriages of the Pathrusim and Casluhim produced the Philistines. According to Amos ix. 7, they sojourned for a time at Caphtor as Israel did in Egypt until God brought them out from there.

Caphtorim. If Caphtor is identified with Crete the Caphtorim were its natives.

13. *Zidon.* The name of one of the two most famous cities of Phoenicia.

Heth. The Hittites who inhabited the country between the Orontes and the Euphrates in Northern Syria, but had a colony in Canaan.

14. *the Jebusite.* The inhabitants of Jerusalem until dispossessed by David (2 Sam. v. 6ff.).

the Amorite. The people of Sihon in Transjordan.

the Girgashite. Of the peoples who inhabited Canaan before the Israelite conquest.

15. *the Hivite.* In the territory that lies in the extreme north of Canaan *under Hermon in the land of Mizpah* (Josh. xi. 3).

the Arkite, and the Sinite. Both inhabited the Lebanon region.

Sinite; 16. and the Arvadite, and
the Zemarite, and the Hamathite.
17. The sons of Shem: Elam, and
Asshur, and Arpachshad, and Lud,
and Aram, and Uz, and Hul, and
Gether, and Meshech. 18. And
Arpachshad begot Shelah, and
Shelah begot Eber. 19. And unto
Eber were born two sons: the name
of the one was Peleg; for in his days
the earth was divided; and his
brother's name was Joktan. 20. And
Joktan begot Almodad, and Sheleph,

16 וְאֶת־הַסִּינִי׃ וְאֶת־הָאַרְוָדִי
וְאֶת־הַצְּמָרִי וְאֶת־הַחֲמָתִי׃
17 בְּנֵי שֵׁם עֵילָם וְאַשּׁוּר
וְאַרְפַּכְשַׁד וְלוּד וַאֲרָם וְעוּץ
18 וְחוּל וְגֶתֶר וָמֶשֶׁךְ׃ וְאַרְפַּכְשַׁד
יָלַד אֶת־שָׁלַח וְשֶׁלַח יָלַד
19 אֶת־עֵבֶר׃ וּלְעֵבֶר יֻלַּד שְׁנֵי
בָנִים שֵׁם הָאֶחָד פֶּלֶג כִּי בְיָמָיו
נִפְלְגָה הָאָרֶץ וְשֵׁם אָחִיו
20 יָקְטָן׃ וְיָקְטָן יָלַד אֶת־
אַלְמוֹדָד וְאֶת־שָׁלֶף וְאֶת־

v. 17. סגול בס״פ

16. *the Arvadite.* On the Mediterranean coast, north of Gebal.

the Zemarite, and the Hamathite. The former lived to the south of the Arvadites, the latter on the Orontes in the north.

17-23. Twenty-six peoples from Shem, exclusive of the descendants of Peleg, an ancestor of Abraham, who are enumerated in verses 25ff. (cf. Gen. x. 22-29).

17. *Elam.* It has been suggested that in blood and speech the Elamites did not belong to the Semitic races, and their only claim to inclusion in this list must be the place of their domicile which was among the Semitic peoples.

Asshur. The Assyrians.

Arpachshad. The name occurs in verse 24; Gen. x. 22, 24, xi. 10ff. It may be noted that the Hebrew for *chshad* (the second half of the noun) represents the first part of *Casdim*, 'the Chaldeans,' and Arpachshad may be intended as the originator of that people who are not otherwise mentioned in the list.

Lud. To be distinguished from *Ludim* in verse 11 who were a Hamitic people. It has been conjectured that it equals *Lubdu*, a region between the Tigris and Euphrates.

Aram. The Aramæans or Syrians whose capital was Damascus; they were constantly at war with the Northern Kingdom of Israel.

Uz . . . Meshech. In Gen. x. 23, these four appear as the *sons of Aram* who was himself a son of Shem. By *sons of Shem* here must therefore be understood 'grandsons.' The identification of these four peoples is doubtful.

Meshech. The reading in Gen. x. 23 is *Mash*, consisting in Hebrew of the first two consonants of the name as it appears here.

18. *Eber.* The meaning of the Hebrew is 'on the (other) side,' usually in connection with the Jordan, *eber hayyarden.* Here it may indicate the people beyond the Euphrates.

19. *Peleg.* Meaning 'division': *in his days the earth was divided*, the peoples were dispersed over the earth.

20-23. The thirteen sons of Joktan represent tribes of South Arabia or of the west coast of the Red Sea facing it.

and Hazarmaveth, and Jerah; 21. and Hadoram, and Uzal, and Diklah; 22. and Ebal, and Abimael, and Sheba; 23. and Ophir, and Havilah, and Jobab. All these were the sons of Joktan.

24. Shem, Arpachshad, Shelah; 25. Eber, Peleg, Reu; 26. Serug, Nahor, Terah; 27. Abram—the same is Abraham. 28. The sons of Abraham: Isaac, and Ishmael.

29. These are their generations: the first-born of Ishmael, Nebaioth; then Kedar, and Adbeel, and Mibsam, 30. Mishma, and Dumah, Massa, Hadad, and Tema, 31. Jetur, Naphish, and Kedem. These are the sons of Ishmael.

21 חֲצַרְמָוֶת וְאֶת־יָרַח׃ וְאֶת־
הֲדוֹרָם וְאֶת־אוּזָל וְאֶת־
22 דִּקְלָה׃ וְאֶת־עֵיבָל וְאֶת־
23 אֲבִימָאֵל וְאֶת־שְׁבָא׃ וְאֶת־
אוֹפִיר וְאֶת־חֲוִילָה וְאֶת־
יוֹבָב כָּל־אֵלֶּה בְּנֵי יָקְטָן׃
24 25 שֵׁם אַרְפַּכְשַׁד שָׁלַח׃ עֵבֶר
26 פֶּלֶג רְעוּ׃ שְׂרוּג נָחוֹר תָּרַח׃
27 28 אַבְרָם הוּא אַבְרָהָם׃ בְּנֵי
אַבְרָהָם יִצְחָק וְיִשְׁמָעֵאל׃
29 אֵלֶּה תֹּלְדוֹתָם בְּכוֹר יִשְׁמָעֵאל
נְבָיוֹת וְקֵדָר וְאַדְבְּאֵל
30 וּמִבְשָׂם׃ מִשְׁמָע וְדוּמָה מַשָּׂא
31 חֲדַד וְתֵימָא׃ יְטוּר נָפִישׁ
וָקֵדְמָה אֵלֶּה הֵם בְּנֵי
יִשְׁמָעֵאל׃

20. *Hazarmaveth.* The modern *Hadramaut*, to the east of Aden.

22. *Ebal.* In Gen. x. 28 *Obal*, said to be in Yemen.

23. *Ophir.* Famous for its gold (cf. Isa. xiii. 12); its location is unknown.

Havilah. Cf. Gen. ii. 11, xxv. 18.

24-27. The ten generations from Noah (cf. verse 4) to Abraham (cf. Gen. xi. 10-26).

27. *the same is Abraham.* A reference to Gen. xvii. 5.

28. Abraham's sons by Sarah and Hagar respectively.

29-31. The tribes of Ishmael (cf. Gen. xxv. 12-18).

29. *Nebaioth.* The tribe of one of Esau's wives (Gen. xxviii. 9, xxxvi. 3); mentioned also in Isa. lx. 7.

Kedar. Famous for its archers (Isa. xxi. 16f.).

Adbeel. Thought to be the tribe *Idibi'il* named by Tiglath-pileser III in an inscription.

30. *Dumah.* On the south border of the Syrian desert (cf. Isa. xxi. 11).

Massa. A city or tribe *Mas'aa* is also mentioned by Tiglath-pileser as paying him tribute.

Tema. Cf. Isa. xxi. 14; the modern *Teima* in north-west Arabia.

31. *Jetur, Naphish.* Mentioned again in v. 19. They lived in the south part of Anti-Libanus.

32. And the sons of Keturah,
Abraham's concubine: she bore
Zimran, and Jokshan, and Medan,
and Midian, and Ishbak, and Shuah,
And the sons of Jokshan: Sheba,
and Dedan. 33. And the sons of
Midian: Ephah, and Epher, and
Hanoch, and Abida, and Eldaah.
All these were the sons of Keturah.
34. And Abraham begot Isaac.
The sons of Isaac: Esau, and Israel.
35. The sons of Esau: Eliphaz,
Reuel, and Jeush, and Jalam, and
Korah. 36. The sons of Eliphaz:
Teman, and Omar, Zephi, and
Gatam, Kenaz, and Timna, and
Amalek. 37. The sons of Reuel:
Nahath, Zerah, Shammah, and Miz-
zah.
38. And the sons of Seir: Lotan,

32 וּבְנֵי קְטוּרָה פִּילֶגֶשׁ אַבְרָהָם
יָלְדָה אֶת־זִמְרָן וְיָקְשָׁן וּמְדָן
וּמִדְיָן וְיִשְׁבָּק וְשׁוּחַ וּבְנֵי יָקְשָׁן
33 שְׁבָא וּדְדָן׃ וּבְנֵי מִדְיָן עֵיפָה
וָעֵפֶר וַחֲנוֹךְ וַאֲבִידָע
וְאֶלְדָּעָה כָּל־אֵלֶּה בְּנֵי
קְטוּרָה׃
34 וַיּוֹלֶד אַבְרָהָם אֶת־יִצְחָק בְּנֵי
יִצְחָק עֵשָׂו וְיִשְׂרָאֵל׃
35 בְּנֵי עֵשָׂו אֱלִיפַז רְעוּאֵל וִיעוּשׁ
36 וְיַעְלָם וְקֹרַח׃ בְּנֵי אֱלִיפָז
תֵּימָן וְאוֹמָר צְפִי וְגַעְתָּם קְנַז
37 וְתִמְנָע וַעֲמָלֵק׃ בְּנֵי רְעוּאֵל
נַחַת זֶרַח שַׁמָּה וּמִזָּה׃
38 וּבְנֵי שֵׂעִיר לוֹטָן וְשׁוֹבָל

32f. Abraham's sons by Keturah (cf. Gen. xxv. 1-4).

32. *Abraham's concubine.* This verse explains that Keturah, who in Gen. xxv. 1 is described as his *wife,* was only one of several concubines (cf. Gen. xxv. 6), and that consequently none of her descendants could claim the rights that were given to Isaac, the only son of Abraham by his wife Sarah.

Midian. The Midianites, who inhabited the east side of the Gulf of Akaba, are often mentioned in the Bible as antagonistic to Israel.

Sheba, and Dedan. See on verse 9.

33. *Ephah.* Associated with Midian in Isa. lx. 6.

Hanoch. See on verse 3.

34. The three Hebrew patriarchs and Esau.

35-42. The tribes of Esau and Seir.

35-37. The sons of Esau who were fathers of the Edomean tribes (cf. Gen. xxxvi. 4f., 11f.).

36. *Teman.* Cf. Amos i. 12 where it is another name for *Edom* (*Seir*).

Zephi. In Gen. xxxvi. 11 *Zepho.*

Timna. In Gen. xxxvi. 12 Timna is the name of a concubine of Eliphaz, unless the name is joined to the preceding verse as the sixth of his sons.

Amalek. He was the son of Timna, a concubine of Eliphaz, or her name is not stated (cf. the preceding note).

38-42. The clans of Seir, the aboriginal inhabitants of Edom before it was occupied by the descendants of Esau (cf. Gen. xxxvi. 20-27).

38. *sons of Seir.* Gen. xxxvi. 20 adds: *the Horite, the inhabitants of the land.*

and Shobal, and Zibeon, and Anah, and Dishon, and Ezer, and Dishan. 39. And the sons of Lotan: Hori, and Homam; and Timna was Lotan's sister. 40. The sons of Shobal: Alian, and Manahath, and Ebal, Shephi, and Onam. And the sons of Zibeon: Aiah, and Anah. 41. The sons of Anah: Dishon. And the sons of Dishon: Hamran, and Eshban, and Ithran, and Cheran. 42. The sons of Ezer: Bilhan, and Zaavan, Jaakan. The sons of Dishan: Uz, and Aran.

43. Now these are the kings that reigned in the land of Edom, before there reigned any king over the children of Israel: Bela the son of Beor; and the name of his city was Dinhabah. 44. And Bela died, and Jobab the son of Zerah of Bozrah reigned in his stead. 45. And Jobab died, and Husham of the land of the Temanites reigned in his stead. 46. And Husham died, and Hadad the son of Bedad, who smote Midian in the field of Moab, reigned in his stead; and the name of his city was Avith. 47. And Hadad died, and Samlah of Masrekah reigned in his stead. 48. And Samlah died, and Shaul of Rehoboth

וְצִבְעוֹן וַעֲנָה וְדִישֹׁן וְאֵצֶר
39 וְדִישָׁן׃ וּבְנֵי לוֹטָן חֹרִי וְהוֹמָם
40 וַאֲחוֹת לוֹטָן תִּמְנָע׃ בְּנֵי שׁוֹבָל
עַלְיָן וּמָנַחַת וְעֵיבָל שְׁפִי וְאוֹנָם
41 וּבְנֵי צִבְעוֹן אַיָּה וַעֲנָה׃ בְּנֵי
עֲנָה דִּישׁוֹן וּבְנֵי דִישׁוֹן חַמְרָן
42 וְאֶשְׁבָּן וְיִתְרָן וּכְרָן׃ בְּנֵי־
אֵצֶר בִּלְהָן וְזַעֲוָן יַעֲקָן בְּנֵי
דִישָׁן עוּץ וַאֲרָן׃
43 וְאֵלֶּה הַמְּלָכִים אֲשֶׁר מָלְכוּ
בְּאֶרֶץ אֱדוֹם לִפְנֵי מְלָךְ־
מֶלֶךְ לִבְנֵי יִשְׂרָאֵל בֶּלַע בֶּן־
בְּעוֹר וְשֵׁם עִירוֹ דִּנְהָבָה׃
44 וַיָּמָת בָּלַע וַיִּמְלֹךְ תַּחְתָּיו יוֹבָב
45 בֶּן־זֶרַח מִבָּצְרָה׃ וַיָּמָת יוֹבָב
וַיִּמְלֹךְ תַּחְתָּיו חוּשָׁם מֵאֶרֶץ
46 הַתֵּימָנִי׃ וַיָּמָת חוּשָׁם וַיִּמְלֹךְ
תַּחְתָּיו הֲדַד בֶּן־בְּדַד הַמַּכֶּה
אֶת־מִדְיָן בִּשְׂדֵה מוֹאָב וְשֵׁם
47 עִירוֹ עֲיוֹת׃ וַיָּמָת הֲדָד וַיִּמְלֹךְ
תַּחְתָּיו שַׂמְלָה מִמַּשְׂרֵקָה׃
48 וַיָּמָת שַׂמְלָה וַיִּמְלֹךְ תַּחְתָּיו

v. 46. עוית ק׳

39. *Homam.* In Gen. xxxvi. 22 *Hemam.*

40. *Alian.* In Gen. xxxvi. 23 *Alvan.*

Shephi. In Gen. xxxvi. 23 *Shepho.*

41. *the sons.* Gen. xxxvi. 25 adds a daughter, *Oholibamah.*

Hamran. In Gen. xxxvi. 25 *Hemdan.*

42. *Jaakan.* In Gen. xxxvi. 27 *Akan.*

43-51a. The kings of Edom (cf. Gen. xxxvi. 31-39).

46. *who smote Midian.* When they invaded Moab.

in the field of Moab. Having proceeded there to the aid of Moab.

by the River reigned in his stead.
49. And Shaul died, and Baal-hanan
the son of Achbor reigned in his
stead. 50. And Baal-hanan died,
and Hadad reigned in his stead; and
the name of his city was Pai; and his
wife's name was Mehetabel, the
daughter of Matred, the daughter of
Mezahab. 51. And Hadad died.

And the chiefs of Edom were: the
chief of Timna, the chief of Alvah,
the chief of Jetheth; 52. the chief of
Oholibamah, the chief of Elah, the
chief of Pinon; 53. the chief of
Kenaz, the chief of Teman, the
chief of Mibzar; 54. the chief of
Magdiel, the chief of Iram. These
are the chiefs of Edom.

49 שָׁאוּל מֵרְחֹבוֹת הַנָּהָר׃ וַיָּמָת
שָׁאוּל וַיִּמְלֹךְ תַּחְתָּיו בַּעַל
50 חָנָן בֶּן־עַכְבּוֹר׃ וַיָּמָת בַּעַל
חָנָן וַיִּמְלֹךְ תַּחְתָּיו הֲדַד וְשֵׁם
עִירוֹ פָּעִי וְשֵׁם אִשְׁתּוֹ
מְהֵיטַבְאֵל בַּת־מַטְרֵד בַּת
51 מֵי זָהָב׃ וַיָּמָת הֲדָד
וַיִּהְיוּ אַלּוּפֵי אֱדוֹם אַלּוּף
תִּמְנָע אַלּוּף עַלְיָה אַלּוּף
52 יְתֵת׃ אַלּוּף אָהֳלִיבָמָה אַלּוּף
53 אֵלָה אַלּוּף פִּינֹן׃ אַלּוּף קְנַז
אַלּוּף תֵּימָן אַלּוּף מִבְצָר׃
54 אַלּוּף מַגְדִּיאֵל אַלּוּף עִירָם
אֵלֶּה אַלּוּפֵי אֱדוֹם׃

2 CHAPTER II ב

1. These are the sons of Israel:

1 אֵלֶּה בְּנֵי יִשְׂרָאֵל רְאוּבֵן

v. 51. עלוה ק׳

48. *the River*. The Euphrates.

50. *Hadad*. In Gen. xxxvi. 39 *Hadar*.

Pai. In Gen. xxxvi. 39 *Pau*.

51b-54. The Edomean chiefs (cf. Gen. xxxvi. 40-43).

51b. *chiefs of Edom*. The English versions have 'dukes' for *chiefs*. 'Duke' means 'leader of a thousand.' The Hebrew *aluph* may be derived from *eleph* meaning 'thousand' and also 'tribe.' *Aluph* is the head of a tribe or clan.

Timna. The name is that of a man though the form is feminine. According to another opinion, it is the name of a district.

52. *Oholibamah*. Cf. the preceding note.

CHAPTERS II-VIII

THE GENEALOGIES OF THE TRIBES OF ISRAEL

THE tables of the genealogies are given in the following order, those in whom the Chronicler is mainly interested receiving the greater attention. No fewer than 102 verses are devoted to Judah, 81 to Levi, 40 to Benjamin and 20 to Simeon. These are the three tribes of South Canaan together with the tribe of Levi.

Reuben, Simeon, Levi, and Judah, Issachar, and Zebulun; 2. Dan, Joseph, and Benjamin, Naphtali, Gad, and Asher.

3. The sons of Judah: Er, and Onan, and Shelah; which three were born unto him of Bath-shua the Canaanitess. And Er, Judah's first-born, was wicked in the sight of the LORD; and He slew him. 4. And Tamar his daughter-in-law bore him Perez and Zerah. All the sons of Judah were five.

5. The sons of Perez: Hezron, and Hamul. 6. And the sons of Zerah: Zimri, and Ethan, and Heman, and Calcol, and Dara: five of them in all. 7. And the sons of Carmi: Achar, the troubler of Israel, who committed a trespass concerning the devoted thing. 8. And the sons of Ethan: Azariah.

שִׁמְעוֹן לֵוִי וִיהוּדָה יִשָּׂשכָר
2 וּזְבֻלוּן׃ דָּן יוֹסֵף וּבִנְיָמִן
נַפְתָּלִי גָּד וְאָשֵׁר׃
3 בְּנֵי יְהוּדָה עֵר וְאוֹנָן וְשֵׁלָה
שְׁלוֹשָׁה נוֹלַד לוֹ מִבַּת־שׁוּעַ
הַכְּנַעֲנִית וַיְהִי עֵר ׀ בְּכוֹר
יְהוּדָה רַע בְּעֵינֵי יְהוָה
4 וַיְמִיתֵהוּ׃ וְתָמָר כַּלָּתוֹ יָלְדָה
לּוֹ אֶת־פֶּרֶץ וְאֶת־זָרַח כָּל־
בְּנֵי יְהוּדָה חֲמִשָּׁה׃
5 בְּנֵי פֶרֶץ חֶצְרוֹן וְחָמוּל׃
6 וּבְנֵי זֶרַח זִמְרִי וְאֵיתָן וְהֵימָן
וְכַלְכֹּל וָדָרַע כֻּלָּם חֲמִשָּׁה׃
7 וּבְנֵי כַּרְמִי עָכָר עוֹכֵר יִשְׂרָאֵל
8 אֲשֶׁר מָעַל בַּחֵרֶם׃ וּבְנֵי אֵיתָן
עֲזַרְיָה׃

ii. 1f., the sons of Israel or Jacob; ii. 3-iv. 23, the families of Judah; iv. 24-43, the families of Simeon; v. 1-26, Reuben, Gad and half Manasseh; v. 27-vi. 66, Levi; vii. 1-5, Issachar; vii. 6-12, Benjamin; vii. 13, Naphtali; vii. 14-19, Manasseh; vii. 20-29, Ephraim; vii. 30-40, Asher; viii. 1-40, Benjamin. There is no specific mention of Zebulun and Dan.

CHAPTER II

DESCENDANTS OF JUDAH

1f. The sons of Israel; the heading of the section to the end of chapter viii.

3f. The sons of Judah (cf. Gen. xxxviii. 2-7, 29f.). Judah, being the most important tribe, is described first.

5. The sons of Perez (cf. Gen. xlvi. 12).

6-8. The descendants of Zerah. No record of this genealogy occurs elsewhere in the Bible.

6. *Zimri.* Identified with *Zabdi* of Josh. vii. 1.

Ethan . . . Dara. Cf. 1 Kings v. 11, where the four names occur as wise men of renown with *Darda* for *Dara* and *Mahol* as the name of the father for *Zerah.* Mahol may have been a descendant of Zerah and an ancestor of the four who are named.

7. *Carmi.* A son of Zabdi (or Zimri, see on verse 6) son of Zerah.

Achar. *Achan* of Josh. vii. 1. The name here means 'troubler,' as the text goes on to explain.

9. The sons also of Hezron, that were born unto him: Jerahmeel, and Ram, and Chelubai. 10. And Ram begot Amminadab; and Amminadab begot Nahshon, prince of the children of Judah; 11. and Nahshon begot Salma, and Salma begot Boaz; 12. and Boaz begot Obed, and Obed begot Jesse; 13. and Jesse begot his first-born Eliab, and Abinadab the second, and Shimea the third; 14. Nethanel the fourth, Raddai the fifth; 15. Ozem the sixth, David the

9 וּבְנֵי חֶצְרוֹן אֲשֶׁר נוֹלַד־לוֹ
אֶת־יְרַחְמְאֵל וְאֶת־רָם וְאֶת־
10 כְּלוּבָי׃ וְרָם הוֹלִיד אֶת־
עַמִּינָדָב וְעַמִּינָדָב הוֹלִיד
אֶת־נַחְשׁוֹן נְשִׂיא בְּנֵי יְהוּדָה׃
11 וְנַחְשׁוֹן הוֹלִיד אֶת־שַׂלְמָא
וְשַׂלְמָא הוֹלִיד אֶת־בֹּעַז׃
12 וּבֹעַז הוֹלִיד אֶת־עוֹבֵד
13 וְעוֹבֵד הוֹלִיד אֶת־יִשָׁי׃ וְאִישַׁי
הוֹלִיד אֶת־בְּכֹרוֹ אֶת־
אֱלִיאָב וַאֲבִינָדָב הַשֵּׁנִי
14 וְשִׁמְעָא הַשְּׁלִישִׁי׃ נְתַנְאֵל
15 הָרְבִיעִי רַדַּי הַחֲמִישִׁי׃ אֹצֶם
הַשִּׁשִּׁי דָּוִיד הַשְּׁבִעִי׃

v. 13. כצ״ל

committed a trespass. The incident is recorded in Josh. vii.

9. The sons of Hezron.

Jerahmeel . . . Ram. The genealogy of the younger son, Ram, is given first (verses 10-17) because it included the royal family of David. The genealogy of Jerahmeel follows in verses 25-41 after the first part of that of Caleb (verses 18-24), to whom precedence is given on account of his greater importance as compared with his eldest brother. Caleb's genealogy is resumed in verses 42-55.

Chelubai. A form of the name of *Caleb* mentioned in verses 18 and 42.

10-17. The descendants of Ram, including David. Cf. David's genealogy, showing his descent from Judah, in Ruth iv. 18-22.

10. *Nahshon, prince . . . Judah.* Cf. Num. i. 7, ii. 3, vii. 12.

11. *Salma.* In Ruth iv. 21 *Salmon.*

13. *Jesse.* The Hebrew name in this verse has the unusual addition of an *aleph* before the initial *yad.* Such an addition sometimes occurs elsewhere in other words.

Shimea. Another form of the name *Shammah* in 1 Sam. xvi. 9.

14. *Nethanel . . . Raddai.* These two brothers of David as well as *Ozem* (verse 15) are named only in this Book.

15. *David the seventh.* From 1 Sam. xvi. 10f., xvii. 12 we learn that Jesse had eight sons. It is suggested that one of the eight had died childless, in consequence of which his name was omitted here.

seventh. 16. And their sisters were Zeruiah and Abigail. And the sons of Zeruiah: Abishai, and Joab, and Asahel, three. 17. And Abigail bore Amasa; and the father of Amasa was Jether the Ishmaelite.

18. And Caleb the son of Hezron begot children of Azubah his wife—and of Jerioth—and these were her sons: Jesher, and Shobab, and Ardon. 19. And Azubah died, and Caleb took unto him Ephrath, who bore him Hur. 20. And Hur begot Uri, and Uri begot Bezalel.

21. And afterward Hezron went in to the daughter of Machir the father of Gilead; whom he took to

16 וְאַחְיֽוֹתֵיהֶם צְרוּיָה וַאֲבִיגָיִל
וּבְנֵי צְרוּיָה אַבְשַׁי וְיוֹאָב
17 וַעֲשָׂה־אֵל שְׁלֹשָׁה׃ וַאֲבִיגַיִל
יָלְדָה אֶת־עֲמָשָׂא וַאֲבִי
עֲמָשָׂא יֶתֶר הַיִּשְׁמְעֵאלִי׃
18 וְכָלֵב בֶּן־חֶצְרוֹן הוֹלִיד אֶת־
עֲזוּבָה אִשָּׁה וְאֶת־יְרִיעוֹת
וְאֵלֶּה בָנֶיהָ יֵשֶׁר וְשׁוֹבָב
19 וְאַרְדּוֹן׃ וַתָּמָת עֲזוּבָה וַיִּקַּח־
לוֹ כָלֵב אֶת־אֶפְרָת וַתֵּלֶד
20 לוֹ אֶת־חוּר׃ וְחוּר הוֹלִיד
אֶת־אוּרִי וְאוּרִי הוֹלִיד אֶת־
בְּצַלְאֵל׃
21 וְאַחַר בָּא חֶצְרוֹן אֶל־בַּת־
מָכִיר אֲבִי גִלְעָד וְהוּא לְקָחָהּ

16. *Zeruiah and Abigail.* The first of David's sisters is named on account of the distinguished rôle played by her sons, Joab and his brothers, in the reign of David. She having been mentioned, the other (cf. 2 Sam. xvii. 25) is also included.

17. *Jether the Ishmaelite.* In 2 Sam. xvii. 25 the reading is *Ithra the Jesraelite.* In the Hebrew there is only a slight difference between the spelling of *Jether* and *Ithra. Ishmaelite,* according to some commentators, indicates that he lived in the land of Ishmael.

18-24. The first part of the genealogy of Caleb.

18-20. The descendants of Caleb who were the ancestors of Bezalel (verse 20), the builder of the Tabernacle (cf. Exod. xxxi. 2ff.).

18. *and of Jerioth.* A phrase in parenthesis. The text is rather obscure and is perhaps to be understood as, 'begot children of Azubah, a wife (so the Hebrew literally), and of Jerioth,' the latter being a concubine (cf. verses 46, 48 for other concubines of Caleb).

her sons. The possessive pronoun *her* refers to Azubah; the children of Jerioth are not included in the list.

20. *and Hur . . . Bezalel.* Cf. Exod. xxxi. 2.

21-24. Another branch of Caleb's descendants.

21. *afterward.* After the birth of Hezron's three sons (cf. verse 9).

went in to the daughter. The expression *went in to* implies that the woman was a concubine (cf. the following notes).

Machir. The eldest son of Manasseh (cf. Num. xxvi. 29).

wife when he was threescore years old; and she bore him Segub. 22. And Segub begot Jair, who had three and twenty cities in the land of Gilead. 23. And Geshur and Aram took Havvoth-jair from them, with Kenath, and the villages thereof, even threescore cities. All these were the sons of Machir the father of Gilead. 24. And after that Hezron was dead in Caleb-ephrath, then Abiah Hezron's wife bore him Ashhur the father of Tekoa.

25. And the sons of Jerahmeel the first-born of Hezron were Ram the first-born, and Bunah, and Oren, and Ozem, Ahijah. 26. And Jerah-

וְהוּא בֶּן־שִׁשִּׁים שָׁנָה וַתֵּלֶד לוֹ
22 אֶת־שְׂגוּב׃ וּשְׂגוּב הוֹלִיד
אֶת־יָאִיר וַיְהִי־לוֹ עֶשְׂרִים
וְשָׁלוֹשׁ עָרִים בְּאֶרֶץ הַגִּלְעָד׃
23 וַיִּקַּח גְּשׁוּר־וַאֲרָם אֶת־חַוֹּת
יָאִיר מֵאִתָּם אֶת־קְנָת וְאֶת־
בְּנֹתֶיהָ שִׁשִּׁים עִיר כָּל־אֵלֶּה
24 בְּנֵי מָכִיר אֲבִי־גִלְעָד׃ וְאַחַר
מוֹת־חֶצְרוֹן בְּכָלֵב אֶפְרָתָה
וְאֵשֶׁת חֶצְרוֹן אֲבִיָּה וַתֵּלֶד לוֹ
אֶת־אַשְׁחוּר אֲבִי תְקוֹעַ׃
25 וַיִּהְיוּ בְנֵי־יְרַחְמְאֵל בְּכוֹר
חֶצְרוֹן הַבְּכוֹר ׀ רָם וּבוּנָה
26 וָאֹרֶן וָאֹצֶם אֲחִיָּה׃ וַתְּהִי אִשָּׁה

threescore years old. Not only did the daughter of Machir consent to take a man of that age, but she accepted the status of concubine for the dignity which was destined to be associated with the family of David (Rashi).

22. *Segub begot Jair.* In Judg. x. 3f. *Jair* is the name of one of the judges of Israel who owned thirty cities. The name also occurs in Num. xxxii. 41 as a *son* of Manasseh; but *son* is often used in the Bible with the meaning 'descendant.' According to the Rabbis, Jair in this verse was not the son of Manasseh but of Segub who married a Gileadite woman, the owner of the twenty-three cities. She pre-deceased him and he inherited her cities.

Gilead. The land occupied by the Israelites in Transjordan and not, as sometimes, the Gilead which was south of the Jarmuk.

23. *Geshur.* A kingdom on the north-east of the territory of Manasseh in Transjordan.

Aram. Presumed to be the people whose capital was Damascus. Like Aram, Geshur was an Aramean kingdom, and the conquest of these territories of Manasseh by Arameans could only have been achieved before the reign of Ahab, in whose time they had extended their conquests as far as Ramoth-gilead (cf. 1 Kings xxii. 3).

all these. Referring to Segub and Jair mentioned in verses 21f. and to their descendants.

24. *Caleb-ephrath.* Possibly Bethlehem is intended (cf. Ruth iv. 11).

bore him. After his death.

father of Tekoa. The governor of the town or the ancestor of its population.

25-41. The Jerahmeelites.

25f. The sons of Jerahmeel; this is a resumption of the genealogy of verse 9.

meel had another wife, whose name was Atarah; she was the mother of Onam.

27. And the sons of Ram the first-born of Jerahmeel were Maaz, and Jamin, and Eker. 28. And the sons of Onam were Shammai, and Jada; and the sons of Shammai: Nadab, and Abishur. 29. And the name of the wife of Abishur was Abihail; and she bore him Ahban, and Molid. 30. And the sons of Nadab: Seled, and Appaim; but Seled died without children. 31. And the sons of Appaim: Ishi. And the sons of Ishi: Sheshan. And the sons of Sheshan: Ahlai. 32. And the sons of Jada the brother of Shammai: Jether, and Jonathan: and Jether died without children. 33. And the sons of Jonathan: Peleth, and Zaza. These were the sons of Jerahmeel.

34. Now Sheshan had no sons, but daughters. And Sheshan had a servant, an Egyptian, whose name was Jarha. 35. So Sheshan gave his daughter to Jarha his servant to wife; and she bore him Attai. 36. And Attai begot Nathan, and Nathan begot Zabad; 37. and Zabad begot Ephlal, and Ephlal begot

אַחֶרֶת לִירַחְמְאֵל וּשְׁמָהּ
עֲטָרָה הִיא אֵם אוֹנָם׃
27 וַיִּהְיוּ בְנֵי־רָם בְּכוֹר יְרַחְמְאֵל
28 מַעַץ וְיָמִין וָעֵקֶר׃ וַיִּהְיוּ בְנֵי־
אוֹנָם שַׁמַּי וְיָדָע וּבְנֵי שַׁמַּי נָדָב
29 וַאֲבִישׁוּר׃ וְשֵׁם אֵשֶׁת אֲבִישׁוּר
אֲבִיהָיִל וַתֵּלֶד לוֹ אֶת־אַחְבָּן
30 וְאֶת־מוֹלִיד׃ וּבְנֵי נָדָב סֶלֶד
וְאַפָּיִם וַיָּמָת סֶלֶד לֹא בָנִים׃
31 וּבְנֵי אַפַּיִם יִשְׁעִי וּבְנֵי יִשְׁעִי
32 שֵׁשָׁן וּבְנֵי שֵׁשָׁן אַחְלָי׃ וּבְנֵי
יָדָע אֲחִי שַׁמַּי יֶתֶר וְיוֹנָתָן וַיָּמָת
33 יֶתֶר לֹא בָנִים׃ וּבְנֵי יוֹנָתָן
פֶּלֶת וְזָזָא אֵלֶּה הָיוּ בְּנֵי
יְרַחְמְאֵל׃
34 וְלֹא־הָיָה לְשֵׁשָׁן בָּנִים כִּי אִם־
בָּנוֹת וּלְשֵׁשָׁן עֶבֶד מִצְרִי וּשְׁמוֹ
35 יַרְחָע׃ וַיִּתֵּן שֵׁשָׁן אֶת־בִּתּוֹ
לְיַרְחָע עַבְדּוֹ לְאִשָּׁה וַתֵּלֶד
36 לוֹ אֶת־עַתָּי׃ וְעַתַּי הוֹלִיד
אֶת־נָתָן וְנָתָן הוֹלִיד אֶת־
37 זָבָד׃ וְזָבָד הוֹלִיד אֶת־
אֶפְלָל וְאֶפְלָל הוֹלִיד אֶת־

27-33. The descendants of Jerahmeel's sons.

31. *the sons of Sheshan. Sons* must here be used in the sense of 'offspring' since verse 34 states that he *had no sons.*
Ahlai. The name of a daughter of Sheshan who is mentioned on account of the family she raised and because she was his heiress (verse 35). In the view of others, *Ahlai* is a gentilic name.

34-41. The descendants of Sheshan through his daughter Ahlai.

Obed; 38. and Obed begot Jehu, and Jehu begot Azariah; 39. and Azariah begot Helez, and Helez begot Eleasah; 40. and Eleasah begot Sisamai, and Sisamai begot Shallum; 41. and Shallum begot Jekamiah, and Jekamiah begot Elishama.

42. And the sons of Caleb the brother of Jerahmeel were Mesha his first-born, who was the father of Ziph, and the sons of Mareshah the father of Hebron. 43. And the sons of Hebron: Korah, and Tappuah, and Rekem, and Shema. 44. And Shema begot Raham, the father of Jorkeam; and Rekem begot Shammai. 45. And the son of Shammai was Maon; and Maon was the father of Beth-zur. 46. And Ephah, Caleb's concubine, bore Haran, and Moza, and Gazez; and Haran begot Gazez. 47. And the sons of Jahdai: Regem, and Jotham, and Geshan, and Pelet, and Ephah, and Shaaph. 48. Maacah, Caleb's concubine, bore

38 עוֹבֵד׃ וְעוֹבֵד הֹלִיד אֶת־
יֵהוּא וְיֵהוּא הֹלִיד אֶת־
39 עֲזַרְיָה׃ וַעֲזַרְיָה הֹלִיד אֶת־
חָלֶץ וְחֶלֶץ הֹלִיד אֶת־
40 אֶלְעָשָׂה׃ וְאֶלְעָשָׂה הֹלִיד
אֶת־סִסְמָי וְסִסְמָי הֹלִיד
41 אֶת־שַׁלּוּם׃ וְשַׁלּוּם הוֹלִיד
אֶת־יְקַמְיָה וִיקַמְיָה הֹלִיד
אֶת־אֱלִישָׁמָע׃
42 וּבְנֵי כָלֵב אֲחִי יְרַחְמְאֵל מֵישָׁע
בְּכֹרוֹ הוּא אֲבִי־זִיף וּבְנֵי
43 מָרֵשָׁה אֲבִי חֶבְרוֹן׃ וּבְנֵי
חֶבְרוֹן קֹרַח וְתַפֻּחַ וְרֶקֶם
44 וָשָׁמַע׃ וְשֶׁמַע הוֹלִיד אֶת־
רַחַם אֲבִי יָרְקֳעָם וְרֶקֶם
45 הוֹלִיד אֶת־שַׁמָּי׃ וּבֶן־שַׁמַּי
מָעוֹן וּמָעוֹן אֲבִי בֵית־צוּר׃
46 וְעֵיפָה פִּילֶגֶשׁ כָּלֵב יָלְדָה
אֶת־חָרָן וְאֶת־מוֹצָא וְאֶת־
47 גָּזֵז וְחָרָן הֹלִיד אֶת־גָּזֵז׃ וּבְנֵי
יָהְדָּי רֶגֶם וְיוֹתָם וְגֵישָׁן וָפֶלֶט
48 וְעֵיפָה וָשָׁעַף׃ פִּלֶגֶשׁ כָּלֵב

v. 39. קמץ בז״ק v. 47. בנ״א הי׳ בסגול

42-55. Second part of Caleb's genealogy (cf. verses 18-20, 21-24).

42. Caleb. i.e. *Chelubai* of verse 9 and *Caleb the son of Hezron* (verse 18).

father of Ziph. i.e. governor of the town Ziph (Josh xv. 24, 55).

sons of Mareshah. i.e. inhabitants of the place Mareshah (2 Chron. xi. 8).

father of Hebron. Here, too, *father* signifies 'governor.' The names of persons and places are mingled in this section.

47. *Jahdai.* He was one of the sons of

Sheber and Tirhanah. 49. And
[the wife of] Shaaph the father of
Madmannah bore Sheva the father
of Machbenah and the father of
Gibea. And the daughter of Caleb
was Achsah. 50. These were the
sons of Caleb.

The sons of Hur the first-born of
Ephrath: Shobal the father of
Kiriath-jearim; 51. Salma the father
of Bethlehem, Hareph the father of
Beth-gader. 52. And Shobal the
father of Kiriath-jearim had sons:
Haroeh, and half of the Menuhoth.
53. And the families of Kiriath-
jearim: the Ithrites, and the Pu-
thites, and the Shumathites, and the
Mishraites; of them came the
Zorathites, and the Eshtaolites.

54. The sons of Salma: Beth-
lehem, and the Netophathites,
Atroth-beth-joab, and half of the
Manahathites, the Zorites. 55. And

מַעֲכָה יָלַד שֶׁבֶר וְאֶת־
49 תִּרְחֲנָה׃ וַתֵּלֶד שַׁעַף אֲבִי
מַדְמַנָּה אֶת־שְׁוָא אֲבִי מַכְבֵּנָה
וַאֲבִי גִבְעָא וּבַת־כָּלֵב
50 עַכְסָה׃ אֵלֶּה הָיוּ בְּנֵי כָלֵב
בֶּן־חוּר בְּכוֹר אֶפְרָתָה שׁוֹבָל
51 אֲבִי קִרְיַת יְעָרִים׃ שַׂלְמָא
אֲבִי בֵּית־לָחֶם חָרֵף אֲבִי
52 בֵית־גָּדֵר׃ וַיִּהְיוּ בָנִים
לְשׁוֹבָל אֲבִי קִרְיַת יְעָרִים
הָרֹאֶה חֲצִי הַמְּנֻחוֹת׃
53 וּמִשְׁפְּחוֹת קִרְיַת יְעָרִים
הַיִּתְרִי וְהַפּוּתִי וְהַשֻּׁמָתִי
וְהַמִּשְׁרָעִי מֵאֵלֶּה יָצְאוּ
הַצָּרְעָתִי וְהָאֶשְׁתָּאֻלִי׃
54 בְּנֵי שַׂלְמָא בֵּית לֶחֶם וּנְטוֹפָתִי
עַטְרוֹת בֵּית יוֹאָב וַחֲצִי
55 הַמָּנַחְתִּי הַצָּרְעִי׃ וּמִשְׁפְּחוֹת

v. 49. בנ״א עכסא   v. 51. קמץ בז״ק

Ephah (verse 46) who is here mentioned apparently under an alternative name.

48. *Maacah . . . bore.* The verb in Hebrew has the masculine form instead of the expected feminine.

49. *and [the wife of] Shaaph . . . bore.* Or, 'she (i.e. Maacah) bore also Shaaph, the father of Madmannah, Sheva the father of,' etc. (R.V.).

Achsah. The daughter of Caleb son of Jephunneh (cf. Josh. xv. 16; Judg. i. 12) was also named Achsah.

50. *these were the sons of Caleb.* The phrase refers to the preceding names and is a repetition of the beginning of verse 42.

father. See on verse 42.

52. *Haroeh, and half of the Menuhoth.* The latter obviously cannot be the name of a person; hence the alternative rendering: 'who supervised half of the resting-places.' Shobal was in charge of half the caravan stations in the land of Judah.

54. *Beth-lehem.* A name of one of Salma's sons or 'the inhabitants of Beth-lehem,' some or most of whom were his descendants.

Netophathites, etc. Here clans, and not

the families of scribes that dwelt at Jabez: the Tirathites, the Shimeathites, the Sucathites. These are the Kenites that came of Hammath, the father of the house of Rechab.

סוֹפְרִים יֹשְׁבֵו יַעְבֵּץ תִּרְעָתִים
שִׁמְעָתִים שׂוּכָתִים הֵמָּה
הַקִּינִים הַבָּאִים מֵחַמַּת אֲבִי
בֵית־רֵכָב׃

3 CHAPTER III ג

1. Now these were the sons of David, that were born unto him in Hebron: the first-born, Amnon, of Ahinoam the Jezreelitess; the second, Daniel, of Abigail the Carmelitess; 2. the third, Absalom the son of Maacah the daughter of Talmai king of Geshur; the fourth, Adonijah the son of Haggith; 3. the fifth, Shephatiah of Abital; the sixth, Ithream by Eglah his wife. 4. Six were born

וְאֵלֶּה הָיוּ בְּנֵי דָוִיד אֲשֶׁר 1
נוֹלַד־לוֹ בְּחֶבְרוֹן הַבְּכוֹר ׀
אַמְנֹן לַאֲחִינֹעַם הַיִּזְרְעֵאלִית
שֵׁנִי דָּנִיֵּאל לַאֲבִיגַיִל
הַכַּרְמְלִית׃ הַשְּׁלִשִׁי 2
לְאַבְשָׁלוֹם בֶּן־מַעֲכָה בַּת־
תַּלְמַי מֶלֶךְ גְּשׁוּר הָרְבִיעִי
אֲדֹנִיָּה בֶן־חַגִּית׃ הַחֲמִישִׁי 3
שְׁפַטְיָה לַאֲבִיטָל הַשִּׁשִּׁי
יִתְרְעָם לְעֶגְלָה אִשְׁתּוֹ׃ שִׁשָּׁה 4

ישבי ק׳ v. 55.

individuals, are clearly intended. The first name is mentioned again in ix. 16; Neh. xii. 28.

55. *scribes.* Hebrew *sopherim* which is understood by some as the name of a clan.

Jabez. A place name, to be distinguished from the name of a person which occurs in iv. 9.

that came, etc. More lit. 'that came in (who attached themselves to Israel) from Hammath.'

the house of Rechab. A son of Rechab is named in 2 Kings x. 15 and *the house of the Rechabites* in Jer. xxxv. 2.

CHAPTER III

THE HOUSE OF DAVID

The Davidic genealogy is now traced down to the sixth generation of Zerubbabel, *c.* 350 B.C.E.

1-4. The sons of David born in Hebron; the section corresponds to 2 Sam. iii. 2-5.

1. *Daniel.* In 2 Sam. iii. 3 he is called *Chileab* and he was apparently known by two names.

2. *Absalom.* The *lamed* prefixed to the name in Hebrew is not translated. It represents one of the peculiar uses of the dative in this Book.

Geshur. See on ii. 23.

unto him in Hebron; and there he
reigned seven years and six months;
and in Jerusalem he reigned thirty
and three years.
5. And these were born unto him
in Jerusalem: Shimea, and Shobab,
and Nathan, and Solomon, four, of
Bath-shua the daughter of Ammiel;
6. and Ibhar, and Elishama, and
Eliphelet; 7. and Nogah, and
Nepheg, and Japhia; 8. and Elishama, and Eliada, and Eliphelet, nine.
9. All these were the sons of David,
beside the sons of the concubines;
and Tamar was their sister.

נֽוֹלַד־לוֹ בְחֶבְרוֹן וַיִּמְלָךְ־
שָׁם שֶׁבַע שָׁנִים וְשִׁשָּׁה חֳדָשִׁים
וּשְׁלֹשִׁים וְשָׁלוֹשׁ שָׁנָה מָלַךְ
בִּירוּשָׁלָֽםִ׃
5 וְאֵלֶּה נוּלְּדוּ־לוֹ בִּירוּשָׁלָםִ
שִׁמְעָא וְשׁוֹבָב וְנָתָן וּשְׁלֹמֹה
אַרְבָּעָה לְבַת־שׁוּעַ בַּת־
6 עַמִּיאֵל׃ וְיִבְחָר וֶאֱלִישָׁמָע
7 וֶאֱלִיפָֽלֶט׃ וְנֹגַהּ וְנֶפֶג וְיָפִֽיעַ׃
8 וֶאֱלִישָׁמָע וְאֶלְיָדָע וֶאֱלִיפֶלֶט
9 תִּשְׁעָה׃ כֹּל בְּנֵי דָוִיד מִלְּבַד
בְּֽנֵי־פִֽילַגְשִׁים וְתָמָר אֲחוֹתָֽם׃

v. 5. דגש אחר שורק

3. *Eglah his wife.* In 2 Sam. iii. 5 *Eglah David's wife.* According to Talmudic tradition (Sanh. 21a), she was Michal, Saul's daughter, described as *his wife* because she was his first and the one loved best.

4. This verse corresponds to 2 Sam. v. 5.

5-9. David's sons born in Jerusalem; this section corresponds to xiv. 4-7 and 2 Sam. v. 14-16.

5. *Shimea.* In the parallel passages he is named *Shammua.*

Bath-shua the daughter of Ammiel. In 2 Sam. xi. 3 her name is *Bath-sheba the daughter of Eliam.* The slight change in her name and the transposition of letters in her father's may perhaps be due to the Chronicler's consideration for the honour of David. He passes over David's sin with Bath-sheba without any allusion to it.

6. *Elishama.* According to xiv. 5 and 2 Sam. v. 15 *Elishua.* This reading avoids the repetition of *Elishama* in verse 8.

Eliphelet. The name appears as *Elpelet* in xiv. 5 (but see on verse 8) and does not occur at all in the list in 2 Sam. v. 15.

7. *Nogah.* The name is found in xiv. 6 but is wanting in 2 Sam. v. 15.

8. *Elishama.* See on verse 6.

Eliada. In xiv. 7 *Beeliada*, but in 2 Sam. v. 16 *Eliada* as here.

Eliphelet. See on verse 6. Some distinguish between this name which has an *e* before the *l* and the name in verse 6 which has an *a*.

nine. In addition to the four enumerated in verse 5. The repetition of some of the names is due, according to Talmudic tradition, to the fact that when the first bearers of the names had died, their brothers who were born subsequently were called after the departed.

9. *all these were.* The last two words are not in the text.

10. And Solomon's son was
Rehoboam; Abijah his son, Asa his
son, Jehoshaphat his son; 11. Joram
his son, Ahaziah his son, Joash his
son; 12. Amaziah his son, Azariah
his son, Jotham his son; 13. Ahaz
his son, Hezekiah his son, Manasseh
his son; 14. Amon his son, Josiah
his son. 15. And the sons of
Josiah: the first-born Johanan, the
second Jehoiakim, the third Zedekiah, the fourth Shallum. 16. And
the sons of Jehoiakim: Jeconiah his
son, Zedekiah his son.

17. And the sons of Jeconiah—
the same is Assir—Shealtiel his son;
18. and Malchiram, and Pedaiah,
and Shenazzar, Jekamiah, Hoshama,
and Nedabiah. 19. And the sons of

10 וּבֶן־שְׁלֹמֹה רְחַבְעָם אֲבִיָּה
בְּנוֹ אָסָא בְנוֹ יְהוֹשָׁפָט בְּנוֹ׃
11 יוֹרָם בְּנוֹ אֲחַזְיָהוּ בְנוֹ יוֹאָשׁ
12 בְּנוֹ׃ אֲמַצְיָהוּ בְנוֹ עֲזַרְיָה בְנוֹ
13 יוֹתָם בְּנוֹ׃ אָחָז בְּנוֹ חִזְקִיָּהוּ
14 בְנוֹ מְנַשֶּׁה בְנוֹ׃ אָמוֹן בְּנוֹ
15 יֹאשִׁיָּהוּ בְנוֹ׃ וּבְנֵי יֹאשִׁיָּהוּ
הַבְּכוֹר יוֹחָנָן הַשֵּׁנִי יְהוֹיָקִים
הַשְּׁלִשִׁי צִדְקִיָּהוּ הָרְבִיעִי
16 שַׁלּוּם׃ וּבְנֵי יְהוֹיָקִים יְכָנְיָה
בְנוֹ צִדְקִיָּה בְנוֹ׃
17 וּבְנֵי יְכָנְיָה אַסִּר שְׁאַלְתִּיאֵל
18 בְּנוֹ׃ וּמַלְכִּירָם וּפְדָיָה
וְשֶׁנְאַצַּר יְקַמְיָה הוֹשָׁמָע
19 וּנְדַבְיָה׃ וּבְנֵי פְדָיָה זְרֻבָּבֶל

v. 18. פתח באתנח

10-16. The line of the kings of Judah.

10. *Abijah.* In 1 Kings xiv. 31 he is called *Abijam*, but several Hebrew MSS. have the reading *Abijah* there.

his son. i.e. son of Rehoboam. Each name in the list is that of a son of the preceding and father of the one following.

12. *Azariah.* Elsewhere he is named *Uzziah* (cf. Isa. i. 1; 2 Chron. xxvi. 1).

15. *the first-born Johanan.* In 2 Kings xxiii. 30 Josiah's successor is named *Jehoahaz*. Though he was the second son of Josiah (cf. 2 Chron. xxxvi. 2, 5) he is here described as the *first-born* because he ascended the throne before his elder brother, Jehoiakim.

the second. In succession to the throne.

Shallum. He is identified by some with Jehoiachin, and by others with Jehoahaz (cf. Jer. xxii. 11 with 2 Chron. xxxvi. 1).

16. *Zedekiah his son.* Here *son* means 'successor,' since Zedekiah was not Jeconiah's son but his nephew.

17-24. The post-exilic line of the House of David.

17. *the same is Assir.* A.J. agrees with A.V. and R.V. margin, and the first three words are not in the text but supplied. R.V. renders *Assir* as 'the captive,' but there is no definite article in the Hebrew. Jeconiah (or Jehoiachin) was taken captive by the king of Babylon (cf. 2 Kings xxiv. 15), and the significance of *Assir* may be that the offspring was born to Jeconiah '(when he was) a captive,' i.e. in captivity. He was only eighteen when he came to the throne and reigned for three months before going

Pedaiah: Zerubbabel, and Shimei.
And the sons of Zerubbabel: Meshullam, and Hananiah; and Shelomith was their sister; 20. and Hashubah, and Ohel, and Berechiah, and Hasadiah, Jushab-hesed, five. 21. And the sons of Hananiah: Pelatiah, and Jeshaiah; the sons of [Jeshaiah]: Rephaiah; the sons of [Rephaiah]: Arnan; the sons of [Arnan]: Obadiah; the sons of [Obadiah]: Shecaniah. 22. And the sons of Shecaniah: Shemaiah; and the sons of Shemaiah: Hattush, and Igal, and Bariah, and Neariah, and Shaphat, six. 23. And the sons of Neariah: Elioenai, and Hizkiah, and Azrikam, three. 24. And the sons of Elioenai: Hodaviah, and Eliashib, and Pelaiah, and Akkub, and Johanan, and Delaiah, and Anani, seven.

וְשִׁמְעִי וּבֶן־זְרֻבָּבֶל מְשֻׁלָּם
וַחֲנַנְיָה וּשְׁלֹמִית אֲחוֹתָם׃
20 וַחֲשֻׁבָה וָאֹהֶל וּבֶרֶכְיָה
וַחֲסַדְיָה יוּשַׁב חֶסֶד חָמֵשׁ׃
21 וּבֶן־חֲנַנְיָה פְּלַטְיָה וִישַׁעְיָה
בְּנֵי רְפָיָה בְּנֵי אַרְנָן בְּנֵי
22 עֹבַדְיָה בְּנֵי שְׁכַנְיָה׃ וּבְנֵי
שְׁכַנְיָה שְׁמַעְיָה וּבְנֵי שְׁמַעְיָה
חַטּוּשׁ וְיִגְאָל וּבָרִיחַ וּנְעַרְיָה
23 וְשָׁפָט שִׁשָּׁה׃ וּבֶן־נְעַרְיָה
אֶלְיוֹעֵינַי וְחִזְקִיָּה וְעַזְרִיקָם
24 שְׁלֹשָׁה׃ וּבְנֵי אֶלְיוֹעֵינַי
הוֹדַיְוָהוּ וְאֶלְיָשִׁיב וּפְלָיָה
וְעַקּוּב וְיוֹחָנָן וּדְלָיָה וַעֲנָנִי
שִׁבְעָה׃

4 CHAPTER IV ד

1. The sons of Judah: Perez, Hezron,

1 בְּנֵי יְהוּדָה פֶּרֶץ חֶצְרוֹן וְכַרְמִי

v. 24. הודיוהו ק׳

into exile (2 Kings xxiv. 8), so he may well have been childless then.

19. *the sons of Pedaiah: Zerubbabel.* According to this verse, Zerubbabel was a grandson of Shealtiel; but since grandchildren are often described as children, he is named elsewhere *the son of Shealtiel* (Hag. i. 1; Ezra iii. 2, v. 2).

sons of Zerubbabel. The Hebrew noun is singular to be taken in a collective sense.

21. *sons of* [*Jeshaiah*], etc. By the insertion of *Jeshaiah* and the following three names an intelligible meaning is obtained. The ancient versions had the reading: 'and the sons of Hananiah: Pelatiah, and Jeshaiah his son, Rephaiah his son, Arnan his son, Obadiah his son, Shecaniah his son.'

22. *six.* Shemaiah and his five sons are the six descendants of Shecaniah.

CHAPTER IV

MORE GENEALOGIES OF JUDAH AND OF SIMEON

1-23. Supplementary genealogies of the

and Carmi, and Hur, and Shobal.
2. And Reaiah the son of Shobal
begot Jahath; and Jahath begot
Ahumai, and Lahad. These are the
families of the Zorathites.

3. And these were [the sons of] the
father of Etam: Jezreel, and Ishma,
and Idbash; and the name of their
sister was Hazlelponi; 4. and Penuel
the father of Gedor, and Ezer the
father of Hushah. These are the
sons of Hur the first-born of
Ephrath, the father of Beth-lehem.

5. And Ashhur the father of
Tekoa had two wives, Helah and
Naarah. 6. And Naarah bore him
Ahuzam, and Hepher, and Timeni,
and Ahashtari. These were the
sons of Naarah. 7. And the sons of
Helah were Zereth, and Zohar, and
Ethnan. 8. And Koz begot Anub,

2 וְחוּר וְשׁוֹבָל׃ וּרְאָיָה בֶן־
שׁוֹבָל הוֹלִיד אֶת־יַחַת וְיַחַת
הוֹלִיד אֶת־אֲחוּמַי וְאֶת־לָהַד
אֵלֶּה מִשְׁפְּחוֹת הַצָּרְעָתִי׃
3 וְאֵלֶּה אֲבִי עֵיטָם יִזְרְעֶאל
וְיִשְׁמָא וְיִדְבָּשׁ וְשֵׁם אֲחוֹתָם
4 הַצְלֶלְפּוֹנִי׃ וּפְנוּאֵל אֲבִי גְדֹר
וְעֵזֶר אֲבִי חוּשָׁה אֵלֶּה בְנֵי־
חוּר בְּכוֹר אֶפְרָתָה אֲבִי בֵּית
לָחֶם׃
5 וּלְאַשְׁחוּר אֲבִי תְקוֹעַ הָיוּ שְׁתֵּי
6 נָשִׁים חֶלְאָה וְנַעֲרָה׃ וַתֵּלֶד
לוֹ נַעֲרָה אֶת־אֲחֻזָּם וְאֶת־
חֵפֶר וְאֶת־תֵּימְנִי וְאֶת־
הָאֲחַשְׁתָּרִי אֵלֶּה בְּנֵי נַעֲרָה׃
7 וּבְנֵי חֶלְאָה צֶרֶת יִצְחַר
8 וְאֶתְנָן׃ וְקוֹץ הוֹלִיד אֶת־

v. 7. וצחר ק׳

tribe of Judah including the repetition of some of the names mentioned above.

1f. The Zorathite families.

1. *the sons.* i.e. descendants. Perez alone was a son of Judah.

Hezron. He was a son of Perez (ii. 5) and, therefore, Judah's grandson.

Carmi. See on ii. 7.

Hur . . . Shobal. Sons of Caleb (ii. 19, 50) and grandsons of Hezron (ii. 18).

2. *Zorathites.* Cf. ii. 53.

3f. Additional descendants of Hur (cf. ii. 19f., 50).

3. [*the sons of*]. Not in the text but to be understood.

the father of Etam. i.e. 'governor of Etam'; a place of this name occurs in 2 Chron. xi. 6.

4. *first-born of Ephrath.* She was a wife of Caleb (ii. 19).

the father of Beth-lehem. Hur was the father, i.e. ancestor, of Beth-lehem, having been the father of Salma who was the father of Beth-lehem (ii. 50f.).

5-10. The Asshur families.

5. *father of Tekoa.* Or, 'governor of Tekoa,' five miles from Beth-lehem.

8. *Koz.* This name has not been mentioned before, and it has been suggested that it is the second name of

and Zobebah, and the families of
Aharhel the son of Harum. 9. And
Jabez was more honourable than his
brethren; and his mother called his
name Jabez, saying: 'Because I bore
him with pain.' 10. And Jabez called
on the God of Israel, saying: 'Oh
that Thou wouldest bless me indeed,
and enlarge my border, and that
Thy hand might be with me, and
that Thou wouldest work deliverance from evil, that it may not pain
me!' And God granted him that
which he requested.

11. And Chelub the brother of
Shuhah begot Mehir, who was the
father of Eshton. 12. And Eshton
begot Beth-rapha, and Paseah, and
Tehinnah the father of Ir-nahash.
These are the men of Recah.

13. And the sons of Kenaz:
Othniel, and Seraiah; and the sons
of Othniel: Hathath. 14. And Meonothai begot Ophrah; and Seraiah

עָנוּב וְאֶת־הַצֹּבֵבָה וּמִשְׁפְּחֹת
9 אֲחַרְחֵל בֶּן־הָרֻם׃ וַיְהִי
יַעְבֵּץ נִכְבָּד מֵאֶחָיו וְאִמּוֹ
קָרְאָה שְׁמוֹ יַעְבֵּץ לֵאמֹר כִּי
10 יָלַדְתִּי בְּעֹצֶב׃ וַיִּקְרָא יַעְבֵּץ
לֵאלֹהֵי יִשְׂרָאֵל לֵאמֹר אִם־
בָּרֵךְ תְּבָרְכֵנִי וְהִרְבִּיתָ אֶת־
גְּבוּלִי וְהָיְתָה יָדְךָ עִמִּי וְעָשִׂיתָ
מֵּרָעָה לְבִלְתִּי עָצְבִּי וַיָּבֵא
אֱלֹהִים אֶת־אֲשֶׁר שָׁאָל׃
11 וּכְלוּב אֲחִי־שׁוּחָה הוֹלִיד
אֶת־מְחִיר הוּא אֲבִי אֶשְׁתּוֹן׃
12 וְאֶשְׁתּוֹן הוֹלִיד אֶת־בֵּית רָפָא
וְאֶת־פָּסֵחַ וְאֶת־תְּחִנָּה אֲבִי
עִיר־נָחָשׁ אֵלֶּה אַנְשֵׁי רֵכָה׃
13 וּבְנֵי קְנַז עָתְנִיאֵל וּשְׂרָיָה וּבְנֵי
14 עָתְנִיאֵל חֲתַת׃ וּמְעוֹנֹתַי
הוֹלִיד אֶת־עָפְרָה וּשְׂרָיָה

v. 13. פתח בס״פ

one of those enumerated in the preceding two verses.

9. *Jabez*. The note on *Koz* applies also to *Jabez*.

with pain. The root of *Jabez* is *ebz* which by transposition yields the root *ezb*, 'sorrow, pain.'

10. *Oh that . . . bless me indeed*. A Hebrew idiom which is literally 'if to bless Thou wilt bless me.' The reason for this prayer may have been to avert the ominous meaning of his name.

work deliverance. lit. 'Thou wouldest do from evil,' i.e. act so that evil does not befall me.

11f. The Recah families.

11. *Chelub*. Cf. the name *Chelubai* in ii. 9. He, too, has not been previously mentioned.

13-15. The Kenaz families.

13. *Othniel*. He was a nephew of Caleb and the first judge in Israel (Judg. iii. 9ff.).

sons of Othniel: Hathath. The plural *sons* implies that *Hathath* was the name of a family.

14. *Meonothai*. He was possibly a son of Othniel and one of the *Hathath* clan.

begot Joab the father of Ge-
harashim; for they were craftsmen.
15. And the sons of Caleb the son
of Jephunneh: Iru, Elah, and
Naam; and the sons of Elah: Kenaz.
16. And the sons of Jehallelel:
Ziph, and Ziphah, Tiria, and Asarel.
17. And the sons of Ezrah: Jether,
and Mered, and Epher, and Jalon.
And she bore Miriam, and Shammai, and Ishbah the father of
Eshtemoa—18. and his wife Hajehudijah bore Jered the father of Gedor,
and Heber the father of Soco, and
Jekuthiel the father of Zanoah—and
these are the sons of Bithiah the
daughter of Pharaoh, whom Mered
took.
19. And the sons of the wife of
Hodiah, the sister of Naham, were
the father of Keilah the Garmite,
and Eshtemoa the Maacathite. 20.
And the sons of Shimon: Amnon,

הוֹלִיד אֶת־יוֹאָב אֲבִי גֵּיא
15 חֲרָשִׁים כִּי חֲרָשִׁים הָיוּ׃ וּבְנֵי
כָּלֵב בֶּן־יְפֻנֶּה עִירוּ אֵלָה
וָנָעַם וּבְנֵי אֵלָה וּקְנַז׃
16 וּבְנֵי יְהַלֶּלְאֵל זִיף וְזִיפָה
17 תִּירְיָא וַאֲשַׂרְאֵל׃ וּבֶן־עֶזְרָה
יֶתֶר וּמֶרֶד וְעֵפֶר וְיָלוֹן וַתַּהַר
אֶת־מִרְיָם וְאֶת־שַׁמַּי וְאֶת־
18 יִשְׁבָּח אֲבִי אֶשְׁתְּמֹעַ׃ וְאִשְׁתּוֹ
הַיְהֻדִיָּה יָלְדָה אֶת־יֶרֶד אֲבִי
גְדֹר וְאֶת־חֶבֶר אֲבִי שׂוֹכוֹ
וְאֶת־יְקוּתִיאֵל אֲבִי זָנוֹחַ
וְאֵלֶּה בְּנֵי בִּתְיָה בַת־פַּרְעֹה
אֲשֶׁר לָקַח מָרֶד׃
19 וּבְנֵי אֵשֶׁת הוֹדִיָּה אֲחוֹת נַחַם
אֲבִי קְעִילָה הַגַּרְמִי וְאֶשְׁתְּמֹעַ
20 הַמַּעֲכָתִי׃ וּבְנֵי שִׁימוֹן אַמְנוֹן

v. 15. פתח בס״פ

father. Or, 'governor.'

Ge-harashim. The name means 'valley of the craftsmen.' It was located near Lod (Lydda) (cf. Neh. xi. 35).

for they were craftsmen. The occupation of the inhabitants gave the place its name.

15. *sons of Elah: Kenaz.* The Hebrew is *Ukenaz* as distinct from *Kenaz* in verse 13.

16-20. Some brief genealogies disconnected from the main genealogical line.

16. *Ziph.* This is a place name (cf. 1 Sam. xxiii. 15) in Judah.

17. *she bore.* The antecedent of *she* is wanting in this verse and is presumed by some to be Bithia of verse 18, the wife of Mered.

18. *his wife.* The pronoun refers to Mered.

Hajehudijah. i.e. 'the Jewess,' as opposed to *the daughter of Pharaoh,* his Egyptian wife.

and these are. Referring to the three sons named at the end of verse 17.

19. *father of Keilah.* The first word probably signifies 'governor,' Keilah being a town which was rescued by David from Philistine attack (1 Sam. xxiii. 1ff.).

Eshtemoa the Maacathite. Distinguished from the *Eshtemoa* of verse 17.

and Rinnah, Benhanan, and Tilon.
And the sons of Ishi: Zoheth, and
Ben-zoheth.
21. The sons of Shelah the son of
Judah: Er the father of Lecah, and
Ladah the father of Mareshah, and
the families of the house of them
that wrought fine linen, of the house
of Ashbea; 22. and Jokim, and the
men of Cozeba, and Joash, and
Saraph, who had dominion in
Moab, and Jashubi-lehem. And the
records are ancient. 23. These were
the potters, and those that dwelt
among plantations and hedges; there
they dwelt occupied in the king's
work.
24. The sons of Simeon: Nemuel,
and Jamin, Jarib, Zerah, Shaul;
25. Shallum his son, Mibsam his

וְרִנָּה בֶּן־חָנָן וְתִוֹלוֹן וּבְנֵי
יִשְׁעִי זוֹחֵת וּבֶן־זוֹחֵת׃
21 בְּנֵי שֵׁלָה בֶן־יְהוּדָה עֵר אֲבִי
לֵכָה וְלַעְדָּה אֲבִי מָרֵשָׁה
וּמִשְׁפְּחוֹת בֵּית־עֲבֹדַת הַבֻּץ
22 לְבֵית אַשְׁבֵּעַ׃ וְיוֹקִים וְאַנְשֵׁי
כֹזֵבָא וְיוֹאָשׁ וְשָׂרָף אֲשֶׁר־
בָּעֲלוּ לְמוֹאָב וְיָשֻׁבִי לָחֶם
23 וְהַדְּבָרִים עַתִּיקִים׃ הֵמָּה
הַיּוֹצְרִים וְיֹשְׁבֵי נְטָעִים וּגְדֵרָה
עִם־הַמֶּלֶךְ בִּמְלַאכְתּוֹ יָשְׁבוּ
שָׁם׃
24 בְּנֵי שִׁמְעוֹן נְמוּאֵל וְיָמִין יָרִיב
25 זֶרַח שָׁאוּל׃ שַׁלֻּם בְּנוֹ מִבְשָׂם

v. 20. ותילון ק׳

21-23. The Shelah families.

21. *Shelah.* The third son of Judah (ii. 3).

father. i.e. governor.

Lecah. The place has not been identified.

Mareshah. In southern Judah (cf. 2 Chron. xi. 8).

of the house of Ashbea. Or, 'of Beth-ashbea,' a place of unknown location.

22. *and Jokim,* etc. The verse continues the names of Shelah's descendants.

who had dominion in Moab. The date is not stated, but it may be presumed to have occurred in the reign of David. According to the Targum, the verb for *had dominion* (*ba'alu*) means 'married,' Joash being identified with Mahlon and Saraph with Chilion (Ruth i. 2) who married Orpah and Ruth.

and the records are ancient. The significance of this clause is uncertain. It may be the Chronicler's note on his reference to a domination of Moab of which there is no Biblical record.

23. *and those . . . hedges.* This is the rendering of R.V. margin which agrees with the Jewish commentators, but R.V. has 'and the inhabitants of Netaim and Gederah.'

occupied in the king's work. lit. 'with the king in his work'; they laboured on the royal estates.

24-27. The Simeon families. They are recorded immediately after those of Judah because the two tribes were closely connected.

24. *Nemuel,* etc. In Gen. xlvi. 10 and Exod. vi. 15 the list reads: Jemuel, Jamin, Ohad, Jachin, Zohar and Shaul *the son of a Canaanitish woman.* In Num. xxvi. 12 the first name is *Nemuel* as here.

son, Mishma his son. 26. And the sons of Mishma: Hammuel his son, Zaccur his son, Shimei his son. 27. And Shimei had sixteen sons and six daughters; but his brethren had not many children, neither did all their family multiply, like to the children of Judah.

28. And they dwelt at Beer-sheba, and Moladah, and Hazar-shual; 29. and at Bilhah, and at Ezem, and at Tolad; 30. and at Bethuel, and at Hormah, and at Ziklag; 31. and at Beth-marcaboth, and Hazar-susim, and at Beth-biri, and at Shaaraim. These were their cities unto the reign of David. 32. And their villages were Etam, and Ain, Rimmon, and Tochen, and Ashan, five cities; 33. and all their villages that were round about the same cities, unto Baal. These were their habitations, and they have their genealogy.

26 בְּנוֹ מִשְׁמָע בְּנוֹ׃ וּבְנֵי מִשְׁמָע
חַמּוּאֵל בְּנוֹ זַכּוּר בְּנוֹ שִׁמְעִי
27 בְּנוֹ׃ וּלְשִׁמְעִי בָּנִים שִׁשָּׁה עָשָׂר
וּבָנוֹת שֵׁשׁ וּלְאֶחָיו אֵין בָּנִים
רַבִּים וְכֹל מִשְׁפַּחְתָּם לֹא
הִרְבּוּ עַד־בְּנֵי יְהוּדָה׃
28 וַיֵּשְׁבוּ בִּבְאֵר־שֶׁבַע וּמוֹלָדָה
29 וַחֲצַר שׁוּעָל׃ וּבְבִלְהָה
30 וּבְעֶצֶם וּבְתוֹלָד׃ וּבִבְתוּאֵל
31 וּבְחָרְמָה וּבְצִיקְלָג׃ וּבְבֵית
מַרְכָּבוֹת וּבַחֲצַר סוּסִים
וּבְבֵית בִּרְאִי וּבְשַׁעֲרָיִם אֵלֶּה
עָרֵיהֶם עַד־מְלֹךְ דָּוִיד׃
32 וְחַצְרֵיהֶם עֵיטָם וָעַיִן רִמּוֹן
33 וְתֹכֶן וְעָשָׁן עָרִים חָמֵשׁ׃ וְכָל־
חַצְרֵיהֶם אֲשֶׁר סְבִיבוֹת
הֶעָרִים הָאֵלֶּה עַד־בָּעַל זֹאת
מוֹשְׁבֹתָם וְהִתְיַחְשָׂם לָהֶם׃

25. *Mibsam . . . Mishma.* These names were included in the Ishmaelite genealogy (i. 29f.).

27. *their family.* viz. the Simeonites.

like. lit. 'unto,' i.e. to the extent of.

28-33. The Simeonite territory (cf. Josh. xix. 2-8).

29. *Bilhah . . . Tolad.* In Josh. xix. 3f. the names are *Balah* and *Eltolad.*

31. *Hazar-susim,* etc. In Josh. xix. 5f. the names occur as *Hazar-susah, Beth-lebaoth* and *Sharuhen.*

unto the reign of David. Subsequently some of the cities passed out of the possession of the Simeonites whose numbers dwindled.

32. *Etam.* Not included in Josh. xix. 7 which also has *Ether* for *Tochen.*

five cities. i.e. 'open cities' or 'villages,' *chatserim* as they are described at the beginning of the verse.

33. *unto Baal.* In Josh. xix. 8 *to Baalath-beer, as far as Ramah of the South.*

34-43. Simeonite migrations and exploits.

34. And Meshobab, and Jamlech, and Joshah the son of Amaziah; 35. and Joel, and Jehu the son of Joshibiah, the son of Seraiah, the son of Asiel; 36. and Elioenai, and Jaakobah, and Jeshohaiah, and Asaiah, and Adiel, and Jesimiel, and Benaiah; 37. and Ziza the son of Shiphi, the son of Allon, the son of Jedaiah, the son of Shimri, the son of Shemaiah; 38. these mentioned by name were princes in their families; and their fathers' houses increased greatly. 39. And they went to the entrance of Gedor, even unto the east side of the valley, to seek pasture for their flocks. 40. And they found fat pasture and good, and the land was wide, and quiet, and peaceable; for they that dwelt there aforetime were of Ham. 41. And these written by name came in the days of Hezekiah king of Judah, and smote their tents, and the Meunim that were found there,

34 וּמְשׁוֹבָב וְיַמְלֵךְ וְיוֹשָׁה בֶּן־
35 אֲמַצְיָה׃ וְיוֹאֵל וְיֵהוּא בֶּן־
יוֹשִׁבְיָה בֶּן־שְׂרָיָה בֶּן־
36 עֲשִׂיאֵל׃ וְאֶלְיוֹעֵינַי וְיַעֲקֹבָה
וִישׁוֹחָיָה וַעֲשָׂיָה וַעֲדִיאֵל
37 וִישִׂימִאֵל וּבְנָיָה׃ וְזִיזָא בֶּן־
שִׁפְעִי בֶן־אַלּוֹן בֶּן־יְדָיָה בֶּן־
38 שִׁמְרִי בֶּן־שְׁמַעְיָה׃ אֵלֶּה
הַבָּאִים בְּשֵׁמוֹת נְשִׂיאִים
בְּמִשְׁפְּחוֹתָם וּבֵית אֲבוֹתֵיהֶם
39 פָּרְצוּ לָרוֹב׃ וַיֵּלְכוּ לִמְבוֹא
גְדֹר עַד לְמִזְרַח הַגָּיְא לְבַקֵּשׁ
40 מִרְעֶה לְצֹאנָם׃ וַיִּמְצְאוּ
מִרְעֶה שָׁמֵן וָטוֹב וְהָאָרֶץ
רַחֲבַת יָדַיִם וְשֹׁקֶטֶת וּשְׁלֵוָה
כִּי מִן־חָם הַיֹּשְׁבִים שָׁם
41 לְפָנִים׃ וַיָּבֹאוּ אֵלֶּה
הַכְּתוּבִים בְּשֵׁמוֹת בִּימֵי ׀
יְחִזְקִיָּהוּ מֶלֶךְ־יְהוּדָה וַיַּכּוּ
אֶת־אָהֳלֵיהֶם וְאֶת־
הַמְּעִינִים אֲשֶׁר נִמְצְאוּ שָׁמָּה

v. 36. בקצת ספרים ש׳ ימנית v. 41. המעונים ק׳

38. *mentioned by name.* lit. 'that came by names.'

39. *and they went.* Because they had *increased greatly*, they required more land.

Gedor. The locality, which was probably in the south of Judah, has not been identified.

40. *for they . . . of Ham.* A Canaanite tribe which was not attacked by Israel during the conquest of the land and, therefore, felt safe and expected no raids.

41. *these written by name.* They who are enumerated in verses 34ff.

in the days of Hezekiah. No other record of this campaign has been preserved.

the Meunim. Mentioned again in 2 Chron. xxvi. 7; cf. *the children of Meunim*

and destroyed them utterly, unto this day, and dwelt in their stead; because there was pasture there for their flocks. 42. And some of them, even of the sons of Simeon, five hundred men, went to mount Seir, having for their captains Pelatiah, and Neariah, and Rephaiah, and Uzziel, the sons of Ishi. 43. And they smote the remnant of the Amalekites that escaped, and dwelt there unto this day.

וַיַּחֲרִימֻם עַד־הַיּוֹם הַזֶּה
וַיֵּשְׁבוּ תַּחְתֵּיהֶם כִּי־מִרְעֶה
42 לְצֹאנָם שָׁם׃ וּמֵהֶם ׀ מִן־בְּנֵי
שִׁמְעוֹן הָלְכוּ לְהַר שֵׂעִיר
אֲנָשִׁים חֲמֵשׁ מֵאוֹת וּפְלַטְיָה
וּנְעַרְיָה וּרְפָיָה וְעֻזִּיאֵל בְּנֵי
43 יִשְׁעִי בְּרֹאשָׁם׃ וַיַּכּוּ אֶת־
שְׁאֵרִית הַפְּלֵטָה לַעֲמָלֵק
וַיֵּשְׁבוּ שָׁם עַד הַיּוֹם הַזֶּה׃

5 CHAPTER V ה

1. And the sons of Reuben the first-born of Israel—for he was the first-born; but, forasmuch as he defiled his father's couch, his birthright was given unto the sons of Joseph the son of Israel, yet not so that he was to be reckoned in the genealogy as first-born. 2. For Judah prevailed above his brethren, and of him came he that is the prince; but the birthright was Joseph's—3. the sons of Reuben the first-born of Israel: Hanoch, and Pallu, Hezron, and

1 וּבְנֵי רְאוּבֵן בְּכוֹר־יִשְׂרָאֵל
כִּי־הוּא הַבְּכוֹר וּבְחַלְּלוֹ
יְצוּעֵי אָבִיו נִתְּנָה בְּכֹרָתוֹ לִבְנֵי
יוֹסֵף בֶּן־יִשְׂרָאֵל וְלֹא
2 לְהִתְיַחֵשׂ לַבְּכֹרָה׃ כִּי יְהוּדָה
גָּבַר בְּאֶחָיו וּלְנָגִיד מִמֶּנּוּ
3 וְהַבְּכֹרָה לְיוֹסֵף׃ בְּנֵי רְאוּבֵן
בְּכוֹר יִשְׂרָאֵל חֲנוֹךְ וּפַלּוּא

included among the *Nethinim* who returned to Judea (Ezra ii. 50; Neh. vii. 52). They were apparently an Edomite tribe who dwelt in the south of the Dead Sea.

42. *having for their captains.* lit. 'at their head.'

43. *that escaped.* From Saul's war of extermination (1 Sam. xv. 4ff.).

dwelt there. In mount Seir or the land of Edom. The Amalekites were descendants of Esau or Edom (cf. Gen. xxxvi. 1, 12).

CHAPTER V

THE TRIBES OF TRANSJORDAN

1-10. The families of Reuben.

1. *he defiled,* etc. Cf. Gen. xxxv. 22, xlix. 4.

not so that he. viz. Joseph; although the *birthright* was transferred to him, he could not be described as the *first-born.* The genealogy of Reuben who was in fact the first-born is therefore dealt with first.

Carmi. 4. The sons of Joel: Shemaiah his son, Gog his son, Shimei his son; 5. Micah his son, Reaiah his son, Baal his son; 6. Beerah his son, whom Tillegath-pilneser king of Assyria carried away captive; he was prince of the Reubenites. 7. And his brethren by their families, when the genealogy of their generations was reckoned: the chief Jeiel, and Zechariah, 8. and Bela the son of Azaz, the son of Shema, the son of Joel, who dwelt in Aroer, even unto Nebo and Baal-meon; 9. and eastward he dwelt even unto the entrance of the wilderness from the river Euphrates; because their cattle were multiplied in the land of Gilead. 10. And in the days of Saul they made war with the Hagrites, who fell by their hand; and they dwelt in their tents throughout all the land east of Gilead.

11. And the sons of Gad dwelt over against them, in the land of Bashan unto Salcah: 12. Joel the

4 חֶצְרוֹן וְכַרְמִי׃ בְּנֵי יוֹאֵל
שְׁמַעְיָה בְנוֹ גּוֹג בְּנוֹ שִׁמְעִי בְנוֹ׃
5 מִיכָה בְנוֹ רְאָיָה בְנוֹ בַּעַל בְּנוֹ׃
6 בְּאֵרָה בְנוֹ אֲשֶׁר הֶגְלָה תִּלְּגַת
פִּלְנְאֶסֶר מֶלֶךְ אַשֻּׁר הוּא נָשִׂיא
7 לָראוּבֵנִי׃ וְאֶחָיו לְמִשְׁפְּחֹתָיו
בְּהִתְיַחֵשׂ לְתֹלְדוֹתָם הָרֹאשׁ
8 יְעִיאֵל וּזְכַרְיָהוּ׃ וּבֶלַע בֶּן־
עָזָז בֶּן־שֶׁמַע בֶּן־יוֹאֵל הוּא
יוֹשֵׁב בַּעֲרֹעֵר וְעַד־נְבוֹ וּבַעַל
9 מְעוֹן׃ וְלַמִּזְרָח יָשַׁב עַד־
לְבוֹא מִדְבָּרָה לְמִן־הַנָּהָר
פְּרָת כִּי מִקְנֵיהֶם רָבוּ בְּאֶרֶץ
10 גִּלְעָד׃ וּבִימֵי שָׁאוּל עָשׂוּ
מִלְחָמָה עִם־הַהַגְרִאִים
וַיִּפְּלוּ בְּיָדָם וַיֵּשְׁבוּ בְּאָהֳלֵיהֶם
עַל־כָּל־פְּנֵי מִזְרָח לַגִּלְעָד׃
11 וּבְנֵי־גָד לְנֶגְדָּם יָשְׁבוּ בְּאֶרֶץ
12 הַבָּשָׁן עַד־סַלְכָה׃ יוֹאֵל

2. ***Judah prevailed above his brethren.*** Cf. what Jacob said of him in Gen. xlix. 8.
he that is the prince. King David.

3. The same four names occur in Gen. xlvi. 9; Exod. vi. 14.

6. *Tillegath-pilneser.* In 2 Kings xv. 29 the name is spelt *Tiglath-pileser.* The carrying of Beerah into captivity is not recorded elsewhere.

8. *Aroer.* The modern *Ar'air,* near the valley of Arnon. It formerly belonged to Sihon king of the Amorites, but it was allotted by Moses to the Reubenites (Josh. xiii. 15).

Baal-meon. Called *Beth-baal-meon* in Josh. xiii. 17.

10. *made war with the Hagrites.* An Arab tribe, descendants of Hagar. Fuller details of the battle are given in verses 18-22.

11-17. The families of Gad.

11. *over against them.* viz. the Reubenites.

the land of Bashan. In Transjordan

chief, and Shapham the second, and Janai, and Shaphat in Bashan; 13. and their brethren of their fathers' houses: Michael, and Meshullam, and Sheba, and Jorai, and Jacan, and Zia, and Eber, seven. 14. These were the sons of Abihail the son of Huri, the son of Jaroah, the son of Gilead, the son of Michael, the son of Jehishai, the son of Jahdo, the son of Buz; 15. Ahi the son of Abdiel, the son of Guni, chief of their fathers' houses. 16. And they dwelt in Gilead in Bashan, and in the towns thereof, and in all the open lands of the plain, upon their borders. 17. All these were reckoned by genealogies in the days of Jotham king of Judah, and in the days of Jeroboam king of Israel.

18. The sons of Reuben, and the Gadites, and the half-tribe of Manasseh, as many as were valiant men, men able to bear buckler and sword, and to shoot with bow, and skilful in war, were forty and four

הָרֹאשׁ וְשָׁפָם הַמִּשְׁנֶה וְיַעְנַי
וְשָׁפָט בַּבָּשָׁן׃ וַאֲחֵיהֶם לְבֵית 13
אֲבוֹתֵיהֶם מִיכָאֵל וּמְשֻׁלָּם
וְשֶׁבַע וְיוֹרַי וְיַעְכָּן וְזִיעַ וָעֵבֶר
שִׁבְעָה׃ אֵלֶּה ׀ בְּנֵי אֲבִיחַיִל 14
בֶּן־חוּרִי בֶּן־יָרוֹחַ בֶּן־גִּלְעָד
בֶּן־מִיכָאֵל בֶּן־יְשִׁישַׁי בֶּן־
יַחְדּוֹ בֶּן־בּוּז׃ אֲחִי בֶּן 15
עַבְדִּיאֵל בֶּן־גּוּנִי רֹאשׁ לְבֵית
אֲבוֹתָם׃ וַיֵּשְׁבוּ בַּגִּלְעָד בַּבָּשָׁן 16
וּבִבְנֹתֶיהָ וּבְכָל־מִגְרְשֵׁי שָׁרוֹן
עַל־תּוֹצְאוֹתָם׃ כֻּלָּם 17
הִתְיַחְשׂוּ בִּימֵי יוֹתָם מֶלֶךְ־
יְהוּדָה וּבִימֵי יָרָבְעָם מֶלֶךְ־
יִשְׂרָאֵל׃
בְּנֵי־רְאוּבֵן וְגָדִי וַחֲצִי שֵׁבֶט־ 18
מְנַשֶּׁה מִן־בְּנֵי־חַיִל אֲנָשִׁים
נֹשְׂאֵי מָגֵן וְחֶרֶב וְדֹרְכֵי קֶשֶׁת
וּלְמוּדֵי מִלְחָמָה אַרְבָּעִים

between mount Hermon on the north and the river Jabbok on the south, the western boundary being the Sea of Galilee.

Salcah. The ruins of Salkhad, east of Botsra and south of Jebel Hauran, are thought to mark its site.

14. *Jehishai.* A misprint in A.J. for *Jeshishai.*

16. *in Gilead in Bashan.* This can only mean that the tribe of Gad inhabited part of Gilead, Reuben's territory (verse 9), as well as Bashan (verse 11).

17. *in the days of Jotham . . . and . . . Jeroboam.* The latter years of the reign of Jeroboam II (785-745) coincided with the regency of Jotham, when his father Azariah was a leper, which ended in 739 (cf. 2 Kings xv. 5).

18-22. The war with the Hagrites.

18. *as many as were.* lit. 'from.'

forty and four thousand seven hundred and threescore. This number of warriors from the Transjordan tribes crossed the Jordan from the east to the west in the

thousand seven hundred and threescore, that were able to go forth to
war. 19. And they made war with
the Hagrites, with Jetur, and
Naphish, and Nodab. 20. And they
were helped against them, and the
Hagrites were delivered into their
hand, and all that were with them;
for they cried to God in the battle,
and He was entreated of them,
because they put their trust in Him.
21. And they took away their cattle:
of their camels fifty thousand, and
of sheep two hundred and fifty
thousand, and of asses two thousand;
and of souls of men a hundred
thousand. 22. For there fell many
slain, because the war was of God.
And they dwelt in their stead until
the captivity.

23. And the children of the half-
tribe of Manasseh dwelt in the land,
from Bashan unto Baal-hermon and
Senir and mount Hermon, where
they increased. 24. And these were
the heads of their fathers' houses:
Epher, and Ishi, and Eliel, and

וְאַרְבָּעָה אֶלֶף וּשְׁבַע־מֵאוֹת
19 וְשִׁשִּׁים יֹצְאֵי צָבָא׃ וַיַּעֲשׂוּ
מִלְחָמָה עִם־הַהַגְרִיאִים
20 וִיטוּר וְנָפִישׁ וְנוֹדָב׃ וַיֵּעָזְרוּ
עֲלֵיהֶם וַיִּנָּתְנוּ בְיָדָם
הַהַגְרִיאִים וְכֹל שֶׁעִמָּהֶם כִּי
לֵאלֹהִים זָעֲקוּ בַּמִּלְחָמָה
וְנַעְתּוֹר לָהֶם כִּי־בָטְחוּ בוֹ׃
21 וַיִּשְׁבּוּ מִקְנֵיהֶם גְּמַלֵּיהֶם
חֲמִשִּׁים אֶלֶף וְצֹאן מָאתַיִם
וַחֲמִשִּׁים אֶלֶף וַחֲמוֹרִים
אַלְפָּיִם וְנֶפֶשׁ אָדָם מֵאָה
22 אָלֶף׃ כִּי־חֲלָלִים רַבִּים
נָפָלוּ כִּי מֵהָאֱלֹהִים הַמִּלְחָמָה
וַיֵּשְׁבוּ תַחְתֵּיהֶם עַד־הַגֹּלָה׃
23 וּבְנֵי חֲצִי שֵׁבֶט מְנַשֶּׁה יָשְׁבוּ
בָּאָרֶץ מִבָּשָׁן עַד־בַּעַל
חֶרְמוֹן וּשְׂנִיר וְהַר־חֶרְמוֹן
24 הֵמָּה רָבוּ׃ וְאֵלֶּה רָאשֵׁי בֵית־
אֲבוֹתָם וְעֵפֶר וְיִשְׁעִי וֶאֱלִיאֵל

days of Joshua to assist in the conquest of the land (Josh. iv. 13).

19. *Jetur*, etc. Three of Ishmael's sons bore the names of *Jetur*, *Naphish* and *Kedem* (i. 31).

20. *they were helped.* By God.

21. *souls of men.* Taken captive.

22. *the war was of God.* i.e. commanded by Him, as was said of the war against the Amalekites (1 Sam. xv. 2f.).

23f. Manasseh of Transjordan.

23. *Baal-hermon.* Possibly the town Banias on the east slope of mount Hermon. In Judg. iii. 3 the name is that of a mountain.

Senir. This was the name the Amorites gave to Hermon (Deut. iii. 9).

where they increased. The first word is not in the text.

24. *Epher.* The Hebrew is *weëpher*, R.V. 'even Epher.'

Azriel, and Jeremiah, and Hodaviah, and Jahdiel, mighty men of valour, famous men, heads of their fathers' houses.

25. And they broke faith with the God of their fathers, and went astray after the gods of the peoples of the land, whom God destroyed before them. 26. And the God of Israel stirred up the spirit of Pul king of Assyria, and the spirit of Tillegath-pilneser king of Assyria, and he carried them away, even the Reubenites, and the Gadites, and the half-tribe of Manasseh, and brought them unto Halah, and Habor, and Hara, and to the river of Gozan, unto this day.

27. The sons of Levi: Gershon, Kohath, and Merari. 28. And the sons of Kohath: Amram, Izhar, and Hebron, and Uzziel. 29. And the

וְעַזְרִיאֵל וְיִרְמְיָה וְהוֹדַוְיָה
וְיַחְדִּיאֵל אֲנָשִׁים גִּבּוֹרֵי חַיִל
אַנְשֵׁי שֵׁמוֹת רָאשִׁים לְבֵית
אֲבוֹתָם׃
25 וַיִּמְעֲלוּ בֵּאלֹהֵי אֲבֹתֵיהֶם וַיִּזְנוּ
אַחֲרֵי אֱלֹהֵי עַמֵּי־הָאָרֶץ
אֲשֶׁר־הִשְׁמִיד אֱלֹהִים
26 מִפְּנֵיהֶם׃ וַיָּעַר אֱלֹהֵי יִשְׂרָאֵל
אֶת־רוּחַ ׀ פּוּל מֶלֶךְ־אַשּׁוּר
וְאֶת־רוּחַ תִּלְּגַת פִּלְנֶסֶר מֶלֶךְ
אַשּׁוּר וַיַּגְלֵם לָראוּבֵנִי וְלַגָּדִי
וְלַחֲצִי שֵׁבֶט מְנַשֶּׁה וַיְבִיאֵם
לַחְלַח וְחָבוֹר וְהָרָא וּנְהַר גּוֹזָן
עַד הַיּוֹם הַזֶּה׃
27 בְּנֵי לֵוִי גֵּרְשׁוֹן קְהָת וּמְרָרִי׃
28 וּבְנֵי קְהָת עַמְרָם יִצְהָר
29 וְחֶבְרוֹן וְעֻזִּיאֵל׃ וּבְנֵי עַמְרָם

25f. The captivity of the Transjordan tribes.

26. *Pul . . . Tillegath-pilneser.* For the latter, see on verse 6, and for the former, cf. 2 Kings xv. 19. From the Babylonian inscriptions it appears that both names refer to the same king who was originally known as *Pulu,* from which is derived the Hebrew *Pul.* It has been conjectured that he assumed the second name when he usurped the Assyrian throne in 745 B.C.E. He reigned until 727.

Halah . . . Gozan. In 2 Kings xvii. 6 the reading is *Halah and in Habor, on the river of Gozan, and in the cities of the Medes. Halah* is a district in northern Mesopotamia. *Habor* is the river called by the Greeks *Chaboras,* a northern tributary of the Euphrates. *Hara* is unknown, and *Gozan* is a river in Mesopotamia.

27-41. (In the English version, vi. 1-15.) The genealogy of Levi including the High Priests down to the captivity. The list is not exhaustive.

27. *sons of Levi . . . Merari.* So also in Gen. xlvi. 11; Exod. vi. 16; Num. iii. 17, xxvi. 57.

28. *sons of Kohath . . . Uzziel.* So Exod. vi. 18; Num. iii. 19. The descendants of Kohath are here given before those of his elder brother Gershon (vi. 1ff.) as a remark of respect to Moses and Aaron who are included.

children of Amram: Aaron, and Moses, and Miriam. And the sons of Aaron: Nadab and Abihu, Eleazar and Ithamar. 30. Eleazar begot Phinehas, Phinehas begot Abishua; 31. and Abishua begot Bukki, and Bukki begot Uzzi; 32. and Uzzi begot Zerahiah, and Zerahiah begot Meraioth; 33. Meraioth begot Amariah, and Amariah begot Ahitub; 34. and Ahitub begot Zadok, and Zadok begot Ahimaaz; 35. and Ahimaaz begot Azariah, and Azariah begot Johanan; 36. and Johanan begot Azariah—he it is that executed the priest's office in the house that Solomon built in Jerusalem—37. and Azariah begot Amariah, and Amariah begot Ahitub; 38. and Ahitub

אַהֲרֹן וּמֹשֶׁה וּמִרְיָם וּבְנֵי
אַהֲרֹן נָדָב וַאֲבִיהוּא אֶלְעָזָר
30 וְאִיתָמָר׃ אֶלְעָזָר הוֹלִיד
אֶת־פִּינְחָס פִּינְחָס הֹלִיד
31 אֶת־אֲבִישׁוּעַ׃ וַאֲבִישׁוּעַ
הוֹלִיד אֶת־בֻּקִּי וּבֻקִּי הוֹלִיד
32 אֶת־עֻזִּי׃ וְעֻזִּי הוֹלִיד אֶת־
זְרַחְיָה וּזְרַחְיָה הוֹלִיד אֶת־
33 מְרָיוֹת׃ מְרָיוֹת הוֹלִיד אֶת־
אֲמַרְיָה וַאֲמַרְיָה הוֹלִיד אֶת־
34 אֲחִיטוּב׃ וַאֲחִיטוּב הוֹלִיד
אֶת־צָדוֹק וְצָדוֹק הוֹלִיד
35 אֶת־אֲחִימָעַץ׃ וַאֲחִימַעַץ
הוֹלִיד אֶת־עֲזַרְיָה וַעֲזַרְיָה
36 הוֹלִיד אֶת־יוֹחָנָן׃ וְיוֹחָנָן
הוֹלִיד אֶת־עֲזַרְיָה הוּא אֲשֶׁר
כִּהֵן בַּבַּיִת אֲשֶׁר־בָּנָה
37 שְׁלֹמֹה בִּירוּשָׁלִָם׃ וַיּוֹלֶד
עֲזַרְיָה אֶת־אֲמַרְיָה וַאֲמַרְיָה
הוֹלִיד אֶת־אֲחִיטוּב׃

29. *Aaron, and Moses.* So in Exod. vi. 20. Aaron was the elder and is given precedence. Elsewhere Moses usually appears first on account of his greater importance.

Nadab . . . Ithamar. So Exod. vi. 23. On the premature death of the two elder sons, cf. Lev. x. 1ff.

30. *Phinehas.* For his religious zeal and God's reward for it, cf. Num. xxv. 7ff.; for his military and civic leadership, cf. Num. xxxi. 6; Josh. xxii. 13ff.

34. *Zadok.* In 2 Sam. viii. 17 Zadok and Abiathar are mentioned as David's *priests.*

Ahimaaz. In David's flight from Absalom, Ahimaaz acted as his informant (2 Sam. xv. 27, xviii. 19ff.).

36. *Azariah . . . priest's office.* The allusion is held by some commentators to be to the incident described in 2 Chron. xxvi. 17ff.

37. *Amariah.* A High Priest of that

begot Zadok, and Zadok begot Shallum; 39. and Shallum begot Hilkiah, and Hilkiah begot Azariah; 40. and Azariah begot Seraiah, and Seraiah begot Jehozadak; 41. and Jehozadak went into captivity, when the LORD carried away Judah and Jerusalem by the hand of Nebuchadnezzar.

38 וַאֲחִיטוּב הוֹלִיד אֶת־צָדוֹק
וְצָדוֹק הוֹלִיד אֶת־שַׁלּוּם׃
39 וְשַׁלּוּם הוֹלִיד אֶת־חִלְקִיָּה
וְחִלְקִיָּה הוֹלִיד אֶת־עֲזַרְיָה׃
40 וַעֲזַרְיָה הוֹלִיד אֶת־שְׂרָיָה
וּשְׂרָיָה הוֹלִיד אֶת־יְהוֹצָדָק׃
41 וִיהוֹצָדָק הָלַךְ בְּהַגְלוֹת יְהוָה
אֶת־יְהוּדָה וִירוּשָׁלִָם בְּיַד
נְבֻכַדְנֶאצַּר׃

6 CHAPTER VI ו

1. The sons of Levi: Gershom, Kohath, and Merari. 2. And these are the names of the sons of Gershom: Libni, and Shimei. 3. And the sons of Kohath were Amram, and Izhar, and Hebron, and Uzziel.

1 בְּנֵי לֵוִי גֵּרְשֹׁם קְהָת וּמְרָרִי׃
2 וְאֵלֶּה שְׁמוֹת בְּנֵי־גֵרְשׁוֹם לִבְנִי
3 וְשִׁמְעִי׃ וּבְנֵי קְהָת עַמְרָם
וְיִצְהָר וְחֶבְרוֹן וְעֻזִּיאֵל׃

name officiated during the reign of Jehoshaphat (2 Chron. xix. 11), but he could not have been this Amariah if the identification of Azariah in the previous verse is correct.

39. *Hilkiah.* He was the High Priest who discovered the Book of the Law in Josiah's reign (cf. 2 Kings xxii. 8).

40. *Jehozadak.* His son Jeshua (Joshua) was the first High Priest after the return from Babylon and the religious leader of the people (cf. Hag. i. 1; Ezra iii. 2, 8, v. 2).

41. *went into captivity.* The last two words are not in the text.

Judah and Jerusalem. i.e. the inhabitants of the land of Judah and in particular those of Jerusalem the capital.

by the hand of Nebuchadnezzar. In the year 587 B.C.E. after the hopeless revolt of king Zedekiah.

CHAPTER VI

THE LEVITICAL FAMILIES AND THEIR CITIES

1-15. (In the English version vi. 16-30.) The descendants of Levi (cf. Exod. vi. 16-24; Num. iii. 17-21).

1-4. Levi's sons and grandsons. Verses 1 and 3 are a repetition of v. 27f. and the others are an expansion of the previous record.

1. *Gershom.* In v. 27 the name is spelt *Gershon*, the *mem* and *nun* being interchangeable. The latter is the more common form to distinguish him from Gershom the son of Moses (Exod. ii. 22).

4. The sons of Merari: Mahli, and
Mushi. And these are the families
of the Levites according to their
fathers' houses.
5. Of Gershom: Libni his son,
Jahath his son, Zimmah his son;
6. Joah his son, Iddo his son, Zerah
his son, Jeatherai his son.
7. The sons of Kohath: Amminadab his son, Korah his son, Assir
his son; 8. Elkanah his son, and
Ebiasaph his son, and Assir his son;
9. Tahath his son, Uriel his son,
Uzziah his son, and Shaul his son.
10. And the sons of Elkanah:
Amasai, and Ahimoth. 11. As for
Elkanah: the sons of Elkanah:
Zophai his son, and Nahath his son;
12. Eliab his son, Jeroham his son,
Elkanah his son. 13. And the sons
of Samuel: the first-born Vashni;
then Abiah.
14. The sons of Merari: Mahli;
Libni his son, Shimei his son, Uzzah
his son; 15. Shimea his son, Haggiah
his son, Asaiah his son.

4 בְּנֵי מְרָרִי מַחְלִי וּמֻשִׁי וְאֵלֶּה
מִשְׁפְּחוֹת הַלֵּוִי לַאֲבֹתֵיהֶם׃
5 לְגֵרְשׁוֹם לִבְנִי בְנוֹ יַחַת בְּנוֹ
6 זִמָּה בְנוֹ׃ יוֹאָח בְּנוֹ עִדּוֹ בְנוֹ
זֶרַח בְּנוֹ יְאָתְרַי בְּנוֹ׃
7 בְּנֵי קְהָת עַמִּינָדָב בְּנוֹ קֹרַח
8 בְּנוֹ אַסִּיר בְּנוֹ׃ אֶלְקָנָה בְנוֹ
9 וְאֶבְיָסָף בְּנוֹ וְאַסִּיר בְּנוֹ׃ תַּחַת
בְּנוֹ אוּרִיאֵל בְּנוֹ עֻזִּיָּה בְנוֹ
10 וְשָׁאוּל בְּנוֹ׃ וּבְנֵי אֶלְקָנָה
11 עֲמָשַׂי וַאֲחִימוֹת׃ אֶלְקָנָה בְּנוֹ*
אֶלְקָנָה צוֹפַי בְּנוֹ וְנַחַת בְּנוֹ׃
12 אֱלִיאָב בְּנוֹ יְרֹחָם בְּנוֹ אֶלְקָנָה
13 בְנוֹ׃ וּבְנֵי שְׁמוּאֵל הַבְּכֹר וַשְׁנִי
וַאֲבִיָּה׃
14 בְּנֵי מְרָרִי מַחְלִי לִבְנִי בְנוֹ
15 שִׁמְעִי בְנוֹ עֻזָּה בְנוֹ׃ שִׁמְעָא
בְנוֹ חַגִּיָּה בְנוֹ עֲשָׂיָה בְנוֹ׃

בני ק׳ v. 11.

5f. The descendants of Gershom.

7-13. The descendants of Kohath.

7. *Amminadab.* According to Exod. vi. 23 he was Aaron's father-in-law. On the strength of verse 23 and Num. xvi. 1 it seems that he also bore the name *Izhar*.

8. *Elkanah . . . Ebiasaph.* They, as well as *Assir* (verses 7f.), were the sons of Korah (cf. Exod. vi. 24). This verse is consequently an expansion of verse 7. On another view *Assir* in this verse is the son of Ebiasaph and is to be distinguished from *Assir* in the preceding verse.

11. *Elkanah.* The husband of Hannah and father of Samuel.

13. *Samuel.* The prophet of that name. According to 1 Sam. i. 1 he was an Ephraimite, but the Chronicler gives him Levitical descent to justify his ministry in the Sanctuary.

Vashni . . . Abiah. The first was also named *Joel* (cf. verse 18 and 1 Sam. viii. 2). *Abiah* in A.J. is a misprint for *Abijah*.

14f. The descendants of Merari.

14. *Libni . . . Shimei.* They bore the same names as the sons of Gershom (verse 2).

16. And these are they whom
David set over the service of song
in the house of the LORD, after that
the ark had rest. 17. And they
ministered with song before the
tabernacle of the tent of meeting,
until Solomon had built the house
of the LORD in Jerusalem; and they
took their station at their service
according to their order. 18. And
these are they that took their station,
and their sons. Of the sons of the
Kohathites: Heman the singer, the
son of Joel, the son of Samuel;
19. the son of Elkanah, the son of
Jeroham, the son of Eliel, the son
of Toah; 20. the son of Zuph, the
son of Elkanah, the son of Mahath,
the son of Amasai; 21. the son of
Elkanah, the son of Joel, the son of
Azariah, the son of Zephaniah;
22. the son of Tahath, the son of
Assir, the son of Ebiasaph, the son
of Korah; 23. the son of Izhar, the
son of Kohath, the son of Levi, the
son of Israel. 24. And his brother
Asaph, who stood on his right hand;

16 וְאֵלֶּה אֲשֶׁר הֶעֱמִיד דָּוִיד עַל־
יְדֵי־שִׁיר בֵּית יְהוָה מִמְּנוֹחַ
17 הָאָרוֹן: וַיִּהְיוּ מְשָׁרְתִים לִפְנֵי
מִשְׁכַּן אֹהֶל־מוֹעֵד בַּשִּׁיר
עַד־בְּנוֹת שְׁלֹמֹה אֶת־
בֵּית יְהוָה בִּירוּשָׁלָםִ וַיַּעַמְדוּ
כְמִשְׁפָּטָם עַל־עֲבוֹדָתָם:
18 וְאֵלֶּה הָעֹמְדִים וּבְנֵיהֶם מִבְּנֵי
הַקְּהָתִי הֵימָן הַמְשׁוֹרֵר בֶּן־
19 יוֹאֵל בֶּן־שְׁמוּאֵל: בֶּן־
אֶלְקָנָה בֶּן־יְרֹחָם בֶּן־
20 אֱלִיאֵל בֶּן־תּוֹחַ: בֶּן־צִיף*
בֶּן־אֶלְקָנָה בֶּן־מַחַת בֶּן־
21 עֲמָשָׂי: בֶּן־אֶלְקָנָה בֶּן־יוֹאֵל
22 בֶּן־עֲזַרְיָה בֶּן־צְפַנְיָה: בֶּן־
תַּחַת בֶּן־אַסִּיר בֶּן־אֶבְיָסָף
23 בֶּן־קֹרַח: בֶּן־יִצְהָר בֶּן־
קְהָת בֶּן־לֵוִי בֶּן־יִשְׂרָאֵל:
24 וְאָחִיו אָסָף הָעֹמֵד עַל־יְמִינוֹ

v. 20. צוף ק׳

16-33. The genealogy of Heman, Asaph and Ethan, David's chief musicians.

16. *service of.* lit. 'hands of.'

the ark had rest. In its permanent home, Jerusalem, where it had been brought by David with music and great rejoicing (cf. 2 Sam. vi. 12ff.).

17. *the tent of meeting.* Where David deposited the ark (2 Sam. vi. 17).

18-23. The central choir under the direction of Heman, a descendant of Kohath, a son of Levi.

18. *Joel, the son of Samuel.* See on verse 13.

22. *the son of Korah.* Cf. *the sons of Korah died not* (Num. xxvi. 11) in the rebellion against Moses. A number of Psalms are entitled *of the sons of Korah.*

24-28. Asaph's choir, on the right of Heman. Asaph was also a descendant of Levi through his son Gershom.

24. *his brother.* i.e. his kinsman.

even Asaph the son of Berechiah, the son of Shimea; 25. the son of Michael, the son of Baaseiah, the son of Malchijah; 26. the son of Ethni, the son of Zerah, the son of Adaiah; 27. the son of Ethan, the son of Zimmah, the son of Shimei; 28. the son of Jahath, the son of Gershom, the son of Levi. 29. And on the left hand their brethren the sons of Merari: Ethan the son of Kishi, the son of Abdi, the son of Malluch; 30. the son of Hashabiah, the son of Amaziah, the son of Hilkiah; 31. the son of Amzi, the son of Bani, the son of Shemer; 32. the son of Mahli, the son of Mushi, the son of Merari, the son of Levi. 33. And their brethren the Levites were appointed for all the service of the tabernacle of the house of God.

34. But Aaron and his sons offered upon the altar of burnt-offering, and upon the altar of incense, for all the work of the most holy place, and to make atonement for Israel, according to all that Moses the servant of

אָסָף בֶּן־בֶּרֶכְיָהוּ בֶּן־
25 שִׁמְעָא׃ בֶּן־מִיכָאֵל בֶּן־
26 בַּעֲשֵׂיָה בֶּן־מַלְכִּיָּה׃ בֶּן־
אֶתְנִי בֶן־זֶרַח בֶּן־עֲדָיָה׃
27 בֶּן־אֵיתָן בֶּן־זִמָּה בֶּן־שִׁמְעִי׃
28 בֶּן־יַחַת בֶּן־גֵּרְשֹׁם בֶּן־לֵוִי׃
29 וּבְנֵי מְרָרִי אֲחֵיהֶם עַל־
הַשְּׂמֹאול אֵיתָן בֶּן־קִישִׁי בֶּן־
30 עַבְדִּי בֶּן־מַלּוּךְ׃ בֶּן־חֲשַׁבְיָה
31 בֶּן־אֲמַצְיָה בֶּן־חִלְקִיָּה׃ בֶּן־
אַמְצִי בֶּן־בָּנִי בֶּן־שָׁמֶר׃
32 בֶּן־מַחְלִי בֶּן־מוּשִׁי בֶּן־
33 מְרָרִי בֶּן־לֵוִי׃ וַאֲחֵיהֶם
הַלְוִיִּם נְתוּנִים לְכָל־עֲבוֹדַת
מִשְׁכַּן בֵּית הָאֱלֹהִים׃
34 וְאַהֲרֹן וּבָנָיו מַקְטִירִים עַל־
מִזְבַּח הָעוֹלָה וְעַל־מִזְבַּח
הַקְּטֹרֶת לְכֹל מְלֶאכֶת קֹדֶשׁ
הַקֳּדָשִׁים וּלְכַפֵּר עַל־
יִשְׂרָאֵל כְּכֹל אֲשֶׁר־צִוָּה מֹשֶׁה

29-32. Ethan's choir on the left of Heman. Ethan was a descendant of Merari, the third son of Levi.

29. *their brethren.* See on verse 24.

32. *Mahli, the son of Mushi.* According to verse 4 Mahli was a brother of *Mushi*. The *Mahli* in this verse, a son of *Mushi*, was named after his father's brother.

33. The duties of the other Levites who were not members of the three choirs and acted as gate-keepers and helped with the sacrifices.

34. The Aaronites' duties.

the altar of burnt-offering. Cf. Exod. xxvii. 1ff.

the altar of incense. Cf. Exod. xxx. 1ff.

the work of the most holy place. Which the Levites were not allowed to enter.

make atonement. Cf. Lev. iv. 20, 26, etc., xvi. 1ff.

God had commanded. 35. And these are the sons of Aaron: Eleazar his son, Phinehas his son, Abishua his son; 36. Bukki his son, Uzzi his son, Zerahiah his son; 37. Meraioth his son, Amariah his son, Ahitub his son; 38. Zadok his son, Ahimaaz his son.

39. Now these are their dwelling-places according to their encampments in their borders: to the sons of Aaron, of the families of the Kohathites, for theirs was the [first] lot, 40. to them they gave Hebron in the land of Judah, and the open land round about it; 41. but the fields of the city, and the villages thereof, they gave to Caleb the son of Jephunneh. 42. And to the sons of Aaron they gave the city of refuge, Hebron; Libnah also with the open land about it, and Jattir,

35 עֶבֶד הָאֱלֹהִים׃ וְאֵלֶּה בְּנֵי
אַהֲרֹן אֶלְעָזָר בְּנוֹ פִּינְחָס בְּנוֹ
36 אֲבִישׁוּעַ בְּנוֹ׃ בֻּקִּי בְנוֹ עֻזִּי
37 בְנוֹ זְרַחְיָה בְנוֹ׃ מְרָיוֹת בְּנוֹ
אֲמַרְיָה בְנוֹ אֲחִיטוּב בְּנוֹ׃
38 צָדוֹק בְּנוֹ אֲחִימַעַץ בְּנוֹ׃
39 וְאֵלֶּה מוֹשְׁבוֹתָם לְטִירוֹתָם
בִּגְבוּלָם לִבְנֵי אַהֲרֹן
לְמִשְׁפַּחַת הַקְּהָתִי כִּי לָהֶם
40 הָיָה הַגּוֹרָל׃ וַיִּתְּנוּ לָהֶם
אֶת־חֶבְרוֹן בְּאֶרֶץ יְהוּדָה
וְאֶת־מִגְרָשֶׁיהָ סְבִיבֹתֶיהָ׃
41 וְאֶת־שְׂדֵה הָעִיר וְאֶת־
חֲצֵרֶיהָ נָתְנוּ לְכָלֵב בֶּן־יְפֻנֶּה׃
42 וְלִבְנֵי אַהֲרֹן נָתְנוּ אֶת־עָרֵי
הַמִּקְלָט אֶת־חֶבְרוֹן וְאֶת־
לִבְנָה וְאֶת־מִגְרָשֶׁיהָ וְאֶת־

35-38. A line of priests from Aaron to Ahimaaz. Cf. v. 30-34 of which this section is almost a repetition.

39-66. The forty-eight priestly and Levitical cities.

39-45 (corresponding to Josh. xxi. 10-19). The thirteen priestly cities.

39. *encampments.* The Hebrew *tirah* means 'a circular enclosure' such as is used by nomads.

the [first] lot. The word *first* is added from Josh. xxi. 10.

40. *the open land.* As pasturage for their cattle.

41. *they gave to Caleb.* In accordance with the command of Moses (cf. Judg. i. 20).

42. *and to the sons of Aaron.* The description begun in verse 39 is resumed after the interruption of the last verse which deals with Caleb who was not a priest.

the city of refuge. viz. Hebron (so Josh. xxi. 13, cf. also Josh. xx. 7); the other cities enumerated in the verse were not for refuge. The Hebrew here has the plural (*cities*) but in Joshua the singular.

Libnah. In the south-west of the territory of Judah.

and Eshtemoa with the open land about it; 43. and Hilen with the open land about it, Debir with the open land about it; 44. and Ashan with the open land about it, and Beth-shemesh with the open land about it; 45. and out of the tribe of Benjamin: Geba with the open land about it, and Alemeth with the open land about it, and Anathoth with the open land about it. All their cities throughout their families were thirteen cities.

46. And unto the rest of the sons of Kohath were given by lot, out of the family of the tribe, out of the half-tribe, the half of Manasseh, ten cities. 47. And to the sons of Gershom, according to their families, out of the tribe of Issachar, and out

יַתִּר וְאֶת־אֶשְׁתְּמֹעַ וְאֶת־
43 מִגְרָשֶׁיהָ׃ וְאֶת־חִילֵן וְאֶת־
מִגְרָשֶׁיהָ אֶת־דְּבִיר וְאֶת־
44 מִגְרָשֶׁיהָ׃ וְאֶת־עָשָׁן וְאֶת־
מִגְרָשֶׁיהָ וְאֶת־בֵּית שֶׁמֶשׁ
45 וְאֶת־מִגְרָשֶׁיהָ׃ וּמִמַּטֵּה בִנְיָמִן
אֶת־גֶּבַע וְאֶת־מִגְרָשֶׁיהָ וְאֶת־
עָלֶמֶת וְאֶת־מִגְרָשֶׁיהָ וְאֶת־
עֲנָתוֹת וְאֶת־מִגְרָשֶׁיהָ כָּל־
עָרֵיהֶם שְׁלֹשׁ־עֶשְׂרֵה עִיר
בְּמִשְׁפְּחוֹתֵיהֶם׃
46 וְלִבְנֵי קְהָת הַנּוֹתָרִים
מִמִּשְׁפַּחַת הַמַּטֶּה מִמַּחֲצִית
מַטֵּה חֲצִי מְנַשֶּׁה בַּגּוֹרָל עָרִים
47 עֶשֶׂר׃ וְלִבְנֵי גֵרְשׁוֹם
לְמִשְׁפְּחוֹתָם מִמַּטֵּה יִשָּׂשכָר

Eshtemoa. South of Hebron, now known as *es-Semu'a*.

43. *Hilen.* In Josh. xxi. 15 *Holon.*

Debir. In the Judean hills, south-west of Hebron. It was formerly called *Kiriath-sannah* (Josh. xv. 49) and *Kiriath-sepher* (Judg. i. 11).

44. *Ashan.* In Josh. xxi. 16 *Ain*, after which is added *and Juttah and the open land about it.*

Beth-shemesh. In the north-west of Judah, on the edge of the hill-country, now known as *Ain Shems.*

45. *of the tribe of Benjamin.* The cities mentioned before were taken from the tribes of Judah and Simeon (verse 50).

Geba. In Josh. xxi. 17 *Gibeon and the open land about it* precedes *Geba* which was about six miles from Jerusalem.

Alemeth. *Almon* in Josh. xxi. 18.

Anathoth. The birth-place of Jeremiah (Jer. i. 1), the modern *Anatha*, three miles north-east of Jerusalem.

thirteen cities. So also in Josh. xxi. 19, where thirteen cities are enumerated. Here only eleven of the cities are named, Juttah and Gibeon being omitted.

46-48 (corresponding to Josh. xxi. 20-39). The thirty-five cities given to the families of Kohath, Gershom and Merari. In Josh. the cities are named; here their totals only are stated.

46. *the rest of the sons of Kohath.* Who were not of the Aaronite descendants of Kohath listed above.

were given. Not in the text.

of the tribe of Asher, and out of the tribe of Naphtali, and out of the tribe of Manasseh in Bashan, thirteen cities. 48. Unto the sons of Merari were given by lot, according to their families, out of the tribe of Reuben, and out of the tribe of Gad, and out of the tribe of Zebulun, twelve cities.

49. So the children of Israel gave to the Levites the cities with the open land about them. 50. And they gave by lot out of the tribe of the children of Judah, and out of the tribe of the children of Simeon, and out of the tribe of the children of Benjamin, these cities which are mentioned by name.

51. And some of the families of the sons of Kohath had cities of their borders out of the tribe of Ephraim. 52. And they gave unto them the city of refuge, Shechem in the hill-country of Ephraim with the open land about it; Gezer also with the open land about it; 53. and Jokmeam with the open land about it, and Beth-horon with the open land

וּמִמַּטֵּה אָשֵׁר וּמִמַּטֵּה נַפְתָּלִי
וּמִמַּטֵּה מְנַשֶּׁה בַּבָּשָׁן עָרִים
48 שְׁלֹשׁ עֶשְׂרֵה׃ לִבְנֵי מְרָרִי
לְמִשְׁפְּחוֹתָם מִמַּטֵּה רְאוּבֵן
וּמִמַּטֵּה־גָד וּמִמַּטֵּה זְבוּלֻן
בַּגּוֹרָל עָרִים שְׁתֵּים עֶשְׂרֵה׃
49 וַיִּתְּנוּ בְנֵי־יִשְׂרָאֵל לַלְוִיִּם
אֶת־הֶעָרִים וְאֶת־מִגְרְשֵׁיהֶם׃
50 וַיִּתְּנוּ בַגּוֹרָל מִמַּטֵּה בְנֵי־
יְהוּדָה וּמִמַּטֵּה בְנֵי־שִׁמְעוֹן
וּמִמַּטֵּה בְּנֵי בִנְיָמִן אֵת הֶעָרִים
הָאֵלֶּה אֲשֶׁר־יִקְרְאוּ אֶתְהֶם
בְּשֵׁמוֹת׃
51 וּמִמִּשְׁפְּחוֹת בְּנֵי קְהָת וַיְהִי
עָרֵי גְבוּלָם מִמַּטֵּה אֶפְרָיִם׃
52 וַיִּתְּנוּ לָהֶם אֶת־עָרֵי הַמִּקְלָט
אֶת־שְׁכֶם וְאֶת־מִגְרָשֶׁהָ
בְּהַר אֶפְרָיִם וְאֶת־גֶּזֶר וְאֶת־
53 מִגְרָשֶׁהָ׃ וְאֶת־יָקְמְעָם וְאֶת־
מִגְרָשֶׁהָ וְאֶת־בֵּית חוֹרוֹן

47. *Manasseh in Bashan.* The half tribe in Transjordan.

48. *were given.* Not in the text.

49f. Résumé of part of the record.

50. *mentioned by name.* In the preceding and following verses.

51-55 (corresponding to Josh. xxi. 20-26). A fuller account of the cities of the non-priestly Kohathites.

52. *the city of refuge, Shechem.* The city of Gezer named in this verse was not a city of refuge. The Hebrew here has the plural, but the corresponding passage in Josh. xxi. 21 has *city* in the singular. *Shechem* is the modern *Nablus* in Central Palestine.

Gezer. Its site was discovered in 1873 and is known as *Tel Jezer* about eighteen miles north-west of Jerusalem.

53. *Jokmeam.* In Josh. xxi. 22 *Kibzaim.* *Beth-horon.* The modern *Beitur.* There

about it; 54. and Aijalon with the open land about it, and Gath-rimmon with the open land about it; 55. and out of the half-tribe of Manasseh: Aner with the open land about it, and Bileam with the open land about it, for the rest of the family of the sons of Kohath.

56. Unto the sons of Gershom were given, out of the family of the half-tribe of Manasseh, Golan in Bashan with the open land about it, and Ashtaroth with the open land about it; 57. and out of the tribe of Issachar: Kedesh with the open land about it, Dobrath with the open land about it; 58. and Ramoth with the open land about it, and Anem with the open land about it; 59. and out of the tribe of Asher: Mashal

54 וְאֶת־מִגְרָשֶׁהָ׃ וְאֶת־אַיָּלוֹן
וְאֶת־מִגְרָשֶׁהָ וְאֶת־גַּת־רִמּוֹן
55 וְאֶת־מִגְרָשֶׁהָ׃ וּמִמַּחֲצִית
מַטֵּה מְנַשֶּׁה אֶת־עָנֵר
וְאֶת־מִגְרָשֶׁהָ וְאֶת־
בִּלְעָם וְאֶת־מִגְרָשֶׁהָ
לְמִשְׁפַּחַת לִבְנֵי־קְהָת
הַנּוֹתָרִים׃
56 לִבְנֵי גֵּרְשׁוֹם מִמִּשְׁפַּחַת חֲצִי
מַטֵּה מְנַשֶּׁה אֶת־גּוֹלָן בַּבָּשָׁן
וְאֶת־מִגְרָשֶׁהָ וְאֶת־עַשְׁתָּרוֹת
57 וְאֶת־מִגְרָשֶׁהָ׃ וּמִמַּטֵּה
יִשָּׂשכָר אֶת־קֶדֶשׁ וְאֶת־
מִגְרָשֶׁהָ אֶת־דָּבְרַת וְאֶת־
58 מִגְרָשֶׁהָ׃ וְאֶת־רָאמוֹת וְאֶת־
מִגְרָשֶׁהָ וְאֶת־עָנֵם וְאֶת־
59 מִגְרָשֶׁהָ׃ וּמִמַּטֵּה אָשֵׁר אֶת־

was a lower and upper Beth-horon as there is now a lower and upper Beitur.

54. *Aijalon . . . Gath-rimmon.* Both these cities were in the territory of Dan as stated in Josh. xxi. 23.

55. *the half-tribe of Manasseh.* Whose territory was on the western side of the Jordan. The other half in Transjordan is referred to in the next verse.

Aner. In Josh. xxi. 25 *Taanach* (so also in vii. 29), in the plain of Esdraelon.

Bileam. It is named *Ibleam* in Judg. i. 27 and *Gath-rimmon* in Josh. xxi. 25.

56-61 (corresponding to Josh. xxi. 27-32). A fuller account of the Gershomite cities.

56. *were given.* Not in the text.

Golan. In the district between mount Hermon and the river Jarmuk in Transjordan, known as *Jolan* or *Jaulan.* It was a city of refuge (Josh. xxi. 27).

Ashtaroth. The capital of Og, king of Bashan (Deut. i. 4).

57. *Kedesh.* In Josh. xxi. 28 *Kishion.*

Dobrath. Close to the foot of mount Tabor and now known as *Daburiyeh.*

58. *Ramoth.* In Josh. xxi. 29 *Jarmuth.*

Anem. In Josh. xxi. 29 *En-gannim,* presumed to be *Jenin,* a large village on the edge of the valley which opens into the plain of Esdraelon.

with the open land about it, and Abdon with the open land about it; 60. and Hukok with the open land about it, and Rehob with the open land about it; 61. and out of the tribe of Naphtali: Kedesh in Galilee with the open land about it, and Hammon with the open land about it, and Kiriathaim with the open land about it.

62. Unto the rest [of the Levites], the sons of Merari, were given, out of the tribe of Zebulun, Rimmono with the open land about it, Tabor with the open land about it; 63. and beyond the Jordan at Jericho, on the east side of the Jordan, were given them, out of the tribe of Reuben, Bezer in the wilderness with the open land about it, and Jahaz with the open land about it, 64. and Kedemoth with the open land about

מָשָׁל וְאֶת־מִגְרָשֶׁהָ וְאֶת־
60 עַבְדּוֹן וְאֶת־מִגְרָשֶׁהָ׃ וְאֶת־
חוּקֹק וְאֶת־מִגְרָשֶׁהָ וְאֶת־
61 רְחֹב וְאֶת־מִגְרָשֶׁהָ׃ וּמִמַּטֵּה
נַפְתָּלִי אֶת־קֶדֶשׁ בַּגָּלִיל
וְאֶת־מִגְרָשֶׁהָ וְאֶת־חַמּוֹן
וְאֶת־מִגְרָשֶׁהָ וְאֶת־קִרְיָתַיִם
וְאֶת־מִגְרָשֶׁהָ׃
62 לִבְנֵי מְרָרִי הַנּוֹתָרִים מִמַּטֵּה
זְבֻלוּן אֶת־רִמּוֹנוֹ וְאֶת־
מִגְרָשֶׁהָ אֶת־תָּבוֹר וְאֶת־
63 מִגְרָשֶׁהָ׃ וּמֵעֵבֶר לְיַרְדֵּן
יְרֵחוֹ לְמִזְרַח הַיַּרְדֵּן מִמַּטֵּה
רְאוּבֵן אֶת־בֶּצֶר בַּמִּדְבָּר
וְאֶת־מִגְרָשֶׁהָ וְאֶת־יַהְצָה
64 וְאֶת־מִגְרָשֶׁהָ׃ וְאֶת־
קְדֵמוֹת וְאֶת־מִגְרָשֶׁהָ וְאֶת־

59. *Mashal.* In Josh. xxi. 30 *Mishal.*

60. *Hukok.* In Josh. xxi. 31 *Helkath.*

61. *Kedesh in Galilee.* Also known as *Kedesh-naphtali* (Judg. iv. 6), a city of refuge (Josh. xxi. 32) overlooking the Waters of Merom (Huleh), the modern *Kedes.*

Hammon . . . Kiriathaim. In Josh. xxi. 32 *Hammoth-dor . . . Kartan.*

62-66 (corresponding to Josh. xxi. 34-39). The cities of the Merarites.

62. *the rest* [*of the Levites*]. The words in brackets are implied since the cities so far enumerated belonged to the Kohathite and Gershomite Levites, not to the Merarites.

were given. Not in the text.

Rimmono . . . Tabor. The corresponding verses, Josh. xxi. 34f., contain four cities: *Jokneam*, *Kartan*, *Dimnah* and *Nahalal.* *Tabor* is the well-known mountain in Zebulun. A city of the name of *Tabor* still stood on the mountain in 218 B.C.E. A modern Jewish settlement *Kephar Tabor* is now situated at the foot of the mountain.

63. *were given them.* Not in the text.

Bezer. A city of refuge *in the table-land* (Deut. iv. 43).

Jahaz. Cf. Judg. xi. 20; Isa. xv.4.

64. *Kedemoth.* Perhaps in the vicinity of the upper reaches of the Arnon.

it, and Mephaath with the open land about it; 65. and out of the tribe of Gad: Ramoth in Gilead with the open land about it, and Mahanaim with the open land about it, 66. and Heshbon with the open land about it, and Jazer with the open land about it.

מֵיפַעַת וְאֶת־מִגְרָשֶׁהָ׃
65 וּמִמַּטֵּה־גָד אֶת־רָאמוֹת
בַּגִּלְעָד וְאֶת־מִגְרָשֶׁהָ וְאֶת־
66 מַחֲנַיִם וְאֶת־מִגְרָשֶׁהָ׃ וְאֶת־
חֶשְׁבּוֹן וְאֶת־מִגְרָשֶׁהָ וְאֶת־
יַעְזֵיר וְאֶת־מִגְרָשֶׁהָ׃

7 CHAPTER VII ז

1. And of the sons of Issachar: Tola, and Puah, Jashub, and Shimron, four. 2. And the sons of Tola: Uzzi, and Rephaiah, and Jeriel, and Jahmai, and Ibsam, and Shemuel, heads of their fathers' houses, mighty men of valour according to their generations, even of Tola; their number in the days of David was two and twenty thousand and six hundred. 3. And the sons of Uzzi: Izrahiah; and the sons of Izrahiah: Michael, and Obadiah,

1 וְלִבְנֵי יִשָּׂשכָר תּוֹלָע וּפוּאָה
2 יָשִׁיב וְשִׁמְרוֹן אַרְבָּעָה׃ וּבְנֵי
תוֹלָע עֻזִּי וּרְפָיָה וִירִיאֵל
וְיַחְמַי וְיִבְשָׂם וּשְׁמוּאֵל רָאשִׁים
לְבֵית־אֲבוֹתָם לְתוֹלָע גִּבּוֹרֵי
חַיִל לְתֹלְדוֹתָם מִסְפָּרָם בִּימֵי
דָוִיד עֶשְׂרִים־וּשְׁנַיִם אֶלֶף
3 וְשֵׁשׁ מֵאוֹת׃ וּבְנֵי עֻזִּי יִזְרַחְיָה
וּבְנֵי יִזְרַחְיָה מִיכָאֵל וְעֹבַדְיָה

v. 1. ישוב ק׳

Mephaath. A Moabite city (Jer. xlviii. 21) in the neighbourhood of Jahaz.

65. *Ramoth in Gilead.* Also called *Ramath-mizpeh* (Josh. xiii. 26) and *Ramoth-gilead* (1 Kings iv. 13).

Mahanaim. Cf. Gen. xxxii. 2.

66. *Heshbon.* To the north-east of mount Nebo.

Jazer. North-east of Heshbon.

CHAPTER VII

THE GENEALOGY OF OTHER TRIBES

1-5. The families of Issachar and the number of their fighting men.

1. *the sons of Issachar.* Cf. Gen. xlvi. 13; Num. xxvi. 23f.

Puah. In Gen. and Num. *Puvah.*

Jashub. So in Num., but Gen. has *Iob.* The Rabbis account for the change of name to *Jashub* (from a root meaning 'to settle down') on the ground that the family settled down to the study of Torah (cf. *And of the children of Issachar, men that had understanding of the times, to know what Israel ought to do,* xii. 32).

2. *in the days of David.* Cf. xxi. 1ff.

two and twenty thousand and six hundred. This was the number of the fighting men of the house of Tola alone.

and Joel, Isshiah, five; all of them chief men. 4. And with them, by their generations, after their fathers' houses, were bands of the host for war, six and thirty thousand; for they had many wives and sons. 5. And their brethren among all the families of Issachar, mighty men of valour, reckoned in all by genealogy, were fourscore and seven thousand.

6. [The sons of] Benjamin: Bela, and Becher, and Jediael, three. 7. And the sons of Bela: Ezbon, and Uzzi, and Uzziel, and Jerimoth, and Iri, five; heads of fathers' houses, mighty men of valour; and they were reckoned by genealogy twenty and two thousand and thirty and four. 8. And the sons of Becher: Zemirah, and Joash, and Eliezer, and Elioenai, and Omri, and Jeremoth, and Abijah, and Anathoth, and Alemeth. All these were the sons

וְיוֹאֵל יִשִּׁיָּה חֲמִשָּׁה רָאשִׁים
4 כֻּלָּם׃ וַעֲלֵיהֶם לְתֹלְדוֹתָם
לְבֵית אֲבוֹתָם גְּדוּדֵי צְבָא
מִלְחָמָה שְׁלֹשִׁים וְשִׁשָּׁה אָלֶף
כִּי־הִרְבּוּ נָשִׁים וּבָנִים׃
5 וַאֲחֵיהֶם לְכֹל מִשְׁפְּחוֹת
יִשָּׂשכָר גִּבּוֹרֵי חֲיָלִים שְׁמוֹנִים
וְשִׁבְעָה אֶלֶף הִתְיַחְשָׂם לַכֹּל׃
6 בִּנְיָמִן בֶּלַע וָבֶכֶר וִידִיעֲאֵל
7 שְׁלֹשָׁה׃ וּבְנֵי בֶלַע אֶצְבּוֹן
וְעֻזִּי וְעֻזִּיאֵל וִירִימוֹת וְעִירִי
חֲמִשָּׁה רָאשֵׁי בֵּית אָבוֹת
גִּבּוֹרֵי חֲיָלִים וְהִתְיַחְשָׂם
עֶשְׂרִים וּשְׁנַיִם אֶלֶף וּשְׁלֹשִׁים
8 וְאַרְבָּעָה׃ וּבְנֵי בֶכֶר זְמִירָה
וְיוֹעָשׁ וֶאֱלִיעֶזֶר וְאֶלְיוֹעֵינַי
וְעָמְרִי וִירֵמוֹת וַאֲבִיָּה
וַעֲנָתוֹת וְעָלָמֶת כָּל־אֵלֶּה בְּנֵי

3. *five.* This number is made up of the father Izrahiah and his four sons.

all of them. All the five.

4. *six and thirty thousand.* Exclusive of the number stated in verse 2.

5. *fourscore and seven thousand.* This was the total military strength of Issachar in the reign of David. In the time of Moses the number was 54,400 (Num. ii. 6) and later 64,300 (Num. xxvi. 25).

6-12. The families of Benjamin and their fighting men.

6. [*the sons of*]. Implied but not expressed; the first three letters of the Hebrew for *Benjamin*, if repeated, supply the Hebrew for *the sons of*.

Bela, and Becher, and Jediael. Contrast viii. 2. The first two names are also found in Gen. xlvi. 21. The third *Jediael* ('known to God') is substituted for the objectionable name *Ashbel* in Gen. and Num. xxvi. 38 which means 'man of Baal.' Seven other sons of Benjamin are enumerated in Gen. who are not included in the list of the Chronicler.

7. *sons of Bela.* Different names for the sons of Bela are found in viii. 3-5 and Num. xxvi. 40.

of Becher. 9. And they were reckoned by genealogy, after their generations, heads of their fathers' houses, mighty men of valour, twenty thousand and two hundred. 10. And the sons of Jediael: Bilhan; and the sons of Bilhan: Jeush, and Benjamin, and Ehud, and Chenaanah, and Zethan, and Tarshish, and Ahishahar. 11. And these were sons of Jediael, even heads of their fathers' houses, mighty men of valour, seventeen thousand and two hundred, that were able to go forth in the host for war. 12. Shuppim also, and Huppim, the sons of Ir, Hushim, the son of another.

13. The sons of Naphtali: Jahziel, and Guni, and Jezer, and Shallum, the sons of Bilhah.

14. The sons of Manasseh: Asriel, whom his wife bore—his concubine the Aramitess bore Machir the father of Gilead; 15. and Machir took

9 בָּכֶר׃ וְהִתְיַחְשָׂם לְתֹלְדוֹתָם
רָאשֵׁי בֵּית אֲבוֹתָם גִּבּוֹרֵי חָיִל
10 עֶשְׂרִים אֶלֶף וּמָאתָיִם׃ וּבְנֵי
יְדִיעֲאֵל בִּלְהָן וּבְנֵי בִלְהָן
יעיש וּבִנְיָמִן וְאֵהוּד וּכְנַעֲנָה
וְזֵיתָן וְתַרְשִׁישׁ וַאֲחִישָׁחַר׃
11 כָּל־אֵלֶּה בְּנֵי יְדִיעֲאֵל
לְרָאשֵׁי הָאָבוֹת גִּבּוֹרֵי חֲיָלִים
שִׁבְעָה־עָשָׂר אֶלֶף וּמָאתָיִם
12 יֹצְאֵי צָבָא לַמִּלְחָמָה׃ וְשֻׁפִּם
וְחֻפִּם בְּנֵי עִיר חֻשִׁם בְּנֵי אַחֵר׃
13 בְּנֵי נַפְתָּלִי יַחֲצִיאֵל וְגוּנִי וְיֵצֶר
וְשַׁלּוּם בְּנֵי בִלְהָה׃
14 בְּנֵי מְנַשֶּׁה אַשְׂרִיאֵל אֲשֶׁר
יָלָדָה פִּילַגְשׁוֹ הָאֲרַמִּיָּה יָלְדָה
אֶת־מָכִיר אֲבִי גִלְעָד׃

v. 10 יעוש ק׳

10. *Ehud.* A judge, Ehud the son of Gera, is described as a Benjamite (Judg. iii. 15).

11. This verse and verses 7 and 9 show that the total armed strength of Benjamin was 59,434.

12. Other families of Benjamin. For *Shuppim* Gen. xlvi. 21 has *Muppim*, Num. xxvi. 39 *Shephupham*, and viii. 5 *Shephuphan*. For *Huppim* Num. has *Hupham* and 2 Chron. *Huram*.

Ir. In verse 7 *Iri*.

Hushim, the son of another. The Jewish commentators understand *acher* (*another*) as a name. Possibly it means 'another tribe,' the reference being to Dan whose genealogy is otherwise omitted. In Gen. xlvi. 23 *Hushim* is the only son of Dan mentioned; in Num. xxvi. 42 the form of the name is *Shusham*.

13. The families of Naphtali.

Jahziel . . . Shallum. In Gen. xlvi. 24 and Num. xxvi. 48f. these names appear as *Jahzeel . . . Shillem*.

14-29. Genealogy of Manasseh and Ephraim.

14-19. The families of Manasseh in Transjordan.

14. *the sons of Manasseh: Asriel.* He was not Manasseh's son but great-grandson, being the son of Gilead who was the son of Machir son of Manasseh (cf. Num. xxvi. 29ff.); but later descendants are often described as *sons*.

his wife bore. lit. 'she bore.'

a wife of Huppim and Shuppim, whose sister's name was Maacah—and the name of the second was Zelophehad; and Zelophehad had daughters. 16. And Maacah the wife of Machir bore a son, and she called his name Peresh; and the name of his brother was Sheresh; and his sons were Ulam and Rekem. 17. And the sons of Ulam: Bedan. These were the sons of Gilead the son of Machir, the son of Manasseh. 18. And his sister Hammolecheth bore Ish-hod, and Abiezer, and Mahlah. 19. And the sons of Shemida were Ahian, and Shechem, and Likhi, and Aniam.

20. And the sons of Ephraim: Shuthelah—and Bered was his son, and Tahath his son, and Eleadah his son, and Tahath his son, 21. and Zabad his son, and Shuthelah his son—and Ezer, and Elead, whom the men of Gath that were born in the

15 וּמָכִ֞יר לָקַ֤ח אִשָּׁה֙ לְחֻפִּ֣ים
וּלְשֻׁפִּ֔ים וְשֵׁ֤ם אֲחֹתוֹ֙ מַֽעֲכָ֔ה
וְשֵׁ֥ם הַשֵּׁנִ֖י צְלָפְחָ֑ד וַתִּהְיֶ֥נָה
16 לִצְלָפְחָ֖ד בָּנֽוֹת׃ וַתֵּ֨לֶד
מַעֲכָ֤ה אֵֽשֶׁת־מָכִיר֙ בֵּ֔ן
וַתִּקְרָ֤א שְׁמוֹ֙ פֶּ֔רֶשׁ וְשֵׁ֥ם אָחִ֖יו
17 שָׁ֑רֶשׁ וּבָנָ֖יו אוּלָ֥ם וָרָֽקֶם׃ וּבְנֵ֥י
אוּלָ֖ם בְּדָ֑ן אֵ֚לֶּה בְּנֵ֣י גִלְעָ֔ד
18 בֶּן־מָכִ֖יר בֶּן־מְנַשֶּֽׁה׃ וַֽאֲחֹתוֹ֙
הַמֹּ*֔לֶכֶת יָלְדָה֙ אֶת־אִ֣ישׁ הוֹד
וְאֶת־אֲבִיעֶ֖זֶר וְאֶת־
19 מַחְלָֽה׃ וַיִּהְי֖וּ בְּנֵ֣י שְׁמִידָ֑ע
אַחְיָ֣ן וָשֶׁ֔כֶם וְלִקְחִ֖י וַאֲנִיעָֽם׃
20 וּבְנֵ֣י אֶפְרַ֔יִם שׁוּתָ֑לַח וּבֶ֥רֶד
בְּנ֖וֹ וְתַ֥חַת בְּנ֖וֹ וְאֶלְעָדָ֥ה בְנֽוֹ׃
21 וְתַ֥חַת בְּנֽוֹ׃ וְזָבָ֥ד בְּנ֖וֹ וְשׁוּתֶ֣לַח
בְּנ֑וֹ וְעֵ֣זֶר וְאֶלְעָ֔ד וַהֲרָג֗וּם

v. 18. סגול באתנח

15. *a wife of Huppim and Shuppim*. i.e. his wife was their sister, or he married a member of these two families from the tribe of Benjamin (verse 12).

whose sister's name. i.e. the sister of Machir.

the second. i.e. the second son of Manasseh.

Zelophehad had daughters. Meaning that he had daughters only and no sons, as recorded in Num. xxvi. 33.

16. *his sons*. It is uncertain whether this means the sons of *Peresh* or *Sheresh*, probably the former.

17. *these were the sons of Gilead*. The demonstrative pronoun refers to Asriel and Zelophehad in verses 14f.

18f. The families of Manasseh in Canaan.

18. *Abiezer*. The judge Gideon belonged to this family (Judg. vi. 11).

20-27. The families of Ephraim.

20. The names in the verse correspond with *Shutelah*, *Becher*, *Tahan* and *Eran* in Num. xxvi. 35f.

his son. The pronoun refers to Ephraim. Except for Shutelah, the others were his grandsons.

21. *the men of Gath*, etc. i.e. Canaanites who were of Philistine origin.

land slew, because they came down to take away their cattle. 22. And Ephraim their father mourned many days, and his brethren came to comfort him. 23. And he went in to his wife, and she conceived, and bore a son, and he called his name Beriah, because it went evil with his house. 24. And his daughter was Sheerah, who built Beth-horon the nether and the upper, and Uzzen-sheerah. 25. And Rephah was his son, and Resheph, and Telah his son, and Tahan his son; 26. Ladan his son, Ammihud his son, Elishama his son; 27. Nun his son, Joshua his son. 28. And their possessions and habitations were Beth-el and the towns thereof, and eastward Naaran, and westward Gezer, with the towns thereof; Shechem also and the towns thereof, unto Aiah and the towns thereof; 29. and by the borders of the children of Manasseh, Beth-shean and the towns thereof, Taanach and

אַנְשֵׁי־גַת הַנּוֹלָדִים בָּאָרֶץ כִּי
יָרְדוּ לָקַחַת אֶת־מִקְנֵיהֶם׃
22 וַיִּתְאַבֵּל אֶפְרַיִם אֲבִיהֶם יָמִים
רַבִּים וַיָּבֹאוּ אֶחָיו לְנַחֲמוֹ׃
23 וַיָּבֹא אֶל־אִשְׁתּוֹ וַתַּהַר וַתֵּלֶד
בֵּן וַיִּקְרָא אֶת־שְׁמוֹ בְּרִיעָה
24 כִּי בְרָעָה הָיְתָה בְּבֵיתוֹ׃ וּבִתּוֹ
שֶׁאֱרָה וַתִּבֶן אֶת־בֵּית־חוֹרוֹן
הַתַּחְתּוֹן וְאֶת־הָעֶלְיוֹן וְאֵת
25 אֻזֵּן שֶׁאֱרָה׃ וְרֶפַח בְּנוֹ וְרֶשֶׁף
26 וְתֶלַח בְּנוֹ וְתַחַן בְּנוֹ׃ לַעְדָּן
בְּנוֹ עַמִּיהוּד בְּנוֹ אֱלִישָׁמָע
27 בְּנוֹ׃ נֹון בְּנוֹ יְהוֹשֻׁעַ בְּנוֹ׃
28 וַאֲחֻזָּתָם וּמֹשְׁבוֹתָם בֵּית אֵל
וּבְנֹתֶיהָ וְלַמִּזְרָח נַעֲרָן
וְלַמַּעֲרָב גֶּזֶר וּבְנֹתֶיהָ וּשְׁכֶם
וּבְנֹתֶיהָ עַד־עַיָּה וּבְנֹתֶיהָ׃
29 וְעַל־יְדֵי בְנֵי־מְנַשֶּׁה בֵּית־
שְׁאָן וּבְנֹתֶיהָ תַּעְנַךְ וּבְנֹתֶיהָ

23. *it went evil.* Hebrew *bera'ah* (lit. 'in evil'), a play upon the name *Beriah.*

24. *Beth-horon.* See on vi. 53.

27. *Nun.* The name is here vocalized as *Non.*

28f. The settlements of Ephraim and Manasseh.

28. *Beth-el.* The modern *Beitin,* ten miles north of Jerusalem, on the border between the territories of Ephraim and Benjamin. It was allotted to the latter by Joshua (Josh. xviii. 22) but was taken from the Canaanites by the Ephraimites (Judg. i. 22ff.) who retained possession of it.

Naaran. Called *Naarah* in Josh. xvi. 7; the modern *Tel Jisr.*

Gezer . . . Shechem. See on vi. 52. *Aiah* has not been identified.

29. *by the borders.* lit. 'by the hands,' at the side.

Beth-shean. Also called *Beth-shan* (1 Sam. xxxi. 10, 12), the modern *Beisan,* in the Jordan valley.

the towns thereof, Megiddo and the towns thereof, Dor and the towns thereof. In these dwelt the children of Joseph the son of Israel.

30. The sons of Asher: Imnah, and Ishvah, and Ishvi, and Beriah, and Serah their sister. 31. And the sons of Beriah: Heber, and Malchiel, who was the father of Birzaith. 32. And Heber begot Japhlet, and Shomer, and Hotham, and Shua their sister. 33. And the sons of Japhlet: Pasach, and Bimhal, and Asvath. These are the children of Japhlet. 34. And the sons of Shemer: Ahi, and Rohgah, and Hubbah, and Aram. 35. And the sons of Helem his brother: Zophah, and Imna, and Shelesh, and Amal. 36. The sons of Zophah: Suah, and Harnepher, and Shual, and Beri, and Imrah; 37. Bezer, and Hod, and Shamma, and Shilsha, and Ithran, and Beera. 38. And the sons of Jether: Jephunneh, and Pispa, and Ara. 39. And the sons of Ulla: Arah, and Hanniel, and Rizia.

מְגִדּוֹ וּבְנוֹתֶיהָ דּוֹר וּבְנוֹתֶיהָ
בְּאֵלֶּה יָשְׁבוּ בְּנֵי יוֹסֵף בֶּן־
יִשְׂרָאֵל׃
30 בְּנֵי אָשֵׁר יִמְנָה וְיִשְׁוָה וְיִשְׁוִי
31 וּבְרִיעָה וְשֶׂרַח אֲחוֹתָם׃ וּבְנֵי
בְרִיעָה חֶבֶר וּמַלְכִּיאֵל הוּא
32 אֲבִי בִרְזָוִת׃ וְחֶבֶר הוֹלִיד
אֶת־יַפְלֵט וְאֶת־שׁוֹמֵר וְאֶת־
חוֹתָם וְאֵת שׁוּעָא אֲחוֹתָם׃
33 וּבְנֵי יַפְלֵט פָּסַךְ וּבִמְהָל
34 וְעַשְׁוָת אֵלֶּה בְּנֵי יַפְלֵט׃ וּבְנֵי
שָׁמֶר אֲחִי וְרוֹהְגָּה יְחֻבָּה
35 וַאֲרָם׃ וּבֶן־הֵלֶם אָחִיו צוֹפַח
36 וְיִמְנָע וְשֵׁלֶשׁ וְעָמָל׃ בְּנֵי צוֹפַח
סוּחַ וְחַרְנֶפֶר וְשׁוּעָל וּבֵרִי
37 וְיִמְרָה׃ בֶּצֶר וָהוֹד וְשַׁמָּא
38 וְשִׁלְשָׁה וְיִתְרָן וּבְאֵרָא׃ וּבְנֵי
39 יֶתֶר יְפֻנֶּה וּפִסְפָּא וַאֲרָא׃ וּבְנֵי
עֻלָּא אָרַח וְחַנִּיאֵל וְרִצְיָא׃

v. 31. ברזית ק׳ v. 34. יתיר ר׳ v. 34. וחבה ק׳

Taanach . . . Megiddo. In the Valley of Jezreel and still known by these names.

Dor. The modern *Tantura.*

the children of Joseph. The tribes of Manasseh in Canaan and Ephraim.

30-40. The families of Asher.

30f. The names, except *Birzaith* which occurs only here, correspond to those in Gen. xlvi. 17 and Num. xxvi. 44ff., but in the latter *Ihvah* is omitted.

31. *Birzaith.* The name signifies 'the well of the olive'; but the Midrash understood it as 'the son of the olive' and states that he was so called because his daughters were beautiful and married priests (or kings) who were anointed with oil.

35. *the sons of Helem.* The Hebrew has the singular; each of the following was his son.

his brother. He was the brother of each of those named in verse 34.

40. All these were the children of Asher, heads of the fathers' houses, choice and mighty men of valour, chief of the princes. And the number of them reckoned by genealogy for service in war was twenty and six thousand men.

40 כָּל־אֵלֶּה בְנֵי־אָשֵׁר רָאשֵׁי
בֵית־הָאָבוֹת בְּרוּרִים גִּבּוֹרֵי
חֲיָלִים רָאשֵׁי הַנְּשִׂיאִים
וְהִתְיַחְשָׂם בַּצָּבָא בַּמִּלְחָמָה
מִסְפָּרָם אֲנָשִׁים עֶשְׂרִים וְשִׁשָּׁה
אָלֶף׃

8 CHAPTER VIII ח

1. And Benjamin begot Bela his first-born, Ashbel the second, and Aharah the third; 2. Nohah the fourth, and Rapha the fifth. 3. And Bela had sons, Addar, and Gera, and Abihud; 4. and Abishua, and Naaman, and Ahoah; 5. and Gera, and Shephuphan, and Huram. 6. And these are the sons of Ehud—these are the heads of fathers' houses of the inhabitants of Geba, and they were carried captive to Manahath; 7. and Naaman, and Ahijah, and Gera, were they that carried them captive—and he begot Uzza, and Ahihud.

1 וּבִנְיָמִן הוֹלִיד אֶת־בֶּלַע
בְּכֹרוֹ אַשְׁבֵּל הַשֵּׁנִי וְאַחְרַח
2 הַשְּׁלִישִׁי׃ נוֹחָה הָרְבִיעִי
3 וְרָפָא הַחֲמִישִׁי׃ וַיִּהְיוּ בָנִים
לְבָלַע אַדָּר וְגֵרָא וַאֲבִיהוּד׃
4 5 וַאֲבִישׁוּעַ וְנַעֲמָן וַאֲחוֹחַ׃ וְגֵרָא
6 וּשְׁפוּפָן וְחוּרָם׃ וְאֵלֶּה בְּנֵי
אֵחוּד אֵלֶּה הֵם רָאשֵׁי אָבוֹת
לְיוֹשְׁבֵי גֶבַע וַיַּגְלוּם אֶל־
7 מָנָחַת׃ וְנַעֲמָן וַאֲחִיָּה וְגֵרָא
הוּא הֶגְלָם וְהוֹלִיד אֶת־עֻזָּא

40. *twenty and six thousand.* The number probably refers to the time of David or only to the clan of Heber. Higher totals are given of the tribe of Asher in xii. 7 (40,000), in Num. i. 41 (41,500) and Num. xxvi. 47 (53,400).

CHAPTER VIII

THE FAMILIES OF BENJAMIN

THE purpose of the chapter is to trace the ancestry of Saul, the first king of Israel, and to present a complete genealogy the Chronicler repeats the beginnings of the tribe to which he belonged.

1-5. The sons of Benjamin (see on vii. 6-12).

3. *Addar.* In Gen. xlvi. 21 *Ard* occurs as a son of Benjamin.

6-28. The descendants of Ehud.

6. *Ehud.* It has been suggested that this is another name for *Bela* in verse 3.

Geba. See on vi. 45.

Manahath. Not mentioned elsewhere and unidentified.

7. *were they.* lit. 'was he,' the subject possibly being Ehud and the object

8. And Shaharaim begot children in the field of Moab, after he had sent them away, to wit, Hushim and Baara his wives; 9. he begot of Hodesh his wife, Jobab, and Zibia, and Mesha, and Malcam; 10. and Jeuz, and Sachiah, and Mirmah. These were his sons, heads of fathers' houses. 11. And of Hushim he begot Abitub, and Elpaal.

12. And the sons of Elpaal: Eber, and Misham, and Shemed, who built Ono, and Lod, with the towns thereof; 13. and Beriah, and Shema, who were heads of fathers' houses of the inhabitants of Aijalon, who put to flight the inhabitants of Gath. 14. And Ahio, Shashak, and Jeremoth; 15. and Zebadiah, and Arad, and Eder; 16. and Michael, and Ishpah, and Joha, were the sons of

8 וְאֶת־אֲחִיחֻד׃ וְשַׁחֲרַיִם
הוֹלִיד בִּשְׂדֵה מוֹאָב מִן־
שִׁלְחוֹ אֹתָם חוּשִׁים וְאֶת־
9 בַּעֲרָא נָשָׁיו׃ וַיּוֹלֶד מִן־חֹדֶשׁ
אִשְׁתּוֹ אֶת־יוֹבָב וְאֶת־צִבְיָא
וְאֶת־מֵישָׁא וְאֶת־מַלְכָּם׃
10 וְאֶת־יְעוּץ וְאֶת־שָׂכְיָה וְאֶת־
מִרְמָה אֵלֶּה בָנָיו רָאשֵׁי
11 אָבוֹת׃ וּמֵחֻשִׁים הוֹלִיד אֶת־
אֲבִיטוּב וְאֶת־אֶלְפָּעַל׃
12 וּבְנֵי אֶלְפַּעַל עֵבֶר וּמִשְׁעָם
וָשֶׁמֶד הוּא בָּנָה אֶת־אוֹנוֹ
13 וְאֶת־לֹד וּבְנֹתֶיהָ׃ וּבְרִעָה
וָשֶׁמַע הֵמָּה רָאשֵׁי הָאָבוֹת
לְיוֹשְׁבֵי אַיָּלוֹן הֵמָּה הִבְרִיחוּ
14 אֶת־יוֹשְׁבֵי גַת׃ וְאַחְיוֹ שָׁשָׁק
15 וִירֵמוֹת׃ וּזְבַדְיָה וַעֲרָד
16 וָעֶדֶר׃ וּמִיכָאֵל וְיִשְׁפָּה וְיוֹחָא

פתח בס״פ v. 13.

referring to Naaman, etc. The pronoun *he* is emphasized in the text, and the meaning may be that after some of his sons had been carried into captivity, he took the rest of his family to the same place so that they should all live together. After that two more sons were born to him.

8. *Shaharaim.* He must have been a Benjamite although his name has not been previously recorded.

after he had sent them away. lit. 'from his sending them'; an obscure phrase which has not yet been elucidated. The suggestion of some Jewish commentators that the Hebrew *shilcho otham* was the first of his three wives is improbable.

to wit. Not in the text.

11. *Abitub.* He was either childless or his descendants are omitted from the list.

12. *who built.* The subject may be *Elpaal* or *Shemed.*

Ono. Mentioned together with *Lod* (Lydda) in Ezra ii. 33; Neh. vii. 37, xi. 35; the modern *Kefr Ana,* north-west of Lydda.

13. *Aijalon.* See on vi. 54.

put to flight. In an attack by the Philistines.

Beriah. 17. And Zebadiah, and
Meshullam, and Hizki, and Heber;
18. and Ishmerai, and Izliah, and
Jobab, were the sons of Elpaal.
19. And Jakim, and Zichri, and
Zabdi; 20. and Elienai, and Zillethai,
and Eliel; 21. and Adaiah, and
Beraiah, and Shimrath, were the
sons of Shimei. 22. And Ishpan,
and Ebed, and Eliel; 23. and Abdon,
and Zichri, and Hanan; 24. and
Hananiah, and Elam, and Antho-
thiah; 25. and Iphdeiah, and Penuel,
were the sons of Shashak. 26. And
Shamsherai, and Shehariah, and
Athaliah; 27. and Jaareshiah, and
Elijah, and Zichri, were the sons of
Jeroham. 28. These were heads of
fathers' houses throughout their
generations, chief men; these dwelt
in Jerusalem.

29. And in Gibeon there dwelt
the father of Gibeon [, Jeiel], whose
wife's name was Maacah; 30. and
his first-born son Abdon, and Zur,
and Kish, and Baal, and Nadab;
31. and Gedor, and Ahio, and
Zecher. 32. And Mikloth begot
Shimeah. And they also dwelt

17 בְּנֵי בְרִיעָה׃ וּזְבַדְיָה וּמְשֻׁלָּם
18 וְחִזְקִי וָחָבֶר׃ וְיִשְׁמְרַי
וְיִזְלִיאָה וְיוֹבָב בְּנֵי אֶלְפָּעַל׃
19 20 וְיָקִים וְזִכְרִי וְזַבְדִּי׃ וֶאֱלִיעֵינַי
21 וְצִלְּתַי וֶאֱלִיאֵל׃ וַעֲדָיָה
וּבְרָאיָה וְשִׁמְרָת בְּנֵי שִׁמְעִי׃
22 וְיִשְׁפָּן וָעֶבֶר וֶאֱלִיאֵל׃
23 24 וְעַבְדּוֹן וְזִכְרִי וְחָנָן׃ וַחֲנַנְיָה
25 וְעֵילָם וְעַנְתֹתִיָּה׃ וְיִפְדְיָה
26 וּפְנִיאֵל בְּנֵי שָׁשָׁק׃ וְשַׁמְשְׁרַי
27 וּשְׁחַרְיָה וַעֲתַלְיָה׃ וְיַעֲרֶשְׁיָה
28 וְאֵלִיָּה וְזִכְרִי בְּנֵי יְרֹחָם׃ אֵלֶּה
רָאשֵׁי אָבוֹת לְתֹלְדוֹתָם
רָאשִׁים אֵלֶּה יָשְׁבוּ בִּירוּשָׁלָם׃
29 וּבְגִבְעוֹן יָשְׁבוּ אֲבִי גִבְעוֹן וְשֵׁם
30 אִשְׁתּוֹ מַעֲכָה׃ וּבְנוֹ הַבְּכוֹר
עַבְדּוֹן וְצוּר וְקִישׁ וּבַעַל
31 וְנָדָב׃ וּגְדוֹר וְאַחְיוֹ וָזָכֶר׃
32 וּמִקְלוֹת הוֹלִיד אֶת־שִׁמְאָה

ופנואל ק׳ v. 25.

18. *the sons of Elpaal.* i.e. his descendants.

20. *Elienai.* A variant of *Elioenai* in iii. 23.

21. *Shimei.* In verse 13 *Shema.*

27. *Jeroham.* In verse 14 *Jeremoth.*

28. *these dwelt in Jerusalem.* The phrase is repeated in ix. 34 (cf. ix. 3).

29-40. The genealogy of Saul and his family. Cf. the parallel passage, with slight variations, in ix. 35-44.

29. *Gibeon.* A Levitical city in the territory of Benjamin, six miles north of Jerusalem.

the father of Gibeon [, Jeiel]. The latter name is added from ix. 35.

30. In ix. 36 *and Ner* is added after *Baal.*

31. *Zecher.* In ix. 37 *Zechariah, and Mikloth.*

32. *Shimeah.* In ix. 38 *Shimeam.*

they also dwelt, etc. The family of *Shimeah* and some of their relatives lived

with their brethren in Jerusalem,
over against their brethren.
33. And Ner begot Kish; and
Kish begot Saul; and Saul begot
Jonathan, and Malchi-shua, and
Abinadab, and Eshbaal. 34. And
the son of Jonathan was Merib-
baal; and Merib-baal begot Micah.
35. And the sons of Micah: Pithon,
and Melech, and Taarea, and Ahaz.
36. And Ahaz begot Jehoaddah; and
Jehoaddah begot Alemeth, and Azmaveth, and Zimri; and Zimri begot
Moza; 37. and Moza begot Binea;
Raphah was his son, Eleasah his son,
Azel his son. 38. And Azel had six
sons, whose names are these: Azrikam, Bocru, and Ishmael, and
Sheariah, and Obadiah, and Hanan.
All these were the sons of Azel.

וְאַף הֵמָּה נֶגֶד אֲחֵיהֶם יָשְׁבוּ
בִירוּשָׁלַםִ עִם־אֲחֵיהֶם׃
33 וְנֵר הוֹלִיד אֶת־קִישׁ וְקִישׁ
הוֹלִיד אֶת־שָׁאוּל וְשָׁאוּל
הוֹלִיד אֶת־יְהוֹנָתָן וְאֶת־
מַלְכִּי־שׁוּעַ וְאֶת־אֲבִינָדָב
34 וְאֶת־אֶשְׁבָּעַל׃ וּבֶן־יְהוֹנָתָן
מְרִיב בָּעַל וּמְרִיב בַּעַל
35 הוֹלִיד אֶת־מִיכָה׃ וּבְנֵי
מִיכָה פִּיתוֹן וָמֶלֶךְ וְתַאְרֵעַ
36 וְאָחָז׃ וְאָחָז הוֹלִיד אֶת־
יְהוֹעַדָּה וִיהוֹעַדָּה הוֹלִיד
אֶת־עָלֶמֶת וְאֶת־עַזְמָוֶת
וְאֶת־זִמְרִי וְזִמְרִי הוֹלִיד אֶת־
37 מוֹצָא׃ וּמוֹצָא הוֹלִיד אֶת־
בִּנְעָא רָפָה בְנוֹ אֶלְעָשָׂה בְנוֹ
38 אָצֵל בְּנוֹ׃ וּלְאָצֵל שִׁשָּׁה בָנִים
וְאֵלֶּה שְׁמוֹתָם עַזְרִיקָם ׀ בֹּכְרוּ
וְיִשְׁמָעֵאל וּשְׁעַרְיָה וְעֹבַדְיָה
וְחָנָן כָּל־אֵלֶּה בְּנֵי אָצֵל׃

in Jerusalem, whereas other families of the clan resided in other towns, such as Gibeon.

33. *Ner begot Kish.* Some links in the chain are evidently omitted, because according to 1 Sam. ix. 1 the father of Kish was *Abiel*.

Abinadab. He is called by this name in 1 Sam. xxxi. 2 but *Ishvi* in 1 Sam. xiv. 49.

Eshbaal. The name is *Ish-bosheth* in 2 Sam. ii. 8. The nouns *bosheth* and *baal* are sometimes interchanged in the Bible, the former meaning 'shame' and the latter being the name of an idol.

34. *Merib-baal.* In ix. 40 the Hebrew form of the name is *Meri-baal*; he is identical with Mephibosheth (2 Sam. iv. 4, ix. 6).

35. *Taarea.* In ix. 41 *Taharea.*

36. *Jehoaddah.* In ix. 42 *Jarah.*

37. *Raphah.* In ix. 43 *Rephaiah.*

39. And the sons of Eshek his brother: Ulam his first-born, Jeush the second, and Eliphelet the third. 40. And the sons of Ulam were mighty men of valour, archers; and had many sons, and sons' sons, a hundred and fifty. All these were of the sons of Benjamin.

39 וּבְנֵי עֵשֶׁק אָחִיו אוּלָם בְּכֹרוֹ
יְעוּשׁ הַשֵּׁנִי וֶאֱלִיפֶלֶט
40 הַשְּׁלִישִׁי׃ וַיִּהְיוּ בְנֵי־אוּלָם
אֲנָשִׁים גִּבֹּרֵי־חַיִל דֹּרְכֵי
קֶשֶׁת וּמַרְבִּים בָּנִים וּבְנֵי בָנִים
מֵאָה וַחֲמִשִּׁים כָּל־אֵלֶּה מִבְּנֵי
בִנְיָמִן׃

9 CHAPTER IX ט

1. So all Israel were reckoned by genealogies; and, behold, they are written in the book of the kings of Israel; and Judah was carried away captive to Babylon because of their transgression. 2. Now the first inhabitants that dwelt in their possessions in their cities were, Israelites, the priests, the Levites, and the Nethinim. 3. And in Jerusalem dwelt of the children of Judah, and

1 וְכָל־יִשְׂרָאֵל הִתְיַחְשׂוּ וְהִנָּם
כְּתוּבִים עַל־סֵפֶר מַלְכֵי
יִשְׂרָאֵל וִיהוּדָה הָגְלוּ לְבָבֶל
2 בְּמַעֲלָם׃ וְהַיּוֹשְׁבִים
הָרִאשֹׁנִים אֲשֶׁר בַּאֲחֻזָּתָם
בְּעָרֵיהֶם יִשְׂרָאֵל הַכֹּהֲנִים
3 הַלְוִיִּם וְהַנְּתִינִים׃ וּבִירוּשָׁלִַם
יָשְׁבוּ מִן־בְּנֵי יְהוּדָה וּמִן־בְּנֵי

39f. These verses do not occur in chapter ix.

CHAPTER IX

1-34. The heads of the inhabitants of Jerusalem.

1. *so all Israel*, etc. lit. 'and all Israel'; the intention may be that the Chronicler points out that the foregoing lists are not exhaustive, nothing, e.g., having been said of the tribes of Zebulun and Naphtali, and the record of the genealogies existed in full and were to be found in the work which he specifies.

Judah was carried away. The mention of the exile of Judah indicates that the following lists refer to the post-exilic period.

2. *the first inhabitants.* After the return from Babylon.

Israelites. The laymen other than priests and Levites.

the Nethinim. These included the Gibeonites (cf. Josh. ix. 23) and other inferior Temple servants who were probably also of foreign extraction. The *Nethinim* are mentioned elsewhere in the Books of Ezra and Nehemiah only. A fourth category, the *children of Solomon's servants*, is added to the three enumerated here in Neh. xi. 3.

3. *in Jerusalem dwelt.* The Holy City

of the children of Benjamin, and of the children of Ephraim and Manasseh: 4. Uthai the son of Ammihud, the son of Omri, the son of Imri, the son of Bani, of the children of Perez the son of Judah. 5. And of the Shilonites: Asaiah the first-born and his sons. 6. And of the sons of Zerah: Jeuel, and their brethren, six hundred and ninety. 7. And of the sons of Benjamin: Sallu the son of Meshullam, the son of Hodaviah, the son of Hassenuah; 8. and Ibneiah the son of Jeroham, and Elah the son of Uzzi, the son of Michri, and Meshullam the son of Shephatiah, the son of Reuel, the son of Ibneiah; 9. and their brethren, according to their generations, nine hundred and fifty and six. All these men were heads of fathers' houses by their fathers' houses.

בִּנְיָמִן וּמִן־בְּנֵי אֶפְרַיִם
4 וּמְנַשֶּׁה׃ עוּתַי בֶּן־עַמִּיהוּד
בֶּן־עָמְרִי בֶּן־אִמְרִי בֶן־
בָּנִימִן־בְּנֵי פֶרֶץ בֶּן־יְהוּדָה׃
5 וּמִן־הַשִּׁילֹנִי עֲשָׂיָה הַבְּכוֹר
6 וּבָנָיו׃ וּמִן־בְּנֵי זֶרַח יְעוּאֵל
וַאֲחֵיהֶם שֵׁשׁ־מֵאוֹת וְתִשְׁעִים׃
7 וּמִן־בְּנֵי בִּנְיָמִן סַלּוּא בֶּן־
מְשֻׁלָּם בֶּן־הוֹדַוְיָה בֶּן־
8 הַסְּנֻאָה׃ וְיִבְנְיָה בֶּן־יְרֹחָם
וְאֵלָה בֶן־עֻזִּי בֶּן־מִכְרִי
וּמְשֻׁלָּם בֶּן־שְׁפַטְיָה בֶּן־
9 רְעוּאֵל בֶּן־יִבְנִיָּה׃ וַאֲחֵיהֶם
לְתֹלְדוֹתָם תְּשַׁע מֵאוֹת
וַחֲמִשִּׁים וְשִׁשָּׁה כָּל־אֵלֶּה
אֲנָשִׁים רָאשֵׁי אָבוֹת לְבֵית
אֲבֹתֵיהֶם׃

v. 4. בני מן ק׳

was underpopulated, and according to Neh. xi. 1, lots were cast *to bring one of ten to dwell in Jerusalem.*

and of the children of Ephraim and Manasseh. These words are omitted from the corresponding verse in Neh. xi. 4.

4-6. The Judahites.

4. *Uthai.* In Neh. xi. 4 *Athaiah.* Both words are more alike in the Hebrew and represent the same name.

the son of Ammihud, etc. In Neh. xi. 4f. the names are quite different.

5. *Shilonites.* i.e. sons of Shelah (cf. iv. 21).

6. *Zerah.* Cf. ii. 4.

and of the sons . . . brethren. These words are not in Neh. xi. 6 which has instead, *all the sons of Perez that dwelt in Jerusalem were.*

their brethren. The brethren of Asaiah (verse 5) and Jeuel.

six hundred and ninety. The number is that of the *Shilonites* and *the sons of Zerah.* The total of *the sons of Perez* in Neh. xi. 6 is *four hundred threescore and eight valiant men.*

7-9. The Benjamites. Cf. Neh. xi. 7-9 where several variations in names and number as well as omissions and additions occur.

10. And of the priests: Jedaiah, and Jehoiarib, and Jachin; 11. and Azariah the son of Hilkiah, the son of Meshullam, the son of Zadok, the son of Meraioth, the son of Ahitub, the ruler of the house of God; 12. and Adaiah the son of Jeroham, the son of Pashhur, the son of Malchijah, and Maasai the son of Adiel, the son of Jahzerah, the son of Meshullam, the son of Meshillemith, the son of Immer; 13. and their brethren, heads of their fathers' houses, a thousand and seven hundred and threescore; very able men for the work of the service of the house of God.

14. And of the Levites: Shemaiah

10 וּמִן־הַכֹּהֲנִים יְדַעְיָה וִיהוֹיָרִיב
11 וְיָכִין׃ וַעֲזַרְיָה בֶּן־חִלְקִיָּה
בֶּן־מְשֻׁלָּם בֶּן־צָדוֹק בֶּן־
מְרָיוֹת בֶּן־אֲחִיטוּב נְגִיד בֵּית
12 הָאֱלֹהִים׃ וַעֲדָיָה בֶּן־יְרֹחָם
בֶּן־פַּשְׁחוּר בֶּן־מַלְכִּיָּה
וּמַעְשַׂי בֶּן־עֲדִיאֵל בֶּן־
יַחְזֵרָה בֶּן־מְשֻׁלָּם בֶּן־
13 מְשִׁלֵּמִית בֶּן־אִמֵּר׃ וַאֲחֵיהֶם
רָאשִׁים לְבֵית אֲבוֹתָם אֶלֶף
וּשְׁבַע מֵאוֹת וְשִׁשִּׁים גִּבּוֹרֵי חֵיל
מְלֶאכֶת עֲבוֹדַת בֵּית־
הָאֱלֹהִים׃
14 וּמִן־הַלְוִיִּם שְׁמַעְיָה בֶּן־

10-13. The priests.

10. *Jehoiarib.* In Neh. xi. 10 *the son of Joiarib.* The Maccabees belonged to the priestly course of this family (cf. 1 Macc. ii. 1).

11. *Azariah.* The same as *Seraiah* in Neh. xi. 11.

the ruler of the house of God. An official who acted as custodian of the Temple, not the High Priest.

12. *Maasai the son of Adiel.* In Neh. xi. 13 *Amashai the son of Azarel.*

13. The number 1,760 in this verse apparently includes the members of the five courses mentioned in verses 10, 12 (Jedaiah, Jehoiarib, Jachin, Malchijah and Immer). If Azariah (or, Seraiah) in verse 11 represents a course which, after the return from Babylon, had replaced one of the courses enumerated in xxiv. 7-18, the total 1,760 would include six courses. On either alternative it is difficult to reconcile the total here with that of Neh. xi. 12-14 where it is stated: *and their brethren that did the work of the house, eight hundred twenty and two . . . and his brethren, chiefs of fathers' houses, two hundred forty and two . . . and their brethren, mighty men of valour, a hundred twenty and eight,* a total of 1,192. It has been suggested that the number in Neh. refers only to those who were under the control of the chiefs there mentioned while the number in Chron. includes all the priests.

very able men. In Neh. xi. 14 the same Hebrew words are rendered *mighty men of valour.* In verse 26, *the four chief porters* is lit. 'the four mighty men (*gibborë*) of the porters,' i.e. their overseers, and the noun probably has the same meaning here, 'overseers of the host' of Temple ministers.

14-16. The Levites (cf. Neh. xi. 15-18).

the son of Hasshub, the son of Azrikam, the son of Hashabiah, of the sons of Merari; 15. and Bakbakkar, Heresh, and Galal, and Mattaniah the son of Mica, the son of Zichri, the son of Asaph; 16. and Obadiah the son of Shemaiah, the son of Galal, the son of Jeduthun, and Berechiah the son of Asa, the son of Elkanah, that dwelt in the villages of the Netophathites.

17. And the porters: Shallum, and Akkub, and Talmon, and Ahiman, and their brother Shallum the chief; 18. who hitherto waited in the king's gate eastward; they were the porters for the camp of the children of Levi. 19. And Shallum the son of Kore, the son of Ebiasaph, the son of Korah, and his brethren, of his father's house, the Korahites, were over the work of the service,

חַשּׁוּב בֶּן־עַזְרִיקָם בֶּן־
חֲשַׁבְיָה מִן־בְּנֵי מְרָרִי׃
15 וּבַקְבַּקַּר חֶרֶשׁ וְגָלָל וּמַתַּנְיָה
בֶּן־מִיכָא בֶּן־זִכְרִי בֶּן־
16 אָסָף׃ וְעֹבַדְיָה בֶּן־שְׁמַעְיָה
בֶּן־גָּלָל בֶּן־ידותון וּבֶרֶכְיָה
בֶּן־אָסָא בֶּן־אֶלְקָנָה הַיּוֹשֵׁב
בְּחַצְרֵי נְטוֹפָתִי׃
17 וְהַשֹּׁעֲרִים שַׁלּוּם וְעַקּוּב
וְטַלְמֹן וַאֲחִימָן וַאֲחִיהֶם
18 שַׁלּוּם הָרֹאשׁ׃ וְעַד־הֵנָּה
בְּשַׁעַר הַמֶּלֶךְ מִזְרָחָה הֵמָּה
הַשֹּׁעֲרִים לְמַחֲנוֹת בְּנֵי לֵוִי׃
19 וְשַׁלּוּם בֶּן־קוֹרֵא בֶּן־אֶבְיָסָף
בֶּן־קֹרַח וְאֶחָיו לְבֵית־אָבִיו
הַקָּרְחִים עַל מְלֶאכֶת

14. *of the Levites.* Their number is given in Neh. xi. 18 as 284.

of the sons of Merari. In Neh. xi. 15 *the son of Bunni.*

15. *Bakbakkar, Heresh, and Galal.* The reading in Neh. xi. 17 is *Bakbukiah, the second among his brethren.*

Zichri. loc. cit. *Zabdi.*

16. *Obadiah the son of Shemaiah.* In Neh. xi. 17 *Abda the son of Shammua.*

and Berechiah . . . Netophathites. Wanting in the corresponding passage in Neh. For the last named, see on ii. 54.

17-26a. The dispositions of the gatekeepers (cf. xxvi. 1-19; Neh. xi. 19).

17. *Shallum . . . Ahiman.* These two names are wanting in Neh. xi. 19.

Shallum the chief. Also absent from Neh. Shallum, Akkub and Talmon are the names of families, not of individuals (cf. Neh. vii. 45).

18. *hitherto.* i.e. since their ordination by David until the days of the Second Temple.

waited. Not in the text.

the king's gate. In 2 Kings xvi. 18 there is a reference to *the king's entry* to the Temple.

eastward. That the gate was on the east side appears also from Ezek. xlvi. 1f.

the camp of the children of Levi. On the Temple mount.

keepers of the gates of the Tent; and their fathers had been over the camp of the LORD, keepers of the entry; 20. and Phinehas the son of Eleazar was ruler over them in time past, the LORD being with him. 21. Zechariah the son of Meshelemiah was porter of the door of the tent of meeting. 22. All these that were chosen to be porters in the gates were two hundred and twelve. These were reckoned by genealogy in their villages, whom David and Samuel the seer did ordain in their set office. 23. So they and their children had the oversight of the gates of the house of the LORD, even the house of the Tent, by wards. 24. On the four sides were the porters, toward the east, west, north, and south. 25. And their brethren, in their villages, were to come in every seven days from time to time to be with them; 26. for the

הָעֲבֹדָה שֹׁמְרֵי הַסִּפִּים לָאֹהֶל
וַאֲבֹתֵיהֶם עַל־מַחֲנֵה יְהוָה
20 שֹׁמְרֵי הַמָּבוֹא׃ וּפִינְחָס בֶּן־
אֶלְעָזָר נָגִיד הָיָה עֲלֵיהֶם
21 לְפָנִים יְהוָה ׀ עִמּוֹ׃ זְכַרְיָה
בֶּן מְשֶׁלֶמְיָה שֹׁעֵר פֶּתַח לְאֹהֶל
22 מוֹעֵד׃ כֻּלָּם הַבְּרוּרִים
לְשֹׁעֲרִים בַּסִּפִּים מָאתַיִם
וּשְׁנֵים עָשָׂר הֵמָּה בְחַצְרֵיהֶם
הִתְיַחְשָׂם הֵמָּה יִסַּד דָּוִיד
וּשְׁמוּאֵל הָרֹאֶה בֶּאֱמוּנָתָם׃
23 וְהֵם וּבְנֵיהֶם עַל־הַשְּׁעָרִים
לְבֵית־יְהוָה לְבֵית הָאֹהֶל
24 לְמִשְׁמָרוֹת׃ לְאַרְבַּע רוּחוֹת
יִהְיוּ הַשֹּׁעֲרִים מִזְרָח יָמָּה
25 צָפוֹנָה וָנֶגְבָּה׃ וַאֲחֵיהֶם
בְּחַצְרֵיהֶם לָבוֹא לְשִׁבְעַת
הַיָּמִים מֵעֵת אֶל־עֵת עִם־

19. *keepers of the gates of the Tent.* In which the ark was deposited before the erection of the Temple. The duty of the Korahites was to prevent any unauthorized person from approaching it.

20. *Phinehas . . . was ruler over them.* He was the High Priest when the Israelites crossed the Jordan into Canaan.

21. *Zechariah,* etc. Cf. xxvi. 14.

22. The discrepancies between the numbers here and in Neh. may be due to differences in the forms of calculation or the classes which are included.

Samuel. This Book is the only source that associates him with David in the organization of the services of the Temple. The work of the latter in this connection is referred to in xxiii. 6ff., xxv. 1ff.

23. *had the oversight.* Not in the text.

the house of the LORD. When the Temple had been built.

the house of the Tent. In the days of David before the Temple was erected.

by wards. i.e. each group served in turn for a specified period (cf. verse 25).

24. *on the four sides.* Cf. xxvi. 14-18 for the details.

25. *from time to time.* Defines the pre-

four chief porters were in a set office. These were the Levites.

They were also over the chambers and over the treasuries in the house of God. 27. And they lodged round about the house of God, because the charge thereof was upon them, and to them pertained the opening thereof morning by morning. 28. And certain of them had charge of the vessels of service; for by tale were they brought in and by tale were they taken out. 29. Some of them also were appointed over the furniture, and over all the holy vessels, and over the fine flour, and the wine, and the oil, and the frankincense, and the spices. 30. And some of the sons of the priests prepared the confection of the spices. 31. And Mattithiah, one

26 אֵלֶּה׃ כִּי בֶאֱמוּנָה הֵמָּה
אַרְבַּעַת גִּבֹּרֵי הַשֹּׁעֲרִים הֵם
הַלְוִיִּם
וְהָיוּ עַל־הַלְּשָׁכוֹת וְעַל־
הָאוֹצְרוֹת בֵּית הָאֱלֹהִים׃
27 וּסְבִיבוֹת בֵּית־הָאֱלֹהִים יָלִינוּ
כִּי־עֲלֵיהֶם מִשְׁמֶרֶת וְהֵם
עַל־הַמַּפְתֵּחַ וְלַבֹּקֶר לַבֹּקֶר׃
28 וּמֵהֶם עַל־כְּלֵי הָעֲבֹדָה כִּי
בְמִסְפָּר יְבִיאוּם וּבְמִסְפָּר
29 יוֹצִיאוּם׃ וּמֵהֶם מְמֻנִּים עַל־
הַכֵּלִים וְעַל כָּל־כְּלֵי הַקֹּדֶשׁ
וְעַל־הַסֹּלֶת וְהַיַּיִן וְהַשֶּׁמֶן
30 וְהַלְּבוֹנָה וְהַבְּשָׂמִים׃ וּמִן־
בְּנֵי הַכֹּהֲנִים רֹקְחֵי הַמִּרְקַחַת
31 לַבְּשָׂמִים׃ וּמַתִּתְיָה מִן־

ceding words: from a certain hour at the beginning of the seven-day period until the same hour at its end.

26a. *chief porters.* See on verse 13.

26b-32. Other services performed by the gate-keepers.

26b. *the chambers.* In these the tithes and sacred vessels were stored (cf. 2 Chron. xxxi. 11f.; Neh. xiii. 4ff.).

27. *to them.* To the chief gate-keepers or to the Levites who were in charge of the stores.

the opening thereof. The Hebrew *maphtëach* may also be rendered 'key' (as, e.g., in Judg. iii. 25): 'they were over the key,' i.e. they kept the key and it was their duty to open the chambers every morning.

28. *certain of them.* Of the Levites.

vessels of service. The reference is probably to the gold and silver utensils whose number was carefully checked.

29. *the furniture.* lit. 'the vessels,' i.e. appurtenances other than the gold and silver utensils.

the fine flour . . . oil. Used for the meal-offerings and drink-offerings.

frankincense. For the cups used in connection with the showbread (cf. Lev. xxiv. 7).

spices. That were burned on the golden altar or mixed in a confection (verse 30).

30. *confection.* Described in Exod. xxx. 23ff.

31. *Shallum.* Cf. verse 19.

הַלְוִיִּם הוּא הַבְּכוֹר לְשַׁלֻּם
הַקָּרְחִי בֶּאֱמוּנָה עַל מַעֲשֵׂה
הַחֲבִתִּים׃ וּמִן־בְּנֵי הַקְּהָתִי 32
מִן־אֲחֵיהֶם עַל־לֶחֶם
הַמַּעֲרֶכֶת לְהָכִין שַׁבַּת שַׁבָּת׃
וְאֵלֶּה הַמְשֹׁרְרִים רָאשֵׁי אָבוֹת 33
לַלְוִיִּם בַּלְּשָׁכֹת פְּטִירִים כִּי־
יוֹמָם וָלַיְלָה עֲלֵיהֶם
בַּמְּלָאכָה׃ אֵלֶּה רָאשֵׁי 34
הָאָבוֹת לַלְוִיִּם לְתֹלְדוֹתָם
רָאשִׁים אֵלֶּה יָשְׁבוּ בִירוּשָׁלִָם׃
וּבְגִבְעוֹן יָשְׁבוּ אֲבִי־גִבְעוֹן 35
יְעוּאֵל וְשֵׁם אִשְׁתּוֹ מַעֲכָה׃
וּבְנוֹ הַבְּכוֹר עַבְדּוֹן וְצוּר וְקִישׁ 36
וּבַעַל וְנֵר וְנָדָב׃ וּגְדוֹר וְאַחְיוֹ 37
וּזְכַרְיָה וּמִקְלוֹת׃ וּמִקְלוֹת 38
הוֹלִיד אֶת־שִׁמְאָם וְאַף־
הֵם נֶגֶד אֲחֵיהֶם יָשְׁבוּ
בִירוּשָׁלִַם עִם־אֲחֵיהֶם׃

of the Levites, who was the first-born of Shallum the Korahite, had the set office over the things that were baked on griddles. 32. And some of their brethren, of the sons of the Kohathites, were over the showbread, to prepare it every sabbath.

33. And these are the singers, heads of fathers' houses of the Levites, who dwelt in the chambers and were free from other service; for they were employed in their work day and night. 34. These were heads of fathers' houses of the Levites, by their generations, chief men; these dwelt at Jerusalem.

35. And in Gibeon there dwelt the father of Gibeon, Jeiel, whose wife's name was Maacah; 36. and his first-born son Abdon, and Zur, and Kish, and Baal, and Ner, and Nadab; 37. and Gedor, and Ahio, and Zechariah, and Mikloth. 38. And Mikloth begot Shimeam. And they also dwelt with their brethren in Jerusalem, over against their brethren.

v. 32. הב׳ בפתח v. 33. פטורים ק׳ v. 35. יעיאל ק׳

the set office. The noun *emunah*, lit. 'faithfulness,' in the sense of 'trust, charge' is only found in this Book.

baked on griddles. A tenth part of an ephah was offered daily, half of it in the morning and the other half in the evening.

32. *the showbread . . . every sabbath.* Cf. Lev. xxiv. 8.

33. *these are the singers.* It is difficult to determine to whom the demonstrative *these* refers. Some connect it with verses 15f. which contain a list of singers (cf. Neh. xi. 17), others with vi. 18-32.

who dwelt. These words and *from other service* are not in the text.

and night. Cf. Ps. cxxxiv. 1.

35-38 (repeated from viii. 29-32). The Benjamites in Gibeon and Jerusalem. The repetition here serves as an introduction to Saul's fall in battle when the throne was vacated for David.

39. And Ner begot Kish; and Kish begot Saul; and Saul begot Jonathan, and Malchi-shua, and Abinadab, and Eshbaal. 40. And the son of Jonathan was Merib-baal; and Merib-baal begot Micah. 41. And the sons of Micah: Pithon, and Melech, and Taharea [, and Ahaz]. 42. And Ahaz begot Jarah; and Jarah begot Alemeth, and Azmaveth, and Zimri; and Zimri begot Moza. 43. And Moza begot Binea; and Rephaiah his son, Eleasah his son, Azel his son. 44. And Azel had six sons, whose names are these: Azrikam, Bocru, and Ishmael, and Sheariah, and Obadiah, and Hanan; these were the sons of Azel.

39 וְנֵר הוֹלִיד אֶת־קִישׁ וְקִישׁ
הוֹלִיד אֶת־שָׁאוּל וְשָׁאוּל
הוֹלִיד אֶת־יְהוֹנָתָן וְאֶת־
מַלְכִּי־שׁוּעַ וְאֶת־אֲבִינָדָב
40 וְאֶת־אֶשְׁבָּעַל׃ וּבֶן־יְהוֹנָתָן
מְרִיב בָּעַל וּמְרִי־בַעַל
41 הוֹלִיד אֶת־מִיכָה׃ וּבְנֵי
מִיכָה פִּיתֹן וָמֶלֶךְ וְתַחְרֵעַ׃
42 וְאָחָז הוֹלִיד אֶת־יַעְרָה
וְיַעְרָה הוֹלִיד אֶת־עָלֶמֶת
וְאֶת־עַזְמָוֶת וְאֶת־זִמְרִי וְזִמְרִי
43 הוֹלִיד אֶת־מוֹצָא׃ וּמוֹצָא
הוֹלִיד אֶת־בִּנְעָא וּרְפָיָה בְנוֹ
אֶלְעָשָׂה בְנוֹ אָצֵל בְּנוֹ׃
44 וּלְאָצֵל שִׁשָּׁה בָנִים וְאֵלֶּה
שְׁמוֹתָם עַזְרִיקָם ׀ בֹּכְרוּ
וְיִשְׁמָעֵאל וּשְׁעַרְיָה וְעֹבַדְיָה
וְחָנָן אֵלֶּה בְּנֵי אָצֵל׃

10 CHAPTER X י

1. Now the Philistines fought against Israel; and the men of Israel fled from before the Philis-

1 וּפְלִשְׁתִּים נִלְחֲמוּ בְיִשְׂרָאֵל
וַיָּנָס אִישׁ־יִשְׂרָאֵל מִפְּנֵי

39-44 (repeated from viii. 33-38).

41. [*and Ahaz*]. Added from viii. 35.

X-XXIX—THE HISTORY OF DAVID

CHAPTER X

1-12 (with variations corresponding to 1 Sam. xxxi. 1-13). The death and burial of Saul.

1. *men of Israel.* The Hebrew has the singular 'man' in a collective sense.

Gilboa. It is in the south-east of the plain of Esdraelon.

tines, and fell down slain in mount Gilboa. 2. And the Philistines followed hard after Saul and after his sons; and the Philistines slew Jonathan, and Abinadab, and Malchi-shua, the sons of Saul. 3. And the battle went sore against Saul, and the archers overtook him; and he was in anguish by reason of the archers. 4. Then said Saul unto his armour-bearer: 'Draw thy sword, and thrust me through therewith; lest these uncircumcised come and make a mock of me.' But his armour-bearer would not; for he was sore afraid. Therefore Saul took his sword, and fell upon it. 5. And when his armour-bearer saw that Saul was dead, he likewise fell upon his sword, and died. 6. So Saul died, and his three sons; and all his house died together. 7. And when all the men of Israel that were in the valley saw that [Israel] fled, and that Saul and his sons were dead,

פְלִשְׁתִּים וַיִּפְּלוּ חֲלָלִים בְּהַר
2 גִּלְבֹּעַ׃ וַיַּדְבְּקוּ פְלִשְׁתִּים
אַחֲרֵי שָׁאוּל וְאַחֲרֵי בָנָיו וַיַּכּוּ
פְלִשְׁתִּים אֶת־יוֹנָתָן וְאֶת־
אֲבִינָדָב וְאֶת־מַלְכִּי־שׁוּעַ
3 בְּנֵי שָׁאוּל׃ וַתִּכְבַּד הַמִּלְחָמָה
עַל־שָׁאוּל וַיִּמְצָאֻהוּ הַמּוֹרִים
בַּקֶּשֶׁת וַיָּחֶל מִן־הַיּוֹרִים׃
4 וַיֹּאמֶר שָׁאוּל אֶל־נֹשֵׂא כֵלָיו
שְׁלֹף חַרְבְּךָ ׀ וְדָקְרֵנִי בָהּ
פֶּן־יָבֹאוּ הָעֲרֵלִים הָאֵלֶּה
וְהִתְעַלְּלוּ־בִי וְלֹא אָבָה נֹשֵׂא
כֵלָיו כִּי יָרֵא מְאֹד וַיִּקַּח שָׁאוּל
אֶת־הַחֶרֶב וַיִּפֹּל עָלֶיהָ׃
5 וַיַּרְא נֹשֵׂא־כֵלָיו כִּי־מֵת
שָׁאוּל וַיִּפֹּל גַּם־הוּא עַל־
6 הַחֶרֶב וַיָּמֹת׃ וַיָּמָת שָׁאוּל
וּשְׁלֹשֶׁת בָּנָיו וְכָל־בֵּיתוֹ יַחְדָּו
7 מֵתוּ׃ וַיִּרְאוּ כָּל־אִישׁ יִשְׂרָאֵל
אֲשֶׁר־בָּעֵמֶק כִּי נָסוּ וְכִי־מֵתוּ

3. *overtook him.* Better, 'got him in range,' lit. 'found him.'

in anguish. Because he was unable to escape the attack upon him by the archers.

4. *make a mock of me.* By humiliating him if he fell into their hands alive.

he was sore afraid. To lay his hand on an anointed king.

5. *his sword.* So in 1 Sam. xxxi. 5. The text here reads 'the sword.'

6. *and all his house died together.* In 1 Sam. xxxi. 6: *and his armour-bearer and all his men, that same day together.* By *his house* is meant the servants of his household or more probably his body-guard.

7. *in the valley.* Of Jezreel (cf. Hos. i. 5), later known as the plain of Esdraelon. According to 1 Sam. xxxi. 7, those who

they forsook their cities, and fled; and the Philistines came and dwelt in them.

8. And it came to pass on the morrow, when the Philistines came to strip the slain, that they found Saul and his sons fallen in mount Gilboa. 9. And they stripped him, and took his head, and his armour, and sent into the land of the Philistines round about, to carry the tidings unto their idols, and to the people. 10. And they put his armour in the house of their gods, and fastened his head in the house of Dagon. 11. And when all Jabesh-gilead heard all that the Philistines had done to Saul, 12. all the valiant men arose, and took away the body

שָׁאוּל וּבָנָיו וַיַּעַזְבוּ עָרֵיהֶם
וַיָּנֻסוּ וַיָּבֹאוּ פְלִשְׁתִּים וַיֵּשְׁבוּ
בָּהֶם׃
8 וַיְהִי מִמָּחֳרָת וַיָּבֹאוּ פְלִשְׁתִּים
לְפַשֵּׁט אֶת־הַחֲלָלִים וַיִּמְצְאוּ
אֶת־שָׁאוּל וְאֶת־בָּנָיו נֹפְלִים
9 בְּהַר גִּלְבֹּעַ׃ וַיַּפְשִׁיטֻהוּ וַיִּשְׂאוּ
אֶת־רֹאשׁוֹ וְאֶת־כֵּלָיו וַיְשַׁלְּחוּ
בְאֶרֶץ־פְּלִשְׁתִּים סָבִיב
לְבַשֵּׂר אֶת־עֲצַבֵּיהֶם וְאֶת־
10 הָעָם׃ וַיָּשִׂימוּ אֶת־כֵּלָיו בֵּית
אֱלֹהֵיהֶם וְאֶת־גֻּלְגָּלְתּוֹ תָקְעוּ
11 בֵּית דָּגוֹן׃ וַיִּשְׁמְעוּ כֹּל יָבֵישׁ
גִּלְעָד אֵת כָּל־אֲשֶׁר־עָשׂוּ
12 פְלִשְׁתִּים לְשָׁאוּל׃ וַיָּקוּמוּ
כָּל־אִישׁ חַיִל וַיִּשְׂאוּ אֶת־

lived on the eastern side of the Jordan also fled.

dwelt in them. Only for a short time; Abner reconquered the territory for Saul's son, Ish-bosheth, whom he made king over a number of localities including Jezreel (cf. 2 Sam. ii. 9).

9. *took his head, and his armour.* In 1 Sam. xxxi. 9 more detailed facts are given: *cut off his head and stripped off his armour.*

unto their idols. In 1 Sam.: *unto the house of their idols.*

10. *in the house of their gods.* The *gods* were the *Ashtaroth,* named in 1 Sam. xxxi. 10. The noun is the plural form of *Ashtoreth,* a goddess associated with warlike exploits.

fastened his head in the house of Dagon. From 1 Sam. it is learnt that they *fastened his body to the wall of Beth-shan,* i.e. apparently the body without the head. The name *Dagon* may be derived from *dag* (fish); the idol according to tradition had the head and arms of a man and the body and tail of a fish. Other authorities hold that *Dagon* was the god of the cornfields, *dagan* meaning 'corn.'

11. *all Jabesh-gilead.* In 1 Sam. xxxi. 11 the reading is: *the inhabitants of Jabesh-gilead.* This city had been delivered from the Ammonites by Saul at the beginning of his reign (cf. 1 Sam. xi. 1ff.). For David's appreciation of the action of the men of Jabesh-gilead, cf. 2 Sam. ii. 5ff.

12. *all the valiant men arose.* 1 Sam.

of Saul, and the bodies of his sons, and brought them to Jabesh, and buried their bones under the terebinth in Jabesh, and fasted seven days.

13. So Saul died for his transgression which he committed against the LORD, because of the word of the LORD, which he kept not; and also for that he asked counsel of a ghost, to inquire thereby, 14. and inquired not of the LORD; therefore He slew him, and turned the kingdom unto David the son of Jesse.

גּוּפַת שָׁאוּל וְאֵת גּוּפֹת בָּנָיו
וַיְבִיאוּם יָבֵישָׁה וַיִּקְבְּרוּ אֶת־
עַצְמוֹתֵיהֶם תַּחַת הָאֵלָה
בְּיָבֵשׁ וַיָּצוּמוּ שִׁבְעַת יָמִים׃
13 וַיָּמָת שָׁאוּל בְּמַעֲלוֹ אֲשֶׁר־
מָעַל בַּיהוָה עַל־דְּבַר יְהוָה
אֲשֶׁר לֹא־שָׁמָר וְגַם־לִשְׁאוֹל
14 בָּאוֹב לִדְרוֹשׁ׃ וְלֹא־דָרַשׁ
בַּיהוָה וַיְמִיתֵהוּ וַיַּסֵּב אֶת־
הַמְּלוּכָה לְדָוִיד בֶּן־יִשָׁי׃

11 CHAPTER XI יא

1. Then all Israel gathered themselves to David unto Hebron,

1 וַיִּקָּבְצוּ כָל־יִשְׂרָאֵל אֶל־
דָּוִיד חֶבְרוֹנָה לֵאמֹר הִנֵּה

xxxi. 12 adds: *and went all night.* The distance they covered was about twenty miles.

his sons. In 1 Sam. this is followed by: *from the wall of Beth-shan.*

and brought them to Jabesh. In 1 Sam. the reading is: *and they came to Jabesh,* the difference in Hebrew between *brought* and *came* being very slight.

and buried their bones. Sam. adds: *and burnt them.*

terebinth. In 1 Sam. xxxi. 13: *tamarisk-tree.*

fasted seven days. This kind of fast involved abstinence from all food and drink during the day, but food and drink were taken after night-fall.

13f. Moral reflection on the violent death of Saul (not in 1 Sam.).

13. *because of the word of the LORD,* etc. As narrated in 1 Sam. xiii. 9ff., xv. 2ff.

he asked counsel of a ghost. The allusion is to the raising of the spirit of Samuel by the woman of En-dor (cf. 1 Sam. xxviii. 7ff.).

14. *inquired not of the LORD.* Cf. xiii. 3. The inquiry which he made of God before engaging in his last battle (1 Sam. xxviii. 6) is disregarded, since it remained unanswered because of his unworthiness.

CHAPTER XI

1-3 (corresponding to 2 Sam. v. 1-3). David is anointed king over all Israel. The Chronicler passes over the details contained in 2 Sam. i-iv which cover a period of seven years (cf. 2 Sam. v. 5), and proceeds at once to David's choice as king over the whole of the people.

1. *unto Hebron.* Where David was reigning as king over Judah.

saying: 'Behold, we are thy bone and thy flesh. 2. In times past, even when Saul was king, it was thou that didst lead out and bring in Israel; and the LORD thy God said unto thee: Thou shalt feed My people Israel, and thou shalt be prince over My people Israel.' 3. So all the elders of Israel came to the king to Hebron; and David made a covenant with them in Hebron before the LORD; and they anointed David king over Israel, according to the word of the LORD by the hand of Samuel.

4. And David and all Israel went to Jerusalem—the same is Jebus—

2 עַצְמְךָ וּבְשָׂרְךָ אֲנָחְנוּ׃ גַּם־
תְּמוֹל גַּם־שִׁלְשׁוֹם גַּם בִּהְיוֹת
שָׁאוּל מֶלֶךְ אַתָּה הַמּוֹצִיא
וְהַמֵּבִיא אֶת־יִשְׂרָאֵל וַיֹּאמֶר
יְהוָה אֱלֹהֶיךָ לְךָ אַתָּה תִרְעֶה
אֶת־עַמִּי אֶת־יִשְׂרָאֵל וְאַתָּה
תִּהְיֶה נָגִיד עַל עַמִּי יִשְׂרָאֵל׃
3 וַיָּבֹאוּ כָּל־זִקְנֵי יִשְׂרָאֵל אֶל־
הַמֶּלֶךְ חֶבְרוֹנָה וַיִּכְרֹת לָהֶם
דָּוִיד בְּרִית בְּחֶבְרוֹן לִפְנֵי
יְהוָה וַיִּמְשְׁחוּ אֶת־דָּוִיד
לְמֶלֶךְ עַל־יִשְׂרָאֵל כִּדְבַר
יְהוָה בְּיַד־שְׁמוּאֵל׃
4 וַיֵּלֶךְ דָּוִיד וְכָל־יִשְׂרָאֵל
יְרוּשָׁלִַם הִיא יְבוּס וְשָׁם

we are thy bone and thy flesh. An expression of kinship, devotion and loyalty.

2. *in times past.* lit. 'also yesterday, also the day before yesterday.'

didst lead out and bring in. Took a prominent part in national affairs (cf. 1 Sam. xviii. 13, 16).

the LORD thy God said, etc. Cf. verses 3 and 10; 1 Sam. xvi. 1ff.

3. *all the elders of Israel came.* The elders had the authority of the people to appoint a king.

made a covenant. Similar to the covenant later made by Jehoiada *between the LORD and the king* (Joash) *and the people, that they should be the LORD'S people* (2 Kings xi. 17). According to others, the covenant mentioned here was a charter guaranteeing Israel the same rights as those enjoyed by Judah and assuring them of the king's protection.

in Hebron. See on verse 1.

before the LORD. i.e. a solemn covenant or, possibly, before the ark which was there for the occasion.

according to the word . . . Samuel. This is added by the Chronicler to the statement in 2 Sam. v. 3, his object being to emphasize the Divine choice of David.

4-9 (corresponding to 2 Sam. v. 6-10). David captures Jerusalem which is made a royal city.

4. *David and all Israel.* In 2 Sam. v. 6: *the king and his men*, i.e. his bodyguard.

the same is Jebus. Not in 2 Sam. The city consisted of two parts: a citadel (*the stronghold of Zion*, verse 5) and a lower section (*the city round about*, verse 8). The former was inhabited by Jebusites and the latter probably by both Jebusites

and the Jebusites, the inhabitants of the land, were there. 5. And the inhabitants of Jebus said to David: 'Thou shalt not come in hither.' Nevertheless David took the stronghold of Zion; the same is the city of David. 6. And David said: 'Whosoever smiteth the Jebusites first shall be chief and captain.' And Joab the son of Zeruiah went up first, and was made chief. 7. And David dwelt in the stronghold; therefore they called it the city of David. 8. And he built the city round about, from Millo even round about; and Joab repaired the rest of the city. 9. And David waxed greater and greater; for the LORD of hosts was with him.

5 הַיְבוּסִי יֹשְׁבֵי הָאָרֶץ׃ וַיֹּאמְרוּ
יֹשְׁבֵי יְבוּס לְדָוִיד לֹא תָבוֹא
הֵנָּה וַיִּלְכֹּד דָּוִיד אֶת־מְצֻדַת
6 צִיּוֹן הִיא עִיר דָּוִיד׃ וַיֹּאמֶר
דָּוִיד כָּל־מַכֵּה יְבוּסִי
בָּרִאשׁוֹנָה יִהְיֶה לְרֹאשׁ וּלְשָׂר
וַיַּעַל בָּרִאשׁוֹנָה יוֹאָב בֶּן־
7 צְרוּיָה וַיְהִי לְרֹאשׁ׃ וַיֵּשֶׁב
דָּוִיד בַּמְצָד עַל־כֵּן קָרְאוּ־
8 לוֹ עִיר דָּוִיד׃ וַיִּבֶן הָעִיר
מִסָּבִיב מִן־הַמִּלּוֹא וְעַד־
הַסָּבִיב וְיוֹאָב יְחַיֶּה אֶת־שְׁאָר
9 הָעִיר׃ וַיֵּלֶךְ דָּוִיד הָלוֹךְ
וְגָדוֹל וַיהוָה צְבָאוֹת עִמּוֹ׃

and Benjamites. It was the citadel that David captured.

the inhabitants of the land. The Jebusites were one of the original seven nations that lived in Canaan before the entry of the Israelites (cf. Deut. vii. 1).

5. *thou shalt not come in hither.* The completion of the boast is given in 2 Sam. v. 6: *except thou take away the blind and the lame,* implying that the city was so well fortified that even a garrison of blind and lame men could hold it against an invader.

the stronghold of Zion. Situated in the south-east of the old city of Jerusalem; but later tradition identified it with the south-west hill of the city.

6. *whosoever smiteth . . . made chief.* This statement is simpler and clearer than the wording in 2 Sam. v. 8.

Joab . . . was made chief. This appointment is not mentioned in the corresponding passage in Sam. On the other hand, from 2 Sam. ii. 13 it appears that Joab was already commander during the wars between David and the house of Saul. It is possible that Joab was at first only one of the commanders of David but was made commander-in-chief after his exploit in the capture of Jerusalem.

8. *Millo.* In Hebrew it is always prefixed by the definite article. It was part of the fortifications of Jerusalem (cf. 2 Chron. xxxii. 5). The literal meaning of the word is 'filling up'; its location is uncertain.

and Joab repaired the rest of the city. Not in Sam. The verb probably means 'restored,' lit. 'kept alive.' The *rest of the city* accordingly signifies the buildings other than the citadel. Less probably, some take the verb in its literal sense and understand the phrase to mean that Joab

10. Now these are the chief of the mighty men whom David had, who held strongly with him in his kingdom, together with all Israel, to make him king, according to the word of the LORD concerning Israel. 11. And this is the number of the mighty men whom David had: Jashobeam, the son of a Hachmonite, the chief of the captains; he lifted up his spear against three hundred and slew them at one time.

12. And after him was Eleazar the son of Dodo, the Ahohite, who was one of the three mighty men. 13. He was with David at Pas-dammim, and there the Philistines

10 וְאֵלֶּה רָאשֵׁי הַגִּבֹּרִים אֲשֶׁר
לְדָוִיד הַמִּתְחַזְּקִים עִמּוֹ
בְמַלְכוּתוֹ עִם־כָּל־יִשְׂרָאֵל
לְהַמְלִיכוֹ כִּדְבַר יְהוָה עַל־
11 יִשְׂרָאֵל׃ וְאֵלֶּה מִסְפַּר
הַגִּבֹּרִים אֲשֶׁר לְדָוִיד יָשָׁבְעָם
בֶּן־חַכְמוֹנִי רֹאשׁ הַשָּׁלוֹשִׁים*
הוּא־עוֹרֵר אֶת־חֲנִיתוֹ עַל־
שְׁלשׁ־מֵאוֹת חָלָל בְּפַעַם
אֶחָת׃
12 וְאַחֲרָיו אֶלְעָזָר בֶּן־דּוֹדוֹ
הָאֲחוֹחִי הוּא בִּשְׁלוֹשָׁה
13 הַגִּבֹּרִים׃ הוּא־הָיָה עִם־
דָּוִיד בַּפַּס דַּמִּים וְהַפְּלִשְׁתִּים

v. 11. השלישים ק׳

spared the inhabitants who consisted of both Jebusites and Benjamites (cf. Judg. i. 21).

10-41a (corresponding to 2 Sam. xxiii. 8-39). David's mighty men.

10. Superscription of the list.

who held strongly, etc. Although awkwardly expressed, the meaning appears to be that the mighty men who are mentioned supported David when he was only king of Judah and helped to secure the recognition of his kingship over all Israel, which was his destiny as willed by God.

11-14 (corresponding to 2 Sam. xxiii. 8-12). Two of the bravest of the heroes (three in Sam.) are named and their exploits described.

11. *the number*. In 2 Sam. xxiii. 8: *the names.*

Jashobeam, the son of a Hachmonite. In xxvii. 2 his father's name is given as *Zabdiel*; and in Sam. his own name is *Josheb-basshebeth a Tahchemonite.*

the captains. The meaning of the *kethib* is 'the thirty (mighty men).'

he lifted up his spear. lit. 'he aroused his spear,' stirred it into action. The corresponding text in Sam. is: *the same was Adino the Eznite.*

three hundred. In Sam.: *eight hundred.* The figures may refer to different exploits.

12. *of the three mighty men.* Who are enumerated in Sam.

13. *he was with David.* The pronoun is presumed to refer to *Shammah* to whom the exploit is ascribed in Sam. (See, however, on verse 14).

Pas-dammim. In the south-west of Judah. In 1 Sam. xvii. 1 it is called *Ephes-dammim.*

were gathered together to battle, where was a plot of ground full of barley; and the people fled from before the Philistines. 14. But they stood in the midst of the plot, and defended it, and slew the Philistines; and the LORD saved them by a great victory.

15. And three of the thirty chiefs went down to the rock to David, unto the cave of Adullam; and the host of the Philistines were encamped in the valley of Rephaim. 16. And David was then in the stronghold, and the garrison of the Philistines was then in Beth-lehem. 17. And David longed, and said: 'Oh that one would give me water to drink of the well of Beth-lehem, which is by the gate!' 18. And the three broke through the host of the Philistines, and drew water out of

נֶאֶסְפוּ־שָׁם לַמִּלְחָמָה וַתְּהִי
חֶלְקַת הַשָּׂדֶה מְלֵאָה שְׂעוֹרִים
וְהָעָם נָסוּ מִפְּנֵי פְלִשְׁתִּים׃
וַיִּתְיַצְּבוּ בְתוֹךְ־הַחֶלְקָה 14
וַיַּצִּילוּהָ וַיַּכּוּ אֶת־פְּלִשְׁתִּים
וַיּוֹשַׁע יְהוָה תְּשׁוּעָה גְדוֹלָה׃
וַיֵּרְדוּ שְׁלוֹשָׁה מִן־הַשְּׁלוֹשִׁים 15
רֹאשׁ עַל־הַצֻּר אֶל־דָּוִיד
אֶל־מְעָרַת עֲדֻלָּם וּמַחֲנֵה
פְלִשְׁתִּים חֹנָה בְּעֵמֶק רְפָאִים׃
וְדָוִיד אָז בַּמְּצוּדָה וּנְצִיב 16
פְּלִשְׁתִּים אָז בְּבֵית לָחֶם׃
וַיִּתְאָו דָּוִיד וַיֹּאמַר מִי יַשְׁקֵנִי 17
מַיִם מִבּוֹר בֵּית־לֶחֶם
אֲשֶׁר בַּשָּׁעַר׃ וַיִּבְקְעוּ 18
הַשְּׁלֹשָׁה בְּמַחֲנֵה פְלִשְׁתִּים
וַיִּשְׁאֲבוּ־מַיִם מִבּוֹר בֵּית־

barley. In 2 Sam. xxiii. 11 the reading is: *lentils.* The Hebrew equivalents of the two words have the same consonants in a different order except that one has a *resh* and the other a *daleth.*

14. *but they stood.* The subject may possibly refer to Eleazar (verse 12) and Shammah (2 Sam. xxiii. 11) or to David and Eleazar. In Sam. the subject is Shammah and the verb is in the singular.

15-19 (corresponding to 2 Sam. xxiii. 13-17). The heroic deed of three unnamed mighty men.

15. *to the rock* (hatstsur). In Sam.: *in the harvest time* (katsir).

the cave of Adullam. Where David took refuge in his flight from Saul (1 Sam. xxii. 1).

the valley of Rephaim. The plain, south of Jerusalem, which extends to Beth-lehem.

16. *in the stronghold.* It has been suggested that the stronghold of Adullam is meant, a prominent hill in the Shephelah identified with Aid-el-Ma, about twelve miles south-west of Beth-lehem.

the garrison (netsib). Or, 'the governor.' In Sam. the text has *mutstsab* which can only mean *garrison.*

17. *oh that one . . . drink.* An idiomatic expression for 'would that I could drink.'

the well of Beth-lehem, that was by the gate, and took it, and brought it to David; but David would not drink thereof, but poured it out unto the LORD, 19. and said: 'My God forbid it me, that I should do this; shall I drink the blood of these men that have put their lives in jeopardy? for with the jeopardy of their lives they brought it.' Therefore he would not drink it. These things did the three mighty men.

20. And Abishai, the brother of Joab, he was chief of the three; for he lifted up his spear against three hundred and slew them, and had a name among the three. 21. Of the three in the second rank he was the most honourable, and was made their captain; howbeit he attained not to the first three.

22. Benaiah the son of Jehoiada, the son of a valiant man of Kabzeel, who had done mighty deeds, he

לֶחֶם אֲשֶׁר בַּשַּׁעַר וַיִּשְׂאוּ וַיָּבִאוּ
אֶל־דָּוִיד וְלֹא־אָבָה דָוִיד
לִשְׁתּוֹתָם וַיְנַסֵּךְ אֹתָם לַיהוָה׃
19 וַיֹּאמֶר חָלִילָה לִּי מֵאֱלֹהַי
מֵעֲשׂוֹת זֹאת הֲדַם הָאֲנָשִׁים
הָאֵלֶּה אֶשְׁתֶּה בְנַפְשׁוֹתָם כִּי
בְנַפְשׁוֹתָם הֱבִיאוּם וְלֹא אָבָה
לִשְׁתּוֹתָם אֵלֶּה עָשׂוּ שְׁלֹשֶׁת
הַגִּבּוֹרִים׃
20 וְאַבְשַׁי אֲחִי־יוֹאָב הוּא הָיָה
רֹאשׁ הַשְּׁלוֹשָׁה וְהוּא עוֹרֵר
אֶת־חֲנִיתוֹ עַל־שְׁלֹשׁ מֵאוֹת
חָלָל וְלֹא־שֵׁם בַּשְּׁלוֹשָׁה׃
21 מִן־הַשְּׁלוֹשָׁה בַשְּׁנַיִם נִכְבָּד
וַיְהִי לָהֶם לְשָׂר וְעַד־הַשְּׁלֹשָׁה
לֹא־בָא׃
22 בְּנָיָה בֶן־יְהוֹיָדָע בֶּן־אִישׁ־
חַיִל רַב־פְּעָלִים מִן־קַבְצְאֵל

v. 20. ולו ק׳

18. ***David would not drink.*** The reason is given in the following verse.

poured it out. The Hebrew verb is the technical term used in connection with drink-offerings.

19. ***my God forbid it me.*** lit. 'far be it for me, from my God.'

that have put their lives in jeopardy. lit. 'with their lives,' at the (possible) cost of their lives.

20-25 (corresponding to 2 Sam. xxiii. 18-23). The exploits of Abishai and Benaiah.

20. ***Abishai.*** The Hebrew has the form *Abshai.* He was David's nephew.

the brother of Joab. Being commander-in-chief over the whole army, Joab is not included in the list of the mighty men.

among the three. i.e. *of the second rank,* as stated in the next verse. This trio is in contrast to that mentioned in verses 11f., viz. Jashobeam, Eleazar and, probably, Shammah.

22. ***Kabzeel.*** In the south of Judah (cf. Josh. xv. 21); its site has not been identified.

smote the two altar-hearths of Moab; he went down also and slew a lion in the midst of a pit in time of snow. 23. And he slew an Egyptian, a man of great stature, five cubits high; and in the Egyptian's hand was a spear like a weaver's beam; and he went down to him with a staff, and plucked the spear out of the Egyptian's hand, and slew him with his own spear. 24. These things did Benaiah the son of Jehoiada, and had a name among the three mighty men. 25. Behold, he was more honourable than the thirty, but he attained not to the first three; and David set him over his guard.

26. Also the mighty men of valour: Asahel the brother of Joab, Elhanan the son of Dodo of Beth-

הוּא הִכָּה אֵת שְׁנֵי אֲרִיאֵל
מוֹאָב וְהוּא יָרַד וְהִכָּה אֶת־
הָאֲרִי בְּתוֹךְ הַבּוֹר בְּיוֹם
23 הַשָּׁלֶג׃ וְהוּא הִכָּה אֶת־הָאִישׁ
הַמִּצְרִי אִישׁ מִדָּה ׀ חָמֵשׁ
בָּאַמָּה וּבְיַד הַמִּצְרִי חֲנִית
כִּמְנוֹר אֹרְגִים וַיֵּרֶד אֵלָיו
בַּשָּׁבֶט וַיִּגְזֹל אֶת־הַחֲנִית מִיַּד
הַמִּצְרִי וַיַּהַרְגֵהוּ בַּחֲנִיתוֹ׃
24 אֵלֶּה עָשָׂה בְּנָיָהוּ בֶּן־יְהוֹיָדָע
וְלוֹ שֵׁם בִּשְׁלוֹשָׁה הַגִּבֹּרִים׃
25 מִן־הַשְּׁלוֹשִׁים הִנּוֹ נִכְבָּד הוּא
וְאֶל־הַשְּׁלֹשָׁה לֹא־בָא
וַיְשִׂימֵהוּ דָוִיד עַל־מִשְׁמַעְתּוֹ׃
26 וְגִבּוֹרֵי הַחֲיָלִים עֲשָׂהאֵל אֲחִי
יוֹאָב אֶלְחָנָן בֶּן־דּוֹדוֹ מִבֵּית

altar-hearths. On which burned the sacred fire of the Moabites. It was a brave feat to penetrate enemy territory as far as their temple. 'But the use of the word *smote* in connection with inanimate objects is unusual. The Targum and Jewish commentators interpret the word as a compound of *ari*, "lion," and *el*, "God," i.e. "two lion-hearted men of Moab." The Arabs and Persians apply the term "lion of God" to celebrated warriors' (Goldman, *Samuel*, Soncino ed., *ad loc.*).

in time of snow. When hunger drove the lion from its lair to a village in search of food.

23. *a man of great stature.* lit. 'a man of measure.' In 2 Sam. xxiii. 21: *a goodly man*, or 'a man of (striking) appearance.'

a staff. Or, 'rod, club.' Shepherds used it as a means of defence against wild beasts; it was pointed at one end and so a thrust stabbed the attacking animal.

24. *had a name . . . three.* See on verse 20.

25. Cf. verse 21.

guard. lit. 'obedience,' the king's guard that obediently carried out his orders. The reference is to the royal bodyguard consisting of the Cherethites and the Pelethites (cf. 2 Sam. viii. 18).

26-41a (corresponding to 2 Sam. xxiii. 24-39). A list of thirty heroes to which are added (in 41b-47) sixteen names of men of lesser importance who are not mentioned in Sam.

lehem; 27. Shammoth the Harorite,
Helez the Pelonite; 28. Ira the son
of Ikkesh the Tekoite, Abiezer the
Anathothite; 29. Sibbecai the Hushathite, Ilai the Ahohite; 30. Mahrai
the Netophathite, Heled the son of
Baanah the Netophathite; 31. Ithai
the son of Ribai of Gibeah of the
children of Benjamin, Benaiah the
Pirathonite; 32. Hurai of Nahale-
gaash, Abiel the Arbathite; 33. Azmaveth the Baharumite, Eliahba the
Shaalbonite; 34. the sons of Hashem
the Gizonite, Jonathan the son of

27 לָֽחֶם׃ שַׁמּוֹת הַהֲרוֹרִי חֶלֶץ
28 הַפְּלוֹנִי׃ עִירָא בֶּן־עִקֵּשׁ
הַתְּקוֹעִי אֲבִיעֶזֶר הָֽעַנְּתוֹתִי׃
29 סִבְּכַי הַחֻשָׁתִי עִילַי הָֽאֲחוֹחִי׃
30 מַהְרַי הַנְּטוֹפָתִי חֵלֶד בֶּן־
31 בַּעֲנָה הַנְּטוֹפָתִי׃ אִיתַי בֶּן־
רִיבַי מִגִּבְעַת בְּנֵי בִנְיָמִן בְּנָיָה
32 הַפִּרְעָתֹנִי׃ חוּרַי מִנַּחֲלֵי גָעַשׁ
33 אֲבִיאֵל הָֽעַרְבָתִי׃ עַזְמָוֶת
הַבַּֽחֲרוּמִי אֶלְיַחְבָּא
34 הַשַּֽׁעַלְבֹנִי׃ בְּנֵי הָשֵׁם הַגִּזוֹנִי

27. *Shammoth the Harorite.* In 2 Sam. xxiii. 25: *Shammah the Harodite.* Harod was in or near the valley of Jezreel (cf. Judg. vii. 1). *Elika the Harodite* of Sam. is not included in Chron.

Helez the Pelonite. In 2 Sam. xxiii. 26: *Helez the Paltite.* According to xxvii. 10, he belonged to the tribe of Ephraim.

28. *the Tekoite.* Tekoa, the native town of the prophet Amos, was twelve miles south of Jerusalem.

the Anathotite. Anathoth was a town in the portion of Benjamin, now known as Anota, about two miles north-east of Jerusalem, the birth-place of Jeremiah.

29. *Sibbecai.* So also in xxvii. 11; the reading in 2 Sam. xxiii. 27 is *Mebunnai.*

the Hushathite. Hushah was probably a place near Beth-lehem.

Ilai. In 2 Sam. xxiii. 28: *Zalmon.*

30. *Mahrai the Netophathite.* In xxvii. 13 the same name occurs with the addition *of the Zerahites. Netophathite* may mean one from the *villages of the Netophathites* (cf. ix. 16), or from Netopha, a Judean village in the vicinity of Beth-lehem (cf. ii. 54).

Heled. Heldai in xxvii. 15; *Heleb* in 2 Sam. xxiii. 29.

31. *Ithai.* In 2 Sam. xxiii. 29: *Ittai.*

Pirathonite. Pirathon was an Ephraimite town (cf. Judg. xii. 15).

32. *Hurai.* The form is *Hiddai* in 2 Sam. xxiii. 30. Neither name occurs elsewhere in the Bible.

Nahale-gaash. Or, 'brooks of Gaash.' Gaash was a mountain in the hill-country of Ephraim (cf. Judg. ii. 9).

Abiel. In 2 Sam. xxiii. 31: *Abi-albon.*

Arbathite. From Beth-arabah, a town in Judah or Benjamin (cf. Josh. xv. 6, 61), or on the border between the two tribes.

33. *the Baharumite.* Or, *Barhumite,* as in 2 Sam. xxiii. 31, an inhabitant of Bahurim, a town in Benjamin (cf. 2 Sam. iii. 16).

Shaalbonite. From *Shaalbim* (cf. Judg. i. 35), or *Shaalabbin* (cf. Josh. xix. 42), a town of Dan.

34. *the sons of Hashem the Gizonite.* In 2 Sam. xxiii. 32: *the sons of Jashen.*

Jonathan the son of Shageh the Hararite. The corresponding passage in 2 Sam.

Shageh the Hararite; 35. Ahiam the son of Sacar the Hararite, Eliphal the son of Ur; 36. Hepher the Mecherathite, Ahijah the Pelonite; 37. Hezro the Carmelite, Naarai the son of Ezbai; 38. Joel the brother of Nathan, Mibhar the son of Hagri; 39. Zelek the Ammonite, Nahrai the Berothite, the armour-bearer of Joab the son of Zeruiah; 40. Ira the Ithrite, Gareb the Ithrite; 41. Uriah the Hittite, Zabad the son of Ahlai; 42. Adina the son of Shiza the Reubenite, a chief of the Reubenites, and thirty with him; 43. Hanan the son of Maacah, and Joshaphat the Mithnite; 44. Uzzia the Ashterathite, Shama and Jeiel the sons of Hotham the Aroerite;

יוֹנָתָן בֶּן־שָׁגֵא הַהֲרָרִי׃
35 אֲחִיאָם בֶּן־שָׂכָר הַהֲרָרִי
36 אֱלִיפַל בֶּן־אוּר׃ חֵפֶר
37 הַמְּכֵרָתִי אֲחִיָּה הַפְּלֹנִי׃ חֶצְרוֹ
הַכַּרְמְלִי נַעֲרַי בֶּן־אֶזְבָּי׃
38 יוֹאֵל אֲחִי נָתָן מִבְחָר בֶּן־
39 הַגְרִי׃ צֶלֶק הָעַמּוֹנִי נַחְרַי
הַבֵּרֹתִי נֹשֵׂא כְּלֵי יוֹאָב בֶּן־
40 צְרוּיָה׃ עִירָא הַיִּתְרִי גָּרֵב
41 הַיִּתְרִי׃ אוּרִיָּה הַחִתִּי זָבָד
42 בֶּן־אַחְלָי׃ עֲדִינָא בֶן־שִׁיזָא
הָרְאוּבֵנִי רֹאשׁ לָרְאוּבֵנִי
43 וְעָלָיו שְׁלוֹשִׁים׃ חָנָן בֶּן־
44 מַעֲכָה וְיוֹשָׁפָט הַמִּתְנִי׃ עֻזִּיָּא
הָעַשְׁתְּרָתִי שָׁמָע וִיעוּאֵל בְּנֵי

v. 44. ויעיאל ק׳

xxiii. 32f. reads: *Jonathan; Shammah the Hararite.*

35. *Sacar.* In Sam.: *Sharar.*

Eliphal the son of Ur. The reading in 2 Sam. xxiii. 34 is: *Eliphelet the son of Ahasbai, the son of the Maachathite.*

36. *Hepher the Mecherathite, Ahijah the Pelonite.* In 2 Sam. xxiii. 34: *Eliam the son of Ahithophel the Gilonite.*

37. *Hezro.* In Sam.: *Hezrai.*

the Carmelite. From Carmel, a town in the hill-country of Judah near Hebron.

Naarai. In Sam.: *Paarai.*

the son of Ezbai. In Sam.: *the Arbite.*

38. The corresponding verse in 2 Sam. xxiii. 36 reads: *Igal the son of Nathan of Zobah, Bani the Gadite.*

39. *the Berothite.* In 2 Sam. xxiii. 37: *the Beerothite,* from Beeroth, a town in Benjamin.

40. *the Ithrite.* Of the family of Jether.

41*a. Uriah the Hittite.* So in 2 Sam. xxiii. 39, where the list concludes with this name and is followed by the remark: *thirty and seven in all.* Another sixteen names are added in the following list.

41b-47. A list of mighty men who are not included in Sam.

42. *and thirty with him.* i.e. his immediate followers.

44. *the Ashterathite.* An inhabitant of Ashtaroth (vi. 56).

the Aroerite. Either from Aroer in Moab (cf. v. 8; Josh. xiii. 16) or in Judah (cf. 1 Sam. xxx. 28).

45. Jediael the son of Shimri, and Joha his brother, the Tizite; 46. Eliel the Mahavite, and Jeribai, and Joshaviah, the sons of Elnaam, and Ithmah the Moabite; 47. Eliel, and Obed, and Jaasiel the Mezobaite.

45 חוֹתָם הָעֲרֹעֵרִי׃ יְדִיעֲאֵל
בֶּן־שִׁמְרִי וְיֹחָא אָחִיו הַתִּיצִי׃
46 אֱלִיאֵל הַמַּחֲוִים וִירִיבַי
וְיוֹשַׁוְיָה בְּנֵי אֶלְנָעַם וְיִתְמָה
47 הַמּוֹאָבִי׃ אֱלִיאֵל וְעוֹבֵד
וְיַעֲשִׂיאֵל הַמְּצֹבָיָה׃

12 CHAPTER XII יב

1. Now these are they that came to David to Ziklag, while he was yet shut up because of Saul the son of Kish; and they were among the mighty men, his helpers in war. 2. They were armed with bows, and could use both the right hand and the left in slinging stones and in shooting arrows from the bow; they were of Saul's brethren of Benjamin. 3. The chief was Ahiezer, then Joash, the sons of Shemaah the Gibeathite; and Jeziel, and Pelet, the sons of Azmaveth; and Beracah,

1 וְאֵלֶּה הַבָּאִים אֶל־דָּוִיד
לְצִיקְלַג עוֹד עָצוּר מִפְּנֵי
שָׁאוּל בֶּן־קִישׁ וְהֵמָּה
בַּגִּבּוֹרִים עֹזְרֵי הַמִּלְחָמָה׃
2 נֹשְׁקֵי קֶשֶׁת מַיְמִינִים
וּמַשְׂמִאלִים בָּאֲבָנִים וּבַחִצִּים
בַּקָּשֶׁת מֵאֲחֵי שָׁאוּל מִבִּנְיָמִן׃
3 הָרֹאשׁ אֲחִיעֶזֶר וְיוֹאָשׁ בְּנֵי
הַשְּׁמָעָה הַגִּבְעָתִי וִיזוּאֵל
וָפֶלֶט בְּנֵי עַזְמָוֶת וּבְרָכָה

v. 3. ויזיאל ק׳

CHAPTER XII

1-23. David's followers when he fled from Saul. The record throws light on Saul's defeat at Gilboa, since it shows that his army was deprived of a valuable source of strength through his hostility to David. This section has no parallel in Sam.

1-8. Benjamite warriors who joined David at Ziklag. Discontent with Saul's rule was so deep that even members of his own tribe deserted him for David at Ziklag, who at the time took refuge with the Philistine, Achish, an enemy of their king (1 Sam. xxvii. 2ff.).

1. *Ziklag.* About eleven miles south-east of Gaza in Philistia.

while he was yet shut up, etc. i.e. unable to move freely in the land of Israel owing to Saul's hatred.

2. *could use both the right hand*, etc. Cf. Judg. xx. 16, where seven hundred Benjamites are said to have been *left-handed;* and *every one could sling stones at a hair-breadth, and not miss.*

Saul's brethren. i.e. tribesmen.

3. *the Gibeathite.* From Gibeah, the modern Tel-el-Ful, four miles north of Jerusalem.

and Jehu the Anathothite; 4. and Ishmaiah the Gibeonite, a mighty man among the thirty, and over the thirty; and Jeremiah, and Jahaziel, and Johanan, and Jozabad the Gederathite; 5. Eluzai, and Jerimoth, and Bealiah, and Shemariah, and Shephatiah the Hariphite; 6. Elkanah, and Isshiah, and Azarel, and Joezer, and Jashobeam, the Korahites; 7. and Joelah, and Zebadiah, the sons of Jeroham of the troop.

8. And of the Gadites there separated themselves unto David to the stronghold in the wilderness, mighty men of valour, men trained for war, that could handle shield

4 וְיֵהוּא הָעַנְּתֹתִי׃ וְיִשְׁמַעְיָה
הַגִּבְעוֹנִי גִּבּוֹר בַּשְּׁלֹשִׁים וְעַל־
הַשְּׁלֹשִׁים וְיִרְמְיָה וְיַחֲזִיאֵל
וְיוֹחָנָן וְיוֹזָבָד הַגְּדֵרָתִי׃
5 אֶלְעוּזַי וִירִימוֹת וּבְעַלְיָה
וּשְׁמַרְיָהוּ וּשְׁפַטְיָהוּ הַחֲרוּ*פִי׃
6 אֶלְקָנָה וְיִשִּׁיָּהוּ וַעֲזַרְאֵל
וְיוֹעֶזֶר וְיָשָׁבְעָם הַקָּרְחִים׃
7 וְיוֹעֵאלָה וּזְבַדְיָה בְּנֵי יְרֹחָם
מִן־הַגְּדוֹר*׃
8 וּמִן־הַגָּדִי נִבְדְּלוּ אֶל־דָּוִיד
לַמְצַד מִדְבָּרָה גִּבֹּרֵי הַחַיִל
אַנְשֵׁי צָבָא לַמִּלְחָמָה עֹרְכֵי

v. 5. החריפי ק' v. 7. בנ"א הגדוד

the Anathothite. See on xi. 28.

4. *Ishmaiah the Gibeonite.* On the Gibeonites' hatred of Saul, cf. 2 Sam. xxi. 1ff. It is therefore not surprising that a Gibeonite should have gone over to David.

among the thirty, and over the thirty. This can have no reference to *the thirty* of 2 Sam. xxiii where Ishmaiah's name is not mentioned; nor does the name occur among the mighty men enumerated in chapter xi. The phrase must either refer to another list or is a superlative description of Ishmaiah's valour. He was not only as heroic as any of the thirty; he was even superior to them.

the Gederathite. From Gederah, a town in the Judean Shephelah (Josh. xv. 36), possibly the ruin Jedireh, nine miles south of Ludd; or (since a Benjamite town is more likely) the village Jedirah north of Jerusalem.

the Hariphite. In Neh. vii. 24 *the children of Hariph* are mentioned.

6. *the Korahites.* These are probably the descendants of Caleb of the tribe of Judah (cf. ii. 43). It is unlikely that the Levitical Korahites are here intended.

7. *of the troop.* This rendering presupposes the reading *gedud* which is found in many Hebrew MSS. and the Targum. Another reading is *Gedor*, a Judahite town (cf. Josh. xv. 58). It may be assumed that some Benjamites lived in cities of Judah.

8-15. Gadite followers of David. As the Gadites joined David while he was in *the stronghold in the wilderness*, this passage precedes chronologically verses 1-8, since he dwelt in the stronghold before he came to Ziklag (cf. verse 1).

8. *separated themselves.* From the other Gadites on the eastern side of the Jordan, who were partisans of Saul, to join David on the western side.

like the faces of lions. Of fierce and terrifying appearance.

and spear; whose faces were like the faces of lions, and they were as swift as the roes upon the mountains: 9. Ezer the chief, Obadiah the second, Eliab the third; 10. Mashmannah the fourth, Jeremiah the fifth; 11. Attai the sixth, Eliel the seventh; 12. Johanan the eighth, Elzabad the ninth; 13. Jeremiah the tenth, Machbannai the eleventh. 14. These of the sons of Gad were captains of the host; he that was least was equal to a hundred, and the greatest to a thousand. 15. These are they that went over the Jordan in the first month, when it had overflown all its banks; and they put to flight all them of the valleys, both toward the east, and toward the west.

16. And there came of the children of Benjamin and Judah to the stronghold unto David. 17. And David went out to meet them, and answered and said unto them: 'If

צִנָּה וָרֹמַח וּפְנֵי אַרְיֵה פְּנֵיהֶם
וְכִצְבָאיִם עַל־הֶהָרִים
9 לְמַהֵר׃ עֵזֶר הָרֹאשׁ עֹבַדְיָה
הַשֵּׁנִי אֱלִיאָב הַשְּׁלִישִׁי׃
10 מִשְׁמַנָּה הָרְבִיעִי יִרְמְיָה
11 הַחֲמִשִׁי׃ עַתַּי הַשִּׁשִּׁי אֱלִיאֵל
12 הַשְּׁבִעִי׃ יוֹחָנָן הַשְּׁמִינִי
13 אֶלְזָבָד הַתְּשִׁיעִי׃ יִרְמְיָהוּ
הָעֲשִׂירִי מַכְבַּנַּי עַשְׁתֵּי עָשָׂר׃
14 אֵלֶּה מִבְּנֵי־גָד רָאשֵׁי הַצָּבָא
אֶחָד לְמֵאָה הַקָּטָן וְהַגָּדוֹל
15 לְאָלֶף׃ אֵלֶּה הֵם אֲשֶׁר עָבְרוּ
אֶת־הַיַּרְדֵּן בַּחֹדֶשׁ הָרִאשׁוֹן
וְהוּא מְמַלֵּא עַל־כָּל־גִּדְיֹתָיו
וַיַּבְרִיחוּ אֶת־כָּל־הָעֲמָקִים
לַמִּזְרָח וְלַמַּעֲרָב׃
16 וַיָּבֹאוּ מִן־בְּנֵי בִנְיָמִן וִיהוּדָה
17 עַד־לַמְצָד לְדָוִיד׃ וַיֵּצֵא
דָוִיד לִפְנֵיהֶם וַיַּעַן וַיֹּאמֶר

v. 15. גדותיו ק׳

swift as the roes. Cf. David's lament over Saul and Jonathan (2 Sam. i. 23).

10. *Jeremiah the fifth.* In verse 14 the same name occurs in connection with *the tenth*, but there is a slight difference of spellings in the Hebrew which distinguishes one from the other.

14. *he that was least*, etc. Better, 'the smallest (or, weakest) (was a match) for a hundred, and the greatest (or, strongest) for a thousand' (cf. Lev. xxvi. 8; Deut. xxxii. 30).

15. *the first month.* Called Nisan, in the spring when the snows on the mountains melt and the Jordan is at its flood (cf. Josh. iii. 15).

all them of the valleys. i.e. the inhabitants of the valleys who, in support of Saul, opposed the passage of the Gadites to join David.

16-18. Additional recruits, under the leadership of Amasai, from the tribes of Judah and Benjamin.

17. *David went out.* From the stronghold.

ye be come peaceably unto me to
help me, my heart shall be knit unto
you; but if ye be come to betray me
to mine adversaries, seeing there is
no wrong in my hands, the God of
our fathers look thereon, and give
judgment.' 18. Then the spirit
clothed Amasai, who was chief of
the captains:

Thine are we, David,
And on thy side, thou son of Jesse;
Peace, peace be unto thee,
And peace be to thy helpers;
For thy God helpeth thee.

Then David received them, and
made them captains of the band.
19. Of Manasseh also there fell
away some to David, when he came
with the Philistines against Saul to
battle, but they helped them not;
for the lords of the Philistines upon
advisement sent him away, saying:
'He will fall away to his master Saul
to the jeopardy of our heads.'

לָהֶם אִם־לְשָׁלוֹם בָּאתֶם אֵלַי
לְעָזְרֵנִי יִהְיֶה־לִּי עֲלֵיכֶם
לֵבָב לְיָחַד וְאִם־לְרַמּוֹתַנִי
לְצָרַי בְּלֹא חָמָס בְּכַפַּי יֵרֶא
18 אֱלֹהֵי אֲבוֹתֵינוּ וְיוֹכַח׃ וְרוּחַ
לָבְשָׁה אֶת־עֲמָשַׂי רֹאשׁ
הַשָּׁלוֹשִׁים
לְךָ דָוִיד
וְעִמְּךָ בֶן־יִשַׁי
שָׁלוֹם ׀ שָׁלוֹם לְךָ
וְשָׁלוֹם לְעֹזְרֶךָ
כִּי עֲזָרְךָ אֱלֹהֶיךָ
וַיְקַבְּלֵם דָּוִיד וַיִּתְּנֵם בְּרָאשֵׁי
הַגְּדוּד׃
19 וּמִמְּנַשֶּׁה נָפְלוּ עַל־דָּוִיד
בְּבֹאוֹ עִם־פְּלִשְׁתִּים עַל־
שָׁאוּל לַמִּלְחָמָה וְלֹא עֲזָרֻם
כִּי בְעֵצָה שִׁלְּחֻהוּ סַרְנֵי
פְלִשְׁתִּים לֵאמֹר בְּרָאשֵׁינוּ

v. 18. השלישים ק׳

shall be knit unto you. Or, 'shall be at one with you.'

18. *the spirit.* The text has 'a spirit' from God.

clothed. i.e. enveloped; the same verb is used of Gideon (Judg. vi. 34).

Amasai. Doubtless to be identified with *Amasa* in 2 Sam. xvii. 25, xx. 4ff.

on thy side. More lit. 'with thee' we take our stand.

helpeth thee. lit. 'hath helped thee,' as proved by David's survival from Saul's attempts upon his life.

19-22. Recruits from the tribe of Manasseh.

19. *when he came with the Philistines.* As narrated in 1 Sam. xxviii. 1f., xxix. 1ff.

but they. The subject is David and his followers.

upon advisement. lit. 'by advice,' after considering the matter.

he will fall away . . . our heads. Or,

20. As he went to Ziklag, there fell to him of Manasseh, Adnah, and Jozabad, and Jediael, and Michael, and Jozabad, and Elihu, and Zillethai, captains of thousands that were of Manasseh. 21. And they helped David against the troop, for they were all mighty men of valour, and were captains in the host. 22. For from day to day men came to David to help him, until there was a great host, like the host of God.

23. And these are the numbers of the heads of them that were armed for war, who came to David to Hebron, to turn the kingdom of Saul to him, according to the word of the LORD. 24. The children of Judah that bore shield and spear were six thousand and eight hun-

יִפּוֹל אֶל־אֲדֹנָיו שָׁאוּל׃
20 בְּלֶכְתּוֹ אֶל־צִיקְלַג נָפְלוּ
עָלָיו ׀ מִמְּנַשֶּׁה עַדְנָה וְיוֹזָבָד
וִידִיעֲאֵל וּמִיכָאֵל וְיוֹזָבָד
וֶאֱלִיהוּא וְצִלְּתָי רָאשֵׁי
21 הָאֲלָפִים אֲשֶׁר לִמְנַשֶּׁה׃ וְהֵמָּה
עָזְרוּ עִם־דָּוִיד עַל־הַגְּדוּד
כִּי־גִבּוֹרֵי חַיִל כֻּלָּם וַיִּהְיוּ
22 שָׂרִים בַּצָּבָא׃ כִּי לְעֶת־יוֹם
בְּיוֹם יָבֹאוּ עַל־דָּוִיד לְעָזְרוֹ
עַד־לְמַחֲנֶה גָדוֹל כְּמַחֲנֵה
אֱלֹהִים׃
23 וְאֵלֶּה מִסְפְּרֵי רָאשֵׁי הֶחָלוּץ
לַצָּבָא בָּאוּ עַל־דָּוִיד
חֶבְרוֹנָה לְהָסֵב מַלְכוּת שָׁאוּל
24 אֵלָיו כְּפִי יְהוָה׃ בְּנֵי יְהוּדָה
נֹשְׂאֵי צִנָּה וָרֹמַח שֵׁשֶׁת אֲלָפִים
וּשְׁמוֹנֶה מֵאוֹת חֲלוּצֵי צָבָא׃

v. 20. בנ״א עדנח

'at the price of our heads he will desert to his master Saul' (cf. 1 Sam. xxix. 4). The underlying thought is that David would seek to win back the favour of Saul by an act of treachery against the Philistines.

20. *as he went.* i.e. returned (cf. 1 Sam. xxx. 1).

Jozabad. The name occurs twice, borne by different men.

captains of thousands. These divisions were civil as well as military, tribes consisting of 'thousands,' each 'thousand' being subdivided into 'hundreds' (cf. Num. xxxi. 14, 48).

21. *helped David.* lit. 'with David.'

against the troop. Of Amalekites who burned Ziklag during David's absence (1 Sam. xxx. 1ff.).

22. *for from day to day.* The first word in the Hebrew is rendered by some as 'indeed.'

the host of God. i.e. a huge host; the phrase may have been taken from Gen. xxxii. 2.

23-40. The warriors who came to Hebron to make David king.

24. *shield.* The Hebrew *tsinnah* denoted the large shield which covered the whole body in contrast with the small shield

dred, armed for war. 25. Of the children of Simeon, mighty men of valour for the war, seven thousand and one hundred. 26. Of the children of Levi four thousand and six hundred. 27. And Jehoiada was the leader of the house of Aaron, and with him were three thousand and seven hundred; 28. and Zadok, a young man mighty of valour, and of his father's house twenty and two captains. 29. And of the children of Benjamin, the brethren of Saul, three thousand; for hitherto the greatest part of them had kept their allegiance to the house of Saul. 30. And of the children of Ephraim twenty thousand and eight hundred, mighty men of valour, famous men in their fathers' houses. 31. And of the half-tribe of Manasseh eighteen thousand, who were mentioned by name, to come and make David king. 32. And of the children of Issachar

25 מִן־בְּנֵי שִׁמְעוֹן גִּבּוֹרֵי חַיִל
לַצָּבָא שִׁבְעַת אֲלָפִים וּמֵאָה׃
26 מִן־בְּנֵי הַלֵּוִי אַרְבַּעַת אֲלָפִים
27 וְשֵׁשׁ מֵאוֹת׃ וִיהוֹיָדָע הַנָּגִיד
לְאַהֲרֹן וְעִמּוֹ שְׁלֹשֶׁת אֲלָפִים
28 וּשְׁבַע מֵאוֹת׃ וְצָדוֹק נַעַר
גִּבּוֹר חַיִל וּבֵית־אָבִיו שָׂרִים
29 עֶשְׂרִים וּשְׁנָיִם׃ וּמִן־בְּנֵי
בִנְיָמִן אֲחֵי שָׁאוּל שְׁלֹשֶׁת
אֲלָפִים וְעַד־הֵנָּה מַרְבִּיתָם
שֹׁמְרִים מִשְׁמֶרֶת בֵּית שָׁאוּל׃
30 וּמִן־בְּנֵי אֶפְרַיִם עֶשְׂרִים אֶלֶף
וּשְׁמוֹנֶה מֵאוֹת גִּבּוֹרֵי חַיִל אַנְשֵׁי
31 שֵׁמוֹת לְבֵית אֲבוֹתָם׃ וּמֵחֲצִי
מַטֵּה מְנַשֶּׁה שְׁמוֹנָה עָשָׂר אָלֶף
אֲשֶׁר נִקְּבוּ בְּשֵׁמוֹת לָבוֹא
32 לְהַמְלִיךְ אֶת־דָּוִיד׃ וּמִבְּנֵי

(*magen*) which served as a protection against arrows.

six thousand and eight hundred. The small number of the soldiers of Judah and Simeon, as compared with that of the other tribes, may be accounted for on the assumption that the main body of the warriors of the two tribes was already at Hebron where David had been king over these tribes for seven years.

27. *Jehoiada.* Possibly the father of Benaiah (cf. xi. 22), and *leader* may signify the head of the clan.

28. *Zadok.* In xxvii. 17 he is described as the *ruler* over the Aaronites. He later became High Priest.

29. *hitherto.* Up to the time of David's coronation (cf. 2 Sam. v. 1ff.) which is now described.

kept their allegiance to. lit. 'kept the charge of'; the phrase is commonly used of the priests and Levites officiating in the Temple.

30. *famous men.* lit. 'men of names.'

31. *of the half-tribe of Manasseh.* Which dwelt west of the Jordan. The other half on the eastern side is mentioned in verse 37.

mentioned by name. Evidently a record was made of those who joined the delegation.

men that had understanding of the times, to know what Israel ought to do; the heads of them were two hundred; and all their brethren were at their commandment. 33. Of Zebulun, such as were able to go out in the host, that could set the battle in array, with all manner of instruments of war, fifty thousand; and that could order the battle array, and were not of double heart. 34. And of Naphtali a thousand captains, and with them with shield and spear thirty and seven thousand. 35. And of the Danites that could set the battle in array, twenty and eight thousand and six hundred. 36. And of Asher, such as were able to go out in the host, that could set the battle in array, forty thousand. 37. And on the other side of the Jordan, of the Reubenites, and the Gadites, and of the half-tribe of Manasseh, with all manner of instruments of war for the battle, a hundred and twenty thousand. 38. All these, being men of war, that could order the battle array, came with a whole heart to Hebron, to make David king over all Israel; and all the rest also of Israel were of one

יִשָּׂשכָר יוֹדְעֵי בִינָה לָעִתִּים
לָדַעַת מַה־יַּעֲשֶׂה יִשְׂרָאֵל
רָאשֵׁיהֶם מָאתַיִם וְכָל־
33 אֲחֵיהֶם עַל־פִּיהֶם׃ מִזְּבֻלוּן
יוֹצְאֵי צָבָא עֹרְכֵי מִלְחָמָה
בְּכָל־כְּלֵי מִלְחָמָה חֲמִשִּׁים
אֶלֶף וְלַעֲדֹר בְּלֹא־לֵב וָלֵב׃
34 וּמִנַּפְתָּלִי שָׂרִים אָלֶף וְעִמָּהֶם
בְּצִנָּה וַחֲנִית שְׁלֹשִׁים וְשִׁבְעָה
35 אָלֶף׃ וּמִן־הַדָּנִי עֹרְכֵי
מִלְחָמָה עֶשְׂרִים־וּשְׁמוֹנָה
36 אֶלֶף וְשֵׁשׁ מֵאוֹת׃ וּמֵאָשֵׁר
יוֹצְאֵי צָבָא לַעֲרֹךְ מִלְחָמָה
37 אַרְבָּעִים אָלֶף׃ וּמֵעֵבֶר
לַיַּרְדֵּן מִן־הָרְאוּבֵנִי וְהַגָּדִי
וַחֲצִי ׀ שֵׁבֶט מְנַשֶּׁה בְּכֹל כְּלֵי
צְבָא מִלְחָמָה מֵאָה וְעֶשְׂרִים
38 אָלֶף׃ כָּל־־אֵלֶּה אַנְשֵׁי
מִלְחָמָה עֹדְרֵי מַעֲרָכָה
בְּלֵבָב שָׁלֵם בָּאוּ חֶבְרוֹנָה
לְהַמְלִיךְ אֶת־דָּוִיד עַל־
כָּל־יִשְׂרָאֵל וְגַם כָּל־שֵׁרִית
יִשְׂרָאֵל לֵב אֶחָד לְהַמְלִיךְ׃

v. 38. כצ״ל

32. *had understanding of the times.* Explained either as 'skilled in astrology' or 'experienced, prudent men' (cf. *wise men, who knew the times*, Esth. i. 13).

at their commandment. lit. 'upon their mouth,' acted according to their bidding.

33. *and were not of double heart.* lit. 'without a heart and a heart.' They fought wholeheartedly, or were united in their aim to fight, on David's side.

heart to make David king. 39. And they were there with David three days, eating and drinking; for their brethren had made preparation for them. 40. Moreover they that were nigh unto them, even as far as Issachar and Zebulun and Naphtali, brought bread on asses, and on camels, and on mules, and on oxen, victual of meal, cakes of figs, and clusters of raisins, and wine, and oil, and oxen, and sheep in abundance; for there was joy in Israel.

39 אֶת־דָּוִיד׃ וַיִּהְיוּ־שָׁם עִם־
דָּוִיד יָמִים שְׁלוֹשָׁה אֹכְלִים
וְשׁוֹתִים כִּי־הֵכִינוּ לָהֶם
40 אֲחֵיהֶם׃ וְגַם הַקְּרוֹבִים־
אֲלֵיהֶם עַד־יִשָּׂשכָר וּזְבֻלוּן
וְנַפְתָּלִי מְבִיאִים לֶחֶם
בַּחֲמוֹרִים וּבַגְּמַלִּים וּבַפְּרָדִים
׀ וּבַבָּקָר מַאֲכָל קֶמַח
דְּבֵלִים וְצִמֻּקִים וְיַיִן וְשֶׁמֶן
וּבָקָר וְצֹאן לָרֹב כִּי שִׂמְחָה
בְּיִשְׂרָאֵל׃

13 CHAPTER XIII יג

1. And David consulted with the captains of thousands and of hundreds, even with every leader. 2. And David said unto all the assembly of Israel: 'If it seem good unto you, and if it be of the LORD our God, let us send abroad everywhere unto our brethren that are

1 וַיִּוָּעַץ דָּוִיד עִם־שָׂרֵי
הָאֲלָפִים וְהַמֵּאוֹת לְכָל־
2 נָגִיד׃ וַיֹּאמֶר דָּוִיד לְכֹל ׀
קְהַל יִשְׂרָאֵל אִם־עֲלֵיכֶם
טוֹב וּמִן־יְהוָה אֱלֹהֵינוּ
נִפְרְצָה נִשְׁלְחָה עַל־אַחֵינוּ

Cf. verse 38, *with a whole heart . . . of one heart.*

39. *their brethren.* Of the tribe of Judah.

40. *that were nigh unto them.* To the men of Hebron.

even as far as Issachar, etc. i.e. even the warriors who came from these tribes were supplied by the other members of their tribe.

there was joy. In the accession of a king who had proved his worth in many trials.

CHAPTER XIII

REMOVAL OF THE ARK FROM KIRIATH-JEARIM

THE chapter, which corresponds to 2 Sam. vi. 1-11, resumes the history of David's reign interrupted by the register of the heroes in xi. 10-xii. Having captured the stronghold of Zion and made it his capital, David decided to bring the ark there and so establish Jerusalem as the religious as well as political centre of the nation.

left in all the land of Israel, and with them to the priests and Levites that are in their cities that have open land about them, that they may gather themselves unto us; 3. and let us bring back the ark of our God to us; for we sought not unto it in the days of Saul.' 4. And all the assembly said that they would do so; for the thing was right in the eyes of all the people. 5. So David assembled all Israel together, from Shihor the brook of Egypt even unto the entrance of Hamath, to bring the ark of God from Kiriath-jearim.

6. And David went up, and all Israel, to Baalah, that is, to Kiriath-jearim, which belonged to Judah, to bring up from thence the ark of God,

הַנִּשְׁאָרִים בְּכֹל אַרְצוֹת
יִשְׂרָאֵל וְעִמָּהֶם הַכֹּהֲנִים
וְהַלְוִיִּם בְּעָרֵי מִגְרְשֵׁיהֶם
3 וְיִקָּבְצוּ אֵלֵינוּ׃ וְנָסֵבָּה אֶת־
אֲרוֹן אֱלֹהֵינוּ אֵלֵינוּ כִּי־לֹא
4 דְרַשְׁנֻהוּ בִּימֵי שָׁאוּל׃ וַיֹּאמְרוּ
כָל־הַקָּהָל לַעֲשׂוֹת כֵּן כִּי־
יָשַׁר הַדָּבָר בְּעֵינֵי כָל־הָעָם׃
5 וַיַּקְהֵל דָּוִיד אֶת־כָּל־
יִשְׂרָאֵל מִן־שִׁיחוֹר מִצְרַיִם
וְעַד־לְבוֹא חֲמָת לְהָבִיא
אֶת־אֲרוֹן הָאֱלֹהִים מִקִּרְיַת
יְעָרִים׃
6 וַיַּעַל דָּוִיד וְכָל־יִשְׂרָאֵל
בַּעֲלָתָה אֶל־קִרְיַת יְעָרִים
אֲשֶׁר לִיהוּדָה לְהַעֲלוֹת מִשָּׁם
אֵת אֲרוֹן הָאֱלֹהִים ׀ יְהוָה

1. *David consulted*, etc. Not mentioned in Sam.

2. *land of Israel.* The text has 'lands,' i.e. the various districts of the kingdom.

the priests and Levites. In Sam. there is no reference to the Levites in connection with the transference of the ark.

cities that have open land. Cf. Num. xxxv. 2ff.

3. *the ark.* It contained the tables of stone with the ten commandments (cf. 2 Chron. v. 10).

sought not unto it. i.e. made no enquiries of God what to do in an emergency.

5. *Shihor.* The modern Wadi el-Arish which, at a distance of fifty miles south-west of Gaza, divides Egypt from Palestine (cf. Josh. xiii. 3; xv. 4).

the entrance of Hamath. A mountain pass between Hermon and Lebanon south of Hamath, which is the modern Hama on the river Orontes. It was the northern frontier of Israel (cf. Josh. xiii. 5).

6. *to Baalah, that is, to Kiriath-jearim.* The city was situated on mount Jearim, nine miles west of Jerusalem, and is identified with the modern Kuriet Eneb to the north of the mountain, or Khuret Erma to the south of it.

the LORD that sitteth upon the cherubim, whereon is called the Name. 7. And they set the ark of God upon a new cart, [and brought it] out of the house of Abinadab; and Uzza and Ahio drove the cart. 8. And David and all Israel played before God with all their might; even with songs, and with harps, and with psalteries, and with timbrels, and with cymbals, and with trumpets. 9. And when they came unto the threshing-floor of Chidon, Uzza put forth his hand to hold the ark; for the oxen stumbled. 10. And the anger of the LORD was kindled against Uzza, and He smote him, because he put forth his hand to the ark; and there he died before God. 11. And David was displeased, because the LORD had broken forth upon Uzza; and that place was called Perez-uzza unto this day.

יוֹשֵׁב הַכְּרוּבִים אֲשֶׁר־נִקְרָא
7 שֵׁם׃ וַיַּרְכִּיבוּ אֶת־אֲרוֹן
הָאֱלֹהִים עַל־עֲגָלָה חֲדָשָׁה
מִבֵּית אֲבִינָדָב וְעֻזָּא וְאַחְיוֹ
8 נֹהֲגִים בָּעֲגָלָה׃ וְדָוִיד וְכָל־
יִשְׂרָאֵל מְשַׂחֲקִים לִפְנֵי
הָאֱלֹהִים בְּכָל־עֹז וּבְשִׁירִים
וּבְכִנֹּרוֹת וּבִנְבָלִים וּבְתֻפִּים
וּבִמְצִלְתַּיִם וּבַחֲצֹצְרוֹת׃
9 וַיָּבֹאוּ עַד־גֹּרֶן כִּידֹן וַיִּשְׁלַח
עֻזָּא אֶת־יָדוֹ לֶאֱחֹז אֶת־
הָאָרוֹן כִּי שָׁמְטוּ הַבָּקָר׃
10 וַיִּחַר־אַף יְהוָה בְּעֻזָּא וַיַּכֵּהוּ
עַל אֲשֶׁר־שָׁלַח יָדוֹ עַל־
הָאָרוֹן וַיָּמָת שָׁם לִפְנֵי
11 אֱלֹהִים׃ וַיִּחַר לְדָוִיד כִּי־
פָרַץ יְהוָה פֶּרֶץ בְּעֻזָּא וַיִּקְרָא
לַמָּקוֹם הַהוּא פֶּרֶץ עֻזָּא עַד

sitteth upon the cherubim. God's presence was associated with the ark (cf. Exod. xxv. 22).

whereon is called the Name. Cf. 2 Sam. vi. 2: *whereupon is called the Name, even the name of the LORD of hosts that sitteth upon the cherubim.*

7. *a new cart.* Which had not been used before for common work and so perhaps defiled.

the house of Abinadab. Where the ark had been kept for many years (cf. 1 Sam. vii. 1f.).

8. *played.* The Hebrew verb means 'made merry' with dancing.

9. *Chidon.* In 2 Sam. vi. 6: *Nacon.*

to hold the ark. In Sam.: *and took hold of it.*

stumbled. Better, 'let it go.' The Targum understood the verb as 'shook it.'

10. *smote him . . . ark.* In 2 Sam. vi. 7: *smote him there for his error.*

before God. In Sam.: *by the ark of God.*

11. *was displeased.* More lit. 'was wroth,' presumably against those who did not instruct the drivers of the cart on the care to be exercised in dealing with the ark (cf. Num. iv. 15).

12. And David was afraid of God that day, saying: 'How shall I bring the ark of God home to me?' 13. So David removed not the ark unto him into the city of David, but carried it aside into the house of Obed-edom the Gittite. 14. And the ark of God remained with the family of Obed-edom in his house three months; and the LORD blessed the house of Obed-edom, and all that he had.

הַיּוֹם הַזֶּה׃ וַיִּרָא דָוִיד אֶת־ 12
הָאֱלֹהִים בַּיּוֹם הַהוּא לֵאמֹר
הֵיךְ אָבִיא אֵלַי אֵת אֲרוֹן
הָאֱלֹהִים׃ וְלֹא־הֵסִיר דָּוִיד 13
אֶת־הָאָרוֹן אֵלָיו אֶל־עִיר
דָּוִיד וַיַּטֵּהוּ אֶל־בֵּית־עֹבֵד
אֱדֹם הַגִּתִּי׃ וַיֵּשֶׁב אֲרוֹן 14
הָאֱלֹהִים עִם־בֵּית עֹבֵד
אֱדֹם בְּבֵיתוֹ שְׁלֹשָׁה חֳדָשִׁים
וַיְבָרֶךְ יְהוָה אֶת־בֵּית עֹבֵד־
אֱדֹם וְאֶת־כָּל־אֲשֶׁר־לוֹ׃

14 CHAPTER XIV יד

1. And Huram king of Tyre sent messengers to David, and cedar-trees, and masons, and carpenters, to build him a house. 2. And David perceived that the LORD had

וַיִּשְׁלַח חִירָם מֶלֶךְ־צֹר 1
מַלְאָכִים אֶל־דָּוִיד וַעֲצֵי
אֲרָזִים וְחָרָשֵׁי קִיר וְחָרָשֵׁי
עֵצִים לִבְנוֹת לוֹ בָּיִת׃ וַיֵּדַע 2

v. 1. חורם ק׳

Perez-uzza. Meaning 'the breach of Uzza.'

13. *Obed-edom the Gittite*. He was a Levite who lived for a time in Gath (cf. xv. 18, 24 where Obed-edom is included among the Levites and doorkeepers for the ark). He is perhaps described as a *Gittite* because he was born in Gath-rimmon, a Levitical city (Josh. xxi. 24f.).

14. *the LORD blessed*. The Targum specifies the blessing as 'sons and grandsons.'

CHAPTER XIV

THIS chapter is parallel to 2 Sam. v. 11-25. It is to be noted that the order of the narrative in Chron. differs from that in Sam., first place being given to the removal of the ark and second to the events narrated here. The unsuccessful attempts to transfer the ark to the city of David which follow each other in Sam. are here interrupted by what is related in this chapter.

1f. Hiram's supply of craftsmen and materials for David's building operations.

1. *Huram*. Elsewhere the name is *Hiram* or *Hirom*.

2. *David perceived*, etc. He found

established him king over Israel, for his kingdom was exalted exceedingly, for His people Israel's sake.

3. And David took more wives at Jerusalem; and David begot more sons and daughters. 4. And these are the names of the children whom he had in Jerusalem: Shammua, and Shobab, Nathan, and Solomon; 5. and Ibhar, and Elishua, and Elpelet; 6. and Nogah, and Nepheg, and Japhia; 7. and Elishama, and Beeliada, and Eliphelet.

8. And when the Philistines heard that David was anointed king over all Israel, all the Philistines went up to seek David; and David heard of

דָּוִיד כִּי־הֱכִינוֹ יְהוָה לְמֶלֶךְ
עַל־יִשְׂרָאֵל כִּי־נִשֵּׂאת
לְמַעְלָה מַלְכוּתוֹ בַּעֲבוּר עַמּוֹ
יִשְׂרָאֵל׃
3 וַיִּקַּח דָּוִיד עוֹד נָשִׁים
בִּירוּשָׁלָםִ וַיּוֹלֶד דָּוִיד עוֹד
4 בָּנִים וּבָנוֹת׃ וְאֵלֶּה שְׁמוֹת
הַיְלוּדִים אֲשֶׁר הָיוּ־לוֹ
בִּירוּשָׁלָםִ שַׁמּוּעַ וְשׁוֹבָב נָתָן
5 וּשְׁלֹמֹה׃ וְיִבְחָר וֶאֱלִישׁוּעַ
6 וְאֶלְפָּלֶט׃ וְנֹגַהּ וְנֶפֶג וְיָפִיעַ׃
7 וֶאֱלִישָׁמָע וּבְעֶלְיָדָע
וֶאֱלִיפָלֶט׃
8 וַיִּשְׁמְעוּ פְלִשְׁתִּים כִּי־נִמְשַׁח
דָּוִיד לְמֶלֶךְ עַל־כָּל־
יִשְׂרָאֵל וַיַּעֲלוּ כָל־פְּלִשְׁתִּים
לְבַקֵּשׁ אֶת־דָּוִיד וַיִּשְׁמַע דָּוִיד

evidence in the desire of the king of Tyre to be on friendly terms with him.

for His people Israel's sake. David in his modesty attributed his success to Israel and not to his own merits.

3-7. David's family born in Jerusalem.

3. *more wives.* In 2 Sam. v. 13: *more concubines and wives.* As far as possible the Chronicler avoids mention of anything which is discreditable to David.

4. *Shammua.* In iii. 5 the name is *Shimea;* and the four sons are said to have been born to Bath-shua, otherwise known as Bath-sheba.

and Solomon. Though mentioned here last, Solomon was the eldest.

7. *Beeliada.* In iii. 8 and 2 Sam. v. 16: *Eliada.*

8-12. Defeat of the Philistines at Baal-perazim.

8. *was anointed king.* The anointing probably refers to that which took place in Hebron (cf. 2 Sam. v. 3).

over all Israel. In 2 Sam. v. 17 *all* is omitted.

all the Philistines . . . David. So long as he was king only over Judah, his limited power could be tolerated by the Philistines; but as king *over all Israel* he became a menace they sought to remove.

went up. To the hill-country of Judah from the lowlands where their country lay.

it, and went out to meet them. 9. Now the Philistines had come and made a raid in the valley of Rephaim. 10. And David inquired of God, saying: 'Shall I go up against the Philistines? and wilt Thou deliver them into my hand?' And the LORD said unto him: 'Go up; for I will deliver them into thy hand.' 11. So they came up to Baal-perazim, and David smote them there; and David said: 'God hath broken mine enemies by my hand, like the breach of waters.' Therefore they called the name of that place Baal-perazim. 12. And they left their gods there; and David gave commandment, and they were burned with fire.

13. And the Philistines yet again made a raid in the valley. 14. And David inquired again of God; and God said unto him: 'Thou shalt not go up after them; turn away from

9 וַיֵּצֵא לִפְנֵיהֶם׃ וּפְלִשְׁתִּים
בָּאוּ וַיִּפְשְׁטוּ בְּעֵמֶק רְפָאִים׃
10 וַיִּשְׁאַל דָּוִיד בֵּאלֹהִים לֵאמֹר
הַאֶעֱלֶה עַל־־פְּלִשְׁתִּיִּים
וּנְתַתָּם בְּיָדִי וַיֹּאמֶר לוֹ יְהוָה
11 עֲלֵה וּנְתַתִּים בְּיָדֶךָ׃ וַיַּעֲלוּ
בְּבַעַל־פְּרָצִים וַיַּכֵּם שָׁם
דָּוִיד וַיֹּאמֶר דָּוִיד פָּרַץ
הָאֱלֹהִים אֶת־אוֹיְבַי בְּיָדִי
כְּפֶרֶץ מָיִם עַל־כֵּן קָרְאוּ
שֵׁם־הַמָּקוֹם הַהוּא בַּעַל
12 פְּרָצִים׃ וַיַּעַזְבוּ־שָׁם אֶת־
אֱלֹהֵיהֶם וַיֹּאמֶר דָּוִיד וַיִּשָּׂרְפוּ
בָּאֵשׁ׃
13 וַיֹּסִיפוּ עוֹד פְּלִשְׁתִּים וַיִּפְשְׁטוּ
14 בָּעֵמֶק׃ וַיִּשְׁאַל עוֹד דָּוִיד
בֵּאלֹהִים וַיֹּאמֶר לוֹ הָאֱלֹהִים
לֹא תַעֲלֶה אַחֲרֵיהֶם הָסֵב

v. 10. יתיר י׳

David . . . went out to meet them. He did not wait for the onslaught but advanced to the attack. In 2 Sam. v. 17 the reading is: *went down to the hold.*

9. *made a raid.* The verb may mean 'spread out.'

the valley of Rephaim. A valley near Jerusalem across which runs the road from Jaffa.

10. *inquired of God.* By means of the Urim and Thummim or the ephod (cf. 1 Sam. xxiii. 6, 9, xxx. 7f.).

11. *Baal-perazim.* Doubtless the same as *mount Perazim* in Isa. xxviii. 21, the site of which is unknown.

like the breach of waters. Like rushing waters bursting through a dam.

Baal-perazim. The meaning is 'Lord, or place, of breakings.'

12. *David gave commandment . . . fire.* In 2 Sam. v. 21: *David and his men took them away.* The disposal of the idols as described here is in conformity with the law in Deut. vii. 5, 25.

13-17. A further defeat of the Philistines.

13. *made a raid.* See on verse 9.

in the valley. In 2 Sam. v. 22: *in the valley of Rephaim.*

14. *thou shalt not go up after them,* etc.

them, and come upon them over against the mulberry-trees. 15. And it shall be, when thou hearest the sound of marching in the tops of the mulberry-trees, that then thou shalt go out to battle; for God is gone out before thee to smite the host of the Philistines.' 16. And David did as God commanded him; and they smote the host of the Philistines from Gibeon even to Gezer. 17. And the fame of David went out into all lands; and the LORD brought the fear of him upon all nations.

מֵעֲלֵיהֶם וּבָאתָ לָהֶם מִמּוּל
15 הַבְּכָאִים׃ וִיהִי כְּשָׁמְעֲךָ אֶת־
קוֹל הַצְּעָדָה בְּרָאשֵׁי
הַבְּכָאִים אָז תֵּצֵא בַמִּלְחָמָה
כִּי־יָצָא הָאֱלֹהִים לְפָנֶיךָ
לְהַכּוֹת אֶת־מַחֲנֵה פְלִשְׁתִּים׃
16 וַיַּעַשׂ דָּוִיד כַּאֲשֶׁר צִוָּהוּ
הָאֱלֹהִים וַיַּכּוּ אֶת־מַחֲנֵה
פְלִשְׁתִּים מִגִּבְעוֹן וְעַד־גָּזְרָה׃
17 וַיֵּצֵא שֵׁם־דָּוִיד בְּכָל־
הָאֲרָצוֹת וַיהוָה נָתַן אֶת־
פַּחְדּוֹ עַל־כָּל־הַגּוֹיִם׃

15 CHAPTER XV טו

1. And [David] made him houses in the city of David; and he prepared

1 וַיַּעַשׂ־לוֹ בָתִּים בְּעִיר דָּוִיד

The attack should not be frontal but made on the flank. In 2 Sam. v. 23 the Hebrew for *after them* is embodied in the following clause which is rendered: *make a circuit behind them,* i.e. attack them in the rear.

from them. The Hebrew is lit. 'from upon them,' which may imply that David occupied a strategic position from which he intended to launch his attack.

over against. Or, 'parallel to.'

mulberry-trees. R.V. margin has 'balsam-trees.'

15. *the sound of marching.* The sound of rustling in the trees was to be the signal to make the assault. 'Ralbag, however, gives a more practical explanation of the stratagem: the trees would conceal David's advance from the Philistines and their rustling drown the sound of his men's attack' (Goldman, *Samuel*, Soncino ed., *ad loc.*).

thou shalt go out to battle. In 2 Sam. v. 24: *thou shalt bestir thyself.*

16. *from Gibeon even to Gezer.* A distance of about sixteen miles. The former is probably the place where the flight of the Philistines began; the latter the city into which they escaped. For *Gibeon*, 2 Sam. v. 25 reads *Geba.* The place must have been in the vicinity of Jerusalem, but there are several towns of the name *Gibeon* in the valley through which the Philistines fled. Gezer is the modern Tel-Jezer, nineteen miles north-west of Jerusalem.

17. The verse is not paralleled in Sam.

a place for the ark of God, and pitched for it a tent. 2. Then David said: 'None ought to carry the ark of God but the Levites; for them hath the LORD chosen to carry the ark of the LORD, and to minister unto Him for ever.' 3. And David assembled all Israel at Jerusalem, to bring up the ark of the LORD unto its place, which he had prepared for it. 4. And David gathered together the sons of Aaron, and the Levites; 5. of the sons of Kohath: Uriel the chief, and his brethren a hundred and twenty; 6. of the sons of Merari:

וַיָּכֶן מָקוֹם לַאֲרוֹן הָאֱלֹהִים
2 וַיֶּט־לוֹ אֹהֶל׃ אָז אָמַר דָּוִיד
לֹא לָשֵׂאת אֶת־אֲרוֹן
הָאֱלֹהִים כִּי אִם־הַלְוִיִּם כִּי־
בָם | בָּחַר יְהוָה לָשֵׂאת אֶת־
אֲרוֹן הָאֱלֹהִים וּלְשָׁרְתוֹ עַד־
3 עוֹלָם׃ וַיַּקְהֵל דָּוִיד אֶת־
כָּל־יִשְׂרָאֵל אֶל־יְרוּשָׁלִָם
לְהַעֲלוֹת אֶת־אֲרוֹן יְהוָה
אֶל־מְקוֹמוֹ אֲשֶׁר־הֵכִין לוֹ׃
4 וַיֶּאֱסֹף דָּוִיד אֶת־בְּנֵי אַהֲרֹן
5 וְאֶת־הַלְוִיִּם׃ לִבְנֵי קְהָת
אוּרִיאֵל הַשָּׂר וְאֶחָיו מֵאָה
6 וְעֶשְׂרִים׃ לִבְנֵי מְרָרִי עֲשָׂיָה

CHAPTER XV

THE ARK BROUGHT TO JERUSALEM

THE narrative, which extends to xvi. 3, differs in some particulars from the account in 2 Sam. vi. The section, verses 1-24, has no counterpart in Sam.

1-15. General preparations for the conveyance of the ark.

1. *pitched for it a tent.* This was not the old tent of meeting which stood in Gibeon (cf. 2 Chron. i. 3) but a new tent put up to receive the ark.

2. *then.* After the preparation described in the previous verse and having in mind the death of Uzza because he *put forth his hand to the ark* (xiii. 10).

none . . . but the Levites. Only the Levites should carry the ark (cf. Num. i. 50), and no cart (xiii. 7) must be used. By strict conformity to the regulations of the Torah, David hoped that no mishap would occur this time.

3. *to bring up.* From the house of Obed-edom the Gittite where it had been deposited (xiii. 13f.).

4-13. Eight hundred and sixty-two Levites belonging to six different families are summoned by David to convey the ark under the direction of six of their leaders and two priests.

5. *of the sons of Kohath.* According to Exod. vi. 18 (repeated in vi. 3) Kohath had four sons, Amram, Izhar, Hebron and Uzziel. The families of the last two appear below (verses 9f.); Uzziel may be represented by Elizaphan (verse 8), one of his descendants; while Amram is represented by Uriel (in this verse) and by the priests (verse 11) who were descended from his son Aaron.

6. *Merari.* He was a brother of Kohath and the third son of Levi (Exod. vi. 16).

Asaiah the chief, and his brethren
two hundred and twenty; 7. of the
sons of Gershom: Joel the chief, and
his brethren a hundred and thirty;
8. of the sons of Elizaphan: Shemaiah the chief, and his brethren two
hundred; 9. of the sons of Hebron:
Eliel the chief, and his brethren fourscore; 10. of the sons of Uzziel:
Amminadab the chief, and his
brethren a hundred and twelve.
11. And David called for Zadok and
Abiathar the priests, and for the
Levites, for Uriel, Asaiah, and Joel,
Shemaiah, and Eliel, and Amminadab, 12. and said unto them: 'Ye are
the heads of the fathers' houses of
the Levites; sanctify yourselves,
both ye and your brethren, that ye
may bring up the ark of the LORD,
the God of Israel, unto the place that
I have prepared for it. 13. For
because ye [bore it] not at the first,
the LORD our God made a breach
upon us, for that we sought Him not
according to the ordinance.' 14. So

הַשָּׂר וְאֶחָיו מָאתַיִם וְעֶשְׂרִים׃
7 לִבְנֵי גֵרְשׁוֹם יוֹאֵל הַשָּׂר וְאֶחָיו
8 מֵאָה וּשְׁלֹשִׁים׃ לִבְנֵי אֱלִיצָפָן
שְׁמַעְיָה הַשָּׂר וְאֶחָיו מָאתָיִם׃
9 לִבְנֵי חֶבְרוֹן אֱלִיאֵל הַשָּׂר
10 וְאֶחָיו שְׁמוֹנִים׃ לִבְנֵי עֻזִּיאֵל
עַמִּינָדָב הַשָּׂר וְאֶחָיו מֵאָה
11 וּשְׁנֵים עָשָׂר׃ וַיִּקְרָא דָוִיד
לְצָדוֹק וּלְאֶבְיָתָר הַכֹּהֲנִים
וְלַלְוִיִּם לְאוּרִיאֵל עֲשָׂיָה
וְיוֹאֵל שְׁמַעְיָה וֶאֱלִיאֵל
12 וְעַמִּינָדָב׃ וַיֹּאמֶר לָהֶם אַתֶּם
רָאשֵׁי הָאָבוֹת לַלְוִיִּם
הִתְקַדְּשׁוּ אַתֶּם וַאֲחֵיכֶם
וְהַעֲלִיתֶם אֵת אֲרוֹן יְהוָה
אֱלֹהֵי יִשְׂרָאֵל אֶל־הֲכִינוֹתִי
13 לוֹ׃ כִּי לְמַבָּרִאשׁוֹנָה לֹא אַתֶּם
פָּרַץ יְהוָה אֱלֹהֵינוּ בָּנוּ כִּי־
לֹא דְרַשְׁנֻהוּ כַּמִּשְׁפָּט׃

7. *Gershom.* The eldest son of Levi (Exod. vi. 16 where his name is *Gershon*).

9f. *Hebron . . . Uzziel.* The third and fourth son respectively of Kohath (see on verse 5).

Amminadab. He is mentioned as a son of Kohath in vi. 7.

11. *Zadok and Abiathar.* In 2 Sam. xv. 35 and elsewhere they are named together. Abiathar was later deposed by Solomon (1 Kings ii. 27).

the priests. The two chief priests only are here named. The remainder are detailed in verse 24.

12. *of the Levites.* The term also includes the priests.

sanctify yourselves. By washing the body and garments, avoiding intercourse with women and keeping away from all defilement (cf. Exod. xix. 10, 15).

the place that. Not in the text and implied.

13. *made a breach upon us.* Cf. xiii. 10f.

the priests and the Levites sanctified themselves to bring up the ark of the LORD, the God of Israel. 15. And the children of the Levites bore the ark of God upon their shoulders with the bars thereon, as Moses commanded according to the word of the LORD.

16. And David spoke to the chief of the Levites to appoint their brethren the singers, with instruments of music, psalteries and harps and cymbals, sounding aloud and lifting up the voice with joy. 17. So the Levites appointed Heman the son of Joel; and of his brethren, Asaph the son of Berechiah; and of the sons of Merari their brethren, Ethan the son of Kushaiah; 18. and with them their brethren of the second degree, Zechariah, Ben, and Jaaziel, and Shemiramoth, and Jehiel, and Unni, Eliab, and Benaiah, and Maaseiah, and Mattithiah, and Eliphalehu, and Mikneiah, and Obed-edom, and Jeiel, the door-

14 וַיִּתְקַדְּשׁוּ הַכֹּהֲנִים וְהַלְוִיִּם
לְהַעֲלוֹת אֶת־אֲרוֹן יְהוָה
15 אֱלֹהֵי יִשְׂרָאֵל׃ וַיִּשְׂאוּ בְנֵי־
הַלְוִיִּם אֵת אֲרוֹן הָאֱלֹהִים
כַּאֲשֶׁר צִוָּה מֹשֶׁה כִּדְבַר יְהוָה
בִּכְתֵפָם בַּמֹּטוֹת עֲלֵיהֶם׃
16 וַיֹּאמֶר דָּוִיד לְשָׂרֵי הַלְוִיִּם
לְהַעֲמִיד אֶת־אֲחֵיהֶם
הַמְשֹׁרְרִים בִּכְלֵי־שִׁיר
נְבָלִים וְכִנֹּרוֹת וּמְצִלְתָּיִם
מַשְׁמִיעִים לְהָרִים־בְּקוֹל
17 לְשִׂמְחָה׃ וַיַּעֲמִידוּ הַלְוִיִּם אֵת
הֵימָן בֶּן־יוֹאֵל וּמִן־אֶחָיו
אָסָף בֶּן־בֶּרֶכְיָהוּ וּמִן־בְּנֵי
מְרָרִי אֲחֵיהֶם אֵיתָן בֶּן־
18 קוּשָׁיָהוּ׃ וְעִמָּהֶם אֲחֵיהֶם
הַמִּשְׁנִים זְכַרְיָהוּ בֵּן וְיַעֲזִיאֵל
וּשְׁמִירָמוֹת וִיחִיאֵל ׀ וְעֻנִּי
אֱלִיאָב וּבְנָיָהוּ וּמַעֲשֵׂיָהוּ
וּמַתִּתְיָהוּ וֶאֱלִיפְלֵהוּ וּמִקְנֵיָהוּ
וְעֹבֵד אֱדֹם וִיעִיאֵל

15. ***upon their shoulders.*** Not in a cart.
with the bars thereon. Cf. Exod. xxv. 13ff.
as Moses commanded. Cf. Num. vii. 9.

16-24. The musical and other arrangements. The order of the procession seems to have been as follows: the musicians, the ark, the king and his retinue.

16. ***the chief of.*** lit. 'the chiefs of,' probably those enumerated in verses 5-10.

18. ***their brethren.*** The names which follow are repeated with some variations in verses 20f.
Ben. An unusual proper noun, the word meaning 'son.' Some Hebrew MSS. omit it as in verse 20.

keepers. 19. So the singers, Heman,
Asaph, and Ethan [, were appointed],
with cymbals of brass to sound
aloud; 20. and Zechariah, and Aziel,
and Shemiramoth, and Jehiel, and
Unni, and Eliab, and Maaseiah, and
Benaiah, with psalteries set to
Alamoth; 21. and Mattithiah, and
Eliphalehu, and Mikneiahu, and
Obed-edom, and Jeiel, and Azaziah,
with harps on the Sheminith, to lead.
22. And Chenaniah, chief of the
Levites, was over the song; he was
master in the song, because he was
skilful. 23. And Berechiah and
Elkanah were doorkeepers for the
ark. 24. And Shebaniah, and Joshaphat, and Nethanel, and Amasai, and
Zechariah, and Benaiah, and Eliezer,
the priests, did blow with the
trumpets before the ark of God; and
Obed-edom and Jehiah were doorkeepers for the ark.

19 הַשֹּׁעֲרִים: וְהַמְשֹׁרְרִים הֵימָן
אָסָף וְאֵיתָן בִּמְצִלְתַּיִם נְחֹשֶׁת
20 לְהַשְׁמִיעַ: וּזְכַרְיָה וַעֲזִיאֵל
וּשְׁמִירָמוֹת וִיחִיאֵל וְעֻנִּי
וֶאֱלִיאָב וּמַעֲשֵׂיָהוּ וּבְנָיָהוּ
בִּנְבָלִים עַל־עֲלָמוֹת:
21 וּמַתִּתְיָהוּ וֶאֱלִיפְלֵהוּ וּמִקְנֵיָהוּ
וְעֹבֵד אֱדֹם וִיעִיאֵל וַעֲזַזְיָהוּ
בְּכִנֹּרוֹת עַל־הַשְּׁמִינִית
22 לְנַצֵּחַ: וּכְנַנְיָהוּ שַׂר־הַלְוִיִּם
בְּמַשָּׂא יָסֹר בַּמַּשָּׂא כִּי מֵבִין
23 הוּא: וּבֶרֶכְיָה וְאֶלְקָנָה
24 שֹׁעֲרִים לָאָרוֹן: וּשְׁבַנְיָהוּ
וְיוֹשָׁפָט וּנְתַנְאֵל וַעֲמָשַׂי
וּזְכַרְיָהוּ וּבְנָיָהוּ וֶאֱלִיעֶזֶר
הַכֹּהֲנִים מַחְצְצְרִים
בַּחֲצֹצְרוֹת לִפְנֵי אֲרוֹן
הָאֱלֹהִים וְעֹבֵד אֱדֹם וִיחִיָּה
שֹׁעֲרִים לָאָרוֹן:

v. 24. יתיר צ'

19-21. The three divisions of the singers, with cymbals and other musical instruments.

20. *set to Alamoth.* Again in the superscription of Ps. xlvi. The last word may mean 'young women,' and the most probable explanation is instruments with a high pitched tone. The suggestion that the reference is to a female choir cannot be entertained because nowhere is such a choir mentioned as functioning in the Temple.

21. *on the Sheminith.* Cf. the superscription of Ps. vi. The literal meaning is 'upon the eighth,' i.e. either 'a deep octave' or 'in the bass,' possibly an octave lower than the psalteries or the viol.

22. *over the song.* The Hebrew *massa* signifies not only 'burden' but also 'lifting up,' hence 'lifting up the voice in song.' Others understand it as 'over the transport.'

24. *did blow with the trumpets.* These were different from the *shophar* which was a curved horn, usually of a ram.

25. So David, and the elders of Israel, and the captains over thousands, went to bring up the ark of the covenant of the LORD out of the house of Obed-edom with joy. 26. And it came to pass, when God helped the Levites that bore the ark of the covenant of the LORD, that they sacrificed seven bullocks and seven rams. 27. And David was clothed with a robe of fine linen, and all the Levites that bore the ark, and the singers, and Chenaniah the master of the singers in the song; and David had upon him an ephod of linen. 28. Thus all Israel brought up the ark of the covenant of the LORD with shouting, and with sound of the horn, and with trumpets, and with cymbals, sounding aloud with psalteries and harps. 29. And it

25 וַיְהִי דָוִיד וְזִקְנֵי יִשְׂרָאֵל וְשָׂרֵי
הָאֲלָפִים הַהֹלְכִים לְהַעֲלוֹת
אֶת־אֲרוֹן בְּרִית־יְהוָה
מִן־בֵּית עֹבֵד־אֱדֹם
26 בְּשִׂמְחָה׃ וַיְהִי בֶּעְזֹר
הָאֱלֹהִים אֶת־הַלְוִיִּם נֹשְׂאֵי
אֲרוֹן בְּרִית־יְהוָה וַיִּזְבְּחוּ
שִׁבְעָה־פָרִים וְשִׁבְעָה
27 אֵילִים׃ וְדָוִיד מְכֻרְבָּל ׀
בִּמְעִיל בּוּץ וְכָל־הַלְוִיִּם
הַנֹּשְׂאִים אֶת־הָאָרוֹן
וְהַמְשֹׁרְרִים וּכְנַנְיָה הַשַּׂר*
הַמַּשָּׂא הַמְשֹׁרְרִים וְעַל־דָּוִיד
28 אֵפוֹד בָּד׃ וְכָל־יִשְׂרָאֵל
מַעֲלִים אֶת־אֲרוֹן בְּרִית־
יְהוָה בִּתְרוּעָה וּבְקוֹל שׁוֹפָר
וּבַחֲצֹצְרוֹת וּבִמְצִלְתָּיִם
מַשְׁמִעִים בִּנְבָלִים וְכִנֹּרוֹת׃

הש׳ בפתח v. 27.

The trumpet was a long, straight silver tube with a mouth like that of a cornet. The former was used mainly in war (cf. Amos iii. 6), the latter on joyful occasions and feast days (cf. Num. x. 1ff.).

Jehiah. He is the same as *Jehiel* in verse 18.

25-xvi. 3. The bringing up of the ark and the accompanying festivities (parallel to 2 Sam. vi. 12-20).

25. *so David . . . went.* lit. 'and it was David . . . that went.'

26. *when God helped . . . rams.* In 2 Sam. vi. 13: *when they that bore the ark of the LORD had gone six paces, he* (David) *sacrificed an ox and a fatling.*

27. *and all the Levites . . . song.* i.e. all these, like David, wore robes of fine linen.

and David had upon him. In addition to *a robe of fine linen.*

an ephod. A short skirt, or a kind of tunic worn round the waist. A linen ephod was the regular attire of priests (cf. 1 Sam. xxii. 18). The High Priest had a special ephod, highly elaborate and costly, as described in Exod. xxviii. 6ff. Rabbinic tradition declares that David wore the same kind of ephod as the High Priest.

came to pass, as the ark of the covenant of the LORD came to the city of David, that Michal the daughter of Saul looked out at the window, and saw king David dancing and making merry; and she despised him in her heart.

29 וַיְהִי אֲרוֹן בְּרִית־יְהוָה בָּא
עַד־עִיר דָּוִיד וּמִיכַל בַּת־
שָׁאוּל נִשְׁקְפָה ׀ בְּעַד הַחַלּוֹן
וַתֵּרֶא אֶת־הַמֶּלֶךְ דָּוִיד
מְרַקֵּד וּמְשַׂחֵק וַתִּבֶז לוֹ
בְּלִבָּהּ׃

16 CHAPTER XVI טז

1. And they brought in the ark of God, and set it in the midst of the tent that David had pitched for it, and they offered burnt-offerings and peace-offerings before God.
2. And when David had made an end of offering the burnt-offering and the peace-offerings, he blessed the people in the name of the LORD.
3. And he dealt to every one of Israel, both man and woman, to every one a loaf of bread, and a cake made in a pan, and a sweet cake.

1 וַיָּבִיאוּ אֶת־אֲרוֹן הָאֱלֹהִים
וַיַּצִּיגוּ אֹתוֹ בְּתוֹךְ הָאֹהֶל אֲשֶׁר
נָטָה־לוֹ דָּוִיד וַיַּקְרִיבוּ עֹלוֹת
וּשְׁלָמִים לִפְנֵי הָאֱלֹהִים׃
2 וַיְכַל דָּוִיד מֵהַעֲלוֹת הָעֹלָה
וְהַשְּׁלָמִים וַיְבָרֶךְ אֶת־הָעָם
3 בְּשֵׁם יְהוָה׃ וַיְחַלֵּק לְכָל־
אִישׁ יִשְׂרָאֵל מֵאִישׁ וְעַד־אִשָּׁה
לְאִישׁ כִּכַּר־לֶחֶם וְאֶשְׁפָּר
וַאֲשִׁישָׁה׃

29. *making merry.* Perhaps the signification of the verb is 'leaping as in sport.'

despised him in her heart. Out of respect for David, the Chronicler does not include Michal's insulting rebuke in 2 Sam. vi. 20.

CHAPTER XVI

1-3. Offering of sacrifices, national rejoicing and royal gifts to the people.

1. *the tent.* See on xv. 1.

they offered. The subject is the king and the people. In 2 Sam. vi. 17 only *David offered.*

2. *blessed the people.* As did his son Solomon (cf. 2 Chron. vi. 3).

3. *a loaf of bread.* A flat cake baked in the oven.

a cake made in a pan. The noun *eshpar* occurs again only in the parallel passage, 2 Sam. vi. 19, and its meaning is uncertain. Another suggested rendering is 'a portion (of meat or wine).'

a sweet cake. Others translate 'a cake of raisins' or 'a flagon of wine.'

4-6. Levites appointed to minister before the ark.

4. And he appointed certain of the Levites to minister before the ark of the LORD, and to celebrate and to thank and praise the LORD, the God of Israel: 5. Asaph the chief, and second to him Zechariah, Jeiel, and Shemiramoth, and Jehiel, and Mattithiah, and Eliab, and Benaiah, and Obed-edom, and Jeiel, with psalteries and with harps; and Asaph with cymbals, sounding aloud; 6. and Benaiah and Jahaziel the priests with trumpets continually, before the ark of the covenant of God.

7. Then on that day did David first ordain to give thanks unto the LORD, by the hand of Asaph and his brethren.

8 O give thanks unto the LORD, call upon His name;
Make known His doings among the peoples.
9 Sing unto Him, sing praises unto Him;
Speak ye of all His marvellous works.
10 Glory ye in His holy name;

4 וַיִּתֵּן לִפְנֵי אֲרוֹן יְהוָה מִן־
הַלְוִיִּם מְשָׁרְתִים וּלְהַזְכִּיר
וּלְהוֹדוֹת וּלְהַלֵּל לַיהוָה
5 אֱלֹהֵי יִשְׂרָאֵל׃ אָסָף הָרֹאשׁ
וּמִשְׁנֵהוּ זְכַרְיָה יְעִיאֵל
וּשְׁמִירָמוֹת וִיחִיאֵל וּמַתִּתְיָה
וֶאֱלִיאָב וּבְנָיָהוּ וְעֹבֵד אֱדֹם
וִיעִיאֵל בִּכְלֵי נְבָלִים
וּבְכִנֹּרוֹת וְאָסָף בַּמְצִלְתַּיִם
6 מַשְׁמִיעַ׃ וּבְנָיָהוּ וְיַחֲזִיאֵל
הַכֹּהֲנִים בַּחֲצֹצְרוֹת תָּמִיד
לִפְנֵי אֲרוֹן בְּרִית־הָאֱלֹהִים׃
7 בַּיּוֹם הַהוּא אָז נָתַן דָּוִיד
בָּרֹאשׁ לְהֹדוֹת לַיהוָה בְּיַד־
אָסָף וְאֶחָיו׃
8 הוֹדוּ לַיהוָה קִרְאוּ בִשְׁמוֹ
הוֹדִיעוּ בָעַמִּים עֲלִילֹתָיו׃
9 שִׁירוּ לוֹ זַמְּרוּ־לוֹ
שִׂיחוּ בְּכָל־נִפְלְאֹתָיו׃
10 הִתְהַלְלוּ בְּשֵׁם קָדְשׁוֹ

4. *to minister.* lit. '(as) ministers.'

to celebrate. The literal meaning of *lehazkir* is 'to make mention,' 'to call to mind,' 'to commemorate.' The verb is used as a musical term in Psalms of praise and thanksgiving (cf. the headings of Pss. xxxviii and lxx) and may here signify 'to chant.'

8-36. A Psalm of thanksgiving.

8-22. This section corresponds to Ps. cv. 1-15 which has apparently been incorporated in this Book.

8. This verse is also found in Isa. xii. 4.

call upon His name. Or, 'proclaim His name'; testify publicly to His greatness.

among the peoples. His treatment of Israel is a lesson and a warning to all the nations, and it is for Israel to propagate this knowledge among them.

9. *sing praises.* Or, 'make melody.'

marvellous works. God's saving acts.

Let the heart of them rejoice that seek the LORD.
11 Seek ye the LORD and His strength;
Seek His face continually.
12 Remember His marvellous works that He hath done,
His wonders, and the judgments of His mouth;
13 O ye seed of Israel His servant,
Ye children of Jacob, His chosen ones.
14 He is the LORD our God;
His judgments are in all the earth.
15 Remember His covenant for ever,
The word which He commanded to a thousand generations;
16 [The covenant] which He made with Abraham,

יִשְׂמַח לֵב מְבַקְשֵׁי יְהוָה׃
דִּרְשׁוּ יְהוָה וְעֻזּוֹ 11
בַּקְּשׁוּ פָנָיו תָּמִיד׃
זִכְרוּ נִפְלְאֹתָיו אֲשֶׁר עָשָׂה 12
מֹפְתָיו וּמִשְׁפְּטֵי־פִיהוּ׃
זֶרַע יִשְׂרָאֵל עַבְדּוֹ 13
בְּנֵי יַעֲקֹב בְּחִירָיו׃
הוּא יְהוָה אֱלֹהֵינוּ 14
בְּכָל־הָאָרֶץ מִשְׁפָּטָיו׃
זִכְרוּ לְעוֹלָם בְּרִיתוֹ 15
דָּבָר צִוָּה לְאֶלֶף דּוֹר׃
אֲשֶׁר כָּרַת אֶת־אַבְרָהָם 16

10. *His holy name.* Holiness is the essence of God's nature from which the attributes of justice and mercy emanate.

rejoice. In their confidence that their petitions will be granted.

11. *seek ye.* Or, 'inquire ye,' to gain a knowledge of His majesty and *His strength.*

seek His face continually. The Hebrew verb is different from that of *seek ye* above, and is the same as that in verse 10. A man should always be conscious that he is in the presence (*face*) of God. Cf. *I have set the LORD always before me* (Ps. xvi. 8).

12. *remember.* A similar exhortation occurs in Deut. xxxii. 7 and elsewhere. A recollection of the *marvellous works* and *wonders* of the past is a source of inspiration for the present.

His wonders. The plagues of Egypt. Cf. Ps. cv. 27 where the same word is used and followed by a description of most of the ten plagues.

judgments. Executed upon the Egyptians (cf. Exod. vi. 6).

13. *seed of Israel.* In Ps. cv. 6 the reading is *Abraham.*

His chosen ones. Chosen to spread the knowledge of God and His commandments, and to lead a saintly life in accordance with the precepts of Torah.

14. *He is the LORD our God.* God has assumed a special and intimate relationship to Israel whom He had chosen; yet He is also a universal God: *His judgments are in all the earth.* All nations are subject to His rule. He is *the Judge of all the earth* (Gen. xviii. 25).

15-18. God's covenant with the patriarchs.

15. *remember.* In Ps. cv. 8: *He hath remembered,* or 'He remembereth.'

the word which He commanded. i.e. the promise He made and confirmed.

a thousand generations. The number is not to be taken literally. It merely signifies many generations.

16. *made with Abraham.* Cf. Gen. xvii. 2ff.

And His oath unto Isaac;
17 And He established it unto Jacob for a statute,
To Israel for an everlasting covenant;
18 Saying: 'Unto thee will I give the land of Canaan,
The lot of your inheritance.'
19 When ye were but a few men in number,
Yea, very few, and sojourners in it,
20 And when they went about from nation to nation,
And from one kingdom to another people,
21 He suffered no man to do them wrong,
Yea, for their sake He reproved kings:
22 'Touch not Mine anointed ones,
And do My prophets no harm.'

וּשְׁבוּעָתוֹ לְיִצְחָק׃
17 וַיַּעֲמִידֶהָ לְיַעֲקֹב לְחֹק
לְיִשְׂרָאֵל בְּרִית עוֹלָם׃
18 לֵאמֹר לְךָ אֶתֵּן אֶרֶץ־כְּנָעַן
חֶבֶל נַחֲלַתְכֶם׃
19 בִּהְיוֹתְכֶם מְתֵי מִסְפָּר
כִּמְעַט וְגָרִים בָּהּ׃
20 וַיִּתְהַלְּכוּ מִגּוֹי אֶל־גּוֹי
וּמִמַּמְלָכָה אֶל־עַם אַחֵר׃
21 לֹא־הִנִּיחַ לְאִישׁ לְעָשְׁקָם
וַיּוֹכַח עֲלֵיהֶם מְלָכִים׃
22 אַל־תִּגְּעוּ בִּמְשִׁיחָי
וּבִנְבִיאַי אַל־תָּרֵעוּ׃

v. 18. קמץ בז"ק v. 22. קמץ בז"ק

unto Isaac. Cf. Gen. xxvi. 3. The covenant made with Abraham was renewed with Isaac to exclude the other sons of Abraham. The Hebrew for *Isaac* has one different letter in Ps. cv. 9. Here it is the normal form.

17. *unto Jacob.* Cf. Gen. xxviii. 13ff. Esau, the elder son of Isaac, was thus excluded.

statute. In Ps. ii. 7 the same Hebrew word is rendered *decree.*

18. *unto thee.* This was addressed to each patriarch or to the people as a whole.

the lot of your inheritance. Each nation has been given its inheritance from God (cf. Deut. xxxii. 8); *the land of Canaan* has been allotted to Israel.

19-22. Divine protection in their wanderings.

19. *when ye were.* Addressed to the patriarchs or to the entire people. The parallel verse, Ps. cv. 12 reads: *when they were.*

few men in number. Cf. Gen. xxxiv. 30 where Jacob uses a similar expression in describing his family and followers.

sojourners. The land was not yet theirs.

20. *they went about,* etc. Each of the patriarchs had to leave Canaan for a period. A famine drove Abraham to Egypt (Gen. xii. 10) and Isaac to the Philistines (Gen. xxvi. 1), while Jacob was compelled to flee to Haran (Gen. xxviii. 10).

and from one kingdom. The conjunction is wanting in Ps. cv. 20. *Kingdom* may refer to Egypt; *people* to the Canaanites and the other neighbouring peoples.

21. *reproved kings.* Cf. Gen. xii. 17, xx. 3.

22. *touch not.* Cf. Gen. xxvi. 11.

Mine anointed ones. viz. the patriarchs. If they were not themselves *anointed,* they were the progenitors of *a kingdom of priests* (Exod. xix. 6) and of the anointed

23 Sing unto the LORD, all the earth;
Proclaim His salvation from day to day.
24 Declare His glory among the nations,
His marvellous works among all the peoples.
25 For great is the LORD, and highly to be praised;
He also is to be feared above all gods.
26 For all the gods of the peoples are things of nought;
But the LORD made the heavens.
27 Honour and majesty are before Him;
Strength and gladness are in His place.
28 Ascribe unto the LORD, ye kindreds of the peoples,
Ascribe unto the LORD glory and strength.

23 שִׁירוּ לַיהוָה כָּל־הָאָרֶץ
בַּשְּׂרוּ מִיּוֹם־אֶל־יוֹם
יְשׁוּעָתוֹ׃
24 סַפְּרוּ בַגּוֹיִם אֶת־כְּבוֹדוֹ
בְּכָל־הָעַמִּים נִפְלְאֹתָיו׃
25 כִּי גָדוֹל יְהוָה וּמְהֻלָּל מְאֹד
וְנוֹרָא הוּא עַל־כָּל־אֱלֹהִים׃
26 כִּי כָּל־אֱלֹהֵי
הָעַמִּים אֱלִילִים
וַיהוָה שָׁמַיִם עָשָׂה׃
27 הוֹד וְהָדָר לְפָנָיו
עֹז וְחֶדְוָה בִּמְקֹמוֹ׃
28 הָבוּ לַיהוָה מִשְׁפְּחוֹת עַמִּים
הָבוּ לַיהוָה כָּבוֹד וָעֹז׃

kings and High Priests of Israel and Judah.

My prophets. Men who commune with God. Abraham is termed a *prophet* in Gen. xx. 7.

23-33 (corresponding to Ps. xcvi with the omission of 1a, 2a, 10a and 13b). A call to universal worship of God.

23. *sing . . . all the earth.* By *all the earth* the dwellers on it are meant. Hence the masculine plural form of the verb, whereas the Hebrew for *earth* is a feminine noun in the singular.

proclaim, etc. Or, 'announce the good tidings that His salvation is renewed daily.' Man is always dependent on God's help and must endeavour to deserve it.

25. *He also is.* The second word is the rendering of the conjunction *waw* which is wanting in Ps. xcvi. 4.

to be feared above all gods. The meaning is that God is *to be feared* because He is *above all* the so-called *gods* which are in reality *things of nought.*

26. *things of nought.* Imaginary beings that lack reality.

the LORD made the heavens. But *the gods that have not made the heavens . . . shall perish* (Jer. x. 11).

27. *honour and majesty . . . before Him.* i.e. are His attributes. These are visualized as ministering angels in attendance *before Him.* In Ps. civ. 1 these attributes are said to be God's robes.

strength and gladness are in His place. In Ps. xcvi. 6 the reading is: *strength and beauty are in His sanctuary.* Elsewhere these qualities are applied to the ark (cf. Ps. lxxviii. 61); here they are associated with the Temple as a whole.

28f. A call to the nations to worship God.

29 Ascribe unto the LORD the glory due unto His name;
Bring an offering, and come before Him;
Worship the LORD in the beauty of holiness.
30 Tremble before Him, all the earth;
The world also is established that it cannot be moved.
31 Let the heavens be glad, and let the earth rejoice;
And let them say among the nations: 'The LORD reigneth.'
32 Let the sea roar, and the fulness thereof;
Let the field exult, and all that is therein;
33 Then shall the trees of the wood sing for joy,
Before the LORD, for He is come to judge the earth.
34 O give thanks unto the LORD; for He is good;
For His mercy endureth for ever.

הָבוּ לַיהוָה כְּבוֹד שְׁמוֹ 29
שְׂאוּ מִנְחָה וּבֹאוּ לְפָנָיו
הִשְׁתַּחֲווּ לַיהוָה
בְּהַדְרַת־קֹדֶשׁ׃
חִילוּ מִלְּפָנָיו כָּל־הָאָרֶץ 30
אַף־תִּכּוֹן תֵּבֵל בַּל־תִּמּוֹט׃
יִשְׂמְחוּ הַשָּׁמַיִם וְתָגֵל הָאָרֶץ 31
וְיֹאמְרוּ בַגּוֹיִם יְהוָה מָלָךְ׃
יִרְעַם הַיָּם וּמְלוֹאוֹ 32
יַעֲלֹץ הַשָּׂדֶה וְכָל־אֲשֶׁר־בּוֹ׃
אָז יְרַנְּנוּ עֲצֵי הַיָּעַר 33
מִלִּפְנֵי יְהוָה
כִּי־בָא לִשְׁפּוֹט אֶת־הָאָרֶץ׃
הוֹדוּ לַיהוָה כִּי טוֹב 34
כִּי לְעוֹלָם חַסְדּוֹ׃

29. *come before Him.* In Ps. xcvi. 8: *come into His courts.*

the beauty of holiness. Or, 'in holy adornment.'

30-33. Nature is invited to pay homage to Him.

30. *the world . . . moved.* In Ps. xcvi. 10 this clause is preceded by *say among the nations: 'The LORD reigneth,'* and is followed by *He will judge the peoples with equity.*

31. *and let them say . . . reigneth.* In Ps. xcvi. 10, *say* is in the imperative; and the clause precedes *the world also . . . moved* (see on verse 30).

reigneth. Or, 'hath become king.'

32. *let the sea roar.* Better, 'let the sea glory, or, praise' (cf. I. W. Slotki, A.J.S.L.L., vol. XXXVII, pp. 149ff.).

fulness thereof. All the creatures that live in it.

the field. The open country as opposed to built-up land.

33. *the trees.* In Ps. xcvi. 12: *all the trees.*

for He is come. In Ps. the clause is repeated.

to judge the earth. God's judgment is welcomed with joy, for *with righteousness shall He judge the poor* (Isa. xi. 4). God as Judge brings terror to the arrogant and the wicked but gladness to the oppressed whose cause He pleads; and all Nature rejoices with them.

34-36 (corresponding to Ps. cvi. 1, 47f.). Praise and doxology.

34. *good.* i.e. considerate, long-suffering and gracious.

His mercy endureth for ever. Cf. *showing*

35 And say ye: 'Save us, O God of our salvation,
And gather us together and deliver us from the nations,
That we may give thanks unto Thy holy name,
That we may triumph in Thy praise.'
36 Blessed be the LORD, the God of Israel,
From everlasting even to everlasting.
And all the people said: 'Amen,' and praised the LORD.
37. So he left there, before the ark
of the covenant of the LORD, Asaph
and his brethren, to minister before
the ark continually, as every day's
work required; 38. and Obed-edom
with their brethren, threescore and
eight; Obed-edom also the son of
Jedithun and Hosah to be doorkeepers; 39. and Zadok the priest,
and his brethren the priests, before
the tabernacle of the LORD in the

35 וְאִמְרוּ הוֹשִׁיעֵנוּ אֱלֹהֵי יִשְׁעֵנוּ
וְקַבְּצֵנוּ וְהַצִּילֵנוּ מִן־הַגּוֹיִם
לְהוֹדוֹת לְשֵׁם קָדְשֶׁךָ
לְהִשְׁתַּבֵּחַ בִּתְהִלָּתֶךָ׃
36 בָּרוּךְ יְהוָה אֱלֹהֵי יִשְׂרָאֵל
מִן־הָעוֹלָם וְעַד־הָעֹלָם
וַיֹּאמְרוּ כָל־הָעָם אָמֵן
וְהַלֵּל לַיהוָה׃
37 וַיַּעֲזָב־שָׁם לִפְנֵי אֲרוֹן בְּרִית־
יְהוָה לְאָסָף וּלְאֶחָיו לְשָׁרֵת
לִפְנֵי הָאָרוֹן תָּמִיד לִדְבַר־
38 יוֹם בְּיוֹמוֹ׃ וְעֹבֵד אֱדֹם
וַאֲחֵיהֶם שִׁשִּׁים וּשְׁמוֹנָה וְעֹבֵד
אֱדֹם בֶּן־יְדִיתוּן וְחֹסָה
39 לְשֹׁעֲרִים׃ וְאֵת ׀ צָדוֹק הַכֹּהֵן
וְאֶחָיו הַכֹּהֲנִים לִפְנֵי מִשְׁכַּן

v. 38. ידותון ק׳ ב״א

mercy unto the thousandth generation (Exod. xx. 6).

35. *and say ye.* This clause is wanting in Ps. cvi. 47.

O God of our salvation. In Ps.: *O LORD our God.*

and gather us together and deliver us. The Hebrew for the last three words is wanting in Ps.

36. *and all the people said.* In Ps. cvi. 48: *and let all the people say.*

and praised the LORD. Or, 'and praise to the Lord.' In Ps. this clause is replaced by the word *Hallelujah,* which concludes the doxology of Book IV of the Psalms.

37-43. Appointments to the ministration before the ark and the tabernacle.

37. *before the ark.* Which was now in the City of David (cf. verse 1), the new and steadily rising religious centre of the nation.

as every day's work required. i.e. in the morning and evening (cf. verse 40).

38. *Obed-edom with their brethren.* One would expect the pronoun to be in the singular (so the LXX) unless it refers to *Asaph and his brethren* in verse 37.

39. *Zadok the priest.* As no sacrifices were yet offered in the new centre, there was no need to appoint priests there.

the tabernacle. Which was built by Moses. On the entry into Canaan it was put up at Shiloh from where it was moved to Nob; and from there, apparently after the slaughter of the priests

high place that was at Gibeon, 40. to offer burnt-offerings unto the LORD upon the altar of burnt-offering continually morning and evening, even according to all that is written in the Law of the LORD, which He commanded unto Israel; 41. and with them Heman and Jeduthun, and the rest that were chosen, who were mentioned by name, to give thanks to the LORD, because His mercy endureth for ever; 42. and with them Heman and Jeduthun, to sound aloud with trumpets and cymbals, and with instruments for the songs of God; and the sons of Jeduthun to be at the gate. 43. And all the people departed every man to his house; and David returned to bless his house.

יְהוָה בַּבָּמָה אֲשֶׁר בְּגִבְעוֹן׃
40 לְהַעֲלוֹת עֹלוֹת לַיהוָה עַל־
מִזְבַּח הָעֹלָה תָּמִיד לַבֹּקֶר
וְלָעָרֶב וּלְכָל־הַכָּתוּב
בְּתוֹרַת יְהוָה אֲשֶׁר צִוָּה עַל־
41 יִשְׂרָאֵל׃ וְעִמָּהֶם הֵימָן
וִידוּתוּן וּשְׁאָר הַבְּרוּרִים אֲשֶׁר
נִקְּבוּ בְּשֵׁמוֹת לְהוֹדוֹת לַיהוָה
42 כִּי לְעוֹלָם חַסְדּוֹ׃ וְעִמָּהֶם
הֵימָן וִידוּתוּן חֲצֹצְרוֹת
וּמְצִלְתַּיִם לְמַשְׁמִיעִים וּכְלֵי
שִׁיר הָאֱלֹהִים וּבְנֵי יְדוּתוּן
43 לַשָּׁעַר׃ וַיֵּלְכוּ כָל־הָעָם אִישׁ
לְבֵיתוֹ וַיִּסֹּב דָּוִיד לְבָרֵךְ אֶת־
בֵּיתוֹ׃

17 CHAPTER XVII יז

1. And it came to pass, when David dwelt in his house, that David said

1 וַיְהִי כַּאֲשֶׁר יָשַׁב דָּוִיד בְּבֵיתוֹ

(cf. 1 Sam. xxii. 16ff.), it was moved again to Gibeon.

40. *morning and evening.* Cf. Exod. xxix. 38f.

even according to all that is written, etc. Or, 'and according to all,' etc.; i.e. all the other duties connected with the various services of the Sanctuary.

41. *Heman and Jeduthun.* The latter is also called Ethan. In xv. 17, 19 Heman, Asaph and Ethan are mentioned but not Jeduthun, while here Asaph (verse 37), Heman and Jeduthun are named and Ethan is omitted.

because His mercy endureth for ever. This was the refrain of their hymns.

42. *and with them Heman and Jeduthun.* The repetition here of the first clause of the preceding verse is necessary for the resumption of the description of the duties of Heman and Jeduthun, which was interrupted in verse 41 by *and the rest*, etc.

to be at the gate. The verb is implied.

43. The verse, with slight variations, corresponds to 2 Sam. vi. 19b-20a. On the omission of Michal's uncomplimentary remark to David which follows in Sam., see on xv. 29.

to Nathan the prophet: 'Lo, I dwell in a house of cedar, but the ark of the covenant of the LORD dwelleth under curtains.' 2. And Nathan said unto David: 'Do all that is in thy heart; for God is with thee.' 3. And it came to pass the same night, that the word of God came to Nathan, saying: 4. 'Go and tell David My servant: Thus saith the LORD: Thou shalt not build Me a house to dwell in; 5. for I have not dwelt in a house since the day that I brought up Israel, unto this day;

וַיֹּאמֶר דָּוִיד אֶל־נָתָן הַנָּבִיא
הִנֵּה אָנֹכִי יוֹשֵׁב בְּבֵית הָאֲרָזִים
וַאֲרוֹן בְּרִית־יְהוָה תַּחַת
2 יְרִיעוֹת׃ וַיֹּאמֶר נָתָן אֶל־
דָּוִיד כֹּל אֲשֶׁר בִּלְבָבְךָ עֲשֵׂה
3 כִּי הָאֱלֹהִים עִמָּךְ׃ וַיְהִי
בַּלַּיְלָה הַהוּא וַיְהִי דְּבַר
4 אֱלֹהִים אֶל־נָתָן לֵאמֹר׃ לֵךְ
וְאָמַרְתָּ אֶל־דָּוִיד עַבְדִּי כֹּה
אָמַר יְהוָה לֹא אַתָּה תִּבְנֶה־לִּי
5 הַבַּיִת לָשָׁבֶת׃ כִּי לֹא יָשַׁבְתִּי
בְּבַיִת מִן־הַיּוֹם אֲשֶׁר הֶעֱלֵיתִי
אֶת־יִשְׂרָאֵל עַד הַיּוֹם הַזֶּה

CHAPTER XVII

THIS chapter has its parallel in 2 Sam. vii. David's desire to build a Temple. The Divine answer, and David's thanks and prayer.

1f. David's implied intention and the prophet's encouragement.

1. *in his house.* In 2 Sam. vii. 1 is added: *and the LORD had given him rest from all his enemies round about.* This addition would obviously be out of harmony with David's wars described in chapters xviii-xx which follow.

the ark of the covenant. The last word refers to the two tables of the covenant which Moses had deposited in the ark (1 Kings viii. 9).

dwelleth under curtains. The verb is implied. In Sam.: *dwelleth within curtains.* By *curtains* is to be understood a tent. David does not specifically state that he desires to build a Temple, but his intention is indicated in his statement.

2. *unto David.* In 2 Sam. vii. 3: *to the king.*

do. In Sam.: *go, do.*

all that is in thy heart. i.e. 'all thou wishest,' the heart being the seat of the desires and emotions.

God is with thee. Sam. reads *the LORD* for *God.* This substitution is frequent in Chron.

3-15. The Divine message through Nathan to David.

3. *the same night.* This is amplified in the Midrash: David, God said to the prophet, is prompt and efficient; you must go at once and stop him before he engages the builders or makes a rash vow. That is why God spoke to Nathan *in the same night.*

4. *thou shalt not build Me a house to dwell in.* In 2 Sam. vii. 5: *shalt thou build Me a house for Me to dwell in?* The question implies a negative answer.

5. *I brought up Israel.* Out of Egypt, as

but have [gone] from tent to tent, and from one tabernacle [to another]. 6. In all places wherein I have walked among all Israel, spoke I a word with any of the judges of Israel, whom I commanded to feed My people, saying: Why have ye not built Me a house of cedar? 7. Now therefore thus shalt thou say unto My servant David: Thus saith the LORD of hosts: I took thee from the sheepcote, from following the sheep, that thou shouldest be prince over My people Israel; 8. and I have been with thee whithersoever thou wentest, and have cut off all thine enemies from before thee; and I will make thee a name, like unto the name of the great ones that are in the earth. 9. And I will appoint a place for My people Israel, and will plant them, that they may dwell in their own place, and be disquieted no more; neither shall the children of wickedness waste them any more, as at the first, 10. even from the day that I commanded judges to be over My

וָאֶהְיֶה מֵאֹהֶל אֶל־אֹהֶל
6 וּמִמִּשְׁכָּן׃ בְּכֹל אֲשֶׁר־
הִתְהַלַּכְתִּי בְּכָל־יִשְׂרָאֵל
הֲדָבָר דִּבַּרְתִּי אֶת־אַחַד
שֹׁפְטֵי יִשְׂרָאֵל אֲשֶׁר צִוִּיתִי
לִרְעוֹת אֶת־עַמִּי לֵאמֹר לָמָּה
לֹא־בְנִיתֶם לִי בֵּית אֲרָזִים׃
7 וְעַתָּה כֹּה תֹאמַר לְעַבְדִּי
לְדָוִיד כֹּה אָמַר יְהוָה צְבָאוֹת
אֲנִי לְקַחְתִּיךָ מִן־הַנָּוֶה מִן
אַחֲרֵי הַצֹּאן לִהְיוֹת נָגִיד עַל
8 עַמִּי יִשְׂרָאֵל׃ וָאֶהְיֶה עִמְּךָ
בְּכֹל אֲשֶׁר הָלַכְתָּ וָאַכְרִית
אֶת־כָּל־אוֹיְבֶיךָ מִפָּנֶיךָ
וְעָשִׂיתִי לְךָ שֵׁם כְּשֵׁם הַגְּדוֹלִים
9 אֲשֶׁר בָּאָרֶץ׃ וְשַׂמְתִּי מָקוֹם
לְעַמִּי יִשְׂרָאֵל וּנְטַעְתִּיהוּ וְשָׁכַן
תַּחְתָּיו וְלֹא יִרְגַּז עוֹד וְלֹא־
יוֹסִיפוּ בְנֵי־עַוְלָה לְבַלֹּתוֹ
10 כַּאֲשֶׁר בָּרִאשׁוֹנָה׃ וּלְמִיָּמִים
אֲשֶׁר צִוִּיתִי שֹׁפְטִים עַל־עַמִּי

explicitly stated in the corresponding verse in Sam.

but have [*gone*] . . . [*to another*]. In 2 Sam. vii. 6: *but have walked in a tent and in a tabernacle.*

6. *the judges.* In 2 Sam. vii. 7: *the tribes;* the difference in Hebrew is slight, viz. *shophetë* and *shibtë.*

8. *a name.* In 2 Sam. vii. 9: *a great name.*

9. *plant them.* lit. 'plant him,' i.e. the nation.

their own place. lit. 'his own place.'

waste them. In 2 Sam. vii. 10: *afflict them.*

10. *even from the day.* So also in the translation of 2 Sam. vii. 11; but the Hebrew has the noun *day* here in the plural.

people Israel; and I will subdue all
thine enemies. Moreover I tell thee
that the LORD will build thee a
house. 11. And it shall come to
pass, when thy days are fulfilled
that thou must go to be with thy
fathers, that I will set up thy seed
after thee, who shall be of thy sons;
and I will establish his kingdom.
12. He shall build Me a house, and
I will establish his throne for ever.
13. I will be to him for a father, and
he shall be to Me for a son; and
I will not take My mercy away from
him, as I took it from him that was
before thee; 14. but I will settle him
in My house and in My kingdom for

יִשְׂרָאֵל וְהִכְנַעְתִּי אֶת־כָּל־
אוֹיְבֶיךָ וָאַגִּד לָךְ וּבַיִת יִבְנֶה־
11 לְּךָ יְהוָה׃ וְהָיָה כִּי־מָלְאוּ
יָמֶיךָ לָלֶכֶת עִם־אֲבֹתֶיךָ
וַהֲקִימוֹתִי אֶת־זַרְעֲךָ אַחֲרֶיךָ
אֲשֶׁר יִהְיֶה מִבָּנֶיךָ וַהֲכִינוֹתִי
12 אֶת־מַלְכוּתוֹ׃ הוּא יִבְנֶה־לִּי
בָּיִת וְכֹנַנְתִּי אֶת־כִּסְאוֹ עַד־
13 עוֹלָם׃ אֲנִי אֶהְיֶה־לּוֹ לְאָב
וְהוּא יִהְיֶה־לִּי לְבֵן וְחַסְדִּי
לֹא־אָסִיר מֵעִמּוֹ כַּאֲשֶׁר
הֲסִירוֹתִי מֵאֲשֶׁר הָיָה לְפָנֶיךָ׃
14 וְהַעֲמַדְתִּיהוּ בְּבֵיתִי
וּבְמַלְכוּתִי עַד־הָעוֹלָם

I will subdue all thine enemies. In Sam.: *I will cause thee to rest from all thine enemies.*

moreover I tell thee . . . house. In Sam.: *moreover the LORD telleth thee that the LORD will make thee a house.* The *house* in either case means a dynasty. David wanted to build for God a house of stone and wood; God will build him one of kings.

11. *and it shall come to pass.* This clause is wanting in 2 Sam. vii. 12.

when thy days are fulfilled. The Hebrew verb is in the perfect, but in Sam. in the imperfect.

that thou must go to be with thy fathers. In Sam.: *and thou shalt sleep with thy fathers.*

who shall be of thy sons. In Sam.: *that shall proceed out of thy body.* The allusion is to Solomon who at the time was unborn.

12. *build Me a house.* In 2 Sam. vii. 13: *build a house for My name.*

his throne. In Sam.: *the throne of his kingdom.*

13. *for a son.* 2 Sam. vii. 14 adds: *if he commit iniquity, I will chasten him with the rod of men, and with the stripes of the children of men.* The Chronicler was averse from striking such an ominous note.

I will not take My mercy away from him. In 2 Sam. vii. 15: *but My mercy shall not depart from him.*

as I took it from him that was before thee. In Sam.: *as I took it from Saul, whom I put away before thee.*

14. *but I will settle him . . . for ever.* In 2 Sam. vii. 16: *and thy house and thy kingdom shall be made sure for ever before thee.*

ever; and his throne shall be established for ever.' 15. According to all these words, and according to all this vision, so did Nathan speak unto David.

16. Then David the king went in, and sat before the LORD; and he said: 'Who am I, O LORD God, and what is my house, that Thou hast brought me thus far? 17. And this was a small thing in Thine eyes, O God; but Thou hast spoken of Thy servant's house for a great while to come, and hast regarded me after the manner of a man of high degree, O LORD God. 18. What can David say yet more unto Thee concerning the honour which is done to Thy servant? for Thou knowest Thy

וְכִסְאוֹ יִהְיֶה נָכוֹן עַד־עוֹלָם׃
15 כְּכֹל הַדְּבָרִים הָאֵלֶּה וּכְכֹל
הֶחָזוֹן הַזֶּה כֵּן דִּבֶּר נָתָן אֶל־
דָּוִיד׃
16 וַיָּבֹא הַמֶּלֶךְ דָּוִיד וַיֵּשֶׁב לִפְנֵי
יְהוָה וַיֹּאמֶר מִי־אֲנִי יְהוָה
אֱלֹהִים וּמִי בֵיתִי כִּי הֲבִיאֹתַנִי
17 עַד־הֲלֹם׃ וַתִּקְטַן זֹאת
בְּעֵינֶיךָ אֱלֹהִים וַתְּדַבֵּר עַל־
בֵּית־עַבְדְּךָ לְמֵרָחוֹק
וּרְאִיתַנִי כְּתוֹר הָאָדָם
18 הַמַּעֲלָה יְהוָה אֱלֹהִים׃ מַה־
יּוֹסִיף עוֹד דָּוִיד אֵלֶיךָ לְכָבוֹד
אֶת־עַבְדֶּךָ וְאַתָּה אֶת־

his throne. In Sam.: *thy throne.* The Chronicler refers the promise to the future kingdom of Solomon while 2 Sam. applies the final assurance to David. It is 'David's dynasty,' not that of Solomon or any other of his descendants.

16-27. David's prayer and thanksgiving.

16. *went in.* Into the tent he erected for the ark (cf. xvi. 1), the new Sanctuary.

sat before the LORD. Nowhere else in the Bible is mention made of sitting during prayer. Hence it has been suggested that the verb *yashab*, here translated *sat*, means, as elsewhere (cf. Lev. xxiii. 42), 'tarried' in prayer (so the Targum). It is also possible that David sat for a while in meditation before beginning his prayer, a custom still observed by pious Jews.

brought me thus far. From the sheepfolds to a throne.

17. *this was a small thing.* In 2 Sam. vii. 19 *yet* is added after *was.* What God had so far done for him was insignificant as compared with His promise of an enduring dynasty.

O God. In Sam.: *O LORD God.*

hast spoken. This is followed by *also* in Sam.

and hast regarded me . . . of high degree. In Sam.: *and this too after the manner of great men.* David humbly avers that he is unworthy of the great honour bestowed upon him.

18. *what can David say yet more.* The verbs *can* and *say* are implied, but in 2 Sam. vii. 20 the second verb is included in the text.

concerning . . . servant. These words are omitted in Sam.

Thou knowest Thy servant. That his heart is full of gratitude which cannot be

servant. 19. O LORD, for Thy servant's sake, and according to Thine own heart, hast Thou wrought all this greatness, to make known all these great things. 20. O LORD, there is none like Thee, neither is there any God beside Thee, according to all that we have heard with our ears. 21. And who is like Thy people Israel, a nation one in the earth, whom God went to redeem unto Himself for a people, to make Thee a name by great and tremendous things, in driving out nations from before Thy people, whom Thou didst redeem out of Egypt? 22. For Thy people Israel didst Thou make Thine own people for ever; and Thou, LORD, becamest their God. 23. And now, O LORD, let the word that Thou hast spoken concerning Thy servant, and concerning his house, be established for ever, and do as Thou hast spoken.

19 עַבְדְּךָ יָדָעְתָּ: יְהוָה בַּעֲבוּר
עַבְדְּךָ וּכְלִבְּךָ עָשִׂיתָ אֵת כָּל־
הַגְּדוּלָּה הַזֹּאת לְהֹדִיעַ אֶת־
20 כָּל־הַגְּדֻלּוֹת: יְהוָה אֵין
כָּמוֹךָ וְאֵין אֱלֹהִים זוּלָתֶךָ
בְּכֹל אֲשֶׁר־שָׁמַעְנוּ בְּאָזְנֵינוּ:
21 וּמִי כְּעַמְּךָ יִשְׂרָאֵל גּוֹי אֶחָד
בָּאָרֶץ אֲשֶׁר הָלַךְ הָאֱלֹהִים
לִפְדּוֹת לוֹ עָם לָשׂוּם לְךָ שֵׁם
גְּדֻלּוֹת וְנֹרָאוֹת לְגָרֵשׁ מִפְּנֵי
עַמְּךָ אֲשֶׁר־פָּדִיתָ מִמִּצְרַיִם
22 גּוֹיִם: וַתִּתֵּן אֶת־עַמְּךָ יִשְׂרָאֵל
׀ לְךָ לְעָם עַד־עוֹלָם וְאַתָּה
יְהוָה הָיִיתָ לָהֶם לֵאלֹהִים:
23 וְעַתָּה יְהוָה הַדָּבָר אֲשֶׁר
דִּבַּרְתָּ עַל־עַבְדְּךָ וְעַל־
בֵּיתוֹ יֵאָמֵן עַד־עוֹלָם וַעֲשֵׂה

adequately expressed in words. In Sam. *O LORD God* is added at the end of the verse.

19. *O LORD, for Thy servant's sake.* In 2 Sam. vii. 21 *word's* takes the place of *servant's* and the exclamation *O LORD* is omitted.

to make known all these great things. In 2 Sam. vii. 21: *to make Thy servant know it.*

20. *O LORD, there is none like Thee.* This is preceded in 2 Sam. vii. 22 by: *therefore Thou art great*, and *O LORD* is followed by *God.*

21. *God went.* The verb is here in the singular and *God* has the definite article. In 2 Sam. vii. 23 the verb is in the plural and *God* is without the article.

to make Thee a name. In Sam.: *and to make Him a name.*

by great and tremendous things, in driving out nations. In Sam.: *and to do for Thy land great things and tremendous, even for you.*

didst redeem out of Egypt. In Sam.: *didst redeem to Thee out of Egypt, the nations and their gods.*

22. *didst Thou make*, etc. In 2 Sam. vii. 24: *didst Thou establish to Thyself to be a people unto Thee for ever.*

23. *be established.* In 2 Sam. vii. 25: *confirm Thou it.*

24. Yea, let it be established, and let Thy name be magnified for ever, that it may be said: The LORD of hosts is the God of Israel, even a God to Israel; and the house of David Thy servant shall be established before Thee. 25. For Thou, O my God, hast revealed to Thy servant that Thou wilt build him a house; therefore hath Thy servant taken heart to pray before Thee. 26. And now, O LORD, Thou alone art God, and hast promised this good thing unto Thy servant; 27. and now it hath pleased Thee to bless the house of Thy servant, that it may continue for ever before Thee; for Thou, O LORD, hast blessed, and so let [Thy servant] be blessed for ever.'

כַּאֲשֶׁר דִּבַּרְתָּ׃ וְיֵאָמֵן וְיִגְדַּל 24
שִׁמְךָ עַד־עוֹלָם לֵאמֹר יְהוָה
צְבָאוֹת אֱלֹהֵי יִשְׂרָאֵל אֱלֹהִים
לְיִשְׂרָאֵל וּבֵית־דָּוִיד עַבְדְּךָ
נָכוֹן לְפָנֶיךָ׃ כִּי ׀ אַתָּה אֱלֹהַי 25
גָּלִיתָ אֶת־אֹזֶן עַבְדְּךָ לִבְנוֹת
לוֹ בָּיִת עַל־כֵּן מָצָא עַבְדְּךָ
לְהִתְפַּלֵּל לְפָנֶיךָ׃ וְעַתָּה 26
יְהוָה אַתָּה־הוּא הָאֱלֹהִים
וַתְּדַבֵּר עַל־עַבְדְּךָ הַטּוֹבָה
הַזֹּאת׃ וְעַתָּה הוֹאַלְתָּ לְבָרֵךְ 27
אֶת־בֵּית עַבְדְּךָ לִהְיוֹת
לְעוֹלָם לְפָנֶיךָ כִּי־אַתָּה יְהוָה
בֵּרַכְתָּ וּמְבֹרָךְ לְעוֹלָם׃

18 CHAPTER XVIII יח

1. And after this it came to pass,

וַיְהִי אַחֲרֵי־כֵן וַיַּךְ דָּוִיד אֶת־ 1

v. 23. פתח בס״פ

24. *yea, let it be established.* Omitted in 2 Sam. vii. 26.

the LORD of hosts . . . to Israel. In Sam.: *the LORD of hosts is God over Israel.*

David Thy servant. In Sam. *David* follows *servant.*

25. *for Thou, O my God, hast revealed.* 2 Sam. vii. 27 reads: *for Thou, O LORD of hosts, the God of Israel, hast revealed.*

to Thy servant. lit. 'the ear of Thy servant.'

that Thou wilt build him a house. In Sam.: *saying: I will build thee a house.*

hath Thy servant taken heart. The last word which occurs in Sam. is here implied.

to pray before Thee. In Sam.: *to pray this prayer unto Thee.*

26. *Thou alone art God.* 2 Sam. vii. 28 inserts *and Thy words are truth.*

27. *and now it hath pleased Thee to bless.* In 2 Sam. vii. 29: *now therefore let it please Thee to bless.*

Thou, O LORD, hast blessed. In Sam.: *for Thou, O LORD God, hast spoken it.*

and so let [*Thy servant*] *be blessed for ever.* In Sam.: *and through Thy blessing let the house of Thy servant be blessed for ever.*

that David smote the Philistines,
and subdued them, and took Gath
and its towns out of the hand of the
Philistines.

2. And he smote Moab; and the
Moabites became servants to David,
and brought presents.

3. And David smote Hadarezer
king of Zobah by Hamath, as he
went to establish his dominion at the
river Euphrates. 4. And David
took from him a thousand chariots,
and seven thousand horsemen, and
twenty thousand footmen; and
David houghed all the chariot

פְּלִשְׁתִּים וַיַּכְנִיעֵם וַיִּקַּח אֶת־
גַּת וּבְנֹתֶיהָ מִיַּד פְּלִשְׁתִּים׃
2 וַיַּךְ אֶת־מוֹאָב וַיִּהְיוּ מוֹאָב
עֲבָדִים לְדָוִיד נֹשְׂאֵי מִנְחָה׃
3 וַיַּךְ דָּוִיד אֶת־הֲדַרְעֶזֶר
מֶלֶךְ־צוֹבָה חֲמָתָה בְּלֶכְתּוֹ
לְהַצִּיב יָדוֹ בִּנְהַר פְּרָת׃
4 וַיִּלְכֹּד דָּוִיד מִמֶּנּוּ אֶלֶף רֶכֶב
וְשִׁבְעַת אֲלָפִים פָּרָשִׁים
וְעֶשְׂרִים אֶלֶף אִישׁ רַגְלִי
וַיְעַקֵּר דָּוִיד אֶת־כָּל־הָרֶכֶב

CHAPTER XVIII

WITH some variations this chapter corresponds to 2 Sam. viii.

1-13 (corresponding to 2 Sam. viii. 1-14). A summary of David's campaigns.

1. The Philistine war.

after this. After David, in compliance with the Divine message, had abandoned the plan for building the Temple (Rashi); but there is not necessarily a chronological sequence in the two chapters.

took Gath and its towns. In 2 Sam. viii. 1: *David took Metheg-ammah.* Gath was one of the five principal cities of the Philistines. It lies now in ruins in the vicinity of Tel-es-Safieh, a prominent hill in the plain on the west of the Judean hills.

2. The Moabite war.

and he smote Moab. 2 Sam. viii. 2 adds the information that David put two-thirds of the Moabites to death, which the Chronicler omitted as not to his credit.

brought presents. Paid tribute as a subjugated people.

3f. The war with Zobah.

3. *Hadarezer.* In 2 Sam. viii. 3: *Hadadezer the son of Rehob.* The form of the name *Hadadezer* conforms to the spelling in the inscriptions.

Zobah by Hamath. Zobah was a small state in the vicinity of Damascus, and by capturing it David extended his frontiers as far as Hamath and the Euphrates. Hamath was an important city on the Orontes, the modern Hama.

as he went. The subject is David.

to establish his dominion. In 2 Sam. viii. 3 the Hebrew may mean 'to recover his dominion' (so R.V.). It is possible that Saul had already gained some territory in the region of Zobah (cf. 1 Sam. xiv. 47), which was later lost and now recovered by David. The literal meaning of the Hebrew for *his dominion* is 'his hand, or, power.'

4. *a thousand chariots, and seven thousand horsemen.* In 2 Sam. viii. 4: *a thousand and seven hundred horsemen*, but the LXX of Sam. agrees with the text here.

David houghed. By cutting the sinews of their legs the horses were disabled.

horses, but reserved of them for a hundred chariots. 5. And when the Arameans of Damascus came to succour Hadarezer king of Zobah, David smote of the Arameans two and twenty thousand men. 6. Then David put [garrisons] in Aram Damascus; and the Arameans became servants to David, and brought presents. And the LORD gave victory to David whithersoever he went. 7. And David took the shields of gold that were on the servants of Hadarezer, and brought them to Jerusalem. 8. And from Tibhath, and from Cun, cities of Hadarezer, David took very much brass, wherewith Solomon made the brazen sea and the pillars, and the vessels of brass.

5 וַיּוֹתֵר מִמֶּנּוּ מֵאָה רָכֶב׃ וַיָּבֹא
אֲרַם דַּרְמֶשֶׂק לַעְזוֹר
לַהֲדַרְעֶזֶר מֶלֶךְ צוֹבָה וַיַּךְ
דָּוִיד בַּאֲרָם עֶשְׂרִים־וּשְׁנַיִם
6 אֶלֶף אִישׁ׃ וַיָּשֶׂם דָּוִיד בַּאֲרַם
דַּרְמֶשֶׂק וַיְהִי אֲרָם לְדָוִיד
עֲבָדִים נֹשְׂאֵי מִנְחָה וַיּוֹשַׁע
יְהוָה לְדָוִיד בְּכֹל אֲשֶׁר הָלָךְ׃
7 וַיִּקַּח דָּוִיד אֵת שִׁלְטֵי הַזָּהָב
אֲשֶׁר הָיוּ עַל־עַבְדֵי הֲדַרְעָזֶר
8 וַיְבִיאֵם יְרוּשָׁלָםִ׃ וּמִטִּבְחַת
וּמִכּוּן עָרֵי הֲדַרְעֶזֶר לָקַח
דָּוִיד נְחֹשֶׁת רַבָּה מְאֹד בָּהּ ׀
עָשָׂה שְׁלֹמֹה אֶת־יָם הַנְּחֹשֶׁת
וְאֶת־הָעַמּוּדִים וְאֵת כְּלֵי
הַנְּחֹשֶׁת׃

5-8. The war with Damascus and the spoils of Hadadezer.

5. *Damascus.* The Hebrew form here is *Darmesek*, in Sam. and Gen. xiv. 15 *Dammesek*, in 2 Kings xvi. 10 *Dummesek*. The additional *r* is not unusual in Hebrew. The city has a very long history and was always famed for its prosperity. Surrounded by a green belt of orchards, it lies in the fertile plain west of mount Hermon.

came to succour. By leading his army from Damascus behind David's rear and thus threatening to cut him off from his base.

6. *David put [garrisons].* The noun in brackets is here implied, but included in 2 Sam. viii. 6. Some render the word as 'officers, governors.'

7. *shields.* The meaning of *shelet* is doubtful and some authorities understand it as 'arms' or 'suits of armour.'

8. *Tibhath.* In 2 Sam. viii. 8: *Betah*; neither has been identified.

Cun. In Sam.: *Berothai.* Cun, it has been suggested, is the same as Cunna-Cunnae which lies between Heliopolis and Laodicea, or the modern Kuna near Bereitan.

brass. The meaning of *nechosheth* is really 'copper' or 'bronze.'

wherewith Solomon made, etc. This is an addition to the text in Sam. in vindication of David's reputation. It indicates that David did not appropriate the spoils for his own use but reserved them for the requirements of the Temple when it would be erected.

9. And when Tou king of Hamath heard that David had smitten all the host of Hadarezer king of Zobah, 10. he sent Hadoram his son to king David, to salute him, and to bless him—because he had fought against Hadarezer and smitten him; for Hadarezer had wars with Tou—and [he had with him] all manner of vessels of gold and silver and brass. 11. These also did king David dedicate unto the LORD, with the silver and the gold that he carried away from all the nations; from Edom, and from Moab, and from the children of Ammon, and from the Philistines, and from Amalek. 12. Moreover Abishai the son of

9 וַיִּשְׁמַע תֹּעוּ מֶלֶךְ חֲמָת כִּי
הִכָּה דָוִיד אֶת־כָּל־חֵיל
הֲדַרְעֶזֶר מֶלֶךְ־צוֹבָה׃
10 וַיִּשְׁלַח אֶת־הֲדוֹרָם־בְּנוֹ אֶל־
הַמֶּלֶךְ דָּוִיד לִשְׁאָול־־לוֹ
לְשָׁלוֹם וּלְבָרְכוֹ עַל אֲשֶׁר
נִלְחַם בַּהֲדַרְעֶזֶר וַיַּכֵּהוּ כִּי־
אִישׁ מִלְחֲמוֹת תֹּעוּ הָיָה
הֲדַרְעָזֶר וְכֹל כְּלֵי זָהָב וָכֶסֶף
11 וּנְחֹשֶׁת׃ גַּם־אֹתָם הִקְדִּישׁ
הַמֶּלֶךְ דָּוִיד לַיהוָה עִם־
הַכֶּסֶף וְהַזָּהָב אֲשֶׁר נָשָׂא
מִכָּל־הַגּוֹיִם מֵאֱדוֹם וּמִמּוֹאָב
וּמִבְּנֵי עַמּוֹן וּמִפְּלִשְׁתִּים
12 וּמֵעֲמָלֵק׃ וְאַבְשַׁי בֶּן־צְרוּיָה

v. 10. יתיר ו

9-11. The gifts of Tou and the spoils of other peoples.

9. *Tou.* In 2 Sam. viii. 9 the name is *Toi*, but the LXX reads *Tou* also there.

Hamath. See on verse 3.

king of Zobah. Not in Sam.

10. *Hadoram.* In 2 Sam. viii. 10: *Joram.*

to bless him. i.e. 'to offer his congratulations' on his triumph.

had wars. lit. 'a man of wars.'

and [he had with him]. In Sam. the text reads: *and he brought with him*, lit. 'in his hand were.'

all manner of vessels of gold and silver and brass. The spontaneous sending of tribute was an acknowledgment of David's suzerainty without loss of all independence; it implied a claim upon David for help and protection in the event of an attack.

11. *these also.* viz. not only the spoils of the peoples he defeated but also the gifts he received from Tou.

that he carried away from all the nations. In 2 Sam. viii. 11: *that he dedicated of all the nations which he subdued.*

from Edom. In 2 Sam. viii. 12: *of Aram.*

and from Amalek. In Sam. there is the addition: *and of the spoil of Hadadezer, son of Rehob, king of Zobah.* As regards Amalek, the only record of a war of David with that people is 1 Sam. xxx, but according to that account David distributed the spoils among his men and the elders of Judah. The spoils of Amalek mentioned here and in Sam. must probably refer to another of David's encounters with the Amalekites.

12f. The Edomite war.

Zeruiah smote of the Edomites in the Valley of Salt eighteen thousand. 13. And he put garrisons in Edom; and all the Edomites became servants to David. And the LORD gave victory to David whithersoever he went.

14. And David reigned over all Israel; and he executed justice and righteousness unto all his people. 15. And Joab the son of Zeruiah was over the host; and Jehoshaphat the son of Ahilud was recorder. 16. And Zadok the son of Ahitub, and Abimelech the son of Abiathar, were priests; and Shavsha was scribe;

הִכָּה אֶת־אֱדוֹם בְּגֵיא הַמֶּלַח
13 שְׁמוֹנָה עָשָׂר אָלֶף׃ וַיָּשֶׂם
בֶּאֱדוֹם נְצִיבִים וַיִּהְיוּ כָל־
אֱדוֹם עֲבָדִים לְדָוִיד וַיּוֹשַׁע
יְהוָה אֶת־דָּוִיד בְּכֹל אֲשֶׁר
הָלָךְ׃
14 וַיִּמְלֹךְ דָּוִיד עַל־כָּל־יִשְׂרָאֵל
וַיְהִי עֹשֶׂה מִשְׁפָּט וּצְדָקָה
15 לְכָל־עַמּוֹ׃ וְיוֹאָב בֶּן־צְרוּיָה
עַל־הַצָּבָא וִיהוֹשָׁפָט בֶּן־
16 אֲחִילוּד מַזְכִּיר׃ וְצָדוֹק בֶּן־
אֲחִיטוּב וַאֲבִימֶלֶךְ בֶּן־
אֶבְיָתָר כֹּהֲנִים וְשַׁוְשָׁא סוֹפֵר׃

12. *Abishai the son of Zeruiah smote of the Edomites.* The Hebrew form of the name is 'Abshai.' In 2 Sam. viii. 13 the credit for the victory is ascribed to David, and *the Arameans* takes the place of *the Edomites.* There the verse begins with the words: *and David got him a name when he returned from smiting the Arameans in the Valley of Salt.* In Ps. lx. 2 credit for what is apparently the same victory is given to Joab and the defeated enemy is again *Edom.* The number of the fallen according to Chron. and Sam. is 18,000, but according to the Psalm 12,000. If the references are to the same war, it must be assumed that David, Abishai and Joab each contributed to the victory in the various phases of the campaign. According to the Rabbis there were two wars.

the Valley of Salt. Identified with the Wadi es-Seba, the marshy flat at the southern end of the Dead Sea. According to another opinion it is the modern Wadi el-Milch in the neighbourhood of Beer-sheba.

13. *put garrisons in Edom.* 2 Sam. viii. 14 adds: *throughout all Edom put he garrisons.*

14-17 (corresponding to 2 Sam. viii. 15-18). David's administration and officers.

14. *he executed justice,* etc. David was the chief magistrate and was personally accessible to all his people.

15. *over the host.* i.e. commander-in-chief.

recorder. lit. 'one who reminds.' The official's function was to remind the king of all important business that required his attention.

16. *Abimelech.* In 2 Sam. viii. 17: *Ahimelech.*

Shavsha. In Sam.: *Seraiah.*

scribe. The king's secretary who kept the State records, corresponded with foreign kings and acted as the royal historian.

17. and Benaiah the son of Jehoiada was over the Cherethites and the Pelethites; and the sons of David were chief about the king.

17 וּבְנָיָהוּ בֶּן־יְהוֹיָדָע עַל־
הַכְּרֵתִי וְהַפְּלֵתִי וּבְנֵי־דָוִיד
הָרִאשֹׁנִים לְיַד הַמֶּלֶךְ׃

19 CHAPTER XIX יט

1. And it came to pass after this, that Nahash the king of the children of Ammon died, and his son reigned in his stead. 2. And David said: 'I will show kindness unto Hanun the son of Nahash, because his father showed kindness to me.' So David sent messengers to comfort him concerning his father. And David's servants came into the land of the children of Ammon to Hanun, to comfort him. 3. But the princes of the children of Ammon said to Hanun: 'Thinkest thou that David doth honour thy father, that he hath sent comforters unto thee? are not his servants come unto thee to search, and to overthrow, and to spy out the land?' 4. So Hanun

1 וַיְהִי אַחֲרֵי־כֵן וַיָּמָת נָחָשׁ מֶלֶךְ
בְּנֵי־עַמּוֹן וַיִּמְלֹךְ בְּנוֹ תַּחְתָּיו׃
2 וַיֹּאמֶר דָּוִיד אֶעֱשֶׂה־חֶסֶד ׀
עִם־חָנוּן בֶּן־נָחָשׁ כִּי־עָשָׂה
אָבִיו עִמִּי חֶסֶד וַיִּשְׁלַח דָּוִיד
מַלְאָכִים לְנַחֲמוֹ עַל־אָבִיו
וַיָּבֹאוּ עַבְדֵי דָוִיד אֶל־אֶרֶץ
בְּנֵי־עַמּוֹן אֶל־חָנוּן לְנַחֲמוֹ׃
3 וַיֹּאמְרוּ שָׂרֵי בְנֵי־עַמּוֹן לְחָנוּן
הַמְכַבֵּד דָּוִיד אֶת־אָבִיךָ
בְּעֵינֶיךָ כִּי־שָׁלַח לְךָ מְנַחֲמִים
הֲלֹא בַּעֲבוּר לַחְקֹר וְלַהֲפֹךְ
וּלְרַגֵּל הָאָרֶץ בָּאוּ עֲבָדָיו

17. *Cherethites . . . Pelethites.* David's bodyguard, composed of foreign mercenaries; they were probably of Philistine origin.

chief about the king. lit. 'the first at the king's hand,' his executive officers to see that his commands were carried out. In 2 Sam. viii. 18: *chief ministers,* lit. 'priests.' The Chronicler deliberately avoided the use of the term in a secular sense.

CHAPTER XIX

1-19 (corresponding to 2 Sam. x. 1-19). David's war with the Ammonites and their Syrian allies. The account of his generosity to Jonathan's son (2 Sam. ix), the incident with Bath-sheba (2 Sam. xi. f.) and, generally, his relations with Saul are omitted.

1-5. David's friendly delegation to Hanun and the latter's insult.

1. *Nahash.* An Ammonite king of the same name warred against Saul (cf. 1 Sam. xi), and it is probable that he was on friendly terms with David during the time the latter was persecuted by Saul.

3. *the land.* In 2 Sam. x. 3 the reading is *the city,* i.e. the capital.

took David's servants, and shaved them, and cut off their garments in the middle, even to their hips, and sent them away. 5. Then there went certain persons, and told David how the men were served. And he sent to meet them; for the men were greatly ashamed. And the king said: 'Tarry at Jericho until your beards be grown, and then return.'

6. And when the children of Ammon saw that they had made themselves odious to David, Hanun and the children of Ammon sent a thousand talents of silver to hire them chariots and horsemen out of Aram-naharaim, and out of Aram-maacah, and out of Zobah. 7. So they hired them thirty and two thousand chariots, and the king of Maacah and his people; who came and encamped before Medeba. And the children of Ammon gathered

אֵלֶיךָ׃ וַיִּקַּח חָנוּן אֶת־עַבְדֵי 4
דָוִיד וַיְגַלְּחֵם וַיִּכְרֹת אֶת־
מַדְוֵיהֶם בַּחֵצִי עַד־הַמִּפְשָׂעָה
וַיְשַׁלְּחֵם׃ וַיֵּלְכוּ וַיַּגִּידוּ לְדָוִיד 5
עַל־הָאֲנָשִׁים וַיִּשְׁלַח
לִקְרָאתָם כִּי־הָיוּ הָאֲנָשִׁים
נִכְלָמִים מְאֹד וַיֹּאמֶר הַמֶּלֶךְ
שְׁבוּ בִירֵחוֹ עַד אֲשֶׁר־יְצַמַּח
זְקַנְכֶם וְשַׁבְתֶּם׃
וַיִּרְאוּ בְּנֵי עַמּוֹן כִּי הִתְבָּאֲשׁוּ 6
עִם־דָּוִיד וַיִּשְׁלַח חָנוּן וּבְנֵי
עַמּוֹן אֶלֶף כִּכַּר־כֶּסֶף לִשְׂכֹּר
לָהֶם מִן־אֲרַם נַהֲרַיִם וּמִן־
אֲרַם מַעֲכָה וּמִצּוֹבָה רֶכֶב
וּפָרָשִׁים׃ וַיִּשְׂכְּרוּ לָהֶם שְׁנַיִם 7
וּשְׁלֹשִׁים אֶלֶף רֶכֶב וְאֶת־
מֶלֶךְ מַעֲכָה וְאֶת־עַמּוֹ וַיָּבֹאוּ
וַיַּחֲנוּ לִפְנֵי מֵידְבָא וּבְנֵי עַמּוֹן

4. *shaved them.* 2 Sam. x. 4: *shaved off the one half of their beards.* This was regarded in the Orient as a grave insult.

to their hips. In 2 Sam. x. 4: *to their buttocks.* This was the mark of slavery (cf. Isa. xx. 4). Freemen wore a long flowing robe. The noun *miphsa'ah* is not found elsewhere and means 'the stepping part (of the body)' and may signify buttocks or hips.

5. *how the men were served.* lit. 'concerning the men.'

tarry at Jericho, etc. This would keep the ambassadors away from public gaze in the capital, spare their outraged feelings and reduce the publicity of the national affront until David decided how he would avenge the deliberate insult.

6f. Hanun's preparations for war.

6. *Aram-naharaim . . . Aram-maacah.* In 2 Sam. x. 6: *the Arameans of Beth-rehob . . . the Arameans of Zobah.*

7. *thirty and two thousand chariots.* 2 Sam. x. 6 does not mention the number of the chariots, but gives the total of footmen as 33,000.

Medeba. On the table-land in the territory of Reuben in Moab, south of Heshbon, which was suitable for the deploying of chariots.

themselves together from their cities, and came to battle. 8. And when David heard of it, he sent Joab, and all the host of the mighty men. 9. And the children of Ammon came out, and put the battle in array at the gate of the city; and the kings that were come were by themselves in the field.

10. Now when Joab saw that the battle was set against him before and behind, he chose of all the choice men of Israel, and put them in array against the Arameans. 11. And the rest of the people he committed into the hand of Abishai his brother, and they put themselves in array against the children of Ammon. 12. And he said: 'If the Arameans be too strong for me, then thou shalt help me; but if the children of Ammon be too strong for thee, then I will help thee. 13. Be of good courage, and let us prove strong for our

נֶאֶסְפוּ מֵעָרֵיהֶם וַיָּבֹאוּ
8 לַמִּלְחָמָה׃ וַיִּשְׁמַע דָּוִיד
וַיִּשְׁלַח אֶת־יוֹאָב וְאֵת כָּל־
9 צָבָא הַגִּבּוֹרִים׃ וַיֵּצְאוּ בְּנֵי
עַמּוֹן וַיַּעַרְכוּ מִלְחָמָה פֶּתַח
הָעִיר וְהַמְּלָכִים אֲשֶׁר־בָּאוּ
לְבַדָּם בַּשָּׂדֶה׃
10 וַיַּרְא יוֹאָב כִּי־הָיְתָה פְנֵי־
הַמִּלְחָמָה אֵלָיו פָּנִים וְאָחוֹר
וַיִּבְחַר מִכָּל־בָּחוּר בְּיִשְׂרָאֵל
11 וַיַּעֲרֹךְ לִקְרַאת אֲרָם׃ וְאֵת
יֶתֶר הָעָם נָתַן בְּיַד אַבְשַׁי אָחִיו
וַיַּעַרְכוּ לִקְרַאת בְּנֵי עַמּוֹן׃
12 וַיֹּאמֶר אִם־תֶּחֱזַק מִמֶּנִּי אֲרָם
וְהָיִיתָ לִּי לִתְשׁוּעָה וְאִם־בְּנֵי
עַמּוֹן יֶחֶזְקוּ מִמְּךָ וְהוֹשַׁעְתִּיךָ׃
13 חֲזַק וְנִתְחַזְּקָה בְּעַד־עַמֵּנוּ

8f. The battle is joined.

8. David despatched Joab to the front while he kept himself in readiness for the bigger battle (verse 17) which he expected.

9. The opposing force was divided in two sections. The Ammonites kept to the *gate of the city* (probably the capital, Rabbah), while their allies formed a line of battle at some distance *in the field* (the open country) so as to attack David's men from the rear (verse 10).

10-15. Joab and Abishai defeat the Ammonites and their allies.

10. *set against him before and behind.* The Arameans contrived to outflank the Israelite army.

he chose, etc. To extricate his army from their perilous position, he placed himself at the head of a band of picked men and directed his attack against the Syrians, the more formidable enemy, leaving it to his brother (verse 11) to deal with the weaker enemy, the Ammonites.

11. *Abishai.* The Hebrew form of the name here is 'Abshai.'

they put themselves. The pronoun refers to Abishai and his men.

12. *thou shalt help me.* lit. 'thou wilt be a salvation to me,' i.e. come to my rescue.

people, and for the cities of our God;
and the LORD do that which seemeth
Him good.' 14. So Joab and the
people that were with him drew
nigh unto the battle to meet the
Arameans; and they fled before him.
15. And when the children of
Ammon saw that the Arameans were
fled, they likewise fled before Abishai
his brother, and entered into the
city. Then Joab came to Jerusalem.
16. And when the Arameans saw
that they were put to the worse
before Israel, they sent messengers,
and brought out the Arameans that
were beyond the River, with Shophach the captain of the host of
Hadarezer at their head. 17. And
it was told David; and he gathered
all Israel together, and passed over

וּבְעַד עָרֵי אֱלֹהֵינוּ וַיהוָה
14 הַטּוֹב בְּעֵינָיו יַעֲשֶׂה׃ וַיִּגַּשׁ
יוֹאָב וְהָעָם אֲשֶׁר־עִמּוֹ לִפְנֵי
אֲרָם לַמִּלְחָמָה וַיָּנוּסוּ מִפָּנָיו׃
15 וּבְנֵי עַמּוֹן רָאוּ כִּי־נָס אֲרָם
וַיָּנוּסוּ גַם־הֵם מִפְּנֵי אַבְשַׁי
אָחִיו וַיָּבֹאוּ הָעִירָה וַיָּבֹא יוֹאָב
יְרוּשָׁלִָם׃
16 וַיַּרְא אֲרָם כִּי נִגְּפוּ לִפְנֵי
יִשְׂרָאֵל וַיִּשְׁלְחוּ מַלְאָכִים
וַיּוֹצִיאוּ אֶת־אֲרָם אֲשֶׁר
מֵעֵבֶר הַנָּהָר וְשׁוֹפַךְ שַׂר־
17 צְבָא הֲדַרְעֶזֶר לִפְנֵיהֶם׃ וַיֻּגַּד
לְדָוִיד וַיֶּאֱסֹף אֶת־כָּל־
יִשְׂרָאֵל וַיַּעֲבֹר הַיַּרְדֵּן וַיָּבֹא

13. *for the cities of our God.* The cities in which God is worshipped by Israel, His people. Should the enemy prove victorious in battle, the cities of Israel would be overrun and idol-worship introduced.

the LORD do . . . good. An expression of complete resignation to the will of God.

14. *to meet the Arameans.* lit. 'before the Arameans.'

they fled. The subject is the Arameans; they could not withstand Joab's fierce onslaught.

15. There was no need for Abishai to launch his attack on the Ammonites, because they lost heart when they saw the headlong flight of their allies before Joab.

entered into the city. i.e. retreated in haste within the fortified positions of their city.

then Joab came to Jerusalem. The war was over with victory to the army of Israel.

16-19. The Arameans renew the war, suffer decisive defeat and sue for peace.

16. *they sent messengers,* etc. According to 2 Sam. x. 16, it was Hadadezer who sent for the Arameans who *came to Helam* (see on verse 17).

the River. The Euphrates.

Shophach. In 2 Sam. x. 16: *Shobach.*

at their head. lit. 'before them.' The entire army was under the supreme command of Shophach.

17. *he gathered all Israel.* The whole fighting strength of the people was required to deliver the final and decisive blow.

the Jordan, and came upon them, and set the battle in array against them. So when David had put the battle in array against the Arameans, they fought with him. 18. And the Arameans fled before Israel; and David slew of the Arameans the men of seven thousand chariots, and forty thousand footmen, and killed Shophach the captain of the host. 19. And when the servants of Hadarezer saw that they were put to the worse before Israel, they made peace with David, and served him; neither would the Arameans help the children of Ammon any more.

אֲלֵהֶם וַיַּעֲרֹךְ אֲלֵהֶם וַיַּעֲרֹךְ
דָּוִיד לִקְרַאת אֲרָם מִלְחָמָה
18 וַיִּלָּחֲמוּ עִמּוֹ׃ וַיָּנָס אֲרָם
מִלִּפְנֵי יִשְׂרָאֵל וַיַּהֲרֹג דָּוִיד
מֵאֲרָם שִׁבְעַת אֲלָפִים רֶכֶב
וְאַרְבָּעִים אֶלֶף אִישׁ רַגְלִי וְאֵת
שׁוֹפַךְ שַׂר־הַצָּבָא הֵמִית׃
19 וַיִּרְאוּ עַבְדֵי הֲדַרְעֶזֶר כִּי נִגְּפוּ
לִפְנֵי יִשְׂרָאֵל וַיַּשְׁלִימוּ עִם־
דָּוִיד וַיַּעַבְדֻהוּ וְלֹא־אָבָה
אֲרָם לְהוֹשִׁיעַ אֶת־בְּנֵי־עַמּוֹן
עוֹד׃

20 CHAPTER XX כ

1. And it came to pass, at the time of the return of the year, at the time when kings go out to battle, that

1 וַיְהִי לְעֵת תְּשׁוּבַת הַשָּׁנָה לְעֵת
צֵאת הַמְּלָכִים וַיִּנְהַג יוֹאָב

passed over the Jordan. Carrying the war into the enemy's domain.

came upon them. 2 Sam. x. 17 has: *came to Helam* (reading *Chelam* instead of *alehem*), where the Aramean army assembled.

18. *men of seven thousand chariots.* The first two words are implied. In 2 Sam. x. 18: *seven hundred drivers of chariots.*

forty thousand footmen. In Sam.: *forty thousand horsemen.* The numbers in Chron. and Sam. may be supplementary.

19. *when the servants of Hadarezer.* In 2 Sam. x. 19: *all the kings that were* is inserted between *when* and *the servants.*

the servants. i.e. subject people, vassals.

made peace with David, and served him. In Sam.: *made peace with Israel, and served them.*

neither would the Arameans. In Sam.: *so the Arameans feared.*

CHAPTER XX

1-3. The account given of the subjugation of the Ammonites corresponds to 2 Sam. xi. 1, xii. 26-31 where fuller details are recorded, including the incident with Bath-sheba which the Chronicler passes over in silence out of respect for David.

1. *at the time of the return of the year.* The phrase has been interpreted as 'a year later' or 'the spring.'

kings go out to battle. The last two words are not in the text. After the season of the early rains, kings usually embarked on a campaign which was held up during the winter.

Joab led forth the power of the
army, and wasted the country of the
children of Ammon, and came and
besieged Rabbah. But David tarried at Jerusalem. And Joab smote
Rabbah, and overthrew it. 2. And
David took the crown of Malcam
from off his head, and found it to
weigh a talent of gold, and there
were precious stones in it; and it
was set upon David's head; and he
brought forth the spoil of the city,
exceeding much. 3. And he brought
forth the people that were therein,
and cut them with saws, and with
harrows of iron, and with axes.
And thus did David unto all the

אֶת־חֵיל הַצָּבָא וַיַּשְׁחֵת ׀ אֶת־
אֶרֶץ בְּנֵי־עַמּוֹן וַיָּבֹא וַיָּצַר
אֶת־רַבָּה וְדָוִיד יֹשֵׁב
בִּירוּשָׁלִָם וַיַּךְ יוֹאָב אֶת־רַבָּה
2 וַיֶּהֶרְסֶהָ׃ וַיִּקַּח דָּוִיד אֶת־
עֲטֶרֶת־מַלְכָּם מֵעַל רֹאשׁוֹ
וַיִּמְצָאֶהָ ׀ מִשְׁקַל כִּכַּר־זָהָב
וּבָהּ אֶבֶן יְקָרָה וַתְּהִי עַל־
רֹאשׁ דָּוִיד וּשְׁלַל הָעִיר הוֹצִיא
3 הַרְבֵּה מְאֹד׃ וְאֶת־הָעָם
אֲשֶׁר־בָּהּ הוֹצִיא וַיָּשַׂר
בַּמְּגֵרָה וּבַחֲרִיצֵי הַבַּרְזֶל
וּבַמְּגֵרוֹת וְכֵן יַעֲשֶׂה דָוִיד לְכֹל

the power of the army. Or, 'the host of war.'

Rabbah. The capital of the country of the Ammonites, situated in a fertile basin about twenty-eight miles east of the Jordan. It was once known as Philadelphia and colonized by Greeks. Now it is called Amman and is the capital of Transjordan. Its citadel is built on a hill to the north of the city.

David tarried at Jerusalem. This introduces in Sam. the story of David and Bath-sheba (2 Sam. xi. 2ff.).

Joab smote Rabbah, and overthrew it. According to 2 Sam. xii. 26ff., Joab, having captured a section of Rabbah, *the city of waters* (probably the lower city), *sent messengers to David* with the good news, and invited him to *gather the rest of the people together* for the final attack, *lest I take the city, and it be called after my name.* David, acting on Joab's advice, had the glory of completing the capture by taking the citadel which seems to have been dependent for its water-supply on the lower section, *the city of waters.*

2. *Malcam.* The national god of Ammon (cf. 1 Kings xi. 5, where the form of the name is *Milcom*). The literal meaning of the word here is 'their king.'

a talent of gold. About fifty-four pounds avoirdupois.

precious stones. Better, 'a precious stone.'

it was set. The pronoun refers to the precious stone (so the Targum) which was apparently set in David's crown. He could not have worn a crown of the weight specified.

he brought forth the spoil. He carried it in triumphal procession.

3. *cut them with saws.* For *wayyasar* 2 Sam. xii. 31 reads *wayyasem: put them under saws*, i.e. made them to work with saws. The verb which is used here is of uncertain meaning.

and with harrows . . . axes. The noun for *axes* is the same as for *saws.* It is not

cities of the children of Ammon. And David and all the people returned to Jerusalem.

4. And it came to pass after this, that there arose war at Gezer with the Philistines; then Sibbecai the Hushathite slew Sippai, of the sons of the giants; and they were subdued. 5. And there was again war with the Philistines; and Elhanan the son of Jair slew Lahmi the brother of Goliath the Gittite, the staff of whose spear was like a weaver's beam. 6. And there was again war at Gath, where was a man of great stature, whose fingers and toes were four and twenty, six [on each hand], and six [on each foot]; and he also was born unto the giant. 7. And when he taunted

עָרֵי בְנֵי־עַמּוֹן וַיָּשָׁב דָּוִיד
וְכָל־הָעָם יְרוּשָׁלָם׃
4 וַיְהִי אַחֲרֵי־כֵן וַתַּעֲמֹד
מִלְחָמָה בְּגֶזֶר עִם־פְּלִשְׁתִּים
אָז הִכָּה סִבְּכַי הַחֻשָׁתִי אֶת־
סִפַּי מִילִדֵי הָרְפָא וַיִּכָּנֵעוּ׃
5 וַתְּהִי־עוֹד מִלְחָמָה אֶת־
פְּלִשְׁתִּים וַיַּךְ אֶלְחָנָן בֶּן־יָעוֹר
אֶת־לַחְמִי אֲחִי גָּלְיָת הַגִּתִּי
וְעֵץ חֲנִיתוֹ כִּמְנוֹר אֹרְגִים׃
6 וַתְּהִי־עוֹד מִלְחָמָה בְּגַת וַיְהִי
׀ אִישׁ מִדָּה וְאֶצְבְּעֹתָיו שֵׁשׁ־
וָשֵׁשׁ עֶשְׂרִים וְאַרְבַּע וְגַם־הוּא
7 נוֹלַד לְהָרָפָא׃ וַיְחָרֵף אֶת־

v. 4. ס"א הרפאים v. 5. יעיר ק'

necessary to interpret David's act as the torture of his captives. It may only refer to compulsory service with the implements mentioned, or to forced labour analogous to that of the children of Israel in Egypt. The wanton insult and callous treatment which David's friendly and well-intentioned delegation received from the Ammonites called for severe retaliation.

4-8 (corresponding to 2 Sam. xxi. 18-22). The destruction of Philistine giants. The Chronicler passes over the incident of Amnon and Tamar, the rebellion of Absalom and Sheba, the vengeance of the Gibeonites on Saul's family and David's narrow escape from death at the hand of the Philistine giant, Ishbi-benob. These episodes were regarded by the Chronicler as irrelevant to the history of David as he wished to portray it or uncomplimentary to the king.

4. *at Gezer.* It lay on an isolated hill in the northern Shephelah and is the modern Tel Jezer. In 2 Sam. xxi. 18 the place is named *Gob*, which is an unknown locality.

Sippai. In Sam.: *Saph.*

5. *war with the Philistines.* In 2 Sam. xxi. 19, *Gob* is named as the scene of the battle.

the son of Jair . . . the Gittite. In Sam.: *the son of Jaare-oregim the Beth-lehemite slew Goliath the Gittite.* The mention of *Goliath* in this encounter with David the king, as well as in the contest which occurred when David was a young man, presents no difficulty if it is assumed that the word is not a proper name but a descriptive title like 'Pharaoh,' 'Rabshakeh,' 'Sultan.' On the other hand, it may be only a coincidence that David's two opponents bore the same name.

6. *a man of great stature.* In 2 Sam. xxi. 20: *a champion.* Here the Hebrew

Israel, Jonathan the son of Shimea
David's brother slew him. 8. These
were born unto the giant in Gath;
and they fell by the hand of David,
and by the hand of his servants.

יִשְׂרָאֵל וַיַּכֵּהוּ יְהֽוֹנָתָן בֶּן־
8 שִׁמְעָא אֲחִי דָוִיד׃ אֵל נוּלְּדוּ
לְהָרָפָא בְּגַת וַיִּפְּלוּ בְיַד־
דָּוִיד וּבְיַד־עֲבָדָיו׃

21 CHAPTER XXI כא

1. And Satan stood up against Israel,
and moved David to number Israel.
2. And David said to Joab and to
the princes of the people: 'Go,
number Israel from Beer-sheba even
to Dan; and bring me word, that I

1 וַיַּעֲמֹד שָׂטָן עַל־יִשְׂרָאֵל וַיָּסֶת
אֶת־דָּוִיד לִמְנוֹת אֶת־
2 יִשְׂרָאֵל׃ וַיֹּאמֶר דָּוִיד אֶל־
יוֹאָב וְאֶל־שָׂרֵי הָעָם לְכוּ
סִפְרוּ אֶת־יִשְׂרָאֵל מִבְּאֵר
שֶׁבַע וְעַד־דָּן וְהָבִיאוּ אֵלַי

v. 8. דגש אחר שורק

word is *middah* and in Sam. *madon* which Kimchi, followed by R.V., also understands as 'stature.'

8. *these.* 2 Sam. xxi. 22 adds: *four.*

CHAPTER XXI

1-27 (corresponding to 2 Sam. xxiv. 1-25). The census and the ensuing plague. The Chronicler omits David's hymn of thanksgiving and 'last words' (2 Sam. xxii. 1-xxiii. 7).

1. *and Satan stood up against Israel.* In 2 Sam. xxiv. 1 the text reads: *and again the anger of the LORD was kindled against Israel.* Satan is the name given to the supernatural being who was believed to be hostile to man and instigated him to commit evil. The literal meaning is 'adversary.' The Chronicler avoids ascribing David's act to the will of God as in Sam.

moved David to number. Israel must not be numbered except at the Divine command (cf. Num. i. 1ff., iii. 14ff., xxvi. 1ff.), and even then the persons were not counted directly. Each individual donated half a shekel as *a ransom for his soul . . . that there be no plague among them* (Exod. xxx. 12). By counting the coins the number of the people was obtained.

2. *David said to Joab.* As the census was for a military purpose, to ascertain the number of men *that drew sword* (verse 5), it was entrusted to Joab *the captain of the host* (2 Sam. xxiv. 2) and the officers.

go, number. This is preceded in 2 Sam. xxiv. 2 by: *go now to and fro through all the tribes of Israel.*

from Beer-Sheba. A town in the extreme southern limit of the country, the modern Bir-es-Seba, about twenty-eight miles south-west of Hebron.

to Dan. In the extreme north, the modern Tel el-Kadi. In Sam. the order of the towns is reversed: *from Dan even to Beer-sheba.* The latter is the usual order, but the Chronicler prefers to begin with the south, i.e. the kingdom of Judah, which he regards as of superior importance.

may know the sum of them.' 3. And
Joab said: 'The LORD make His
people a hundred times so many
more as they are; but, my lord the
king, are they not all my lord's
servants? why doth my lord require
this thing? why will he be a cause of
guilt unto Israel?' 4. Nevertheless
the king's word prevailed against
Joab. Wherefore Joab departed,
and went throughout all Israel, and
came to Jerusalem. 5. And Joab
gave up the sum of the numbering
of the people unto David. And all
they of Israel were a thousand
thousand and a hundred thousand
men that drew sword; and Judah
was four hundred threescore and ten
thousand men that drew sword.
6. But Levi and Benjamin he did

3 וְאֵדְעָה אֶת־מִסְפָּרָם׃ וַיֹּאמֶר
יוֹאָב יוֹסֵף יְהוָה עַל־עַמּוֹ ׀
כָּהֵם מֵאָה פְעָמִים הֲלֹא אֲדֹנִי
הַמֶּלֶךְ כֻּלָּם לַאדֹנִי לַעֲבָדִים
לָמָּה יְבַקֵּשׁ זֹאת אֲדֹנִי לָמָּה
יִהְיֶה לְאַשְׁמָה לְיִשְׂרָאֵל׃
4 וּדְבַר־הַמֶּלֶךְ חָזַק עַל־יוֹאָב
וַיֵּצֵא יוֹאָב וַיִּתְהַלֵּךְ בְּכָל־
5 יִשְׂרָאֵל וַיָּבֹא יְרוּשָׁלִָם׃ וַיִּתֵּן
יוֹאָב אֶת־מִסְפַּר מִפְקַד־
הָעָם אֶל־דָּוִיד וַיְהִי כָל־
יִשְׂרָאֵל אֶלֶף אֲלָפִים וּמֵאָה
אֶלֶף אִישׁ שֹׁלֵף חֶרֶב וִיהוּדָה
אַרְבַּע מֵאוֹת וְשִׁבְעִים אֶלֶף
6 אִישׁ שֹׁלֵף חָרֶב׃ וְלֵוִי וּבִנְיָמִן

and bring me word. The object is implied in the text. In Sam. the clause is wanting.

3. *the LORD*, etc. Cf. Deut. i. 11.

a cause of guilt. The first noun is not in the Hebrew and is to be understood. Joab apparently realized the danger which was involved in David's plan.

4. *prevailed against Joab.* 2 Sam. xxiv. 4 adds: *and against the captains of the host.*

wherefore Joab departed. In Sam.: *and Joab and the captains of the host went out from the presence of the king.*

and went throughout all Israel. In Sam. the clause is omitted and the text has instead: *to number the people of Israel,* followed by details of the route and the time the census occupied (2 Sam. xxiv. 5-8).

and came to Jerusalem. After a period of *nine months and twenty days* (2 Sam. xxiv. 8).

5. The number of Israel was 1,100,000 and of Judah 470,000. In 2 Sam. xxiv. 9 the figures are respectively 800,000 and 500,000. It has been suggested that the larger number in Chron. embraces the grand total, inclusive of Judah (*all they of Israel*). This view is supported by the omission of *all* in the text of Sam. In the case of Judah the smaller number in Chron. may include only *men that drew sword*, while the larger number in Sam. gives the total of the tribe. The phrase, *that drew sword*, which occurs in Chron. is omitted in Sam.

6. *was abominable to Joab.* Hence the exclusion of these tribes from the census. According to Num. i. 49, the tribe of Levi was not to be numbered among the

not number among them; for the
king's word was abominable to Joab.
7. And God was displeased with
this thing; therefore He smote Israel.
8. And David said unto God: 'I have
sinned greatly, in that I have done
this thing; but now, put away, I
beseech Thee, the iniquity of Thy
servant; for I have done very
foolishly.' 9. And the LORD spoke
unto Gad, David's seer, saying:
10. 'Go and speak unto David,
saying: Thus saith the LORD: I offer
thee three things; choose thee one
of them, that I may do it unto thee.'
11. So Gad came to David, and said
unto him: 'Thus saith the LORD:
Take which thou wilt: 12. either
three years of famine; or three

לֹא פָקַד בְּתוֹכָם כִּי־נִתְעַב
דְּבַר־הַמֶּלֶךְ אֶת־יוֹאָב׃
7 וַיֵּרַע בְּעֵינֵי הָאֱלֹהִים עַל־
הַדָּבָר הַזֶּה וַיַּךְ אֶת־יִשְׂרָאֵל׃
8 וַיֹּאמֶר דָּוִיד אֶל־הָאֱלֹהִים
חָטָאתִי מְאֹד אֲשֶׁר עָשִׂיתִי
אֶת־הַדָּבָר הַזֶּה וְעַתָּה
הַעֲבֶר־נָא אֶת־עֲווֹן עַבְדְּךָ
9 כִּי נִסְכַּלְתִּי מְאֹד׃ וַיְדַבֵּר
יְהוָה אֶל־גָּד חֹזֵה דָוִיד
10 לֵאמֹר׃ לֵךְ וְדִבַּרְתָּ אֶל־
דָּוִיד לֵאמֹר כֹּה אָמַר יְהוָה
שָׁלוֹשׁ אֲנִי נֹטֶה עָלֶיךָ בְּחַר־
לְךָ אַחַת מֵהֵנָּה וְאֶעֱשֶׂה־לָּךְ׃
11 וַיָּבֹא גָד אֶל־דָּוִיד וַיֹּאמֶר לוֹ
כֹּה־אָמַר יְהוָה קַבֶּל־לָךְ׃
12 אִם־שָׁלוֹשׁ שָׁנִים רָעָב וְאִם־

other tribes, probably because the Levites were exempt from military service. They were, however, to be numbered separately (cf. Num. iii. 15). The reason that Joab did not number the Benjamites, according to the Jewish commentators, was because the tribe had suffered great losses on a previous occasion (cf. Judg. xx. 46) and he wished to spare them further diminution when God punished the people for the census. This verse is not paralleled in Sam.

7. *and God was displeased . . . Israel.* There is no corresponding passage in 2 Sam. xxiv. 10a which has instead: *and David's heart smote him after that he had numbered the people.*

He smote Israel. With a plague.

8. *put away . . . the iniquity.* The phrase may signify 'avert . . . (the penalty of) the iniquity.'

9. *and the LORD spoke.* In 2 Sam. xxiv. 11 the text is: *and when David rose up in the morning, the word of the LORD came.*

unto Gad. In Sam.: *the prophet Gad.* He is described as *seer* again in xxix. 29 and 2 Chron. xxix. 25.

10. *I offer.* For the verb *noteh* 2 Sam. xxiv. 12 has *notel* which means *I lay.*

three things. i.e. punishments for the sin of numbering the people.

11. *take which thou wilt.* lit. 'take for thyself.' This clause is wanting in 2 Sam. xxiv. 13.

months to be swept away before thy
foes, while the sword of thine
enemies overtaketh thee; or else
three days the sword of the LORD,
even pestilence in the land, and the
angel of the LORD destroying
throughout all the borders of Israel.
Now therefore consider what answer
I shall return to Him that sent me.'
13. And David said unto Gad: 'I am
in a great strait; let me fall now into
the hand of the LORD, for very great
are His mercies; and let me not fall
into the hand of man.'

14. So the LORD sent a pestilence
upon Israel; and there fell of Israel
seventy thousand men. 15. And
God sent an angel unto Jerusalem to
destroy it; and as he was about to
destroy, the LORD beheld, and He
repented Him of the evil, and said to
the destroying angel: 'It is enough;
now stay thy hand.' And the angel

שְׁלֹשָׁה חֳדָשִׁים נִסְפֶּה מִפְּנֵי־
צָרֶיךָ וְחֶרֶב אוֹיְבֶיךָ ׀ לְמַשֶּׂגֶת
וְאִם־שְׁלֹשֶׁת יָמִים חֶרֶב יְהֹוָה
׀ וְדֶבֶר בָּאָרֶץ וּמַלְאַךְ יְהֹוָה
מַשְׁחִית בְּכָל־גְּבוּל יִשְׂרָאֵל
וְעַתָּה רְאֵה מָה־אָשִׁיב אֶת־
13 שֹׁלְחִי דָּבָר׃ וַיֹּאמֶר דָּוִיד
אֶל־גָּד צַר־לִי מְאֹד אֶפְּלָה־
נָּא בְיַד־יְהֹוָה כִּי־רַבִּים
רַחֲמָיו מְאֹד וּבְיַד־אָדָם אַל־
אֶפֹּל׃
14 וַיִּתֵּן יְהֹוָה דֶּבֶר בְּיִשְׂרָאֵל וַיִּפֹּל
מִיִּשְׂרָאֵל שִׁבְעִים אֶלֶף אִישׁ׃
15 וַיִּשְׁלַח הָאֱלֹהִים ׀ מַלְאָךְ ׀
לִירוּשָׁלִַם לְהַשְׁחִיתָהּ
וּכְהַשְׁחִית רָאָה יְהֹוָה וַיִּנָּחֶם
עַל־הָרָעָה וַיֹּאמֶר לַמַּלְאָךְ
הַמַּשְׁחִית רַב עַתָּה הֶרֶף יָדֶךָ

12. *three years of famine.* In Sam.: *seven years of famine.*

three months to be swept away. In Sam.: *wilt thou flee three months.*

while the sword . . . overtaketh. In Sam. this is replaced by: *while they pursue thee.*

the sword of the LORD. Omitted in Sam.

and the angel . . . of Israel. Also omitted in Sam.

now therefore consider. In Sam.: *now advise thee, and consider.*

13. *let me fall.* In 2 Sam. xxiv. 14: *let us fall.* David regarded famine and pestilence as lesser evils than war, since God is more merciful than man.

14. *a pestilence upon Israel.* 2 Sam. xxiv. 15 adds: *from the morning even to the time appointed.*

and there fell of Israel. In Sam.: *and there died of the people from Dan even to Beer-sheba,* i.e. throughout all the land.

15. *and God sent . . . Jerusalem.* In 2 Sam. xxiv. 16: *and when the angel stretched out his hand toward Jerusalem.* He first destroyed the provincial towns.

and as he was about . . . the LORD beheld. Omitted in Sam.

of the LORD was standing by the threshing-floor of Ornan the Jebusite. 16. And David lifted up his eyes, and saw the angel of the LORD standing between the earth and the heaven, having a drawn sword in his hand stretched out over Jerusalem. Then David and the elders, clothed in sackcloth, fell upon their faces. 17. And David said unto God: 'Is it not I that commanded the people to be numbered? even I it is that have sinned and done very wickedly; but these sheep, what have they done? let Thy hand, I pray Thee, O LORD my God, be against me, and against my father's house; but not against Thy people, that they should be plagued.'

18. Then the angel of the LORD commanded Gad to say to David, that David should go up, and rear an altar unto the LORD in the threshing-floor of Ornan the Jebusite. 19. And David went up at the saying of Gad, which he spoke in the name

וּמַלְאַךְ יְהוָה עֹמֵד עִם־גֹּרֶן
16 אָרְנָן הַיְבוּסִי׃ וַיִּשָּׂא דָוִיד
אֶת־עֵינָיו וַיַּרְא אֶת־מַלְאַךְ
יְהוָה עֹמֵד בֵּין הָאָרֶץ וּבֵין
הַשָּׁמַיִם וְחַרְבּוֹ שְׁלוּפָה בְּיָדוֹ
נְטוּיָה עַל־יְרוּשָׁלָםִ וַיִּפֹּל
דָּוִיד וְהַזְּקֵנִים מְכֻסִּים בַּשַּׂקִּים
17 עַל־פְּנֵיהֶם׃ וַיֹּאמֶר דָּוִיד
אֶל־הָאֱלֹהִים הֲלֹא אֲנִי
אָמַרְתִּי לִמְנוֹת בָּעָם וַאֲנִי־
הוּא אֲשֶׁר־חָטָאתִי וְהָרֵעַ
הֲרֵעוֹתִי וְאֵלֶּה הַצֹּאן מֶה עָשׂוּ
יְהוָה אֱלֹהַי תְּהִי נָא יָדְךָ בִּי
וּבְבֵית אָבִי וּבְעַמְּךָ לֹא
לְמַגֵּפָה׃
18 וּמַלְאַךְ יְהוָה אָמַר אֶל־גָּד
לֵאמֹר לְדָוִיד כִּי ׀ יַעֲלֶה דָוִיד
לְהָקִים מִזְבֵּחַ לַיהוָה בְּגֹרֶן
19 אָרְנָן הַיְבֻסִי׃ וַיַּעַל דָּוִיד
בִּדְבַר־גָּד אֲשֶׁר דִּבֶּר בְּשֵׁם

the destroying angel. In Sam.: *the angel that destroyed the people.*

was standing by. In Sam.: *was by.*

Ornan. In Sam.: *Araunah.* His threshing-floor was situated on mount Moriah on which the Temple was later built (cf. 2 Chron. iii. 1).

16. The detailed description in this verse corresponds to five Hebrew words in 2 Sam. xxiv. 17 translated: *when he saw the angel that smote the people.*

17. A shorter version of David's prayer is given in 2 Sam. xxiv. 17.

18. *then the angel.* In 2 Sam. xxiv. 18 the angel is not mentioned.

go up. The hill on which the threshing-floor was located.

19. *which he spoke in the name of the LORD.* In 2 Sam. xxiv. 19: *as the LORD commanded.*

20. *and Ornan turned back.* In 2 Sam. xxiv. 20: *and Araunah looked back.*

of the LORD. 20. And Ornan turned back, and saw the angel; and his four sons that were with him hid themselves. Now Ornan was threshing wheat. 21. And as David came to Ornan, Ornan looked and saw David, and went out of the threshing-floor, and bowed down to David with his face to the ground. 22. Then David said to Ornan: 'Give me the place of this threshing-floor, that I may build thereon an altar unto the LORD; for the full price shalt thou give it me; that the plague may be stayed from the people.' 23. And Ornan said unto David: 'Take it to thee, and let my lord the king do that which is good in his eyes; lo, I give thee the oxen for burnt-offerings, and the threshing-instruments for wood, and the wheat for the meal-offering; I give it all.' 24. And king David said to Ornan: 'Nay, but I will verily buy it for the full price; for I will not take that which is thine for the LORD,

יְהוָה׃ וַיָּשָׁב אָרְנָן וַיַּרְא אֶת־ 20
הַמַּלְאָךְ וְאַרְבַּעַת בָּנָיו עִמּוֹ
מִתְחַבְּאִים וְאָרְנָן דָּשׁ חִטִּים׃
וַיָּבֹא דָוִיד עַד־אָרְנָן וַיַּבֵּט 21
אָרְנָן וַיַּרְא אֶת־דָּוִיד וַיֵּצֵא
מִן־הַגֹּרֶן וַיִּשְׁתַּחוּ לְדָוִיד
אַפַּיִם אָרְצָה׃ וַיֹּאמֶר דָּוִיד 22
אֶל־אָרְנָן תְּנָה־לִּי מְקוֹם
הַגֹּרֶן וְאֶבְנֶה־בּוֹ מִזְבֵּחַ לַיהוָה
בְּכֶסֶף מָלֵא תְּנֵהוּ לִי וְתֵעָצַר
הַמַּגֵּפָה מֵעַל הָעָם׃ וַיֹּאמֶר 23
אָרְנָן אֶל־דָּוִיד קַח־לָךְ וְיַעַשׂ
אֲדֹנִי הַמֶּלֶךְ הַטּוֹב בְּעֵינָיו
רְאֵה נָתַתִּי הַבָּקָר לָעֹלוֹת
וְהַמּוֹרִגִּים לָעֵצִים וְהַחִטִּים
לַמִּנְחָה הַכֹּל נָתָתִּי׃ וַיֹּאמֶר 24
הַמֶּלֶךְ דָּוִיד לְאָרְנָן לֹא כִּי־
קָנֹה אֶקְנֶה בְּכֶסֶף מָלֵא כִּי
לֹא־אֶשָּׂא אֲשֶׁר־לְךָ לַיהוָה

saw the angel. In Sam.: *saw the king and his servants coming on toward him.* In Hebrew the words for *angel* and *king* consist of the same consonants with the addition of one letter to the former.

and his four sons . . . wheat. Not in Sam. They hid themselves from looking upon an angel, which act endangered the life of the beholder (cf. Judg. vi. 22f., xiii. 22).

21. This verse corresponds to 2 Sam. xxiv. 20.

22. *the place of this threshing-floor.* The noun *place* is understood by some to imply an area larger than the actual threshing-floor which may not have sufficed as a site of the Temple, though sufficiently large for the altar. In 2 Sam. xxiv. 21 David's request is preceded by a question from Araunah: *wherefore is the lord my king come to his servant?*

23. *and the threshing-instruments for wood.* In 2 Sam. xxiv. 22 *and the furniture of the oxen* is inserted before *for wood,* while *and the wheat for the meal-offering* is wanting.

nor offer a burnt-offering without cost.' 25. So David gave to Ornan for the place six hundred shekels of gold by weight. 26. And David built there an altar unto the LORD, and offered burnt-offerings and peace-offerings, and called upon the LORD; and He answered him from heaven by fire upon the altar of burnt-offering. 27. And the LORD commanded the angel; and he put up his sword back into the sheath thereof.

28. At that time, when David saw that the LORD had answered him in the threshing-floor of Ornan the Jebusite, then he sacrificed there. 29. For the tabernacle of the LORD, which Moses made in the wilderness, and the altar of burnt-offering, were

25 וְהַעֲלוֹת עוֹלָה חִנָּם׃ וַיִּתֵּן
דָּוִיד לְאָרְנָן בַּמָּקוֹם שִׁקְלֵי
26 זָהָב מִשְׁקַל שֵׁשׁ מֵאוֹת׃ וַיִּבֶן
שָׁם דָּוִיד מִזְבֵּחַ לַיהוָה וַיַּעַל
עֹלוֹת וּשְׁלָמִים וַיִּקְרָא אֶל־
יְהוָה וַיַּעֲנֵהוּ בָאֵשׁ מִן־הַשָּׁמַיִם
27 עַל מִזְבַּח הָעֹלָה׃ וַיֹּאמֶר
יְהוָה לַמַּלְאָךְ וַיָּשֶׁב חַרְבּוֹ
אֶל־נְדָנָהּ׃
28 בָּעֵת הַהִיא בִּרְאוֹת דָּוִיד
כִּי־עָנָהוּ יְהוָה בְּגֹרֶן אָרְנָן
29 הַיְבוּסִי וַיִּזְבַּח שָׁם׃ וּמִשְׁכַּן
יְהוָה אֲשֶׁר־עָשָׂה מֹשֶׁה
בַמִּדְבָּר וּמִזְבַּח הָעֹלָה בָּעֵת

25. *six hundred shekels of gold.* About one thousand two hundred pounds. According to 2 Sam. xxiv. 24 David bought *the threshing-floor and the oxen for fifty shekels of silver,* a sum equal to about seven pounds. The Talmud (Zeb. 116b) explains that the latter sum was collected from each of the twelve tribes which produced a total of six hundred. This, however, does not remove the discrepancy between *shekels of gold* and *shekels of silver.* An alternative Rabbinical explanation is that the fifty shekels of silver were paid (as stated in Sam.) for *the threshing-floor and the oxen,* while the six hundred shekels of gold were paid, as stated here, for the entire site.

26. *built there an altar.* On this spot Solomon's altar of burnt-offerings was afterwards erected; it is now occupied by the mosque known as the Dome of the Rock.

He answered . . . by fire. Which consumed the offerings as on the day of Aaron's consecration (Lev. ix. 24), a sign of God's favour and acceptance of the sanctification of the place. This clause is not in Sam.

27. *and the LORD commanded . . . thereof.* In 2 Sam. xxiv. 25: *so the LORD was entreated for the land, and the plague was stayed from Israel.*

28-xxii. 1. Selection of the Temple site. Verse 28 is a protasis to which xxii. 1 is the apodosis, while verses 29f. are a parenthesis. The passage, which has no parallel in Sam., forms a connecting link between the preceding narrative and the preparations for the building of the Temple in the following chapter.

28. *then he sacrificed.* Render, 'and he had sacrificed there,' this verse being the protasis.

29. *for the tabernacle.* This begins the parenthesis.

at that time in the high place at Gibeon. 30. But David could not go before it to inquire of God; for he was terrified because of the sword of the angel of the LORD.

30 הַהִיא בַּבָּמָה בְּגִבְעוֹן׃ וְלֹא־
יָכֹל דָּוִיד לָלֶכֶת לְפָנָיו לִדְרֹשׁ
אֱלֹהִים כִּי נִבְעַת מִפְּנֵי חֶרֶב
מַלְאַךְ יְהוָה׃

22 CHAPTER XXII כב

1. Then David said: 'This is the house of the LORD God, and this is the altar of burnt-offering for Israel.'

2. And David commanded to gather together the strangers that were in the land of Israel; and he set masons to hew wrought stones to build the house of God. 3. And David prepared iron in abundance for the nails for the doors of the gates, and for the couplings; and brass in abundance without weight; 4. and cedar-trees without number; for the Zidonians and they of Tyre

1 וַיֹּאמֶר דָּוִיד זֶה הוּא בֵּית יְהוָה
הָאֱלֹהִים וְזֶה־מִזְבֵּחַ לְעֹלָה
לְיִשְׂרָאֵל׃
2 וַיֹּאמֶר דָּוִיד לִכְנוֹס אֶת־
הַגֵּרִים אֲשֶׁר בְּאֶרֶץ יִשְׂרָאֵל
וַיַּעֲמֵד חֹצְבִים לַחְצוֹב אַבְנֵי
גָזִית לִבְנוֹת בֵּית הָאֱלֹהִים׃
3 וּבַרְזֶל ׀ לָרֹב לַמִּסְמְרִים
לְדַלְתוֹת הַשְּׁעָרִים
וְלַמְחַבְּרוֹת הֵכִין דָּוִיד
4 וּנְחֹשֶׁת לָרֹב אֵין מִשְׁקָל׃ וַעֲצֵי
אֲרָזִים לְאֵין מִסְפָּר כִּי־
הֵבִיאוּ הַצִּידֹנִים וְהַצֹּרִים עֲצֵי

30. *he was terrified*, etc. For this reason he offered his sacrifices on the altar which he set up in Ornan's threshing-floor and not in Gibeon.

CHAPTER XXII

1. This verse is the apodosis to xxi. 28.

2-5. Preparation of materials for the Temple.

2. *the strangers.* The descendants of the Canaanite nations whom the Israelites, on conquering the land, had allowed to remain (cf. 2 Chron. viii. 7ff.).

masons to hew. This kind of work was normally undertaken by slaves.

wrought stones. Cut to the required size at the quarry (cf. 1 Kings vi. 7).

3. *the couplings.* Which joined one board to another.

4. *and cedar-trees*, etc. Further supplies were sent in the reign of Solomon (cf. 1 Kings v. 22ff.).

brought cedar-trees in abundance to David. 5. And David said: 'Solomon my son is young and tender, and the house that is to be builded for the LORD must be exceeding magnificent, of fame and of glory throughout all countries; I will therefore make preparation for him.' So David prepared abundantly before his death.

6. Then he called for Solomon his son, and charged him to build a house for the LORD, the God of Israel. 7. And David said to Solomon: 'My son, as for me, it was in my heart to build a house unto the name of the LORD my God. 8. But the word of the LORD came to me, saying: Thou hast shed blood abundantly, and hast made great wars; thou shalt not build a house unto My name, because thou hast shed much blood upon the earth in My sight. 9. Behold, a son shall be born to thee, who shall be a man of rest; and I will give him rest from all his enemies round about; for his name shall be Solomon, and I will give peace and quietness unto Israel

5 אֲרָזִים לָרֹב לְדָוִיד׃ וַיֹּאמֶר
דָּוִיד שְׁלֹמֹה בְנִי נַעַר וָרָךְ
וְהַבַּיִת לִבְנוֹת לַיהוָה לְהַגְדִּיל
׀ לְמַעְלָה לְשֵׁם וּלְתִפְאֶרֶת
לְכָל־הָאֲרָצוֹת אָכִינָה נָּא לוֹ
וַיָּכֶן דָּוִיד לָרֹב לִפְנֵי מוֹתוֹ׃
6 וַיִּקְרָא לִשְׁלֹמֹה בְנוֹ וַיְצַוֵּהוּ
לִבְנוֹת־בַּיִת לַיהוָה אֱלֹהֵי
7 יִשְׂרָאֵל׃ וַיֹּאמֶר דָּוִיד
לִשְׁלֹמֹה בְּנוֹ אֲנִי הָיָה עִם־
לְבָבִי לִבְנוֹת בַּיִת לְשֵׁם יְהוָה
8 אֱלֹהָי׃ וַיְהִי עָלַי דְּבַר־יְהוָה
לֵאמֹר דָּם לָרֹב שָׁפַכְתָּ
וּמִלְחָמוֹת גְּדֹלוֹת עָשִׂיתָ לֹא־
תִבְנֶה בַיִת לִשְׁמִי כִּי דָמִים
רַבִּים שָׁפַכְתָּ אַרְצָה לְפָנָי׃
9 הִנֵּה־בֵן נוֹלָד לָךְ הוּא יִהְיֶה
אִישׁ מְנוּחָה וַהֲנִיחוֹתִי לוֹ
מִכָּל־אוֹיְבָיו מִסָּבִיב כִּי
שְׁלֹמֹה יִהְיֶה שְׁמוֹ וְשָׁלוֹם וָשֶׁקֶט

v. 7. בני ק'

5. *make preparation for him.* By collecting the required materials.

6-16. David's charge to Solomon.

7. *to Solomon: 'My son.'* So the *kerē*; the *kethib* means 'to Solomon his son' (so R.V.).

8. *but the word of the LORD came to me,* etc. This Divine message is not recorded elsewhere. His son Solomon, when addressing Hiram king of Tyre, asserted that David *could not build a house for the name of the LORD his God for the wars which were about him on every side* (I Kings v. 17). The two statements are not necessarily contradictory. Solomon may have thought it sufficient to give only one reason. There was no need, he may have felt, to repeat a Divine message to the heathen king.

9. *his name shall be Solomon.* i.e. 'peaceful,' the name *Shelomoh* being connected with *shalom*, 'peace.'

I will give peace . . . in his days. This

in his days. 10. He shall build a house for My name; and he shall be to Me for a son, and I will be to him for a father; and I will establish the throne of his kingdom over Israel for ever. 11. Now, my son, the LORD be with thee; and prosper thou, and build the house of the LORD thy God, as He hath spoken concerning thee. 12. Only the LORD give thee discretion and understanding, and give thee charge concerning Israel; that so thou mayest keep the law of the LORD thy God. 13. Then shalt thou prosper, if thou observe to do the statutes and the ordinances which the LORD charged Moses with concerning Israel; be strong, and of good courage; fear not, neither be dismayed. 14. Now, behold, in my straits I have prepared for the house of the LORD a hundred thousand talents of gold, and a thousand thousand talents of silver; and of

אֶתֵּן עַל־יִשְׂרָאֵל בְּיָמָיו׃
10 הוּא־יִבְנֶה בַיִת לִשְׁמִי וְהוּא
יִהְיֶה־לִּי לְבֵן וַאֲנִי־לוֹ לְאָב
וַהֲכִינוֹתִי אֶת־כִּסֵּא מַלְכוּתוֹ
עַל־יִשְׂרָאֵל עַד־עוֹלָם׃
11 עַתָּה בְנִי יְהִי יְהוָה עִמָּךְ
וְהִצְלַחְתָּ וּבָנִיתָ בֵּית יְהוָה
אֱלֹהֶיךָ כַּאֲשֶׁר דִּבֶּר עָלֶיךָ׃
12 אַךְ יִתֶּן־לְךָ יְהוָה שֵׂכֶל וּבִינָה
וִיצַוְּךָ עַל־יִשְׂרָאֵל וְלִשְׁמוֹר
13 אֶת־תּוֹרַת יְהוָה אֱלֹהֶיךָ׃ אָז
תַּצְלִיחַ אִם־תִּשְׁמוֹר לַעֲשׂוֹת
אֶת־הַחֻקִּים וְאֶת־הַמִּשְׁפָּטִים
אֲשֶׁר צִוָּה יְהוָה אֶת־מֹשֶׁה
עַל־יִשְׂרָאֵל חֲזַק וֶאֱמָץ אַל־
14 תִּירָא וְאַל־תֵּחָת׃ וְהִנֵּה
בְעָנְיִי הֲכִינוֹתִי לְבֵית־יְהוָה
זָהָב כִּכָּרִים מֵאָה־אֶלֶף
וְכֶסֶף אֶלֶף אֲלָפִים כִּכָּרִים

v. 13. קמץ בז״ק

was true during the earlier portion of his reign. In his later years the peace of the land was disturbed (cf. 1 Kings xi. 14ff., 23ff., 26ff.).

10. Cf. the corresponding passage in 2 Sam. vii. 13-16.

for ever. i.e. for a long time.

12. *the law.* Hebrew *torah* which signifies 'teaching, instruction.'

13. *be strong . . . neither be dismayed.* A similar exhortation was addressed by Moses to Joshua (cf. Josh. i. 9).

14. *in my straits.* The Hebrew noun means 'affliction.' David accumulated the building materials with great pains while he was distracted and troubled by enemies.

a hundred thousand talents, etc. The sum is said by some commentators to be 'incredibly large' and 'exaggerated'; but the fact is that it is impossible to estimate with any degree of certainty what the 'talent' was worth. Both Babylonian and Phoenician systems of weights seem to have been current in Canaan, and the value of the talent of the former (as that

brass and iron without weight, for it is in abundance; timber also and stone have I prepared; and thou mayest add thereto. 15. Moreover there are workmen with thee in abundance, hewers and workers of stone and timber, and all men that are skilful in any manner of work; 16. of the gold, the silver, and the brass, and the iron, there is no number. Arise and be doing, and the LORD be with thee.'

17. David also commanded all the princes of Israel to help Solomon his son: 18. 'Is not the LORD your God with you? and hath He not given you rest on every side? for He hath delivered the inhabitants of the land into my hand; and the land is subdued before the LORD, and before His people. 19. Now set your heart and your soul to seek after the LORD your God; arise therefore, and build ye the sanctuary of the LORD God, to bring the ark of the covenant of the LORD, and the holy vessels of God, into the house that is to be built to the name of the LORD.'

וְלַנְּחֹשֶׁת וְלַבַּרְזֶל אֵין מִשְׁקָל
כִּי לָרֹב הָיָה וְעֵצִים וַאֲבָנִים
הֲכִינוֹתִי וַעֲלֵיהֶם תּוֹסִיף׃
15 וְעִמְּךָ לָרֹב עֹשֵׂי מְלָאכָה
חֹצְבִים וְחָרָשֵׁי אֶבֶן וָעֵץ וְכָל־
16 חָכָם בְּכָל־מְלָאכָה׃ לַזָּהָב
לַכֶּסֶף וְלַנְּחֹשֶׁת וְלַבַּרְזֶל אֵין
מִסְפָּר קוּם וַעֲשֵׂה וִיהִי יְהוָה
עִמָּךְ׃
17 וַיְצַו דָּוִיד לְכָל־שָׂרֵי יִשְׂרָאֵל
18 לַעְזֹר לִשְׁלֹמֹה בְנוֹ׃ הֲלֹא
יְהוָה אֱלֹהֵיכֶם עִמָּכֶם וְהֵנִיחַ
לָכֶם מִסָּבִיב כִּי | נָתַן בְּיָדִי אֵת
יֹשְׁבֵי הָאָרֶץ וְנִכְבְּשָׁה הָאָרֶץ
19 לִפְנֵי יְהוָה וְלִפְנֵי עַמּוֹ׃ עַתָּה
תְּנוּ לְבַבְכֶם וְנַפְשְׁכֶם לִדְרוֹשׁ
לַיהוָה אֱלֹהֵיכֶם וְקוּמוּ וּבְנוּ
אֶת־מִקְדַּשׁ יְהוָה הָאֱלֹהִים
לְהָבִיא אֶת־אֲרוֹן בְּרִית־
יְהוָה וּכְלֵי קֹדֶשׁ הָאֱלֹהִים
לַבַּיִת הַנִּבְנֶה לְשֵׁם־יְהוָה׃

of the shekel also) was double that of the latter. Each system, furthermore, appears to have had a heavier and a lighter scale, the former again being double the latter. Before the system adopted by the Chronicler is established (for it may have been neither of the two mentioned), it is presumptuous to speak of incredibility or exaggeration.

17-19. David's charge to the princes.

18. *the inhabitants of the land.* He probably had the Jebusites in mind (cf. xi. 4) from whom he had captured Jerusalem.

19. *build ye.* i.e. co-operate with Solomon in the building of the Temple.

23 CHAPTER XXIII כג

1. Now David was old and full of days; and he made Solomon his son king over Israel. 2. And he gathered together all the princes of Israel, with the priests and the Levites. 3. And the Levites were numbered from thirty years old and upward; and their number by their polls, man by man, was thirty and eight thousand. 4. Of these, twenty and four thousand were to oversee the work of the house of the LORD; and six thousand were officers and judges; 5. and four thousand were doorkeepers; and four thousand praised the LORD 'with the instruments which I made to praise therewith.'

6. And David divided them into courses according to the sons of Levi: Gershon, Kohath, and Merari.

1 וְדָוִיד זָקֵן וְשָׂבַע יָמִים וַיַּמְלֵךְ
אֶת־שְׁלֹמֹה בְנוֹ עַל־יִשְׂרָאֵל׃
2 וַיֶּאֱסֹף אֶת־כָּל־שָׂרֵי יִשְׂרָאֵל
3 וְהַכֹּהֲנִים וְהַלְוִיִּם׃ וַיִּסָּפְרוּ
הַלְוִיִּם מִבֶּן שְׁלֹשִׁים שָׁנָה
וָמָעְלָה וַיְהִי מִסְפָּרָם
לְגֻלְגְּלֹתָם לִגְבָרִים שְׁלֹשִׁים
4 וּשְׁמוֹנָה אָלֶף׃ מֵאֵלֶּה לְנַצֵּחַ
עַל־מְלֶאכֶת בֵּית־יְהוָה
עֶשְׂרִים וְאַרְבָּעָה אָלֶף
וְשֹׁטְרִים וְשֹׁפְטִים שֵׁשֶׁת
5 אֲלָפִים׃ וְאַרְבַּעַת אֲלָפִים
שֹׁעֲרִים וְאַרְבַּעַת אֲלָפִים
מְהַלְלִים לַיהוָה בַּכֵּלִים אֲשֶׁר
עָשִׂיתִי לְהַלֵּל׃
6 וַיֶּחָלְקֵם דָּוִיד מַחְלְקוֹת לִבְנֵי
לֵוִי לְגֵרְשׁוֹן קְהָת וּמְרָרִי׃

CHAPTER XXIII

1. David nominated Solomon as his successor. The Chronicler treats the succession in a summary manner and gives no account of the intrigue which attended it as related in 1 Kings i. 5ff.

2-5. Census and functions of the Levites.

2. *gathered together.* Probably for the purpose of communicating to them his decision that Solomon would follow him on the throne. This gathering was followed by a larger assembly for a public proclamation, described in xxviiif.

3. *from thirty years old.* Levites from the age of twenty were numbered *for the service of the house of the LORD* (verse 24), but a maturer age was required for the more responsible positions. According to Num. iv. 3 the Levites entered on their duties when thirty years old; but it is possible that the minimum was reduced to twenty when their numbers were insufficient for the work.

5. *with the instruments which I made to praise therewith.* The words are a quotation from a statement by David (cf. 2 Chron. xxix. 26 for a reference to his instruments).

6. The main divisions of the Levite families (cf. vi. 1).

7. Of the Gershonites: Ladan, and Shimei. 8. The sons of Ladan: Jehiel the chief, and Zetham, and Joel, three. 9. The sons of Shimei: Shelomith, and Haziel, and Haran, three. These were the heads of the fathers' houses of Ladan. 10. And the sons of Shimei: Jahath, Zina, and Jeush, and Beriah. These four were the sons of Shimei. 11. And Jahath was the chief, and Zizah the second; but Jeush and Beriah had not many sons; therefore they became a fathers' house in one reckoning.

12. The sons of Kohath: Amram, Izhar, Hebron, and Uzziel, four. 13. The sons of Amram: Aaron and Moses; and Aaron was separated, that he should be sanctified as most holy, he and his sons for ever, to offer before the LORD, to minister unto Him, and to bless in His name for ever. 14. But as for Moses the man of God, his sons are named among the tribe of Levi. 15. The sons of Moses: Gershom, and

7 8 לַגֵּרְשֻׁנִּי לַעְדָּן וְשִׁמְעִי׃ בְּנֵי
לַעְדָּן הָרֹאשׁ יְחִיאֵל וְזֵתָם
9 וְיוֹאֵל שְׁלֹשָׁה׃ בְּנֵי שִׁמְעִי
שְׁלֹמוֹת וַחֲזִיאֵל וְהָרָן שְׁלֹשָׁה
אֵלֶּה רָאשֵׁי הָאָבוֹת לְלַעְדָּן׃
10 וּבְנֵי שִׁמְעִי יַחַת זִינָא וִיעוּשׁ
וּבְרִיעָה אֵלֶּה בְנֵי־שִׁמְעִי
11 אַרְבָּעָה׃ וַיְהִי־יַחַת הָרֹאשׁ
וְזִיזָה הַשֵּׁנִי וִיעוּשׁ וּבְרִיעָה
לֹא־הִרְבּוּ בָנִים וַיִּהְיוּ לְבֵית
אָב לִפְקֻדָּה אֶחָת׃
12 בְּנֵי קְהָת עַמְרָם יִצְהָר חֶבְרוֹן
13 וְעֻזִּיאֵל אַרְבָּעָה׃ בְּנֵי עַמְרָם
אַהֲרֹן וּמֹשֶׁה וַיִּבָּדֵל אַהֲרֹן
לְהַקְדִּישׁוֹ קֹדֶשׁ קָדָשִׁים הוּא־
וּבָנָיו עַד־עוֹלָם לְהַקְטִיר
לִפְנֵי יְהוָה לְשָׁרְתוֹ וּלְבָרֵךְ
14 בִּשְׁמוֹ עַד־עוֹלָם׃ וּמֹשֶׁה אִישׁ
הָאֱלֹהִים בָּנָיו יִקָּרְאוּ עַל־
15 שֵׁבֶט הַלֵּוִי׃ בְּנֵי מֹשֶׁה גֵּרְשׁוֹם

v. 9. שלמית ק׳

7-11. The courses of the Gershonites.

7. *Ladan.* So again in xxvi. 21. Elsewhere he is named *Libni* (vi. 14; Exod. vi. 17).

9. *Shimei.* He may have been a descendant of Ladan and is to be distinguished from the *Shimei* in verses 7, 10.

10. *Shimei.* The Gershonite (verse 7). *Zina.* In verse 11 the name appears as *Zizah.*

12-20. The courses of the Kohathites.

12. Cf. vi. 2; Exod. vi. 18.

13f. Aaron's sons were separated from the other Levites and sanctified as priests, but the sons of Moses remained Levites.

13. *that he should be sanctified as most holy.* A.V. and R.V. less probably 'that he should sanctify the most holy things.' *to bless in His name.* Cf. Num. vi. 22ff.

Eliezer. 16. The sons of Gershom: Shebuel the chief. 17. And the sons of Eliezer were: Rehabiah the chief. And Eliezer had no other sons; but the sons of Rehabiah were very many. 18. The sons of Izhar: Shelomith the chief. 19. The sons of Hebron: Jeriah the chief, Amariah the second, Jahaziel the third, and Jekameam the fourth. 20. The sons of Uzziel: Micah the chief, and Isshiah the second.

21. The sons of Merari: Mahli, and Mushi. The sons of Mahli: Eleazar, and Kish. 22. And Eleazar died, and had no sons, but daughters only; and their brethren the sons of Kish took them to wife. 23. The sons of Mushi: Mahli, and Eder, and Jeremoth, three.

24. These were the sons of Levi after their fathers' houses, even the heads of the fathers' houses, according to their muster, in the number of names by their polls, who did the work for the service of the house of the LORD, from twenty years old and upward. 25. For David said:

16 וֶאֱלִיעֶזֶר׃ בְּנֵי גֵרְשׁוֹם שְׁבוּאֵל
17 הָרֹאשׁ׃ וַיִּהְיוּ בְנֵי־אֱלִיעֶזֶר
רְחַבְיָה הָרֹאשׁ וְלֹא־הָיָה
לֶאֱלִיעֶזֶר בָּנִים אֲחֵרִים וּבְנֵי
18 רְחַבְיָה רָבוּ לְמָעְלָה׃ בְּנֵי
19 יִצְהָר שְׁלֹמִית הָרֹאשׁ׃ בְּנֵי
חֶבְרוֹן יְרִיָּהוּ הָרֹאשׁ אֲמַרְיָה
הַשֵּׁנִי יַחֲזִיאֵל הַשְּׁלִישִׁי
20 וִיקַמְעָם הָרְבִיעִי׃ בְּנֵי עֻזִּיאֵל
מִיכָה הָרֹאשׁ וְיִשִּׁיָּה הַשֵּׁנִי׃
21 בְּנֵי מְרָרִי מַחְלִי וּמוּשִׁי בְּנֵי
22 מַחְלִי אֶלְעָזָר וְקִישׁ׃ וַיָּמָת
אֶלְעָזָר וְלֹא־הָיוּ לוֹ בָּנִים כִּי
אִם־בָּנוֹת וַיִּשָּׂאוּם בְּנֵי־קִישׁ
23 אֲחֵיהֶם׃ בְּנֵי מוּשִׁי מַחְלִי
וְעֵדֶר וִירֵמוֹת שְׁלוֹשָׁה׃
24 אֵלֶּה בְנֵי־לֵוִי לְבֵית
אֲבוֹתֵיהֶם רָאשֵׁי הָאָבוֹת
לִפְקוּדֵיהֶם בְּמִסְפַּר שֵׁמוֹת
לְגֻלְגְּלֹתָם עֹשֵׂה הַמְּלָאכָה
לַעֲבֹדַת בֵּית יְהוָה מִבֶּן
25 עֶשְׂרִים שָׁנָה וָמָעְלָה׃ כִּי אָמַר

16. *Shebuel.* In xxiv. 20: *Shubael.*

18. *Shelomith.* In xxiv. 22: *Shelomoth.*

21-23. The courses of the Merarites.

21. *the sons of Merari.* Cf. Exod. vi. 19.

22. *their brethren.* Their kinsmen.

23. *Jeremoth.* In xxiv. 30: *Jerimoth.*

24-32. The qualifying age and Temple duties of the Levites.

24. *the fathers' houses.* The last word is implied.

from twenty years. See on verse 3.

'The LORD, the God of Israel, hath given rest unto His people, and He dwelleth in Jerusalem for ever; 26. and also the Levites shall no more have need to carry the tabernacle and all the vessels of it for the service thereof.' 27. For by the last ordinances of David the sons of Levi were numbered from twenty years old and upward. 28. For their station was at the side of the sons of Aaron for the service of the house of the LORD, in the courts, and in the chambers, and in the purifying of all holy things, even the work of the service of the house of God; 29. for the showbread also, and for the fine flour for a meal-offering, whether of unleavened wafers, or of that which is baked on the griddle, or of that which is soaked, and for all manner of measure and size; 30. and to stand every morning to thank and praise the LORD, and likewise at even; 31. and to offer all burnt-offerings

דָּוִיד הֵנִיחַ יְהוָה אֱלֹהֵי־
יִשְׂרָאֵל לְעַמּוֹ וַיִּשְׁכֹּן
26 בִּירוּשָׁלִַם עַד־לְעוֹלָם׃ וְגַם
לַלְוִיִּם אֵין־לָשֵׂאת אֶת־
הַמִּשְׁכָּן וְאֶת־כָּל־כֵּלָיו
27 לַעֲבֹדָתוֹ׃ כִּי בְדִבְרֵי דָוִיד
הָאַחֲרוֹנִים הֵמָּה מִסְפַּר בְּנֵי־
לֵוִי מִבֶּן עֶשְׂרִים שָׁנָה
28 וּלְמָעְלָה׃ כִּי מַעֲמָדָם לְיַד
בְּנֵי־אַהֲרֹן לַעֲבוֹדַת בֵּית
יְהוָה עַל־הַחֲצֵרוֹת וְעַל־
הַלְּשָׁכוֹת וְעַל־טָהֳרַת
לְכָל־קֹדֶשׁ וּמַעֲשֵׂה עֲבֹדַת
29 בֵּית הָאֱלֹהִים׃ וּלְלֶחֶם
הַמַּעֲרֶכֶת וּלְסֹלֶת לְמִנְחָה
וְלִרְקִיקֵי הַמַּצּוֹת וְלַמַּחֲבַת
וְלַמֻּרְבֶּכֶת וּלְכָל־מְשׂוּרָה
30 וּמִדָּה׃ וְלַעֲמֹד בַּבֹּקֶר בַּבֹּקֶר
לְהֹדוֹת וּלְהַלֵּל לַיהוָה וְכֵן
31 לָעֶרֶב׃ וּלְכֹל הַעֲלוֹת עֹלוֹת

26. *to carry the tabernacle,* etc. As described in Num. iii. 21ff.

28. *for their station was,* etc. Since the duties of the Levites would be increased when the Temple was erected, a larger number of attendants was required. Hence the lowering by David of the age qualifying for service.

29. *the showbread.* Cf. Lev. xxiv. 5ff.

the fine flour for a meal-offering, etc. Cf. Lev. vi. 13f.

all manner of measure and size. viz. the quantities required for the various offerings.

30. *to stand every morning,* etc. Described in xxv. 1ff.

31. *to offer.* The offering of the animals was performed only by the priests. This verse is also governed by *and to stand* at the beginning of the previous verse. The Levites assisted the priests with the offerings and rendered the music which accompanied them.

unto the LORD, on the sabbaths, on the new moons, and in the appointed seasons, in number according to the ordinance concerning them, continually, before the LORD; 32. and that they should keep the charge of the tent of meeting, and the charge of the holy place, and the charge of the sons of Aaron their brethren, for the service of the house of the LORD.

לַיהוָה לַשַּׁבָּתוֹת לֶחֳדָשִׁים
וְלַמֹּעֲדִים בְּמִסְפָּר כְּמִשְׁפָּט
עֲלֵיהֶם תָּמִיד לִפְנֵי יְהוָה׃
32 וְשָׁמְרוּ אֶת־מִשְׁמֶרֶת אֹהֶל־
מוֹעֵד וְאֵת מִשְׁמֶרֶת הַקֹּדֶשׁ
וּמִשְׁמֶרֶת בְּנֵי אַהֲרֹן אֲחֵיהֶם
לַעֲבֹדַת בֵּית יְהוָה׃

24 CHAPTER XXIV כד

1. And the courses of the sons of Aaron were these. The sons of Aaron: Nadab and Abihu, Eleazar and Ithamar. 2. But Nadab and Abihu died before their father, and had no children; therefore Eleazar and Ithamar executed the priest's office. 3. And David with Zadok of the sons of Eleazar, and Ahimelech of the sons of Ithamar, divided them according to their ordering in their service. 4. And there were more chief men found of the sons of

1 וְלִבְנֵי אַהֲרֹן מַחְלְקוֹתָם בְּנֵי
אַהֲרֹן נָדָב וַאֲבִיהוּא אֶלְעָזָר
2 וְאִיתָמָר׃ וַיָּמָת נָדָב וַאֲבִיהוּא
לִפְנֵי אֲבִיהֶם וּבָנִים לֹא־הָיוּ
לָהֶם וַיְכַהֲנוּ אֶלְעָזָר וְאִיתָמָר׃
3 וַיֶּחָלְקֵם דָּוִיד וְצָדוֹק מִן־
בְּנֵי אֶלְעָזָר וַאֲחִימֶלֶךְ מִן־
בְּנֵי אִיתָמָר לִפְקֻדָּתָם
4 בַּעֲבֹדָתָם׃ וַיִּמָּצְאוּ בְנֵי־
אֶלְעָזָר רַבִּים לְרָאשֵׁי

32. *and the charge of the sons of Aaron.* Details are given in Num. xviii. 1ff.

CHAPTER XXIV

1-19. Organization of the courses of priests.

1. *the sons of Aaron.* Cf. v. 29; Exod. vi. 23.

2. *died before their father.* They were devoured by fire which descended from heaven as a punishment because they *offered strange fire before the LORD* (Lev. x. 1f.).

3. *Ahimelech of the sons of Ithamar.* He is the same person as *Ahimelech the son of Abiathar* (verse 6; in xviii. 16 *Abimelech the son of Abiathar*). Abiathar was the father of Ahimelech and a descendant of Ithamar.

their ordering. i.e. the order described below, their precedence (cf. verse 19).

Eleazar than of the sons of Ithamar; and thus were they divided: of the sons of Eleazar there were sixteen, heads of fathers' houses; and of the sons of Ithamar, according to their fathers' houses, eight. 5. Thus were they divided by lot, one sort with another; for they were princes of the sanctuary and princes of God, both of the sons of Eleazar, and of the sons of Ithamar. 6. And Shemaiah the son of Nethanel the scribe, who was of the Levites, wrote them in the presence of the king, and the princes, and Zadok the priest, and Ahimelech the son of Abiathar, and the heads of the fathers' houses of the priests and of the Levites: one fathers' house being taken for Eleazar, and proportionately for Ithamar.

7. Now the first lot came forth to Jehoiarib, the second to Jedaiah;

הַגְּבָרִ֔ים מִן־בְּנֵ֖י אִיתָמָ֑ר
וַֽיַּחְלְק֗וּם לִבְנֵ֨י אֶלְעָזָ֜ר
רָאשִׁ֤ים לְבֵית־אָבוֹת֙ שִׁשָּׁ֣ה
עָשָׂ֔ר וְלִבְנֵ֧י אִיתָמָ֛ר לְבֵ֥ית
5 אֲבוֹתָ֖ם שְׁמוֹנָֽה׃ וַיַּחְלְק֥וּם
בְּגוֹרָל֖וֹת אֵ֣לֶּה עִם־אֵ֑לֶּה כִּֽי־
הָי֧וּ שָׂרֵי־קֹ֙דֶשׁ֙ וְשָׂרֵ֣י הָאֱלֹהִ֔ים
מִבְּנֵ֥י אֶלְעָזָ֖ר וּבִבְנֵ֥י אִיתָמָֽר׃
6 וַֽיִּכְתְּבֵ֡ם שְׁמַֽעְיָה֩ בֶן־נְתַנְאֵ֨ל
הַסּוֹפֵ֜ר מִן־הַלֵּוִ֗י לִפְנֵ֨י הַמֶּ֜לֶךְ
וְהַשָּׂרִ֗ים וְצָד֣וֹק הַכֹּהֵ֔ן
וַאֲחִימֶ֙לֶךְ֙ בֶּן־אֶבְיָתָ֔ר וְרָאשֵׁ֣י
הָֽאָבוֹת לַכֹּהֲנִ֖ים וְלַלְוִיִּ֑ם
בֵּית־אָ֣ב אֶחָ֗ד אָחֻז֙ לְאֶלְעָזָ֔ר
וְאָחֻ֖ז ׀ אָחֻ֖ז לְאִיתָמָֽר׃
7 וַיֵּצֵ֞א הַגּוֹרָ֤ל הָרִאשׁוֹן֙
לִיה֣וֹיָרִ֔יב לִידַֽעְיָ֖ה הַשֵּׁנִֽי׃

4. *thus were they divided*, etc. Originally, when the tabernacle was at Shiloh, there were altogether sixteen courses, equally divided between the descendants of Eleazar and Ithamar. Now that there were more chief men of Eleazar, David divided each of their eight courses into two, producing a total of sixteen, while the eight courses of Ithamar remained unchanged.

5. *divided by lot*. To determine the order of their periods of service.

one sort with another. The courses of Eleazar with those of Ithamar.

for they were princes, etc. Hence the selection by lot. David did not venture to decide the order of their priority.

6. *wrote them*. On the ballot papers which were then put in a box.

one fathers' house being taken, etc. The drawing from the box was done alternately, one for Eleazar and one for Ithamar.

proportionately for Ithamar. As there were sixteen courses of Eleazar and only eight of Ithamar (see on verse 4), the alternate drawings extended to the first sixteen only (eight of each). With the last eight, the drawings only concerned the courses of Eleazar and determined their order.

8. the third to Harim, the fourth to
Seorim; 9. the fifth to Malchijah,
the sixth to Mijamin; 10. the seventh
to Hakkoz, the eighth to Abijah;
11. the ninth to Jeshua, the tenth to
Shecaniah; 12. the eleventh to
Eliashib, the twelfth to Jakim;
13. the thirteenth to Huppah, the
fourteenth to Jeshebeab; 14. the
fifteenth to Bilgah, the sixteenth to
Immer; 15. the seventeenth to
Hezir, the eighteenth to Happizzez;
16. the nineteenth to Pethahiah, the
twentieth to Jehezkel; 17. the one
and twentieth to Jachin, the two and
twentieth to Gamul; 18. the three
and twentieth to Delaiah, the four
and twentieth to Maaziah. 19. These
were the orderings of them in their
service, to come into the house of
the LORD according to the ordinance
given unto them by the hand of
Aaron their father, as the LORD, the
God of Israel, had commanded him.
20. And of the rest of the sons of
Levi: of the sons of Amram,

8 לְחָרִם הַשְּׁלִשִׁי לִשְׂעֹרִים
9 הָרְבִעִי: לְמַלְכִּיָּה הַחֲמִישִׁי
10 לְמִיָּמִן הַשִּׁשִּׁי: לְהַקּוֹץ
הַשְּׁבִעִי לַאֲבִיָּה הַשְּׁמִינִי:
11 לְיֵשׁוּעַ הַתְּשִׁעִי לִשְׁכַנְיָהוּ
12 הָעֲשִׂרִי: לְאֶלְיָשִׁיב עַשְׁתֵּי
עָשָׂר לְיָקִים שְׁנֵים עָשָׂר:
13 לְחֻפָּה שְׁלֹשָׁה עָשָׂר לְיֶשֶׁבְאָב
14 אַרְבָּעָה עָשָׂר: לְבִלְגָּה
חֲמִשָּׁה עָשָׂר לְאִמֵּר שִׁשָּׁה
15 עָשָׂר: לְחֵזִיר שִׁבְעָה עָשָׂר
לְהַפִּצֵּץ שְׁמוֹנָה עָשָׂר:
16 לִפְתַחְיָה תִּשְׁעָה עָשָׂר
17 לִיחֶזְקֵאל הָעֶשְׂרִים: לְיָכִין
אֶחָד וְעֶשְׂרִים לְגָמוּל שְׁנַיִם
18 וְעֶשְׂרִים: לִדְלָיָהוּ שְׁלֹשָׁה
וְעֶשְׂרִים לְמַעַזְיָהוּ אַרְבָּעָה
19 וְעֶשְׂרִים: אֵלֶּה פְקֻדָּתָם
לַעֲבֹדָתָם לָבוֹא לְבֵית־יְהוָה
כְּמִשְׁפָּטָם בְּיַד אַהֲרֹן אֲבִיהֶם
כַּאֲשֶׁר צִוָּהוּ יְהוָה אֱלֹהֵי
יִשְׂרָאֵל:
20 וְלִבְנֵי לֵוִי הַנּוֹתָרִים לִבְנֵי

19. *according to the ordinance given unto them.* Lit. 'according to their ordinance.'

20-31. A supplementary list of Levites. The list, as compared with that of xxiii. 6-23, repeats some of the names, omits others, notably all the Gershonites (xxiii. 6-11), and contains also some additional and altered names.

20. *the rest of the sons of Levi.* i.e. those not included among the priests enumerated above, who were also, through Aaron, the sons of Levi.

Shubael; of the sons of Shubael, Jehdeiah. 21. Of Rehabiah: of the sons of Rehabiah, Isshiah the chief. 22. Of the Izharites, Shelomoth; of the sons of Shelomoth, Jahath. 23. And Benai, Jeriah, Amariah the second, Jahaziel the third, Jekameam the fourth. 24. The sons of Uzziel, Micah; of the sons of Micah, Shamir. 25. The brother of Micah, Isshiah; of the sons of Isshiah, Zechariah. 26. The sons of Merari: Mahli and Mushi; the sons of Jaaziah, his son, 27. even the sons of Merari through Jaaziah his son: Shoham, and Zaccur, and Ibri. 28. Of Mahli: Eleazar, who had no sons. 29. Of Kish: the sons of Kish, Jerahmeel. 30. And the sons of Mushi: Mahli, and Eder, and Jerimoth. These were the sons of the Levites after their fathers' houses. 31. These likewise cast lots even as their brethren the sons of Aaron in the presence of David the king, and Zadok, and Ahimelech, and the heads of the fathers' houses of the priests and of the Levites; the fathers' houses of the chief even as those of his younger brother.

עַמְרָם֙ שׁוּבָאֵ֔ל לִבְנֵ֥י שׁוּבָאֵ֖ל
21 יֶחְדְּיָֽהוּ׃ לִרְחַבְיָ֑הוּ לִבְנֵי֙
רְחַבְיָ֔הוּ הָרֹ֖אשׁ יִשִּׁיָּֽה׃
22 לַיִּצְהָרִי֙ שְׁלֹמ֔וֹת לִבְנֵ֥י שְׁלֹמ֖וֹת
23 יָֽחַת׃ וּבָנָ֕י יְרִיָּ֑הוּ אֲמַרְיָ֙הוּ֙
הַשֵּׁנִ֔י יַחֲזִיאֵל֙ הַשְּׁלִישִׁ֔י יְקַמְעָ֖ם
24 הָרְבִיעִֽי׃ בְּנֵ֥י עֻזִּיאֵ֖ל מִיכָ֑ה
25 לִבְנֵ֥י מִיכָ֖ה שָׁמְֽוֹר׃ אֲחִ֣י מִיכָ֔ה
26 יִשִּׁיָּ֑ה לִבְנֵ֥י יִשִּׁיָּ֖ה זְכַרְיָֽהוּ׃ בְּנֵ֤י
מְרָרִי֙ מַחְלִ֣י וּמוּשִׁ֔י בְּנֵ֥י יַעֲזִיָּ֖הוּ
27 בְנֽוֹ׃ בְּנֵ֤י מְרָרִי֙ לְיַעֲזִיָּ֣הוּ בְּנ֑וֹ
28 וְשֹׁ֥הַם וְזַכּ֖וּר וְעִבְרִֽי׃ לְמַחְלִ֖י
אֶלְעָזָ֑ר וְלֹא־הָ֥יָה ל֖וֹ בָּנִֽים׃
29 לְקִ֕ישׁ בְּנֵי־קִ֖ישׁ יְרַחְמְאֵֽל׃
30 וּבְנֵ֣י מוּשִׁ֔י מַחְלִ֥י וָעֵ֖דֶר
וִירִימ֑וֹת אֵ֛לֶּה בְּנֵ֥י הַלְוִיִּ֖ם
31 לְבֵ֥ית אֲבֹתֵיהֶֽם׃ וַיַּפִּ֨ילוּ גַם־
הֵ֜ם גּוֹרָל֗וֹת לְעֻמַּ֣ת ׀ אֲחֵיהֶ֣ם
בְּנֵֽי־אַהֲרֹ֗ן לִפְנֵי֙ דָּוִ֣יד הַמֶּ֔לֶךְ
וְצָד֣וֹק וַאֲחִימֶ֔לֶךְ וְרָאשֵׁ֣י
הָאָב֔וֹת לַכֹּהֲנִ֖ים וְלַלְוִיִּ֑ם
אָב֣וֹת הָרֹ֔אשׁ לְעֻמַּ֖ת אָחִ֥יו
הַקָּטָֽן׃

v. 24. שמיר ק׳

Shubael. In xxiii. 16: *Shebuel.*

22. *Shelomoth.* In xxiii. 18: *Shelomith.*

23. *and Benai, Jeriah.* Cf. xxiii. 19 where the reading is: *the sons of Hebron: Jeriah the chief.*

26. *his son.* This is joined to verse 27. A.V. and R.V. understand it as a name, 'Beno,' here and in the next verse.

30. *Jerimoth.* In xxiii. 23: *Jeremoth.*

25 CHAPTER XXV כה

1. Moreover David and the captains of the host separated for the service certain of the sons of Asaph, and of Heman, and of Jeduthun, who should prophesy with harps, with psalteries, and with cymbals; and the number of them that did the work according to their service was: 2. of the sons of Asaph: Zaccur, and Joseph, and Nethaniah, and Asarelah, the sons of Asaph; under the hand of Asaph, who prophesied according to the direction of the king. 3. Of Jeduthun: the sons of Jeduthun: Gedaliah, and Zeri, and Jeshaiah, Hashabiah, and Mattithiah, six; under the hands of their father Jeduthun with the harp, who prophesied in giving thanks and praising the LORD. 4. Of Heman: the sons of Heman: Bukkiah, Mattaniah, Uzziel, Shebuel, and Jerimoth, Hananiah, Hanani, Eliathah, Giddalti, and Romamti-ezer, Joshbekashah, Mallothi, Hothir, Mahazioth; 5. all these were the sons of Heman the king's seer in the things

1 וַיַּבְדֵּל דָּוִיד וְשָׂרֵי הַצָּבָא
לַעֲבֹדָה לִבְנֵי אָסָף וְהֵימָן
וִידוּתוּן הַנְּבִיאִים בְּכִנֹּרוֹת
בִּנְבָלִים וּבִמְצִלְתָּיִם וַיְהִי
מִסְפָּרָם אַנְשֵׁי מְלָאכָה
2 לַעֲבֹדָתָם׃ לִבְנֵי אָסָף זַכּוּר
וְיוֹסֵף וּנְתַנְיָה וַאֲשַׂרְאֵלָה בְּנֵי
אָסָף עַל יַד־אָסָף הַנִּבָּא עַל־
3 יְדֵי הַמֶּלֶךְ׃ לִידוּתוּן בְּנֵי
יְדוּתוּן גְּדַלְיָהוּ וּצְרִי וִישַׁעְיָהוּ
חֲשַׁבְיָהוּ וּמַתִּתְיָהוּ שִׁשָּׁה עַל
יְדֵי אֲבִיהֶם יְדוּתוּן בַּכִּנּוֹר
הַנִּבָּא עַל־הוֹדוֹת וְהַלֵּל
4 לַיהוָה׃ לְהֵימָן בְּנֵי הֵימָן
בֻּקִּיָּהוּ מַתַּנְיָהוּ עֻזִּיאֵל שְׁבוּאֵל
וִירִימוֹת חֲנַנְיָה חֲנָנִי אֱלִיאָתָה
גִּדַּלְתִּי וְרֹמַמְתִּי עֶזֶר יָשְׁבְּקָשָׁה
מַלּוֹתִי הוֹתִיר מַחֲזִיאוֹת׃
5 כָּל־אֵלֶּה בָנִים לְהֵימָן חֹזֵה

יתיר י׳ v. 1.

CHAPTER XXV

1-7. The appointment of the singers.

1. *separated.* i.e. set apart, appointed.

who should prophesy. The meaning of the verb in this connection is 'sing,' give thanks and offer praises to God in the ecstatic manner of prophets (cf. 1 Sam. x. 5).

2. *Asarelah.* In verse 14: *Jesarelah.*

3. *Zeri.* In verse 11: *Izri.*

six. Five sons and their father. Some insert the name *Shimei* (cf. verse 17) to make up six sons.

4. *Uzziel.* In verse 18: *Azarel.*

Shebuel. In verse 20: *Shubael.*

Jerimoth. In verse 22: *Jeremoth.*

5. *the king's seer.* This title is given to Heman here, to Gad in xxi. 9, and to

pertaining to God, to lift up the
horn. And God gave to Heman
fourteen sons and three daughters.
6. All these were under the hands
of their fathers for song in the house
of the LORD, with cymbals, psalteries, and harps, for the service of
the house of God, according to the
direction of the king—Asaph, Jeduthun, and Heman. 7. And the
number of them, with their brethren
that were instructed in singing unto
the LORD, even all that were skilful,
was two hundred fourscore and
eight. 8. And they cast lots ward
against [ward], as well the small as
the great, the teacher as the scholar.
9. Now the first lot came forth for
Asaph to Joseph;

הַמֶּלֶךְ בְּדִבְרֵי הָאֱלֹהִים
לְהָרִים קָרֶן וַיִּתֵּן הָאֱלֹהִים
לְהֵימָן בָּנִים אַרְבָּעָה עָשָׂר
6 וּבָנוֹת שָׁלוֹשׁ׃ כָּל־אֵלֶּה עַל־
יְדֵי אֲבִיהֶם בַּשִּׁיר בֵּית יְהוָה
בִּמְצִלְתַּיִם נְבָלִים וְכִנֹּרוֹת
לַעֲבֹדַת בֵּית הָאֱלֹהִים עַל
יְדֵי הַמֶּלֶךְ אָסָף וִידוּתוּן
7 וְהֵימָן׃ וַיְהִי מִסְפָּרָם עִם־
אֲחֵיהֶם מְלֻמְּדֵי־שִׁיר לַיהוָה
כָּל־הַמֵּבִין מָאתַיִם שְׁמוֹנִים
8 וּשְׁמוֹנָה׃ וַיַּפִּילוּ גּוֹרָלוֹת
מִשְׁמֶרֶת לְעֻמַּת כַּקָּטֹן כַּגָּדוֹל
מֵבִין עִם־תַּלְמִיד׃
9 וַיֵּצֵא הַגּוֹרָל הָרִאשׁוֹן לְאָסָף
לְיוֹסֵף

Jeduthun in 2 Chron. xxxv. 15. Asaph is called *the seer* in 2 Chron. xxix. 30.

in the things pertaining to God. i.e. in the arrangements of Divine worship in the Temple. Another rendering is: 'by the command of God' (cf. 2 Chron. xxix. 15).

to lift up the horn. To exalt the grandeur of song in Divine worship; or, simply, 'to blow the horn,' 'to make loud blasts.'

fourteen sons. Enumerated in verse 4.

6. *of their fathers.* viz. *Asaph, Jeduthun and Heman* mentioned at the end of the verse, who acted *according to the direction of the king.*

7. *two hundred fourscore and eight.* This is the total for the twenty-four courses enumerated in verses 9-31, each consisting of twelve Levites. The twenty-four courses of the Levites corresponded to the number of priestly courses (cf. xxiv. 7-18).

8-31. Order of precedence of the courses.

8. *as well the small as the great.* Better, 'the small like the great,' i.e. a small family received the same treatment and consideration as a large.

the teacher as the scholar. Or, 'the skilled as the learner,' two contrasting categories to denote all concerned.

9-31. The order of precedence shows that Asaph received courses 1, 3, 5, 7; Jeduthun 2, 4, 8, 10, 12, 14; and Heman 6, 9, 11, 13, 15-24.

9. *he and his brethren and sons were twelve.* This applies to the two courses in the

The second to Gedaliah; he and his brethren and sons were twelve;

גְּדַלְיָהוּ הַשֵּׁנִי הוּא־וְאֶחָיו וּבָנָיו שְׁנֵים עָשָׂר׃

10. The third to Zaccur, his sons and his brethren, twelve;

10 הַשְּׁלִשִׁי זַכּוּר בָּנָיו וְאֶחָיו שְׁנֵים עָשָׂר׃

11. The fourth to Izri, his sons and his brethren, twelve;

11 הָרְבִיעִי לַיִּצְרִי בָּנָיו וְאֶחָיו שְׁנֵים עָשָׂר׃

12. The fifth to Nethaniah, his sons and his brethren, twelve;

12 הַחֲמִישִׁי נְתַנְיָהוּ בָּנָיו וְאֶחָיו שְׁנֵים עָשָׂר׃

13. The sixth to Bukkiah, his sons and his brethren, twelve;

13 הַשִּׁשִּׁי בֻקִּיָּהוּ בָּנָיו וְאֶחָיו שְׁנֵים עָשָׂר׃

14. The seventh to Jesarelah, his sons and his brethren, twelve;

14 הַשְּׁבִעִי יְשַׂרְאֵלָה בָּנָיו וְאֶחָיו שְׁנֵים עָשָׂר׃

15. The eighth to Jeshaiah, his sons and his brethren, twelve;

15 הַשְּׁמִינִי יְשַׁעְיָהוּ בָּנָיו וְאֶחָיו שְׁנֵים עָשָׂר׃

16. The ninth to Mattaniah, his sons and his brethren, twelve;

16 הַתְּשִׁיעִי מַתַּנְיָהוּ בָּנָיו וְאֶחָיו שְׁנֵים עָשָׂר׃

17. The tenth to Shimei, his sons and his brethren, twelve;

17 הָעֲשִׂירִי שִׁמְעִי בָּנָיו וְאֶחָיו שְׁנֵים עָשָׂר׃

18. The eleventh to Azarel, his sons and his brethren, twelve;

18 עַשְׁתֵּי־עָשָׂר עֲזַרְאֵל בָּנָיו וְאֶחָיו שְׁנֵים עָשָׂר׃

19. The twelfth to Hashabiah, his sons and his brethren, twelve;

19 הַשְּׁנֵים עָשָׂר לַחֲשַׁבְיָה בָּנָיו וְאֶחָיו שְׁנֵים עָשָׂר׃

20. For the thirteenth, Shubael, his sons and his brethren, twelve;

20 לִשְׁלֹשָׁה עָשָׂר שׁוּבָאֵל בָּנָיו וְאֶחָיו שְׁנֵים עָשָׂר׃

21. For the fourteenth, Mattithiah,

21 לְאַרְבָּעָה עָשָׂר מַתִּתְיָהוּ בָּנָיו

verse, Joseph and Gedaliah, consisting of twelve members.

11ff. For the variants in some of the names, see on verses 3ff.

his sons and his brethren, twelve;

22. For the fifteenth to Jeremoth, his sons and his brethren, twelve;

23. For the sixteenth to Hananiah, his sons and his brethren, twelve;

24. For the seventeenth to Joshbekashah, his sons and his brethren, twelve;

25. For the eighteenth to Hanani, his sons and his brethren, twelve;

26. For the nineteenth to Mallothi, his sons and his brethren, twelve;

27. For the twentieth to Eliathah, his sons and his brethren, twelve;

28. For the one and twentieth to Hothir, his sons and his brethren, twelve;

29. For the two and twentieth to Giddalti, his sons and his brethren, twelve;

30. For the three and twentieth to Mahazioth, his sons and his brethren, twelve;

31. For the four and twentieth to Romamti-ezer, his sons and his brethren, twelve.

וְאֶחָיו שְׁנֵים עָשָׂר׃
22 לַחֲמִשָּׁה עָשָׂר לִירֵמוֹת בָּנָיו
וְאֶחָיו שְׁנֵים עָשָׂר׃
23 לְשִׁשָּׁה עָשָׂר לַחֲנַנְיָהוּ בָּנָיו
וְאֶחָיו שְׁנֵים עָשָׂר׃
24 לְשִׁבְעָה עָשָׂר לְיָשְׁבְּקָשָׁה בָּנָיו
וְאֶחָיו שְׁנֵים עָשָׂר׃
25 לִשְׁמוֹנָה עָשָׂר לַחֲנָנִי בָּנָיו
וְאֶחָיו שְׁנֵים עָשָׂר׃
26 לְתִשְׁעָה עָשָׂר לְמַלּוֹתִי בָּנָיו
וְאֶחָיו שְׁנֵים עָשָׂר׃
27 לְעֶשְׂרִים לֶאֱלִיָּתָה בָּנָיו וְאֶחָיו
שְׁנֵים עָשָׂר׃
28 לְאֶחָד וְעֶשְׂרִים לְהוֹתִיר בָּנָיו
וְאֶחָיו שְׁנֵים עָשָׂר׃
29 לִשְׁנַיִם וְעֶשְׂרִים לְגִדַּלְתִּי בָּנָיו
וְאֶחָיו שְׁנֵים עָשָׂר׃
30 לִשְׁלֹשָׁה וְעֶשְׂרִים לְמַחֲזִיאוֹת
בָּנָיו וְאֶחָיו שְׁנֵים עָשָׂר׃
31 לְאַרְבָּעָה וְעֶשְׂרִים לְרוֹמַמְתִּי
עֶזֶר בָּנָיו וְאֶחָיו שְׁנֵים עָשָׂר׃

26 CHAPTER XXVI כו

1. For the courses of the doorkeepers: of the Korahites: Meshelemiah the son of Kore, of the sons of

1 לְמַחְלְקוֹת לְשֹׁעֲרִים לַקָּרְחִים
מְשֶׁלֶמְיָהוּ בֶן־קֹרֵא מִן־בְּנֵי

v. 27. למדנחאי בא׳ תחת ה׳ v. 31. קמץ בז״ק

CHAPTER XXVI

1-11. The genealogies of the doorkeepers.

1. *Meshelemiah . . . Asaph.* Cf. ix. 19: ***Shallum the son of Kore, the son of Eliasaph.***

Asaph. 2. And Meshelemiah had sons: Zechariah the first-born, Jediael the second, Zebadiah the third, Jathniel the fourth; 3. Elam the fifth, Jehohanan the sixth, Eliehoenai the seventh. 4. And Obed-edom had sons: Shemaiah the first-born, Jehozabad the second, Joah the third, and Sacar the fourth, and Nethanel the fifth; 5. Ammiel the sixth, Issachar the seventh, Peullethai the eighth; for God blessed him. 6. Also unto Shemaiah his son were sons born, that ruled over the house of their father; for they were mighty men of valour. 7. The sons of Shemaiah: Othni, and Rephael and Obed and Elzabad his brethren, valiant men; Elihu also, and Semachiah. 8. All these were of the sons of Obed-edom: they and their sons and their brethren, able men in strength for the service; threescore and two of Obed-edom. 9. And Meshelemiah had sons and brethren, valiant men, eighteen.

2 אָסָף׃ וְלִמְשֶׁלֶמְיָהוּ בָּנִים
זְכַרְיָהוּ הַבְּכוֹר יְדִיעֲאֵל הַשֵּׁנִי
זְבַדְיָהוּ הַשְּׁלִישִׁי יַתְנִיאֵל
3 הָרְבִיעִי׃ עֵילָם הַחֲמִישִׁי
יְהוֹחָנָן הַשִּׁשִּׁי אֶלְיְהוֹעֵינַי
4 הַשְּׁבִיעִי׃ וּלְעֹבֵד אֱדֹם בָּנִים
שְׁמַעְיָה הַבְּכוֹר יְהוֹזָבָד הַשֵּׁנִי
יוֹאָח הַשְּׁלִישִׁי וְשָׂכָר הָרְבִיעִי
5 וּנְתַנְאֵל הַחֲמִישִׁי׃ עַמִּיאֵל
הַשִּׁשִּׁי יִשָּׂשכָר הַשְּׁבִיעִי
פְּעֻלְּתַי הַשְּׁמִינִי כִּי בֵרֲכוֹ
6 אֱלֹהִים׃ וְלִשְׁמַעְיָה בְנוֹ נוֹלַד
בָּנִים הַמִּמְשָׁלִים לְבֵית
אֲבִיהֶם כִּי־גִבּוֹרֵי חַיִל הֵמָּה׃
7 בְּנֵי שְׁמַעְיָה עָתְנִי וּרְפָאֵל
וְעוֹבֵד אֶלְזָבָד אֶחָיו בְּנֵי־חָיִל
8 אֱלִיהוּ וּסְמַכְיָהוּ׃ כָּל־
אֵלֶּה מִבְּנֵי ׀ עֹבֵד אֱדֹם הֵמָּה
וּבְנֵיהֶם וַאֲחֵיהֶם אִישׁ־חַיִל
בַּכֹּחַ לַעֲבֹדָה שִׁשִּׁים וּשְׁנַיִם
9 לְעֹבֵד אֱדֹם׃ וְלִמְשֶׁלֶמְיָהוּ
בָּנִים וְאַחִים בְּנֵי־חָיִל שְׁמוֹנָה

v. 9. קמץ בלא אס"ף

2. *Zechariah the first-born.* Cf. ix. 21.

4. *Obed-edom.* David deposited the ark in his house where it remained for three months (xiii. 13f.). That Obed-edom was a door-keeper is also mentioned in xv. 24, xvi. 38.

5. *for God blessed him.* The pronoun refers to Obed-edom (cf. xiii. 14).

7. *his brethren.* The pronoun *his* refers to *Othni.*

8. *able men.* The Hebrew singular indicates the ability and strength of each of them.

9. *and Meshelemiah had sons,* etc. This verse is a supplement to verses 1-3.

10. Also Hosah, of the children of Merari, had sons: Shimri the chief —for though he was not the first-born, yet his father made him chief —11. Hilkiah the second, Tebaliah the third, Zechariah the fourth; all the sons and brethren of Hosah were thirteen.

12. These courses of the doorkeepers, even the chief men, had wards over against their brethren, to minister in the house of the LORD. 13. And they cast lots, as well the small as the great, according to their fathers' houses, for every gate. 14. And the lot eastward fell to Shelemiah. Then for Zechariah his son, a discreet counsellor, they cast lots; and his lot came out northward. 15. To Obed-edom southward; and to his sons the Storehouse. 16. To Shuppim and Hosah westward, by the gate of Shallecheth, at the causeway that goeth up, ward

10 עָשָׂר׃ וּלְחֹסָה מִן־בְּנֵי־
מְרָרִי בָּנִים שִׁמְרִי הָרֹאשׁ כִּי
לֹא־הָיָה בְכוֹר וַיְשִׂימֵהוּ
11 אָבִיהוּ לְרֹאשׁ׃ חִלְקִיָּהוּ הַשֵּׁנִי
טְבַלְיָהוּ הַשְּׁלִישִׁי זְכַרְיָהוּ
הָרְבִעִי כָּל־בָּנִים וְאַחִים
לְחֹסָה שְׁלֹשָׁה עָשָׂר׃
12 לְאֵלֶּה מַחְלְקוֹת הַשֹּׁעֲרִים
לְרָאשֵׁי הַגְּבָרִים מִשְׁמָרוֹת
לְעֻמַּת אֲחֵיהֶם לְשָׁרֵת בְּבֵית
13 יְהוָה׃ וַיַּפִּילוּ גוֹרָלוֹת כַּקָּטָן
כַּגָּדוֹל לְבֵית אֲבוֹתָם לְשַׁעַר
14 וָשָׁעַר׃ וַיִּפֹּל הַגּוֹרָל מִזְרָחָה
לְשֶׁלֶמְיָהוּ וּזְכַרְיָהוּ בְנוֹ יוֹעֵץ
בְּשֶׂכֶל הִפִּילוּ גוֹרָלוֹת וַיֵּצֵא
15 גוֹרָלוֹ צָפוֹנָה׃ לְעֹבֵד אֱדֹם
נֶגְבָּה וּלְבָנָיו בֵּית הָאֲסֻפִּים׃
16 לְשֻׁפִּים וּלְחֹסָה לַמַּעֲרָב עִם
שַׁעַר שַׁלֶּכֶת בַּמְסִלָּה הָעוֹלָה

10. *Hosah.* He appears as a doorkeeper in association with Obed-edom in xvi. 38.

11. The thirteen doorkeepers mentioned here, the eighteen in verse 9 and the sixty-two in verse 8, make a total of ninety-three, all of whom were chiefs (cf. verse 12). The number of all the doorkeepers was four thousand (cf. xxiii. 5).

12-19. The appointments of the doorkeepers.

12. *over against their brethren.* viz. the singers. The number of doorkeepers was the same as of singers (cf. xxiii. 5).

13. *they cast lots*, etc. Cf. xxv. 8.

14. *Shelemiah.* In verses 1f. he is named *Meshelemiah.*

Zechariah. He is also mentioned in verse 2 as the son of Meshelemiah.

a discreet counsellor. lit. 'a counsellor with prudence.'

16. *the gate of Shallecheth.* Not named elsewhere in the Bible.

the causeway that goeth up. Or, 'the ascending highway.'

against ward. 17. Eastward were
six Levites, northward four a day,
southward four a day, and for the
Storehouse two and two. 18. For
the Precinct westward, four at the
causeway, and two at the Precinct.
19. These were the courses of the
doorkeepers; of the sons of the
Korahites, and of the sons of Merari.
20. And of the Levites, Ahijah was
over the treasuries of the house of
God, and over the treasuries of the
hallowed things. 21. The sons of
Ladan, the sons of the Gershonites
belonging to Ladan, the heads of the
fathers' houses belonging to Ladan
the Gershonite: Jehieli. 22. The
sons of Jehieli: Zetham, and Joel his
brother, over the treasuries of the
house of the LORD. 23. Of the
Amramites, of the Izharites, of the
Hebronites, of the Uzzielites;
24. Shebuel the son of Gershom,
the son of Moses, was ruler over the

17 מִשְׁמָר לְעֻמַּת מִשְׁמָר: לַמִּזְרָח
הַלְוִיִּם שִׁשָּׁה לַצָּפוֹנָה לַיּוֹם
אַרְבָּעָה לַנֶּגְבָּה לַיּוֹם אַרְבָּעָה
וְלָאֲסֻפִּים שְׁנַיִם שְׁנָיִם:
18 לַפַּרְבָּר לַמַּעֲרָב אַרְבָּעָה
19 לַמְסִלָּה שְׁנַיִם לַפַּרְבָּר: אֵלֶּה
מַחְלְקוֹת הַשֹּׁעֲרִים לִבְנֵי
הַקָּרְחִי וְלִבְנֵי מְרָרִי:
20 וְהַלְוִיִּם אֲחִיָּה עַל־אוֹצְרוֹת
בֵּית הָאֱלֹהִים וּלְאֹצְרוֹת
21 הַקֳּדָשִׁים: בְּנֵי לַעְדָּן בְּנֵי
הַגֵּרְשֻׁנִּי לְלַעְדָּן רָאשֵׁי הָאָבוֹת
22 לְלַעְדָּן הַגֵּרְשֻׁנִּי יְחִיאֵלִי: בְּנֵי
יְחִיאֵלִי זֵתָם וְיוֹאֵל אָחִיו עַל־
23 אֹצְרוֹת בֵּית יְהוָה: לָעַמְרָמִי
לַיִּצְהָרִי לַחֶבְרוֹנִי לָעָזִּיאֵלִי:
24 וּשְׁבֻאֵל בֶּן־גֵּרְשׁוֹם בֶּן־מֹשֶׁה

ward against ward. i.e. the two wards performed their duties alternately, or they had their respective stations facing each other.

17. *for the Storehouse two and two.* i.e. two Levites at each side of the Storehouse or at each door.

18. *the Precinct.* A colonnade or an open chamber on the west side of the Temple area. The word, *parbar*, is probably identical with *parwarim* in 2 Kings xxiii. 11, derived from the Persian, meaning 'possessing light (of the sun).'

20-28. The officers over the Temple treasuries.

20. *treasuries of the house of God.* The funds for acquiring materials to build the Temple and later to maintain the fabric. *treasuries of the hallowed things.* The revenues from which the sacrificial animals were purchased.

21. *Ladan.* Cf. xxiii. 7.

22. *Zetham, and Joel his brother.* According to xxiii. 8, Jehiel, Zetham and Joel were brothers. The text has been interpreted in the sense: 'the sons of Jehieli, together with Zetham and Joel, his (Jehieli's) brother.'

23. *the Amramites*, etc. They were the descendants of the four sons of Kohath (cf. xxiii. 12).

treasuries. 25. And his brethren by Eliezer: Rehabiah his son, and Jeshaiah his son, and Joram his son, and Zichri his son, and Shelomith his son. 26. This Shelomith and his brethren were over all the treasuries of the dedicated things, which David the king, and the heads of the fathers' houses, the captains over thousands and hundreds, and the captains of the host, had dedicated. 27. Out of the spoil won in battles did they dedicate to repair the house of the LORD. 28. And all that Samuel the seer, and Saul the son of Kish, and Abner the son of Ner, and Joab the son of Zeruiah, had dedicated; whosoever had dedicated any thing, it was under the hand of Shelomith, and his brethren.

29. Of the Izharites, Chenaniah and his sons were for the outward business over Israel, for officers and judges. 30. Of the Hebronites, Hashabiah and his brethren, men of valour, a thousand and seven hun-

25 נָגִיד עַל־הָאֹצָרוֹת׃ וְאֶחָיו
לֶאֱלִיעֶזֶר רְחַבְיָהוּ בְנוֹ
וִישַׁעְיָהוּ בְנוֹ וְיֹרָם בְּנוֹ וְזִכְרִי
26 בְנוֹ וּשְׁלֹמוֹת בְּנוֹ׃ הוּא ׀
שְׁלֹמוֹת וְאֶחָיו עַל כָּל־
אֹצְרוֹת הַקֳּדָשִׁים אֲשֶׁר
הִקְדִּישׁ דָּוִיד הַמֶּלֶךְ וְרָאשֵׁי
הָאָבוֹת לְשָׂרֵי־הָאֲלָפִים
27 וְהַמֵּאוֹת וְשָׂרֵי הַצָּבָא׃ מִן־
הַמִּלְחָמוֹת וּמִן־הַשָּׁלָל
הִקְדִּישׁוּ לְחַזֵּק לְבֵית יְהוָה׃
28 וְכֹל הַהִקְדִּישׁ שְׁמוּאֵל הָרֹאֶה
וְשָׁאוּל בֶּן־קִישׁ וְאַבְנֵר בֶּן־
נֵר וְיוֹאָב בֶּן־צְרוּיָה כֹּל־
הַמַּקְדִּישׁ עַל יַד־שְׁלֹמִית
וְאֶחָיו׃
29 לַיִּצְהָרִי כְּנַנְיָהוּ וּבָנָיו
לַמְּלָאכָה הַחִיצוֹנָה עַל־
יִשְׂרָאֵל לְשֹׁטְרִים וּלְשֹׁפְטִים׃
30 לַחֶבְרוֹנִי חֲשַׁבְיָהוּ וְאֶחָיו בְּנֵי־
חַיִל אֶלֶף וּשְׁבַע־מֵאוֹת עַל

v. 25. ושלומית ק׳

25. *his brethren.* i.e. the kinsmen of Shebuel.

26. *Shelomith.* The text has *Shelomoth* which corresponds to the *kethib* in the preceding verse.

David . . . had dedicated. Cf. xviii. 11.

27. *out of the spoil won in battles.* lit. 'out of the battles and out of the spoil.'

29-32. Officers for the outward business.

29. *the outward business.* The Jewish commentators understood the phrase to indicate matters connected with the building of the Temple which had to be attended to outside Jerusalem, e.g. the hewing of timber and quarrying of stones. The words which follow, *for officers and*

dred, had the oversight of Israel beyond the Jordan westward; for all the business of the LORD, and for the service of the king. 31. Of the Hebronites was Jerijah the chief, even of the Hebronites, according to their generations by fathers' houses. In the fortieth year of the reign of David they were sought for, and there were found among them mighty men of valour at Jazer of Gilead. 32. And his brethren, men of valour, were two thousand and seven hundred, heads of fathers' houses, whom king David made overseers over the Reubenites, and the Gadites, and the half-tribe of the Manassites, for every matter pertaining to God, and for the affairs of the king.

פְּקֻדַּת יִשְׂרָאֵל מֵעֵבֶר לַיַּרְדֵּן
מַעְרָבָה לְכֹל מְלֶאכֶת יְהוָֹה
31 וְלַעֲבֹדַת הַמֶּלֶךְ׃ לַחֶבְרוֹנִי
יְרִיָּה הָרֹאשׁ לַחֶבְרוֹנִי
לְתֹלְדֹתָיו לְאָבוֹת בִּשְׁנַת
הָאַרְבָּעִים לְמַלְכוּת דָּוִיד
נִדְרָשׁוּ וַיִּמָּצֵא בָהֶם גִּבּוֹרֵי חַיִל
32 בְּיַעְזֵיר גִּלְעָד׃ וְאֶחָיו בְּנֵי־
חַיִל אַלְפַּיִם וּשְׁבַע מֵאוֹת
רָאשֵׁי הָאָבוֹת וַיַּפְקִידֵם דָּוִיד
הַמֶּלֶךְ עַל־הָרְאוּבֵנִי וְהַגָּדִי
וַחֲצִי שֵׁבֶט הַמְנַשִּׁי לְכָל־דְּבַר
הָאֱלֹהִים וּדְבַר הַמֶּלֶךְ׃

27 CHAPTER XXVII כז

1. Now the children of Israel after their number, to wit, the heads of fathers' houses and the captains of thousands and of hundreds, and their officers that served the king, in any matter of the courses which came in and went out month by month throughout all the months of the year, of every course were

1 וּבְנֵי יִשְׂרָאֵל ׀ לְמִסְפָּרָם רָאשֵׁי
הָאָבוֹת ׀ וְשָׂרֵי הָאֲלָפִים ׀
וְהַמֵּאוֹת וְשֹׁטְרֵיהֶם הַמְשָׁרְתִים
אֶת־הַמֶּלֶךְ לְכֹל ׀ דְּבַר
הַמַּחְלְקוֹת הַבָּאָה וְהַיֹּצֵאת
חֹדֶשׁ בְּחֹדֶשׁ לְכֹל חָדְשֵׁי הַשָּׁנָה
הַמַּחֲלֹקֶת הָאַחַת עֶשְׂרִים

כצ״ל v. 31. כצ״ל v. 1.

judges, seem rather to suggest administrative positions throughout the community.

31. *Jazer.* See on vi. 66.

32. *his brethren.* The brethren of Jerijah.

CHAPTER XXVII

1-15. Military organization.

1. *which came in and went out.* Came on and went off duty, serving for a period of one month.

twenty and four thousand. 2. Over the first course for the first month was Jashobeam the son of Zabdiel; and in his course were twenty and four thousand. 3. Of the children of Perez was he, and the chief of all the captains of the host for the first month. 4. And over the course of the second month was Dodai the Ahohite, and his course, and Mikloth the ruler; and in his course were twenty and four thousand. 5. The third captain of the host for the third month was Benaiah the son of Jehoiada, the priest, chief; and in his course were twenty and four thousand. 6. This is that Benaiah, who was the mighty man of the thirty, and over the thirty; and of his course was Ammizabad his son. 7. The fourth captain for the fourth month was Asahel the brother of Joab, and Zebadiah his son after

2 וְאַרְבָּעָה אָלֶף׃ עַל הַמַּחֲלֹקֶת
הָרִאשׁוֹנָה לַחֹדֶשׁ הָרִאשׁוֹן
יָשָׁבְעָם בֶּן־זַבְדִּיאֵל וְעַל
מַחֲלֻקְתּוֹ עֶשְׂרִים וְאַרְבָּעָה
3 אָלֶף׃ מִן־בְּנֵי־פֶרֶץ הָרֹאשׁ
לְכָל־שָׂרֵי הַצְּבָאוֹת לַחֹדֶשׁ
4 הָרִאשׁוֹן׃ וְעַל מַחֲלֹקֶת ׀
הַחֹדֶשׁ הַשֵּׁנִי דּוֹדַי הָאֲחוֹחִי
וּמַחֲלֻקְתּוֹ וּמִקְלוֹת הַנָּגִיד וְעַל
מַחֲלֻקְתּוֹ עֶשְׂרִים וְאַרְבָּעָה
5 אָלֶף׃ שַׂר הַצָּבָא הַשְּׁלִישִׁי
לַחֹדֶשׁ הַשְּׁלִישִׁי בְּנָיָהוּ בֶן־
יְהוֹיָדָע הַכֹּהֵן רֹאשׁ וְעַל
מַחֲלֻקְתּוֹ עֶשְׂרִים וְאַרְבָּעָה
6 אָלֶף׃ הוּא בְנָיָהוּ גִּבּוֹר
הַשְּׁלֹשִׁים וְעַל־הַשְּׁלֹשִׁים
וּמַחֲלֻקְתּוֹ עַמִּיזָבָד בְּנוֹ׃
7 הָרְבִיעִי לַחֹדֶשׁ הָרְבִיעִי
עֲשָׂהאֵל אֲחִי יוֹאָב וּזְבַדְיָה

2. *over the first course . . . Jashobeam.* He (cf. xi. 11) was the commander of the first division which, like the others, consisted of 24,000 men.

3. *of the children of Perez was he.* Jashobeam belonged to the family of Perez (cf. ii. 4f.).

4. *Dodai the Ahohite.* Cf. xi. 12, *Dodo. and his course, and Mikloth the ruler.* Mikloth was the deputy commander of the course. The name, presumably of a different person, occurs in viii. 32.

5. *Benaiah.* Some of his heroic acts are recorded in xi. 22f.

chief. The title refers to Benaiah.

6. *the mighty man of the thirty.* Cf. xi. 25.

of his course, etc. The intention may be that Ammizabad was Benaiah's second in command.

7. *the fourth captain.* The noun is implied.

Asahel. Cf. xi. 26.

Zebadiah . . . after him. Asahel was

him; and in his course were twenty and four thousand. 8. The fifth captain for the fifth month was Shamhuth the Izrahite; and in his course were twenty and four thousand. 9. The sixth captain for the sixth month was Ira the son of Ikkesh the Tekoite; and in his course were twenty and four thousand. 10. The seventh captain for the seventh month was Helez the Pelonite, of the children of Ephraim; and in his course were twenty and four thousand. 11. The eighth captain for the eighth month was Sibbecai the Hushathite, of the Zerahites; and in his course were twenty and four thousand. 12. The ninth captain for the ninth month was Abiezer the Anathothite, of the Benjamites; and in his course were twenty and four thousand. 13. The tenth captain for the tenth month was Mahrai, the Netophathite, of the Zerahites; and in his course were twenty and four thousand. 14. The eleventh captain for the eleventh month was Benaiah the Pirathonite,

בְּנוֹ אַחֲרָיו וְעַל מַחֲלֻקְתּוֹ
עֶשְׂרִים וְאַרְבָּעָה אָלֶף׃
8 הַחֲמִישִׁי לַחֹדֶשׁ הַחֲמִישִׁי הַשַּׂר
שַׁמְהוּת הַיִּזְרָח וְעַל מַחֲלֻקְתּוֹ
9 עֶשְׂרִים וְאַרְבָּעָה אָלֶף׃ הַשִּׁשִּׁי
לַחֹדֶשׁ הַשִּׁשִּׁי עִירָא בֶּן־עִקֵּשׁ
הַתְּקוֹעִי וְעַל מַחֲלֻקְתּוֹ
עֶשְׂרִים וְאַרְבָּעָה אָלֶף׃
10 הַשְּׁבִיעִי לַחֹדֶשׁ הַשְּׁבִיעִי חֶלֶץ
הַפְּלוֹנִי מִן־בְּנֵי אֶפְרָיִם וְעַל
מַחֲלֻקְתּוֹ עֶשְׂרִים וְאַרְבָּעָה
11 אָלֶף׃ הַשְּׁמִינִי לַחֹדֶשׁ הַשְּׁמִינִי
סִבְּכַי הַחֻשָׁתִי לַזַּרְחִי וְעַל
מַחֲלֻקְתּוֹ עֶשְׂרִים וְאַרְבָּעָה
12 אָלֶף׃ הַתְּשִׁיעִי לַחֹדֶשׁ
הַתְּשִׁיעִי אֲבִיעֶזֶר הָעַנְּתוֹתִי
לַבִּנְיָמִינִי וְעַל מַחֲלֻקְתּוֹ
עֶשְׂרִים וְאַרְבָּעָה אָלֶף׃
13 הָעֲשִׂירִי לַחֹדֶשׁ הָעֲשִׂירִי
מַהְרַי הַנְּטוֹפָתִי לַזַּרְחִי וְעַל
מַחֲלֻקְתּוֹ עֶשְׂרִים וְאַרְבָּעָה
14 אָלֶף׃ עַשְׁתֵּי־עָשָׂר לְעַשְׁתֵּי
עָשָׂר הַחֹדֶשׁ בְּנָיָה הַפִּרְעָתוֹנִי

v. 8. השׂ׳ בפתח   v. 12. לבן ימיני ק׳

slain by Abner (cf. 2 Sam. ii. 23) and Zebadiah succeeded him.

8. *Shamhuth the Izrahite.* Perhaps identical with *Shammoth the Hororite* (xi. 27).

9. *Ira.* Cf. xi. 28.

10. *Helez.* Cf. xi. 27.

11. *Sibbecai.* Cf. xi. 29.

12. *Abiezer.* Cf. xi. 28.

13. *Mahrai.* Cf. xi. 30.

14. *Benaiah the Pirathonite.* Cf. xi. 31.

of the children of Ephraim; and in his course were twenty and four thousand. 15. The twelfth captain for the twelfth month was Heldai the Netophathite, of Othniel; and in his course were twenty and four thousand.

16. Furthermore over the tribes of Israel: of the Reubenites was Eliezer the son of Zichri the ruler; of the Simeonites, Shephatiah the son of Maacah; 17. of Levi, Hashabiah the son of Kemuel; of Aaron, Zadok; 18. of Judah, Elihu, one of the brethren of David; of Issachar, Omri the son of Michael; 19. of Zebulun, Ishmaiah the son of Obadiah; of Naphtali, Jerimoth the son of Azriel; 20. of the children of Ephraim, Hoshea the son of Azaziah; of the half-tribe of Manasseh, Joel the son of Pedaiah; 21. of the half-tribe of Manasseh in Gilead, Iddo the son of Zechariah; of Benjamin, Jaasiel the son of Abner; 22. of Dan, Azarel the son of Jeroham. These were the captains of the tribes of Israel.

מִן־בְּנֵי אֶפְרָיִם וְעַל מַחֲלֻקְתּוֹ
עֶשְׂרִים וְאַרְבָּעָה אָלֶף׃
15 הַשְּׁנֵים עָשָׂר לִשְׁנֵים עָשָׂר
הַחֹדֶשׁ חֶלְדַּי הַנְּטוֹפָתִי
לְעָתְנִיאֵל וְעַל מַחֲלֻקְתּוֹ
עֶשְׂרִים וְאַרְבָּעָה אָלֶף׃
16 וְעַל שִׁבְטֵי יִשְׂרָאֵל לָרְאוּבֵנִי
נָגִיד אֱלִיעֶזֶר בֶּן־זִכְרִי
לַשִּׁמְעוֹנִי שְׁפַטְיָהוּ בֶּן־
17 מַעֲכָה׃ לְלֵוִי חֲשַׁבְיָה בֶן־
קְמוּאֵל לְאַהֲרֹן צָדוֹק׃
18 לִיהוּדָה אֱלִיהוּ מֵאֲחֵי דָוִיד
לְיִשָּׂשכָר עָמְרִי בֶּן־מִיכָאֵל׃
19 לִזְבוּלֻן יִשְׁמַעְיָהוּ בֶּן־עֹבַדְיָהוּ
לְנַפְתָּלִי יְרִימוֹת בֶּן־
20 עַזְרִיאֵל׃ לִבְנֵי אֶפְרַיִם הוֹשֵׁעַ
בֶּן־עֲזַזְיָהוּ לַחֲצִי שֵׁבֶט מְנַשֶּׁה
21 יוֹאֵל בֶּן־פְּדָיָהוּ׃ לַחֲצִי
הַמְנַשֶּׁה גִּלְעָדָה יִדּוֹ בֶּן־
זְכַרְיָהוּ לְבִנְיָמִן יַעֲשִׂיאֵל בֶּן־
22 אַבְנֵר׃ לְדָן עֲזַרְאֵל בֶּן־
יְרֹחָם אֵלֶּה שָׂרֵי שִׁבְטֵי

15. *Heldai.* Cf. xi. 30: *Heled the son of Baanah.*

of Othniel. i.e. of the descendants of Othniel, brother and son-in-law of Caleb (cf. Judg. i. 13, iii. 9).

16-24. The rulers of the tribes. It is to be noted that Gad and Asher are omitted, the reason being unknown.

17. *Zadok.* He was in control of the priests (cf. xii. 29).

18. *Elihu.* Perhaps a variant of *Eliab* (1 Sam. xvi. 6).

21. *in Gilead.* The tribe of Manasseh was divided into two sections. One half dwelt on the western side of the Jordan

23. But David took not the number of them from twenty years old and under; because the LORD had said He would increase Israel like to the stars of heaven. 24. Joab the son of Zeruiah began to number, but finished not; and there came wrath for this upon Israel; neither was the number put into the account in the chronicles of king David.

25. And over the king's treasuries was Azmaveth the son of Adiel; and over the treasuries in the fields, in the cities, and in the villages, and in the towers, was Jonathan the son of Uzziah; 26. and over them that did the work of the field for tillage of the ground was Ezri the son of Chelub; 27. and over the vineyards was Shimei the Ramathite; and over the increase of the vineyards for the wine-cellars was Zabdi the Shiphmite; 28. and over the olive-trees and the sycomore-trees that were in the

23 יִשְׂרָאֵל׃ וְלֹא־נָשָׂא דָוִיד
מִסְפָּרָם לְמִבֶּן עֶשְׂרִים שָׁנָה
וּלְמָטָּה כִּי אָמַר יְהוָה
לְהַרְבּוֹת אֶת־יִשְׂרָאֵל
24 כְּכוֹכְבֵי הַשָּׁמָיִם׃ יוֹאָב בֶּן־
צְרוּיָה הֵחֵל לִמְנוֹת וְלֹא כִלָּה
וַיְהִי בָזֹאת קֶצֶף עַל־יִשְׂרָאֵל
וְלֹא עָלָה הַמִּסְפָּר בְּמִסְפַּר
דִּבְרֵי הַיָּמִים לַמֶּלֶךְ דָּוִיד׃
25 וְעַל אֹצְרוֹת הַמֶּלֶךְ עַזְמָוֶת
בֶּן־עֲדִיאֵל וְעַל־הָאֹצָרוֹת
בַּשָּׂדֶה בֶּעָרִים וּבַכְּפָרִים
וּבַמִּגְדָּלוֹת יְהוֹנָתָן בֶּן־עֻזִּיָּהוּ׃
26 וְעַל עֹשֵׂי מְלֶאכֶת הַשָּׂדֶה
לַעֲבֹדַת הָאֲדָמָה עֶזְרִי בֶּן־
27 כְּלוּב׃ וְעַל־הַכְּרָמִים שִׁמְעִי
הָרָמָתִי וְעַל שֶׁבַּכְּרָמִים
לְאֹצְרוֹת הַיַּיִן זַבְדִּי הַשִּׁפְמִי׃
28 וְעַל־הַזֵּיתִים וְהַשִּׁקְמִים אֲשֶׁר

v. 25. חצי הספר בפסוקים

and the other on its eastern side in Gilead, including Bashan.

23f. The two verses refer back to the census (xxi) and the reason that numerical details are excluded from *the chronicles of king David.*

23. *from twenty years old and under.* Below the age of military service (Num. i. 3).

24. *neither was the number put,* etc. A summary of the figures is given in xxi. 5 and with variants in 2 Sam. xxiv. 9.

25-31. The twelve officers over the king's possessions.

25. *the king's treasuries.* i.e. those in the royal palace. There were others outside the capital.

the fields. The Hebrew is singular in a collective sense.

26. *tillage of the ground.* The Hebrew for *tillage* is literally 'labour' which includes ploughing, sowing and reaping.

27. *the increase of the vineyards.* lit. 'what is in the vineyards.'

Lowland was Baal-hanan the Gederite; and over the cellars of oil was Joash; 29. and over the herds that fed in Sharon was Shirtai the Sharonite; and over the herds that were in the valleys was Shaphat the son of Adlai; 30. and over the camels was Obil the Ishmaelite; and over the asses was Jehdeiah the Meronothite; 31. and over the flocks was Jaziz the Hagrite. All these were the rulers of the substance which was king David's.

32. Also Jonathan David's uncle was a counsellor, a man of understanding, and a scribe; and Jehiel the son of Hachmoni was with the king's sons; 33. and Ahithophel was the king's counsellor; and Hushai the Archite was the king's friend;

בַּשְּׁפֵלָה בַּעַל חָנָן הַגְּדֵרִי
וְעַל־אֹצְרוֹת הַשֶּׁמֶן יוֹעָשׁ׃
29 וְעַל־הַבָּקָר הָרֹעִים בַּשָּׁרוֹן
שִׁטְרַי הַשָּׁרוֹנִי וְעַל־הַבָּקָר
בָּעֲמָקִים שָׁפָט בֶּן־עַדְלָי׃
30 וְעַל־הַגְּמַלִּים אוֹבִיל
הַיִּשְׁמְעֵלִי וְעַל־הָאֲתֹנוֹת
31 יֶחְדְּיָהוּ הַמֵּרֹנֹתִי׃ וְעַל־הַצֹּאן
יָזִיז הַהַגְרִי כָּל־אֵלֶּה שָׂרֵי
הָרְכוּשׁ אֲשֶׁר לַמֶּלֶךְ דָּוִיד׃
32 וִיהוֹנָתָן דּוֹד־דָּוִיד יוֹעֵץ
אִישׁ־מֵבִין וְסוֹפֵר הוּא
וִיחִיאֵל בֶּן־חַכְמוֹנִי עִם־בְּנֵי
33 הַמֶּלֶךְ׃ וַאֲחִיתֹפֶל יוֹעֵץ
לַמֶּלֶךְ וְחוּשַׁי הָאַרְכִּי רֵעַ

v. 29. שרטי ק׳

28. *the Lowland.* Better, 'the Shephelah,' the plain on the south-west of the Judean hills bordering on the Mediterranean. It was famous for its sycomore-trees, a species of fig-trees known as the fig-mulberry. Others limit the Shephelah to the low undulating ground west and south-west from the hill-country of Judah.

29. *Sharon.* The fertile maritime plain along the Mediterranean between the north of the Shephelah and mount Carmel.

30. *Obil.* It has been pointed out that in Arabic the noun *abil* signifies 'one who feeds camels.'

31. *substance.* The Hebrew *rechush* denotes both movable and immovable property.

32-34. David's counsellors. Cf. xviii. 15-17; 2 Sam. viii. 16-18, xx. 23-26.

32. *Jonathan David's uncle.* David had a nephew named Jonathan (cf. xx. 7), but nowhere is it recorded that an uncle bore that name. Possibly the word *dod* is used loosely for a near relative.

was with the king's sons. He acted as their tutor.

33. *Ahithophel.* David's counsellor whose advice *was as if a man inquired of the word of God* (2 Sam. xvi. 23). During Absalom's rebellion he deserted David to join Absalom and when his advice was not followed he took his life (2 Sam. xvii. 23).

Hushai. The counsellor who remained loyal to David during the rebellion and frustrated Ahithophel's counsel (2 Sam. xv. 32ff., xvii. 5ff.).

34. and after Ahithophel was Jehoiada the son of Benaiah, and Abiathar; and the captain of the king's host was Joab.

הַמֶּלֶךְ׃ וְאַחֲרֵי אֲחִיתֹפֶל 34
יְהוֹיָדָע בֶּן־בְּנָיָהוּ וְאֶבְיָתָר
וְשַׂר־צָבָא לַמֶּלֶךְ יוֹאָב׃

28 CHAPTER XXVIII כח

1. And David assembled all the
princes of Israel, the princes of the
tribes, and the captains of the
companies that served the king by
course, and the captains of thousands, and the captains of hundreds,
and the rulers over all the substance
and cattle of the king and of his sons,
with the officers, and the mighty
men, even all the mighty men of
valour, unto Jerusalem. 2. Then
David the king stood up upon his
feet, and said: 'Hear me, my
brethren, and my people; as for me,
it was in my heart to build a house
of rest for the ark of the covenant of

1 וַיַּקְהֵל דָּוִיד אֶת־כָּל־שָׂרֵי
יִשְׂרָאֵל שָׂרֵי הַשְּׁבָטִים וְשָׂרֵי
הַמַּחְלְקוֹת הַמְשָׁרְתִים אֶת־
הַמֶּלֶךְ וְשָׂרֵי הָאֲלָפִים וְשָׂרֵי
הַמֵּאוֹת וְשָׂרֵי כָל־רְכוּשׁ־
וּמִקְנֶה לַמֶּלֶךְ וּלְבָנָיו עִם־
הַסָּרִיסִים וְהַגִּבּוֹרִים וּלְכָל־
2 גִּבּוֹר חָיִל אֶל־יְרוּשָׁלִָם׃ וַיָּקָם
דָּוִיד הַמֶּלֶךְ עַל־רַגְלָיו
וַיֹּאמֶר שְׁמָעוּנִי אַחַי וְעַמִּי אֲנִי
עִם־לְבָבִי לִבְנוֹת בֵּית מְנוּחָה

the king's friend. A similar title is given to Hushai in 2 Sam. xvi. 16. In Egypt, 'the friend of the king' or 'the well-beloved friend of the king' was a title of honour; and the Greek kings of Syria bestowed a similar title upon their favourites (cf. 1 Macc. ii. 18).

34. *after Ahithophel.* His successor when he died.

Jehoiada. Evidently named after his grandfather (cf. xviii. 17).

Abiathar. He was a chief priest with Zadok (cf. xv. 11), unless this was a different person.

CHAPTER XXVIII

1-8. David's address to the assembled leaders of Israel, and the public presentation of Solomon as his successor.

1. *the princes of the tribes,* etc. They were enumerated in the previous chapter.

unto Jerusalem. These words are to be attached to the verb assembled.

2. *stood up.* As a mark of reverence to God Whom he invokes as a Witness (cf. verse 8, *in the hearing of our God*). As king and as a man advanced in years, he could have claimed the privilege of delivering his address while sitting.

my brethren. This may have been addressed to his kinsmen, the tribe of Judah. On the other hand, he may have referred to the whole assembly as his *brethren.*

my people. On the first interpretation, this alludes to the men of the other tribes.

the footstool of our God. For the phrase, cf. Isa. lxvi. 1 where it applies to the

the LORD, and for the footstool of our God; and I had made ready for the building. 3. But God said unto me: Thou shalt not build a house for My name, because thou art a man of war, and hast shed blood. 4. Howbeit the LORD, the God of Israel, chose me out of all the house of my father to be king over Israel for ever; for He hath chosen Judah to be prince, and in the house of Judah, the house of my father, and among the sons of my father He took pleasure in me to make me king over all Israel; 5. and of all my sons—for the LORD hath given me many sons—He hath chosen Solomon my son to sit upon the throne of the kingdom of the LORD over Israel. 6. And He said unto me: Solomon thy son, he shall build My house and My courts; for I have chosen him to be to Me for a son, and I will be to him for a father. 7. And I will establish his kingdom for ever, if he be constant to do My commandments and Mine ordi-

לַאֲרוֹן בְּרִית־יְהוָה וְלַהֲדֹם
רַגְלֵי אֱלֹהֵינוּ וַהֲכִינוֹתִי
לִבְנוֹת׃ וְהָאֱלֹהִים אָמַר לִי 3
לֹא־תִבְנֶה בַיִת לִשְׁמִי כִּי אִישׁ
מִלְחָמוֹת אַתָּה וְדָמִים שָׁפָכְתָּ׃
וַיִּבְחַר יְהוָה אֱלֹהֵי יִשְׂרָאֵל בִּי 4
מִכֹּל בֵּית־אָבִי לִהְיוֹת לְמֶלֶךְ
עַל־יִשְׂרָאֵל לְעוֹלָם כִּי
בִיהוּדָה בָּחַר לְנָגִיד וּבְבֵית
יְהוּדָה בֵּית אָבִי וּבִבְנֵי אָבִי
בִּי רָצָה לְהַמְלִיךְ עַל־כָּל־
יִשְׂרָאֵל׃ וּמִכָּל־בָּנַי כִּי רַבִּים 5
בָּנִים נָתַן לִי יְהוָה וַיִּבְחַר
בִּשְׁלֹמֹה בְנִי לָשֶׁבֶת עַל־כִּסֵּא
מַלְכוּת יְהוָה עַל־יִשְׂרָאֵל׃
וַיֹּאמֶר לִי שְׁלֹמֹה בִנְךָ הוּא־ 6
יִבְנֶה בֵיתִי וַחֲצֵרוֹתָי כִּי־
בָחַרְתִּי בוֹ לִי לְבֵן וַאֲנִי
אֶהְיֶה־לּוֹ לְאָב׃ וַהֲכִינוֹתִי 7
אֶת־מַלְכוּתוֹ עַד־לְעוֹלָם
אִם־יֶחֱזַק לַעֲשׂוֹת מִצְוֺתַי

earth. Here we have the thought of God 'sitting upon the cherubim' (cf. xiii. 6).

3. Cf. xxii. 8.

4. *to be king . . . for ever.* The allusion is to his dynasty, and *for ever* signifies 'for a long period.'

to be prince. Or, 'leader' among the tribes.

5. *the LORD hath given me many sons.* Cf. iii. 1-9.

the throne of the kingdom of the LORD. God was the King of Israel in the supreme sense.

6. *he shall build My house.* Cf. xxii. 10.

7. *I will establish his kingdom,* etc. Cf. xvii. 11.

if he be constant. lit. 'if he be strong' (cf. verses 10, 20).

nances, as at this day. 8. Now therefore, in the sight of all Israel, the congregation of the LORD, and in the hearing of our God, observe and seek out all the commandments of the LORD your God; that ye may possess this good land, and leave it for an inheritance to your children after you for ever.

9. And thou, Solomon my son, know thou the God of thy father, and serve Him with a whole heart and with a willing mind; for the LORD searcheth all hearts, and understandeth all the imaginations of the thoughts; if thou seek Him, He will be found of thee; but if thou forsake Him, He will cast thee off for ever. 10. Take heed now; for the LORD hath chosen thee to build a house for the sanctuary; be strong, and do it.'

11. Then David gave to Solomon his son the pattern of the porch [of the temple], and of the houses thereof, and of the treasuries thereof, and of the upper rooms thereof, and

8 וּמִשְׁפָּטַי כַּיּוֹם הַזֶּה׃ וְעַתָּה
לְעֵינֵי כָל־יִשְׂרָאֵל קְהַל־
יְהוָה וּבְאָזְנֵי אֱלֹהֵינוּ שִׁמְרוּ
וְדִרְשׁוּ כָּל־מִצְוֹת יְהוָה
אֱלֹהֵיכֶם לְמַעַן תִּירְשׁוּ אֶת־
הָאָרֶץ הַטּוֹבָה וְהִנְחַלְתֶּם
לִבְנֵיכֶם אַחֲרֵיכֶם עַד־
עוֹלָם׃
9 וְאַתָּה שְׁלֹמֹה־בְנִי דַּע אֶת־
אֱלֹהֵי אָבִיךָ וְעָבְדֵהוּ בְּלֵב
שָׁלֵם וּבְנֶפֶשׁ חֲפֵצָה כִּי כָל־
לְבָבוֹת דּוֹרֵשׁ יְהוָה וְכָל־יֵצֶר
מַחֲשָׁבוֹת מֵבִין אִם־תִּדְרְשֶׁנּוּ
יִמָּצֵא לָךְ וְאִם־תַּעַזְבֶנּוּ
10 יַזְנִיחֲךָ לָעַד׃ רְאֵה ׀ עַתָּה
כִּי־יְהוָה בָּחַר בְּךָ לִבְנוֹת־
בַּיִת לַמִּקְדָּשׁ חֲזַק וַעֲשֵׂה׃
11 וַיִּתֵּן דָּוִיד לִשְׁלֹמֹה בְנוֹ אֶת־
תַּבְנִית הָאוּלָם וְאֶת־בָּתָּיו
וְגַנְזַכָּיו וַעֲלִיֹּתָיו וַחֲדָרָיו

8. *in the hearing of our God.* 'I exhort you' is implied before these words.

9f. David exhorts and encourages Solomon.

9. *know thou the God of thy father.* By *know* is meant the concept of God which results from inquiry and reasoning, while the addition of *God of thy father* implies belief in tradition handed down from generation to generation. One should endeavour to arrive at the knowledge of God by rational processes aided by the influence of tradition.

with a whole heart. With single-mindedness, complete loyalty.

10. *be strong, and do it.* Cf. Moses' exhortation to his successor, Joshua (Josh. i. 6).

11-19. Solomon receives the plans of the Temple from his father.

11. *the houses thereof.* The different sections of the edifice.

of the inner chambers thereof, and of the place of the ark-cover; 12. and the pattern of all that he had by the spirit, for the courts of the house of the LORD, and for all the chambers round about, for the treasuries of the house of God, and for the treasuries of the hallowed things; 13. also for the courses of the priests and the Levites, and for all the work of the service of the house of the LORD, and for all the vessels of service in the house of the LORD: 14. of gold by weight for the vessels of gold, for all vessels of every kind of service; of silver for all the vessels of silver by weight, for all vessels of every kind of service; 15. by weight also for the candlesticks of gold, and for the lamps thereof, of gold, by weight for every candlestick and for the lamps thereof; and for the candlesticks of silver, silver by weight for every candlestick and for the lamps thereof, according to the use of every candlestick; 16. and the gold by weight for the tables of

הַפְּנִימִים וּבֵית הַכַּפֹּרֶת׃
12 וְתַבְנִית כֹּל אֲשֶׁר הָיָה בָרוּחַ
עִמּוֹ לְחַצְרוֹת בֵּית־יְהוָה
וּלְכָל־הַלְּשָׁכוֹת סָבִיב
לְאֹצְרוֹת בֵּית הָאֱלֹהִים
וּלְאֹצְרוֹת הַקֳּדָשִׁים׃
13 וּלְמַחְלְקוֹת הַכֹּהֲנִים וְהַלְוִיִּם
וּלְכָל־מְלֶאכֶת עֲבוֹדַת בֵּית־
יְהוָה וּלְכָל־כְּלֵי עֲבוֹדַת
14 בֵּית־יְהוָה׃ לַזָּהָב בַּמִּשְׁקָל
לַזָּהָב לְכָל־כְּלֵי עֲבוֹדָה
וַעֲבוֹדָה לְכֹל כְּלֵי הַכֶּסֶף
בְּמִשְׁקָל לְכָל־כְּלֵי עֲבוֹדָה
15 וַעֲבוֹדָה׃ וּמִשְׁקָל לִמְנֹרוֹת
הַזָּהָב וְנֵרֹתֵיהֶם זָהָב
בְּמִשְׁקַל־מְנוֹרָה וּמְנוֹרָה
וְנֵרֹתֶיהָ וְלִמְנֹרוֹת הַכֶּסֶף
בְּמִשְׁקָל לִמְנוֹרָה וְנֵרֹתֶיהָ
כַּעֲבוֹדַת מְנוֹרָה וּמְנוֹרָה׃
16 וְאֶת־הַזָּהָב מִשְׁקָל לְשֻׁלְחֲנוֹת

the place of the ark-cover. lit. 'the house of the ark-cover,' i.e. the Holy of Holies.

12. *that he had by the spirit.* The plan of the Temple, like that of the tabernacle of Moses (cf. Exod. xxv. 9), was Divinely inspired.

the treasuries, etc. See on xxvi. 20.

13. *also for the courses*, etc. This refers to the rooms set aside for their lodging and official duties (Rashi); to the rota of those who have to officiate (Metsudath David). Modern commentators similarly differ in their interpretation.

14. *for the vessels of gold.* The first three words are implied.

every kind of service. lit. 'service and service.'

of silver for all the vessels of silver. The first two words are to be understood and are not in the text.

15. *silver by weight.* The first word is not in the Hebrew.

showbread, for every table; and silver for the tables of silver; 17. and the flesh-hooks, and the basins and the jars, of pure gold; and for the golden bowls by weight for every bowl; and for the silver bowls by weight for every bowl; 18. and for the altar of incense refined gold by weight; and gold for the pattern of the chariot, even the cherubim, that spread out their wings, and covered the ark of the covenant of the LORD. 19. 'All this [do I give thee] in writing, as the LORD hath made me wise by His hand upon me, even all the works of this pattern.'

20. And David said to Solomon his son: 'Be strong and of good courage, and do it; fear not, nor be dismayed; for the LORD God, even my God, is with thee; He will not

הַמַּעֲרֶכֶת לְשֻׁלְחַן וְשֻׁלְחָן
וְכֶסֶף לְשֻׁלְחֲנוֹת הַכָּסֶף׃
17 וְהַמִּזְלָגוֹת וְהַמִּזְרָקוֹת וְהַקְּשָׂוֺת
זָהָב טָהוֹר וְלִכְפוֹרֵי הַזָּהָב
בְּמִשְׁקָל לִכְפוֹר וּכְפוֹר
וְלִכְפוֹרֵי הַכֶּסֶף בְּמִשְׁקָל
18 לִכְפוֹר וּכְפוֹר׃ וּלְמִזְבַּח
הַקְּטֹרֶת זָהָב מְזֻקָּק בַּמִּשְׁקָל
וּלְתַבְנִית הַמֶּרְכָּבָה הַכְּרֻבִים
זָהָב לְפֹרְשִׂים וְסֹכְכִים עַל־
19 אֲרוֹן בְּרִית־יְהוָה׃ הַכֹּל
בִּכְתָב מִיַּד יְהוָה עָלַי הִשְׂכִּיל
כֹּל מַלְאֲכוֹת הַתַּבְנִית׃
20 וַיֹּאמֶר דָּוִיד לִשְׁלֹמֹה בְנוֹ חֲזַק
וֶאֱמַץ וַעֲשֵׂה אַל־תִּירָא וְאַל־
תֵּחָת כִּי יְהוָה אֱלֹהִים אֱלֹהַי

16. *tables of showbread . . . tables of silver.* Elsewhere (except 2 Chron. iv. 19) only one table of showbread and one candlestick for the interior of the Temple are mentioned, while the reference to the *tables of silver* occurs only here. According to Jewish commentators, upon them the carcase of the sacrificed animal was flayed.

17. *the flesh-hooks.* Forks used for extracting the flesh of the sacrifices from the pots.

the basins. For sprinkling the blood of the animal against the altar.

the jars. For pouring out the drink-offerings.

bowls. According to Rabbinic tradition, the priests wiped the blood from their fingers on the edge of these bowls.

18. *the chariot, even the cherubim.* The two nouns are in apposition, the latter explaining the former (cf. Ps. xviii. 11, *He rode upon a cherub*).

that spread out their wings. Cf. Exod. xxv. 20. The last two words are implied.

19. [*do I give thee*]. The speaker is David.

in writing. All the plans enumerated were written down.

by His hand upon me. David claimed that his scheme was not his own invention, but the result of Divine guidance (cf. verse 12).

20f. David's encouragement and assurance to Solomon.

20. *the LORD God, even my God.* The implication is, as *my God* inspired me and enabled me to prepare the plans, so will

fail thee, nor forsake thee, until all the work for the service of the house of the LORD be finished. 21. And, behold, there are the courses of the priests and the Levites, for all the service of the house of God; and there shall be with thee in all manner of work every willing man that hath skill, for any manner of service; also the captains and all the people will be wholly at thy commandment.'

עִמָּךְ לֹא יַרְפְּךָ וְלֹא יַעַזְבֶךָּ
עַד־לִכְלוֹת כָּל־מְלֶאכֶת
21 עֲבוֹדַת בֵּית־יְהוָה׃ וְהִנֵּה
מַחְלְקוֹת הַכֹּהֲנִים וְהַלְוִיִּם
לְכָל־עֲבוֹדַת בֵּית הָאֱלֹהִים
וְעִמְּךָ בְכָל־מְלָאכָה לְכָל־
נָדִיב בַּחָכְמָה לְכָל־עֲבוֹדָה
וְהַשָּׂרִים וְכָל־הָעָם לְכָל־
דְּבָרֶיךָ׃

29 CHAPTER XXIX כט

1. And David the king said unto all the congregation: 'Solomon my son, whom alone God hath chosen, is yet young and tender, and the work is great; for the palace is not for man, but for the LORD God. 2. Now I have prepared with all my might for the house of my God the gold for the things of gold, and the silver for

1 וַיֹּאמֶר דָּוִיד הַמֶּלֶךְ לְכָל־
הַקָּהָל שְׁלֹמֹה בְנִי אֶחָד בָּחַר־
בּוֹ אֱלֹהִים נַעַר וָרָךְ
וְהַמְּלָאכָה גְדוֹלָה כִּי לֹא
לְאָדָם הַבִּירָה כִּי לַיהוָה
2 אֱלֹהִים׃ וּבְכָל־כֹּחִי הֲכִינוֹתִי
לְבֵית־אֱלֹהַי הַזָּהָב ׀ לַזָּהָב

He be with you and enable you to carry them into effect.

21. *every willing man.* The preposition *lamed* before the Hebrew for *every* is not to be translated 'to' as elsewhere. It is the *lamed* that occasionally introduces a nominative.

will be wholly at thy commandment. lit. 'to all thy words.'

CHAPTER XXIX

1-5. David appeals to the community for liberal offerings.

1. *whom alone.* The relative pronoun is understood; the literal meaning is 'one.'

the palace. The word *birah* is usually applied to a Persian palace or fortress. The Temple is the *palace* of God Who is the King of kings.

but for the LORD God. Therefore it is the duty of the people to erect an edifice which in its splendour would be worthy of Him.

2. *with all my might.* Cf. *in my straits* (xxii. 14).

onyx stones. A stone with the colour of

the things of silver, and the brass for the things of brass, the iron for the things of iron, and wood for the things of wood; onyx stones, and stones to be set, glistering stones, and of divers colours, and all manner of precious stones, and marble stones in abundance. 3. Moreover also, because I have set my affection on the house of my God, seeing that I have a treasure of mine own of gold and silver, I give it unto the house of my God, over and above all that I have prepared for the holy house, 4. even three thousand talents of gold, of the gold of Ophir, and seven thousand talents of refined silver, wherewith to overlay the walls of the houses; 5. of gold for the things of gold, and of silver for the things of silver, and for all manner of work to be made by the hands of artificers. Who then offereth willingly to consecrate himself this day unto the LORD?'

וְהַכֶּסֶף לַכֶּסֶף וְהַנְּחֹשֶׁת
לַנְּחֹשֶׁת הַבַּרְזֶל לַבַּרְזֶל
וְהָעֵצִים לָעֵצִים אַבְנֵי־שֹׁהַם
וּמִלּוּאִים אַבְנֵי־פוּךְ וְרִקְמָה
וְכֹל אֶבֶן יְקָרָה וְאַבְנֵי־שַׁיִשׁ
3 לָרֹב׃ וְעוֹד בִּרְצוֹתִי בְּבֵית
אֱלֹהַי יֶשׁ־לִי סְגֻלָּה זָהָב וָכָסֶף
נָתַתִּי לְבֵית־אֱלֹהַי לְמַעְלָה
מִכָּל־הֲכִינוֹתִי לְבֵית
4 הַקֹּדֶשׁ׃ שְׁלֹשֶׁת אֲלָפִים כִּכְּרֵי
זָהָב מִזְּהַב אוֹפִיר וְשִׁבְעַת
אֲלָפִים כִּכַּר־כֶּסֶף מְזֻקָּק
5 לָטוּחַ קִירוֹת הַבָּתִּים׃ לַזָּהָב
לַזָּהָב וְלַכֶּסֶף לַכֶּסֶף וּלְכָל־
מְלָאכָה בְּיַד חָרָשִׁים וּמִי
מִתְנַדֵּב לְמַלֹּאות יָדוֹ הַיּוֹם
לַיהוָה׃

5. ו' יתיר ו' על פי המסורה

leek, the green beryl; or, flesh-coloured with white streaks. For their use and of *stones to be set*, cf. Exod. xxviii. 17, 20. *glistering*. An old form for 'glistening.' The word *puch* occurs in Isa. liv. 11, *I will set thy stones in* fair colours.

of divers colours. The Hebrew *rikmah* probably signifies 'embroidered hangings' or 'variegated woven stuff.'

marble stones. i.e. white marble.

3. *that I have prepared for the holy house*. To encourage the chiefs of the people to contribute liberally, David announces that, in addition to the materials he had collected for the Temple from various sources, he is donating a substantial part of his private fortune, because he has set his affection on the house of God.

4. The royal gifts enumerated in this verse amount in value to thirteen million pounds sterling in gold and half a million pounds in silver.

Ophir. Identified with India or the south-east coast of Arabia. Its gold was famed for its pure quality.

wherewith to overlay. This refers only to the gold (cf. 2 Chron. iii. 4ff.). The silver was not used for this purpose.

the walls of the houses. viz. *the porch that was before* [*the house*], *the greater house* and *the most holy place* (2 Chron. iii. 4, 5, 8).

5. *to be made*. Not in the text.

to consecrate himself. lit. 'to fill his hand,' an idiom used also for con-

6. Then the princes of the fathers' houses, and the princes of the tribes of Israel, and the captains of thousands and of hundreds, with the rulers over the king's work, offered willingly; 7. and they gave for the service of the house of God of gold five thousand talents and ten thousand darics, and of silver ten thousand talents, and of brass eighteen thousand talents, and of iron a hundred thousand talents. 8. And they with whom precious stones were found gave them to the treasure of the house of the LORD, under the hand of Jehiel the Gershonite. 9. Then the people rejoiced, for that they offered willingly, because with a whole heart they offered willingly to the LORD; and David the king also rejoiced with great joy.

10. Wherefore David blessed the LORD before all the congregation; and David said: 'Blessed be Thou,

6 וַיִּתְנַדְּבוּ שָׂרֵי הָאָבוֹת וְשָׂרֵי |
שִׁבְטֵי יִשְׂרָאֵל וְשָׂרֵי הָאֲלָפִים
וְהַמֵּאוֹת וּלְשָׂרֵי מְלֶאכֶת
7 הַמֶּלֶךְ׃ וַיִּתְּנוּ לַעֲבוֹדַת בֵּית־
הָאֱלֹהִים זָהָב כִּכָּרִים
חֲמֵשֶׁת־אֲלָפִים וַאֲדַרְכֹנִים
רִבּוֹ וְכֶסֶף כִּכָּרִים עֲשֶׂרֶת
אֲלָפִים וּנְחֹשֶׁת רִבּוֹ וּשְׁמוֹנַת
אֲלָפִים כִּכָּרִים וּבַרְזֶל מֵאָה־
8 אֶלֶף כִּכָּרִים׃ וְהַנִּמְצָא אִתּוֹ
אֲבָנִים נָתְנוּ לְאוֹצַר בֵּית־
יְהוָה עַל יַד־יְחִיאֵל הַגֵּרְשֻׁנִּי׃
9 וַיִּשְׂמְחוּ הָעָם עַל־הִתְנַדְּבָם
כִּי בְּלֵב שָׁלֵם הִתְנַדְּבוּ לַיהוָה
וְגַם דָּוִיד הַמֶּלֶךְ שָׂמַח שִׂמְחָה
גְדוֹלָה׃
10 וַיְבָרֶךְ דָּוִיד אֶת־יְהוָה לְעֵינֵי
כָּל־הַקָּהָל וַיֹּאמֶר דָּוִיד

secration to the priesthood. They who contribute whole-heartedly to the erection of the Temple are comparable to the priests who minister in it.

6-9. The generous donations of the national leaders.

6. *the rulers over the king's work.* They are enumerated in xxvii. 25-31.

7. The value of the gold donated by the princes and captains amounts to above twenty-two million pounds sterling or about ten million; the estimate depends on the sense of the word translated *darics.* The daric was a Persian gold coin worth about twenty-two shillings. It is uncertain whether the Hebrew *adarkon* (again in Ezra viii. 27, *darkemon* in Ezra ii. 69; Neh. vii. 70f.) is the daric or, as A.V. translates, the 'dram' (drachma) which was worth less than ten shillings.

8. *gave them.* The pronoun is implied. *Jehiel the Gershonite.* Cf. xxiii. 8, and also xxvi. 21f. where his name is *Jehieli.*

9. *with a whole heart.* See on xxviii. 9.

10-19. David's blessing, thanksgiving and prayer. Verses 10-13 have been incorporated in the morning service of the Jewish liturgy (cf. ed. Singer, p. 33).

O LORD, the God of Israel our
father, for ever and ever. 11. Thine,
O LORD, is the greatness, and the
power, and the glory, and the
victory, and the majesty; for all that
is in the heaven and in the earth is
Thine; Thine is the kingdom,
O LORD, and Thou art exalted as
head above all. 12. Both riches and
honour come of Thee, and Thou
rulest over all; and in Thy hand is
power and might; and in Thy hand
it is to make great, and to give
strength unto all. 13. Now therefore, our God, we thank Thee, and
praise Thy glorious name. 14. But
who am I, and what is my people,
that we should be able to offer so
willingly after this sort? for all
things come of Thee, and of Thine
own have we given Thee. 15. For
we are strangers before Thee, and
sojourners, as all our fathers were:
our days on the earth are as a
shadow, and there is no abiding.
16. O LORD our God, all this store

בָּרוּךְ אַתָּה יְהוָה אֱלֹהֵי
יִשְׂרָאֵל אָבִינוּ מֵעוֹלָם וְעַד־
11 עוֹלָם׃ לְךָ יְהוָה הַגְּדֻלָּה
וְהַגְּבוּרָה וְהַתִּפְאֶרֶת וְהַנֵּצַח
וְהַהוֹד כִּי־כֹל בַּשָּׁמַיִם
וּבָאָרֶץ לְךָ יְהוָה הַמַּמְלָכָה
וְהַמִּתְנַשֵּׂא לְכֹל ׀ לְרֹאשׁ׃
12 וְהָעֹשֶׁר וְהַכָּבוֹד מִלְּפָנֶיךָ
וְאַתָּה מוֹשֵׁל בַּכֹּל וּבְיָדְךָ כֹּחַ
וּגְבוּרָה וּבְיָדְךָ לְגַדֵּל וּלְחַזֵּק
13 לַכֹּל׃ וְעַתָּה אֱלֹהֵינוּ מוֹדִים
אֲנַחְנוּ לָךְ וּמְהַלְלִים לְשֵׁם
14 תִּפְאַרְתֶּךָ׃ וְכִי מִי אֲנִי וּמִי
עַמִּי כִּי־נַעְצֹר כֹּחַ לְהִתְנַדֵּב
כָּזֹאת כִּי־מִמְּךָ הַכֹּל וּמִיָּדְךָ
15 נָתַנּוּ לָךְ׃ כִּי־גֵרִים אֲנַחְנוּ
לְפָנֶיךָ וְתוֹשָׁבִים כְּכָל־
אֲבוֹתֵינוּ כַּצֵּל יָמֵינוּ עַל־
16 הָאָרֶץ וְאֵין מִקְוֶה׃ יְהוָה

11. *is Thine.* Not in the text.

12. *come of Thee.* lit. 'from before Thee.'

14. *what is my people.* lit. 'who is,' etc.

that we should be able. lit. 'that we should close in (or, retain) strength.'

and of Thine own. lit. 'and of Thine hand.'

have we given Thee. All that David and his people have given is not their property. They have only returned to God what was originally His. Commenting on this verse, a rabbi exhorted, 'Give unto Him of what is His, seeing that thou and what thou hast are His' (Aboth iii. 8).

15. *strangers . . . sojourners.* As aliens are dependent upon the goodwill of the ruler of the land in which they dwell temporarily, so the people of Israel must rely upon God's bounty and protection. For the language, cf. Ps. xxxix. 13.

and there is no abiding. lit. 'and there is no hope' of escaping death.

16. *store.* lit. 'abundance.'

that we have prepared to build Thee a house for Thy holy name cometh of Thy hand, and is all Thine own. 17. I know also, my God, that Thou triest the heart, and hast pleasure in uprightness. As for me, in the uprightness of my heart I have willingly offered all these things; and now have I seen with joy Thy people, that are present here, offer willingly unto Thee. 18. O LORD, the God of Abraham, of Isaac, and of Israel, our fathers, keep this for ever, even the imagination of the thoughts of the heart of Thy people, and direct their heart unto Thee; 19. and give unto Solomon my son a whole heart, to keep Thy commandments, Thy testimonies, and Thy statutes, and to do all these things, and to build the palace, for which I have made provision.'

20. And David said to all the congregation: 'Now bless the LORD your God.' And all the congregation blessed the LORD, the God of their fathers, and bowed down their

אֱלֹהֵינוּ כֹּל הֶהָמוֹן הַזֶּה אֲשֶׁר
הֲכִינֹנוּ לִבְנוֹת־לְךָ בַיִת לְשֵׁם
קָדְשֶׁךָ מִיָּדְךָ הִיא וּלְךָ הַכֹּל׃
17 וְיָדַעְתִּי אֱלֹהַי כִּי אַתָּה בֹּחֵן
לֵבָב וּמֵישָׁרִים תִּרְצֶה אֲנִי
בְּיֹשֶׁר לְבָבִי הִתְנַדַּבְתִּי כָל־
אֵלֶּה וְעַתָּה עַמְּךָ הַנִּמְצְאוּ־
פֹה רָאִיתִי בְשִׂמְחָה
18 לְהִתְנַדֶּב־לָךְ׃ יְהוָֹה אֱלֹהֵי
אַבְרָהָם יִצְחָק וְיִשְׂרָאֵל
אֲבֹתֵינוּ שָׁמְרָה־זֹּאת לְעוֹלָם
לְיֵצֶר מַחְשְׁבוֹת לְבַב עַמֶּךָ
19 וְהָכֵן לְבָבָם אֵלֶיךָ׃ וְלִשְׁלֹמֹה
בְּנִי תֵּן לֵבָב שָׁלֵם לִשְׁמוֹר
מִצְוֹתֶיךָ עֵדְוֹתֶיךָ וְחֻקֶּיךָ
וְלַעֲשׂוֹת הַכֹּל וְלִבְנוֹת הַבִּירָה
אֲשֶׁר־הֲכִינוֹתִי׃
20 וַיֹּאמֶר דָּוִיד לְכָל־הַקָּהָל
בָּרְכוּ־נָא אֶת־יְהוָֹה אֱלֹהֵיכֶם
וַיְבָרְכוּ כָל־הַקָּהָל לַיהוָֹה
אֱלֹהֵי אֲבֹתֵיהֶם וַיִּקְּדוּ

v. 16. הוא ק׳

cometh of Thy hand. The verb is implied.

17. *offer willingly.* The Hebrew is lit. 'to offer willingly,' and a verb like 'and are desirous' is to be understood.

18. *keep this for ever,* etc. i.e. may they always be as generous and devoted as they are now.

even the imagination. The preposition *lamed* indicates the accusative; and *imagination* is in apposition to the preceding *this.*

direct their heart unto Thee. That it may respond to every call to serve Thee.

19. *the palace.* See on verse 1.

20-25. The people's homage and rejoicing and Solomon's accession to the throne.

heads, and prostrated themselves before the LORD, and before the king. 21. And they sacrificed sacrifices unto the LORD, and offered burnt-offerings unto the LORD, on the morrow after that day, even a thousand bullocks, a thousand rams, and a thousand lambs, with their drink-offerings, and sacrifices in abundance for all Israel; 22. and did eat and drink before the LORD on that day with great gladness. And they made Solomon the son of David king the second time, and anointed him unto the LORD to be prince, and Zadok to be priest. 23. Then Solomon sat on the throne of the LORD as king instead of David his father, and prospered; and all Israel hearkened to him. 24. And all the princes, and the mighty men, and all the sons likewise of king David, submitted themselves unto Solomon the king. 25. And the LORD magnified Solomon exceedingly in the sight of all Israel, and bestowed upon him such royal

וַיִּשְׁתַּחֲווּ לַיהוָה וְלַמֶּלֶךְ׃
21 וַיִּזְבְּחוּ לַיהוָה ׀ זְבָחִים וַיַּעֲלוּ
עֹלוֹת לַיהוָה לְמָחֳרַת הַיּוֹם
הַהוּא פָּרִים אֶלֶף אֵילִים אֶלֶף
כְּבָשִׂים אֶלֶף וְנִסְכֵּיהֶם
וּזְבָחִים לָרֹב לְכָל־יִשְׂרָאֵל׃
22 וַיֹּאכְלוּ וַיִּשְׁתּוּ לִפְנֵי יְהוָה בַּיּוֹם
הַהוּא בְּשִׂמְחָה גְדוֹלָה
וַיַּמְלִיכוּ שֵׁנִית לִשְׁלֹמֹה בֶן־
דָּוִיד וַיִּמְשְׁחוּ לַיהוָה לְנָגִיד
23 וּלְצָדוֹק לְכֹהֵן׃ וַיֵּשֶׁב שְׁלֹמֹה
עַל־כִּסֵּא יְהוָה ׀ לְמֶלֶךְ
תַּחַת־דָּוִיד אָבִיו וַיַּצְלַח
וַיִּשְׁמְעוּ אֵלָיו כָּל־יִשְׂרָאֵל׃
24 וְכָל־הַשָּׂרִים וְהַגִּבֹּרִים וְגַם
כָּל־בְּנֵי הַמֶּלֶךְ דָּוִיד נָתְנוּ יָד
25 תַּחַת שְׁלֹמֹה הַמֶּלֶךְ׃ וַיְגַדֵּל
יְהוָה אֶת־שְׁלֹמֹה לְמַעְלָה
לְעֵינֵי כָּל־יִשְׂרָאֵל וַיִּתֵּן עָלָיו

v. 23. פתח באתנח

20. *before the LORD, and before the king.* They worshipped God and paid homage to David.

21. *sacrifices in abundance for all Israel.* These were peace-offerings the flesh of which lay Israelites were allowed to eat.

22. *the second time.* The first occasion is briefly recorded in xxiii. 1 and, in fuller detail, in 1 Kings i. 32ff.

and Zadok to be priest. According to 1 Kings ii. 35, Solomon appointed Zadok in place of Abiathar whom he had deposed.

23. *the throne of the LORD.* See on xxviii. 5. Here the thought may be that He decrees who shall occupy the throne.

24. *all the sons.* This may be an allusion to Adonijah whose attempt to usurp the throne failed; he too submitted to Solomon (cf. 1 Kings i. 53).

submitted themselves. lit. 'gave a hand,' an indication of the acceptance of his kingship.

25. *exceedingly.* lit. 'above.'

any king before him in Israel. The

majesty as had not been on any king before him in Israel.

26. Now David the son of Jesse reigned over all Israel. 27. And the time that he reigned over Israel was forty years: seven years reigned he in Hebron, and thirty and three years reigned he in Jerusalem. 28. And he died in a good old age, full of days, riches, and honour; and Solomon his son reigned in his stead. 29. Now the acts of David the king, first and last, behold, they are written in the words of Samuel the seer, and in the words of Nathan the prophet, and in the words of Gad the seer; 30. with all his reign and his might, and the times that went over him, and over Israel, and over all the kingdoms of the countries.

הוֹד מַלְכוּת אֲשֶׁר לֹא־הָיָה
עַל־כָּל־מֶלֶךְ לְפָנָיו עַל־
יִשְׂרָאֵל׃
26 וְדָוִיד בֶּן־יִשָׁי מָלַךְ עַל־כָּל־
27 יִשְׂרָאֵל׃ וְהַיָּמִים אֲשֶׁר מָלַךְ
עַל־יִשְׂרָאֵל אַרְבָּעִים שָׁנָה
בְּחֶבְרוֹן מָלַךְ שֶׁבַע שָׁנִים
וּבִירוּשָׁלִַם מָלַךְ שְׁלֹשִׁים
28 וְשָׁלוֹשׁ׃ וַיָּמָת בְּשֵׂיבָה טוֹבָה
שְׂבַע יָמִים עֹשֶׁר וְכָבוֹד וַיִּמְלֹךְ
29 שְׁלֹמֹה בְנוֹ תַּחְתָּיו׃ וְדִבְרֵי
דָּוִיד הַמֶּלֶךְ הָרִאשֹׁנִים
וְהָאַחֲרֹנִים הִנָּם כְּתוּבִים עַל־
דִּבְרֵי שְׁמוּאֵל הָרֹאֶה וְעַל־
דִּבְרֵי נָתָן הַנָּבִיא וְעַל־דִּבְרֵי
30 גָּד הַחֹזֶה׃ עִם כָּל־מַלְכוּתוֹ
וּגְבוּרָתוֹ וְהָעִתִּים אֲשֶׁר עָבְרוּ
עָלָיו וְעַל־יִשְׂרָאֵל וְעַל כָּל־
מַמְלְכוֹת הָאֲרָצוֹת׃

v. 26. קמץ בז״ק

comparison is with Saul, Ishbosheth and David. Another possible translation is: 'which was not on any king *more than* on him' (the preposition *liphnē* is so used in Job xxxiv. 19). The comparison will then be with the kings who preceded and followed him.

26-30. Closing summary of David's reign.

27. This verse corresponds to 1 Kings ii. 11. Elsewhere in Chron. the seven years' reign in Hebron is passed over.

29. *first and last.* In the early and late periods of his reign.

Samuel the seer. Cf. 1 Sam. ix. 9, 19.

the words of Nathan . . . the words of Gad. These records are not extant and only extracts from them were embodied in this Book.

30. *the times.* i.e. the varying experiences.

all the kingdoms of the countries. With which David had had relations.

SECOND CHRONICLES

1 CHAPTER I א

1. AND Solomon the son of David
was strengthened in his kingdom,
and the LORD his God was with him,
and magnified him exceedingly.
2. And Solomon spoke unto all
Israel, to the captains of thousands
and of hundreds, and to the judges,
and to every prince in all Israel, the
heads of the fathers' houses. 3. So
Solomon, and all the congregation
with him, went to the high place
that was at Gibeon; for there was
the tent of meeting of God, which
Moses the servant of the LORD had
made in the wilderness. 4. But the
ark of God had David brought up
from Kiriath-jearim to the place
that David had prepared for it; for
he had pitched a tent for it at
Jerusalem. 5. Moreover the brazen

1 וַיִּתְחַזֵּק שְׁלֹמֹה בֶן־דָּוִיד עַל־
מַלְכוּתוֹ וַיהוָה אֱלֹהָיו עִמּוֹ
2 וַיְגַדְּלֵהוּ לְמָעְלָה׃ וַיֹּאמֶר
שְׁלֹמֹה לְכָל־יִשְׂרָאֵל לְשָׂרֵי
הָאֲלָפִים וְהַמֵּאוֹת וְלַשֹּׁפְטִים
וּלְכֹל נָשִׂיא לְכָל־יִשְׂרָאֵל
3 רָאשֵׁי הָאָבוֹת׃ וַיֵּלְכוּ שְׁלֹמֹה
וְכָל־הַקָּהָל עִמּוֹ לַבָּמָה אֲשֶׁר
בְּגִבְעוֹן כִּי־שָׁם הָיָה אֹהֶל
מוֹעֵד הָאֱלֹהִים אֲשֶׁר עָשָׂה
מֹשֶׁה עֶבֶד־יְהוָה בַּמִּדְבָּר׃
4 אֲבָל אֲרוֹן הָאֱלֹהִים הֶעֱלָה
דָוִיד מִקִּרְיַת יְעָרִים בַּהֵכִין
לוֹ דָּוִיד כִּי נָטָה־לוֹ אֹהֶל
5 בִּירוּשָׁלִָם׃ וּמִזְבַּח הַנְּחֹשֶׁת

CHAPTERS I-IX

THE REIGN OF SOLOMON

CHAPTER I

1-6 (cf. I Kings iii. 4). The assembly at Gibeon and the sacrifices offered there.

1. *was strengthened.* Or, 'strengthened himself'; the allusion may be to the suppression of the persons who threatened the stability of his throne (cf. I Kings ii. 46).

in his kingdom. lit. 'upon his kingdom.'

magnified him exceedingly. Cf. I Chron. xxix. 25.

2. *Solomon spoke unto all Israel*, etc. He requested them to accompany him on his pilgrimage to the high place at Gibeon where the tabernacle of Moses stood (verse 3), for the religious ceremony which was to inaugurate his reign.

3. *Gibeon.* See on I Chron. viii. 29.

the tent of meeting. See on I Chron. xvi. 39.

4. *Kiriath-jearim.* See on I Chron. xiii. 6.

to the place. Not in the text.

he had pitched a tent for it. Cf. I Chron. xv. 1.

altar, that Bezalel the son of Uri, the son of Hur, had made, had been put before the tabernacle of the LORD; and Solomon and the congregation sought unto it. 6. And Solomon offered there, upon the brazen altar before the LORD, which was at the tent of meeting, he offered a thousand burnt-offerings upon it.

7. In that night did God appear unto Solomon, and said unto him: 'Ask what I shall give thee.' 8. And Solomon said unto God: 'Thou hast shown great kindness unto David my father, and hast made me king in his stead. 9. Now, O LORD God, let Thy promise unto David my father be established; for Thou hast made me king over a people like the dust of the earth in multitude. 10. Give me now wisdom and knowledge, that I may go out and

אֲשֶׁר עָשָׂה בְּצַלְאֵל בֶּן־אוּרִי
בֶן־חוּר שָׂם לִפְנֵי מִשְׁכַּן יְהוָה
וַיִּדְרְשֵׁהוּ שְׁלֹמֹה וְהַקָּהָל׃
6 וַיַּעַל שְׁלֹמֹה שָׁם עַל־מִזְבַּח
הַנְּחֹשֶׁת לִפְנֵי יְהוָה אֲשֶׁר
לְאֹהֶל מוֹעֵד וַיַּעַל עָלָיו עֹלוֹת
אָלֶף׃
7 בַּלַּיְלָה הַהוּא נִרְאָה אֱלֹהִים
לִשְׁלֹמֹה וַיֹּאמֶר לוֹ שְׁאַל מָה
8 אֶתֶּן־לָךְ׃ וַיֹּאמֶר שְׁלֹמֹה
לֵאלֹהִים אַתָּה עָשִׂיתָ עִם־
דָּוִיד אָבִי חֶסֶד גָּדוֹל
9 וְהִמְלַכְתַּנִי תַּחְתָּיו׃ עַתָּה
יְהוָה אֱלֹהִים יֵאָמֵן דְּבָרְךָ
עִם דָּוִיד אָבִי כִּי אַתָּה
הִמְלַכְתַּנִי עַל־עַם רַב כַּעֲפַר
10 הָאָרֶץ׃ עַתָּה חָכְמָה וּמַדָּע
תֶּן־לִי וְאֵצְאָה לִפְנֵי הָעָם־

5. *Bezalel . . . had made.* Cf. Exod. xxxviii. 1ff.

sought unto it. viz. the brazen altar. Another rendering may be 'inquired of Him.'

6. *upon the brazen altar.* 1 Kings iii. 4 calls it *the great high place*, a description which was obnoxious to the Chronicler.

7-13 (corresponding to 1 Kings iii. 5-15). Solomon's vision.

7. *in that night.* The night following the sacrifices.

did God appear. In 1 Kings iii. 5: *the LORD appeared to Solomon in a dream.*

ask what I shall give thee. i.e. I will grant thy request, whatever it be.

9. *Thy promise.* The promise is probably that made in 1 Chron. xxii. 9f., *behold a son shall be born*, etc. The description of himself by Solomon in 1 Kings iii. 7, *I am but a little child*, is omitted here.

10. *give me now wisdom and knowledge.* In 1 Kings iii. 9: *an understanding heart.*

come in before this people; for who can judge this Thy people, that is so great?' 11. And God said to Solomon: 'Because this was in thy heart, and thou hast not asked riches, wealth, or honour, nor the life of them that hate thee, neither yet hast asked long life, but hast asked wisdom and knowledge for thyself, that thou mayest judge My people, over whom I have made thee king; 12. wisdom and knowledge is granted unto thee, and I will give thee riches, and wealth, and honour, such as none of the kings have had that have been before thee, neither shall there any after thee have the like.' 13. So Solomon came [from his journey] to the high place that was at Gibeon, from before the tent of meeting, unto Jerusalem; and he reigned over Israel.

14. And Solomon gathered chariots and horsemen; and he had a thousand and four hundred chariots, and twelve thousand horse-

הַזֶּה וְאָבוֹאָה כִּי־מִי יִשְׁפֹּט
11 אֶת־עַמְּךָ הַזֶּה הַגָּדוֹל׃ וַיֹּאמֶר
אֱלֹהִים לִשְׁלֹמֹה יַעַן אֲשֶׁר
הָיְתָה זֹאת עִם־לְבָבֶךָ וְלֹא
שָׁאַלְתָּ עֹשֶׁר נְכָסִים וְכָבוֹד
וְאֵת נֶפֶשׁ שֹׂנְאֶיךָ וְגַם־יָמִים
רַבִּים לֹא שָׁאָלְתָּ וַתִּשְׁאַל־
לְךָ חָכְמָה וּמַדָּע אֲשֶׁר תִּשְׁפּוֹט
אֶת־עַמִּי אֲשֶׁר הִמְלַכְתִּיךָ
12 עָלָיו׃ הַחָכְמָה וְהַמַּדָּע נָתוּן
לָךְ וְעֹשֶׁר וּנְכָסִים וְכָבוֹד
אֶתֶּן־לָךְ אֲשֶׁר ׀ לֹא־הָיָה כֵן
לַמְּלָכִים אֲשֶׁר לְפָנֶיךָ
13 וְאַחֲרֶיךָ לֹא יִהְיֶה־כֵּן׃ וַיָּבֹא
שְׁלֹמֹה לַבָּמָה אֲשֶׁר־בְּגִבְעוֹן
יְרוּשָׁלִַם מִלִּפְנֵי אֹהֶל מוֹעֵד
וַיִּמְלֹךְ עַל־יִשְׂרָאֵל׃
14 וַיֶּאֱסֹף שְׁלֹמֹה רֶכֶב וּפָרָשִׁים
וַיְהִי־לוֹ אֶלֶף וְאַרְבַּע־מֵאוֹת
רֶכֶב וּשְׁנֵים־עָשָׂר אֶלֶף

go out and come in. i.e. carry out all the duties of a leader.

judge. The Hebrew verb implies not only dispensing justice, but also leading in peace and war.

13. *Solomon came . . . to the high place.* Others understand the preposition *lamed* (which usually has the sense of 'to') to mean here, as in some other passages, 'from' (so R. Jonah quoted with approval by the Be'ur). It was so understood or read by the LXX and Vulgate. This rendering avoids the necessity to insert the phrase *from his journey* which has no corresponding words in the text.

14-17 (corresponding to 1 Kings x. 26-29). Solomon's fabulous wealth; his horses and chariots.

14. *gathered chariots and horsemen.* The Torah forbade a king to gather many horses (cf. Deut. xvii. 16).

men, that he placed in the chariot cities, and with the king at Jerusalem. 15. And the king made silver and gold to be in Jerusalem as stones, and cedars made he to be as the sycomore-trees that are in the Lowland, for abundance. 16. And the horses which Solomon had were brought out of Egypt; also out of Keve, the king's merchants buying them of the men of Keve at a price. 17. And they fetched up, and brought out of Egypt a chariot for six hundred shekels of silver, and a horse for a hundred and fifty; and so for all the kings of the Hittites, and the kings of Aram, did they bring them out by their means.

18. Now Solomon purposed to build a house for the name of the LORD, and a house for his kingdom.

פָּרָשִׁים וַיַּנִּיחֵם בְּעָרֵי הָרֶכֶב
15 וְעִם־הַמֶּלֶךְ בִּירוּשָׁלָם׃ וַיִּתֵּן
הַמֶּלֶךְ אֶת־הַכֶּסֶף וְאֶת־
הַזָּהָב בִּירוּשָׁלַם כָּאֲבָנִים
וְאֵת־הָאֲרָזִים נָתַן כַּשִּׁקְמִים
16 אֲשֶׁר־בַּשְּׁפֵלָה לָרֹב׃ וּמוֹצָא
הַסּוּסִים אֲשֶׁר לִשְׁלֹמֹה
מִמִּצְרָיִם וּמִקְוֵא סֹחֲרֵי הַמֶּלֶךְ
17 מִקְוֵא יִקְחוּ בִּמְחִיר׃ וַיַּעֲלוּ
וַיּוֹצִיאוּ מִמִּצְרַיִם מֶרְכָּבָה
בְּשֵׁשׁ מֵאוֹת כֶּסֶף וְסוּס
בַּחֲמִשִּׁים וּמֵאָה וְכֵן לְכָל־
מַלְכֵי הַחִתִּים וּמַלְכֵי אֲרָם
בְּיָדָם יוֹצִיאוּ׃
18 וַיֹּאמֶר שְׁלֹמֹה לִבְנוֹת בַּיִת
לְשֵׁם יְהוָה וּבַיִת לְמַלְכוּתוֹ׃

v. 16. א׳ במקום ה׳ v. 16. א׳ במקום ה׳

the chariot cities. As the greater part of Canaan was hilly and unsuitable for the movement of chariots, these cities must have been situated in the valley of Esdraelon, in the maritime plain which bordered on the Mediterranean and in the Jordan valley.

15. *the sycomore-trees . . . Lowland.* See on I Chron. xxvii. 28.

16. *were brought out of Egypt.* Which was a market for horses reared elsewhere, possibly in Asia Minor and Armenia. Egypt was an agricultural country and lacked spacious breeding grounds required for that purpose.

Keve. The name for Cilicia in the Assyrian inscriptions.

them of the men of Keve. The first four words are implied.

17. *shekels.* Not in the text.

the Hittites. The ancient Hittite empire lay between the rivers Orontes (in Syria) and the Euphrates, though small colonies of Hittites settled in Canaan. In the days of Solomon the Hittite empire was at the height of its power, but in the eighth century B.C.E. it was finally subdued by the Assyrians and disappeared from history.

by their means. By means of Solomon's merchants. The kings of the Hittites and of Aram purchased their horses and chariots through these merchants.

18. Solomon's determination to construct the Temple and other buildings.

purposed. lit. 'said' in his heart.

a house for his kingdom. Cf. I Kings vii. 1ff.

2 CHAPTER II ב

1. And Solomon counted out threescore and ten thousand men to bear burdens, and fourscore thousand men that were hewers in the mountains, and three thousand and six hundred to oversee them. 2. And Solomon sent to Huram the king of Tyre, saying: 'As thou didst deal with David my father, and didst send him cedars to build him a house to dwell therein [, even so deal with me]. 3. Behold, I am about to build a house for the name of the Lord my God, to dedicate it to Him, and to burn before Him incense of sweet spices, and for the continual showbread, and for the burnt-offerings morning and evening, on the sabbaths, and on the new moons, and on the appointed seasons of the Lord our God. This is an

1 וַיִּסְפֹּר שְׁלֹמֹה שִׁבְעִים אֶלֶף
אִישׁ סַבָּל וּשְׁמוֹנִים אֶלֶף אִישׁ
חֹצֵב בָּהָר וּמְנַצְּחִים עֲלֵיהֶם
שְׁלֹשֶׁת אֲלָפִים וְשֵׁשׁ מֵאוֹת׃
2 וַיִּשְׁלַח שְׁלֹמֹה אֶל־חוּרָם
מֶלֶךְ־צֹר לֵאמֹר כַּאֲשֶׁר
עָשִׂיתָ עִם־דָּוִיד אָבִי
וַתִּשְׁלַח־לוֹ אֲרָזִים לִבְנוֹת לוֹ
3 בַּיִת לָשֶׁבֶת בּוֹ׃ הִנֵּה אֲנִי
בוֹנֶה־בַּיִת לְשֵׁם ׀ יְהוָה אֱלֹהָי
לְהַקְדִּישׁ לוֹ לְהַקְטִיר לְפָנָיו
קְטֹרֶת־סַמִּים וּמַעֲרֶכֶת תָּמִיד
וְעֹלוֹת לַבֹּקֶר וְלָעֶרֶב
לַשַּׁבָּתוֹת וְלֶחֳדָשִׁים וּלְמוֹעֲדֵי
יְהוָה אֱלֹהֵינוּ לְעוֹלָם זֹאת

v. 3. קמץ בלא אס״ף

CHAPTER II

1 (corresponding to 1 Kings v. 29f.). Solomon's levy of workmen and overseers.

hewers in the mountains. The Hebrew has the singular. The mountains are assumed to be the hill-country of Canaan which yields a fine quality of limestone. Soft when quarried and hardening gradually under exposure, it was eminently suitable for building purposes.

three thousand and six hundred. The number here and in verse 17, which exceeds that given in 1 Kings v. 30 by three hundred, probably includes superior officers who exercised control over the overseers.

2-9 (corresponding to 1 Kings v. 16-20). Solomon's proposal to Huram.

2. *sent.* A letter, copies of which as well as that of Huram (verses 10-15), according to Josephus (*Antiquities* VIII. ii. 8), were preserved in the Jewish and Tyrian records.

Huram. Or, *Hiram* and *Hirom* (1 Kings v. 16, 24). He ascended the throne of Tyre in 968 B.C.E., three years after Solomon's accession to the throne of Israel.

didst send him cedars. Cf. 1 Chron. xiv. 1.

3. *the continual showbread.* Cf. 1 Chron. ix. 32.

is an ordinance. Not in the text.

ordinance for ever to Israel. 4. And the house which I build is great; for great is our God above all gods. 5. But who is able to build Him a house, seeing the heaven and the heaven of heavens cannot contain Him? who am I then, that I should build Him a house, save only to offer before Him? 6. Now therefore send me a man skilful to work in gold, and in silver, and in brass, and in iron, and in purple, and crimson, and blue, and that hath skill to grave all manner of gravings, to be with the skilful men that are with me in Judah and in Jerusalem, whom David my father did provide. 7. Send me also cedar-trees, cypress-trees, and sandal-wood, out of Lebanon; for I know that thy servants have skill to cut timber in Lebanon; and, behold, my servants shall be with thy servants, 8. even to prepare me timber in abundance;

4 עַל־יִשְׂרָאֵל׃ וְהַבַּיִת אֲשֶׁר־
אֲנִי בוֹנֶה גָּדוֹל כִּי־גָדוֹל
5 אֱלֹהֵינוּ מִכָּל־הָאֱלֹהִים׃ וּמִי
יַעֲצָר־כֹּחַ לִבְנוֹת־לוֹ בַיִת כִּי
הַשָּׁמַיִם וּשְׁמֵי הַשָּׁמַיִם לֹא
יְכַלְכְּלֻהוּ וּמִי אֲנִי אֲשֶׁר
אֶבְנֶה־לּוֹ בַיִת כִּי אִם־
6 לְהַקְטִיר לְפָנָיו׃ וְעַתָּה
שְׁלַח־לִי אִישׁ־חָכָם לַעֲשׂוֹת
בַּזָּהָב וּבַכֶּסֶף וּבַנְּחֹשֶׁת
וּבַבַּרְזֶל וּבָאַרְגְּוָן וְכַרְמִיל
וּתְכֵלֶת וְיֹדֵעַ לְפַתֵּחַ פִּתּוּחִים
עִם־הַחֲכָמִים אֲשֶׁר עִמִּי
בִּיהוּדָה וּבִירוּשָׁלִַם אֲשֶׁר
7 הֵכִין דָּוִיד אָבִי׃ וּשְׁלַח־לִי
עֲצֵי אֲרָזִים בְּרוֹשִׁים
וְאַלְגּוּמִּים מֵהַלְּבָנוֹן כִּי אֲנִי
יָדַעְתִּי אֲשֶׁר עֲבָדֶיךָ יוֹדְעִים
לִכְרוֹת עֲצֵי לְבָנוֹן וְהִנֵּה עֲבָדַי
8 עִם־עֲבָדֶיךָ׃ וּלְהָכִין לִי

v. 7. דגש אחר שורק

4. *great is our God*, etc. A similar expression is found in Exod. xviii. 11.

5. *who is able.* See on 1 Chron. xxix. 14.

seeing the heaven, etc. Cf. vi. 18.

who am I then . . . offer before Him? It is impossible for a human being to provide a habitation for God Who is omnipresent. Solomon declares that he is not so presumptuous as to think that he can do it. The Temple he intends to build is to serve only as a place for worship, to offer sacrifices and burn incense before God.

6. *David . . . did provide.* Cf. 1 Chron. xxii. 15.

7. *cypress-trees.* Another rendering is 'fir-trees.'

sandal-wood. Or, 'ebony.' Here the noun is *algumim* but in 1 Kings x. 11f. *almugim*, where it is stated that the wood was imported from Ophir.

for the house which I am about to build shall be great and wonderful. 9. And, behold, I will give to thy servants, the hewers that cut timber, twenty thousand measures of beaten wheat, and twenty thousand measures of barley, and twenty thousand baths of wine, and twenty thousand baths of oil.'

10. Then Huram the king of Tyre answered in writing, which he sent to Solomon: 'Because the LORD loveth His people, He hath made thee king over them.' 11. Huram said moreover: 'Blessed be the LORD, the God of Israel, that made heaven and earth, who hath given to David the king a wise son, endued with discretion and understanding, that should build a house for the LORD, and a house for his kingdom. 12. And now I have sent a skilful man, endued with understanding, even Huram my master craftsman, 13. the son of a woman of the daughters of Dan, and his father

עֵצִים לָרֹב כִּי הַבַּיִת אֲשֶׁר־
9 אֲנִי בוֹנֶה גָּדוֹל וְהַפְלֵא׃ וְהִנֵּה
לַחֹטְבִים לְכֹרְתֵי הָעֵצִים
נָתַתִּי חִטִּים ׀ מַכּוֹת לַעֲבָדֶיךָ
כֹּרִים עֶשְׂרִים אֶלֶף וּשְׂעֹרִים
כֹּרִים עֶשְׂרִים אָלֶף וְיַיִן בַּתִּים
עֶשְׂרִים אֶלֶף וְשֶׁמֶן בַּתִּים
עֶשְׂרִים אָלֶף׃
10 וַיֹּאמֶר חוּרָם מֶלֶךְ־צֹר
בִּכְתָב וַיִּשְׁלַח אֶל־שְׁלֹמֹה
בְּאַהֲבַת יְהוָה אֶת־עַמּוֹ נְתָנְךָ
11 עֲלֵיהֶם מֶלֶךְ׃ וַיֹּאמֶר חוּרָם
בָּרוּךְ יְהוָה אֱלֹהֵי יִשְׂרָאֵל
אֲשֶׁר עָשָׂה אֶת־הַשָּׁמַיִם וְאֶת־
הָאָרֶץ אֲשֶׁר נָתַן לְדָוִיד הַמֶּלֶךְ
בֵּן חָכָם יוֹדֵעַ שֵׂכֶל וּבִינָה
אֲשֶׁר יִבְנֶה־בַּיִת לַיהוָה וּבַיִת
12 לְמַלְכוּתוֹ׃ וְעַתָּה שָׁלַחְתִּי
אִישׁ־חָכָם יוֹדֵעַ בִּינָה לְחוּרָם
13 אָבִי׃ בֶּן־אִשָּׁה מִן־בְּנוֹת דָּן

9. *I will give.* lit. 'I gave'; the use of the perfect indicates determination or intention to give.

measures. The Hebrew is *korim*, a *kor* being about eleven bushels.

beaten wheat. The phrase occurs only here; in 1 Kings v. 25: *wheat for food.*

barley . . . wine. These are not mentioned in Kings.

twenty thousand baths of oil. In Kings: *twenty measures of beaten oil*, but the LXX and Josephus (*Antiquities* VIII. ii. 9) read there the same quantity as here. The *bath* was a tenth of a *kor*, a little more than eight gallons.

10-15 (corresponding to 1 Kings v. 21-23). Huram accedes to Solomon's request.

12. *my master craftsman.* The Hebrew *abi* is literally 'my father'; but the noun *ab* also signifies 'chief, master.'

13. *the son of a woman . . . of Dan.* In

was a man of Tyre, skilful to work in gold, and in silver, in brass, in iron, in stone, and in timber, in purple, in blue, and in fine linen, and in crimson; also to grave any manner of graving, and to devise any device; to do whatever may be set before him, with thy skilful men, and with the skilful men of my lord David thy father. 14. Now therefore the wheat and the barley, the oil and the wine, which my lord hath spoken of, let him send unto his servants; 15. and we will cut wood out of Lebanon, as much as thou shalt need; and we will bring it to thee in floats by sea to Joppa; and thou shalt carry it up to Jerusalem.'

16. And Solomon numbered all the strangers that were in the land of Israel, after the numbering wherewith David his father had numbered them; and they were found a hundred and fifty thousand and three thousand and six hundred. 17. And he set threescore and ten thousand of them to bear burdens,

וְאָבִ֣יו אִישׁ־צֹרִ֗י יוֹדֵ֡עַ לַעֲשׂ֣וֹת
בַּזָּהָב֩ וּבַכֶּ֨סֶף בַּנְּחֹ֜שֶׁת בַּבַּרְזֶ֗ל
בָּאֲבָנִ֣ים וּבָעֵצִ֡ים בָּֽאַרְגָּמָ֣ן
בַּתְּכֵ֜לֶת וּבַבּ֣וּץ וּבַכַּרְמִ֗יל
וּלְפַתֵּ֙חַ֙ כָּל־פִּתּ֔וּחַ וְלַחְשֹׁ֖ב
כָּל־מַחֲשָׁ֑בֶת אֲשֶׁ֣ר יִנָּֽתֶן־ל֔וֹ
עִם־חֲכָמֶ֔יךָ וְחַכְמֵ֕י אֲדֹנִ֖י
14 דָּוִ֥יד אָבִֽיךָ׃ וְעַתָּ֗ה הַחִטִּ֤ים
וְהַשְּׂעֹרִים֙ הַשֶּׁ֣מֶן וְהַיַּ֔יִן אֲשֶׁר֙
אָמַ֣ר אֲדֹנִ֔י יִשְׁלַ֖ח לַעֲבָדָֽיו׃
15 וַאֲנַ֜חְנוּ נִכְרֹ֣ת עֵצִ֗ים מִן־
הַלְּבָנוֹן֙ כְּכָל־צָרְכֶּ֔ךָ וּנְבִיאֵ֥ם
לְךָ֛ רַפְסֹד֖וֹת עַל־יָ֣ם יָפ֑וֹ
וְאַתָּ֛ה תַּעֲלֶ֥ה אֹתָ֖ם יְרוּשָׁלִָֽם׃
16 וַיִּסְפֹּ֣ר שְׁלֹמֹ֗ה כָּל־הָאֲנָשִׁ֤ים
הַגֵּירִים֙ אֲשֶׁ֣ר בְּאֶ֣רֶץ יִשְׂרָאֵ֔ל
אַחֲרֵ֣י הַסְּפָ֔ר אֲשֶׁ֥ר סְפָרָ֖ם
דָּוִ֣יד אָבִ֑יו וַיִּמָּצְא֗וּ מֵאָ֨ה
וַחֲמִשִּׁ֥ים אֶ֙לֶף֙ וּשְׁלֹ֣שֶׁת אֲלָפִ֔ים
17 וְשֵׁ֖שׁ מֵאֽוֹת׃ וַיַּ֨עַשׂ מֵהֶ֜ם
שִׁבְעִ֨ים אֶ֜לֶף סַבָּ֗ל וּשְׁמֹנִ֥ים

1 Kings vii. 14: *he was the son of a widow of the tribe of Naphtali.* His mother was of the tribe of Dan while his father, and therefore he himself, was of the tribe of Naphtali.

a man of Tyre. i.e. he lived in Tyre while in the service of Huram.

14. *unto his servants.* Huram calls his men the servants of Solomon as a mark of respect. He similarly describes David as *my lord* in verse 13.

15. *Joppa.* The modern Jaffa, which was the port of Jerusalem until superseded by the new city Tel-Aviv.

16f. The alien porters and hewers and their overseers.

16. *David . . . had numbered them.* As recorded in 1 Chron. xxii. 2.

and fourscore thousand to be hewers in the mountains, and three thousand and six hundred overseers to set the people at work.

אֶלֶף חֹצֵב בָּהָר וּשְׁלֹשֶׁת
אֲלָפִים וְשֵׁשׁ מֵאוֹת מְנַצְּחִים
לְהַעֲבִיד אֶת־הָעָם׃

3 CHAPTER III ג

1. Then Solomon began to build the house of the LORD at Jerusalem in mount Moriah, where [the LORD] appeared unto David his father; for which provision had been made in the Place of David, in the threshing-floor of Ornan the Jebusite. 2. And he began to build in the second day of the second month, in the fourth year of his reign. 3. Now these are the foundations which Solomon laid for the building of the house of God. The length by cubits after the ancient measure was threescore cubits, and the breadth twenty cubits. 4. And the porch that was before [the house], the length of it,

1 וַיָּחֶל שְׁלֹמֹה לִבְנוֹת אֶת־
בֵּית־יְהוָה בִּירוּשָׁלִַם בְּהַר
הַמּוֹרִיָּה אֲשֶׁר נִרְאָה לְדָוִיד
אָבִיהוּ אֲשֶׁר הֵכִין בִּמְקוֹם
דָּוִיד בְּגֹרֶן אָרְנָן הַיְבוּסִי׃
2 וַיָּחֶל לִבְנוֹת בַּחֹדֶשׁ הַשֵּׁנִי בַּשֵּׁנִי
בִּשְׁנַת אַרְבַּע לְמַלְכוּתוֹ׃
3 וְאֵלֶּה הוּסַד שְׁלֹמֹה לִבְנוֹת
אֶת־בֵּית הָאֱלֹהִים הָאֹרֶךְ
אַמּוֹת בַּמִּדָּה הָרִאשׁוֹנָה אַמּוֹת
שִׁשִּׁים וְרֹחַב אַמּוֹת עֶשְׂרִים׃
4 וְהָאוּלָם אֲשֶׁר עַל־פְּנֵי הָאֹרֶךְ

17. The preceding verse shows that the porters and hewers mentioned here, which is a repetition of verse 1, belonged to the alien population that lived in Solomon's kingdom.

CHAPTER III

1f. (corresponding to 1 Kings vi. 1). The place of the Temple and the date of its building.

1. *mount Moriah.* Cf. Gen. xxii. 2 where Abraham is commanded to offer Isaac on a mountain in the land of Moriah. The name occurs nowhere else in the Bible.

appeared. God's Presence was indicated by the fire which came down from heaven on the altar built by David (1 Chron. xxi. 26).

threshing-floor of Ornan. Cf. 1 Chron. xxi. 15ff.

2. *in the second day*, etc. 1 Kings vi. 1 records that it took place in the *four hundred and eightieth year* after the exodus from Egypt, *in the month Ziv, which is the second month.*

3-7 (corresponding to 1 Kings vi. 2f., 15, 21, 29f.). The measurements of the Temple and the porch.

3. *after the ancient measure.* i.e. the 'sacred' cubit which was used by Moses in the construction of the tabernacle.

according to the breadth of the house, was twenty cubits, and the height a hundred and twenty; and he overlaid it within with pure gold. 5. And the greater house he covered with cypress-wood, which he overlaid with fine gold, and wrought thereon palm-trees and chains. 6. And he garnished the house with precious stones for beauty; and the gold was gold of Parvaim. 7. He overlaid also the house, the beams, the thresholds, and the walls thereof, and the doors thereof, with gold; and graved cherubim on the walls.

8. And he made the most holy place; the length thereof, according

עַל־פְּנֵי רֹחַב־הַבַּיִת אַמּוֹת
עֶשְׂרִים וְהַגֹּבַהּ מֵאָה וְעֶשְׂרִים
וַיְצַפֵּהוּ מִפְּנִימָה זָהָב טָהוֹר׃
5 וְאֵת ׀ הַבַּיִת הַגָּדוֹל חִפָּה עֵץ
בְּרוֹשִׁים וַיְחַפֵּהוּ זָהָב טוֹב
וַיַּעַל עָלָיו תִּמֹרִים וְשַׁרְשְׁרֹת׃
6 וַיְצַף אֶת־הַבַּיִת אֶבֶן יְקָרָה
לְתִפְאָרֶת וְהַזָּהָב זְהַב פַּרְוָיִם׃
7 וַיְחַף אֶת־הַבַּיִת הַקֹּרוֹת
הַסִּפִּים וְקִירוֹתָיו וְדַלְתוֹתָיו
זָהָב וּפִתַּח כְּרוּבִים עַל־
הַקִּירוֹת׃
8 וַיַּעַשׂ אֶת־בֵּית־קֹדֶשׁ

According to Rabbinical tradition, it was six handbreadths in length whereas the secular cubit measured five. A handbreadth was about three and a half inches. The area covered by the building was therefore 105 feet by 35 feet.

4. *the height a hundred and twenty.* The height of the *porch* is not stated in 1 Kings vi. 3 but that of the Temple was thirty cubits (1 Kings vi. 2). The porch (which was a hundred cubits high in Herod's Temple) extended in the form of a tower ninety cubits above the building, and, in the opinion of Jewish commentators, accommodated the *upper rooms thereof* mentioned in 1 Chron. xxviii. 11.

5. *the greater house.* i.e. the *hechal*, between the porch and the *debir* or Holy of Holies. According to 1 Kings vi. 17, it was forty cubits long, the breadth being presumably the same as of the porch, viz. twenty cubits.

and chains. Which linked the palm-trees. In 1 Kings vi. 29 the carvings were *figures of cherubim and palm-trees and open flowers.*

6. *he garnished the house,* etc. Not in Kings.

Parvaim. Identified with the gold mine of Sak el-Farwain or with Farma, both in the Yemen.

7. *cherubim.* See on verse 5 and cf. Ezek. xli. 18. On the cherubim in the Holy of Holies and the figures wrought on the veil which hung between it and the *hechal*, cf. verses 10-14; Exod. xxv. 18ff., xxvi. 31. They symbolized the Divine Presence.

8-13. The Holy of Holies and the cherubim.

8. *the most holy place.* lit. 'the house of the Holy of Holies'; it is also known as the *debir*, lit. 'the hinder part,' because it

to the breadth of the house, was twenty cubits, and the breadth thereof twenty cubits; and he overlaid it with fine gold, amounting to six hundred talents. 9. And the weight of the nails was fifty shekels of gold. And he overlaid the upper chambers with gold.

10. And in the most holy place he made two cherubim of image work; and they overlaid them with gold. 11. And the wings of the cherubim were twenty cubits long: the wing of the one cherub was five cubits, reaching to the wall of the house; and the other wing was likewise five cubits, reaching to the wing of the other cherub. 12. And the wing of the other cherub was five cubits, reaching to the wall of the house and the other wing was five cubits also, joining to the wing of the other cherub. 13. The wings of these cherubim spread themselves forth twenty cubits; and they stood on

הַקֳּדָשִׁים אָרְכּוֹ עַל־פְּנֵי
רֹחַב־הַבַּיִת אַמּוֹת עֶשְׂרִים
וְרָחְבּוֹ אַמּוֹת עֶשְׂרִים וַיְחַפֵּהוּ
זָהָב טוֹב לְכִכָּרִים שֵׁשׁ מֵאוֹת׃
9 וּמִשְׁקָל לְמִסְמְרוֹת לִשְׁקָלִים
חֲמִשִּׁים זָהָב וְהָעֲלִיּוֹת חִפָּה
זָהָב׃
10 וַיַּעַשׂ בְּבֵית־קֹדֶשׁ הַקֳּדָשִׁים
כְּרוּבִים שְׁנַיִם מַעֲשֵׂה
צַעֲצֻעִים וַיְצַפּוּ אֹתָם זָהָב׃
11 וְכַנְפֵי הַכְּרוּבִים אָרְכָּם אַמּוֹת
עֶשְׂרִים כְּנַף הָאֶחָד לְאַמּוֹת
חָמֵשׁ מַגַּעַת לְקִיר הַבַּיִת
וְהַכָּנָף הָאַחֶרֶת אַמּוֹת חָמֵשׁ
מַגִּיעַ לִכְנַף הַכְּרוּב הָאַחֵר׃
12 וּכְנַף הַכְּרוּב הָאֶחָד אַמּוֹת
חָמֵשׁ מַגִּיעַ לְקִיר הַבָּיִת
וְהַכָּנָף הָאַחֶרֶת אַמּוֹת חָמֵשׁ
דְּבֵקָה לִכְנַף הַכְּרוּב הָאַחֵר׃
13 כַּנְפֵי הַכְּרוּבִים הָאֵלֶּה
פֹּרְשִׂים אַמּוֹת עֶשְׂרִים וְהֵם

was located in the innermost part of the building.

9. *the nails.* Used for fastening the gold sheets to the walls.

the upper chambers. Small rooms for storage situated between the walls.

10. *of image work.* In 1 Kings vi. 23: *of olive-wood,* the two accounts being complementary. The word *tsa'atsu'im* does not occur again in the Bible, and is derived from a root which in Arabic means 'to fashion.'

11. *of the one cherub.* The last word is implied.

13. *spread . . . twenty cubits.* This was their combined length which extended across the entire breadth of the chamber.

inward. lit. 'towards the house'; not towards each other. They formed a barrier as though to protect the place their feet, and their faces were inward.

14. And he made the veil of blue, and purple, and crimson, and fine linen, and wrought cherubim thereon.

15. Also he made before the house two pillars of thirty and five cubits high, and the capital that was on the top of each of them was five cubits.

16. And he made chains in the Sanctuary, and put them on the tops of the pillars; and he made a hundred pomegranates, and put them on the chains. 17. And he set up the pillars before the temple, one on the right hand, and the other on the left; and called the name of that on the right hand Jachin, and the name of that on the left Boaz.

עֹמְדִים עַל־רַגְלֵיהֶם וּפְנֵיהֶם
לַבָּיִת׃
14 וַיַּעַשׂ אֶת־הַפָּרֹכֶת תְּכֵלֶת
וְאַרְגָּמָן וְכַרְמִיל וּבוּץ וַיַּעַל
עָלָיו כְּרוּבִים׃
15 וַיַּעַשׂ לִפְנֵי הַבַּיִת עַמּוּדִים
שְׁנַיִם אַמּוֹת שְׁלֹשִׁים וְחָמֵשׁ
אֹרֶךְ וְהַצֶּפֶת אֲשֶׁר־עַל־
רֹאשׁוֹ אַמּוֹת חָמֵשׁ׃
16 וַיַּעַשׂ שַׁרְשְׁרוֹת בַּדְּבִיר וַיִּתֵּן
עַל־רֹאשׁ הָעַמֻּדִים וַיַּעַשׂ
רִמּוֹנִים מֵאָה וַיִּתֵּן בַּשַּׁרְשְׁרוֹת׃
17 וַיָּקֶם אֶת־הָעַמּוּדִים עַל־פְּנֵי
הַהֵיכָל אֶחָד מִיָּמִין וְאֶחָד
מֵהַשְּׂמֹאול וַיִּקְרָא שֵׁם־
הַיְמָנִי יָכִין וְשֵׁם הַשְּׂמָאלִי
בֹּעַז׃

v. 17. יתיר י׳

from intrusion by an unauthorized person.

14. The veil (cf. Exod. xxvi. 31f.).

he made the veil. Between the *hechal* and the *debir*, the veil being in front of the doors of olive-wood mentioned in 1 Kings vi. 31f.

15-17 (corresponding to 1 Kings vii. 15-22). The pillars named Jachin and Boaz which were set up in front of the porch but detached from it.

15. *thirty and five cubits high.* lit. '(in) length.' In 1 Kings vii. 15 the two pillars are said to be *of eighteen cubits high each* (lit. 'one'). The last word is omitted here, and Jewish commentators explain that the two pillars were cast in one piece having a length of thirty-five cubits. Then it was cut in two, and each pillar supplied with an attachment on top, half a cubit in width, to hold the *capital* which adorned it. In this manner the two verses are harmonized.

17. *before the temple.* i.e. in front of the porch.

on the right hand. Of the entrance.

Jachin. The meaning of the name is 'He (God) will establish.'

Boaz. It signifies 'in Him is strength.' The pillars symbolized God's protection of Israel and His omnipotence. Cf. Exod. xvii. 15, *Moses built an altar, and called the name of it Adonai-nissi* (the LORD is my banner).

4 CHAPTER IV ד

1. Moreover he made an altar of brass, twenty cubits the length thereof, and twenty cubits the breadth thereof, and ten cubits the height thereof.

2. Also he made the molten sea of ten cubits from brim to brim, round in compass, and the height thereof was five cubits; and a line of thirty cubits did compass it round about. 3. And under it was the similitude of oxen, which did compass it round about, for ten cubits, compassing the sea round about. The oxen were in two rows, cast when it was cast. 4. It stood upon twelve oxen, three

1 וַיַּעַשׂ מִזְבַּח נְחֹשֶׁת עֶשְׂרִים
אַמָּה אָרְכּוֹ וְעֶשְׂרִים אַמָּה
רָחְבּוֹ וְעֶשֶׂר אַמּוֹת קוֹמָתוֹ׃
2 וַיַּעַשׂ אֶת־הַיָּם מוּצָק עֶשֶׂר
בָּאַמָּה מִשְּׂפָתוֹ אֶל־שְׂפָתוֹ
עָגוֹל ׀ סָבִיב וְחָמֵשׁ בָּאַמָּה
קוֹמָתוֹ וְקָו שְׁלֹשִׁים בָּאַמָּה
3 יָסֹב אֹתוֹ סָבִיב׃ וּדְמוּת
בְּקָרִים תַּחַת לוֹ סָבִיב ׀ סָבִיב
סוֹבְבִים אֹתוֹ עֶשֶׂר בָּאַמָּה
מַקִּיפִים אֶת־הַיָּם סָבִיב שְׁנַיִם
טוּרִים הַבָּקָר יְצוּקִים
4 בְּמֻצַקְתּוֹ׃ עוֹמֵד עַל־שְׁנֵים

CHAPTER IV

THE EQUIPMENT OF THE TEMPLE

1. *altar of brass.* Its dimensions differed from those of the altar in the tabernacle which were five cubits square by three (Exod. xxvii. 1). The latter had no steps, which were in fact forbidden (cf. Exod. xx. 23). The height of Solomon's altar, ten cubits, made some form of ascent essential. It has been suggested that it resembled the altar described in Ezek. xliii. 13ff.; but more probably it had a *kebesh,* or incline, leading up to it, as described in the Mishnah (Middoth III. 3).

2-5 (corresponding to 1 Kings vii. 23-26). The molten sea.

2. *the molten sea.* lit. 'the sea cast (in metal).' It resembled a very large tank which rested on the backs of figured oxen.

from brim to brim. i.e. in diameter.

a line . . . round about. i.e. the circumference. With a diameter of ten cubits, the circumference would be in fact just under thirty-one and a half cubits, but the writer gives an approximate figure.

3. *under it.* Under the brim of the sea, as specified in 1 Kings vii. 24.

the similitude of oxen. In 1 Kings vii. 24: *there were knops,* and it has been suggested that the *knops* were ornaments, shaped in the form of the heads of oxen.

for ten cubits. Better, with R.V. margin, 'ten in a cubit,' making a total of three hundred of them.

the oxen. viz. the ornaments just mentioned. The oxen on which the sea rested are referred to in the next verse.

cast when it was cast. The ornaments were not riveted on to the sea, but both were cast in one mould. Cf. what is said of the candlestick in Exod. xxv. 31.

looking toward the north, and three looking toward the west, and three looking toward the south, and three looking toward the east; and the sea was set upon them above, and all their hinder parts were inward.
5. And it was a handbreadth thick; and the brim thereof was wrought like the brim of a cup, like the flower of a lily: it received and held three thousand baths.

6. He made also ten lavers, and put five on the right hand, and five on the left, to wash in them; such things as belonged to the burnt-offering they washed in them; but the sea was for the priests to wash in.

7. And he made the ten candlesticks of gold according to the ordinance concerning them; and he set them in the temple, five on the right hand, and five on the left.

8. He made also ten tables, and

עָשָׂר בָּקָר שְׁלֹשָׁה פֹּנִים ׀
צָפוֹנָה וּשְׁלוֹשָׁה פֹּנִים יָמָּה
וּשְׁלֹשָׁה ׀ פֹּנִים נֶגְבָּה וּשְׁלֹשָׁה
פֹּנִים מִזְרָחָה וְהַיָּם עֲלֵיהֶם
מִלְמָעְלָה וְכָל־אֲחֹרֵיהֶם
5 בָּיְתָה׃ וְעָבְיוֹ טֶפַח וּשְׂפָתוֹ
כְּמַעֲשֵׂה שְׂפַת־כּוֹס פֶּרַח
שׁוֹשַׁנָּה מַחֲזִיק בַּתִּים שְׁלֹשֶׁת
אֲלָפִים יָכִיל׃
6 וַיַּעַשׂ כִּיּוֹרִים עֲשָׂרָה וַיִּתֵּן
חֲמִשָּׁה מִיָּמִין וַחֲמִשָּׁה
מִשְּׂמֹאול לְרָחְצָה בָהֶם
אֶת־מַעֲשֵׂה הָעוֹלָה יָדִיחוּ
בָם וְהַיָּם לְרָחְצָה לַכֹּהֲנִים
בּוֹ׃
7 וַיַּעַשׂ אֶת־מְנֹרוֹת הַזָּהָב עֶשֶׂר
כְּמִשְׁפָּטָם וַיִּתֵּן בַּהֵיכָל חָמֵשׁ
מִיָּמִין וְחָמֵשׁ מִשְּׂמֹאול׃
8 וַיַּעַשׂ שֻׁלְחָנוֹת עֲשָׂרָה וַיַּנַּח

4. *inward.* Towards the centre of the sea.

5. *like the flower of a lily.* Bending outwards and widening towards the top, or ornamented like the lily.

three thousand baths. In 1 Kings vii. 26: *two thousand baths.* The two passages are harmonized on the hypothesis that the capacity of the *bath* had changed in the interval between the composition of Kings and Chronicles. For the capacity of a *bath*, see on ii. 9.

6 (corresponding to 1 Kings vii. 38f.). The lavers. These were placed on carriages and are described in detail in 1 Kings vii. 27-39. Cf. verse 14.

for the priests to wash in. According to the Rabbis, this meant complete immersion of the body.

7 (corresponding to 1 Kings vii. 49). The candlesticks.

according to the ordinance. Prescribed in Exod. xxv. 31-37.

he set them in the temple. In 1 Kings vii. 49 more precisely: *before the Sanctuary,* i.e. before the Holy of Holies.

placed them in the temple, five on
the right side, and five on the left.
And he made a hundred basins of
gold.

9. Furthermore he made the court
of the priests, and the great court,
and doors for the court, and overlaid
the doors of them with brass.

10. And he set the sea on the
right side [of the house] eastward,
toward the south.

11. And Huram made the pots,
and the shovels, and the basins. So
Huram made an end of doing the
work that he wrought for king
Solomon in the house of God:
12. the two pillars, and the bowls,

בַּהֵיכָל חֲמִשָּׁה מִיָּמִין וַחֲמִשָּׁה
מִשְּׂמֹאול וַיַּעַשׂ מִזְרְקֵי זָהָב
מֵאָה׃
9 וַיַּעַשׂ חֲצַר הַכֹּהֲנִים וְהָעֲזָרָה
הַגְּדוֹלָה וּדְלָתוֹת לָעֲזָרָה
וְדַלְתוֹתֵיהֶם צִפָּה נְחֹשֶׁת׃
10 וְאֶת־הַיָּם נָתַן מִכֶּתֶף הַיְמָנִית
קֵדְמָה מִמּוּל נֶגְבָּה׃
11 וַיַּעַשׂ חוּרָם אֶת־הַסִּירוֹת
וְאֶת־הַיָּעִים וְאֶת־הַמִּזְרָקוֹת
וַיְכַל חִירָם לַעֲשׂוֹת אֶת־
הַמְּלָאכָה אֲשֶׁר עָשָׂה לַמֶּלֶךְ
שְׁלֹמֹה בְּבֵית הָאֱלֹהִים׃
12 עַמּוּדִים שְׁנַיִם וְהַגֻּלּוֹת

חורם ק׳ v. 11.

8. The tables and basins.
ten tables. These were probably used in connection with the ten candlesticks mentioned in verse 7. For the showbread only one table was required (cf. xiii. 11, xxix. 18), although the plural occurs in connection with it in verse 19 and 1 Chron. xxviii. 16 (see *ad loc.*).
basins. Employed for dashing the blood of the sacrifices against the altar.

9. The courts.
the court of the priests. Into this inner court only the priests were allowed to enter.
the great court. The Hebrew word for court (*azarah*) differs here from the preceding (*chatsër*). It was the outer enclosure which all Israelites could enter and where the people congregated.

10. Position of the molten sea.
toward the south. In 1 Kings vii. 39: *eastward, toward the south,* i.e. in the south-east corner of the inner court.

11 (corresponding to 1 Kings vii. 40). The description of the equipment of the Temple is concluded with a short summary, in the first part of the verse (*and Huram . . . basins*), of the smaller utensils. The second part (*so Huram . . . God*) introduces the inventory of verses 12-16.
the pots. For boiling the flesh of certain sacrifices (cf. 1 Sam. ii. 13f.).
the shovels. For removing the ashes from the altar (cf. Exod. xxvii. 3).
the basins. See on verse 8.

12-16 (corresponding to 1 Kings vii. 41-45). Inventory of the articles made by Huram.

12. *the two pillars.* Cf. iii. 15-17.
the bowls. The lower sections of the capitals.

and the two capitals which were on the top of the pillars; and the two networks to cover the two bowls of the capitals that were on the top of the pillars; 13. and the four hundred pomegranates for the two networks: two rows of pomegranates for each network, to cover the two bowls of the capitals that were upon the top of the pillars. 14. He made also the bases, and the lavers made hè upon the bases; 15. one sea, and the twelve oxen under it. 16. The pots also, and the shovels, and the flesh-hooks, and all the vessels thereof, did Huram his master craftsman make for king Solomon for the house of the LORD of bright brass. 17. In the plain of the Jordan did the king cast them, in the clay ground between Succoth and Zeredah.

וְהַכֹּתָרוֹת עַל־רֹאשׁ
הָעַמֻּדִים שְׁתָּיִם וְהַשְּׂבָכוֹת
שְׁתַּיִם לְכַסּוֹת אֶת־שְׁתֵּי גֻּלּוֹת
הַכֹּתָרוֹת אֲשֶׁר עַל־רֹאשׁ
13 הָעַמּוּדִים׃ וְאֶת־הָרִמּוֹנִים
אַרְבַּע מֵאוֹת לִשְׁתֵּי הַשְּׂבָכוֹת
שְׁנַיִם טוּרִים רִמּוֹנִים לַשְּׂבָכָה
הָאֶחָת לְכַסּוֹת אֶת־שְׁתֵּי גֻּלּוֹת
הַכֹּתָרוֹת אֲשֶׁר עַל־פְּנֵי
14 הָעַמּוּדִים׃ וְאֶת־הַמְּכֹנוֹת
עָשָׂה וְאֶת־הַכִּיֹּרוֹת עָשָׂה
15 עַל־הַמְּכֹנוֹת׃ אֶת־הַיָּם אֶחָד
וְאֶת־הַבָּקָר שְׁנֵים־עָשָׂר
16 תַּחְתָּיו׃ וְאֶת־הַסִּירוֹת וְאֶת־
הַיָּעִים וְאֶת־הַמִּזְלָגוֹת וְאֶת־
כָּל־כְּלֵיהֶם עָשָׂה חוּרָם אָבִיו
לַמֶּלֶךְ שְׁלֹמֹה לְבֵית יְהוָה
17 נְחֹשֶׁת מָרוּק׃ בְּכִכַּר הַיַּרְדֵּן
יְצָקָם הַמֶּלֶךְ בַּעֲבִי הָאֲדָמָה

13. *the top of.* lit. 'the face of.' 1 Kings vii. 41 has *rosh*, 'head, top.'

14. *the bases and the lavers.* The number of each was ten (1 Kings vii. 43).

16. *flesh-hooks.* In 1 Kings vii. 45: *the basins* (as in verse 11). The present verse is assumed to have the intention of adding *flesh-hooks* to the other articles already specified and to supply the information that they were all made of *bright brass.*

Huram his master craftsman. See on ii. 12.

17 (corresponding to 1 Kings vii. 46). The place of the foundry.

the king cast them. i.e. they were cast by the king's order.

clay ground. lit. 'in the thickness of the ground.' The clay in the Jordan valley was eminently suitable for the big moulds required for the work. Traces of ancient brick-fields have been found there in modern times.

Succoth. Situated on the east side of the Jordan; perhaps Tel Deir Alla.

Zeredah. In Kings: *Zarethan;* it cannot

18. Thus Solomon made all these vessels in great abundance; for the weight of the brass could not be found out.

19. And Solomon made all the vessels that were in the house of God, the golden altar also, and the tables whereon was the showbread; **20.** and the candlesticks with their lamps, that they should burn according to the ordinance before the Sanctuary, of pure gold; **21.** and the flowers, and the lamps, and the tongs, of gold, and that perfect gold; **22.** and the snuffers, and the basins, and the pans, and the fire-pans, of pure gold. And as for the entry of the house, the inner doors thereof for the most holy place, and the doors of the house, that is, of the temple, were of gold.

18 בֵּין סֻכּוֹת וּבֵין צְרֵדָתָה׃ וַיַּעַשׂ
שְׁלֹמֹה כָּל־הַכֵּלִים הָאֵלֶּה
לָרֹב מְאֹד כִּי לֹא נֶחְקַר
מִשְׁקַל הַנְּחֹשֶׁת׃
19 וַיַּעַשׂ שְׁלֹמֹה אֵת כָּל־הַכֵּלִים
אֲשֶׁר בֵּית הָאֱלֹהִים וְאֵת מִזְבַּח
הַזָּהָב וְאֶת־הַשֻּׁלְחָנוֹת
20 וַעֲלֵיהֶם לֶחֶם הַפָּנִים׃ וְאֶת־
הַמְּנֹרוֹת וְנֵרֹתֵיהֶם לְבַעֲרָם
כַּמִּשְׁפָּט לִפְנֵי הַדְּבִיר זָהָב
21 סָגוּר׃ וְהַפֶּרַח וְהַנֵּרוֹת
וְהַמֶּלְקַחַיִם זָהָב הוּא מִכְלוֹת
22 זָהָב׃ וְהַמְזַמְּרוֹת וְהַמִּזְרָקוֹת
וְהַכַּפּוֹת וְהַמַּחְתּוֹת זָהָב סָגוּר
וּפֶתַח הַבַּיִת דַּלְתוֹתָיו
הַפְּנִימִיּוֹת לְקֹדֶשׁ הַקֳּדָשִׁים
וְדַלְתֵי הַבַּיִת לַהֵיכָל זָהָב׃

be the *Zeredah* of 1 Kings xi. 26 and identification with the modern Tel es-Saidiyeh has been proposed.

18 (corresponding to 1 Kings vii. 47). The vast quantity of brass.

thus Solomon made . . . abundance. In Kings: *and Solomon left all the vessels unweighed, because they were exceeding many.*

could not be found out. No attempt was made to calculate the weight of the brass on account of the great quantities used in the work.

19-22 (corresponding to 1 Kings vii. 48-50). The golden articles for the Temple.

19. *in the house.* The preposition is not in the text.

the golden altar. For the burning of incense (cf. Exod. xxx. 1ff.).

the tables. See on verse 8.

showbread. lit. 'bread of the presence' (cf. Lev. xxiv. 5ff.).

20. *according to the ordinance.* Cf. Num. viii. 2ff.

21. *the flowers.* The flower-shaped ornaments on the golden candlesticks (cf. Exod. xxxvii. 19).

perfect gold. lit. 'completenesses of gold.'

22. *the inner doors . . . were of gold.*

5 CHAPTER V ה

1. Thus all the work that Solomon
wrought for the house of the LORD
was finished. And Solomon brought
in the things that David his father
had hallowed; even the silver, and
the gold, and all the vessels, and put
them in the treasuries of the house
of God.
2. Then Solomon assembled the
elders of Israel, and all the heads of
the tribes, the princes of the fathers'
houses of the children of Israel, unto
Jerusalem, to bring up the ark of the
covenant of the LORD out of the city
of David, which is Zion. 3. And all
the men of Israel assembled themselves unto the king at the feast,
which was in the seventh month.

1 וַתִּשְׁלַם כָּל־הַמְּלָאכָה אֲשֶׁר־
עָשָׂה שְׁלֹמֹה לְבֵית יְהוָה וַיָּבֵא
שְׁלֹמֹה אֶת־קָדְשֵׁי ׀ דָּוִיד אָבִיו
וְאֶת־הַכֶּסֶף וְאֶת־הַזָּהָב
וְאֶת־כָּל־הַכֵּלִים נָתַן
בְּאֹצְרוֹת בֵּית הָאֱלֹהִים׃
2 אָז יַקְהֵיל שְׁלֹמֹה אֶת־זִקְנֵי
יִשְׂרָאֵל וְאֶת־כָּל־רָאשֵׁי
הַמַּטּוֹת נְשִׂיאֵי הָאָבוֹת לִבְנֵי
יִשְׂרָאֵל אֶל־יְרוּשָׁלָםִ
לְהַעֲלוֹת אֶת־אֲרוֹן בְּרִית־
יְהוָה מֵעִיר דָּוִיד הִיא צִיּוֹן׃
3 וַיִּקָּהֲלוּ אֶל־הַמֶּלֶךְ כָּל־אִישׁ
יִשְׂרָאֵל בֶּחָג הוּא הַחֹדֶשׁ

According to 1 Kings vii. 50, only the hinges were of gold, while the doors were of olive-wood overlaid with gold (1 Kings vi. 31f.).

CHAPTER V

1 (corresponding to 1 Kings vii. 51). The completion of Solomon's work on the Temple. Having brought his plans to a successful conclusion, the king deposited in the treasuries of the Temple the riches which his father had dedicated to God.

the things . . . hallowed. lit. 'the sacred things of David his father' (cf. 1 Chron. xviii. 11).

and put them. The first and third words are implied.

2-10 (corresponding to 1 Kings viii. 1-9). The bringing of the ark into the Sanctuary.

2. *then.* When the construction of the Temple, its furniture and utensils was completed.

the princes of the fathers' houses. The phrase defines *the heads of the tribes.*

Jerusalem . . . Zion. Originally the name *Zion* was restricted to the southern portion of the hill rising on the east side of Jerusalem. Subsequently the name was extended to the northern portion on which the Temple stood, and finally it connoted all Jerusalem.

to bring up. As the hill on which the Temple stood was higher than the hill of Zion, the verb *to bring up* is exactly descriptive.

3. *the feast.* viz. Tabernacles, which

4. And all the elders of Israel came, and the Levites took up the ark. 5. And they brought up the ark, and the tent of meeting, and all the holy vessels that were in the Tent; these did the priests and the Levites bring up. 6. And king Solomon and all the congregation of Israel, that were assembled unto him, were before the ark, sacrificing sheep and oxen, that could not be counted nor numbered for multitude. 7. And the priests brought in the ark of the covenant of the LORD unto its place, into the Sanctuary of the house, to the most holy place, even under the wings of the cherubim. 8. For the cherubim spread forth their wings over the place of the ark, and the cherubim covered the ark and the staves thereof above. 9. And the staves

4 הַשְּׁבִעִי׃ וַיָּבֹאוּ כֹּל זִקְנֵי
יִשְׂרָאֵל וַיִּשְׂאוּ הַלְוִיִּם אֶת־
5 הָאָרוֹן׃ וַיַּעֲלוּ אֶת־הָאָרוֹן
וְאֶת־אֹהֶל מוֹעֵד וְאֶת־כָּל־
כְּלֵי הַקֹּדֶשׁ אֲשֶׁר בָּאֹהֶל הֶעֱלוּ
אֹתָם הַכֹּהֲנִים הַלְוִיִּם׃
6 וְהַמֶּלֶךְ שְׁלֹמֹה וְכָל־עֲדַת
יִשְׂרָאֵל הַנּוֹעָדִים עָלָיו לִפְנֵי
הָאָרוֹן מְזַבְּחִים צֹאן וּבָקָר
אֲשֶׁר לֹא־יִסָּפְרוּ וְלֹא יִמָּנוּ
7 מֵרֹב׃ וַיָּבִיאוּ הַכֹּהֲנִים אֶת־
אֲרוֹן בְּרִית־יְהוָה אֶל־
מְקוֹמוֹ אֶל־דְּבִיר הַבַּיִת אֶל־
קֹדֶשׁ הַקֳּדָשִׁים אֶל־תַּחַת
8 כַּנְפֵי הַכְּרוּבִים׃ וַיִּהְיוּ
הַכְּרוּבִים פֹּרְשִׂים כְּנָפַיִם
עַל־מְקוֹם הָאָרוֹן וַיְכַסּוּ
הַכְּרוּבִים עַל־הָאָרוֹן וְעַל־
9 בַּדָּיו מִלְמָעְלָה׃ וַיַּאֲרִיכוּ

begins on the fifteenth day of the month Tishri *the seventh month*) and ends on the twenty-first. After *the feast* Kings inserts *in the month Ethanim which is.* The Chronicler omitted the name because in his day it was no longer in use.

4. *the Levites.* In 1 Kings viii. 3: *the priests.* The former is sometimes a synonym of the latter, both denoting members of the tribe of Levi.

5. *the tent of meeting.* Made by Moses in the wilderness and at that time in Gibeon (cf. i. 3).

the priests and the Levites. The conjunction is not in the text but occurs in 1 Kings viii. 4. The priests carried the ark, the Levites the tent and holy vessels.

6. *sacrificing*, etc. The offerings were made either at the last stage, before the ark was carried into the Temple, or possibly during halts along the route of the procession. The large number of sacrifices seems to favour the second suggestion, and it also conformed to the precedent of David (cf. 2 Sam. vi. 13).

9. *the ends of the staves.* These pressed

were so long that the ends of the staves were seen from the ark before the Sanctuary; but they could not be seen without; and there they are unto this day. 10. There was nothing in the ark save the two tables which Moses put there at Horeb, when the LORD made a covenant with the children of Israel, when they came out of Egypt.

11. And it came to pass, when the priests were come out of the holy place—for all the priests that were present had sanctified themselves, and did not keep their courses; 12. also the Levites who were the singers, all of them, even Asaph, Heman, Jeduthun, and their sons and their brethren, arrayed in fine linen, with cymbals and psalteries

הַבַּדִּים וַיֵּרָאוּ רָאשֵׁי הַבַּדִּים
מִן־הָאָרוֹן עַל־פְּנֵי הַדְּבִיר
וְלֹא יֵרָאוּ הַחוּצָה וַיְהִי־שָׁם
עַד הַיּוֹם הַזֶּה׃ אֵין בָּאָרוֹן רַק 10
שְׁנֵי הַלֻּחוֹת אֲשֶׁר־נָתַן מֹשֶׁה
בְּחֹרֵב אֲשֶׁר כָּרַת יְהוָה עִם־
בְּנֵי יִשְׂרָאֵל בְּצֵאתָם
מִמִּצְרָיִם׃
וַיְהִי בְּצֵאת הַכֹּהֲנִים מִן־ 11
הַקֹּדֶשׁ כִּי כָּל־הַכֹּהֲנִים
הַנִּמְצְאִים הִתְקַדָּשׁוּ אֵין
לִשְׁמוֹר לְמַחְלְקוֹת׃ וְהַלְוִיִּם 12
הַמְשֹׁרְרִים לְכֻלָּם לְאָסָף
לְהֵימָן לִידֻתוּן וְלִבְנֵיהֶם
וְלַאֲחֵיהֶם מְלֻבָּשִׁים בּוּץ
בִּמְצִלְתַּיִם וּבִנְבָלִים וְכִנֹּרוֹת

against the veil which hung before them between the holy (*hechal*) and the most holy (*debir*) sections of the Temple.

the staves were seen. i.e. were noticeable by their impression upon the veil. The staves were not removed from the ark when it rested (Exod. xxv. 15).

from the ark. 1 Kings viii. 8: *from the holy place.*

they could not be seen without. Because the veil covered them.

and there they are. So in Kings. The verb here is in the singular, and A.V. and R.V. render: 'and there it (the ark) is.'

10. *Moses put there.* The last word occurs in Kings, but is implied here. The reference is to Exod. xl. 20.

made a covenant. lit. 'cut.' The usual Hebrew phrase for the making of a covenant is 'to cut' it, the verb alluding to the animals that were cut when a pact was made (cf. Gen. xv. 9f.).

11-14 (corresponding to 1 Kings viii. 10f.). The descent of the Divine glory. The Chronicler elaborates the description of the scene.

11. *for all the priests.* This begins a parenthesis which ends with *trumpets* (verse 12).

and did not keep their courses. lit. 'not to keep courses.' On this special occasion, the entire body of priests joined in the celebration.

12. *Asaph*, etc. Cf. 1 Chron. xxv. 1ff.

and harps, stood at the east end of the altar, and with them a hundred and twenty priests sounding with trumpets—13. it came even to pass, when the trumpeters and singers were as one, to make one sound to be heard in praising and thanking the LORD; and when they lifted up their voice with the trumpets and cymbals and instruments of music, and praised the LORD: 'for He is good, for His mercy endureth for ever'; that then the house was filled with a cloud, even the house of the LORD, 14. so that the priests could not stand to minister by reason of the cloud; for the glory of the LORD filled the house of God.

עֹמְדִים מִזְרָח לַמִּזְבֵּחַ וְעִמָּהֶם
כֹּהֲנִים לְמֵאָה וְעֶשְׂרִים
13 מַחְצְרְרִים בַּחֲצֹצְרוֹת׃ וַיְהִי
כְאֶחָד לַמְחַצְצְרִים
וְלַמְשֹׁרְרִים לְהַשְׁמִיעַ קוֹל־
אֶחָד לְהַלֵּל וּלְהֹדוֹת לַיהוָה
וּכְהָרִים קוֹל בַּחֲצֹצְרוֹת
וּבִמְצִלְתַּיִם וּבִכְלֵי הַשִּׁיר
וּבְהַלֵּל לַיהוָה כִּי טוֹב כִּי
לְעוֹלָם חַסְדּוֹ וְהַבַּיִת מָלֵא
14 עָנָן בֵּית יְהוָה׃ וְלֹא־יָכְלוּ
הַכֹּהֲנִים לַעֲמוֹד לְשָׁרֵת מִפְּנֵי
הֶעָנָן כִּי־מָלֵא כְבוֹד־יְהוָה
אֶת־בֵּית הָאֱלֹהִים׃

6 CHAPTER VI ו

1 Then spoke Solomon:
The LORD hath said that He would dwell in the thick darkness.
2 But I have built Thee a house of habitation,

1 אָז אָמַר שְׁלֹמֹה
יְהוָה אָמַר לִשְׁכּוֹן בָּעֲרָפֶל׃
2 וַאֲנִי בָּנִיתִי בֵית־זְבֻל לָךְ

v. 12. יתיר ר׳ v. 13. יתיר צ׳

the east end of the altar. Facing the Sanctuary which was in the west.

13. *instruments of music.* Or, 'instruments of the song.'

for He is good . . . ever. Cf. 1 Chron. xvi. 34.

filled with a cloud. A symbol of the Divine Presence (cf. Exod. xl. 34).

14. *to minister.* To offer sacrifices.

CHAPTER VI

1f. (corresponding to 1 Kings viii. 12f.). Introductory poem.

1. *then.* After the cloud had filled the house of God.

the LORD hath said . . . in the thick darkness. In Lev. xvi. 2 God said, *For I appear in the cloud upon the ark-cover.* Cf. *the thick darkness where God was* (Exod. xx. 21 [18 in A.J.]).

And a place for Thee to dwell in
for ever.
3. And the king turned his face, and
blessed all the congregation of Israel;
and all the congregation of Israel
stood. 4. And he said: 'Blessed be
the LORD, the God of Israel, who
spoke with His mouth unto David
my father, and hath with His hands
fulfilled it, saying: 5. Since the day
that I brought forth My people out
of the land of Egypt, I chose no city
out of all the tribes of Israel to build
a house in, that My name might be
there; neither chose I any man to
be prince over My people Israel;
6. but I have chosen Jerusalem, that
My name might be there; and have
chosen David to be over My people
Israel. 7. Now it was in the heart
of David my father to build a house
for the name of the LORD, the God
of Israel. 8. But the LORD said
unto David my father: Whereas it
was in thy heart to build a house for
My name, thou didst well that it

וּמָכ֥וֹן לְשִׁבְתְּךָ֖ עוֹלָמִֽים׃
3 וַיַּסֵּ֤ב הַמֶּ֙לֶךְ֙ אֶת־פָּנָ֔יו וַיְבָ֕רֶךְ
אֵ֖ת כָּל־קְהַ֣ל יִשְׂרָאֵ֑ל וְכָל־
4 קְהַ֥ל יִשְׂרָאֵ֖ל עוֹמֵֽד׃ וַיֹּ֗אמֶר
בָּר֤וּךְ יְהוָה֙ אֱלֹהֵ֣י יִשְׂרָאֵ֔ל
אֲשֶׁ֣ר דִּבֶּ֔ר בְּפִ֔יו אֵ֖ת דָּוִ֣יד אָבִ֑י
5 וּבְיָדָ֥יו מִלֵּ֖א לֵאמֹֽר׃ מִן־
הַיּ֗וֹם אֲשֶׁ֨ר הוֹצֵ֥אתִי אֶת־עַמִּי֮
מֵאֶ֣רֶץ מִצְרַיִם֒ לֹא־בָחַ֣רְתִּי
בְעִ֗יר מִכֹּל֙ שִׁבְטֵ֣י יִשְׂרָאֵ֔ל
לִבְנ֣וֹת בַּ֔יִת לִהְי֥וֹת שְׁמִ֖י שָׁ֑ם
וְלֹא־בָחַ֣רְתִּי בְאִ֔ישׁ לִהְי֥וֹת
נָגִ֖יד עַל־עַמִּ֥י יִשְׂרָאֵֽל׃
6 וָֽאֶבְחַר֙ בִּיר֣וּשָׁלִַ֔ם לִהְי֥וֹת שְׁמִ֖י
שָׁ֑ם וָאֶבְחַ֣ר בְּדָוִ֔יד לִהְי֖וֹת
7 עַל־עַמִּ֥י יִשְׂרָאֵֽל׃ וַיְהִ֕י עִם־
לְבַ֖ב דָּוִ֣יד אָבִ֑י לִבְנ֣וֹת בַּ֔יִת
לְשֵׁ֥ם יְהוָ֖ה אֱלֹהֵ֥י יִשְׂרָאֵֽל׃
8 וַיֹּ֤אמֶר יְהוָה֙ אֶל־דָּוִ֣יד אָבִ֔י
יַ֗עַן אֲשֶׁ֤ר הָיָה֙ עִם־לְבָ֣בְךָ֔
לִבְנ֥וֹת בַּ֖יִת לִשְׁמִ֑י הֱטִיב֔וֹתָ

2. *but I.* In 1 Kings viii. 13: *I have surely.*

3-11 (corresponding to 1 Kings viii. 14-21). Solomon's blessing, and review of the history of the plan to erect the Temple.

3. *turned his face.* Towards the people. The introductory poem (verses 1f.) was spoken while the king's face was turned towards the Sanctuary.

4. *who spoke,* etc. Through the prophet Nathan (cf. 2 Sam. vii. 5ff.).

with His hands. The Hebrew for 'hand' also means 'power' and is used here in this sense.

5. *that My name might be there.* So as

was in thy heart; 9. nevertheless thou
shalt not build the house, but thy
son that shall come forth out of thy
loins, he shall build the house for
My name. 10. And the LORD hath
established His word that He spoke;
for I am risen up in the room of
David my father, and sit on the
throne of Israel, as the LORD
promised, and have built the house
for the name of the LORD, the God
of Israel. 11. And there have I set
the ark, wherein is the covenant of
the LORD, which He made with the
children of Israel.'

12. And he stood before the altar
of the LORD in the presence of all
the congregation of Israel, and
spread forth his hands—13. for
Solomon had made a brazen scaffold,
of five cubits long, and five cubits
broad, and three cubits high, and
had set it in the midst of the court;

9 כִּי־הָיָה עִם־לְבָבֶךָ׃ רַק אַתָּה
לֹא תִבְנֶה הַבָּיִת כִּי בִנְךָ הַיֹּצֵא
מֵחֲלָצֶיךָ הוּא־יִבְנֶה הַבַּיִת
10 לִשְׁמִי׃ וַיָּקֶם יְהוָה אֶת־דְּבָרוֹ
אֲשֶׁר דִּבֵּר וָאָקוּם תַּחַת דָּוִיד
אָבִי וָאֵשֵׁב ׀ עַל־כִּסֵּא יִשְׂרָאֵל
כַּאֲשֶׁר דִּבֶּר יְהוָה וָאֶבְנֶה
הַבַּיִת לְשֵׁם יְהוָה אֱלֹהֵי
11 יִשְׂרָאֵל׃ וָאָשִׂים שָׁם אֶת־
הָאָרוֹן אֲשֶׁר שָׁם בְּרִית יְהוָה
אֲשֶׁר כָּרַת עִם־בְּנֵי יִשְׂרָאֵל׃
12 וַיַּעֲמֹד לִפְנֵי מִזְבַּח יְהוָה נֶגֶד
כָּל־קְהַל יִשְׂרָאֵל וַיִּפְרֹשׂ
13 כַּפָּיו׃ כִּי־עָשָׂה שְׁלֹמֹה כִּיּוֹר
נְחֹשֶׁת וַיִּתְּנֵהוּ בְּתוֹךְ הָעֲזָרָה
חָמֵשׁ אַמּוֹת אָרְכּוֹ וְחָמֵשׁ אַמּוֹת
רָחְבּוֹ וְאַמּוֹת שָׁלוֹשׁ קוֹמָתוֹ

to constitute the *house* as the central place of national worship.

11. *the covenant of the LORD.* The two tables of stone engraven with the Ten Commandments.

which He made. When the Decalogue was communicated to Israel.

12-39 (corresponding to 1 Kings viii. 22-50). Solomon's dedicatory prayer consists, after a description of the king's attitude and position (12f.), of a series of short prayers for the general fulfilment of God's promise (14-17), His constant presence in the Temple and acceptance of all petitions (18-21), Divine punishment for a false oath (22f.), help when the people repent after defeat in battle (24f.), rain in times of drought (26f.), aid in diverse calamities (28-31), answer to the prayers of the stranger (32f.), success in a war ordained by God (34f.), and mercy and forgiveness should Israel be in captivity (36-39).

12f. Solomon's attitude in his prayer.

12. *the altar.* This was the brazen altar for burnt-offerings which stood in the court of the Temple.

spread forth his hands. In an attitude of supplication (cf. Exod. ix. 29; Isa. i. 15).

13. This verse has no parallel in Kings.

scaffold. The Hebrew *kiyyor* is the same word translated *lavers* in iv. 6; perhaps the *scaffold* was shaped like a bowl.

and upon it he stood, and kneeled down upon his knees before all the congregation of Israel, and spread forth his hands toward heaven—14. and he said: 'O LORD, the God of Israel, there is no God like Thee, in the heaven, or in the earth; who keepest covenant and mercy with Thy servants, that walk before Thee with all their heart; 15. who hast kept with Thy servant David my father that which Thou didst promise him; yea, Thou spokest with Thy mouth, and hast fulfilled it with Thy hand, as it is this day. 16. Now therefore, O LORD, the God of Israel, keep with Thy servant David my father that which Thou hast promised him, saying: There shall not fail thee a man in My sight to sit on the throne of Israel; if only thy children take heed to their way, to walk in My law as thou hast walked before Me. 17. Now therefore, O LORD, the God of Israel, let Thy word be verified, which Thou spokest unto Thy servant David.

18. But will God in very truth dwell with men on the earth? behold,

וַיַּעֲמֹ֣ד עָלָ֗יו וַיִּבְרַ֤ךְ עַל־
בִּרְכָּיו֙ נֶ֣גֶד כָּל־קְהַ֣ל יִשְׂרָאֵ֔ל
וַיִּפְרֹ֥שׂ כַּפָּ֖יו הַשָּׁמָֽיְמָה׃
14 וַיֹּאמַ֗ר יְהוָ֞ה אֱלֹהֵ֤י יִשְׂרָאֵל֙
אֵין־כָּמ֣וֹךָ אֱלֹהִ֔ים בַּשָּׁמַ֖יִם
וּבָאָ֑רֶץ שֹׁמֵ֤ר הַבְּרִית֙ וְהַחֶ֔סֶד
לַעֲבָדֶ֕יךָ הַהֹלְכִ֥ים לְפָנֶ֖יךָ
15 בְּכָל־לִבָּֽם׃ אֲשֶׁ֣ר שָׁמַ֗רְתָּ
לְעַבְדְּךָ֙ דָּוִ֣יד אָבִ֔י אֵ֖ת אֲשֶׁר־
דִּבַּ֣רְתָּ ל֑וֹ וַתְּדַבֵּ֥ר בְּפִ֛יךָ
וּבְיָדְךָ֥ מִלֵּ֖אתָ כַּיּ֥וֹם הַזֶּֽה׃
16 וְעַתָּ֞ה יְהוָ֣ה ׀ אֱלֹהֵ֣י יִשְׂרָאֵ֗ל
שְׁ֠מֹר לְעַבְדְּךָ֨ דָוִ֜יד אָבִ֗י אֵת֩
אֲשֶׁ֨ר דִּבַּ֤רְתָּ לוֹ֙ לֵאמֹ֔ר לֹֽא־
יִכָּרֵ֨ת לְךָ֥ אִ֛ישׁ מִלְּפָנַ֖י יוֹשֵׁ֣ב
עַל־כִּסֵּ֣א יִשְׂרָאֵ֑ל רַ֠ק אִם־
יִשְׁמְר֨וּ בָנֶ֤יךָ אֶת־דַּרְכָּם֙
לָלֶ֣כֶת בְּתוֹרָתִ֔י כַּאֲשֶׁ֥ר הָלַ֖כְתָּ
17 לְפָנָֽי׃ וְעַתָּה֙ יְהוָ֣ה אֱלֹהֵ֔י
יִשְׂרָאֵ֑ל יֵאָמֵ֣ן דְּבָרְךָ֔ אֲשֶׁ֥ר
דִּבַּ֖רְתָּ לְעַבְדְּךָ֥ לְדָוִֽיד׃
18 כִּ֚י הַֽאֻמְנָ֔ם יֵשֵׁ֧ב אֱלֹהִ֛ים אֶת־
הָאָדָ֖ם עַל־הָאָ֑רֶץ הִנֵּה֩ שָׁמַ֨יִם

14-17. Prayer for the fulfilment of God's promise in the future as in the past.

16. *to walk in My law.* In 1 Kings viii. 25: *to walk before Me.*

18-21. General petition for God's constant presence in the Temple, and for His acceptance of all prayers, individual and communal.

18. *with men.* Not in 1 Kings viii. 27.

heaven and the heaven of heavens cannot contain Thee; how much less this house which I have builded! 19. Yet have Thou respect unto the prayer of Thy servant, and to his supplication, O LORD my God, to hearken unto the cry and to the prayer which Thy servant prayeth before Thee; 20. that Thine eyes may be open toward this house day and night, even toward the place whereof Thou hast said that Thou wouldest put Thy name there; to hearken unto the prayer which Thy servant shall pray toward this place. 21. And hearken Thou to the supplications of Thy servant, and of Thy people Israel, when they shall pray toward this place; yea, hear Thou from Thy dwelling-place, even from heaven; and when Thou hearest, forgive.

22. If a man sin against his neighbour, and an oath be exacted of him to cause him to swear, and he come and swear before Thine altar in this house; 23. then hear Thou from heaven, and do, and

וּשְׁמֵי הַשָּׁמַיִם לֹא יְכַלְכְּלוּךָ
אַף כִּי־הַבַּיִת הַזֶּה אֲשֶׁר
19 בָּנִיתִי׃ וּפָנִיתָ אֶל־תְּפִלַּת
עַבְדְּךָ וְאֶל־תְּחִנָּתוֹ יְהוָה
אֱלֹהָי לִשְׁמֹעַ אֶל־הָרִנָּה
וְאֶל־הַתְּפִלָּה אֲשֶׁר עַבְדְּךָ
20 מִתְפַּלֵּל לְפָנֶיךָ׃ לִהְיוֹת
עֵינֶיךָ פְּתֻחוֹת אֶל־הַבַּיִת
הַזֶּה יוֹמָם וָלַיְלָה אֶל־הַמָּקוֹם
אֲשֶׁר אָמַרְתָּ לָשׂוּם שִׁמְךָ שָׁם
לִשְׁמוֹעַ אֶל־הַתְּפִלָּה אֲשֶׁר
יִתְפַּלֵּל עַבְדְּךָ אֶל־הַמָּקוֹם
21 הַזֶּה׃ וְשָׁמַעְתָּ אֶל־תַּחֲנוּנֵי
עַבְדְּךָ וְעַמְּךָ יִשְׂרָאֵל אֲשֶׁר
יִתְפַּלְלוּ אֶל־הַמָּקוֹם הַזֶּה
וְאַתָּה תִּשְׁמַע מִמְּקוֹם שִׁבְתְּךָ
מִן־הַשָּׁמַיִם וְשָׁמַעְתָּ וְסָלָחְתָּ׃
22 אִם־יֶחֱטָא אִישׁ לְרֵעֵהוּ
וְנָשָׁא־בוֹ אָלָה לְהַאֲלֹתוֹ וּבָא
אָלָה לִפְנֵי מִזְבַּחֲךָ בַּבַּיִת
23 הַזֶּה׃ וְאַתָּה ׀ תִּשְׁמַע מִן־

20. *day and night.* In 1 Kings viii. 29: *night and day.*

which Thy servant shall pray. This is a reference to future prayers which Solomon would offer. In the preceding verse (*which Thy servant prayeth*) he refers to the petition he is now offering.

21. *even from heaven.* The Temple is only symbolic of the Divine Presence; God's 'abode' is in heaven.

22f. Divine condemnation and punishment for the taking of a false oath.

22. *an oath be exacted.* Cf. Exod. xxii. 7ff.

23. *and do.* i.e. do what is proper to be done, viz. execute judgment.

הַשָּׁמַיִם וְעָשִׂיתָ וְשָׁפַטְתָּ אֶת־
עֲבָדֶיךָ לְהָשִׁיב לְרָשָׁע לָתֵת
דַּרְכּוֹ בְּרֹאשׁוֹ וּלְהַצְדִּיק
צַדִּיק לָתֶת לוֹ כְּצִדְקָתוֹ׃
24 וְאִם־יִנָּגֵף עַמְּךָ יִשְׂרָאֵל לִפְנֵי
אוֹיֵב כִּי יֶחֶטְאוּ־לָךְ וְשָׁבוּ
וְהוֹדוּ אֶת־שְׁמֶךָ וְהִתְפַּלְלוּ
וְהִתְחַנְּנוּ לְפָנֶיךָ בַּבַּיִת הַזֶּה׃
25 וְאַתָּה תִּשְׁמַע מִן־הַשָּׁמַיִם
וְסָלַחְתָּ לְחַטַּאת עַמְּךָ
יִשְׂרָאֵל וַהֲשֵׁיבוֹתָם אֶל־
הָאֲדָמָה אֲשֶׁר־נָתַתָּה לָהֶם
וְלַאֲבֹתֵיהֶם׃
26 בְּהֵעָצֵר הַשָּׁמַיִם וְלֹא־יִהְיֶה
מָטָר כִּי יֶחֶטְאוּ־לָךְ
וְהִתְפַּלְלוּ אֶל־הַמָּקוֹם הַזֶּה
וְהוֹדוּ אֶת־שְׁמֶךָ מֵחַטָּאתָם
27 יְשׁוּבוּן כִּי תַעֲנֵם׃ וְאַתָּה ׀
תִּשְׁמַע הַשָּׁמַיִם וְסָלַחְתָּ
לְחַטַּאת עֲבָדֶיךָ וְעַמְּךָ

judge Thy servants, requiting the wicked, to bring his way upon his own head; and justifying the righteous, to give him according to his righteousness.

24. And if Thy people Israel be smitten down before the enemy, when they sin against Thee, and shall turn again and confess Thy name, and pray and make supplication before Thee in this house; 25. then hear Thou from heaven, and forgive the sin of Thy people Israel, and bring them back unto the land which Thou gavest to them and to their fathers.

26. When the heaven is shut up, and there is no rain, when they sin against Thee; if they pray toward this place, and confess Thy name, turning from their sin, when Thou dost afflict them; 27. then hear Thou in heaven, and forgive the sin of Thy servants, and of Thy people

24f. Invocation of God's help after defeat in battle and subsequent repentance.

24. *when they sin against Thee.* Defeat in battle was interpreted as the consequence of sin (cf. Josh. vii. 11).

and shall turn again. 1 Kings viii. 33 adds: *to Thee*; they repent.

25. *bring them back.* May the Israelite warriors return safely home and not fall into the enemy's hand.

26f. Prayer in time of drought.

26. *when the heaven is shut up.* The ancients believed that reservoirs containing water existed in heaven (cf. Gen. vii. 11). The closing of the heavens consequently meant a drought (cf. Deut. xi. 17).

when Thou dost afflict them. R.V. margin renders: 'because Thou answerest them.'

Israel, when Thou dost direct them on the good way wherein they should walk; and send rain upon Thy land, which Thou hast given to Thy people for an inheritance.

28. If there be in the land famine, if there be pestilence, if there be blasting or mildew, locust or caterpillar; if their enemies besiege them in the land of their cities; whatsoever plague or whatsoever sickness there be; 29. what prayer and supplication soever be made by any man, or by all Thy people Israel, who shall know every man his own plague and his own pain, and shall spread forth his hands toward this house; 30. then hear Thou from heaven Thy dwelling-place, and forgive, and render unto every man according to all his ways, whose heart Thou knowest—for Thou, even Thou only knowest the hearts of the children of men—31. that they may fear Thee, to walk in Thy ways, all

יִשְׂרָאֵל כִּי תוֹרֵם אֶל־הַדֶּרֶךְ
הַטּוֹבָה אֲשֶׁר יֵלְכוּ־בָהּ
וְנָתַתָּה מָטָר עַל־אַרְצְךָ
אֲשֶׁר־נָתַתָּה לְעַמְּךָ לְנַחֲלָה׃
28 רָעָב כִּי־יִהְיֶה בָאָרֶץ דֶּבֶר
כִּי־יִהְיֶה שִׁדָּפוֹן וְיֵרָקוֹן
אַרְבֶּה וְחָסִיל כִּי יִהְיֶה כִּי
יָצַר־לוֹ אֹיְבָיו בְּאֶרֶץ שְׁעָרָיו
29 כָּל־נֶגַע וְכָל־מַחֲלָה׃ כָּל־
תְּפִלָּה כָל־תְּחִנָּה אֲשֶׁר יִהְיֶה
לְכָל־הָאָדָם וּלְכֹל עַמְּךָ
יִשְׂרָאֵל אֲשֶׁר יֵדְעוּ אִישׁ נִגְעוֹ
וּמַכְאֹבוֹ וּפָרַשׂ כַּפָּיו אֶל־
30 הַבַּיִת הַזֶּה׃ וְאַתָּה תִּשְׁמַע מִן־
הַשָּׁמַיִם מְכוֹן שִׁבְתֶּךָ וְסָלַחְתָּ
וְנָתַתָּה לָאִישׁ כְּכָל־דְּרָכָיו
אֲשֶׁר תֵּדַע אֶת־לְבָבוֹ כִּי־
אַתָּה לְבַדְּךָ יָדַעְתָּ אֶת־לְבַב
31 בְּנֵי הָאָדָם׃ לְמַעַן יִירָאוּךָ
לָלֶכֶת בִּדְרָכֶיךָ כָּל־הַיָּמִים

28-31. Prayer for help in various troubles and calamities.

28. *blasting.* Injury to crops by storms. *their cities.* lit. 'their gates.'

whatsoever plague. The meaning of the noun here is 'calamity.'

29. *his own plague and his own pain.* In 1 Kings viii. 38: the *plague of his own heart.* The meaning is, each individual, whatever be his affliction, will recognize that it is sent by God upon him for some misdeed committed by him.

30. *for Thou, even Thou.* This begins the parenthesis which ends with *men* at the close of the verse.

31. *that they may fear Thee*, etc. 1 Kings viii. 40 omits *to walk in Thy ways.* Seeing that their sins brought affliction while their return to God brought salvation, they would perceive the guiding hand of Providence and fear to

the days that they live in the land which Thou gavest unto our fathers.

32. Moreover concerning the stranger, that is not of Thy people Israel, when he shall come out of a far country for Thy great name's sake, and Thy mighty hand, and Thine outstretched arm; when they shall come and pray toward this house; 33. then hear Thou from heaven, even from Thy dwelling-place, and do according to all that the stranger calleth to Thee for; that all the peoples of the earth may know Thy name, and fear Thee, as doth Thy people Israel, and that they may know that Thy name is called upon this house which I have built.

34. If Thy people go out to battle against their enemies, by whatsoever way Thou shalt send them, and they pray unto Thee toward this city which Thou hast chosen, and the house which I have built for Thy name; 35. then hear Thou from

אֲשֶׁר־הֵם חַיִּים עַל־פְּנֵי
הָאֲדָמָה אֲשֶׁר נָתַתָּה
לַאֲבֹתֵינוּ׃
32 וְגַם אֶל־הַנָּכְרִי אֲשֶׁר לֹא־
מֵעַמְּךָ יִשְׂרָאֵל הוּא וּבָא ׀
מֵאֶרֶץ רְחוֹקָה לְמַעַן שִׁמְךָ
הַגָּדוֹל וְיָדְךָ הַחֲזָקָה וּזְרוֹעֲךָ
הַנְּטוּיָה וּבָאוּ וְהִתְפַּלְלוּ אֶל־
33 הַבַּיִת הַזֶּה׃ וְאַתָּה תִּשְׁמַע
מִן־הַשָּׁמַיִם מִמְּכוֹן שִׁבְתֶּךָ
וְעָשִׂיתָ כְּכֹל אֲשֶׁר־יִקְרָא
אֵלֶיךָ הַנָּכְרִי לְמַעַן יֵדְעוּ כָל־
עַמֵּי הָאָרֶץ אֶת־שְׁמֶךָ
וּלְיִרְאָה אֹתְךָ כְּעַמְּךָ יִשְׂרָאֵל
וְלָדַעַת כִּי־שִׁמְךָ נִקְרָא עַל־
הַבַּיִת הַזֶּה אֲשֶׁר בָּנִיתִי׃
34 כִּי־יֵצֵא עַמְּךָ לַמִּלְחָמָה עַל־
אֹיְבָיו בַּדֶּרֶךְ אֲשֶׁר תִּשְׁלָחֵם
וְהִתְפַּלְלוּ אֵלֶיךָ דֶּרֶךְ הָעִיר
הַזֹּאת אֲשֶׁר בָּחַרְתָּ בָּהּ וְהַבַּיִת
35 אֲשֶׁר־בָּנִיתִי לִשְׁמֶךָ׃ וְשָׁמַעְתָּ

do evil again. Cf. *For with Thee there is forgiveness, that Thou mayest be feared* (Ps. cxxx. 4).

32f. The stranger's prayer.

32. *for Thy great name's sake.* Because he heard of God's great name (cf. 1 Kings viii. 42).

33. *Thy name is called upon this house.* In this house God is near and accessible, so to speak, to all who pray unto Him within its precincts.

34f. Prayer for success in a war commanded by God.

34. *by whatsoever way Thou shalt send them.* The text refers to a campaign undertaken by the Israelites with the approval of God and at His direction.

toward this city. Being unable to come

heaven their prayer and their supplication, and maintain their cause. 36. If they sin against Thee—for there is no man that sinneth not—and Thou be angry with them, and deliver them to the enemy, so that they carry them away captive unto a land far off or near; 37. yet if they shall bethink themselves in the land whither they are carried captive, and turn, and make supplication unto Thee in the land of their captivity, saying: We have sinned, we have done iniquitously, and have dealt wickedly; 38. if they return unto Thee with all their heart and with all their soul in the land of their captivity, whither they have carried them captive, and pray toward their land, which Thou gavest unto their fathers, and the city which Thou hast chosen, and toward the house which I have built for Thy name; 39. then hear Thou from heaven, even from Thy dwelling-place, their prayer and their supplications, and maintain their cause; and forgive Thy people who have sinned against Thee.

40. Now, O my God, let, I beseech Thee, Thine eyes be open, and let

מִן־הַשָּׁמַיִם אֶת־תְּפִלָּתָם
וְאֶת־תְּחִנָּתָם וְעָשִׂיתָ
36 מִשְׁפָּטָם׃ כִּי יֶחֶטְאוּ־לָךְ כִּי
אֵין אָדָם אֲשֶׁר לֹא־יֶחֱטָא
וְאָנַפְתָּ בָם וּנְתַתָּם לִפְנֵי אוֹיֵב
וְשָׁבוּם שׁוֹבֵיהֶם אֶל־אֶרֶץ
37 רְחוֹקָה אוֹ קְרוֹבָה׃ וְהֵשִׁיבוּ
אֶל־לְבָבָם בָּאָרֶץ אֲשֶׁר
נִשְׁבּוּ־שָׁם וְשָׁבוּ ׀ וְהִתְחַנְּנוּ
אֵלֶיךָ בְּאֶרֶץ שִׁבְיָם לֵאמֹר
38 חָטָאנוּ הֶעֱוִינוּ וְרָשָׁעְנוּ׃ וְשָׁבוּ
אֵלֶיךָ בְּכָל־לִבָּם וּבְכָל־
נַפְשָׁם בְּאֶרֶץ שִׁבְיָם אֲשֶׁר־
שָׁבוּ אֹתָם וְהִתְפַּלְלוּ דֶּרֶךְ
אַרְצָם אֲשֶׁר־נָתַתָּה לַאֲבֹתָם
וְהָעִיר אֲשֶׁר בָּחַרְתָּ וְלַבַּיִת
39 אֲשֶׁר־בָּנִיתִי לִשְׁמֶךָ׃ וְשָׁמַעְתָּ
מִן־הַשָּׁמַיִם מִמְּכוֹן שִׁבְתְּךָ
אֶת־תְּפִלָּתָם וְאֶת־תְּחִנֹּתֵיהֶם
וְעָשִׂיתָ מִשְׁפָּטָם וְסָלַחְתָּ
לְעַמְּךָ אֲשֶׁר חָטְאוּ־לָךְ׃
40 עַתָּה אֱלֹהַי יִהְיוּ־נָא עֵינֶיךָ

to Jerusalem, they would pray with the face towards it from wherever they may be (cf. Dan. vi. 11).

36-39. Repentance and prayer in captivity.

36. *for there is no man that sinneth not.* Cf. Eccles. vii. 20.

so that they carry them away captive. lit. 'and their captors will capture them.'

40-42. Concluding prayer. The closing petition in 1 Kings viii. 52f. is almost entirely different from the version given here.

40. *attent.* i.e. attentive.

Thine ears be attent, unto the prayer that is made in this place.
41 Now therefore arise, O LORD God, into Thy resting-place,
Thou, and the ark of Thy strength;
Let Thy priests, O LORD God, be clothed with salvation,
And let Thy saints rejoice in good.
42 O LORD God, turn not away the face of Thine anointed;
Remember the good deeds of David Thy servant.'

פְּתֻחוֹת וְאָזְנֶיךָ קַשֻּׁבוֹת
לִתְפִלַּת הַמָּקוֹם הַזֶּה׃
41 וְעַתָּה קוּמָה
יְהוָה אֱלֹהִים לְנוּחֶךָ
אַתָּה וַאֲרוֹן עֻזֶּךָ
כֹּהֲנֶיךָ יְהוָה אֱלֹהִים
יִלְבְּשׁוּ תְשׁוּעָה
וַחֲסִידֶיךָ יִשְׂמְחוּ בַטּוֹב׃
42 יְהוָה אֱלֹהִים
אַל־תָּשֵׁב פְּנֵי מְשִׁיחֶךָ
זָכְרָה לְחַסְדֵי דָּוִיד עַבְדֶּךָ׃

7 CHAPTER VII ז

1. Now when Solomon had made an
end of praying, the fire came down
from heaven, and consumed the

1 וּכְכַלּוֹת שְׁלֹמֹה לְהִתְפַּלֵּל
וְהָאֵשׁ יָרְדָה מֵהַשָּׁמַיִם וַתֹּאכַל

מלרע v. 41.

the prayer . . . place. lit. 'the prayer of this place.'

41f. These verses correspond closely, though with variations in phraseology, to Ps. cxxxii. 8-10.

41. *arise, O LORD.* Cf. Num. x. 35.

Thy resting-place. The Temple.

the ark of Thy strength. This may be a reference to the occasional practice of taking the ark into battle which inspired hope of victory.

salvation. Triumph over the oppressor which brings salvation and the vindication of righteousness. In Ps. cxxxii. 9 the reading is *righteousness.*

Thy saints. The Israelites who are loyal to the service of God.

rejoice in good. i.e. in happiness and prosperity. In Ps. cxxxii. 9: *shout for joy.*

42. *turn not away the face.* Do not reject his prayer.

Thine anointed. Solomon the anointed king (cf. 1 Kings i. 39; 1 Chron. xxix. 22).

remember, etc. May his son enjoy their reward.

good deeds. Or, 'acts of mercy, or, kindness.'

CHAPTER VII

1-3. Fire from heaven and the manifestation of the Divine glory. This section has no parallel in Kings.

1. *fire came down*, etc. See 1 Chron. xxi. 26.

burnt-offering and the sacrifices; and the glory of the LORD filled the house. 2. And the priests could not enter into the house of the LORD, because the glory of the LORD filled the LORD's house. 3. And all the children of Israel looked on, when the fire came down, and the glory of the LORD was upon the house; and they bowed themselves with their faces to the ground upon the pavement, and prostrated themselves, and gave thanks unto the LORD: 'for He is good, for His mercy endureth for ever.'

4. And the king and all the people offered sacrifice before the LORD. 5. And king Solomon offered a sacrifice of twenty and two thousand oxen, and a hundred and twenty thousand sheep. So the king and all the people dedicated the house of God. 6. And the priests stood, according to their offices; the Levites also with instruments of music of the LORD, which David the king had made, to give thanks unto the LORD, for His mercy endureth for ever, with the praises of David by their hand; and the priests sounded

הָעֹלָה וְהַזְּבָחִים וּכְבוֹד יְהוָה
2 מָלֵא אֶת־הַבָּיִת׃ וְלֹא יָכְלוּ
הַכֹּהֲנִים לָבוֹא אֶל־בֵּית יְהוָה
כִּי־מָלֵא כְבוֹד־יְהוָה אֶת־
3 בֵּית יְהוָה׃ וְכֹל ׀ בְּנֵי יִשְׂרָאֵל
רֹאִים בְּרֶדֶת הָאֵשׁ וּכְבוֹד
יְהוָה עַל־הַבָּיִת וַיִּכְרְעוּ
אַפַּיִם אַרְצָה עַל־הָרִצְפָּה
וַיִּשְׁתַּחֲווּ וְהוֹדוֹת לַיהוָה כִּי
טוֹב כִּי לְעוֹלָם חַסְדּוֹ׃
4 וְהַמֶּלֶךְ וְכָל־הָעָם זֹבְחִים
5 זֶבַח לִפְנֵי יְהוָה׃ וַיִּזְבַּח הַמֶּלֶךְ
שְׁלֹמֹה אֶת־זֶבַח הַבָּקָר
עֶשְׂרִים וּשְׁנַיִם אֶלֶף וְצֹאן מֵאָה
וְעֶשְׂרִים אָלֶף וַיַּחְנְכוּ אֶת־
בֵּית הָאֱלֹהִים הַמֶּלֶךְ וְכָל־
6 הָעָם׃ וְהַכֹּהֲנִים עַל־
מִשְׁמְרוֹתָם עֹמְדִים וְהַלְוִיִּם
בִּכְלֵי־שִׁיר יְהוָה אֲשֶׁר עָשָׂה
דָּוִיד הַמֶּלֶךְ לְהֹדוֹת לַיהוָה
כִּי־לְעוֹלָם חַסְדּוֹ בְּהַלֵּל
דָּוִיד בְּיָדָם וְהַכֹּהֲנִים
מַחְצְצְרִים* נֶגְדָּם וְכָל־יִשְׂרָאֵל

* v. 6. יתיר צ׳

2. *the priests could not enter.* Cf. v. 14; and of Moses, Exod. xl. 35.

3. *upon the pavement.* As distinct from Solomon who knelt upon the scaffold (vi. 13).

4-7 (corresponding to 1 Kings viii. 62-64). The dedicatory sacrifices of the king and people.

5. The number of oxen and sheep offered is the same as in 1 Kings viii. 63.

6. This verse has no parallel in Kings.

trumpets over against them; and all
Israel stood. 7. Moreover Solomon
hallowed the middle of the court
that was before the house of the
LORD; for there he offered the burnt-
offerings, and the fat of the peace-
offerings; because the brazen altar
which Solomon had made was not
able to receive the burnt-offering,
and the meal-offering, and the fat.
8. So Solomon held the feast at
that time seven days, and all Israel
with him, a very great congregation,
from the entrance of Hamath unto
the Brook of Egypt. 9. And on the
eighth day they held a solemn
assembly; for they kept the dedication of the altar seven days, and the

7 עֹמְדִים׃ וַיְקַדֵּשׁ שְׁלֹמֹה אֶת־
תּוֹךְ הֶחָצֵר אֲשֶׁר לִפְנֵי בֵית־
יְהוָה כִּי־עָשָׂה שָׁם הָעֹלוֹת
וְאֵת חֶלְבֵי הַשְּׁלָמִים כִּי־
מִזְבַּח הַנְּחֹשֶׁת אֲשֶׁר־עָשָׂה
שְׁלֹמֹה לֹא יָכוֹל לְהָכִיל אֶת־
הָעֹלָה וְאֶת־הַמִּנְחָה וְאֶת־
הַחֲלָבִים׃
8 וַיַּעַשׂ שְׁלֹמֹה אֶת־הֶחָג בָּעֵת
הַהִיא שִׁבְעַת יָמִים וְכָל־
יִשְׂרָאֵל עִמּוֹ קָהָל גָּדוֹל מְאֹד
מִלְּבוֹא חֲמָת עַד־נַחַל
9 מִצְרָיִם׃ וַיַּעֲשׂוּ בַּיּוֹם הַשְּׁמִינִי
עֲצָרֶת כִּי ׀ חֲנֻכַּת הַמִּזְבֵּחַ עָשׂוּ
שִׁבְעַת יָמִים וְהֶחָג שִׁבְעַת

the priests sounded trumpets. In accordance with Num. x. 8 (cf. v. 12).

7. *Solomon hallowed.* With the sanctity of the altar.

the middle of the court. This was the court of the priests (cf. iv. 9).

there. On the hallowed floor.

burnt-offerings. These were entirely burnt on the altar.

peace-offerings. Only the fat and certain other parts of the sacrifice were consumed on the altar. The rest was eaten by those who offered the animals.

the brazen altar. Cf. iv. 1. This altar on all other occasions was adequate for the number of sacrifices offered.

was not able. On account of the vast numbers offered on this occasion.

meal-offering. This consisted of fine flour mixed with incense, salt and oil (cf. Lev. ii. 1ff.).

8-10. The concluding feast. The first seven days were spent in the rites of dedication, and the second period of seven days was the occasion of the feast of Tabernacles.

8. *at that time.* In Tishri, the seventh month (cf. v. 3).

seven days. This was the festival of dedication, held from the eighth of Tishri to the fourteenth. Included in the period was the Day of Atonement on the tenth of the month (cf. Num. xxix. 7), but a deviation from the Mosaic law was allowed in the special circumstances.

the entrance of Hamath . . . the Brook of Egypt. The latter is identical with *Shihor* (see on 1 Chron. xiii. 5).

9. *the eighth day.* Of Tabernacles, the

feast seven days. 10. And on the
three and twentieth day of the
seventh month he sent the people
away unto their tents, joyful and glad
of heart for the goodness that the
LORD had shown unto David, and to
Solomon, and to Israel His people.
11. Thus Solomon finished the
house of the LORD, and the king's
house; and all that came into
Solomon's heart to make in the
house of the LORD, and in his own
house, he prosperously effected.
12. And the LORD appeared to
Solomon by night, and said unto
him: 'I have heard thy prayer, and
have chosen this place to Myself for
a house of sacrifice. 13. If I shut up
heaven that there be no rain, or if I

יָמִים׃ וּבְיוֹם עֶשְׂרִים וּשְׁלֹשָׁה 10
לַחֹדֶשׁ הַשְּׁבִיעִי שִׁלַּח אֶת־
הָעָם לְאָהֳלֵיהֶם שְׂמֵחִים
וְטוֹבֵי לֵב עַל־הַטּוֹבָה אֲשֶׁר
עָשָׂה יְהוָה לְדָוִיד וְלִשְׁלֹמֹה
וּלְיִשְׂרָאֵל עַמּוֹ׃
וַיְכַל שְׁלֹמֹה אֶת־בֵּית יְהוָה 11
וְאֶת־בֵּית הַמֶּלֶךְ וְאֵת כָּל־
הַבָּא עַל־לֵב שְׁלֹמֹה לַעֲשׂוֹת
בְּבֵית־יְהוָה וּבְבֵיתוֹ הִצְלִיחַ׃
וַיֵּרָא יְהוָה אֶל־שְׁלֹמֹה 12
בַּלָּיְלָה וַיֹּאמֶר לוֹ שָׁמַעְתִּי
אֶת־תְּפִלָּתֶךָ וּבָחַרְתִּי בַּמָּקוֹם
הַזֶּה לִי לְבֵית זָבַח׃ הֵן אֶעֱצֹר 13
הַשָּׁמַיִם וְלֹא־יִהְיֶה מָטָר וְהֵן־

day following the second period of seven days (cf. Num. xxix. 35f.).

the feast. See on v. 3.

10. *three and twentieth day.* This was the day on which the people departed from Jerusalem to go *unto their tents.* On the preceding day, the eighth day of Tabernacles (cf. 1 Kings viii. 66), they received the king's leave for their departure; and this, according to tradition, is the meaning of the text in 1 Kings viii. 66, *on the eighth day he sent the people away.* The departure to their homes is referred to in the second part of the verse just quoted, *and went unto their tents,* which took place, as here stated, on the following day which was the *three and twentieth day of the seventh month.*

the goodness . . . and to Solomon. The fulfilment of the Divine promise that David's son would reign in peace and security and that he would build the Temple.

and to Israel. Who enjoyed the blessings of Solomon's kingship and God's protection. Their non-observance of the Day of Atonement (see on verse 8) was also forgiven them and, as a Rabbinical tradition tells, 'A heavenly voice announced that their sin was pardoned and all of them were assured of a portion in the World to Come.'

11-22 (corresponding to 1 Kings ix. 1-9). The Divine response to Solomon's prayer.

12. *and have chosen this place.* From these words to the end of verse 16 is an addition of the Chronicler.

13ff. These verses indicate that the king's prayer at the dedication of the

command the locust to devour the
land, or if I send pestilence among
My people; 14. if My people, upon
whom My name is called, shall
humble themselves, and pray, and
seek My face, and turn from their
evil ways; then will I hear from
heaven, and will forgive their sin,
and will heal their land. 15. Now
Mine eyes shall be open, and Mine
ears attent, unto the prayer that is
made in this place. 16. For now
have I chosen and hallowed this
house, that My name may be there
for ever; and Mine eyes and My
heart shall be there perpetually.
17. And as for thee, if thou wilt walk
before Me as David thy father
walked, and do according to all that
I have commanded thee, and wilt
keep My statutes and Mine ordinances; 18. then I will establish the
throne of thy kingdom, according as
I covenanted with David thy father,
saying: There shall not fail thee a
man to be ruler in Israel. 19. But
if ye turn away, and forsake My
statutes and My commandments
which I have set before you, and
shall go and serve other gods, and

אֲצַוֶּה עַל־חָגָב לֶאֱכוֹל
הָאָרֶץ וְאִם־אֲשַׁלַּח דֶּבֶר
14 בְּעַמִּי׃ וְיִכָּנְעוּ עַמִּי אֲשֶׁר
נִקְרָא־שְׁמִי עֲלֵיהֶם וְיִתְפַּלְלוּ
וִיבַקְשׁוּ פָנַי וְיָשֻׁבוּ מִדַּרְכֵיהֶם
הָרָעִים וַאֲנִי אֶשְׁמַע מִן־
הַשָּׁמַיִם וְאֶסְלַח לְחַטָּאתָם
15 וְאֶרְפָּא אֶת־אַרְצָם׃ עַתָּה
עֵינַי יִהְיוּ פְתֻחוֹת וְאָזְנַי קַשֻּׁבוֹת
16 לִתְפִלַּת הַמָּקוֹם הַזֶּה׃ וְעַתָּה
בָּחַרְתִּי וְהִקְדַּשְׁתִּי אֶת־הַבַּיִת
הַזֶּה לִהְיוֹת שְׁמִי שָׁם עַד־
עוֹלָם וְהָיוּ עֵינַי וְלִבִּי שָׁם כָּל־
17 הַיָּמִים׃ וְאַתָּה אִם־תֵּלֵךְ
לְפָנַי כַּאֲשֶׁר הָלַךְ דָּוִיד אָבִיךָ
וְלַעֲשׂוֹת כְּכֹל אֲשֶׁר צִוִּיתִיךָ
וְחֻקַּי וּמִשְׁפָּטַי תִּשְׁמוֹר׃
18 וַהֲקִימוֹתִי אֵת כִּסֵּא מַלְכוּתֶךָ
כַּאֲשֶׁר כָּרַתִּי לְדָוִיד אָבִיךָ
לֵאמֹר לֹא־יִכָּרֵת לְךָ אִישׁ
19 מוֹשֵׁל בְּיִשְׂרָאֵל׃ וְאִם־
תְּשׁוּבוּן אַתֶּם וַעֲזַבְתֶּם חֻקּוֹתַי
וּמִצְוֹתַי אֲשֶׁר נָתַתִּי לִפְנֵיכֶם
וַהֲלַכְתֶּם וַעֲבַדְתֶּם אֱלֹהִים
אֲחֵרִים וְהִשְׁתַּחֲוִיתֶם לָהֶם׃

Temple was received by God with favour.

18. *I covenanted.* lit. 'I cut' (see on v. 10).

there shall not fail. lit. 'there shall not be cut off.'

19. *if ye turn away.* The singular is now changed to the plural because the fate

worship them: 20. then will I pluck them up by the roots out of My land which I have given them; and this house, which I have hallowed for My name, will I cast out of My sight, and I will make it a proverb and a byword among all peoples. 21. And this house, which is so high, every one that passeth by it shall be astonished, and shall say: Why hath the LORD done thus unto this land, and to this house? 22. And they shall answer: Because they forsook the LORD, the God of their fathers, who brought them forth out of the land of Egypt, and laid hold on other gods, and worshipped them, and served them; therefore hath He brought all this evil upon them.'

20 וּנְתַשְׁתִּים מֵעַל אַדְמָתִי אֲשֶׁר־
נָתַתִּי לָהֶם וְאֶת־הַבַּיִת הַזֶּה
אֲשֶׁר־הִקְדַּשְׁתִּי לִשְׁמִי אַשְׁלִיךְ
מֵעַל פָּנָי וְאֶתְּנֶנּוּ לְמָשָׁל
וְלִשְׁנִינָה בְּכָל־הָעַמִּים׃
21 וְהַבַּיִת הַזֶּה אֲשֶׁר־הָיָה עֶלְיוֹן
לְכָל־עֹבֵר עָלָיו יִשֹּׁם וְאָמַר
בַּמֶּה עָשָׂה יְהוָה כָּכָה לָאָרֶץ
22 הַזֹּאת וְלַבַּיִת הַזֶּה׃ וְאָמְרוּ
עַל אֲשֶׁר עָזְבוּ אֶת־יְהוָה ׀
אֱלֹהֵי אֲבֹתֵיהֶם אֲשֶׁר הוֹצִיאָם
מֵאֶרֶץ מִצְרַיִם וַיַּחֲזִיקוּ
בֵּאלֹהִים אֲחֵרִים וַיִּשְׁתַּחֲווּ
לָהֶם וַיַּעַבְדוּם עַל־כֵּן הֵבִיא
עֲלֵיהֶם אֵת כָּל־הָרָעָה
הַזֹּאת׃

8 CHAPTER VIII ח

1. And it came to pass at the end of twenty years, wherein Solomon had

1 וַיְהִי מִקֵּץ ׀ עֶשְׂרִים שָׁנָה אֲשֶׁר

of the nation as well as the dynasty is dealt with.

20. *a proverb and a byword.* Cf. Deut. xxviii. 37. The downfall of Israel will be mentioned in their taunting songs with malicious glee.

21f. The phraseology of these verses bears a close resemblance to Deut. xxix. 23-27.

21. *which is so high.* In the Hebrew the verb is in the perfect. When the passer-by will express his astonishment, *Why hath the LORD, etc.*', the house will lie in ruins and no longer be high.

shall be astonished. At the destruction of God's house and its desolation.

22. *and they shall answer.* lit. 'and they shall say' in answer to their question.

built the house of the LORD, and his own house, 2. that the cities which Huram had given to Solomon, Solomon built them, and caused the children of Israel to dwell there.

3. And Solomon went to Hamath-zobah, and prevailed against it. 4. And he built Tadmor in the wilderness, and all the store-cities, which he built in Hamath. 5. Also he built Beth-horon the upper, and Beth-horon the nether, fortified cities, with walls, gates, and bars; 6. and Baalath, and all the store-cities that Solomon had, and all the

בָּנָה שְׁלֹמֹה אֶת־בֵּית יְהוָה
2 וְאֶת־בֵּיתוֹ׃ וְהֶעָרִים אֲשֶׁר
נָתַן חוּרָם לִשְׁלֹמֹה בָּנָה שְׁלֹמֹה
אוֹתָם וַיּוֹשֶׁב שָׁם אֶת־בְּנֵי
יִשְׂרָאֵל׃
3 וַיֵּלֶךְ שְׁלֹמֹה חֲמָת צוֹבָה וַיֶּחֱזַק
4 עָלֶיהָ׃ וַיִּבֶן אֶת־תַּדְמֹר
בַּמִּדְבָּר וְאֵת כָּל־עָרֵי
הַמִּסְכְּנוֹת אֲשֶׁר בָּנָה בַּחֲמָת׃
5 וַיִּבֶן אֶת־בֵּית חוֹרוֹן הָעֶלְיוֹן
וְאֶת־בֵּית חוֹרוֹן הַתַּחְתּוֹן עָרֵי
מָצוֹר חוֹמוֹת דְּלָתַיִם וּבְרִיחַ׃
6 וְאֶת־בַּעֲלָת וְאֵת כָּל־עָרֵי
הַמִּסְכְּנוֹת אֲשֶׁר־הָיוּ לִשְׁלֹמֹה

CHAPTER VIII

1-6. The cities established by Solomon. The passage occurs with variations in I Kings ix. 10f., 17-19.

1. *twenty years.* Seven years were occupied in building the Temple and thirteen in connection with the royal residences (cf. I Kings vi. 38, vii. 1ff.).

2. *the cities which Huram had given to Solomon.* According to I Kings ix. 11, *Solomon gave Hiram twenty cities in the land of Galilee.* Apparently, there was an exchange of gifts of cities between the two kings, although this is not recorded elsewhere.

Solomon built. The meaning of the verb is 'fortified.'

3-6. Solomon's store-cities.

3. *Hamath-zobah.* Or, 'Hamath of Zobah.' There was a kingdom of Hamath as well as of Zobah (cf. I Chron. xviii. 9) with a city named Hamath in the latter. Apparently there were several cities of this name (cf. Amos vi. 2). No other mention of this campaign occurs in the Bible.

4. *Tadmor in the wilderness.* i.e. Palmyra, a hundred and fifty miles north-east of Damascus. Modern commentators prefer the *kethib* in I Kings ix. 18, *Tamar,* a town on the southern border of Judah near the south-west tip of the Dead Sea.

store-cities. For the storage of produce in times of plenty for years of scarcity.

Hamath. This is probably the kingdom of Hamath which was to the north of Zobah.

5. *Beth-horon,* etc. See on I Chron. vi. 53. *Beth-horon the upper* is not included in I Kings ix. 17.

6. *Baalath.* A city in Dan (cf. Josh.

cities for his chariots, and the cities for his horsemen, and all that Solomon desired to build for his pleasure in Jerusalem, and in Lebanon, and in all the land of his dominion.

7. As for all the people that were left of the Hittites, and the Amorites, and the Perizzites, and the Hivites, and the Jebusites, who were not of Israel; 8. of their children that were left after them in the land, whom the children of Israel consumed not, of them did Solomon raise a levy of bondservants, unto this day. 9. But of the children of Israel did Solomon make no servants for his work; but they were men of war, and chief of his captains, and rulers of his chariots and of his horsemen.

10. And these were the chief officers of king Solomon, even two

וְאֵת כָּל־עָרֵי הָרֶכֶב וְאֵת עָרֵי
הַפָּרָשִׁים וְאֵת ׀ כָּל־חֵשֶׁק
שְׁלֹמֹה אֲשֶׁר חָשַׁק לִבְנוֹת
בִּירוּשָׁלִַם וּבַלְּבָנוֹן וּבְכֹל
אֶרֶץ מֶמְשַׁלְתּוֹ׃
7 כָּל־הָעָם הַנּוֹתָר מִן־הַחִתִּי
וְהָאֱמֹרִי וְהַפְּרִזִּי וְהַחִוִּי
וְהַיְבוּסִי אֲשֶׁר לֹא מִיִּשְׂרָאֵל
8 הֵמָּה׃ מִן־בְּנֵיהֶם אֲשֶׁר נוֹתְרוּ
אַחֲרֵיהֶם בָּאָרֶץ אֲשֶׁר לֹא־
כִלּוּם בְּנֵי יִשְׂרָאֵל וַיַּעֲלֵם
שְׁלֹמֹה לְמַס עַד הַיּוֹם הַזֶּה׃
9 וּמִן־בְּנֵי יִשְׂרָאֵל אֲשֶׁר לֹא־
נָתַן שְׁלֹמֹה לַעֲבָדִים
לִמְלַאכְתּוֹ כִּי־הֵמָּה אַנְשֵׁי
מִלְחָמָה וְשָׂרֵי שָׁלִישָׁיו וְשָׂרֵי
רִכְבּוֹ וּפָרָשָׁיו׃
10 וְאֵלֶּה שָׂרֵי הַנִּצִּיבִים אֲשֶׁר־

v. 10. יתיר י׳

xix. 44), probably on the border of Philistia; but its position is unknown.

cities for his chariots. See on i. 14.

Solomon desired . . . pleasure. lit. 'the desire of Solomon which he desired to build.'

in Lebanon. Where Solomon had an armoury or summer residence (cf. 1 Kings vii. 2, x. 17, 21).

7-9 (corresponding to 1 Kings ix. 20-22). The levy of forced labour.

8. *consumed not.* The Chronicler toned down the phrase *whom the children of Israel were not able utterly to destroy* in 1 Kings ix. 21.

of them did Solomon . . . bondservants. lit. 'and Solomon brought them up as a levy.' The Hebrew *mas* may signify tribute of money or a levy of men for task work.

9. *no servants.* This must mean that Israelites, unlike the others, were not subjected to forced labour continuously, but for limited periods of service, e.g. one month in every three (cf. 1 Kings v. 28).

10 (corresponding to 1 Kings ix. 23). The king's chief officers.

hundred and fifty, that bore rule over the people.

11. And Solomon brought up the daughter of Pharaoh out of the city of David unto the house that he had built for her; for he said: 'No wife of mine shall dwell in the house of David king of Israel, because the places are holy, whereunto the ark of the LORD hath come.'

12. Then Solomon offered burnt-offerings unto the LORD on the altar of the LORD, which he had built before the porch, 13. even as the duty of every day required, offering according to the commandment of Moses, on the sabbaths, and on the new moons, and on the appointed seasons, three times in the year, even in the feast of unleavened bread, and in the feast of weeks, and in the feast of tabernacles. 14. And he appointed, according to the ordinance of David his father, the courses of the priests to their service, and the

לַמֶּלֶךְ שְׁלֹמֹה חֲמִשִּׁים
וּמָאתַיִם הָרֹדִים בָּעָם׃
11 וְאֶת־בַּת־פַּרְעֹה הֶעֱלָה
שְׁלֹמֹה מֵעִיר דָּוִיד לַבַּיִת אֲשֶׁר
בָּנָה־לָהּ כִּי אָמַר לֹא־תֵשֵׁב
אִשָּׁה לִי בְּבֵית דָּוִיד מֶלֶךְ־
יִשְׂרָאֵל כִּי־קֹדֶשׁ הֵמָּה אֲשֶׁר־
בָּאָה אֲלֵיהֶם אֲרוֹן יְהוָה׃
12 אָז הֶעֱלָה שְׁלֹמֹה עֹלוֹת לַיהוָה
עַל מִזְבַּח יְהוָה אֲשֶׁר בָּנָה
13 לִפְנֵי הָאוּלָם׃ וּבִדְבַר־יוֹם
בְּיוֹם לְהַעֲלוֹת כְּמִצְוַת מֹשֶׁה
לַשַּׁבָּתוֹת וְלֶחֳדָשִׁים
וְלַמּוֹעֲדוֹת שָׁלוֹשׁ פְּעָמִים
בַּשָּׁנָה בְּחַג הַמַּצּוֹת וּבְחַג
הַשָּׁבֻעוֹת וּבְחַג הַסֻּכּוֹת׃
14 וַיַּעֲמֵד כְּמִשְׁפַּט דָּוִיד־אָבִיו
אֶת־מַחְלְקוֹת הַכֹּהֲנִים עַל־

two hundred and fifty. The number *five hundred and fifty* in 1 Kings ix. 23 may refer to another period of Solomon's reign when more officers were required.

11 (corresponding to 1 Kings ix. 24). The palace of Pharaoh's daughter.

out of the city of David. Where she lived while her residence and the other buildings were being erected (cf. 1 Kings iii. 1).

for he said, etc. Not in Kings. It is to be noted that the Chronicler does not record this marriage.

the places. Not in the text which is literally 'they are holy,' referring to all the buildings in the city.

12-16 (cf. 1 Kings ix. 25). Organization of the Temple service.

12. *on the altar*. The brazen altar which stood in the courtyard of the Temple. In 1 Kings ix. 25 it is also mentioned that he burned incense upon the (golden) altar. This the Chronicler omits because it was prohibited to anyone but the High Priest (Exod. xxx. 7), and he later narrates that king Uzziah was smitten with leprosy for contravening the law (xxvi. 16ff.).

13. Kings mentions only the sacrifices which Solomon offered *three times in a year* and omits the others.

Levites to their charges, to praise, and to minister before the priests, as the duty of every day required; the doorkeepers also by their courses at every gate; for so had David the man of God commanded. 15. And they departed not from the commandment of the king unto the priests and Levites concerning any matter, or concerning the treasures. 16. So all the work of Solomon was set in order from the day of the foundation of the house of the LORD, and until it was finished. So the house of the LORD was perfected.

17. Then went Solomon to Ezion-geber, and to Eloth, on the sea-shore in the land of Edom. 18. And Huram sent him by the hands of his servants ships, and servants that had knowledge of the sea; and they came

עֲבֹדָתָם וְהַלְוִיִּם עַל־
מִשְׁמְרוֹתָם לְהַלֵּל וּלְשָׁרֵת
נֶגֶד הַכֹּהֲנִים לִדְבַר־יוֹם
בְּיוֹמוֹ וְהַשֹּׁעֲרִים בְּמַחְלְקוֹתָם
לְשַׁעַר וָשָׁעַר כִּי כֵן מִצְוַת
15 דָּוִיד אִישׁ־הָאֱלֹהִים׃ וְלֹא
סָרוּ מִצְוַת הַמֶּלֶךְ עַל־
הַכֹּהֲנִים וְהַלְוִיִּם לְכָל־דָּבָר
16 וְלָאֹצָרוֹת׃ וַתִּכֹּן כָּל־
מְלֶאכֶת שְׁלֹמֹה עַד־הַיּוֹם
מוּסַד בֵּית־יְהוָה וְעַד־כְּלֹתוֹ
שָׁלֵם בֵּית יְהוָה׃
17 אָז הָלַךְ שְׁלֹמֹה לְעֶצְיוֹן־גֶּבֶר
וְאֶל־אֵילוֹת עַל־שְׂפַת הַיָּם
18 בְּאֶרֶץ אֱדוֹם׃ וַיִּשְׁלַח־לוֹ
חוּרָם בְּיַד־עֲבָדָיו אֳונִיּוֹת
וַעֲבָדִים יוֹדְעֵי יָם וַיָּבֹאוּ עִם־

v. 18. יתיר ו׳

14. *according to the ordinance of David.* Cf. 1 Chron. xxiv-xxvi.

to minister befors the priests. Cf. 1 Chron. xxiii. 28.

the man of God. He is so described again in Neh. xii. 24, 36. The description implies that David acted under Divine direction. The Targum paraphrases 'the prophet of the LORD.'

15. *from the commandment.* The preposition is implied.

concerning the treasures. Cf. 1 Chron. xxvi. 20-28.

16. *from the day.* lit. 'unto the day.'

so the house . . . perfected. lit. 'perfect (shalem) the house of the LORD.' 1 Kings ix. 25 has: *so he finished* (*weshillem*) *the house.*

17f. (corresponding to 1 Kings ix. 26-28). Solomon's navy and trade at Ophir.

17. *then went Solomon to.* In Kings: *and king Solomon made a navy of ships in.*

Ezion-geber. Now identified with Tel-el-Kheleifeh; it was evidently a well-known port on the northern tip of the gulf of Akaba.

Eloth. The modern Akaba, at the point of the north-east arm of the Red Sea. In Solomon's time it seems to have superseded in importance the older port of Ezion-geber. In 1 Kings ix. 26, Ezion-geber is described as being *beside Eloth.*

18. *servants that had knowledge of the sea.* Skilled and experienced navigators.

with the servants of Solomon to Ophir, and fetched from thence four hundred and fifty talents of gold, and brought them to king Solomon.

עַבְדֵי שְׁלֹמֹה אוֹפִירָה וַיִּקְחוּ
מִשָּׁם אַרְבַּע־מֵאוֹת וַחֲמִשִּׁים
כִּכַּר זָהָב וַיָּבִיאוּ אֶל־הַמֶּלֶךְ
שְׁלֹמֹה׃

9 CHAPTER IX ט

1. And when the queen of Sheba heard of the fame of Solomon, she came to prove Solomon with hard questions at Jerusalem, with a very great train, and camels that bore spices and gold in abundance, and precious stones; and when she was come to Solomon, she spoke with him of all that was in her heart. 2. And Solomon told her all her questions; and there was not any thing hid from Solomon which he told her not. 3. And when the queen of Sheba had seen the wisdom

1 וּמַלְכַּת־שְׁבָא שָׁמְעָה אֶת־
שֵׁמַע שְׁלֹמֹה וַתָּבוֹא לְנַסּוֹת
אֶת־־שְׁלֹמֹה בְחִידוֹת
בִּירוּשָׁלַםִ בְּחַיִל כָּבֵד מְאֹד
וּגְמַלִּים נֹשְׂאִים בְּשָׂמִים וְזָהָב
לָרֹב וְאֶבֶן יְקָרָה וַתָּבוֹא אֶל־
שְׁלֹמֹה וַתְּדַבֵּר עִמּוֹ אֵת כָּל־
2 אֲשֶׁר הָיָה עִם־לְבָבָהּ׃ וַיַּגֶּד־
לָהּ שְׁלֹמֹה אֶת־כָּל־דְּבָרֶיהָ
וְלֹא־נֶעְלַם דָּבָר מִשְּׁלֹמֹה
3 אֲשֶׁר לֹא הִגִּיד לָהּ׃ וַתֵּרֶא
מַלְכַּת־שְׁבָא אֵת חָכְמַת

Ophir. See on 1 Chron. xxix. 4.

four hundred and fifty talents. In 1 Kings ix. 28: *four hundred and twenty talents*. It has been suggested that 420 Jerusalem talents were equal to 450 Ophir talents. The value was over two and a half million pounds sterling.

CHAPTER IX

1-12 (corresponding to 1 Kings x. 1-13). The queen of Sheba's visit.

1. *Sheba*. An empire and great commercial power in the south-west of Arabia. It is identified by others with Ethiopia or Egypt.

hard questions. lit. 'riddles,' the same noun as in Judg. xiv. 12.

train. The Hebrew word *chayyil* may signify 'army' or 'wealth.' The latter may be its significance here.

all that was in her heart. All the questions she had prepared.

2. *there was not any thing*, etc. Solomon gave her the correct answers to all the questions she addressed to him.

of Solomon, and the house that he had built, 4. and the food of his table, and the sitting of his servants, and the attendance of his ministers, and their apparel; his cup-bearers also, and their apparel; and his ascent by which he went up unto the house of the LORD; there was no more spirit in her. 5. And she said to the king: 'It was a true report that I heard in mine own land of thine acts, and of thy wisdom. 6. Howbeit I believed not their words, until I came, and mine eyes had seen it; and, behold, the half of the greatness of thy wisdom was not told me; thou exceedest the fame that I heard. 7. Happy are thy men, and happy are these thy servants, that stand continually before thee, and hear thy wisdom. 8. Blessed be the LORD thy God, who delighted in thee, to set thee on His throne, to be king for the LORD thy God; because thy God loved Israel,

שְׁלֹמֹה וְהַבַּיִת אֲשֶׁר בָּנָה׃
4 וּמַאֲכַל שֻׁלְחָנוֹ וּמוֹשַׁב עֲבָדָיו
וּמַעֲמַד מְשָׁרְתָיו וּמַלְבּוּשֵׁיהֶם
וּמַשְׁקָיו וּמַלְבּוּשֵׁיהֶם וַעֲלִיָּתוֹ
אֲשֶׁר יַעֲלֶה בֵּית יְהוָה וְלֹא־
5 הָיָה עוֹד בָּהּ רוּחַ׃ וַתֹּאמֶר
אֶל־הַמֶּלֶךְ אֱמֶת הַדָּבָר אֲשֶׁר
שָׁמַעְתִּי בְּאַרְצִי עַל־דְּבָרֶיךָ
6 וְעַל־חָכְמָתֶךָ׃ וְלֹא־
הֶאֱמַנְתִּי לְדִבְרֵיהֶם עַד
אֲשֶׁר־בָּאתִי וַתִּרְאֶינָה עֵינַי
וְהִנֵּה לֹא הֻגַּד־לִי חֲצִי מַרְבִּית
חָכְמָתֶךָ יָסַפְתָּ עַל־הַשְּׁמוּעָה
7 אֲשֶׁר שָׁמַעְתִּי׃ אַשְׁרֵי אֲנָשֶׁיךָ
וְאַשְׁרֵי עֲבָדֶיךָ אֵלֶּה הָעֹמְדִים
לְפָנֶיךָ תָּמִיד וְשֹׁמְעִים אֶת־
8 חָכְמָתֶךָ׃ יְהִי יְהוָה אֱלֹהֶיךָ
בָּרוּךְ אֲשֶׁר ׀ חָפֵץ בְּךָ לְתִתְּךָ
עַל־כִּסְאוֹ לְמֶלֶךְ לַיהוָה
אֱלֹהֶיךָ בְּאַהֲבַת אֱלֹהֶיךָ אֶת־

4. *the sitting of his servants.* The officials who dined at Solomon's table.
the attendance of his ministers. i.e. the excellent service of his well-trained staff of waiters at the banquet.
his ascent by which he went up. For *aliyyatho* (*ascent*) 1 Kings x. 5 reads *olatho: his burnt-offering which he offered.* The noun used here denotes the magnificent retinue which accompanied him when he went to the Temple. The Jewish commentators regard the two nouns as identical in meaning.

there was no more spirit in her. She was amazed and lost in admiration.

5. *thine acts.* Solomon's magnificent buildings, organization and administration.

6. *thou exceedest,* etc. lit. 'thou hast added to the fame that I heard.'

8. *His throne.* 1 Kings x. 9: *the throne of Israel.* The Chronicler repeatedly states that the throne occupied by the Davidic dynasty is God's (cf. 1 Chron.

to establish them for ever, therefore made He thee king over them, to do justice and righteousness.'

9. And she gave the king a hundred and twenty talents of gold, and spices in great abundance, and precious stones; neither was there any such spice as the queen of Sheba gave to king Solomon. 10. And the servants also of Huram, and the servants of Solomon, that brought gold from Ophir, brought sandal-wood and precious stones. 11. And the king made of the sandal-wood paths for the house of the LORD, and for the king's house, and harps and psalteries for the singers; and there were none such seen before in the land of Judah. 12. And king Solomon gave to the queen of Sheba all her desire, whatsoever she asked, beside that which she had brought unto the king. So she

יִשְׂרָאֵל לְהַעֲמִידוֹ לְעוֹלָם
וַיִּתֶּנְךָ עֲלֵיהֶם לְמֶלֶךְ לַעֲשׂוֹת
מִשְׁפָּט וּצְדָקָה׃
9 וַתִּתֵּן לַמֶּלֶךְ מֵאָה וְעֶשְׂרִים ׀
כִּכַּר זָהָב וּבְשָׂמִים לָרֹב מְאֹד
וְאֶבֶן יְקָרָה וְלֹא הָיָה כַּבֹּשֶׂם
הַהוּא אֲשֶׁר נָתְנָה מַלְכַּת־
10 שְׁבָא לַמֶּלֶךְ שְׁלֹמֹה׃ וְגַם
עַבְדֵי חִירָם וְעַבְדֵי שְׁלֹמֹה
אֲשֶׁר־הֵבִיאוּ זָהָב מֵאוֹפִיר
הֵבִיאוּ עֲצֵי אַלְגּוּמִּים וְאֶבֶן
11 יְקָרָה׃ וַיַּעַשׂ הַמֶּלֶךְ אֶת־עֲצֵי
הָאַלְגּוּמִּים מְסִלּוֹת לְבֵית־
יְהוָה וּלְבֵית הַמֶּלֶךְ וְכִנֹּרוֹת
וּנְבָלִים לַשָּׁרִים וְלֹא־נִרְאוּ
כָהֵם לְפָנִים בְּאֶרֶץ יְהוּדָה׃
12 וְהַמֶּלֶךְ שְׁלֹמֹה נָתַן לְמַלְכַּת־
שְׁבָא אֶת־כָּל־חֶפְצָהּ אֲשֶׁר
שָׁאָלָה מִלְּבַד אֲשֶׁר־הֵבִיאָה

v. 10. חורם ק׳ v. 10. דגש אחר שורק v. 11. דגש אחר שורק

xxviii. 5, xxix. 23). The phrase *to be king for the LORD thy God* is not in Kings.

9. *neither was there any such spice.* i.e. in such abundance (so explicitly in 1 Kings x. 10).

10f. These verses are a parenthesis, their subject-matter having been suggested by the spices and gold mentioned in verse 9. The narrative of the queen of Sheba is resumed in verse 12.

10. *servants.* In 1 Kings x. 11: *navy.*

sandal-wood. See on ii. 7.

11. *paths.* In 1 Kings x. 12: *pillars.*

in the land of Judah. In Kings: *unto this day.* The phrase *the land of Judah,* instead of 'the land of Israel,' indicates a post-exilic date.

12. *king Solomon gave,* etc. He not only presented her with gifts equal in value to those which she had brought him, but he added *whatsoever she asked.*

beside that which she had brought unto

turned, and went to her own land, she and her servants.

13. Now the weight of gold that came to Solomon in one year was six hundred and threescore and six talents of gold; 14. beside that which the traffickers and merchants brought; and all the kings of Arabia and the governors of the country brought gold and silver to Solomon. 15. And king Solomon made two hundred targets of beaten gold: six hundred shekels of beaten gold went to one target; 16. three hundred shields of beaten gold also: three hundred shekels of gold went to one shield; and the king put them in the house of the forest of Lebanon.

אֶל־הַמֶּלֶךְ וַתַּהֲפֹךְ וַתֵּלֶךְ
לְאַרְצָהּ הִיא וַעֲבָדֶיהָ׃
וַיְהִי מִשְׁקַל הַזָּהָב אֲשֶׁר־בָּא 13
לִשְׁלֹמֹה בְּשָׁנָה אֶחָת שֵׁשׁ מֵאוֹת
וְשִׁשִּׁים וָשֵׁשׁ כִּכְּרֵי זָהָב׃ לְבַד 14
מֵאַנְשֵׁי הַתָּרִים וְהַסֹּחֲרִים
מְבִיאִים וְכָל־מַלְכֵי עֲרַב
וּפַחוֹת הָאָרֶץ מְבִיאִים זָהָב
וָכֶסֶף לִשְׁלֹמֹה׃ וַיַּעַשׂ הַמֶּלֶךְ 15
שְׁלֹמֹה מָאתַיִם צִנָּה זָהָב שָׁחוּט
שֵׁשׁ מֵאוֹת זָהָב שָׁחוּט יַעֲלֶה
עַל־הַצִּנָּה הָאֶחָת׃ וּשְׁלֹשׁ־ 16
מֵאוֹת מָגִנִּים זָהָב שָׁחוּט שְׁלֹשׁ
מֵאוֹת זָהָב יַעֲלֶה עַל־הַמָּגֵן
הָאֶחָת וַיִּתְּנֵם הַמֶּלֶךְ בְּבֵית
יַעַר הַלְּבָנוֹן׃

the king. In 1 Kings x. 13: *besides that which Solomon gave her of his royal bounty.*

13-28 (corresponding to 1 Kings x. 14-28). Solomon's exceptional wealth, wisdom, power and influence.

13f. His sources of revenue.

13. *six hundred,* etc. Equivalent to about four million pounds sterling in weight.

14. *the traffickers.* lit. 'those who go about.'

Arabia. The word *arab* is read in 1 Kings x. 15 as *(ha-)ereb: the mingled people.*

governors. The noun *pachoth* is a title usually applied to Babylonian and Persian governors of provinces; it may therefore be that governors of foreign countries are referred to here.

15f. The golden targets and shields.

15. *targets.* The *tsinnah* was large in size and protected the warrior's body from three sides.

six hundred shekels. Equal in weight to about twenty pounds.

shekels of. Not in the text.

went to. lit. 'ascended upon,' which probably means was overlaid upon (similarly in the next verse).

16. *shields.* The *magen* was smaller and lighter in weight.

three hundred shekels. In 1 Kings x. 17: *three pounds.*

house . . . Lebanon. Described in 1 Kings vii. 2ff. The targets and shields adorned this residence; later

17. Moreover the king made a great throne of ivory, and overlaid it with pure gold. 18. And there were six steps to the throne, with a footstool of gold, which were fastened to the throne, and arms on either side by the place of the seat, and two lions standing beside the arms. 19. And twelve lions stood there on the one side and on the other upon the six steps; there was not the like made in any kingdom.

20. And all king Solomon's drinking-vessels were of gold, and all the vessels of the house of the forest of Lebanon were of pure gold; silver was nothing accounted of in the days of Solomon. 21. For the king had ships that went to Tarshish with the servants of Huram; once every three years came the ships of Tarshish, bringing gold, and silver, ivory, and apes, and peacocks.

17 וַיַּעַשׂ הַמֶּלֶךְ כִּסֵּא־שֵׁן גָּדוֹל
18 וַיְצַפֵּהוּ זָהָב טָהוֹר׃ וְשֵׁשׁ
מַעֲלוֹת לַכִּסֵּא וְכֶבֶשׁ בַּזָּהָב
לַכִּסֵּא מָאֳחָזִים וְיָדוֹת מִזֶּה
וּמִזֶּה עַל־מְקוֹם הַשָּׁבֶת וּשְׁנַיִם
אֲרָיוֹת עֹמְדִים אֵצֶל הַיָּדוֹת׃
19 וּשְׁנֵים עָשָׂר אֲרָיוֹת עֹמְדִים
שָׁם עַל־שֵׁשׁ הַמַּעֲלוֹת מִזֶּה
וּמִזֶּה לֹא־נַעֲשָׂה כֵן לְכָל־
מַמְלָכָה׃
20 וְכֹל כְּלֵי מַשְׁקֵה הַמֶּלֶךְ שְׁלֹמֹה
זָהָב וְכֹל כְּלֵי בֵית־יַעַר
הַלְּבָנוֹן זָהָב סָגוּר אֵין כֶּסֶף
נֶחְשָׁב בִּימֵי שְׁלֹמֹה לִמְאוּמָה׃
21 כִּי־אֳנִיּוֹת לַמֶּלֶךְ הֹלְכוֹת
תַּרְשִׁישׁ עִם עַבְדֵי חוּרָם אַחַת
לְשָׁלוֹשׁ שָׁנִים תָּבוֹאנָה ׀ אֳנִיּוֹת
תַּרְשִׁישׁ נֹשְׂאוֹת זָהָב וָכֶסֶף
שֶׁנְהַבִּים וְקוֹפִים וְתוּכִּיִּים׃

v. 21. דגש אחר שורק

they were taken as spoil by the king of Egypt (I Kings xiv. 26).

17-19. Solomon's throne of ivory and gold.

18. I Kings x. 19 has an additional detail: *and the top of the throne was round behind*, but omits *with a footstool of gold, which was fastened to the throne.*

arms. lit. 'hands,' supports for the king's arms.

19. *twelve lions.* Made of gold.

on the one side, etc. There were six lions on each side, one on each step.

20. The abundance of gold and cheapness of silver.

nothing accounted of. Because of the abundance of gold.

21. The ships of Tarshish.

the king. viz. Solomon.

that went to Tarshish. In I Kings x. 22: *a navy of Tarshish*, i.e. large-sized ships capable of undertaking the long voyage to that city, viz. Tartessus in the south of Spain.

22. So king Solomon exceeded all the kings of the earth in riches and wisdom. 23. And all the kings of the earth sought the presence of Solomon, to hear his wisdom, which God had put in his heart. 24. And they brought every man his present, vessels of silver, and vessels of gold, and raiment, armour, and spices, horses, and mules, a rate year by year.

25. And Solomon had four thousand stalls for horses and chariots, and twelve thousand horsemen, that he bestowed in the chariot cities, and with the king at Jerusalem. 26. And he ruled over all the kings from the River even unto the land of the Philistines, and to the border of Egypt. 27. And the king made silver to be in Jerusalem as stones, and cedars made he to be as the sycomore-trees that are in the

22 וַיִּגְדַּל הַמֶּלֶךְ שְׁלֹמֹה מִכֹּל
מַלְכֵי הָאָרֶץ לְעֹשֶׁר וְחָכְמָה׃
23 וְכֹל מַלְכֵי הָאָרֶץ מְבַקְשִׁים
אֶת־פְּנֵי שְׁלֹמֹה לִשְׁמֹעַ אֶת־
חָכְמָתוֹ אֲשֶׁר־נָתַן הָאֱלֹהִים
24 בְּלִבּוֹ׃ וְהֵם מְבִיאִים אִישׁ
מִנְחָתוֹ כְּלֵי כֶסֶף וּכְלֵי זָהָב
וּשְׂלָמוֹת נֵשֶׁק וּבְשָׂמִים סוּסִים
וּפְרָדִים דְּבַר־שָׁנָה בְּשָׁנָה׃
25 וַיְהִי לִשְׁלֹמֹה אַרְבַּעַת אֲלָפִים
אֻרְיוֹת סוּסִים וּמַרְכָּבוֹת
וּשְׁנֵים־עָשָׂר אֶלֶף פָּרָשִׁים
וַיַּנִּיחֵם בְּעָרֵי הָרֶכֶב וְעִם־
26 הַמֶּלֶךְ בִּירוּשָׁלִָם׃ וַיְהִי מוֹשֵׁל
בְּכָל־הַמְּלָכִים מִן־הַנָּהָר
וְעַד־אֶרֶץ פְּלִשְׁתִּים וְעַד
27 גְּבוּל מִצְרָיִם׃ וַיִּתֵּן הַמֶּלֶךְ
אֶת־הַכֶּסֶף בִּירוּשָׁלִַם
כָּאֲבָנִים וְאֵת הָאֲרָזִים נָתַן
כַּשִּׁקְמִים אֲשֶׁר־בַּשְּׁפֵלָה

the servants. In Kings: *the navy,* the same alteration as in verse 10.

apes, and peacocks. The nouns in Hebrew are of foreign origin, perhaps Indian.

22-24. Solomon's pre-eminence in wisdom and wealth is universally recognized.

23. *all the kings of the earth.* In 1 Kings x. 24: *all the earth.*

24. *present.* i.e. tribute.

a rate year by year. lit. 'the word (or, matter) of a year in a year.'

25-28. Solomon's horses, chariots and horsemen (cf. i. 14ff.).

25. *four thousand stalls for horses and chariots.* In 1 Kings x. 26: *a thousand and four hundred chariots.*

chariot cities. See on i. 14.

26. *the River.* The Euphrates.

Lowland, for abundance. 28. And they brought horses for Solomon out of Egypt, and out of all lands.

29. Now the rest of the acts of Solomon, first and last, are they not written in the words of Nathan the prophet, and in the prophecy of Ahijah the Shilonite, and in the visions of Jedo the seer concerning Jeroboam the son of Nebat? 30. And Solomon reigned in Jerusalem over all Israel forty years. 31. And Solomon slept with his fathers, they buried him in the city of David his father; and Rehoboam his son reigned in his stead.

28 לָרֹב׃ וּמוֹצִיאִים סוּסִים
מִמִּצְרַיִם לִשְׁלֹמֹה וּמִכָּל־
הָאֲרָצוֹת׃
29 וּשְׁאָר דִּבְרֵי שְׁלֹמֹה הָרִאשֹׁנִים
וְהָאַחֲרוֹנִים הֲלֹא־הֵם
כְּתוּבִים עַל־דִּבְרֵי נָתָן
הַנָּבִיא וְעַל־נְבוּאַת אֲחִיָּה
הַשִּׁילוֹנִי וּבַחֲזוֹת יֶעְדִּי הַחֹזֶה
30 עַל יָרָבְעָם בֶּן־נְבָט׃ וַיִּמְלֹךְ
שְׁלֹמֹה בִירוּשָׁלִַם עַל־כָּל־
יִשְׂרָאֵל אַרְבָּעִים שָׁנָה׃
31 וַיִּשְׁכַּב שְׁלֹמֹה עִם־אֲבֹתָיו
וַיִּקְבְּרֻהוּ בְּעִיר דָּוִיד אָבִיו
וַיִּמְלֹךְ רְחַבְעָם בְּנוֹ תַּחְתָּיו׃

10 CHAPTER X י

1. And Rehoboam went to Shechem; for all Israel were come to Shechem

1 וַיֵּלֶךְ רְחַבְעָם שְׁכֶמָה כִּי שְׁכֶם

v. 29. יעדו ק׳

27. This verse is repeated from i. 15 with the omission of *and gold.*

28. Cf. i. 16.

29-31 (corresponding to 1 Kings xi. 41-43). The end of Solomon's reign; his successor.

29. *the acts.* The Hebrew also means 'words.' Solomon's fame was due to both his acts and his words of wisdom.

first and last. See on 1 Chron. xxix. 29.

in the words of Nathan, etc. Cf. 1 Chron. xxix. 29. In 1 Kings xi. 41: *in the book of the acts of Solomon.*

Ahijah the Shilonite. Cf. 1 Kings xi. 29, xiv. 2ff.

Jedo. Cf. xii. 15, and xiii. 22 where the name is *Iddo.*

30. *forty years.* Perhaps from 971 to 932 B.C.E.

31. *slept with his fathers.* It is computed that at his death Solomon could not have been more than sixty years old.

city of David. Cf. 1 Chron. xi. 7.

to make him king. 2. And it came
to pass, when Jeroboam the son of
Nebat heard of it—for he was in
Egypt, whither he had fled from
the presence of king Solomon—that
Jeroboam returned out of Egypt.
3. And they sent and called him; and
Jeroboam and all Israel came, and
they spoke to Rehoboam, saying:
4. 'Thy father made our yoke
grievous; now therefore make thou
the grievous service of thy father,
and his heavy yoke which he put
upon us, lighter, and we will serve
thee.' 5. And he said unto them:

בָּאוּ כָל־יִשְׂרָאֵל לְהַמְלִיךְ
2 אֹתוֹ׃ וַיְהִי כִּשְׁמֹעַ יָרָבְעָם
בֶּן־נְבָט וְהוּא בְמִצְרַיִם אֲשֶׁר
בָּרַח מִפְּנֵי שְׁלֹמֹה הַמֶּלֶךְ וַיָּשָׁב
3 יָרָבְעָם מִמִּצְרָיִם׃ וַיִּשְׁלְחוּ
וַיִּקְרְאוּ־לוֹ וַיָּבֹא יָרָבְעָם
וְכָל־יִשְׂרָאֵל וַיְדַבְּרוּ אֶל־
4 רְחַבְעָם לֵאמֹר׃ אָבִיךָ
הִקְשָׁה אֶת־עֻלֵּנוּ וְעַתָּה הָקֵל
מֵעֲבוֹדַת אָבִיךָ הַקָּשָׁה וּמֵעֻלּוֹ
הַכָּבֵד אֲשֶׁר־נָתַן עָלֵינוּ
5 וְנַעַבְדֶךָּ׃ וַיֹּאמֶר אֲלֵהֶם עוֹד

CHAPTERS X-XXXVI

THE HISTORY OF JUDAH FROM REHOBOAM TO THE CAPTIVITY

CHAPTER X

REVOLT OF THE NORTHERN TRIBES

1-5 (corresponding to 1 Kings xii. 1-5). The people's demand of the new king.

1. *Rehoboam.* He reigned from 932 to 916 B.C.E.

Shechem. An ancient city in the centre of the Holy Land on the north-east slopes of mount Gerizim in the hill-country of Ephraim. Its Arabic name now is Nablus.

all Israel. The northern tribes as well as the southern.

to make him king. The choice of Shechem for the purpose was due to several reasons. It lay in the territory of Ephraim, the tribe of Jeroboam who was the leader of the disaffected people; it was far removed from Jerusalem where the fame and glories of Rehoboam's father and grandfather might have stirred the sympathies of the people towards the scion of the house of David and weakened the position of the malcontents; and it was, finally, in the heart of the territory inhabited by the aggrieved tribes of the north.

2. *heard of it.* The last two words are implied. Jeroboam heard of the death of Solomon and felt that it was now safe to return to his native land. For the reason of his flight, cf. 1 Kings xi. 26ff.

Jeroboam returned out of Egypt. In 1 Kings xii. 2: *Jeroboam dwelt in Egypt.* The difference between the two verbs in Hebrew is only in their vowels; the consonants are identical.

3. *they sent and called him.* From his residence in Ephraim. According to the reading in Kings, he was recalled from Egypt.

4. *made our yoke grievous.* By the imposition of heavy taxation and forced labour.

make thou . . . lighter. The people's request was not for complete abolition of the oppressive measures but only for an easing of the burden.

'Come again unto me after three days.' And the people departed.

6. And king Rehoboam took counsel with the old men, that had stood before Solomon his father while he yet lived, saying: 'What counsel give ye me to return answer to this people?' 7. And they spoke unto him, saying: 'If thou be kind to this people, and please them, and speak good words to them, then they will be thy servants for ever.' 8. But he forsook the counsel of the old men which they had given him, and took counsel with the young men that were grown up with him, that stood before him. 9. And he said unto them: 'What counsel give ye, that we may return answer to this people, who have spoken to me, saying: Make the yoke that thy father did put upon us lighter?' 10. And the young men that were grown up with him spoke unto him, saying: 'Thus shalt thou say unto

שְׁלֹ֥שֶׁת יָמִ֖ים וְשׁ֣וּבוּ אֵלָ֑י וַיֵּ֖לֶךְ
הָעָֽם׃
6 וַיִּוָּעַ֨ץ הַמֶּ֜לֶךְ רְחַבְעָ֗ם אֶת־
הַזְּקֵנִ֗ים אֲשֶׁר־הָי֤וּ עֹֽמְדִים֙
לִפְנֵי֙ שְׁלֹמֹ֣ה אָבִ֔יו בִּהְיֹת֥וֹ חַ֖י
לֵאמֹ֑ר אֵ֚יךְ אַתֶּ֣ם נֽוֹעָצִ֔ים
לְהָשִׁ֥יב לָֽעָם־הַזֶּ֖ה דָּבָֽר׃
7 וַיְדַבְּר֨וּ אֵלָ֜יו לֵאמֹ֗ר אִם־
תִּֽהְיֶה֩ לְט֨וֹב לְהָעָ֤ם הַזֶּה֙
וּרְצִיתָ֔ם וְדִבַּרְתָּ֥ אֲלֵהֶ֖ם
דְּבָרִ֣ים טוֹבִ֑ים וְהָי֥וּ לְךָ֛
8 עֲבָדִ֖ים כָּל־הַיָּמִֽים׃ וַיַּעֲזֹ֛ב
אֶת־עֲצַ֥ת הַזְּקֵנִ֖ים אֲשֶׁ֣ר
יְעָצֻ֑הוּ וַיִּוָּעַ֗ץ אֶת־הַיְלָדִים֙
אֲשֶׁ֣ר גָּדְל֣וּ אִתּ֔וֹ הָעֹמְדִ֖ים
9 לְפָנָֽיו׃ וַיֹּ֣אמֶר אֲלֵהֶ֗ם מָ֤ה
אַתֶּם֙ נֽוֹעָצִ֔ים וְנָשִׁ֥יב דָּבָ֖ר אֶת־
הָעָ֣ם הַזֶּ֑ה אֲשֶׁ֨ר דִּבְּר֤וּ אֵלַי֙
לֵאמֹ֔ר הָקֵ֣ל מִן־הָעֹ֔ל אֲשֶׁר־
10 נָתַ֥ן אָבִ֖יךָ עָלֵֽינוּ׃ וַיְדַבְּר֣וּ
אִתּ֗וֹ הַיְלָדִים֙ אֲשֶׁ֣ר גָּדְל֣וּ אִתּוֹ֮
לֵאמֹר֒ כֹּֽה־תֹאמַ֣ר לָעָם֩ אֲשֶׁר־

5. *come . . . after three days.* Rehoboam wanted time for consulting his advisers.

6-11 (corresponding to 1 Kings xii. 6-11). The counsellors' advice.

6. *stood before.* i.e. served.

7. *if thou be . . . to them.* In 1 Kings xii. 7: *if thou wilt be a servant unto this people this day, and wilt serve them.*

thy servants. Loyal subjects.

8. *that were grown up with him.* His contemporaries. He was then forty-one years of age (cf. xii. 13).

the people that spoke unto thee, saying: Thy father made our yoke heavy, but make thou it lighter unto us; thus shalt thou say unto them: My little finger is thicker than my father's loins. 11. And now whereas my father did lade you with a heavy yoke, I will add to your yoke; my father chastised you with whips, but I will chastise you with scorpions.'

12. So Jeroboam and all the people came to Rehoboam the third day, as the king bade, saying: 'Come to me again the third day.' 13. And the king answered them roughly; and king Rehoboam forsook the counsel of the old men, 14. and spoke to them after the counsel of the young men, saying: '[My father] made your yoke heavy, but I will add thereto; my father chastised you with whips, but I will chastise you with scorpions.' 15. So the king hearkened not unto the people; for it was brought about of God, that the LORD might establish His word,

דִּבְּרוּ אֵלֶיךָ לֵאמֹר אָבִיךָ
הִכְבִּיד אֶת־עֻלֵּנוּ וְאַתָּה הָקֵל
מֵעָלֵינוּ כֹּה תֹאמַר אֲלֵהֶם
11 קָטָנִּי עָבָה מִמָּתְנֵי אָבִי׃ וְעַתָּה
אָבִי הֶעְמִיס עֲלֵיכֶם עֹל כָּבֵד
וַאֲנִי אֹסִיף עַל־עֻלְּכֶם אָבִי
יִסַּר אֶתְכֶם בַּשּׁוֹטִים וַאֲנִי
בָּעַקְרַבִּים׃
12 וַיָּבֹא יָרָבְעָם וְכָל־הָעָם אֶל־
רְחַבְעָם בַּיּוֹם הַשְּׁלִשִׁי כַּאֲשֶׁר
דִּבֶּר הַמֶּלֶךְ לֵאמֹר שׁוּבוּ אֵלַי
13 בַּיּוֹם הַשְּׁלִשִׁי׃ וַיַּעֲנֵם הַמֶּלֶךְ
קָשָׁה וַיַּעֲזֹב הַמֶּלֶךְ רְחַבְעָם
14 אֵת עֲצַת הַזְּקֵנִים׃ וַיְדַבֵּר
אֲלֵהֶם כַּעֲצַת הַיְלָדִים לֵאמֹר
הִכְבִּיד אֶת־עֻלְּכֶם וַאֲנִי
אֹסִיף עָלָיו אָבִי יִסַּר אֶתְכֶם
בַּשּׁוֹטִים וַאֲנִי בָּעַקְרַבִּים׃
15 וְלֹא־שָׁמַע הַמֶּלֶךְ אֶל־הָעָם
כִּי־הָיְתָה נְסִבָּה מֵעִם
הָאֱלֹהִים לְמַעַן הָקִים יְהוָה

10. *my little finger*, etc. A metaphor which is explained in the next verse.

11. *whips . . . scorpions.* Another metaphor, repeating in different words and emphasizing the first part of the verse. It may be that a 'whip' or flail was one of the insignia of an Israelite, as it was of an Egyptian king. A 'scorpion' is, according to the Peshitta, a kind of lash.

12-15 (corresponding to 1 Kings xii. 12-15). Rehoboam's reply.

14. [*my father*] . . . *heavy.* This reading, with the insertion of *abi*, *my father*, agrees with 1 Kings xii. 14; some MSS. and editions read here: 'I will make your yoke heavy and I will add.'

15. *it was brought about.* lit. 'a turn'; it was fate, providence.

which He spoke by the hand of Ahijah the Shilonite to Jeroboam the son of Nebat.

16. And when all Israel [saw] that the king hearkened not unto them, the people answered the king, saying: 'What portion have we in David? neither have we inheritance in the son of Jesse; every man to your tents, O Israel; now see to thine own house, David.' So all Israel departed unto their tents. 17. But as for the children of Israel that dwelt in the cities of Judah, Rehoboam reigned over them. 18. Then king Rehoboam sent Hadoram, who was over the levy; and the children of Israel stoned him with stones, so that he died. And king Rehoboam made speed to get him up to his chariot, to flee to Jerusalem.

אֶת־דְּבָרוֹ אֲשֶׁר דִּבֶּר בְּיַד
אֲחִיָּהוּ הַשִּׁלוֹנִי אֶל־יָרָבְעָם
בֶּן־נְבָט׃
וְכָל־יִשְׂרָאֵל כִּי לֹא־ 16
שָׁמַע הַמֶּלֶךְ לָהֶם וַיָּשִׁיבוּ
הָעָם ׀ אֶת־הַמֶּלֶךְ ׀ לֵאמֹר
מַה־לָּנוּ חֵלֶק בְּדָוִיד וְלֹא־
נַחֲלָה בְּבֶן־יִשַׁי אִישׁ לְאֹהָלֶיךָ
יִשְׂרָאֵל עַתָּה רְאֵה בֵיתְךָ דָּוִיד
וַיֵּלֶךְ כָּל־יִשְׂרָאֵל לְאֹהָלָיו׃
וּבְנֵי יִשְׂרָאֵל הַיֹּשְׁבִים בְּעָרֵי 17
יְהוּדָה וַיִּמְלֹךְ עֲלֵיהֶם
רְחַבְעָם׃ וַיִּשְׁלַח הַמֶּלֶךְ 18
רְחַבְעָם אֶת־הֲדֹרָם אֲשֶׁר
עַל־הַמַּס וַיִּרְגְּמוּ־בוֹ בְנֵי־
יִשְׂרָאֵל אֶבֶן וַיָּמֹת וְהַמֶּלֶךְ
רְחַבְעָם הִתְאַמֵּץ לַעֲלוֹת
בַּמֶּרְכָּבָה לָנוּס יְרוּשָׁלִָם׃

by . . . Ahijah the Shilonite. Recorded in 1 Kings xi. 29ff. but not in Chron.

16-19 (corresponding to 1 Kings xii. 16-19). The revolt.

16. *all Israel* [*saw*]. The definition of the subject required by the context is the northern tribes. The verb is supplied from 1 Kings xii. 16.

what portion, etc. A forceful way of saying, 'we have no portion.'

David. The founder of the dynasty.

to your tents. Take no part in the coronation and return to your homes.

now see to thine own house, David. The words are ironical: let Rehoboam, the descendant of David, who lost a kingdom, now look after his own household, or after his shrunken State.

18. *Hadoram.* In 1 Kings xii. 18: *Adoram*, and in 1 Kings iv. 6, v. 28: *Adoniram.*

who was over the levy. It was a most inappropriate choice, since he was personally identified with the cause of the people's complaint.

made speed. lit. 'strengthened himself.' The verb expresses the urgent necessity for Rehoboam to leave in order to escape death.

19. So Israel rebelled against the house of David unto this day.

19 וַיִּפְשְׁעוּ יִשְׂרָאֵל בְּבֵית דָּוִיד
עַד הַיּוֹם הַזֶּה׃

11 CHAPTER XI יא

1. And when Rehoboam was come to Jerusalem, he assembled the house of Judah and Benjamin, a hundred and fourscore thousand chosen men, that were warriors, to fight against Israel, to bring the kingdom back to Rehoboam. 2. But the word of the LORD came to Shemaiah the man of God, saying: 3. 'Speak unto Rehoboam the son of Solomon, king of Judah, and to all Israel in Judah and Benjamin, saying: 4. Thus saith the LORD: Ye shall not go up, nor fight against your brethren; return every man to his house, for this thing is of Me.'

1 וַיָּבֹא רְחַבְעָם יְרוּשָׁלִַם
וַיַּקְהֵל אֶת־בֵּית יְהוּדָה
וּבִנְיָמִן מֵאָה וּשְׁמוֹנִים אֶלֶף
בָּחוּר עֹשֵׂה מִלְחָמָה לְהִלָּחֵם
עִם־יִשְׂרָאֵל לְהָשִׁיב אֶת־
2 הַמַּמְלָכָה לִרְחַבְעָם׃ וַיְהִי
דְּבַר־יְהוָה אֶל־שְׁמַעְיָהוּ
3 אִישׁ־הָאֱלֹהִים לֵאמֹר׃ אֱמֹר
אֶל־רְחַבְעָם בֶּן־שְׁלֹמֹה מֶלֶךְ
יְהוּדָה וְאֶל כָּל־יִשְׂרָאֵל
4 בִּיהוּדָה וּבִנְיָמִן לֵאמֹר׃ כֹּה
אָמַר יְהוָה לֹא־תַעֲלוּ וְלֹא־
תִלָּחֲמוּ עִם־אֲחֵיכֶם שׁוּבוּ
אִישׁ לְבֵיתוֹ כִּי מֵאִתִּי נִהְיָה

19. *unto this day.* The split in the kingdom was never healed.

CHAPTERS XI-XII

THE REIGN OF REHOBOAM

CHAPTER XI

1-4 (corresponding to 1 Kings xii. 21-24). Civil war averted by the prophet Shemaiah. The crowning of Jeroboam as king over the northern tribes (1 Kings xii. 20) is omitted by the Chronicler who is only concerned with the kingdom of Judah.

1. *Judah and Benjamin.* Immediately after the revolt, only Judah remained loyal to Rehoboam (1 Kings xii. 20). Benjamin must have joined Judah soon after (1 Kings xii. 21).

2. *Shemaiah.* He ministered throughout the reign of Rehoboam and prophesied at the invasion of Shishak (xii. 5). He is also said to have compiled a history (xii. 15).

3. *Israel.* The Chronicler often refers to the people of the Southern Kingdom by this term (cf. xii. 1, xv. 17).

4. *is of Me.* It is Divine retribution for

So they hearkened unto the words of the LORD, and returned from going against Jeroboam.

5. And Rehoboam dwelt in Jerusalem, and built cities for defence in Judah. 6. He built even Beth-lehem, and Etam, and Tekoa, 7. and Beth-zur, and Soco, and Adullam, 8. and Gath, and Mareshah, and Ziph, 9. and Adoraim, and Lachish, and Azekah, 10. and

הַדָּבָר הַזֶּה וַיִּשְׁמְעוּ אֶת־
דִּבְרֵי יְהוָה וַיָּשֻׁבוּ מִלֶּכֶת
אֶל־יָרָבְעָם׃
5 וַיֵּשֶׁב רְחַבְעָם בִּירוּשָׁלִָם וַיִּבֶן
6 עָרִים לְמָצוֹר בִּיהוּדָה׃ וַיִּבֶן
אֶת־בֵּית־לֶחֶם וְאֶת־עֵיטָם
7 וְאֶת־תְּקוֹעַ׃ וְאֶת־בֵּית־
צוּר וְאֶת־שׂוֹכוֹ וְאֶת־עֲדֻלָּם׃
8 וְאֶת־גַּת וְאֶת־מָרֵשָׁה וְאֶת־
9 זִיף׃ וְאֶת־אֲדוֹרַיִם וְאֶת־
10 לָכִישׁ וְאֶת־עֲזֵקָה׃ וְאֶת־

Solomon's sins and Rehoboam's obduracy.

5-23. Rehoboam's activities and progress. There is no parallel to this passage in Kings.

5-12. His fortifications.

5. *built.* The verb may signify constructed, rebuilt, or fortified. Some of the cities named were ancient and famous long before the time of Rehoboam.

for defence. Mainly, if not solely, against Egyptian invasion, since the fortified cities enumerated were located along the main road from Egypt to Jerusalem or on the western hills of the Shephelah. None of them were on the frontier between Judah and Israel.

6. *Beth-lehem.* North of Hebron and five miles south-west of Jerusalem.

Etam. Two miles to the south-west of Beth-lehem; possibly the modern Ain Atan.

Tekoa. About five miles to the south of Beth-lehem.

7. *Beth-zur.* Four and a half miles north of Hebron, on the road from Jerusalem to Hebron; it is still known by this name.

Soco. Now called esh-Shuweikeh, in the Shephelah.

Adullam. See on 1 Chron. xi. 16.

8. *Gath.* See on 1 Chron. xviii. 1.

Mareshah. To the south of Beit Jibrin (Eleutheropolis) in the Shephelah.

Ziph. Probably the modern Tel-Zif, eight miles south-east of Hebron.

9. *Adoraim.* The modern Dura, five miles south-west of Hebron.

Lachish. One of the most important Judean strongholds in the Shephelah now identified with Tel ed-Duweir. It stood in a commanding position on the road to Egypt, being the furthest city in that direction fortified by Rehoboam.

Azekah. Also in the Shephelah, but the site is unknown. It may be represented by the modern Bir ez-Zag, north of Soco.

10. *Zorah.* The modern Sara in the Shephelah, fourteen miles west of Jeru-

Zorah, and Aijalon, and Hebron, which are in Judah and in Benjamin, fortified cities. 11. And he fortified the strongholds, and put captains in them, and store of victual, and oil and wine. 12. And in every city he put shields and spears, and made them exceeding strong. And Judah and Benjamin adhered to him.

13. And the priests and the Levites that were in all Israel presented themselves to him out of all their border. 14. For the Levites left their open land and their possession, and came to Judah and Jerusalem; for Jeroboam and his sons cast them off, that they should not execute the priest's office unto the LORD; 15. and he appointed him priests for the high places, and for the satyrs, and for the calves which

צָרְעָה וְאֶת־אַיָּלוֹן וְאֶת־
חֶבְרוֹן אֲשֶׁר בִּיהוּדָה וּבְבִנְיָמִן
11 עָרֵי מְצוּרוֹת׃ וַיְחַזֵּק אֶת־
הַמְּצוּרוֹת וַיִּתֵּן בָּהֶם נְגִידִים
וְאֹצְרוֹת מַאֲכָל וְשֶׁמֶן וָיָיִן׃
12 וּבְכָל־עִיר וָעִיר צִנּוֹת
וּרְמָחִים וַיְחַזְּקֵם לְהַרְבֵּה
מְאֹד וַיְהִי־לוֹ יְהוּדָה וּבִנְיָמִן׃
13 וְהַכֹּהֲנִים וְהַלְוִיִּם אֲשֶׁר בְּכָל־
יִשְׂרָאֵל הִתְיַצְּבוּ עָלָיו מִכָּל־
14 גְּבוּלָם׃ כִּי־עָזְבוּ הַלְוִיִּם
אֶת־מִגְרְשֵׁיהֶם וַאֲחֻזָּתָם וַיֵּלְכוּ
לִיהוּדָה וְלִירוּשָׁלִַם כִּי־
הִזְנִיחָם יָרָבְעָם וּבָנָיו מִכַּהֵן
15 לַיהוָה׃ וַיַּעֲמֶד־לוֹ כֹּהֲנִים
לַבָּמוֹת וְלַשְּׂעִירִים וְלָעֲגָלִים

salem. Another opinion locates it in the Negeb.

Aijalon. The modern Yalo, fourteen miles from Jerusalem, almost midway between it and Ramleh. The valley of Aijalon is mentioned in Josh. x. 12 and in the Tel el-Amarna letters.

Hebron. On the Judean hills between Jerusalem and Beer-sheba. It is one of the most ancient and famous of Biblical cities.

11. *he fortified the strongholds.* As lines of defence against an invader. There is no reason to assume that the fortifications were intended to keep in subjection his kinsmen in Judah or his subjects in Benjamin.

12. *he put.* Not in the text.

adhered to him. lit. 'was to him.'

13-17. Migration from the north to Rehoboam's kingdom.

13. *all Israel.* The tribes under the rule of Jeroboam.

14. *Jeroboam . . . cast them off.* He set up his own shrines in which he installed golden calves, and appointed as ministers members of the tribes of Israel other than priests and Levites (cf. 1 Kings xii. 28ff.).

15. *appointed him priests.* Who were not of the tribe of Levi; this was the cause of the migration from his kingdom.

for the satyrs. These are not mentioned in Kings. They were believed to be spirits in animal form; cf. *they shall no more sacrifice their sacrifices unto the satyrs after whom they go astray* (Lev. xvii. 7).

he had made. 16. And after them, out of all the tribes of Israel, such as set their hearts to seek the LORD, the God of Israel, came to Jerusalem to sacrifice unto the LORD, the God of their fathers. 17. So they strengthened the kingdom of Judah, and made Rehoboam the son of Solomon strong, three years; for they walked three years in the way of David and Solomon.

18. And Rehoboam took him a wife, Mahalath the daughter of Jerimoth the son of David, and of Abihail the daughter of Eliab the son of Jesse; 19. and she bore him sons: Jeush, and Shemariah, and Zaham. 20. And after her he took Maacah the daughter of Absalom;

16 אֲשֶׁר עָשָׂה׃ וְאַחֲרֵיהֶם מִכֹּל
שִׁבְטֵי יִשְׂרָאֵל הַנֹּתְנִים אֶת־
לְבָבָם לְבַקֵּשׁ אֶת־יְהוָה
אֱלֹהֵי יִשְׂרָאֵל בָּאוּ יְרוּשָׁלַםִ
לִזְבּוֹחַ לַיהוָה אֱלֹהֵי
17 אֲבוֹתֵיהֶם׃ וַיְחַזְּקוּ אֶת־
מַלְכוּת יְהוּדָה וַיְאַמְּצוּ אֶת־
רְחַבְעָם בֶּן־שְׁלֹמֹה לְשָׁנִים
שָׁלוֹשׁ כִּי הָלְכוּ בְּדֶרֶךְ דָּוִיד
וּשְׁלֹמֹה לְשָׁנִים שָׁלוֹשׁ׃
18 וַיִּקַּח־לוֹ רְחַבְעָם אִשָּׁה אֶת־
מָחֲלַת *בַּן־יְרִימוֹת בֶּן־דָּוִיד
אֲבִיהַיִל בַּת־אֱלִיאָב בֶּן־
19 יִשָׁי׃ וַתֵּלֶד לוֹ בָּנִים אֶת־
יְעוּשׁ וְאֶת־שְׁמַרְיָה וְאֶת־
20 זָהַם׃ וְאַחֲרֶיהָ לָקַח אֶת־
מַעֲכָה בַּת־אַבְשָׁלוֹם וַתֵּלֶד

v. 18. בת ק'

16. *and after them.* The priests and Levites were followed by lay-Israelites who revolted against Jeroboam's idolatry.

17. *three years.* After that period they themselves lapsed from their loyalty to God. They were seduced to idolatry in the fourth year and punishment followed in the fifth (cf. xii. 1ff.).

and Solomon. The Chronicler glosses over the errors of the king he admires.

18-23. The royal family.

18. *the son of David.* No son of his with this name is elsewhere recorded.

and of Abihail. The conjunction is implied. Mahalath was the daughter of Jerimoth and Abihail. Some commentators regard Abihail as the name of another of Rehoboam's wives.

Eliab. David's eldest brother.

19. *and she bore.* The pronoun refers to Mahalath if Abihail was her mother. If, however, Abihail was also a wife of Rehoboam, the pronoun would refer to her.

20. *he.* i.e. Rehoboam.

Maacah the daughter. Absalom had only one daughter and her name was Tamar (2 Sam. xiv. 27); she married Uriel of Gibeah. The noun *bath* may also mean 'granddaughter' (cf. 1 Kings xv. 2 with 2 Chron. xiii. 2).

and she bore him Abijah, and Attai, and Ziza, and Shelomith. 21. And Rehoboam loved Maacah the daughter of Absalom above all his wives and his concubines—for he took eighteen wives, and threescore concubines, and begot twenty and eight sons and threescore daughters. 22. And Rehoboam appointed Abijah the son of Maacah to be chief, even the prince among his brethren; for he was minded to make him king. 23. And he dealt wisely, and dispersed of all his sons throughout all the lands of Judah and Benjamin, unto every fortified city; and he gave them victual in abundance. And he sought for them many wives.

לוֹ אֶת־אֲבִיָּה וְאֶת־עַתַּי
וְאֶת־זִיזָא וְאֶת־שְׁלֹמִית׃
21 וַיֶּאֱהַב רְחַבְעָם אֶת־מַעֲכָה
בַת־אַבְשָׁלוֹם מִכָּל־נָשָׁיו
וּפִילַגְשָׁיו כִּי נָשִׁים שְׁמוֹנֶה־
עֶשְׂרֵה נָשָׂא וּפִילַגְשִׁים שִׁשִּׁים
וַיּוֹלֶד עֶשְׂרִים וּשְׁמוֹנָה בָּנִים
22 וְשִׁשִּׁים בָּנוֹת׃ וַיַּעֲמֵד לָרֹאשׁ
רְחַבְעָם אֶת־אֲבִיָּה בֶן־
מַעֲכָה לְנָגִיד בְּאֶחָיו כִּי
23 לְהַמְלִיכוֹ׃ וַיָּבֶן וַיִּפְרֹץ
מִכָּל־בָּנָיו לְכָל־אַרְצוֹת
יְהוּדָה וּבִנְיָמִן לְכֹל עָרֵי
הַמְּצֻרוֹת וַיִּתֵּן לָהֶם הַמָּזוֹן
לָרֹב וַיִּשְׁאַל הֲמוֹן נָשִׁים׃

12 CHAPTER XII יב

1. And it came to pass, when the kingdom of Rehoboam was established, and he was strong, that he forsook the law of the LORD, and all Israel with him. 2. And it came

1 וַיְהִי כְּהָכִין מַלְכוּת רְחַבְעָם
וּכְחֶזְקָתוֹ עָזַב אֶת־תּוֹרַת
2 יְהוָה וְכָל־יִשְׂרָאֵל עִמּוֹ׃ וַיְהִי

Abijah. In 1 Kings xv. 1: *Abijam.*

22. *he was minded.* Not in the text.

23. *dispersed of all his sons*, etc. They probably acted as the king's agents and kept a firm hold on the people in the remote parts of the kingdom.

the lands. i.e. the districts.

for them. Not in the text. If the words are not implied, the text summarizes or even supplements verse 21.

CHAPTER XII

REHOBOAM'S apostasy and Shishak's invasion.

1-12 (corresponding to 1 Kings xiv. 22-28). The invasion by Shishak.

1. Neglect of God's law by Rehoboam and his subjects had its sequel in an attack upon the land by the king of Egypt.

all Israel. i.e. the kingdom of Judah

to pass in the fifth year of king Rehoboam, that Shishak king of Egypt came up against Jerusalem, because they had dealt treacherously with the LORD, 3. with twelve hundred chariots, and threescore thousand horsemen; and the people were without number that came with him out of Egypt; the Lubim, the Sukkiim, and the Ethiopians. 4. And he took the fortified cities which pertained to Judah, and came unto Jerusalem. 5. Now Shemaiah the prophet came to Rehoboam, and to the princes of Judah, that were gathered together to Jerusalem because of Shishak, and said unto them: 'Thus saith the LORD: Ye have forsaken Me, therefore have I also left you in the hand of Shishak.'

בַּשָּׁנָה הַחֲמִישִׁית לַמֶּלֶךְ
רְחַבְעָם עָלָה שִׁישַׁק מֶלֶךְ־
מִצְרַיִם עַל־יְרוּשָׁלִָם כִּי
מָעֲלוּ בַּיהוָה׃ בְּאֶלֶף 3
וּמָאתַיִם רֶכֶב וּבְשִׁשִּׁים אֶלֶף
פָּרָשִׁים וְאֵין מִסְפָּר לָעָם
אֲשֶׁר־בָּאוּ עִמּוֹ מִמִּצְרַיִם
לוּבִים סֻכִּיִּים וְכוּשִׁים׃
וַיִּלְכֹּד אֶת־עָרֵי הַמְּצֻרוֹת 4
אֲשֶׁר לִיהוּדָה וַיָּבֹא עַד־
יְרוּשָׁלִָם׃ וּשְׁמַעְיָה הַנָּבִיא בָּא 5
אֶל־רְחַבְעָם וְשָׂרֵי יְהוּדָה
אֲשֶׁר־נֶאֶסְפוּ אֶל־יְרוּשָׁלִָם
מִפְּנֵי שִׁישָׁק וַיֹּאמֶר לָהֶם כֹּה־
אָמַר יְהוָה אַתֶּם עֲזַבְתֶּם אֹתִי
וְאַף־אֲנִי עָזַבְתִּי אֶתְכֶם בְּיַד־

(see on xi. 3). Details of their idolatrous acts are given in 1 Kings xiv. 22ff.

2. *Shishak.* He is identified with Sesonchosis or Shoshenk I, the founder of the twenty-second Egyptian dynasty who began his reign about 988 or 950 B.C.E. The success of this expedition is commemorated in an inscription on the wall of the temple of Amon at Karnak.

because they had dealt treacherously. To the Biblical authors Divine punishment is the consequence of sin and deviation from God's ways.

3. This verse supplements the information in Kings.

the Lubim. The Libyans, the north African people from whom Shishak originated.

the Sukkiim. The LXX renders by 'Troglodytes'; they were cave-dwellers on the borders of Egypt, west of the Red Sea.

4. *the fortified cities.* Some of them are included in the list of xi. 6ff.

5. *Shemaiah the prophet.* In xi. 2 he is described as *the man of God.*

therefore have I also left you. The Hebrew verb is the same as *forsaken* and the contrast is better indicated by translating: 'and also I (emphatic in the Hebrew) have forsaken you (by delivering you) into the hand of Shishak.'

6. *princes of Israel.* In verse 5 they are called *the princes of Judah.*

humbled themselves. They admitted their

6. Then the princes of Israel and the king humbled themselves; and they said: 'The LORD is righteous.' 7. And when the LORD saw that they humbled themselves, the word of the LORD came to Shemaiah, saying: 'They have humbled themselves; I will not destroy them; but I will grant them some deliverance, and My wrath shall not be poured out upon Jerusalem by the hand of Shishak. 8. Nevertheless they shall be his servants; that they may know My service, and the service of the kingdoms of the countries.'

9. So Shishak king of Egypt came up against Jerusalem, and took away the treasures of the house of the LORD, and the treasures of the king's house; he took all away; he took away also the shields of gold which Solomon had made. 10. And king Rehoboam made in their stead shields of brass, and committed them to the hands of the captains of the guard, that kept the door of the

6 שִׁישָׁק׃ וַיִּכָּנְעוּ שָׂרֵי־יִשְׂרָאֵל
וְהַמֶּלֶךְ וַיֹּאמְרוּ ׀ צַדִּיק ׀ יְהוָה׃
7 וּבִרְאוֹת יְהוָה כִּי נִכְנָעוּ הָיָה
דְבַר־יְהוָה אֶל־שְׁמַעְיָה ׀
לֵאמֹר נִכְנְעוּ לֹא אַשְׁחִיתֵם
וְנָתַתִּי לָהֶם כִּמְעַט לִפְלֵיטָה
וְלֹא־תִתַּךְ חֲמָתִי בִּירוּשָׁלִַם
8 בְּיַד־שִׁישָׁק׃ כִּי יִהְיוּ־לוֹ
לַעֲבָדִים וְיֵדְעוּ עֲבוֹדָתִי
וַעֲבוֹדַת מַמְלְכוֹת הָאֲרָצוֹת׃
9 וַיַּעַל שִׁישַׁק מֶלֶךְ־מִצְרַיִם
עַל־יְרוּשָׁלִַם וַיִּקַּח אֶת־
אֹצְרוֹת בֵּית־יְהוָה וְאֶת־
אֹצְרוֹת בֵּית הַמֶּלֶךְ אֶת־הַכֹּל
לָקָח וַיִּקַּח אֶת־מָגִנֵּי הַזָּהָב
10 אֲשֶׁר עָשָׂה שְׁלֹמֹה׃ וַיַּעַשׂ
הַמֶּלֶךְ רְחַבְעָם תַּחְתֵּיהֶם מָגִנֵּי
נְחֹשֶׁת וְהִפְקִיד עַל־יַד שָׂרֵי
הָרָצִים הַשֹּׁמְרִים פֶּתַח בֵּית

v. 7. קמץ בפשטא

sin and repented; they showed this outwardly by fasting and wearing sackcloth (cf. 1 Kings xxi. 27, 29).

the LORD is righteous. The implication is that they deserved the calamity which He had sent upon them.

7. *some deliverance.* Or, 'deliverance within a little while' (R.V. margin).

8. *that they may know,* etc. By being made to serve, in consequence of their sins, under the foreign rule of Shishak, they will appreciate the difference between the benign rule of God and the oppressive government of *the kingdoms of the countries.*

9. *against Jerusalem, and took away.* Different interpretations have been placed upon the words. In one view, Shishak entered Jerusalem and plundered the treasuries. Alternatively, he advanced as far as Jerusalem, and Rehoboam bribed him not to attack the city by giving him the treasures with which he departed.

shields of gold. Cf. ix. 16.

10. *the guard.* lit. 'the runners'; one of

king's house. 11. And it was so,
that as oft as the king entered into
the house of the LORD, the guard
came and bore them, and brought
them back into the guard-chamber.
12. And when he humbled himself,
the anger of the LORD turned from
him, that He would not destroy him
altogether; and moreover in Judah
there were good things found.

13. So king Rehoboam strengthened himself in Jerusalem, and
reigned; for Rehoboam was forty
and one years old when he began to
reign, and he reigned seventeen
years in Jerusalem, the city which
the LORD had chosen out of all the
tribes of Israel, to put His name
there; and his mother's name was
Naamah the Ammonitess. 14. And
he did that which was evil, because
he set not his heart to seek the LORD.

15. Now the acts of Rehoboam,
first and last, are they not written in

11 הַמֶּלֶךְ׃ וַיְהִי מִדֵּי־בוֹא
הַמֶּלֶךְ בֵּית יְהוָה בָּאוּ הָרָצִים
וּנְשָׂאוּם וֶהֱשִׁבוּם אֶל־תָּא
12 הָרָצִים׃ וּבְהִכָּנְעוֹ שָׁב מִמֶּנּוּ
אַף־יְהוָה וְלֹא לְהַשְׁחִית
לְכָלָה וְגַם בִּיהוּדָה הָיָה
דְּבָרִים טוֹבִים׃
13 וַיִּתְחַזֵּק הַמֶּלֶךְ רְחַבְעָם
בִּירוּשָׁלִַם וַיִּמְלֹךְ כִּי בֶן־
אַרְבָּעִים וְאַחַת שָׁנָה רְחַבְעָם
בְּמָלְכוֹ וּשְׁבַע עֶשְׂרֵה שָׁנָה ׀
מָלַךְ בִּירוּשָׁלִַם הָעִיר אֲשֶׁר־
בָּחַר יְהוָה לָשׂוּם אֶת־שְׁמוֹ
שָׁם מִכֹּל שִׁבְטֵי יִשְׂרָאֵל וְשֵׁם
14 אִמּוֹ נַעֲמָה הָעַמֹּנִית׃ וַיַּעַשׂ
הָרָע כִּי לֹא הֵכִין לִבּוֹ לִדְרוֹשׁ
אֶת־יְהוָה׃
15 וְדִבְרֵי רְחַבְעָם הָרִאשֹׁנִים
וְהָאַחֲרוֹנִים הֲלֹא־הֵם

their main duties was to run before the king (cf. 2 Sam. xv. 1; 1 Kings i. 5) and act as his bodyguard.

11. *brought them back.* After the parade. Perhaps the reason for their immediate return was to conceal from the people the substitution of brass shields for the original gold, a fact of which they were kept in ignorance as humiliating to the king.

12. *there were good things.* By contrast with the Northern Kingdom, which the Chronicler regarded as irretrievably bad, he considered that the Southern was at heart faithful to God in spite of occasional lapses.

13-16 (corresponding to 1 Kings xiv. 21, 29-31). The chronology and sources of Rehoboam's reign.

13. *strengthened himself.* He recovered the authority which had been shaken by Shishak's attack.

his mother's name. The queen-mother exercised considerable influence in the courts of the Judean kings and their names are usually mentioned.

15. *first and last.* See on 1 Chron. xxix. 29.

the histories of Shemaiah the prophet and of Iddo the seer, after the manner of genealogies? And there were wars between Rehoboam and Jeroboam continually. 16. And Rehoboam slept with his fathers, and was buried in the city of David; and Abijah his son reigned in his stead.

כְּתוּבִים בְּדִבְרֵי שְׁמַעְיָה
הַנָּבִיא וְעִדּוֹ הַחֹזֶה לְהִתְיַחֵשׂ
וּמִלְחֲמוֹת רְחַבְעָם וְיָרָבְעָם
16 כָּל־הַיָּמִים׃ וַיִּשְׁכַּב
רְחַבְעָם עִם־אֲבֹתָיו וַיִּקָּבֵר
בְּעִיר דָּוִיד וַיִּמְלֹךְ אֲבִיָּה בְנוֹ
תַּחְתָּיו׃

13 CHAPTER XIII יג

1. In the eighteenth year of king Jeroboam began Abijah to reign over Judah. 2. Three years reigned he in Jerusalem; and his mother's name was Micaiah the daughter of Uriel of Gibeah. And there was war between Abijah and Jeroboam. 3. And Abijah joined battle with an army of valiant men of war, even

1 בִּשְׁנַת שְׁמוֹנֶה עֶשְׂרֵה לַמֶּלֶךְ
יָרָבְעָם וַיִּמְלֹךְ אֲבִיָּה עַל־
2 יְהוּדָה׃ שָׁלוֹשׁ שָׁנִים מָלַךְ
בִּירוּשָׁלִַם וְשֵׁם אִמּוֹ מִיכָיָהוּ
בַת־אוּרִיאֵל מִן־גִּבְעָה
וּמִלְחָמָה הָיְתָה בֵּין אֲבִיָּה וּבֵין
3 יָרָבְעָם׃ וַיֶּאְסֹר אֲבִיָּה אֶת־
הַמִּלְחָמָה בְּחַיִל גִּבּוֹרֵי

Iddo the seer. Cf. ix. 29.

after the manner of genealogies. The Hebrew *lehithyachēs* may have been the title of the book, or the first striking word in it by which a Hebrew book is commonly named; or it may possibly describe the contents or nature of the work.

16. *Abijah.* He is called *Abijahu* in xiii. 20f.; in Kings the form of the name is *Abijam.*

CHAPTER XIII

THE REIGN OF ABIJAH

1f. (corresponding to 1 Kings xv. 1f.). The length of Abijah's reign (916-914 B.C.E.).

1. *began . . . to reign.* lit. 'and he reigned.'

2. *three years.* In fact it was a little over two years (cf. *eighteenth year of king Jeroboam* with the statement in 1 Kings xv. 9 that Asa came to the throne *in the twentieth year of Jeroboam*).

Micaiah. The name is given as *Maacah* in xi. 20 and 1 Kings xv. 2.

3-20. War between the Southern and Northern Kingdoms. The account has no parallel in Kings.

3. *four hundred thousand,* etc. The Judean warriors were outnumbered by two to one; but the victory was theirs (verses 15ff.) because they fought for a

four hundred thousand chosen men; and Jeroboam set the battle in array against him with eight hundred thousand chosen men, who were mighty men of valour. 4. And Abijah stood up upon mount Zemaraim, which is in the hill-country of Ephraim, and said: 'Hear me, O Jeroboam and all Israel; 5. ought ye not to know that the LORD, the God of Israel, gave the kingdom over Israel to David for ever, even to him and to his sons by a covenant of salt? 6. Yet Jeroboam the son of Nebat, the servant of Solomon the son of David, rose up, and rebelled against his lord. 7. And there were gathered unto him vain men, base fellows that strengthened themselves against Rehoboam the son of Solomon, when Rehoboam was young and faint-hearted, and could not

מִלְחָמָה אַרְבַּע־מֵאוֹת אֶלֶף
אִישׁ בָּחוּר וְיָרָבְעָם עָרַךְ עִמּוֹ
מִלְחָמָה בִּשְׁמוֹנֶה מֵאוֹת אֶלֶף
4 אִישׁ בָּחוּר גִּבּוֹר חָיִל׃ וַיָּקָם
אֲבִיָּה מֵעַל לְהַר צְמָרַיִם אֲשֶׁר
בְּהַר אֶפְרָיִם וַיֹּאמֶר שְׁמָעוּנִי
5 יָרָבְעָם וְכָל־יִשְׂרָאֵל׃ הֲלֹא
לָכֶם לָדַעַת כִּי יְהוָה | אֱלֹהֵי
יִשְׂרָאֵל נָתַן מַמְלָכָה לְדָוִיד
עַל־יִשְׂרָאֵל לְעוֹלָם לוֹ
6 וּלְבָנָיו בְּרִית מֶלַח׃ וַיָּקָם
יָרָבְעָם בֶּן־נְבָט עֶבֶד שְׁלֹמֹה
בֶּן־דָּוִיד וַיִּמְרֹד עַל־אֲדֹנָיו׃
7 וַיִּקָּבְצוּ עָלָיו אֲנָשִׁים רֵקִים
בְּנֵי בְלִיַּעַל וַיִּתְאַמְּצוּ עַל־
רְחַבְעָם בֶּן־שְׁלֹמֹה
וּרְחַבְעָם הָיָה נַעַר וְרַךְ־לֵבָב

regime which loyally carried out the ordinances of God (verses 10ff.), whereas the Northern Kingdom was guilty of idolatry (verses 8f.).

4-12. Abijah's address to the opposing forces.

4. *mount Zemaraim.* Zemaraim is mentioned among the cities of Benjamin (Josh. xviii. 22) and the mount was probably on the border between the territories of Benjamin and Ephraim, the frontier between the Southern and Northern Kingdoms.

hear me, O Jeroboam, etc. The king's intention is to try to win back the tribes of the north to the worship of God.

5. *a covenant of salt.* A sacred and indissoluble covenant (cf. Lev. ii. 13). 'Eating salt' together is recognized by the Arabs as establishing an inviolable bond between host and guest.

7. *base fellows.* lit. 'sons of Belial,' usually explained as 'sons of worthlessness.'

young. The Hebrew *na'ar* probably bears here the meaning 'inexperienced' (cf. the similar use in 1 Kings iii. 7). Rehoboam was forty-one years old when the revolt took place (xii. 13).

faint-hearted. lit. 'tender of heart,' the noun representing the seat of intellect.

could not withstand them. lit. 'and he

withstand them. 8. And now ye think to withstand the kingdom of the LORD in the hand of the sons of David; and ye are a great multitude, and there are with you the golden calves which Jeroboam made you for gods. 9. Have ye not driven out the priests of the LORD, the sons of Aaron, and the Levites, and have made you priests after the manner of the peoples of other lands? so that whosoever cometh to consecrate himself with a young bullock and seven rams, the same becometh a priest of them that are no gods. 10. But as for us, the LORD is our God, and we have not forsaken Him; and we have priests ministering unto the LORD, the sons of Aaron, and the Levites in their work; 11. and they burn unto the LORD every

8 וְלֹא הִתְחַזַּק לִפְנֵיהֶם׃ וְעַתָּה ׀
אַתֶּם אֹמְרִים לְהִתְחַזֵּק לִפְנֵי
מַמְלֶכֶת יְהוָה בְּיַד בְּנֵי דָוִיד
וְאַתֶּם הָמוֹן רָב וְעִמָּכֶם עֶגְלֵי
זָהָב אֲשֶׁר עָשָׂה לָכֶם יָרָבְעָם
9 לֵאלֹהִים׃ הֲלֹא הִדַּחְתֶּם
אֶת־כֹּהֲנֵי יְהוָה אֶת־בְּנֵי
אַהֲרֹן וְהַלְוִיִּם וַתַּעֲשׂוּ לָכֶם
כֹּהֲנִים כְּעַמֵּי הָאֲרָצוֹת כָּל־
הַבָּא לְמַלֵּא יָדוֹ בְּפַר בֶּן־
בָּקָר וְאֵילִם שִׁבְעָה וְהָיָה כֹהֵן
10 לְלֹא אֱלֹהִים׃ וַאֲנַחְנוּ יְהוָה
אֱלֹהֵינוּ וְלֹא עֲזַבְנֻהוּ וְכֹהֲנִים
מְשָׁרְתִים לַיהוָה בְּנֵי אַהֲרֹן
11 וְהַלְוִיִּם בַּמְלָאכֶת׃ וּמַקְטִרִים

did not strengthen himself before them'; so again in the next verse.

8. *the kingdom of the LORD . . . David.* Abijah implies that this fact in itself should convince the rebels that they were acting against the Divine will; yet they relied upon their *great multitude* and *the golden calves which Jeroboam made for you for gods* to resist the dynasty which God had established.

there are with you the golden calves. With you means nothing more than 'in your possession' in your land. It is not to be supposed that they had brought their images on to the field of battle.

9. *driven out.* Cf. xi. 13.

the sons of Aaron. Who alone were the authorized priests.

the Levites. Who were ordained to act as subordinates to the priests.

after the manner, etc. Among other peoples any person could minister to the idols on behalf of his fellows.

to consecrate himself. lit. 'to fill his hand.'

a young bullock and seven rams. At the consecration of Aaron and his sons one bullock and two rams were offered (Exod. xxix. 1). These unauthorized persons, Abijah says in effect, try to make up for their disqualification by bringing seven rams instead of the prescribed two.

them that are no gods. Alluding to the golden calves.

10. *in their work.* Assisting the priests. The pronoun is implied.

11. *and they.* The priests mentioned in the preceding verses.

every morning, etc. In accordance with the ordinance of Exod. xxix. 38ff.

morning and every evening burnt-offerings and sweet incense; the showbread also set they in order upon the pure table; and the candlestick of gold with the lamps thereof, to burn every evening; for we keep the charge of the LORD our God; but ye have forsaken Him. 12. And behold, God is with us at our head, and His priests with the trumpets of alarm to sound an alarm against you. O children of Israel, fight ye not against the LORD, the God of your fathers; for ye shall not prosper.'

13. But Jeroboam caused an ambushment to come about behind them; so they were before Judah, and the ambushment was behind them. 14. And when Judah looked back, behold, the battle was before and behind them; and they cried unto the LORD, and the priests sounded with the trumpets. 15. Then the men of Judah gave a shout; and

לַיהוָה עֹלוֹת בַּבֹּקֶר־בַּבֹּקֶר
וּבָעֶרֶב־בָּעֶרֶב וּקְטֹרֶת־
סַמִּים וּמַעֲרֶכֶת לֶחֶם עַל־
הַשֻּׁלְחָן הַטָּהוֹר וּמְנוֹרַת הַזָּהָב
וְנֵרֹתֶיהָ לְבָעֵר בָּעֶרֶב בָּעֶרֶב
כִּי־שֹׁמְרִים אֲנַחְנוּ אֶת־
מִשְׁמֶרֶת יְהוָה אֱלֹהֵינוּ וְאַתֶּם
12 עֲזַבְתֶּם אֹתוֹ׃ וְהִנֵּה עִמָּנוּ
בָרֹאשׁ הָאֱלֹהִים ׀ וְכֹהֲנָיו
וַחֲצֹצְרוֹת הַתְּרוּעָה לְהָרִיעַ
עֲלֵיכֶם בְּנֵי יִשְׂרָאֵל אַל־
תִּלָּחֲמוּ עִם־יְהוָה אֱלֹהֵי־
אֲבֹתֵיכֶם כִּי־לֹא תַצְלִיחוּ׃
13 וְיָרָבְעָם הֵסֵב אֶת־הַמַּאְרָב
לָבוֹא מֵאַחֲרֵיהֶם וַיִּהְיוּ לִפְנֵי
יְהוּדָה וְהַמַּאְרָב מֵאַחֲרֵיהֶם׃
14 וַיִּפְנוּ יְהוּדָה וְהִנֵּה לָהֶם
הַמִּלְחָמָה פָּנִים וְאָחוֹר
וַיִּצְעֲקוּ לַיהוָה וְהַכֹּהֲנִים
מַחְצֹצְרִים בַּחֲצֹצְרוֹת׃
15 וַיָּרִיעוּ אִישׁ יְהוּדָה וַיְהִי

v. 14. יתיר צ׳

sweet incense. Cf. Exod. xxx. 7.

the showbread . . . order. lit. 'an arrangement of bread.'

the candlestick. Cf. Exod. xxv. 37, xxvii. 20f.

12. *the trumpets of alarm.* Cf. Num. x. 9.

children of Israel. The men of the Northern Kingdom.

13-20. Abijah's victory.

13. *caused an ambushment*, etc. Ignoring the exhortation, Jeroboam planned to attack Abijah's army in front and in the rear.

so they. The main section of Jeroboam's men whom Abijah was addressing.

14. The perilous position of the Judean force enhanced the miracle of its providential deliverance.

15. *gave a shout.* A battle-cry expressing

as the men of Judah shouted, it came
to pass, that God smote Jeroboam
and all Israel before Abijah and
Judah. 16. And the children of
Israel fled before Judah; and God
delivered them into their hand.
17. And Abijah and his people slew
them with a great slaughter; so there
fell down slain of Israel five hundred
thousand chosen men. 18. Thus
the children of Israel were brought
under at that time, and the children
of Judah prevailed, because they
relied upon the LORD, the God of
their fathers. 19. And Abijah pursued after Jeroboam, and took
cities from him, Bethel with the
towns thereof, and Jeshanah with the
towns thereof, and Ephrain with
the towns thereof. 20. Neither did

בְּהָרִיעַ אִישׁ יְהוּדָה וְהָאֱלֹהִים
נָגַף אֶת־יָרָבְעָם וְכָל־
יִשְׂרָאֵל לִפְנֵי אֲבִיָּה וִיהוּדָה׃
16 וַיָּנוּסוּ בְנֵי־יִשְׂרָאֵל מִפְּנֵי
יְהוּדָה וַיִּתְּנֵם אֱלֹהִים בְּיָדָם׃
17 וַיַּכּוּ בָהֶם אֲבִיָּה וְעַמּוֹ מַכָּה
רַבָּה וַיִּפְּלוּ חֲלָלִים מִיִּשְׂרָאֵל
חֲמֵשׁ־מֵאוֹת אֶלֶף אִישׁ בָּחוּר׃
18 וַיִּכָּנְעוּ בְנֵי־יִשְׂרָאֵל בָּעֵת
הַהִיא וַיֶּאֶמְצוּ בְּנֵי יְהוּדָה כִּי
נִשְׁעֲנוּ עַל־יְהוָה אֱלֹהֵי
19 אֲבוֹתֵיהֶם׃ וַיִּרְדֹּף אֲבִיָּה
אַחֲרֵי יָרָבְעָם וַיִּלְכֹּד מִמֶּנּוּ
עָרִים אֶת־בֵּית־אֵל וְאֶת־
בְּנוֹתֶיהָ וְאֶת־יְשָׁנָה וְאֶת־
בְּנוֹתֶיהָ וְאֶת־עֶפְרוֹן וּבְנֹתֶיהָ׃

עפרין ק' v. 19.

confidence in God, as at the battle of Jericho (Josh. vi. 16) where the same Hebrew verb is used.

God smote Jeroboam. The victory was due to God. Without His help Abijah's men, outnumbered and outmanœuvred, would have been overwhelmed and defeated.

17. *five hundred thousand.* It is not necessary to assume that they were all killed in one day; many probably fell in the ensuing flight (verse 19).

18. *were brought under.* i.e. were vanquished.

because they relied upon the LORD. This is the moral which the Chronicler seeks to drive home here and elsewhere (cf. xii. 2, xiv. 10).

19. *Bethel.* One of the cities (see on 1 Chron. vii. 28) where Jeroboam had set up a golden calf (1 Kings xii. 28f.). There is no mention of the capture or destruction of the image, either because it was distasteful to the Chronicler to speak of it (contrast his brief reference to it in xi. 15 with the fuller account in 1 Kings xii. 28ff.), or because the calf was removed from Bethel before the city was taken.

Jeshanah. The modern Ain Sinia, three and a half miles north of Bethel.

Ephrain. This is the reading of the *kerē*; the *kethib* is *Ephron.* It is identified with the modern et-Taiyibeh, four miles north-east of Bethel.

20. *recover strength.* lit. 'retain strength.'

Jeroboam recover strength again in the days of Abijah; and the LORD smote him, and he died. 21. But Abijah waxed mighty, and took unto himself fourteen wives, and begot twenty and two sons, and sixteen daughters. 22. And the rest of the acts of Abijah, and his ways, and his sayings, are written in the commentary of the prophet Iddo.

23. So Abijah slept with his fathers, and they buried him in the city of David, and Asa his son reigned in his stead; in his days the land was quiet ten years.

20 וְלֹא־עָצַר כֹּחַ־יָרָבְעָם עוֹד
בִּימֵי אֲבִיָּהוּ וַיִּגְּפֵהוּ יְהוָה
21 וַיָּמֹת׃ וַיִּתְחַזֵּק אֲבִיָּהוּ וַיִּשָּׂא־
לוֹ נָשִׁים אַרְבַּע עֶשְׂרֵה וַיּוֹלֶד
עֶשְׂרִים וּשְׁנַיִם בָּנִים וְשֵׁשׁ
22 עֶשְׂרֵה בָּנוֹת׃ וְיֶתֶר דִּבְרֵי
אֲבִיָּה וּדְרָכָיו וּדְבָרָיו
כְּתוּבִים בְּמִדְרַשׁ הַנָּבִיא עִדּוֹ׃
23 וַיִּשְׁכַּב אֲבִיָּה עִם־אֲבֹתָיו
וַיִּקְבְּרוּ אֹתוֹ בְּעִיר דָּוִיד
וַיִּמְלֹךְ אָסָא בְנוֹ תַּחְתָּיו בְּיָמָיו
שָׁקְטָה הָאָרֶץ עֶשֶׂר שָׁנִים׃

14 CHAPTER XIV יד

1. And Asa did that which was good and right in the eyes of the LORD his God; 2. for he took away

1 וַיַּעַשׂ אָסָא הַטּוֹב וְהַיָּשָׁר בְּעֵינֵי
2 יְהוָה אֱלֹהָיו׃ וַיָּסַר אֶת־

21-23. The remainder of Abijah's reign after the victory.

21. *fourteen wives.* Evidence of the king's wealth and magnificence.

22. *commentary.* Hebrew *midrash* (from a root meaning 'to seek, enquire'), the term for a didactic exposition or interpretation. A *commentary* (*midrash*) *of the book of the kings* is cited in xxiv. 27.

the prophet Iddo. Cf. ix. 29, xii. 15.

23. In the English versions this verse begins chapter xiv.

the land was quiet. Free from the menace of war.

ten years. The number is not to be understood in its exact sense, but as denoting 'for a period.' Baasa became king of Israel in the third year of Asa's reign (I Kings xv. 33) and *there was war between Asa and Baasa . . . all their days.* The word *all* should not be taken literally.

CHAPTER XIV

THE REIGN OF ASA

HIS reign extended from 914 to 874 B.C.E. As against sixteen verses in Kings, the Chronicler devotes three chapters to Asa's reign.

1-7 (corresponding to I Kings xv. 11-15, 17-22). Asa's religious reformation and defensive measures.

the strange altars, and the high
places, and broke down the pillars,
and hewed down the Asherim;
3. and commanded Judah to seek the
LORD, the God of their fathers, and
to do the law and the commandment.
4. Also he took away out of all the
cities of Judah the high places and
the sun-images; and the kingdom
was quiet before him. 5. And he
built fortified cities in Judah; for the
land was quiet, and he had no war in
those years; because the LORD had
given him rest. 6. For he said unto
Judah: 'Let us build these cities, and

מִזְבְּחוֹת הַנֵּכָר וְהַבָּמוֹת
וַיְשַׁבֵּר אֶת־הַמַּצֵּבוֹת וַיְגַדַּע
3 אֶת־הָאֲשֵׁרִים׃ וַיֹּאמֶר
לִיהוּדָה לִדְרוֹשׁ אֶת־יְהוָה
אֱלֹהֵי אֲבוֹתֵיהֶם וְלַעֲשׂוֹת
4 הַתּוֹרָה וְהַמִּצְוָה׃ וַיָּסַר
מִכָּל־עָרֵי יְהוּדָה אֶת־
הַבָּמוֹת וְאֶת־הַחַמָּנִים
וַתִּשְׁקֹט הַמַּמְלָכָה לְפָנָיו׃
5 וַיִּבֶן עָרֵי מְצוּרָה בִּיהוּדָה כִּי־
שָׁקְטָה הָאָרֶץ וְאֵין־עִמּוֹ
מִלְחָמָה בַּשָּׁנִים הָאֵלֶּה כִּי־
6 הֵנִיחַ יְהוָה לוֹ׃ וַיֹּאמֶר
לִיהוּדָה נִבְנֶה ׀ אֶת־הֶעָרִים

2. *the strange altars.* Dedicated to the worship of foreign gods.

the high places. According to I Kings xv. 14, *the high places were not taken away;* but Chron. may give the record of Asa's personal act while Kings speaks of the people's persistence in this form of worship despite the king's orders.

the pillars. The *matstsebah* was a stone standing upright by the side of an altar as a symbol of the deity worshipped and regarded as sacred. The symbol was, in later times, replaced by images of the god of the shrine. It is assumed to have been a survival of stone-worship.

the Asherim. The plural of *asherah* which was an upright wooden pole placed by the side of an altar as a symbol of a god or goddess. The reverence paid to it may have been a survival of tree-worship, and the god or its symbol was sometimes carved on the pole.

4. *sun-images.* The Hebrew is *chammanim* which may be connected with *chammah,* a word for 'sun.' They were stones used in connection with the high places and probably dedicated to the sun-god (*Ba'al-chamman*), a Carthaginian deity.

5. *he built,* etc. From I Kings xv. 17-22 it is learnt that Asa's defensive measures were the result of the threatened invasion of his kingdom by Baasa, king of Israel. The Chronicler omits the cause as well as the help which, in consideration of a heavy bribe taken from the Temple treasury, Ben-hadad, king of Syria, had rendered to Asa by a raid on Baasa's territory.

for the land was quiet. Until peace was disturbed by Zerah the Ethiopian (verse 8).

6. *these cities.* Referred to in verse 5; the names are not given.

make about them walls, and towers, gates, and bars; the land is yet before us, because we have sought the LORD our God; we have sought Him, and He hath given us rest on every side.' So they built and prospered. 7. And Asa had an army that bore bucklers and spears, out of Judah three hundred thousand; and out of Benjamin, that bore shields and drew bows, two hundred and fourscore thousand; all these were mighty men of valour.

8. And there came out against them Zerah the Ethiopian with an army of a thousand thousand, and three hundred chariots; and he came unto Mareshah. 9. Then Asa went out to meet him, and they set the battle in array in the valley of Zephath at Mareshah. 10. And Asa cried unto the LORD his God, and said: 'LORD, there is none beside Thee to help, between the mighty and him that hath no strength; help us, O LORD our God; for we rely on Thee, and in Thy name are we come

הָאֵלֶּה וְנָסֵב חוֹמָה וּמִגְדָּלִים
דְּלָתַיִם וּבְרִיחִים עוֹדֶנּוּ
הָאָרֶץ לְפָנֵינוּ כִּי דָרַשְׁנוּ אֶת־
יְהוָה אֱלֹהֵינוּ דָּרַשְׁנוּ וַיָּנַח לָנוּ
7 מִסָּבִיב וַיִּבְנוּ וַיַּצְלִיחוּ׃ וַיְהִי
לְאָסָא חַיִל נֹשֵׂא צִנָּה וָרֹמַח
מִיהוּדָה שְׁלֹשׁ מֵאוֹת אֶלֶף
וּמִבִּנְיָמִן נֹשְׂאֵי מָגֵן וְדֹרְכֵי קֶשֶׁת
מָאתַיִם וּשְׁמוֹנִים אֶלֶף כָּל־
אֵלֶּה גִּבּוֹרֵי חָיִל׃
8 וַיֵּצֵא אֲלֵיהֶם זֶרַח הַכּוּשִׁי
בְּחַיִל אֶלֶף אֲלָפִים וּמַרְכָּבוֹת
שְׁלֹשׁ מֵאוֹת וַיָּבֹא עַד־מָרֵשָׁה׃
9 וַיֵּצֵא אָסָא לְפָנָיו וַיַּעַרְכוּ
מִלְחָמָה בְּגֵיא צְפַתָה
10 לְמָרֵשָׁה׃ וַיִּקְרָא אָסָא אֶל־
יְהוָה אֱלֹהָיו וַיֹּאמַר יְהוָה אֵין־
עִמְּךָ לַעְזוֹר בֵּין רַב לְאֵין כֹּחַ
עָזְרֵנוּ יְהוָה אֱלֹהֵינוּ כִּי־עָלֶיךָ
נִשְׁעַנּוּ וּבְשִׁמְךָ בָאנוּ עַל־

8-14. Ethiopian invasion and defeat. This is not recorded in Kings.

8. *against them.* The army described in verse 7.

Zerah the Ethiopian. It is probable that the Hebrew *cushi* is not to be understood as *Ethiopian* but 'Cushite,' descended from Cush the ancestor of a number of Arabian peoples (Gen. x. 7); and *Zerah* may correspond to *Zirrih*, a title meaning 'magnificent' borne by some of their princes.

a thousand thousand. A round number implying a vast host, too large to be counted.

Mareshah. See on xi. 8.

9. *Zephath.* The Hebrew name is 'Zephathah'; the valley leads from the Shephelah into the central region of Judah.

against this multitude. Thou art the LORD our God; let not man prevail against Thee.' 11. So the LORD smote the Ethiopians before Asa, and before Judah; and the Ethiopians fled. 12. And Asa and the people that were with him pursued them unto Gerar; and there fell of the Ethiopians so that none remained alive; for they were shattered before the LORD, and before His host; and they carried away very much booty. 13. And they smote all the cities round about Gerar; for a terror from the LORD came upon them; and they spoiled all the cities; for there was much spoil in them. 14. They smote also the tents of cattle, and carried away sheep in abundance and camels, and returned to Jerusalem.

הֶהָמ֣וֹן הַזֶּ֑ה יְהוָ֤ה אֱלֹהֵ֙ינוּ֙ אַ֔תָּה
11 אַל־יַעְצֹ֥ר עִמְּךָ֖ אֱנֽוֹשׁ׃ וַיִּגֹּ֤ף
יְהוָה֙ אֶת־הַכּ֣וּשִׁ֔ים לִפְנֵ֥י אָסָ֖א
וְלִפְנֵ֣י יְהוּדָ֑ה וַיָּנֻ֖סוּ הַכּוּשִֽׁים׃
12 וַֽיִּרְדְּפֵ֡ם אָסָא֩ וְהָעָ֨ם אֲשֶׁר־
עִמּ֜וֹ עַד־לִגְרָ֗ר וַיִּפֹּ֨ל מִכּוּשִׁ֜ים
לְאֵ֤ין לָהֶם֙ מִֽחְיָ֔ה כִּֽי־נִשְׁבְּר֥וּ
לִפְנֵי־יְהוָ֖ה וְלִפְנֵ֣י מַחֲנֵ֑הוּ
וַיִּשְׂא֥וּ שָׁלָ֖ל הַרְבֵּ֥ה מְאֹֽד׃
13 וַיַּכּ֗וּ אֵ֤ת כָּל־הֶֽעָרִים֙ סְבִיב֣וֹת
גְּרָ֔ר כִּֽי־הָיָ֥ה פַֽחַד־יְהוָ֖ה
עֲלֵיהֶ֑ם וַיָּבֹ֙זּוּ֙ אֶת־כָּל־
הֶ֣עָרִ֔ים כִּֽי־בִזָּ֥ה רַבָּ֖ה הָיְתָ֥ה
14 בָהֶֽם׃ וְגַם־אָהֳלֵ֥י מִקְנֶ֖ה הִכּ֑וּ
וַיִּשְׁבּ֨וּ צֹ֤אן לָרֹב֙ וּגְמַלִּ֔ים וַיָּשֻׁ֖בוּ
יְרוּשָׁלִָֽם׃

15 CHAPTER XV טו

1. And the spirit of God came upon Azariah the son of Oded; 2. and

1 וַעֲזַרְיָ֙הוּ֙ בֶּן־עוֹדֵ֔ד הָיְתָ֥ה

10. *let no man prevail against Thee.* lit. 'let no man restrain with Thee.'

11. *the Ethiopians.* Or, 'the Cushites' (see on verse 8).

12. *Gerar.* Five miles south of Gaza and identified with el-Jerar.

so that none remained alive. Another possible translation is 'so that there was no recovery for them.' The total slaughter of so large an army is an improbability, nor does the wording of the text conform to the phraseology for such a contingency.

13. *they smote all the cities.* Which were probably in league with the invader.

14. *the tents of cattle.* Some Jewish commentators explain the phrase as 'the tents of (the men who looked after the) cattle.'

CHAPTER XV

1-7 (not paralleled in Kings). The prophecy of Azariah.

1. *Azariah the son of Oded.* This is the only reference to him in the Bible.

he went out to meet Asa, and said unto him: 'Hear ye me, Asa, and all Judah and Benjamin: the LORD is with you, while ye are with Him; and if ye seek Him, He will be found of you; but if ye forsake Him, He will forsake you. 3. Now for long seasons Israel was without the true God, and without a teaching priest, and without law; 4. but when in their distress they turned unto the LORD, the God of Israel, and sought Him, He was found of them. 5. And in those times there was no peace to him that went out, nor to him that came in, but great discomfitures were upon all the inhabitants of the lands. 6. And they were broken in pieces, nation against nation, and city against city; for God did discomfit them with all manner of adversity. 7. But be ye strong, and let not your hands be slack; for your work shall be rewarded.'

עָלָיו רוּחַ אֱלֹהִים׃ וַיֵּצֵא לִפְנֵי 2
אָסָא וַיֹּאמֶר לוֹ שְׁמָעוּנִי אָסָא
וְכָל־יְהוּדָה וּבִנְיָמִן יְהוָה
עִמָּכֶם בִּהְיוֹתְכֶם עִמּוֹ וְאִם־
תִּדְרְשֻׁהוּ יִמָּצֵא לָכֶם וְאִם־
תַּעַזְבֻהוּ יַעֲזֹב אֶתְכֶם׃ וְיָמִים 3
רַבִּים לְיִשְׂרָאֵל לְלֹא ׀ אֱלֹהֵי
אֱמֶת וּלְלֹא כֹּהֵן מוֹרֶה וּלְלֹא
תוֹרָה׃ וַיָּשָׁב בַּצַּר־לוֹ עַל־ 4
יְהוָה אֱלֹהֵי יִשְׂרָאֵל וַיְבַקְשֻׁהוּ
וַיִּמָּצֵא לָהֶם׃ וּבָעִתִּים הָהֵם 5
אֵין שָׁלוֹם לַיּוֹצֵא וְלַבָּא כִּי
מְהוּמֹת רַבּוֹת עַל כָּל־יוֹשְׁבֵי
הָאֲרָצוֹת׃ וְכֻתְּתוּ גוֹי־בְּגוֹי 6
וְעִיר בְּעִיר כִּי־אֱלֹהִים
הֲמָמָם בְּכָל־צָרָה׃ וְאַתֶּם 7
חִזְקוּ וְאַל־יִרְפּוּ יְדֵיכֶם כִּי
יֵשׁ שָׂכָר לִפְעֻלַּתְכֶם׃

2. *went out to meet.* lit. 'went out before,' i.e. he deliberately set out to confront the king. Metsudath David connects the incident with the preceding chapter, and times the encounter with Asa's return home from his campaign.

3. *long seasons.* lit. 'many days.'

teaching . . . law. The Hebrew root of both words is the same. A function of the priest was to give teaching (*moreh*) in matters relating to the *law* (*Torah*). Cf. Mal. ii. 7.

4. *but when in their distress they turned.* lit. 'in the distress to him he turned.' The singular is used of the people as a whole.

5. *in those times.* viz. when Israel *was without the true God*, etc. (verse 3).

the lands. See on xi. 23.

6. *they were broken in pieces.* National unity was destroyed by internecine strife.

nation against nation. i.e. one tribe or section of Israel against another. War between tribes is recorded in the Book of Judges (e.g. ix. 26ff., xii. 1ff., xx. 12ff.).

7. *be ye strong.* i.e. firm in your determination to be loyal to God.

8. And when Asa heard these words, even the prophecy of Oded the prophet, he took courage, and put away the detestable things out of all the land of Judah and Benjamin, and out of the cities which he had taken from the hill-country of Ephraim; and he renewed the altar of the LORD, that was before the porch of the LORD. 9. And he gathered all Judah and Benjamin, and them that sojourned with them out of Ephraim and Manasseh, and out of Simeon; for they fell to him out of Israel in abundance, when they saw that the LORD his God was with him. 10. So they gathered themselves together at Jerusalem in the third month, in the fifteenth year of the reign of Asa. 11. And they sacrificed unto the LORD in that day,

וְכִשְׁמֹעַ אָסָא הַדְּבָרִים הָאֵלֶּה 8
וְהַנְּבוּאָה עֹדֵד הַנָּבִיא הִתְחַזַּק
וַיַּעֲבֵר הַשִּׁקּוּצִים מִכָּל־אֶרֶץ
יְהוּדָה וּבִנְיָמִן וּמִן־הֶעָרִים
אֲשֶׁר לָכַד מֵהַר אֶפְרָיִם
וַיְחַדֵּשׁ אֶת־מִזְבַּח יְהוָה אֲשֶׁר
לִפְנֵי אוּלָם יְהוָה׃ וַיִּקְבֹּץ 9
אֶת־כָּל־יְהוּדָה וּבִנְיָמִן
וְהַגָּרִים עִמָּהֶם מֵאֶפְרַיִם
וּמְנַשֶּׁה וּמִשִּׁמְעוֹן כִּי־נָפְלוּ
עָלָיו מִיִּשְׂרָאֵל לָרֹב בִּרְאֹתָם
כִּי־יְהוָה אֱלֹהָיו עִמּוֹ׃
וַיִּקָּבְצוּ יְרוּשָׁלִַם בַּחֹדֶשׁ 10
הַשְּׁלִישִׁי לִשְׁנַת חֲמֵשׁ־עֶשְׂרֵה
לְמַלְכוּת אָסָא׃ וַיִּזְבְּחוּ 11
לַיהוָה בַּיּוֹם הַהוּא מִן־הַשָּׁלָל

8-15 (not paralleled in Kings). Asa's religious reforms.

8. *the prophecy of Oded.* The Hebrew construction is irregular, the preposition *of* being implied and the noun *prophecy* in the absolute form.

Oded the prophet. The reference is doubtless to *Azariah the son of Oded* (verse 1), although some Jewish commentators understand it of another prophecy by Oded which is not recorded in detail.

he took courage. lit. 'strengthened himself.'

the detestable things. Objects of idolatrous worship.

out of the cities, etc. The allusion may be to the cities taken by Abijah (cf. xiii. 19).

the altar, etc. Cf. viii. 12.

9. *them that sojourned with them*, etc. These were the Israelites who migrated to the south because they repudiated the idolatry which was practised in the Northern Kingdom (xi. 16).

Simeon. This tribe, or a part of it, though residing in the south of Judah and entirely cut off from the Northern Kingdom, may have held aloof when the division took place and now joined Judah as the effect of Asa's victories and religious reform.

10. *the third month.* i.e. Sivan (June-July) in which the Feast of Weeks or

of the spoil which they had brought, seven hundred oxen and seven thousand sheep. 12. And they entered into the covenant to seek the LORD, the God of their fathers, with all their heart and with all their soul; 13. and that whosoever would not seek the LORD, the God of Israel, should be put to death, whether small or great, whether man or woman. 14. And they swore unto the LORD with a loud voice, and with shouting, and with trumpets, and with horns. 15. And all Judah rejoiced at the oath; for they had sworn with all their heart, and sought Him with their whole desire; and He was found of them; and the LORD gave them rest round about.

16. And also Maacah the mother of Asa the king, he removed her from being queen, because she had made

הֵבִ֑יאוּ בָּקָר֙ שְׁבַ֣ע מֵא֔וֹת וְצֹ֖אן
12 שִׁבְעַ֥ת אֲלָפִֽים׃ וַיָּבֹ֣אוּ
בַבְּרִ֔ית לִדְר֕וֹשׁ אֶת־יְהוָ֖ה
אֱלֹהֵ֣י אֲבוֹתֵיהֶ֑ם בְּכָל־
13 לְבָבָ֖ם וּבְכָל־נַפְשָֽׁם׃ וְכֹ֨ל
אֲשֶׁ֤ר לֹֽא־יִדְרֹשׁ֙ לַיהוָ֣ה
אֱלֹהֵֽי־יִשְׂרָאֵ֔ל יוּמָ֑ת לְמִן־
קָטֹן֙ וְעַד־גָּד֔וֹל לְמֵאִ֖ישׁ וְעַד־
14 אִשָּֽׁה׃ וַיִּשָּֽׁבְעוּ֙ לַֽיהוָ֔ה בְּק֖וֹל
גָּד֑וֹל וּבִתְרוּעָ֕ה וּבַחֲצֹצְר֖וֹת
15 וּבְשׁוֹפָרֽוֹת׃ וַיִּשְׂמְח֨וּ כָל־
יְהוּדָ֜ה עַל־הַשְּׁבוּעָ֗ה כִּ֤י
בְכָל־לְבָבָם֙ נִשְׁבָּ֔עוּ וּבְכָל־
רְצוֹנָ֣ם בִּקְשֻׁ֔הוּ וַיִּמָּצֵ֖א לָהֶ֑ם
וַיָּ֧נַח יְהוָ֛ה לָהֶ֖ם מִסָּבִֽיב׃
16 וְגַם־מַעֲכָ֞ה אֵ֣ם ׀ אָסָ֣א הַמֶּ֗לֶךְ
הֱסִירָהּ֙ מִגְּבִירָ֔ה אֲשֶׁר־

Pentecost is observed (Deut. xvi. 9ff.). What is described here was a special celebration.

11. *of the spoil.* Taken in Asa's victory over Zerah (xiv. 13f.).

12. *they entered into the covenant.* They bound themselves with a solemn oath (cf. verse 15).

13. *should be put to death.* As commanded in Deut. xvii. 2ff.

whether small or great. An idiomatic expression, lit. 'as from the small unto the great.' The same applies to the phrase, *whether man or woman.*

14. *with shouting.* The Hebrew word *teruah* may denote a cry of joy (cf. 1 Chron. xv. 28) or a trumpet blast. The former is the probable sense here because the mention of *trumpets* follows.

15. *He was found of them.* As the prophet Azariah had assured them (verse 2).

16-19 (corresponding to 1 Kings xv. 13-15). Supplementary religious measures by king Asa.

16. *Maacah the mother of Asa.* She was the daughter of Abishalom and mother of Abijam (1 Kings xv. 2), the father of Asa. She was consequently the king's grandmother. In Hebrew the terms denoting relationship are not employed in an exact sense.

queen. Better, 'queen-mother.' She

an abominable image for an Asherah;
and Asa cut down her image, and
made dust of it, and burnt it at the
brook Kidron. 17. But the high
places were not taken away out of
Israel; nevertheless the heart of Asa
was whole all his days. 18. And he
brought into the house of God the
things that his father had hallowed,
and that he himself had hallowed,
silver, and gold, and vessels. 19. And
there was no more war unto the five
and thirtieth year of the reign of Asa.

עָשְׂתָה לַאֲשֵׁרָה מִפְלֶצֶת
וַיִּכְרֹת אָסָא אֶת־מִפְלַצְתָּהּ
וַיָּדֶק וַיִּשְׂרֹף בְּנַחַל קִדְרוֹן׃
17 וְהַבָּמוֹת לֹא־סָרוּ מִיִּשְׂרָאֵל
רַק לְבַב־אָסָא הָיָה שָׁלֵם
18 כָּל־יָמָיו׃ וַיָּבֵא אֶת־קָדְשֵׁי
אָבִיו וְקָדָשָׁיו בֵּית הָאֱלֹהִים
19 כֶּסֶף וְזָהָב וְכֵלִים׃ וּמִלְחָמָה
לֹא הָיָתָה עַד שְׁנַת־שְׁלֹשִׁים
וְחָמֵשׁ לְמַלְכוּת אָסָא׃

16 CHAPTER XVI טז

1. In the six and thirtieth year of the

1 בִּשְׁנַת שְׁלֹשִׁים וָשֵׁשׁ לְמַלְכוּת

had occupied this influential position both in the reign of her son Abijam and her grandson Asa.

an abominable image. lit. 'a horror'; the image probably had an obscene form.

Asherah. See on xiv. 2.

and made dust of it. Not in 1 Kings xv. 13.

brook Kidron. It flowed on the east of Jerusalem, where such idolatrous objects were usually destroyed or their dust scattered (cf. xxix. 16, xxx. 14; 2 Kings xxiii. 4).

17. *the high places.* Although sacrifices to God were offered upon them, the practice was condemned after the establishment of the central Sanctuary in Jerusalem.

out of Israel. The people of the kingdom of Judah are sometimes described as *Israel* (cf. xi. 3); or the reference may be to the Northern Kingdom. The latter interpretation would remove the contradiction between xiv. 4 (where it is recorded that Asa had removed the high places) and the statement in this verse.

was whole. i.e. of undivided loyalty to God. 1 Kings xv. 14 adds: *with the LORD.*

18. *the things . . . hallowed.* lit. 'the holy things of his father,' i.e. the treasures dedicated to the Temple.

that he himself had hallowed. lit. 'his holy things.' This corresponds to the *kethib* in 1 Kings xv. 15.

19. *there was no more war.* There is an apparent contradiction between this statement and 1 Kings xv. 16, *there was war between Asa and Baasa . . . all their days.* The explanation may be that *all their days* refers only to the years which followed the outbreak of hostilities between them, and not to the whole reign of the two kings. Asa's reign was much longer than Baasa's who ascended the throne in the third year of Asa's kingship.

the five and thirtieth year. See on xvi. 1.

reign of Asa, Baasa king of Israel
went up against Judah, and built
Ramah, that he might not suffer any
to go out or come in to Asa king of
Judah. 2. Then Asa brought out
silver and gold out of the treasures
of the house of the LORD and of the
king's house, and sent to Ben-hadad
king of Aram, that dwelt at
Damascus, saying: 3. 'There is
a league between me and thee,
as there was between my father
and thy father; behold, I have sent
thee silver and gold; go, break
thy league with Baasa king of
Israel, that he may depart from me.'
4. And Ben-hadad hearkened unto
king Asa, and sent the captains of

אָסָא עָלָה בַּעְשָׁא מֶלֶךְ־
יִשְׂרָאֵל עַל־יְהוּדָה וַיִּבֶן אֶת־
הָרָמָה לְבִלְתִּי תֵּת יוֹצֵא וָבָא
לְאָסָא מֶלֶךְ יְהוּדָה׃ וַיֹּצֵא 2
אָסָא כֶּסֶף וְזָהָב מֵאֹצְרוֹת בֵּית
יְהוָה וּבֵית הַמֶּלֶךְ וַיִּשְׁלַח אֶל־
בֶּן־הֲדַד מֶלֶךְ אֲרָם הַיּוֹשֵׁב
בְּדַרְמֶשֶׂק לֵאמֹר׃ בְּרִית בֵּינִי 3
וּבֵינֶךָ וּבֵין אָבִי וּבֵין אָבִיךָ
הִנֵּה שָׁלַחְתִּי לְךָ כֶּסֶף וְזָהָב
לֵךְ הָפֵר בְּרִיתְךָ אֶת־בַּעְשָׁא
מֶלֶךְ יִשְׂרָאֵל וְיַעֲלֶה מֵעָלָי׃
וַיִּשְׁמַע בֶּן־הֲדַד אֶל־הַמֶּלֶךְ 4
אָסָא וַיִּשְׁלַח אֶת־שָׂרֵי

CHAPTER XVI

1-6 (corresponding to I Kings xv. 17-22). Asa's war with Baasa.

1. *in the six and thirtieth year.* A difficulty arises from a comparison with the narrative in Kings, according to which Baasa died and was succeeded by his son ten years earlier, viz. in the *twenty-sixth* year of Asa's reign (I Kings xvi. 8). The Jewish commentators quote the *Seder Olam* which suggests that the thirty-sixth year was reckoned from the existence of the separate kingdom of Judah which corresponded to the sixteenth year of Asa (Rehoboam 17 years, Abijah 3 and Asa 16).

built. i.e. fortified; the town had long been in existence.

Ramah. The modern er-Ram, a border town between the two kingdoms, situated on a hill on the road to, and five miles north of, Jerusalem.

2. *silver and gold.* According to I Kings xv. 18: *all the silver and the gold that were left.* A considerable portion of these treasures had already been taken by Shishak, king of Egypt, during Rehoboam's reign (xii. 9). Asa must have felt his position insecure to seek the aid of Ben-hadad by these means.

that dwelt at. More lit. 'who was dwelling.' Since Damascus was the capital of Aram, the fact that the king was in residence there probably indicates that he was not engaged in a campaign at that time, and so was able to come to Asa's help.

Damascus. The Hebrew form is *Darmesek* (see on I Chron. xviii. 5).

3. *a league.* lit. 'a covenant.'

as there was between. lit. 'and between.'

break thy league. This would enable Ben-hadad to attack Baasa from the north of the kingdom of Israel where its

his armies against the cities of Israel;
and they smote Ijon, and Dan, and
Abel-maim, and all the store-cities
of Naphtali. 5. And it came to
pass, when Baasa heard thereof, that
he left off building Ramah, and let
his work cease. 6. Then Asa the
king took all Judah; and they carried
away the stones of Ramah, and the
timber thereof, wherewith Baasa had
builded; and he built therewith
Geba and Mizpah.

7. And at that time Hanani the

הַחֲיָלִים אֲשֶׁר־לוֹ אֶל־עָרֵי
יִשְׂרָאֵל וַיַּכּוּ אֶת־עִיּוֹן וְאֶת־
דָּן וְאֵת אָבֵל מָיִם וְאֵת כָּל־
מִסְכְּנוֹת עָרֵי נַפְתָּלִי׃ וַיְהִי 5
כִּשְׁמֹעַ בַּעְשָׁא וַיֶּחְדַּל מִבְּנוֹת
אֶת־הָרָמָה וַיַּשְׁבֵּת אֶת־
מְלַאכְתּוֹ׃ וְאָסָא הַמֶּלֶךְ לָקַח 6
אֶת־כָּל־יְהוּדָה וַיִּשְׂאוּ אֶת־
אַבְנֵי הָרָמָה וְאֶת־עֵצֶיהָ אֲשֶׁר
בָּנָה בַּעְשָׁא וַיִּבֶן בָּהֶם אֶת־
גֶּבַע וְאֶת־הַמִּצְפָּה׃
וּבָעֵת הַהִיא בָּא חֲנָנִי הָרֹאֶה 7

boundary adjoined the southern frontier of Aram.

4. All the places attacked were in the northern districts of Israel.

Ijon. A town in the territory of Naphtali whose name survives in the valley by the upper Jordan called Merj Ayun.

Dan. Formerly called Laish; the modern Tel el-Kadi, on one of the middle confluents of the Jordan.

Abel-maim. lit. 'Abel in (or, of) the water'; in 1 Kings xv. 20: *Abel-beth-maacah.* It is now known as Abil, situated near Dan on a hill overlooking the Jordan valley.

and all the store-cities of Naphtali. In Kings: *and all Chinneroth, with all the land of Naphtali.* The district is on the west of the Sea of Galilee and, being very fertile, would naturally contain store-cities.

5. *left off building.* He thereby removed the menace from Asa's kingdom, which was the object of Ben-hadad's attack.

and let his work cease. In 1 Kings xv. 21 the reading is: *and he dwelt in Tirzah.* Having abandoned his plan to live in Ramah, Baasa, like Jeroboam (1 Kings xiv. 17), chose Tirzah as his capital which was in the centre of his kingdom almost equidistant from Aram in the north and Judah in the south.

6. *Asa the king took,* etc. In 1 Kings xv. 22: *king Asa made a proclamation unto all Judah; none was exempted.*

all Judah. All the able-bodied men of his kingdom.

he built. See on verse 1.

Geba. A town in Benjamin (see on 1 Chron. vi. 45).

Mizpah. Also in Benjamin, south-west of Ramah, the modern en-Nebi Samwil, which commands a comprehensive view of southern Palestine, including Jerusalem. Its elevation made it eminently suitable as a fortress.

7-10 (no parallel in Kings). The dire message of Hanani the seer.

7. *Hanani.* He occurs in xix. 2, xx. 34 and 1 Kings xvi. 1 as the father of the prophet Jehu.

seer came to Asa king of Judah, and said unto him: 'Because thou hast relied on the king of Aram, and hast not relied on the LORD thy God, therefore is the host of the king of Aram escaped out of thy hand. 8. Were not the Ethiopians and the Lubim a huge host, with chariots and horsemen exceeding many? yet, because thou didst rely on the LORD, He delivered them into thy hand. 9. For the eyes of the LORD run to and fro throughout the whole earth, to show Himself strong in the behalf of them whose heart is whole toward Him. Herein thou hast done foolishly; for from henceforth thou shalt have wars.' 10. Then Asa was wroth with the seer, and put him in the prison-house; for he was in a rage with him because of this thing. And Asa oppressed some of the people the same time.

11. And, behold, the acts of Asa, first and last, lo, they are written in

אֶל־אָסָא מֶלֶךְ יְהוּדָה
וַיֹּאמֶר אֵלָיו בְּהִשָּׁעֶנְךָ עַל־
מֶלֶךְ אֲרָם וְלֹא נִשְׁעַנְתָּ עַל־
יְהוָה אֱלֹהֶיךָ עַל־כֵּן נִמְלַט
8 חֵיל מֶלֶךְ־אֲרָם מִיָּדֶךָ׃ הֲלֹא
הַכּוּשִׁים וְהַלּוּבִים הָיוּ לְחַיִל
לָרֹב לְרֶכֶב וּלְפָרָשִׁים
לְהַרְבֵּה מְאֹד וּבְהִשָּׁעֶנְךָ עַל־
9 יְהוָה נְתָנָם בְּיָדֶךָ׃ כִּי יְהוָה
עֵינָיו מְשֹׁטְטוֹת בְּכָל־הָאָרֶץ
לְהִתְחַזֵּק עִם־לְבָבָם שָׁלֵם
אֵלָיו נִסְכַּלְתָּ עַל־זֹאת כִּי
מֵעַתָּה יֵשׁ עִמְּךָ מִלְחָמוֹת׃
10 וַיִּכְעַס אָסָא אֶל־הָרֹאֶה
וַיִּתְּנֵהוּ בֵּית הַמַּהְפֶּכֶת כִּי־
בְזַעַף עִמּוֹ עַל־זֹאת וַיְרַצֵּץ
אָסָא מִן־הָעָם בָּעֵת הַהִיא׃
11 וְהִנֵּה דִּבְרֵי אָסָא הָרִאשׁוֹנִים

because . . . therefore, etc. Had Asa trusted in God instead of appealing to Ben-hadad, he would have triumphed over the combined forces of Aram and Israel. As he relied on foreign help and was the cause of the first Syrian invasion of the Northern Kingdom, he lost the opportunity of defeating Aram.

8. *Lubim.* They are not mentioned in the Ethiopian (or, Cushite) invasion of Judah (xiv. 8ff.); but, as they were allied to the Egyptians on the occasion of Shishak's invasion (xii. 3), it may be assumed that they again joined them under Zerah.

9. *run to and fro.* The verb occurs again in a similar connection in Zech. iv. 10.

henceforth thou shalt have wars. There is no record of these wars.

10. *in the prison-house.* Or, 'in the stocks.'

Asa oppressed some of the people. Who were on the side of Hanani and demanded his release.

11-14 (an expansion of 1 Kings xv. 23f.). The last days of Asa's reign.

11. *first and last.* See on 1 Chron. xxix. 29.

the book of the kings of Judah and Israel. 12. And in the thirty and ninth year of his reign Asa was diseased in his feet; his disease was exceeding great; yet in his disease he sought not to the LORD, but to the physicians. 13. And Asa slept with his fathers, and died in the one and fortieth year of his reign. 14. And they buried him in his own sepulchres, which he had hewn out for himself in the city of David, and laid him in the bed which was filled with sweet odours and divers kinds [of spices] prepared by the perfumers' art; and they made a very great burning for him.

וְהָאַחֲרוֹנִים הִנָּם כְּתוּבִים
עַל־סֵפֶר הַמְּלָכִים לִיהוּדָה
12 וְיִשְׂרָאֵל׃ וַיֶּחֱלֶא אָסָא בִּשְׁנַת
שְׁלוֹשִׁים וָתֵשַׁע לְמַלְכוּתוֹ
בְּרַגְלָיו עַד־לְמַעְלָה חָלְיוֹ
וְגַם־בְּחָלְיוֹ לֹא־דָרַשׁ אֶת־
13 יְהוָה כִּי בָּרֹפְאִים׃ וַיִּשְׁכַּב
אָסָא עִם־אֲבֹתָיו וַיָּמָת בִּשְׁנַת
אַרְבָּעִים וְאַחַת לְמָלְכוֹ׃
14 וַיִּקְבְּרֻהוּ בְקִבְרֹתָיו אֲשֶׁר
כָּרָה־לוֹ בְּעִיר דָּוִיד
וַיַּשְׁכִּיבֻהוּ בַּמִּשְׁכָּב אֲשֶׁר מִלֵּא
בְּשָׂמִים וּזְנִים מְרֻקָּחִים
בְּמִרְקַחַת מַעֲשֶׂה וַיִּשְׂרְפוּ־לוֹ
שְׂרֵפָה גְּדוֹלָה עַד־לִמְאֹד׃

17 CHAPTER XVII יז

1. And Jehoshaphat his son reigned

1 וַיִּמְלֹךְ יְהוֹשָׁפָט בְּנוֹ תַּחְתָּיו

of the kings of Judah and Israel. In 1 Kings xv. 23: *of the chronicles of the kings of Judah.*

12. *in the thirty and ninth year of his reign.* In Kings: *in the time of his old age.*

his disease was exceeding great. lit. 'until a high (degree) his disease.' The Talmud (Sotah 10a) relates that he was punished because he imposed forced labour also on the disciples of the sages (*took all Judah*, verse 6).

the physicians. Who were probably a class of magicians.

14. *they buried him in his own sepulchres.* In 1 Kings xv. 24: *and was buried with his fathers.*

which he had hewn out for himself, etc. Omitted in 1 Kings xv. 24.

they made a very great burning. Cf. xxi. 19. The burning was of spices, not the cremation of the king's body (cf. Jer. xxxiv. 5 and see *ad loc.*, Soncino ed.).

CHAPTERS XVII-XX

THE REIGN OF JEHOSHAPHAT

CHAPTER XVII

1-6. Jehoshaphat's precautionary measures, his piety and success.

in his stead, and strengthened
himself against Israel. 2. And he
placed forces in all the fortified
cities of Judah, and set garrisons in
the land of Judah, and in the cities
of Ephraim, which Asa his father had
taken. 3. And the LORD was with
Jehoshaphat, because he walked in
the first ways of his father David,
and sought not unto the Baalim;
4. but sought to the God of his
father, and walked in His commandments, and not after the
doings of Israel. 5. Therefore the
LORD established the kingdom in
his hand; and all Judah brought to
Jehoshaphat presents; and he had
riches and honour in abundance.
6. And his heart was lifted up in the
ways of the LORD; and furthermore
he took away the high places and the
Asherim out of Judah.

2 וַיִּתְחַזֵּ֖ק עַל־יִשְׂרָאֵֽל׃ וַיִּֽתֶּן־
חַ֔יִל בְּכָל־עָרֵ֥י יְהוּדָ֖ה
הַבְּצֻר֑וֹת וַיִּתֵּ֤ן נְצִיבִים֙ בְּאֶ֣רֶץ
יְהוּדָ֔ה וּבְעָרֵי֙ אֶפְרַ֔יִם אֲשֶׁ֥ר
3 לָכַ֖ד אָסָ֥א אָבִֽיו׃ וַיְהִ֥י יְהוָ֖ה
עִם־יְהוֹשָׁפָ֑ט כִּ֣י הָלַ֗ךְ בְּדַרְכֵ֞י
דָּוִ֤יד אָבִיו֙ הָרִ֣אשֹׁנִ֔ים וְלֹ֥א
4 דָרַ֖שׁ לַבְּעָלִֽים׃ כִּ֠י לֵֽאלֹהֵ֤י
אָבִיו֙ דָּרָ֔שׁ וּבְמִצְוֺתָ֖יו הָלָ֑ךְ
5 וְלֹ֖א כְּמַעֲשֵׂ֥ה יִשְׂרָאֵֽל׃ וַיָּכֶן֩
יְהוָ֨ה אֶת־הַמַּמְלָכָ֜ה בְּיָד֗וֹ
וַיִּתְּנ֧וּ כָל־יְהוּדָ֛ה מִנְחָ֖ה
לִיהוֹשָׁפָ֑ט וַֽיְהִי־ל֥וֹ עֹֽשֶׁר
6 וְכָב֖וֹד לָרֹֽב׃ וַיִּגְבַּ֣הּ לִבּ֔וֹ
בְּדַרְכֵ֖י יְהוָ֑ה וְעוֹד֙ הֵסִ֣יר אֶת־
הַבָּמ֔וֹת וְאֶת־הָאֲשֵׁרִ֖ים
מִֽיהוּדָֽה׃

v. 4. קמץ בז"ק

1. *Jehoshaphat . . . reigned.* From 874 to 850 B.C.E.

strengthened himself. By placing garrisons in his fortified and other cities (verse 2).

against Israel. i.e. the Northern Kingdom. Others render: 'in (or, over) Israel,' understanding the noun *Israel* as applicable to Judah (cf. xi. 3).

2. *the cities of Ephraim,* etc. As stated in xv. 8.

3. *the first ways of his father David.* Before his sin with Bathsheba and his act of numbering the people.

the Baalim. A general designation of false gods.

4. *the doings of Israel.* The idolatrous worship of golden calves practised in the Northern Kingdom.

5. *presents.* Gifts to the king on his accession as a mark of loyalty.

riches and honour in abundance. Repeated in xviii. 1.

6. *his heart was lifted up.* This expression, which usually denotes pride, is here used in a laudatory sense. The riches and honour which came to him had no deteriorating effect upon his character but, on the contrary, his heart was elevated in the service of God and the ways of righteousness.

he took away the high places. For the

7. Also in the third year of his reign he sent his princes, even Ben-hail, and Obadiah, and Zechariah, and Nethanel, and Micaiah, to teach in the cities of Judah; 8. and with them the Levites, even Shemaiah, and Nethaniah, and Zebadiah, and Asahel, and Shemiramoth, and Jehonathan, and Adonijah, and Tobijah, and Tob-adonijah, the Levites; and with them Elishama and Jehoram, the priests. 9. And they taught in Judah, having the book of the Law of the LORD with them; and they went about throughout all the cities of Judah, and taught among the people.

10. And a terror from the LORD fell upon all the kingdoms of the lands that were round about Judah, so that they made no war against Jehoshaphat. 11. And some of the Philistines brought Jehoshaphat presents, and silver for tribute; the

7 וּבִשְׁנַת שָׁלוֹשׁ לְמָלְכוֹ שָׁלַח
לְשָׂרָיו לְבֶן־חַיִל וּלְעֹבַדְיָה
וְלִזְכַרְיָה וְלִנְתַנְאֵל וּלְמִיכָיָהוּ
8 לְלַמֵּד בְּעָרֵי יְהוּדָה׃ וְעִמָּהֶם
הַלְוִיִּם שְׁמַעְיָהוּ וּנְתַנְיָהוּ
וּזְבַדְיָהוּ וַעֲשָׂהאֵל וּשְׁמִרָימוֹת
וִיהוֹנָתָן וַאֲדֹנִיָּהוּ וְטוֹבִיָּהוּ
וְטוֹב אֲדוֹנִיָּה הַלְוִיִּם וְעִמָּהֶם
אֱלִישָׁמָע וִיהוֹרָם הַכֹּהֲנִים׃
9 וַיְלַמְּדוּ בִּיהוּדָה וְעִמָּהֶם סֵפֶר
תּוֹרַת יְהוָה וַיָּסֹבּוּ בְּכָל־עָרֵי
יְהוּדָה וַיְלַמְּדוּ בָּעָם׃
10 וַיְהִי ׀ פַּחַד יְהוָה עַל כָּל־
מַמְלְכוֹת הָאֲרָצוֹת אֲשֶׁר
סְבִיבוֹת יְהוּדָה וְלֹא נִלְחֲמוּ
11 עִם־יְהוֹשָׁפָט׃ וּמִן־פְּלִשְׁתִּים
מְבִיאִים לִיהוֹשָׁפָט מִנְחָה

v. 8. ושמירמות ק׳

apparent contradiction between this statement and that of xx. 33 (corresponding to 1 Kings xxii. 44), which declares that *the high places were not taken away*, see on xiv. 2.

the Asherim. See on xiv. 2.

7-9 (no parallel in Kings). A commission of princes, Levites and priests is sent to all parts of the kingdom to arrange for the instruction of the people in the Torah.

7. *in the third year.* The mention of the date is intended to show that Jehoshaphat arranged for the religious instruction of the people early in his reign.

he sent, etc. Five princes formed part of the commission for the purpose of inducing the people to take advantage of the instruction given by the priests and Levites who accompanied them.

to teach. i.e. to make arrangements for the teaching.

8. *the Levites.* Who, with the two priests, were to serve as instructors.

9. *the book of the Law of the LORD.* The five Books of Moses.

10-19 (no parallel in Kings). Jehoshaphat's power and greatness and the size of his army.

10. *fell.* lit. 'was.'

11. *tribute.* lit. 'burden' or 'portion.'

Arabians also brought him flocks, seven thousand and seven hundred rams, and seven thousand and seven hundred he-goats. 12. And Jehoshaphat waxed great exceedingly; and he built in Judah castles and cities of store. 13. And he had many works in the cities of Judah; and men of war, mighty men of valour, in Jerusalem. 14. And this was the numbering of them according to their fathers' houses: of Judah, the captains of thousands: Adnah the captain, and with him mighty men of valour three hundred thousand; 15. and next to him Jehohanan the captain, and with him two hundred and fourscore thousand; 16. and next to him Amasiah the son of Zichri, who willingly offered himself unto the LORD, and with him two hundred thousand mighty men of valour; 17. and of Benjamin: Eliada a mighty man of valour, and with him two hundred thousand armed with bow and shield; 18. and next to him Jehozabad, and with him a hundred and fourscore thousand ready prepared for war. 19. These were they

וְכֶסֶף מַשָּׂא גַּם הָעַרְבִיאִים
מְבִיאִים לוֹ צֹאן אֵילִים שִׁבְעַת
אֲלָפִים וּשְׁבַע מֵאוֹת וּתְיָשִׁים
שִׁבְעַת אֲלָפִים וּשְׁבַע מֵאוֹת׃
12 וַיְהִי יְהוֹשָׁפָט הֹלֵךְ וְגָדֵל עַד־
לְמָעְלָה וַיִּבֶן בִּיהוּדָה
בִּירָנִיּוֹת וְעָרֵי מִסְכְּנוֹת׃
13 וּמְלָאכָה רַבָּה הָיָה לוֹ בְּעָרֵי
יְהוּדָה וְאַנְשֵׁי מִלְחָמָה גִּבּוֹרֵי
14 חַיִל בִּירוּשָׁלִָם׃ וְאֵלֶּה
פְקֻדָּתָם לְבֵית אֲבוֹתֵיהֶם
לִיהוּדָה שָׂרֵי אֲלָפִים עַדְנָה
הַשָּׂר וְעִמּוֹ גִּבּוֹרֵי חַיִל שְׁלֹשׁ
15 מֵאוֹת אָלֶף׃ וְעַל־יָדוֹ יְהוֹחָנָן
הַשָּׂר וְעִמּוֹ מָאתַיִם וּשְׁמוֹנִים
16 אָלֶף׃ וְעַל־יָדוֹ עֲמַסְיָה בֶּן־
זִכְרִי הַמִּתְנַדֵּב לַיהוָה וְעִמּוֹ
17 מָאתַיִם אֶלֶף גִּבּוֹר חָיִל׃ וּמִן־
בִּנְיָמִן גִּבּוֹר חַיִל אֶלְיָדָע וְעִמּוֹ
נֹשְׁקֵי־קֶשֶׁת וּמָגֵן מָאתַיִם
18 אָלֶף׃ וְעַל־יָדוֹ יְהוֹזָבָד וְעִמּוֹ
מֵאָה־וּשְׁמוֹנִים אֶלֶף חֲלוּצֵי
19 צָבָא׃ אֵלֶּה הַמְשָׁרְתִים אֶת־

12. *castles.* As a protection against raids (again of Jotham, xxvii. 4).

13. *many works.* lit. 'great work.' The reference may be to fortifications or military supplies.

15. *next to him.* lit. 'by his hand.'

16. *who willingly offered himself.* The same Hebrew verb as in Judg. v. 9. What is implied is uncertain.

17. *armed with bow and shield.* These were troops skilled in archery (cf. xiv. 7; 1 Chron. xii. 2).

that waited on the king, beside those whom the king put in the fortified cities throughout all Judah.

הַמֶּלֶךְ מִלְּבַד אֲשֶׁר־נָתַן
הַמֶּלֶךְ בְּעָרֵי הַמִּבְצָר בְּכָל־
יְהוּדָה׃

18 CHAPTER XVIII יח

1. Now Jehoshaphat had riches and honour in abundance; and he allied himself with Ahab by marriage. 2. And after a lapse of years he went down to Ahab to Samaria. And Ahab killed sheep and oxen for him in abundance, and for the people that were with him, and persuaded him to go up with him to Ramoth-gilead. 3. And Ahab king of Israel said unto Jehoshaphat king of Judah: 'Wilt thou go with me to Ramoth-gilead?' And he answered him: 'I am as thou art, and my people as thy people; and we will be with thee in the war.'

4. And Jehoshaphat said unto the

1 וַיְהִי לִיהוֹשָׁפָט עֹשֶׁר וְכָבוֹד
2 לָרֹב וַיִּתְחַתֵּן לְאַחְאָב׃ וַיֵּרֶד
לְקֵץ שָׁנִים אֶל־אַחְאָב
לְשֹׁמְרוֹן וַיִּזְבַּח־לוֹ אַחְאָב
צֹאן וּבָקָר לָרֹב וְלָעָם אֲשֶׁר־
עִמּוֹ וַיְסִיתֵהוּ לַעֲלוֹת אֶל־
3 רָמֹת גִּלְעָד׃ וַיֹּאמֶר אַחְאָב ׀
מֶלֶךְ־יִשְׂרָאֵל אֶל־יְהוֹשָׁפָט
מֶלֶךְ יְהוּדָה הֲתֵלֵךְ עִמִּי רָמֹת
גִּלְעָד וַיֹּאמֶר לוֹ כָּמוֹנִי כָמוֹךָ
וּכְעַמְּךָ עַמִּי וְעִמְּךָ בַּמִּלְחָמָה׃
4 וַיֹּאמֶר יְהוֹשָׁפָט אֶל־מֶלֶךְ

CHAPTER XVIII

1-3 (corresponding, with some changes, to 1 Kings xxii. 1-4). Jehoshaphat's alliance with Ahab.

1. *allied himself with Ahab by marriage.* Jehoshaphat's son, Jehoram, married Ahab's granddaughter Athaliah (xxi. 6).

2. *after a lapse of years.* 1 Kings xxii. 1 states that this happened in the third year of the peace which followed the war between Israel and Aram.

he went down, etc. This was probably in response to an invitation from Ahab who desired to propose an alliance of the two kingdoms against Aram.

to go up with him. The last words are not in the text.

Ramoth-gilead. Called *Ramoth in Gilead* in 1 Chron. vi. 65. It was an important fortress city for the possession of which Israel and Aram fought several wars. The site has not been identified with certainty, but it may be the modern es-Salt.

3. *and we will be with thee in the war.* In 1 Kings xxii. 4: *my horses as thy horses*, a polite oriental expression implying a promise of full military help.

king of Israel: 'Inquire, I pray thee, at the word of the LORD to-day.' 5. Then the king of Israel gathered the prophets together, four hundred men, and said unto them: 'Shall we go to Ramoth-gilead to battle, or shall I forbear?' And they said: 'Go up; for God will deliver it into the hand of the king.' 6. But Jehoshaphat said: 'Is there not here besides a prophet of the LORD, that we might inquire of him?' 7. And the king of Israel said unto Jehoshaphat: 'There is yet one man by whom we may inquire of the LORD; but I hate him; for he never prophesieth good concerning me, but always evil; the same is Micaiah the son of Imla.' And Jehoshaphat said: 'Let not the king say so.' 8. Then the king of Israel called an officer, and said: 'Fetch quickly Micaiah the son of Imla.' 9. Now the king of Israel and Jehoshaphat

יִשְׂרָאֵל דְּרָשׁ־נָא כַיּוֹם אֶת־
5 דְּבַר יְהוָה׃ וַיִּקְבֹּץ מֶלֶךְ־
יִשְׂרָאֵל אֶת־הַנְּבִאִים אַרְבַּע
מֵאוֹת אִישׁ וַיֹּאמֶר אֲלֵהֶם
הֲנֵלֵךְ אֶל־רָמֹת גִּלְעָד
לַמִּלְחָמָה אִם־אֶחְדָּל וַיֹּאמְרוּ
עֲלֵה וְיִתֵּן הָאֱלֹהִים בְּיַד
6 הַמֶּלֶךְ׃ וַיֹּאמֶר יְהוֹשָׁפָט הַאֵין
פֹּה נָבִיא לַיהוָה עוֹד וְנִדְרְשָׁה
7 מֵאֹתוֹ׃ וַיֹּאמֶר מֶלֶךְ־יִשְׂרָאֵל
׀ אֶל־יְהוֹשָׁפָט עוֹד אִישׁ־
אֶחָד לִדְרוֹשׁ אֶת־יְהוָה מֵאֹתוֹ
וַאֲנִי שְׂנֵאתִיהוּ כִּי־אֵינֶנּוּ מִתְנַבֵּא
עָלַי לְטוֹבָה כִּי כָל־יָמָיו
לְרָעָה הוּא מִיכָיְהוּ בֶן־יִמְלָא
וַיֹּאמֶר יְהוֹשָׁפָט אַל־יֹאמַר
8 הַמֶּלֶךְ כֵּן׃ וַיִּקְרָא מֶלֶךְ
יִשְׂרָאֵל אֶל־סָרִיס אֶחָד
וַיֹּאמֶר מַהֵר מִיכָהוּ בֶן־
9 יִמְלָא׃ וּמֶלֶךְ יִשְׂרָאֵל

v. 8. מיכיהו ק׳

4-11 (corresponding to 1 Kings xxii. 5-12). Consultation with Ahab's prophets.

4. *to-day.* Or, 'first of all,' lit. 'as the day.'

5. *the prophets.* viz. of Baal who had survived Elijah's campaign against them.

shall we go. In 1 Kings xxii. 6: *shall I go.*

6. *is there not here besides a prophet of the LORD.* Jehoshaphat was not a Baal-worshipper and placed no reliance upon the advice of the men whom Ahab consulted.

7. *Micaiah.* Apart from this incident nothing is known of him. Some identify him with the unnamed prophet of 1 Kings xx. 35ff. who foretold disaster to Ahab for having spared Ben-hadad, to which the king alludes in this verse.

8. *fetch quickly.* lit. 'hurry' to come here.

the king of Judah sat each on his
throne, arrayed in their robes, and
they sat in a threshing-floor at the
entrance of the gate of Samaria;
and all the prophets were prophesying before them. 10. And Zedekiah
the son of Chenaanah made him
horns of iron, and said: 'Thus saith
the LORD: With these shalt thou
gore the Arameans, until they be
consumed.' 11. And all the prophets prophesied so, saying: 'Go up
to Ramoth-gilead, and prosper; for
the LORD will deliver it into the hand
of the king.'

12. And the messenger that went
to call Micaiah spoke to him, saying:
'Behold, the words of the prophets
declare good to the king with one
mouth; let thy word therefore, I
pray thee, be like one of theirs, and
speak thou good.' 13. And Micaiah

וִיהוֹשָׁפָט מֶלֶךְ־יְהוּדָה
יוֹשְׁבִים אִישׁ עַל־כִּסְאוֹ
מְלֻבָּשִׁים בְּגָדִים וְיוֹשְׁבִים
בְּגֹרֶן פֶּתַח שַׁעַר שֹׁמְרוֹן וְכָל־
הַנְּבִיאִים מִתְנַבְּאִים לִפְנֵיהֶם׃
10 וַיַּעַשׂ לוֹ צִדְקִיָּהוּ בֶן־כְּנַעֲנָה
קַרְנֵי בַרְזֶל וַיֹּאמֶר כֹּה־אָמַר
יְהוָה בְּאֵלֶּה תְּנַגַּח אֶת־אֲרָם
11 עַד־כַּלּוֹתָם׃ וְכָל־הַנְּבִיאִים
נִבְּאִים כֵּן לֵאמֹר עֲלֵה רָמֹת
גִּלְעָד וְהַצְלַח וְנָתַן יְהוָה בְּיַד
הַמֶּלֶךְ׃
12 וְהַמַּלְאָךְ אֲשֶׁר־הָלַךְ ׀ לִקְרֹא
לְמִיכָיְהוּ דִּבֶּר אֵלָיו לֵאמֹר
הִנֵּה דִבְרֵי הַנְּבִיאִים פֶּה־
אֶחָד טוֹב אֶל־הַמֶּלֶךְ וִיהִי־
נָא דְבָרְךָ כְּאַחַד מֵהֶם וְדִבַּרְתָּ
13 טּוֹב׃ וַיֹּאמֶר מִיכָיְהוּ חַי־

9. *arrayed in their robes.* lit. 'dressed in (royal) garments.' This is mentioned because of what is narrated in verse 29.

a threshing-floor. Being an elevated and open space, it was suitable for such an assembly, consisting of hundreds of prophets and many onlookers.

were prophesying. i.e. working themselves into a state of frenzy in which they uttered what purported to be inspired messages.

10. *Zedekiah.* One of Ahab's false prophets.

horns of iron. An emblem of offensive military power. Symbolic actions were among the means whereby even the true prophets sought to drive home their warnings to the people (cf. Jer. xxvii. 2ff., xxviii. 10ff.).

with these shalt thou gore. A similar expression occurs in an Egyptian psalm where Rameses II is lauded as 'the strong bull against the Ethiopians; his horn pushes them.'

11. *prophesied so.* In the same strain, foretelling victory over the enemy.

12-22 (corresponding to 1 Kings xxii. 13-23). The visions and warning of Micaiah.

12. *with one mouth.* Unanimously.

said: 'As the LORD liveth, what my God saith, that will I speak.' 14. And when he was come to the king, the king said unto him: 'Micaiah, shall we go to Ramoth-gilead to battle, or shall I forbear?' And he said: 'Go ye up, and prosper; and they shall be delivered into your hand.' 15. And the king said to him: 'How many times shall I adjure thee that thou speak unto me nothing but the truth in the name of the LORD?' 16. And he said: 'I saw all Israel scattered upon the mountains, as sheep that have no shepherd; and the LORD said: These have no master, let them return every man to his house in peace.' 17. And the king of Israel said to Jehoshaphat: 'Did I not tell thee that he would not prophesy good

יְהֹוָה כִּי אֶת־אֲשֶׁר־יֹאמַר
14 אֱלֹהַי אֹתוֹ אֲדַבֵּר׃ וַיָּבֹא אֶל־
הַמֶּלֶךְ וַיֹּאמֶר הַמֶּלֶךְ אֵלָיו
מִיכָה הֲנֵלֵךְ אֶל־רָמֹת גִּלְעָד
לַמִּלְחָמָה אִם־אֶחְדָּל וַיֹּאמֶר
עֲלוּ וְהַצְלִיחוּ וְיִנָּתְנוּ בְּיֶדְכֶם׃
15 וַיֹּאמֶר אֵלָיו הַמֶּלֶךְ עַד־כַּמֶּה
פְעָמִים אֲנִי מַשְׁבִּיעֶךָ אֲשֶׁר
לֹא־תְדַבֵּר אֵלַי רַק אֱמֶת
16 בְּשֵׁם יְהֹוָה׃ וַיֹּאמֶר רָאִיתִי
אֶת־כָּל־יִשְׂרָאֵל נְפוֹצִים
עַל־הֶהָרִים כַּצֹּאן אֲשֶׁר אֵין־
לָהֶן רֹעֶה וַיֹּאמֶר יְהֹוָה לֹא־
אֲדֹנִים לָאֵלֶּה יָשׁוּבוּ אִישׁ־
17 לְבֵיתוֹ בְּשָׁלוֹם׃ וַיֹּאמֶר
מֶלֶךְ־יִשְׂרָאֵל אֶל־יְהוֹשָׁפָט
הֲלֹא אָמַרְתִּי אֵלֶיךָ לֹא־
יִתְנַבֵּא עָלַי טוֹב כִּי אִם־

13. *what my God saith.* The Hebrew may be rendered: 'surely, what my God shall say.' Micaiah was not yet in possession of the message he was to deliver.

14. *Micaiah.* The Hebrew form here is 'Micah.'

go ye up, and prosper . . . hand. A repetition of the assurance given by the other prophets, but spoken in ironical tones which Ahab did not fail to detect (verse 15). It is to be noted that Micaiah does not use the usual prophetic introduction, 'thus saith the LORD.'

15. *how many times shall I adjure thee.* i.e. Ahab is ready to make him swear numberless times until he utters the truth.

16. *that have no shepherd.* An indication that Ahab will lose his life in the battle. The king is commonly described in the East as the 'shepherd' of his people.

let them return. Before catastrophe overtakes them.

17. In his anxiety to remove the despondency which the prophetic vision must have caused, Ahab insinuates that Micaiah was not moved by Divine

concerning me, but evil?' 18. And
he said: 'Therefore hear ye the word
of the LORD: I saw the LORD sitting
upon His throne, and all the host of
heaven standing on His right hand
and on His left. 19. And the LORD
said: Who shall entice Ahab king
of Israel, that he may go up and fall
at Ramoth-gilead? And one spoke
saying after this manner, and another saying after that manner.
20. And there came forth the spirit,
and stood before the LORD, and said:
I will entice him. And the LORD
said unto him: Wherewith? 21. And
he said: I will go forth, and will be a
lying spirit in the mouth of all his
prophets. And He said: Thou shalt
entice him, and shalt prevail also;
go forth, and do so. 22. Now
therefore, behold, the LORD hath
put a lying spirit in the mouth of
these thy prophets; and the LORD
hath spoken evil concerning thee.'
23. Then Zedekiah the son of
Chenaanah came near, and smote
Micaiah upon the cheek, and said:

18 לְרָע׃ וַיֹּאמֶר לָכֵן שִׁמְעוּ
דְבַר־יְהוָה רָאִיתִי אֶת־יְהוָה
יוֹשֵׁב עַל־כִּסְאוֹ וְכָל־צְבָא
הַשָּׁמַיִם עֹמְדִים עַל־יְמִינוֹ
19 וּשְׂמֹאלוֹ׃ וַיֹּאמֶר יְהוָה מִי
יְפַתֶּה אֶת־אַחְאָב מֶלֶךְ־
יִשְׂרָאֵל וְיַעַל וְיִפֹּל בְּרָמֹת
גִּלְעָד וַיֹּאמֶר זֶה אֹמֵר כָּכָה
20 וְזֶה אֹמֵר כָּכָה׃ וַיֵּצֵא הָרוּחַ
וַיַּעֲמֹד לִפְנֵי יְהוָה וַיֹּאמֶר אֲנִי
אֲפַתֶּנּוּ וַיֹּאמֶר יְהוָה אֵלָיו
21 בַּמָּה׃ וַיֹּאמֶר אֵצֵא וְהָיִיתִי
לְרוּחַ שֶׁקֶר בְּפִי כָּל־נְבִיאָיו
וַיֹּאמֶר תְּפַתֶּה וְגַם־תּוּכָל צֵא
22 וַעֲשֵׂה־כֵן׃ וְעַתָּה הִנֵּה נָתַן
יְהוָה רוּחַ שֶׁקֶר בְּפִי נְבִיאֶיךָ
אֵלֶּה וַיהוָה דִּבֶּר עָלֶיךָ רָעָה׃
23 וַיִּגַּשׁ צִדְקִיָּהוּ בֶן־כְּנַעֲנָה וַיַּךְ
אֶת־מִיכָיְהוּ עַל־הַלֶּחִי

v. 21. קמץ בז״ק

inspiration, but by animosity against him. This charge arouses the prophet's indignation, and he reveals a second vision still more condemnatory and terrible in its portent.

18. *he said.* The pronoun refers to Micaiah.

all the host of heaven. The angels attendant upon God.

19. *who shall entice.* Divine enticement of a wicked man, or hardening his heart (as with Pharaoh), is a part of his punishment. Man has it in his power to resist evil, but the sinful delight in being encouraged in their activities.

20. *the spirit.* i.e. the spirit which induces prophecy. The Talmud (Sanh. 89a) asserts that it was the spirit of Naboth avenging his murder by Ahab (1 Kings xxi).

23-27 (corresponding to 1 Kings xxii. 24-28). Assault upon and arrest of Micaiah.

23. *Zedekiah.* The prophet with the horns of iron (verse 10).

'Which way went the spirit of the LORD from me to speak unto thee?' 24. And Micaiah said: 'Behold, thou shalt see on that day, when thou shalt go into an inner chamber to hide thyself.' 25. And the king of Israel said: 'Take ye Micaiah; and carry him back unto Amon the governor of the city, and to Joash the king's son; 26. and say: Thus saith the king: Put this fellow in the prison, and feed him with scant bread and with scant water, until I return in peace.' 27. And Micaiah said: 'If thou return at all in peace, the LORD hath not spoken by me.' And he said: 'Hear, ye peoples, all of you.'

28. So the king of Israel and

וַיֹּאמֶר אֵי זֶה הַדֶּרֶךְ עָבַר
רֽוּחַ־יְהוָה מֵאִתִּי לְדַבֵּר
24 אֹתָֽךְ׃ וַיֹּאמֶר מִיכָיְהוּ הִנְּךָ
רֹאֶה בַּיּוֹם הַהוּא אֲשֶׁר תָּבוֹא
25 חֶדֶר בְּחֶדֶר לְהֵחָבֵֽא׃ וַיֹּאמֶר
מֶלֶךְ יִשְׂרָאֵל קְחוּ אֶת־
מִיכָיְהוּ וַהֲשִׁיבֻהוּ אֶל־אָמוֹן
שַׂר־הָעִיר וְאֶל־יוֹאָשׁ בֶּן־
26 הַמֶּֽלֶךְ׃ וַאֲמַרְתֶּם כֹּה אָמַר
הַמֶּלֶךְ שִׂימוּ זֶה בֵּית הַכֶּלֶא
וְהַאֲכִילֻהוּ לֶחֶם לַחַץ וּמַיִם
לַחַץ עַד שׁוּבִי בְשָׁלֽוֹם׃
27 וַיֹּאמֶר מִיכָיְהוּ אִם־שׁוֹב
תָּשׁוּב בְּשָׁלוֹם לֹא־דִבֶּר יְהוָה
בִּי וַיֹּאמֶר שִׁמְעוּ עַמִּים כֻּלָּֽם׃
28 וַיַּעַל מֶֽלֶךְ־יִשְׂרָאֵל וִיהוֹשָׁפָט

which way. The second word is omitted in 1 Kings xxii. 24 though implied. The question is rhetorical, Zedekiah asserting that he, not Micaiah, was truly inspired.

24. *thou shalt see.* The verb *see* may be used here deliberately instead of 'know' as a taunt against Zedekiah's claim to be a true prophet: on the day of disaster you will indeed be a 'seer,' witnessing the catastrophe which will force you to seek safety in hiding.

on that day. Of defeat.

inner chamber. lit. 'a chamber within a chamber.'

to hide thyself. Zedekiah would conceal himself from the invader and also perhaps from the anger of his own people whom he misled by his false prediction.

25. *carry him back.* From the threshing-floor (verse 9) to the city. The verb may also imply that the prophet had been previously in the custody of Amon and Joash.

26. *this fellow.* lit. 'this,' an expression of contempt.

scant bread. lit. 'bread (which is) affliction' because of its small quantity.

I return. From the battle.

27. *hear, ye peoples, all of you.* lit. 'all of them.' These words are the introduction to the Book of Micah, and it may be that they were inserted here subsequently by one who identified that prophet with Micaiah.

28-34 (corresponding to 1 Kings xxii.

Jehoshaphat the king of Judah went
up to Ramoth-gilead. 29. And the
king of Israel said unto Jehoshaphat:
'I will disguise myself, and go into
battle; but put thou on thy robes.'
So the king of Israel disguised himself; and they went into the battle.
30. Now the king of Aram had
commanded the captains of his
chariots, saying: 'Fight neither with
small nor great, save only with the
king of Israel.' 31. And it came to
pass, when the captains of the
chariots saw Jehoshaphat, that they
said: 'It is the king of Israel.'
Therefore they turned about to
fight against him; but Jehoshaphat
cried out, and the LORD helped him;
and God moved them to depart from
him. 32. And it came to pass, when
the captains of the chariots saw that

מֶלֶךְ־יְהוּדָה אֶל־רָמֹת
29 גִּלְעָד׃ וַיֹּאמֶר מֶלֶךְ יִשְׂרָאֵל
אֶל־יְהוֹשָׁפָט הִתְחַפֵּשׂ וָבוֹא
בַמִּלְחָמָה וְאַתָּה לְבַשׁ בְּגָדֶיךָ
וַיִּתְחַפֵּשׂ מֶלֶךְ יִשְׂרָאֵל וַיָּבֹאוּ
30 בַּמִּלְחָמָה׃ וּמֶלֶךְ אֲרָם צִוָּה
אֶת־שָׂרֵי הָרֶכֶב אֲשֶׁר־לוֹ
לֵאמֹר לֹא תִּלָּחֲמוּ אֶת־הַקָּטֹן
וְאֶת־הַגָּדוֹל כִּי אִם־אֶת־
31 מֶלֶךְ יִשְׂרָאֵל לְבַדּוֹ׃ וַיְהִי
כִּרְאוֹת שָׂרֵי הָרֶכֶב אֶת־
יְהוֹשָׁפָט וְהֵמָּה אָמְרוּ מֶלֶךְ־
יִשְׂרָאֵל הוּא וַיָּסֹבּוּ עָלָיו
לְהִלָּחֵם וַיִּזְעַק יְהוֹשָׁפָט וַיהוָה
עֲזָרוֹ וַיְסִיתֵם אֱלֹהִים מִמֶּנּוּ׃
32 וַיְהִי כִּרְאוֹת שָׂרֵי הָרֶכֶב כִּי

29-35). The battle of Ramoth-gilead and Ahab's death.

29. Although Ahab refused to believe the word of God's prophet, the prediction must have disturbed him. He therefore disguised himself in the belief that changing his royal robes for those of a commoner would make him less conspicuous and ward off the evil decreed against him.

put thou on thy robes. Jehoshaphat, against whom the prophet had not predicted disaster, had no need to follow Ahab's example.

they went. In I Kings xxii. 30: (the king of Israel) *went.*

30. *captains of his chariots.* Their number was thirty-two according to I Kings xxii. 31.

fight neither, etc. While the rest of the army were to meet the attack of the forces of Israel and Judah, his officers in the chariots were to concentrate upon the capture or killing of Ahab.

31. *saw Jehoshaphat.* Who was conspicuous because of his royal robes.

cried out. This was either a call to his men to come to his defence or a cry of prayer to God for help.

and the LORD . . . from him. Not in Kings; the Chronicler evidently understands the 'cry' in the latter sense.

to depart. Not in the text, but implied in the preposition *from.*

32. *saw that it was not the king of Israel.* From a distance they could not distinguish between the two kings, but on

it was not the king of Israel, that
they turned back from pursuing
him. 33. And a certain man drew
his bow at a venture, and smote the
king of Israel between the lower
armour and the breastplate; wherefore he said to the driver of the
chariot: 'Turn thy hand, and carry
me out of the host; for I am sore
wounded.' 34. And the battle increased that day; howbeit the king
of Israel stayed himself up in his
chariot against the Arameans until
the even; and about the time of the
going down of the sun he died.

לֹא־הָיָה מֶלֶךְ יִשְׂרָאֵל וַיָּשׁוּבוּ
מֵאַחֲרָיו׃ וְאִישׁ מָשַׁךְ בַּקֶּשֶׁת 33
לְתֻמּוֹ וַיַּךְ אֶת־מֶלֶךְ יִשְׂרָאֵל
בֵּין הַדְּבָקִים וּבֵין הַשִּׁרְיָן
וַיֹּאמֶר לָרַכָּב הֲפֹךְ יָדְיךָ
וְהוֹצֵאתַנִי מִן־הַמַּחֲנֶה כִּי
הָחֳלֵיתִי׃ וַתַּעַל הַמִּלְחָמָה 34
בַּיּוֹם הַהוּא וּמֶלֶךְ יִשְׂרָאֵל הָיָה
מַעֲמִיד בַּמֶּרְכָּבָה נֹכַח אֲרָם
עַד־הָעָרֶב וַיָּמָת לְעֵת בּוֹא
הַשָּׁמֶשׁ׃

19 CHAPTER XIX יט

1. And Jehoshaphat the king of
Judah returned to his house in
peace to Jerusalem. 2. And Jehu
the son of Hanani the seer went out

וַיָּשָׁב יְהוֹשָׁפָט מֶלֶךְ־יְהוּדָה 1
אֶל־בֵּיתוֹ בְשָׁלוֹם לִירוּשָׁלִָם׃
וַיֵּצֵא אֶל־פָּנָיו יֵהוּא בֶן־חֲנָנִי 2

v. 33. יתיר י'

coming nearer they identified Jehoshaphat.

33. *a certain man.* Jewish tradition identifies him with Naaman, captain of the Aramean army mentioned in 2 Kings v. 1ff. (Midrash to Ps. lxxviii. 45; Josephus, *Antiquities* VIII. xv. 5).

at a venture. lit. 'in his innocence'; he had no idea that the man he aimed at was the king of Israel.

out of the host. From the thick of the battle to a quiet spot within sight (verse 34).

34. *stayed himself up.* In 1 Kings xxii. 35: *was stayed up.* To prevent the news of his fatal wound from spreading panic among the soldiers.

about the time, etc. In Kings details are given of Ahab's death and the flight of the army. But the Chronicler is not interested in matters relating to the Northern Kingdom except in so far as they bear upon Judah.

CHAPTER XIX

The whole chapter has no parallel in Kings.

1-3. Jehoshaphat rebuked by the prophet Jehu.

1. *in peace.* Cf. xviii. 16 where the same Hebrew word, *shalom,* is used. It signifies not only 'peace' but also 'safety' (cf. xviii. 27).

2. *Jehu the son of Hanani.* He denounced

to meet him, and said to king Jehoshaphat: 'Shouldest thou help the wicked, and love them that hate the LORD? for this thing wrath is upon thee from before the LORD.
3. Nevertheless there are good things found in thee, in that thou hast put away the Asheroth out of the land, and hast set thy heart to seek God.'

4. And Jehoshaphat dwelt at Jerusalem; and he went out again among the people from Beer-sheba to the hill-country of Ephraim, and brought them back unto the LORD, the God of their fathers. 5. And he set judges in the land throughout all the fortified cities of Judah, city by city, 6. and said to the judges: 'Consider what ye do; for ye judge not for man, but for the LORD; and

הַחֹזֶה וַיֹּאמֶר אֶל־הַמֶּלֶךְ
יְהוֹשָׁפָט הֲלָרָשָׁע לַעְזֹר
וּלְשֹׂנְאֵי יְהוָה תֶּאֱהָב וּבָזֹאת
עָלֶיךָ קֶּצֶף מִלִּפְנֵי יְהוָה׃
3 אֲבָל דְּבָרִים טוֹבִים נִמְצְאוּ
עִמָּךְ כִּי־בִעַרְתָּ הָאֲשֵׁרוֹת
מִן־הָאָרֶץ וַהֲכִינוֹתָ לְבָבְךָ
לִדְרֹשׁ הָאֱלֹהִים׃
4 וַיֵּשֶׁב יְהוֹשָׁפָט בִּירוּשָׁלִָם וַיָּשָׁב
וַיֵּצֵא בָעָם מִבְּאֵר שֶׁבַע עַד־
הַר אֶפְרַיִם וַיְשִׁיבֵם אֶל־יְהוָה
5 אֱלֹהֵי אֲבוֹתֵיהֶם׃ וַיַּעֲמֵד
שֹׁפְטִים בָּאָרֶץ בְּכָל־עָרֵי
יְהוּדָה הַבְּצֻרוֹת לְעִיר וָעִיר׃
6 וַיֹּאמֶר אֶל־הַשֹּׁפְטִים רְאוּ
מָה־אַתֶּם עֹשִׂים כִּי לֹא לְאָדָם
תִּשְׁפְּטוּ כִּי לַיהוָה וְעִמָּכֶם

Baasa (1 Kings xvi. 1ff.), condemned Asa's alliance with Aram (xvi. 7ff.) and was the historian of Jehoshaphat's reign (xx. 34). He evidently lived to an advanced age.

the wicked. viz. Ahab.

them that hate the LORD. Ahab's followers.

wrath is upon thee. i.e. punishment is imminent. The allusion is to the invasion narrated in the next chapter.

3. *good things.* See on xii. 12.

Asheroth. The plural feminine of *Asherah*, the usual plural having a masculine form, *Asherim* (see on xiv. 2).

4-7. Jehoshaphat appoints judges.

4. *went out again.* The first time may have been the occasion when he sent a commission, in the third year of his reign, to spread a knowledge of the Torah in the cities of Judah (xvii. 7ff.).

from Beer-sheba . . . Ephraim. These were apparently the southern (cf. 1 Chron. xxi. 2) and northern (cf. xvii. 2) limits of his realm.

brought them back. They had evidently lapsed into idolatry.

5. *set judges.* Cf. Deut. xvi. 18.

the fortified cities. Which were the centre for the smaller towns in the district.

6. *for ye judge . . . for the LORD.* The

[He is] with you in giving judgment.
7. Now therefore let the fear of the
LORD be upon you; take heed and
do it; for there is no iniquity with
the LORD our God, nor respect of
persons, nor taking of bribes.'
8. Moreover in Jerusalem did
Jehoshaphat set of the Levites and
the priests, and of the heads of the
fathers' houses of Israel, for the
judgment of the LORD, and for
controversies. And they returned
to Jerusalem. 9. And he charged
them, saying: 'Thus shall ye do in
the fear of the LORD, faithfully, and
with a whole heart. 10. And when-
soever any controversy shall come
to you from your brethren that dwell
in their cities, between blood and
blood, between law and command-

7 בִּדְבַר מִשְׁפָּט׃ וְעַתָּה יְהִי
פַחַד־יְהוָה עֲלֵיכֶם שִׁמְרוּ
וַעֲשׂוּ כִּי־אֵין עִם־יְהוָה
אֱלֹהֵינוּ עַוְלָה וּמַשֹּׂא פָנִים
וּמִקַּח־שֹׁחַד׃
8 וְגַם בִּירוּשָׁלַםִ הֶעֱמִיד
יְהוֹשָׁפָט מִן־הַלְוִיִּם
וְהַכֹּהֲנִים וּמֵרָאשֵׁי הָאָבוֹת
לְיִשְׂרָאֵל לְמִשְׁפַּט יְהוָה
9 וְלָרִיב וַיָּשֻׁבוּ יְרוּשָׁלָםִ׃ וַיְצַו
עֲלֵיהֶם לֵאמֹר כֹּה תַעֲשׂוּן
בְּיִרְאַת יְהוָה בֶּאֱמוּנָה וּבְלֵבָב
10 שָׁלֵם׃ וְכָל־רִיב אֲשֶׁר־יָבוֹא
עֲלֵיכֶם מֵאֲחֵיכֶם ׀ הַיֹּשְׁבִים
בְּעָרֵיהֶם בֵּין־דָּם ׀ לְדָם בֵּין־

judge functioned as the earthly representative of God.

[*He is*] *with you*, etc. This thought should give the judge courage to decide against an influential litigant when the evidence was against him (cf. verse 7).

7. *there is no iniquity with the LORD.* Cf. Deut. xxxii. 4.

nor respect of persons, etc. Cf. Deut. x. 17.

8-11. Appointment of a supreme court of justice in Jerusalem.

8. *judgment of the LORD.* On religious issues or matters which had to be decided according to the precepts of the Torah.

controversies. Civil cases or such as might be settled by arbitration.

they returned to Jerusalem. The intention of the clause is uncertain. The words may perhaps be rendered: 'after having returned to Jerusalem,' the subject being Jehoshaphat and his counsellors who accompanied him on his tour through the kingdom (verse 4). Another possibility is that *they* refers to the men nominated to act as judges in Jerusalem who may have resided in other cities.

9. *with a whole heart.* In the administration of justice, complete conscientiousness is demanded, without fear or favour.

10. Cases committed to Jerusalem by the provincial courts (cf. Deut. xvii. 8ff.).

from your brethren. The judges in the smaller towns.

between blood and blood. Whether a person is guilty of murder or manslaughter (cf. Exod. xxi. 12ff.).

between law and commandment, etc.

ment, statutes and ordinances, ye shall warn them, that they be not guilty towards the LORD, and so wrath come upon you and upon your brethren; thus shall ye do, and ye shall not be guilty. 11. And, behold, Amariah the chief priest is over you in all matters of the LORD; and Zebadiah the son of Ishmael, the ruler of the house of Judah, in all the king's matters; also the officers of the Levites before you. Deal courageously, and the LORD be with the good.'

תּוֹרָה לְמִצְוָה לְחֻקִּים
וּלְמִשְׁפָּטִים וְהִזְהַרְתֶּם אֹתָם
וְלֹא יֶאְשְׁמוּ לַיהוָה וְהָיָה־
קֶצֶף עֲלֵיכֶם וְעַל־אֲחֵיכֶם
11 כֹּה תַעֲשׂוּן וְלֹא תֶאְשָׁמוּ׃ וְהִנֵּה
אֲמַרְיָהוּ כֹהֵן הָרֹאשׁ עֲלֵיכֶם
לְכֹל ׀ דְּבַר יְהוָה וּזְבַדְיָהוּ
בֶן־יִשְׁמָעֵאל הַנָּגִיד לְבֵית־
יְהוּדָה לְכֹל דְּבַר־הַמֶּלֶךְ
וְשֹׁטְרִים הַלְוִיִּם לִפְנֵיכֶם חִזְקוּ
וַעֲשׂוּ וִיהִי יְהוָה עִם־הַטּוֹב׃

20 CHAPTER XX כ

1. And it came to pass after this, that the children of Moab, and the children of Ammon, and with them some of the Ammonites, came against Jehoshaphat to battle.

1 וַיְהִי אַחֲרֵי־כֵן בָּאוּ בְנֵי־
מוֹאָב וּבְנֵי עַמּוֹן וְעִמָּהֶם ׀
מֵהָעַמּוֹנִים עַל־יְהוֹשָׁפָט

Questions of legal interpretation, to decide under which law a particular case had to be determined.

thus shall ye do, etc. Cf. Deut. xvii. 11ff.

11. *Amariah the chief priest.* See on 1 Chron. v. 37.

matters of the LORD. Ecclesiastical or religious questions.

Zebadiah. Possibly the Levite named in xvii. 8.

the king's matters. Civil cases which come within the king's jurisdiction.

the officers of the Levites. Or, 'the Levites shall be officers.'

deal courageously. lit. 'be strong and act.'

the good. The man who walks in His ways and follows His precepts.

CHAPTER XX

1-30. This section has no parallel in Kings.

1f. Threatened invasion of Judah by a triple alliance.

1. *after this.* After Jehoshaphat had established administration of justice throughout his realm.

Ammonites. The Midrash identifies them with the Amalekites who lived round mount Seir (cf. verse 10) and asserts that they were subjects of Jehoshaphat like the Edomeans who

2. Then there came some that told
Jehoshaphat, saying: 'There cometh
a great multitude against thee from
beyond the sea from Aram; and,
behold, they are in Hazazon-tamar'
—the same is En-gedi. 3. And
Jehoshaphat feared, and set himself
to seek unto the LORD; and he
proclaimed a fast throughout all
Judah. 4. And Judah gathered
themselves together, to seek help of
the LORD; even out of all the cities of
Judah they came to seek the LORD.
5. And Jehoshaphat stood in the
congregation of Judah and Jerusalem, in the house of the LORD,
before the new court; 6. and he said:
'O LORD, the God of our fathers,
art not Thou alone God in heaven?
and art not Thou ruler over all the
kingdoms of the nations? and in Thy

2 לַמִּלְחָמָה׃ וַיָּבֹאוּ וַיַּגִּידוּ
לִיהוֹשָׁפָט לֵאמֹר בָּא עָלֶיךָ
הָמוֹן רָב מֵעֵבֶר לַיָּם מֵאֲרָם
וְהִנָּם בְּחַצְצוֹן תָּמָר הִיא עֵין
3 גֶּדִי׃ וַיִּרָא וַיִּתֵּן יְהוֹשָׁפָט אֶת־
פָּנָיו לִדְרוֹשׁ לַיהוָה וַיִּקְרָא־
צוֹם עַל־כָּל־יְהוּדָה׃
4 וַיִּקָּבְצוּ יְהוּדָה לְבַקֵּשׁ מֵיְהוָה
גַּם מִכָּל־עָרֵי יְהוּדָה בָּאוּ
5 לְבַקֵּשׁ אֶת־יְהוָה׃ וַיַּעֲמֹד
יְהוֹשָׁפָט בִּקְהַל יְהוּדָה
וִירוּשָׁלַםִ בְּבֵית יְהוָה לִפְנֵי
6 הֶחָצֵר הַחֲדָשָׁה׃ וַיֹּאמַר יְהוָה
אֱלֹהֵי אֲבֹתֵינוּ הֲלֹא אַתָּה־
הוּא אֱלֹהִים בַּשָּׁמַיִם וְאַתָּה
מוֹשֵׁל בְּכֹל מַמְלְכוֹת הַגּוֹיִם

v. 3. חסר י׳

inhabited the same mount. Afraid of reprisals on their people in the event of defeat, they disguised themselves as their allies, the Ammonites. Metsudath David and modern commentators hold that *Ammonim* here stands for *Meunim* (cf. xxvi. 7; 1 Chron. iv. 41, see *ad loc.*).

2. *beyond the sea.* i.e. the Dead Sea.

from Aram. The invasion was made through that country (Metsudath David). M.T. is supported by the LXX, but most moderns read with a Hebrew MS. *Edom* for *Aram.* The latter (Syria) is many miles away to the north, while Edom is immediately on the south or south-east of the Dead Sea.

Hazazon-tamar. Mentioned in Gen. xiv. 7.

En-gedi. The modern Ain Jidi, fifteen miles from Jerusalem on the west shore of the Dead Sea, from which a pass leads to the interior of the Judean hills.

3f. A fast and solemn assembly are proclaimed.

3. *set himself.* lit. 'set his face.'

proclaimed a fast. As was usual when calamity threatened the people (cf. Joel ii. 15; Jonah iii. 5; Esth. iv. 16).

4. *seek help.* The noun is implied.

5-13. Jehoshaphat's prayer.

5. *the new court.* It was called *new* for a reason which is unknown. Metsudath David suggests that it had been recently repaired.

hand is power and might, so that none is able to withstand Thee. 7. Didst not Thou, O our God, drive out the inhabitants of this land before Thy people Israel, and gavest it to the seed of Abraham Thy friend for ever? 8. And they dwelt therein, and have built Thee a sanctuary therein for Thy name, saying: 9. If evil come upon us, the sword, judgment, or pestilence, or famine, we will stand before this house, and before Thee—for Thy name is in this house—and cry unto Thee in our affliction, and Thou wilt hear and save. 10. And now, behold, the children of Ammon and Moab and mount Seir, whom Thou wouldest not let Israel invade, when they came out of the land of Egypt, but they turned aside from them, and destroyed them not; 11. behold, they render unto us [evil], to come to cast us out of Thy possession, which Thou hast given us to inherit. 12. O our God, wilt Thou not execute judgment on them? for we have no might against this great

וּבְיָדְךָ כֹּחַ וּגְבוּרָה וְאֵין עִמְּךָ
7 לְהִתְיַצֵּב: הֲלֹא | אַתָּה
אֱלֹהֵינוּ הוֹרַשְׁתָּ אֶת־יֹשְׁבֵי
הָאָרֶץ הַזֹּאת מִלִּפְנֵי עַמְּךָ
יִשְׂרָאֵל וַתִּתְּנָהּ לְזֶרַע אַבְרָהָם
8 אֹהַבְךָ לְעוֹלָם: וַיֵּשְׁבוּ־בָהּ
וַיִּבְנוּ לְךָ | בָּהּ מִקְדָּשׁ לְשִׁמְךָ
9 לֵאמֹר: אִם־תָּבוֹא עָלֵינוּ
רָעָה חֶרֶב שְׁפוֹט וְדֶבֶר וְרָעָב
נַעַמְדָה לִפְנֵי הַבַּיִת הַזֶּה
וּלְפָנֶיךָ כִּי שִׁמְךָ בַּבַּיִת הַזֶּה
וְנִזְעַק אֵלֶיךָ מִצָּרָתֵנוּ וְתִשְׁמַע
10 וְתוֹשִׁיעַ: וְעַתָּה הִנֵּה בְנֵי־
עַמּוֹן וּמוֹאָב וְהַר־שֵׂעִיר אֲשֶׁר
לֹא־נָתַתָּה לְיִשְׂרָאֵל לָבוֹא
בָהֶם בְּבֹאָם מֵאֶרֶץ מִצְרָיִם
כִּי סָרוּ מֵעֲלֵיהֶם וְלֹא
11 הִשְׁמִידוּם: וְהִנֵּה־הֵם גֹּמְלִים
עָלֵינוּ לָבוֹא לְגָרְשֵׁנוּ מִיְּרֻשָּׁתְךָ
12 אֲשֶׁר הוֹרַשְׁתָּנוּ: אֱלֹהֵינוּ הֲלֹא
תִשְׁפָּט־בָּם כִּי אֵין בָּנוּ כֹּחַ

7. *didst not Thou . . . drive out.* Cf. Deut. ix. 5.

the seed of Abraham Thy friend. A reminiscence of Isa. xli. 8.

9. *the sword, judgment.* Ignoring the accentuation, R.V. margin renders: 'the sword of judgment.'

in our affliction. lit. 'from our troubles.'

10. *mount Seir.* This corresponds to the *Ammonites* in verse 1.

Thou wouldest not let Israel invade. lit. 'to come into them'; cf. Deut. ii. 4f., 9, 19.

11. *Thy possession.* The land of Judah.

12. Cf. the similarity with Asa's prayer in xiv. 10.

multitude that cometh against us;
neither know we what to do; but our
eyes are upon Thee.' 13. And all
Judah stood before the LORD, with
their little ones, their wives, and
their children.

14. Then upon Jahaziel the son of
Zechariah, the son of Benaiah, the
son of Jeiel, the son of Mattaniah,
the Levite, of the sons of Asaph,
came the spirit of the LORD in the
midst of the congregation; 15. and
he said: 'Hearken ye, all Judah, and
ye inhabitants of Jerusalem, and
thou king Jehoshaphat: thus saith
the LORD unto you: Fear not ye,
neither be dismayed by reason of
this great multitude; for the battle is
not yours, but God's. 16. To-
morrow go ye down against them;
behold, they come up by the ascent
of Ziz; and ye shall find them at the
end of the valley, before the wilderness of Jeruel. 17. Ye shall not need
to fight in this battle; set yourselves,

לִפְנֵי הֶהָמוֹן הָרָב הַזֶּה הַבָּא
עָלֵינוּ וַאֲנַחְנוּ לֹא נֵדַע מַה־
13 נַּעֲשֶׂה כִּי עָלֶיךָ עֵינֵינוּ׃ וְכָל־
יְהוּדָה עֹמְדִים לִפְנֵי יְהוָה גַּם־
טַפָּם נְשֵׁיהֶם וּבְנֵיהֶם׃
14 וְיַחֲזִיאֵל בֶּן־זְכַרְיָהוּ בֶּן־
בְּנָיָה בֶּן־יְעִיאֵל בֶּן־מַתַּנְיָה
הַלֵּוִי מִן־בְּנֵי אָסָף הָיְתָה עָלָיו
רוּחַ יְהוָה בְּתוֹךְ הַקָּהָל׃
15 וַיֹּאמֶר הַקְשִׁיבוּ כָל־יְהוּדָה
וְיֹשְׁבֵי יְרוּשָׁלַםִ וְהַמֶּלֶךְ
יְהוֹשָׁפָט כֹּה־אָמַר יְהוָה לָכֶם
אַתֶּם אַל־תִּירְאוּ וְאַל־תֵּחַתּוּ
מִפְּנֵי הֶהָמוֹן הָרָב הַזֶּה כִּי
לֹא לָכֶם הַמִּלְחָמָה כִּי
16 לֵאלֹהִים׃ מָחָר רְדוּ עֲלֵיהֶם
הִנָּם עֹלִים בְּמַעֲלֵה הַצִּיץ
וּמְצָאתֶם אֹתָם בְּסוֹף הַנַּחַל
17 פְּנֵי מִדְבַּר יְרוּאֵל׃ לֹא לָכֶם
לְהִלָּחֵם בָּזֹאת הִתְיַצְּבוּ עִמְדוּ

13. *stood before the LORD.* In supplication.

with their little ones. Even the young children were brought to the solemn assemblies (cf. Deut. xxix. 10, xxxi. 12).

14-19. God's reassuring response.

14. *Jahaziel.* This chapter records the only appearance of this man who belonged to the Levitical musicians.

15. *the battle is not yours,* etc. Your rescue from danger will be effected by Divine intervention (cf. the phrase used by David against Goliath, 1 Sam. xvii. 47).

16. *the ascent of Ziz . . . the wilderness of Jeruel.* Neither of these localities has been identified. They must have been situated to the north of the Dead Sea, south-east of the wilderness of Tekoa (cf. verse 20).

17. *in this battle.* The noun is implied.

stand ye still, and see the salvation
of the LORD with you, O Judah and
Jerusalem; fear not, nor be dismayed; to-morrow go out against
them; for the LORD is with you.'
18. And Jehoshaphat bowed his head
with his face to the ground; and all
Judah and the inhabitants of Jerusalem fell down before the LORD,
worshipping the LORD. 19. And the
Levites, of the children of the
Kohathites and of the children of
the Korahites, stood up to praise
the LORD, the God of Israel, with an
exceeding loud voice.

20. And they rose early in the
morning, and went forth into the
wilderness of Tekoa; and as they
went forth, Jehoshaphat stood and
said: 'Hear me, O Judah, and ye
inhabitants of Jerusalem; believe in
the LORD your God, so shall ye be
established; believe His prophets,
so shall ye prosper.' 21. And when
he had taken counsel with the people,
he appointed them that should sing
unto the LORD, and praise in the
beauty of holiness, as they went out

וּרְאוּ אֶת־יְשׁוּעַת יְהוָה עִמָּכֶם
יְהוּדָה וִירוּשָׁלִַם אַל־תִּירְאוּ
וְאַל־תֵּחַתּוּ מָחָר צְאוּ
18 לִפְנֵיהֶם וַיהוָה עִמָּכֶם׃ וַיִּקֹּד
יְהוֹשָׁפָט אַפַּיִם אָרְצָה וְכָל־
יְהוּדָה וְיֹשְׁבֵי יְרוּשָׁלִַם נָפְלוּ
לִפְנֵי יְהוָה לְהִשְׁתַּחֲוֺת לַיהוָה׃
19 וַיָּקֻמוּ הַלְוִיִּם מִן־בְּנֵי
הַקְּהָתִים וּמִן־בְּנֵי הַקָּרְחִים
לְהַלֵּל לַיהוָה אֱלֹהֵי יִשְׂרָאֵל
בְּקוֹל גָּדוֹל לְמָעְלָה׃
20 וַיַּשְׁכִּימוּ בַבֹּקֶר וַיֵּצְאוּ
לְמִדְבַּר תְּקוֹעַ וּבְצֵאתָם עָמַד
יְהוֹשָׁפָט וַיֹּאמֶר שְׁמָעוּנִי
יְהוּדָה וְיֹשְׁבֵי יְרוּשָׁלִַם הַאֲמִינוּ
בַּיהוָה אֱלֹהֵיכֶם וְתֵאָמֵנוּ
הַאֲמִינוּ בִנְבִיאָיו וְהַצְלִיחוּ׃
21 וַיִּוָּעַץ אֶל־הָעָם וַיַּעֲמֵד
מְשֹׁרְרִים לַיהוָה וּמְהַלְלִים
לְהַדְרַת־קֹדֶשׁ בְּצֵאת לִפְנֵי

see the salvation of the LORD. Cf. Exod. xiv. 13. The exhortation to rely upon God is one of the conspicuous messages in this Book. See on xiii. 18.

18. *bowed his head,* etc. In gratitude for God's assurance of aid.

19. *Kohathites . . . Korahites.* The latter were a branch of the family first named (cf. 1 Chron. vi. 7).

with an exceeding loud voice. lit. 'with a great voice upwards.'

20-30. The deliverance and capture of spoils, thanksgiving and peace.

20. *wilderness of Tekoa.* i.e. the part of the wilderness of Judah by the city of Tekoa (see on xi. 6).

believe . . . established. The Hebrew, *ha'aminu . . . te'amenu,* is a play upon two forms of the same verb. It occurs again in a negative form in Isa. vii. 9.

21. *in the beauty of holiness.* See on 1 Chron. xvi. 29.

before the army, and say: 'Give thanks unto the LORD, for His mercy endureth for ever.' 22. And when they began to sing and to praise, the LORD set liers-in-wait against the children of Ammon, Moab, and mount Seir, that were come against Judah; and they were smitten. 23. For the children of Ammon and Moab stood up against the inhabitants of mount Seir, utterly to slay and destroy them; and when they had made an end of the inhabitants of Seir, every one helped to destroy another.

24. And when Judah came to the watch-tower of the wilderness, they looked upon the multitude; and, behold, they were dead bodies fallen to the earth, and there were none that escaped. 25. And when Jehoshaphat and his people came to take the spoil of them, they found among them in abundance both riches and dead bodies, and precious jewels, which they stripped off for themselves, more than they could carry away; and they were three days in taking the spoil, it was so much. 26. And on the fourth day they assembled themselves in the

הֶחָלוּץ וְאֹמְרִים הוֹדוּ לַיהוָה
כִּי לְעוֹלָם חַסְדּוֹ׃ וּבְעֵת 22
הֵחֵלּוּ בְרִנָּה וּתְהִלָּה נָתַן יְהוָה
| מְאָרְבִים עַל־בְּנֵי עַמּוֹן
מוֹאָב וְהַר־שֵׂעִיר הַבָּאִים
לִיהוּדָה וַיִּנָּגֵפוּ׃ וַיַּעַמְדוּ בְּנֵי 23
עַמּוֹן וּמוֹאָב עַל־יֹשְׁבֵי הַר־
שֵׂעִיר לְהַחֲרִים וּלְהַשְׁמִיד
וּכְכַלּוֹתָם בְּיוֹשְׁבֵי שֵׂעִיר עָזְרוּ
אִישׁ בְּרֵעֵהוּ לְמַשְׁחִית׃
וִיהוּדָה בָּא עַל־הַמִּצְפֶּה 24
לַמִּדְבָּר וַיִּפְנוּ אֶל־הֶהָמוֹן
וְהִנָּם פְּגָרִים נֹפְלִים אַרְצָה
וְאֵין פְּלֵיטָה׃ וַיָּבֹא יְהוֹשָׁפָט 25
וְעַמּוֹ לָבֹז אֶת־שְׁלָלָם וַיִּמְצְאוּ
בָהֶם לָרֹב וּרְכוּשׁ וּפְגָרִים
וּכְלֵי חֲמֻדוֹת וַיְנַצְּלוּ לָהֶם
לְאֵין מַשָּׂא וַיִּהְיוּ יָמִים שְׁלוֹשָׁה
בֹּזְזִים אֶת־הַשָּׁלָל כִּי רַב־
הוּא׃ וּבַיּוֹם הָרְבִעִי נִקְהֲלוּ 26

give thanks, etc. Cf. 1 Chron. xvi. 34, 41.

22. *the LORD set liers-in-wait*. The probable meaning is that, at the critical moment, the invading force was set upon by men living in that area and was demoralized by the unexpected attack. The danger to Judah was thereby averted, and the Chronicler attributed this to the direct intervention of God.

23. The surprise assault by the ambush created panic among the invaders, and they turned their weapons against one another. This had happened among the Midianites when attacked suddenly by Gideon (Judg. vii. 22).

24. *the watch-tower*. A high point among the hills from which a view was obtained of the battlefield.

25. *dead bodies*. For *pegarim* some Hebrew MSS. read *begadim*, 'garments.'

valley of Beracah; for there they blessed the LORD; therefore the name of that place was called The valley of Beracah, unto this day. 27. Then they returned, every man of Judah and Jerusalem, and Jehoshaphat in the forefront of them, to go back to Jerusalem with joy; for the LORD had made them to rejoice over their enemies. 28. And they came to Jerusalem with psalteries and harps and trumpets unto the house of the LORD. 29. And a terror from God was on all the kingdoms of the countries, when they heard that the LORD fought against the enemies of Israel. 30. So the realm of Jehoshaphat was quiet; for his God gave him rest round about.

31. And Jehoshaphat reigned over Judah; he was thirty and five years old when he began to reign; and he reigned twenty and five years in Jerusalem; and his mother's name was Azubah the daughter of Shilhi. 32. And he walked in the way of Asa his father, and turned not aside from it, doing that which was right

לְעֵמֶק בְּרָכָה כִּי־שָׁם בֵּרְכוּ
אֶת־יְהוָה עַל־כֵּן קָרְאוּ אֶת־
שֵׁם הַמָּקוֹם הַהוּא עֵמֶק בְּרָכָה
27 עַד־הַיּוֹם׃ וַיָּשֻׁבוּ כָּל־אִישׁ
יְהוּדָה וִירוּשָׁלִַם וִיהוֹשָׁפָט
בְּרֹאשָׁם לָשׁוּב אֶל־יְרוּשָׁלִַם
בְּשִׂמְחָה כִּי־שִׂמְּחָם יְהוָה
28 מֵאוֹיְבֵיהֶם׃ וַיָּבֹאוּ יְרוּשָׁלִַם
בִּנְבָלִים וּבְכִנֹּרוֹת וּבַחֲצֹצְרוֹת
29 אֶל־בֵּית יְהוָה׃ וַיְהִי פַּחַד
אֱלֹהִים עַל כָּל־מַמְלְכוֹת
הָאֲרָצוֹת בְּשָׁמְעָם כִּי נִלְחַם
יְהוָה עִם אוֹיְבֵי יִשְׂרָאֵל׃
30 וַתִּשְׁקֹט מַלְכוּת יְהוֹשָׁפָט וַיָּנַח
לוֹ אֱלֹהָיו מִסָּבִיב׃
31 וַיִּמְלֹךְ יְהוֹשָׁפָט עַל־יְהוּדָה
בֶּן־שְׁלֹשִׁים וְחָמֵשׁ שָׁנָה
בְּמָלְכוֹ וְעֶשְׂרִים וְחָמֵשׁ שָׁנָה
מָלַךְ בִּירוּשָׁלִַם וְשֵׁם אִמּוֹ
32 עֲזוּבָה בַּת־שִׁלְחִי׃ וַיֵּלֶךְ
בְּדֶרֶךְ אָבִיו אָסָא וְלֹא־סָר
מִמֶּנָּה לַעֲשׂוֹת הַיָּשָׁר בְּעֵינֵי

26. *the valley of Beracah.* The name signifies 'blessing'; it is preserved in a ruined village between Gedor and Tekoa called Bereikut.

29. *a terror from God.* Better, 'the terror of God'; the victory of Judah deterred other peoples from planning an attack upon a land which was under God's mighty protection.

31-34 (corresponding, with variants, to I Kings xxii. 41-45). A brief summary of Jehoshaphat's reign.

31. *when he began to reign.* lit. 'when he reigned.' In I Kings xxii. 41 the accession is dated *in the fourth year of Ahab king of Israel.* The Chronicler ignores the chronological relationship

in the eyes of the LORD. 33. Howbeit the high places were not taken away; neither as yet had the people set their hearts unto the God of their fathers. 34. Now the rest of the acts of Jehoshaphat, first and last, behold, they are written in the words of Jehu the son of Hanani, which is inserted in the book of the kings of Israel.

35. And after this did Jehoshaphat king of Judah join himself with Ahaziah king of Israel; the same did very wickedly; 36. and he joined him with himself to make ships to go to Tarshish; and they made the ships in Ezion-geber. 37. Then Eliezer the son of Dodavahu of Mareshah prophesied against Jehoshaphat, saying: 'Because thou hast

33 יְהוָה׃ אַךְ הַבָּמוֹת לֹא־סָרוּ
וְעוֹד הָעָם לֹא־הֵכִינוּ לְבָבָם
34 לֵאלֹהֵי אֲבֹתֵיהֶם׃ וְיֶתֶר
דִּבְרֵי יְהוֹשָׁפָט הָרִאשֹׁנִים
וְהָאַחֲרֹנִים הִנָּם כְּתוּבִים
בְּדִבְרֵי יֵהוּא בֶן־חֲנָנִי אֲשֶׁר
הֹעֲלָה עַל־סֵפֶר מַלְכֵי
יִשְׂרָאֵל׃
35 וְאַחֲרֵי־כֵן אֶתְחַבַּר יְהוֹשָׁפָט
מֶלֶךְ־יְהוּדָה עִם אֲחַזְיָה
מֶלֶךְ־יִשְׂרָאֵל הוּא הִרְשִׁיעַ
36 לַעֲשׂוֹת׃ וַיְחַבְּרֵהוּ עִמּוֹ
לַעֲשׂוֹת אֳנִיּוֹת לָלֶכֶת תַּרְשִׁישׁ
וַיַּעֲשׂוּ אֳנִיּוֹת בְּעֶצְיוֹן גָּבֶר׃
37 וַיִּתְנַבֵּא אֱלִיעֶזֶר בֶּן־דֹּדָוָהוּ
מִמָּרֵשָׁה עַל־יְהוֹשָׁפָט לֵאמֹר

with the impious king of the Northern Kingdom.

32. *doing that.* lit. 'to do.'

33. *the high places were not taken away.* Contrast xvii. 6.

neither as yet . . . fathers. 1 Kings xxii. 44 is more specific: *the people still sacrificed and offered in the high places.* The statement that Jehoshaphat made peace with the king of Israel (1 Kings xxii. 45) is omitted by the Chronicler.

34. *first and last.* See on 1 Chron. xxix. 29. 1 Kings xxii. 46 has instead: *and his might that he showed, and how he warred.*

in the words of Jehu . . . Israel. In Kings: *in the book of the chronicles of the kings of Judah. Israel* here is used in its wide sense and includes Judah.

35-37. Jehoshaphat's joint adventure with Ahaziah in building a merchant fleet comes to a disastrous end. There is a different account in 1 Kings xxii. 49f.

35. *the same did very wickedly.* A fact which should have deterred Jehoshaphat from entering into an alliance with him (verse 37).

36. *ships to go to Tarshish.* See on ix. 21. According to 1 Kings xxii. 49, *Jehoshaphat made ships of Tarshish to go to Ophir.*

Ezion-geber. See on viii. 17.

37. *Eliezer the son of Dodavahu.* Nothing is known about this prophet beyond what is related of him here.

Mareshah. See on xi. 8.

joined thyself with Ahaziah, the LORD hath made a breach in thy works.' And the ships were broken, that they were not able to go to Tarshish.

כְּהִתְחַבֶּרְךָ עִם־אֲחַזְיָהוּ פָּרַץ
יְהוָה אֶת־מַעֲשֶׂיךָ וַיִּשָּׁבְרוּ
אֳנִיּוֹת וְלֹא עָצְרוּ לָלֶכֶת אֶל־
תַּרְשִׁישׁ׃

21 CHAPTER XXI כא

1. And Jehoshaphat slept with his
fathers, and was buried with his
fathers in the city of David; and
Jehoram his son reigned in his
stead. 2. And he had brethren the
sons of Jehoshaphat, Azariah, and
Jehiel, and Zechariah, and Azariahu,
and Michael, and Shephatiah; all
these were the sons of Jehoshaphat
king of Israel. 3. And their father
gave them great gifts, of silver, and
of gold, and of precious things, with
fortified cities in Judah; but the
kingdom gave he to Jehoram, because he was the first-born. 4. Now
when Jehoram was risen up over
the kingdom of his father, and had
strengthened himself, he slew all

1 וַיִּשְׁכַּב יְהוֹשָׁפָט עִם־אֲבֹתָיו
וַיִּקָּבֵר עִם־אֲבֹתָיו בְּעִיר
דָּוִיד וַיִּמְלֹךְ יְהוֹרָם בְּנוֹ
2 תַּחְתָּיו׃ וְלוֹ־־אַחִים בְּנֵי
יְהוֹשָׁפָט עֲזַרְיָה וִיחִיאֵל
וּזְכַרְיָהוּ וַעֲזַרְיָהוּ וּמִיכָאֵל
וּשְׁפַטְיָהוּ כָּל־אֵלֶּה בְּנֵי
3 יְהוֹשָׁפָט מֶלֶךְ־יִשְׂרָאֵל׃ וַיִּתֵּן
לָהֶם ׀ אֲבִיהֶם מַתָּנוֹת רַבּוֹת
לְכֶסֶף וּלְזָהָב וּלְמִגְדָּנוֹת עִם־
עָרֵי מְצוּרוֹת בִּיהוּדָה וְאֶת־
הַמַּמְלָכָה נָתַן לִיהוֹרָם כִּי־
4 הוּא הַבְּכוֹר׃ וַיָּקָם יְהוֹרָם
עַל־מַמְלֶכֶת אָבִיו וַיִּתְחַזַּק

hath made a breach in thy works. Fulfilled in the following statement: *and the ships were broken.* The wrecking took place, according to 1 Kings xxii. 49, at Ezion-geber.

CHAPTER XXI

THE REIGN OF JEHORAM

1 (corresponding to 1 Kings xxii. 51). Jehoram succeeds his father. The years of his reign were 850-843 B.C.E.

2-4 (no parallel in Kings). Violent opening of the reign.

2. *king of Israel.* As elsewhere, the Chronicler here designates Judah by the general term *Israel.*

3. *their father gave them.* Bequeathed to them.

his brethren with the sword, and divers also of the princes of Israel. 5. Jehoram was thirty and two years old when he began to reign; and he reigned eight years in Jerusalem. 6. And he walked in the way of the kings of Israel, as did the house of Ahab; for he had the daughter of Ahab to wife; and he did that which was evil in the sight of the LORD. 7. Howbeit the LORD would not destroy the house of David, because of the covenant that He had made with David, and as He promised to give a lamp to him and to his children alway.

8. In his days Edom revolted from under the hand of Judah, and made a king over themselves. 9. Then Jehoram passed over with his captains, and all his chariots with

וַיַּהֲרֹג אֶת־כָּל־אֶחָיו בֶּחָרֶב
וְגַם מִשָּׂרֵי יִשְׂרָאֵל׃ בֶּן־ 5
שְׁלֹשִׁים וּשְׁתַּיִם שָׁנָה יְהוֹרָם
בְּמָלְכוֹ וּשְׁמוֹנֶה שָׁנִים מָלַךְ
בִּירוּשָׁלִָם׃ וַיֵּלֶךְ בְּדֶרֶךְ ׀ 6
מַלְכֵי יִשְׂרָאֵל כַּאֲשֶׁר עָשׂוּ
בֵּית אַחְאָב כִּי בַּת־אַחְאָב
הָיְתָה לּוֹ אִשָּׁה וַיַּעַשׂ הָרַע
בְּעֵינֵי יְהוָה׃ וְלֹא־אָבָה יְהוָה 7
לְהַשְׁחִית אֶת־בֵּית דָּוִיד
לְמַעַן הַבְּרִית אֲשֶׁר כָּרַת
לְדָוִיד וְכַאֲשֶׁר אָמַר לָתֵת לוֹ
נִיר וּלְבָנָיו כָּל־הַיָּמִים׃
בְּיָמָיו פָּשַׁע אֱדוֹם מִתַּחַת יַד־ 8
יְהוּדָה וַיַּמְלִיכוּ עֲלֵיהֶם מֶלֶךְ׃
וַיַּעֲבֹר יְהוֹרָם עִם־שָׂרָיו 9

4. *he slew all his brethren.* To remove the danger of rivals to the throne.

divers also. The first word is not in the text.

5-7 (corresponding to 2 Kings viii. 17-19). Characteristics of Jehoram's reign.

5. *when he began to reign.* lit. 'in his reigning.'

6. *the kings of Israel.* Here the Northern Kingdom is intended.

the daughter of Ahab. viz. Athaliah; cf. xxii. 2 where she is described as *the daughter of Omri. Daughter* is employed for 'granddaughter.'

7. *the house of David.* In 2 Kings viii. 19: *Judah.*

a lamp. A symbol of kingship, the extinction of the light denoting the end of the dynasty.

8-10 (corresponding to 2 Kings viii. 20-22). The revolt of Edom and Libnah.

8. *made a king over themselves.* Hitherto, since the time of David, they were ruled by a deputy appointed by the king of Judah (cf. 1 Chron. xviii. 12f.).

9. The corresponding verse in 2 Kings viii. 21 concludes: *and the people fled to their tents.* Jehoram's attempt to crush the rebellion was unsuccessful; but he and his army, surrounded by an Edomite force, managed to save themselves by breaking through during the night and reaching their homeland.

with his captains. The reading in 2 Kings viii. 21 is: *to Zair*, a town in or near Edom.

him; and he rose up by night, and smote the Edomites that compassed him about, and the captains of the chariots. 10. So Edom revolted from under the hand of Judah unto this day; then did Libnah revolt at the same time from under his hand; because he had forsaken the LORD, the God of his fathers. 11. Moreover he made high places in the mountains of Judah, and made the inhabitants of Jerusalem to go astray, and drew Judah away. 12. And there came a writing to him from Elijah the prophet, saying: 'Thus saith the LORD, the God of David thy father: Because thou hast not walked in the ways of Jehoshaphat thy father, nor in the ways of Asa king of Judah; 13. but hast walked in the way of the kings of Israel, and hast made Judah and the inhabitants of Jerusalem to go astray, like as the house of Ahab made [Israel] to go astray; and also

וְכָל־הָרֶכֶב עִמּוֹ וַיְהִי קָם
לַיְלָה וַיַּךְ אֶת־אֱדוֹם הַסּוֹבֵב
10 אֵלָיו וְאֵת שָׂרֵי הָרָכֶב׃ וַיִּפְשַׁע
אֱדוֹם מִתַּחַת יַד־יְהוּדָה עַד
הַיּוֹם הַזֶּה אָז תִּפְשַׁע לִבְנָה
בָּעֵת הַהִיא מִתַּחַת יָדוֹ כִּי עָזַב
11 אֶת־יְהוָה אֱלֹהֵי אֲבֹתָיו׃ גַּם־
הוּא עָשָׂה בָמוֹת בְּהָרֵי יְהוּדָה
וַיֶּזֶן אֶת־יֹשְׁבֵי יְרוּשָׁלִַם וַיַּדַּח
12 אֶת־יְהוּדָה׃ וַיָּבֹא אֵלָיו
מִכְתָּב מֵאֵלִיָּהוּ הַנָּבִיא לֵאמֹר
כֹּה ׀ אָמַר יְהוָה אֱלֹהֵי דָּוִיד
אָבִיךָ תַּחַת אֲשֶׁר לֹא־הָלַכְתָּ
בְּדַרְכֵי יְהוֹשָׁפָט אָבִיךָ
וּבְדַרְכֵי אָסָא מֶלֶךְ יְהוּדָה׃
13 וַתֵּלֶךְ בְּדֶרֶךְ מַלְכֵי יִשְׂרָאֵל
וַתַּזְנֶה אֶת־יְהוּדָה וְאֶת־יֹשְׁבֵי
יְרוּשָׁלִַם כְּהַזְנוֹת בֵּית אַחְאָב

and the captains of the chariots. This clause may be construed as the object of *smote* or *compassed.*

10. *unto this day.* The time the Book was compiled.

Libnah. A strongly fortified city in the lowland between the Mediterranean coast and the mountains of Judah, not far from Lachish near the Philistine border.

because hs had forsaken, etc. The reason for Jehoram's failure does not occur in Kings.

11-15 (no parallel in Kings). Elijah's letter of denunciation.

11. *drew Judah away.* From the worship of God.

12. *a writing . . . from Elijah.* It would appear from 2 Kings iii. 11ff. that the great prophet had passed from earth before Jehoram came to the throne. The fact is acknowledged by the Jewish commentators who hold that Elijah, from heaven, influenced a contemporary prophet to write down his message and communicate it to the king. Harvey-Jellie, however, does not rule out the possibility that Elijah was at this time still in the land of the living.

13. *thy brethren of thy father's house.* The preposition *of* is implied, *thy father's*

hast slain thy brethren of thy father's house, who were better than thyself; 14. behold, the LORD will smite with a great plague thy people, and thy children, and thy wives, and all thy substance; 15. and thou shalt have great sickness by disease of thy bowels, until thy bowels fall out by reason of the sickness, day by day.'

16. And the LORD stirred up against Jehoram the spirit of the Philistines, and of the Arabians that are beside the Ethiopians; 17. and they came up against Judah, and broke into it, and carried away all the substance that was found in the king's house, and his sons also, and his wives; so that there was never a son left him, save Jehoahaz, the youngest of his sons.

18. And after all this the LORD

וְגַם אֶת־אַחֶיךָ בֵית־אָבִיךָ
14 הַטּוֹבִים מִמְּךָ הָרָגְתָּ׃ הִנֵּה
יְהוָה נֹגֵף מַגֵּפָה גְדוֹלָה בְּעַמֶּךָ
וּבְבָנֶיךָ וּבְנָשֶׁיךָ וּבְכָל־
15 רְכוּשֶׁךָ׃ וְאַתָּה בָּחֳלָיִים
רַבִּים בְּמַחֲלֵה מֵעֶיךָ עַד־
יֵצְאוּ מֵעֶיךָ מִן־הַחֹלִי יָמִים
עַל־יָמִים׃
16 וַיָּעַר יְהוָה עַל־יְהוֹרָם אֶת־
רוּחַ הַפְּלִשְׁתִּים וְהָעַרְבִים
17 אֲשֶׁר עַל־יַד כּוּשִׁים׃ וַיַּעֲלוּ
בִיהוּדָה וַיִּבְקָעוּהָ וַיִּשְׁבּוּ אֵת
כָּל־הָרְכוּשׁ הַנִּמְצָא לְבֵית־
הַמֶּלֶךְ וְגַם־בָּנָיו וְנָשָׁיו וְלֹא
נִשְׁאַר־לוֹ בֵּן כִּי אִם־יְהוֹאָחָז
קְטֹן בָּנָיו׃
18 וְאַחֲרֵי כָּל־זֹאת נְגָפוֹ יְהוָה ׀

house being in the Hebrew in apposition to *thy brethren*.

14. *thy substance.* See I Chron. xxvii. 31.

15. *thou shalt have great sickness.* lit. 'thou in many sicknesses,' i.e. various forms of diseases.

day by day. lit. 'days upon days,' i.e. a protracted ailment.

16f. (no parallel in Kings). A raid by Philistines and Arabians.

16. *the Philistines, and of the Arabians.* Who had paid tribute to Jehoshaphat (xvii. 11).

Ethiopians. See on xiv. 8.

17. *broke into it.* i.e. raided the country. The Hebrew verb means 'to split' and so 'breach a city wall'; but it is here used for penetration into the land of Judah. There is no suggestion that Jerusalem was invaded; if that had happened, it would have been specifically mentioned.

that was found in the king's house. Or, 'belonging to the king's house.' The *house* referred to may have been one of the royal residences outside Jerusalem, in a part of the country which was overrun by the invaders.

Jehoahaz. The meaning of the name is 'the LORD has taken.' The other name by which he was known, Ahaziah, has the same signification, the part denoting 'the LORD' being attached at the end.

smote him in his bowels with an incurable disease.
19. And it came to pass, that in process of time, at the end of two years, his bowels fell out by reason of his sickness, and he died of sore diseases. And his people made no burning for him, like the burning of his fathers.
20. Thirty and two years old was he when he began to reign, and he reigned in Jerusalem eight years; and he departed joyless; and they buried him in the city of David, but not in the sepulchres of the kings.

בְּמֵעָיו לָחֳלִי לְאֵין מַרְפֵּא׃
19 וַיְהִי לְיָמִים ׀ מִיָּמִים וּכְעֵת
צֵאת הַקֵּץ לְיָמִים שְׁנַיִם יָצְאוּ
מֵעָיו עִם־חָלְיוֹ וַיָּמָת
בְּתַחֲלֻאִים רָעִים וְלֹא־עָשׂוּ
לוֹ עַמּוֹ שְׂרֵפָה כִּשְׂרֵפַת
20 אֲבֹתָיו׃ בֶּן־שְׁלֹשִׁים וּשְׁתַּיִם
הָיָה בְמָלְכוֹ וּשְׁמוֹנֶה שָׁנִים
מָלַךְ בִּירוּשָׁלָםִ וַיֵּלֶךְ בְּלֹא
חֶמְדָּה וַיִּקְבְּרֻהוּ בְּעִיר דָּוִיד
וְלֹא בְּקִבְרוֹת הַמְּלָכִים׃

22 CHAPTER XXII כב

1. And the inhabitants of Jerusalem made Ahaziah his youngest son king in his stead; for the band of men that came with the Arabians to the camp

1 וַיַּמְלִיכוּ יוֹשְׁבֵי יְרוּשָׁלַםִ אֶת־
אֲחַזְיָהוּ בְנוֹ הַקָּטֹן תַּחְתָּיו כִּי
כָל־הָרִאשֹׁנִים הָרַג הַגְּדוּד

18-20. Jehoram's ignoble fate.

19. *in process of time.* lit. 'for days from days.'

at the end of two years. lit. 'and about the time of the going out of the end of two years.'

by reason of his sickness. lit. 'with his sickness.' Perhaps the meaning is 'in the course of his sickness.'

made no burning. See on xvi. 14.

20. *thirty and two years,* etc. Repeated from verse 5.

joyless, etc. lit. 'without desire, or, pleasantness'; his death was not regretted by his people, as was evidenced by the manner in which they treated his body.

but not in the sepulchres of the kings. 2 Kings viii. 24 records simply that he *was buried with his fathers.*

CHAPTER XXII

THE REIGN OF AHAZIAH AND ATHALIAH

1-4 (corresponding to 2 Kings viii. 25-27). The brief reign of Ahaziah, 843 B.C.E.

1. *the inhabitants of Jerusalem made,* etc. The specific mention of *the inhabitants of Jerusalem* (which is unusual in connection with a succession) may imply that there was opposition from provincial towns.

Ahaziah. He was also called *Jehoahaz* (see on xxi. 17).

the band of men, etc. Cf. xxi. 16f.

had slain all the eldest. So Ahaziah the son of Jehoram king of Judah reigned. 2. Forty and two years old was Ahaziah when he began to reign; and he reigned one year in Jerusalem; and his mother's name was Athaliah the daughter of Omri. 3. He also walked in the ways of the house of Ahab; for his mother was his counsellor to do wickedly. 4. And he did that which was evil in the sight of the LORD, as did the house of Ahab; for they were his counsellors after the death of his father, to his destruction. 5. He walked also after their counsel, and went with Jehoram the son of Ahab king of Israel to war against Hazael king of Aram at Ramoth-gilead; and the Arameans wounded Joram. 6. And he returned to be healed in Jezreel of the wounds which they had given him at Ramah, when he fought against Hazael king of Aram.

הַבָּא בָעַרְבִים לַמַּחֲנֶה וַיִּמְלֹךְ
אֲחַזְיָהוּ בֶּן־יְהוֹרָם מֶלֶךְ
2 יְהוּדָה׃ בֶּן־אַרְבָּעִים וּשְׁתַּיִם
שָׁנָה אֲחַזְיָהוּ בְּמָלְכוֹ וְשָׁנָה
אַחַת מָלַךְ בִּירוּשָׁלִָם וְשֵׁם
אִמּוֹ עֲתַלְיָהוּ בַּת־עָמְרִי׃
3 גַּם־הוּא הָלַךְ בְּדַרְכֵי בֵּית
אַחְאָב כִּי אִמּוֹ הָיְתָה יוֹעַצְתּוֹ
4 לְהַרְשִׁיעַ׃ וַיַּעַשׂ הָרַע בְּעֵינֵי
יְהוָה כְּבֵית אַחְאָב כִּי הֵמָּה
הָיוּ־לוֹ יוֹעֲצִים אַחֲרֵי מוֹת
5 אָבִיו לְמַשְׁחִית לוֹ׃ גַּם
בַּעֲצָתָם הָלַךְ וַיֵּלֶךְ אֶת־
יְהוֹרָם בֶּן־אַחְאָב מֶלֶךְ
יִשְׂרָאֵל לַמִּלְחָמָה עַל־חֲזָאֵל
מֶלֶךְ־אֲרָם בְּרָמוֹת גִּלְעָד
6 וַיַּכּוּ הָרַמִּים אֶת־יוֹרָם׃ וַיָּשָׁב
לְהִתְרַפֵּא בְיִזְרְעֶאל כִּי
הַמַּכִּים אֲשֶׁר הִכֻּהוּ בָרָמָה
בְּהִלָּחֲמוֹ אֶת־חֲזָהאֵל מֶלֶךְ

2. *forty and two years old.* Ahaziah's age is given as *two and twenty* in 2 Kings viii. 26. According to the *Seder Olam*, the Chronicler's reckoning is from the rise of the house of Omri.

Athaliah the daughter of Omri. See on xxi. 6.

5f. (corresponding to 2 Kings viii. 28f.). Defeat of the army of the two kingdoms at Ramoth-gilead.

6. *Jezreel.* The modern Zer'in, on a hill near Gilboa, on the east side of the plain of Ezdraelon. It was one of the capital cities of the Northern Kingdom.

of the wounds. So in 2 Kings viii. 29. The text here means, 'because the wounds.'

Ramah. A short name for Ramoth-gilead. *Ramah* means 'height' or 'high land,' and the plural form of the noun is *ramoth*. The city was built on several hills, hence *Ramoth* (plural), and the wounding of Ahaziah may have occurred

And Azariah the son of Jehoram king of Judah went down to see Jehoram the son of Ahab in Jezreel, because he was sick.

7. Now the downfall of Ahaziah was of God, in that he went unto Joram; for when he was come, he went out with Jehoram against Jehu the son of Nimshi, whom the LORD had anointed to cut off the house of Ahab. 8. And it came to pass, when Jehu was executing judgment upon the house of Ahab, that he found the princes of Judah, and the sons of the brethren of Ahaziah, ministering to Ahaziah, and slew them. 9. And he sought Ahaziah, and they caught him—now he was hiding in Samaria —and they brought him to Jehu, and slew him; and they buried him, for they said: 'He is the son of

אֲרָ֑ם וַעֲזַרְיָ֨הוּ בֶן־יְהוֹרָ֜ם
מֶ֣לֶךְ יְהוּדָ֗ה יָרַ֞ד לִרְא֨וֹת אֶת־
יְהוֹרָ֧ם בֶּן־אַחְאָ֛ב בְּיִזְרְעֶ֖אל
כִּֽי־חֹלֶ֥ה הֽוּא׃
7 וּמֵֽאֱלֹהִ֗ים הָיְתָה֙ תְּבוּסַ֣ת
אֲחַזְיָ֔הוּ לָב֖וֹא אֶל־יוֹרָ֑ם
וּבְבֹא֗וֹ יָצָ֤א עִם־יְהוֹרָם֙ אֶל־
יֵה֣וּא בֶן־נִמְשִׁ֔י אֲשֶׁ֣ר מְשָׁח֣וֹ
יְהוָ֔ה לְהַכְרִ֖ית אֶת־בֵּ֥ית
8 אַחְאָֽב׃ וַיְהִ֕י כְּהִשָּׁפֵ֥ט יֵה֖וּא
עִם־בֵּ֣ית אַחְאָ֑ב וַיִּמְצָא֩ אֶת־
שָׂרֵ֨י יְהוּדָ֜ה וּבְנֵ֨י אֲחֵ֧י אֲחַזְיָ֛הוּ
מְשָׁרְתִ֥ים לַאֲחַזְיָ֖הוּ וַיַּֽהַרְגֵֽם׃
9 וַיְבַקֵּ֣שׁ אֶת־אֲחַזְיָ֗הוּ וַֽיִּלְכְּדֻ֙הוּ֙
וְה֣וּא מִתְחַבֵּ֣א בְשֹׁמְר֔וֹן
וַיְבִאֻ֣הוּ אֶל־יֵה֗וּא וַיְמִתֻ֘הוּ֮
וַֽיִּקְבְּרֻ֗הוּ כִּ֤י אָֽמְרוּ֙ בֶּן־

on one of the hills, hence *Ramah* (singular).

Azariah. Apparently one of the three names by which Ahaziah was known (cf. xxi. 17).

went down. Probably from Jerusalem, which stood on higher ground, where he seems to have gone after the battle.

7-9 (cf. 2 Kings ix. 21, 27f., x. 13f.). The death of Ahaziah. As compared with the narrative in Kings, the present account is highly condensed and differs in a number of particulars.

7. *downfall.* lit. 'treading, trampling.'

in that he went. lit. 'to come.'

the LORD had anointed. Cf. 2 Kings ix. 1ff.

8. *executing judgment.* viz. God's penalty for the murder of Naboth pronounced by Elijah (1 Kings xxi. 21).

the sons of the brethren. In 2 Kings x. 13: *the brethren*, i.e. kinsmen. Ahaziah's brothers had been killed (verse 1).

ministering to Ahaziah. In Kings, they were going down *to salute the children of the king and the children of the queen*, to pay them a formal visit of respect.

9. *they caught him.* The subject of the verb is Jehu's men.

they buried him. With due honours.

Jehoshaphat, who sought the LORD with all his heart.' And there was none of the house of Ahaziah that had power to hold the kingdom.

10. Now when Athaliah the mother of Ahaziah saw that her son was dead, she arose and destroyed all the seed royal of the house of Judah. 11. But Jehoshabeath, the daughter of the king, took Joash the son of Ahaziah, and stole him away from among the king's sons that were slain, and put him and his nurse in the bed-chamber. So Jehoshabeath, the daughter of king Jehoram, the wife of Jehoiada the priest—for she was the sister of Ahaziah—hid him from Athaliah, so that she slew him not. 12. And he was with them hid

יְהוֹשָׁפָט הוּא אֲשֶׁר־דָּרַשׁ
אֶת־יְהוָה בְּכָל־לְבָבוֹ וְאֵין
לְבֵית אֲחַזְיָהוּ לַעְצֹר כֹּחַ
לְמַמְלָכָה׃
10 וַעֲתַלְיָהוּ אֵם אֲחַזְיָהוּ רָאֲתָה
כִּי־מֵת בְּנָהּ וַתָּקָם וַתְּדַבֵּר
אֶת־כָּל־זֶרַע הַמַּמְלָכָה
11 לְבֵית יְהוּדָה׃ וַתִּקַּח
יְהוֹשַׁבְעַת בַּת־הַמֶּלֶךְ אֶת־
יוֹאָשׁ בֶּן־אֲחַזְיָהוּ וַתִּגְנֹב אֹתוֹ
מִתּוֹךְ בְּנֵי־הַמֶּלֶךְ הַמּוּמָתִים
וַתִּתֵּן אֹתוֹ וְאֶת־מֵינִקְתּוֹ
בַּחֲדַר הַמִּטּוֹת וַתַּסְתִּירֵהוּ
יְהוֹשַׁבְעַת בַּת־הַמֶּלֶךְ יְהוֹרָם
אֵשֶׁת יְהוֹיָדָע הַכֹּהֵן כִּי הִיא
הָיְתָה אֲחוֹת אֲחַזְיָהוּ מִפְּנֵי
12 עֲתַלְיָהוּ וְלֹא הֱמִיתָתְהוּ׃ וַיְהִי
אִתָּם בְּבֵית הָאֱלֹהִים מִתְחַבֵּא

Different treatment was accorded to the bodies of the others which, according to 2 Kings x. 14, were thrown into a pit.

that had power to hold the kingdom. lit. 'to retain power for kingdom.'

10-12 (corresponding to 2 Kings xi. 1-3). Athaliah's usurpation of the throne.

10. *destroyed.* This is the translation of the verb in 2 Kings xi. 1. Here the verb is from the root *dibber* which means 'speak.' The Jewish commentators connect it with the noun *deber*, 'pestilence,' while some modern expositors identify it with the Arabic *dabbara*, 'plot against, waylay.'

all the seed royal. To remove all legal claimants to the throne.

11. *Jehoshabeath.* In 2 Kings xi. 2: *Jehosheba*; both are variants of the same name with the same meaning, 'Jah is an oath.'

daughter of the king. She was the daughter of Athaliah.

took Joash. Who was then one year old.

for she was the sister of Ahaziah. By the same mother; hence her concern for her nephew, Joash.

12. *with them.* viz. Jehoiada and Jeho-

in the house of God six years; and
Athaliah reigned over the land.

שֵׁשׁ שָׁנִים וַעֲתַלְיָה מֹלֶכֶת עַל־
הָאָרֶץ׃

23 CHAPTER XXIII כג

1. And in the seventh year Jehoiada
strengthened himself, and took the
captains of hundreds, Azariah the
son of Jeroham, and Ishmael the son
of Jehohanan, and Azariah the son
of Obed, and Maaseiah the son of
Adaiah, and Elishaphat the son of
Zichri, into covenant with him.
2. And they went about in Judah,
and gathered the Levites out of all
the cities of Judah, and the heads of
fathers' houses of Israel, and they
came to Jerusalem. 3. And all the
congregation made a covenant with
the king in the house of God. And

1 וּבַשָּׁנָה הַשְּׁבִעִית הִתְחַזַּק
יְהוֹיָדָע וַיִּקַּח אֶת־שָׂרֵי
הַמֵּאוֹת לַעֲזַרְיָה בֶן־יְרֹחָם
וּלְיִשְׁמָעֵאל בֶּן־יְהוֹחָנָן
וְלַעֲזַרְיָהוּ בֶן־עוֹבֵד וְאֶת־
מַעֲשֵׂיָהוּ בֶן־עֲדָיָהוּ וְאֶת־
אֱלִישָׁפָט בֶּן־זִכְרִי עִמּוֹ
2 בַבְּרִית׃ וַיָּסֹבּוּ בִּיהוּדָה
וַיִּקְבְּצוּ אֶת־הַלְוִיִּם מִכָּל־
עָרֵי יְהוּדָה וְרָאשֵׁי הָאָבוֹת
לְיִשְׂרָאֵל וַיָּבֹאוּ אֶל־
3 יְרוּשָׁלָם׃ וַיִּכְרֹת כָּל־הַקָּהָל
בְּרִית בְּבֵית הָאֱלֹהִים עִם־

shabeath; in 2 Kings xi. 3: *with her*, i.e. the nurse.

in the house of God. Where he had been taken from the bed-chamber.

CHAPTERS XXIII-XXIV

THE REIGN OF JOASH

CHAPTER XXIII

CORONATION OF JOASH AND OVERTHROW OF ATHALIAH

1-7 (corresponding to 2 Kings xi. 4-8). Jehoiada's conspiracy and plan of action.

1. *strengthened himself.* In 2 Kings xi. 4: *sent.*

captains of hundreds. Kings in greater detail: *captains over hundreds, of the Carites and of the guard.*

Azariah, etc. These names do not occur in Kings.

into covenant with him. Kings adds that the captains were brought *to him into the house of the LORD.*

2. This verse has no parallel in Kings. The variants between the two accounts are not contradictory but add together to provide a complete account of the incident.

of Israel. Here a term for Judah.

3. *all the congregation.* That were assembled in the house of God. In Kings,

he said unto them: 'Behold, the king's son shall reign, as the LORD hath spoken concerning the sons of David. 4. This is the thing that ye shall do: a third part of you, that come in on the sabbath, of the priests and of the Levites, shall be porters of the doors; 5. and a third part shall be at the king's house; and a third part at the gate of the foundation; and all the people shall be in the courts of the house of the LORD. 6. But let none come into the house of the LORD, save the priests, and they that minister of the Levites; they shall come in, for they are holy; but all the people shall keep the charge of the LORD. 7. And the Levites shall compass the king round about, every man with his weapons in his hand; and whosoever cometh into the house, let him be slain; and be ye with the king when he cometh in, and when he goeth out.'

הַמֶּלֶךְ וַיֹּאמֶר לָהֶם הִנֵּה בֶן־
הַמֶּלֶךְ יִמְלֹךְ כַּאֲשֶׁר דִּבֶּר
4 יְהוָה עַל־בְּנֵי דָוִיד׃ זֶה
הַדָּבָר אֲשֶׁר תַּעֲשׂוּ הַשְּׁלִשִׁית
מִכֶּם בָּאֵי הַשַּׁבָּת לַכֹּהֲנִים
וְלַלְוִיִּם לְשֹׁעֲרֵי הַסִּפִּים׃
5 וְהַשְּׁלִשִׁית בְּבֵית הַמֶּלֶךְ
וְהַשְּׁלִשִׁית בְּשַׁעַר הַיְסוֹד
וְכָל־הָעָם בְּחַצְרוֹת בֵּית
6 יְהוָה׃ וְאַל־יָבוֹא בֵית־יְהוָה
כִּי אִם־הַכֹּהֲנִים וְהַמְשָׁרְתִים
לַלְוִיִּם הֵמָּה יָבֹאוּ כִּי־קֹדֶשׁ
הֵמָּה וְכָל־הָעָם יִשְׁמְרוּ
7 מִשְׁמֶרֶת יְהוָה׃ וְהִקִּיפוּ
הַלְוִיִּם אֶת־הַמֶּלֶךְ סָבִיב אִישׁ
וְכֵלָיו בְּיָדוֹ וְהַבָּא אֶל־הַבַּיִת
יוּמָת וִהְיוּ אֶת־הַמֶּלֶךְ בְּבֹאוֹ
וּבְצֵאתוֹ׃

the covenant is entered into by Jehoiada with the officers.

as the LORD hath spoken. Cf. 2 Sam. vii. 16.

4. *this is the thing that ye shall do.* The priests and Levites were classified in groups each of which served in the Temple for a week in turn. The change took place on the Sabbath when one group went off duty and the next in order entered upon its ministrations for the ensuing week.

a third part. The groups were sub-divided in three parties, each performing the task assigned to it as described in the following verses.

shall be porters of the doors. lit. 'for (or, as) porters of the thresholds' of the Temple.

5. *the gate of the foundation.* Probably identical with *the gate Sur* of 2 Kings xi. 6.

6. *all the people shall keep the charge of the LORD.* They shall not enter the courts reserved for the priests and Levites, but perform their act of worship in their own court, 'the Court of the Israelites.'

7. *compass the king.* While he is still concealed within the Temple.

cometh into the house. In 2 Kings xi. 8: *cometh within the ranks.*

8. So the Levites and all Judah did according to all that Jehoiada the priest commanded; and they took every man his men, those that were to come in on the sabbath, with those that were to go out on the sabbath; for Jehoiada the priest dismissed not the courses. 9. And Jehoiada the priest delivered to the captains of hundreds the spears, and bucklers, and shields, that had been king David's, which were in the house of God. 10. And he set all the people, every man with his weapon in his hand, from the right side of the house to the left side of the house, along by the altar and the house, by the king round about. 11. Then they brought out the king's son, and put upon him the

8 וַיַּעֲשׂוּ הַלְוִיִּם וְכָל־יְהוּדָה
כְּכֹל אֲשֶׁר־צִוָּה יְהוֹיָדָע
הַכֹּהֵן וַיִּקְחוּ אִישׁ אֶת־אֲנָשָׁיו
בָּאֵי הַשַּׁבָּת עִם יוֹצְאֵי הַשַּׁבָּת
כִּי לֹא־פָטַר יְהוֹיָדָע הַכֹּהֵן
9 אֶת־הַמַּחְלְקוֹת׃ וַיִּתֵּן יְהוֹיָדָע
הַכֹּהֵן לְשָׂרֵי הַמֵּאוֹת אֶת־
הַחֲנִיתִים וְאֶת־הַמָּגִנּוֹת וְאֶת־
הַשְּׁלָטִים אֲשֶׁר לַמֶּלֶךְ דָּוִיד
10 אֲשֶׁר בֵּית הָאֱלֹהִים׃ וַיַּעֲמֵד
אֶת־כָּל־הָעָם וְאִישׁ | שִׁלְחוֹ
בְיָדוֹ מִכֶּתֶף הַבַּיִת הַיְמָנִית
עַד־כֶּתֶף הַבַּיִת הַשְּׂמָאלִית
לַמִּזְבֵּחַ וְלַבָּיִת עַל־הַמֶּלֶךְ
11 סָבִיב׃ וַיּוֹצִיאוּ אֶת־בֶּן־
הַמֶּלֶךְ וַיִּתְּנוּ עָלָיו אֶת־הַנֵּזֶר

when he cometh in, etc. i.e. the whole time.

8-11 (corresponding to 2 Kings xi. 9-12). The crowning of Joash.

8. *the Levites and all Judah.* In 2 Kings xi. 9: *the captains over hundreds.*

those that were to come in . . . with those that were to go out. Both groups were to be at hand for the emergency.

dismissed not the courses. Their presence was retained to strengthen the force which was in favour of crowning Joash. This is not in Kings.

9. *bucklers.* Not in 2 Kings xi. 10.

that had been king David's. The weapons had been captured by David in his wars and stored in chambers within the Temple precincts.

10. *he set all the people.* In 2 Kings xi. 11: *and the guard stood.* The people, or the guards, were ranged so as to form a ring around Joash when he left the safety of the Temple.

by the altar. Which stood in the Temple court.

and the house. On the outside.

by the king. Who was soon to proceed between the ranks. The phrase may possibly be attached to *and the house* with the meaning 'and the part of the Temple where the king was.'

11. *then they.* The pronoun is impersonal; in 2 Kings xi. 12: *then he*, viz. Jehoiada.

the king's son. Joash is so described to emphasize his title to the crown.

crown and the insignia, and made
him king; and Jehoiada and his sons
anointed him; and they said: 'Long
live the king.'
12. And when Athaliah heard the
noise of the people running and
praising the king, she came to the
people into the house of the LORD;
13. and she looked, and, behold, the
king stood on his platform at the
entrance, and the captains and the
trumpets by the king; and all the
people of the land rejoiced, and blew
with trumpets; the singers also
[played] on instruments of music,
and led the singing of praise.
Then Athaliah rent her clothes, and
said: 'Treason, treason.' 14. And
Jehoiada the priest brought out the
captains of hundreds that were set
over the host, and said unto them:

וְאֶת־הָעֵדוּת וַיַּמְלִיכוּ אֹתוֹ
וַיִּמְשָׁחֻהוּ יְהוֹיָדָע וּבָנָיו
וַיֹּאמְרוּ יְחִי הַמֶּלֶךְ׃
12 וַתִּשְׁמַע עֲתַלְיָהוּ אֶת־קוֹל
הָעָם הָרָצִים וְהַמְהַלְלִים
אֶת־הַמֶּלֶךְ וַתָּבוֹא אֶל־הָעָם
13 בֵּית יְהוָה׃ וַתֵּרֶא וְהִנֵּה הַמֶּלֶךְ
עוֹמֵד עַל־עַמּוּדוֹ בַמָּבוֹא
וְהַשָּׂרִים וְהַחֲצֹצְרוֹת עַל־
הַמֶּלֶךְ וְכָל־עַם הָאָרֶץ
שָׂמֵחַ וְתוֹקֵעַ בַּחֲצֹצְרוֹת
וְהַמְשׁוֹרְרִים בִּכְלֵי הַשִּׁיר
וּמוֹדִיעִים לְהַלֵּל וַתִּקְרַע
עֲתַלְיָהוּ אֶת־בְּגָדֶיהָ וַתֹּאמֶר
14 קֶשֶׁר קָשֶׁר׃ וַיּוֹצֵא יְהוֹיָדָע
הַכֹּהֵן אֶת־שָׂרֵי הַמֵּאוֹת ׀
פְּקוּדֵי הַחַיִל וַיֹּאמֶר אֲלֵהֶם

insignia. The noun is *ha-eduth*, lit. 'the testimony,' i.e. a copy of the Torah. Upon this passage rests the custom of handing a Bible to the British monarch as part of the coronation ceremony.

and Jehoiada and his sons anointed him. An amplification of (they) *anointed him* in Kings.

and they said. Kings inserts: *and they clapped their hands.*

long live the king. lit. 'let (or, may) the king live.'

12-15 (corresponding to 2 Kings xi. 13-16). The execution of Athaliah.

12. *running and praising.* In 2 Kings xi. 13 the Hebrew for *running* precedes *the people* and is rendered *the guard* while *and praising* is wanting.

13. *on his platform.* Better, 'by his pillar' (R.V.), where the king usually took up his position when in the Temple.

at the entrance. In 2 Kings xi. 14: *as the manner was.*

the singers also . . . praise. An addition to the account in Kings.

and led the singing of praise. lit. 'and announcing to praise.'

rent her clothes. In anguish.

14. *brought out.* In 2 Kings xi. 15: *commanded.*

'Have her forth between the ranks;
and whoso followeth her, let him be
slain with the sword'; for the priest
said: 'Slay her not in the house of
the LORD.' 15. So they made way
for her; and she went to the entry
of the horse gate to the king's house;
and they slew her there.

16. And Jehoiada made a covenant
between himself, and all the people,
and the king, that they should be the
LORD's people. 17. And all the
people went to the house of Baal,
and broke it down, and broke his
altars and his images in pieces, and
slew Mattan the priest of Baal before
the altars. 18. And Jehoiada appointed the offices of the house of
the LORD under the hand of the
priests the Levites, whom David had

הוֹצִיאוּהָ אֶל־מִבֵּית הַשְּׂדֵרוֹת
וְהַבָּא אַחֲרֶיהָ יוּמַת בֶּחָרֶב
כִּי אָמַר הַכֹּהֵן לֹא תְמִיתוּהָ
15 בֵּית יְהוָה׃ וַיָּשִׂימוּ לָהּ יָדַיִם
וַתָּבוֹא אֶל־מְבוֹא שַׁעַר־
הַסּוּסִים בֵּית הַמֶּלֶךְ וַיְמִיתוּהָ
שָׁם׃
16 וַיִּכְרֹת יְהוֹיָדָע בְּרִית בֵּינוֹ
וּבֵין כָּל־הָעָם וּבֵין הַמֶּלֶךְ
17 לִהְיוֹת לְעָם לַיהוָה׃ וַיָּבֹאוּ
כָל־הָעָם בֵּית־הַבַּעַל
וַיִּתְּצֻהוּ וְאֶת־מִזְבְּחֹתָיו וְאֶת־
צְלָמָיו שִׁבֵּרוּ וְאֵת מַתָּן כֹּהֵן
הַבַּעַל הָרְגוּ לִפְנֵי הַמִּזְבְּחוֹת׃
18 וַיָּשֶׂם יְהוֹיָדָע פְּקֻדֹּת בֵּית יְהוָה
בְּיַד הַכֹּהֲנִים הַלְוִיִּם אֲשֶׁר

between the ranks. Under armed escort.

whoso followeth her. To attempt to rescue her.

15. ***made way.*** lit. 'set hands.' 'Hands' in the sense of 'space' occurs in the phrase *large enough* (Gen. xxxiv. 21) and *wide* (Ps. civ. 25) lit. 'broad of hands.'

the entry of the horse gate. In 2 Kings xi. 16: *by the way of the horses' entry*, the gate of the palace used by the cavalry.

16-18 (corresponding to 2 Kings xi. 17f.). Religious and political covenant, and the destruction of Baal worship.

16. ***between himself . . . and the king.*** A fuller version of the covenant is given in 2 Kings xi. 17: *between the LORD and the king and the people*, i.e. a religious covenant, and *between the king also and the people*, i.e. a political agreement that the king will rule justly and the people be loyal to him.

17. ***broke it down.*** With the removal of Athaliah, it was but natural for the people to destroy the traces of Baal worship which she had promoted in the kingdom.

slew Mattan. This act is evidence that the revolt against the queen was inspired by a religious, more than a political, motive.

18. ***the offices.*** Or 'guards, overseers,' to replace those who had served in the worship of Baal.

under the hand of the priests . . . the

distributed in the house of the LORD,
to offer the burnt-offerings of the
LORD, as it is written in the Law
of Moses, with rejoicing and with
singing, according to the direction
of David. 19. And he set the
porters at the gates of the house of
the LORD, that none that was
unclean in any thing should enter in.
20. And he took the captains of
hundreds, and the nobles, and the
governors of the people, and all the
people of the land, and brought
down the king from the house of the
LORD; and they came through the
upper gate unto the king's house,
and set the king upon the throne of
the kingdom. 21. So all the people
of the land rejoiced, and the city
was quiet; and they slew Athaliah
with the sword.

חָלַק דָּוִיד עַל־בֵּית יְהוָה
לְהַעֲלוֹת עֹלוֹת יְהוָה כַּכָּתוּב
בְּתוֹרַת מֹשֶׁה בְּשִׂמְחָה וּבְשִׁיר
19 עַל יְדֵי דָוִיד׃ וַיַּעֲמֵד
הַשּׁוֹעֲרִים עַל־שַׁעֲרֵי בֵּית
יְהוָה וְלֹא־יָבוֹא טָמֵא לְכָל־
20 דָּבָר׃ וַיִּקַּח אֶת־שָׂרֵי הַמֵּאוֹת
וְאֶת־הָאַדִּירִים וְאֶת־
הַמּוֹשְׁלִים בָּעָם וְאֵת ׀ כָּל־עַם
הָאָרֶץ וַיּוֹרֶד אֶת־הַמֶּלֶךְ
מִבֵּית יְהוָה וַיָּבֹאוּ בְּתוֹךְ־
שַׁעַר הָעֶלְיוֹן בֵּית הַמֶּלֶךְ
וַיּוֹשִׁיבוּ אֶת־הַמֶּלֶךְ עַל כִּסֵּא
21 הַמַּמְלָכָה׃ וַיִּשְׂמְחוּ כָל־
עַם־הָאָרֶץ וְהָעִיר שָׁקָטָה
וְאֶת־עֲתַלְיָהוּ הֵמִיתוּ בֶחָרֶב׃

direction of David. This is an amplification of the brief statement in 2 Kings xi. 18: *and the priest appointed officers over the house of the LORD.*

19-21 (corresponding to 2 Kings xi. 19f.). The enthronement of Joash.

19. This verse continues the amplification of the account in Kings.

20. *and the nobles, and the governors of the people.* In 2 Kings xi. 19: *and the Carites, and the guard.*

the people of the land. M. Sulzberger, *The Ancient Hebrew Parliament*, maintained that this was a term descriptive of the governing body.

and brought down. The subject is Jehoiada; in Kings: *and they brought down.*

came through the upper gate. In Kings: *came by the way of the gate of the guard.* This gate was built by Solomon and it communicated between the Temple and the palace (cf. 2 Kings xi. 19). It may be identical with *the upper gate of Benjamin* (Jer. xx. 2) in the north wall of the inner court of the Temple.

and set the king upon the throne of the kingdom. This appears in Kings as: *and he sat on the throne of the kings.*

21. *the city was quiet.* If there were any supporters of the executed queen, they created no disturbance. The verse also indicates that there was general approval of what had occurred.

24 CHAPTER XXIV כד

1. Joash was seven years old when he began to reign; and he reigned forty years in Jerusalem; and his mother's name was Zibiah of Beer-sheba. 2. And Joash did that which was right in the eyes of the LORD all the days of Jehoiada the priest. 3. And Jehoiada took for him two wives; and he begot sons and daughters.

4. And it came to pass after this, that Joash was minded to restore the house of the LORD. 5. And he gathered together the priests and the Levites, and said to them: 'Go out unto the cities of Judah, and gather of all Israel money to repair the house of your God from year to year, and see that ye hasten the matter.'

1 בֶּן־שֶׁבַע שָׁנִים יֹאָשׁ בְּמָלְכוֹ
וְאַרְבָּעִים שָׁנָה מָלַךְ
בִּירוּשָׁלָם וְשֵׁם אִמּוֹ צִבְיָה
2 מִבְּאֵר שָׁבַע׃ וַיַּעַשׂ יוֹאָשׁ
הַיָּשָׁר בְּעֵינֵי יְהוָה כָּל־יְמֵי
3 יְהוֹיָדָע הַכֹּהֵן׃ וַיִּשָּׂא־לוֹ
יְהוֹיָדָע נָשִׁים שְׁתָּיִם וַיּוֹלֶד
בָּנִים וּבָנוֹת׃
4 וַיְהִי אַחֲרֵי־כֵן הָיָה עִם־לֵב
יוֹאָשׁ לְחַדֵּשׁ אֶת־בֵּית יְהוָה׃
5 וַיִּקְבֹּץ אֶת־הַכֹּהֲנִים וְהַלְוִיִּם
וַיֹּאמֶר לָהֶם צְאוּ לְעָרֵי יְהוּדָה
וְקִבְצוּ מִכָּל־יִשְׂרָאֵל כֶּסֶף
לְחַזֵּק ׀ אֶת־בֵּית אֱלֹהֵיכֶם
מִדֵּי שָׁנָה בְּשָׁנָה וְאַתֶּם תְּמַהֲרוּ

CHAPTER XXIV

1-3 (corresponding to 2 Kings xii. 1-3). The duration of Joash's reign and the king's pious character. The synchronism with the reign of Jehu in Israel and the people's addiction to the high places (2 Kings xii. 2) are omitted by the Chronicler as irrelevant to the purpose of his account. Verse 3 in this chapter is an addition to the version in Kings.

1. *when he began to reign.* lit. 'in his reigning' or 'when he became king.' The years of his reign were 837-798 B.C.E.

2. *all the days of Jehoiada.* In 2 Kings xii. 3: *all his days wherein Jehoiada the priest instructed him.* Jehoiada acted as regent as well as tutor while the king was young and trained him to be loyal to the Torah, but later in life Joash turned away from the right path.

3. *Jehoiada took for him.* It was his duty to do this, since he was his guardian and stood *in loco parentis.*

4-14 (corresponding to 2 Kings xii. 5-17). The king's scheme for the repair of the Temple.

4. *Joash was minded.* lit. 'it was with the heart of Joash.'

5. *and the Levites.* In 2 Kings xii. 5, Joash only addressed the priests.

go out unto the cities of Judah. 2 Kings xii. 5 makes no reference to collections outside the Temple, but only to *money*

Howbeit the Levites hastened it not.
6. And the king called for Jehoiada the chief, and said unto him: 'Why hast thou not required of the Levites to bring in out of Judah and out of Jerusalem the tax of Moses the servant of the LORD, and of the congregation of Israel, for the tent of the testimony?'
7. For the sons of Athaliah, that wicked woman, had broken up the house of God; and also all the hallowed things of the house of the LORD did they bestow upon the Baalim.

8. So the king commanded, and they made a chest, and set it without at the gate of the house of the LORD.
9. And they made a proclamation through Judah and Jerusalem, to

לַדָּבָר וְלֹא מִהֲרוּ הַלְוִיִּם׃
וַיִּקְרָא הַמֶּלֶךְ לִיהוֹיָדָע 6
הָרֹאשׁ וַיֹּאמֶר לוֹ מַדּוּעַ לֹא־
דָרַשְׁתָּ עַל־הַלְוִיִּם לְהָבִיא
מִיהוּדָה וּמִירוּשָׁלִַם אֶת־
מַשְׂאַת מֹשֶׁה עֶבֶד־יְהוָה
וְהַקָּהָל לְיִשְׂרָאֵל לְאֹהֶל
הָעֵדוּת׃ כִּי עֲתַלְיָהוּ 7
הַמִּרְשַׁעַת בָּנֶיהָ פָרְצוּ אֶת־
בֵּית הָאֱלֹהִים וְגַם כָּל־קָדְשֵׁי
בֵית־יְהוָה עָשׂוּ לַבְּעָלִים׃
וַיֹּאמֶר הַמֶּלֶךְ וַיַּעֲשׂוּ אֲרוֹן 8
אֶחָד וַיִּתְּנֻהוּ בְּשַׁעַר בֵּית־
יְהוָה חוּצָה׃ וַיִּתְּנוּ־קוֹל 9
בִּיהוּדָה וּבִירוּשָׁלִַם לְהָבִיא

that is brought into the house of the LORD. One account may be supplementary to the other.

the Levites hastened it not. 2 Kings xii. 7 reads: *in the three and twentieth year of king Jehoash the priests had not repaired the breaches of the house.*

6. *the tax of Moses.* Cf. Exod. xxx. 11-16. The wording of Kings is different. Here a charge of neglect is made that the annual tax of a half-shekel had not been collected.

and of the congregation. i.e. the tax which was obligatory upon the community.

7. *the sons of Athaliah.* This verse does not occur in Kings. The text is more accurately translated, 'For Athaliah (being) wicked, her sons,' etc.; the evil character of the mother influenced the conduct of her sons.

had broken up. Better, 'had broken into,' made raids upon.

all the hallowed things. Probably the vessels of silver and gold.

did they bestow upon the Baalim. Or, 'did they make into (images) of the Baalim.'

8. *a chest.* To receive contributions. 2 Kings xii. 10 adds that Jehoiada *bored a hole in the lid of it,* through which was inserted *all the money that was brought into the house of the LORD.*

at the gate. 2 Kings xii. 10 has: *beside the altar, on the right side as one cometh into the house of the LORD.*

9f. These verses have no parallel in Kings.

bring in for the LORD the tax that Moses the servant of God laid upon Israel in the wilderness. 10. And all the princes and all the people rejoiced, and brought in, and cast into the chest, until they had made an end. 11. And it was so, that at what time the chest was brought unto the king's officers by the hand of the Levites, and when they saw that there was much money, the king's scribe and the chief priest's officer came and emptied the chest, and took it, and carried it back to its place. Thus they did day by day, and gathered money in abundance. 12. And the king and Jehoiada gave it to such as did the work of the service of the house of the LORD; and they hired masons and carpenters to restore the house of the LORD, and also such as wrought iron and brass to repair the house of the LORD. 13. So the workmen wrought, and the work was perfected by them, and they set up the house of God in

לַיהוָה מַשְׂאַת מֹשֶׁה עֶבֶד־
הָאֱלֹהִים עַל־יִשְׂרָאֵל
בַּמִּדְבָּר׃ וַיִּשְׂמְחוּ כָל־ 10
הַשָּׂרִים וְכָל־הָעָם וַיָּבִיאוּ
וַיַּשְׁלִיכוּ לָאָרוֹן עַד־לְכַלֵּה׃
וַיְהִי בְּעֵת יָבִיא אֶת־הָאָרוֹן 11
אֶל־פְּקֻדַּת הַמֶּלֶךְ בְּיַד
הַלְוִיִּם וְכִרְאוֹתָם כִּי־רַב
הַכֶּסֶף וּבָא סוֹפֵר הַמֶּלֶךְ
וּפְקִיד כֹּהֵן הָרֹאשׁ וִיעָרוּ אֶת־
הָאָרוֹן וְיִשָּׂאֻהוּ וִישִׁבֻהוּ אֶל־
מְקֹמוֹ כֹּה עָשׂוּ לְיוֹם בְּיוֹם
וַיַּאַסְפוּ כֶסֶף לָרֹב׃ וַיִּתְּנֵהוּ 12
הַמֶּלֶךְ וִיהוֹיָדָע אֶל־עוֹשֵׂה
מְלֶאכֶת עֲבוֹדַת בֵּית־יְהוָה
וַיִּהְיוּ שֹׂכְרִים חֹצְבִים וְחָרָשִׁים
לְחַדֵּשׁ בֵּית יְהוָה וְגַם לְחָרָשֵׁי
בַרְזֶל וּנְחֹשֶׁת לְחַזֵּק אֶת־בֵּית
יְהוָה׃ וַיַּעֲשׂוּ עֹשֵׂי הַמְּלָאכָה 13
וַתַּעַל אֲרוּכָה לַמְּלָאכָה
בְּיָדָם וַיַּעֲמִידוּ אֶת־בֵּית

10. ***until they had made an end.*** i.e. until everybody had paid his contribution, or until the chest was filled.

11. ***at what time . . . of the Levites.*** Not in Kings.

unto the king's officers. Or, 'for the oversight of the king.' The Hebrew noun *pekudath* may bear either meaning.

the chief priest's officer. This explains the statement of 2 Kings xii. 11 that the *High Priest* accompanied the king's scribe.

and emptied . . . abundance. The version in Kings has instead: *and they put up in bags and counted the money that was found in the house of the LORD.*

13. ***and the work was perfected by them.*** lit. 'and there went up a healing (restoration) to the work in their hand.'

its state, and strengthened it. 14. And when they had made an end, they brought the rest of the money before the king and Jehoiada, whereof were made vessels for the house of the LORD, even vessels wherewith to minister, and buckets, and pans, and vessels of gold and silver. And they offered burnt-offerings in the house of the LORD continually all the days of Jehoiada.

15. But Jehoiada waxed old and was full of days, and he died; a hundred and thirty years old was he when he died. 16. And they buried him in the city of David among the kings, because he had done good in Israel, and toward God and His house. 17. Now after the death of Jehoiada came the princes of Judah, and prostrated themselves before the king. Then the king hearkened unto them. 18. And they forsook

הָאֱלֹהִים עַל־מַתְכֻּנְתּוֹ
14 וַֽיְאַמְּצֻהוּ׃ וּכְכַלּוֹתָם הֵבִיאוּ
לִפְנֵי הַמֶּלֶךְ וִיהוֹיָדָע אֶת־
שְׁאָר הַכֶּסֶף וַיַּעֲשֵׂהוּ כֵלִים
לְבֵית־יְהוָה כְּלֵי שָׁרֵת
וְהַעֲלוֹת וְכַפּוֹת וּכְלֵי זָהָב
וָכָסֶף וַיִּהְיוּ מַעֲלִים עֹלוֹת
בְּבֵית־יְהוָה תָּמִיד כֹּל יְמֵי
יְהוֹיָדָע׃
15 וַיִּזְקַן יְהוֹיָדָע וַיִּשְׂבַּע יָמִים
וַיָּמֹת בֶּן־מֵאָה וּשְׁלֹשִׁים שָׁנָה
16 בְּמוֹתוֹ׃ וַיִּקְבְּרֻהוּ בְעִיר־
דָּוִיד עִם־הַמְּלָכִים כִּֽי־עָשָׂה
טוֹבָה בְּיִשְׂרָאֵל וְעִם־
17 הָאֱלֹהִים וּבֵיתוֹ׃ וְאַחֲרֵי מוֹת
יְהוֹיָדָע בָּאוּ שָׂרֵי יְהוּדָה
וַיִּֽשְׁתַּחֲווּ לַמֶּלֶךְ אָז שָׁמַע
18 הַמֶּלֶךְ אֲלֵיהֶם׃ וַיַּעַזְבוּ אֶת־

in its state. i.e. its former state before the fabric deteriorated.

14. *whereof were made vessels . . . gold and silver*. This apparently contradicts 2 Kings xii. 14 which states that *there were not made . . . cups of silver, snuffers, basins, trumpets, any vessels of gold, or vessels of silver*. The Talmud (Keth. 106b) resolves the difficulty by explaining that Chron. refers to a time when there was a surplus which could be used for the provision of vessels, and the account in Kings to a time when there was no surplus. Note *the rest of the money* earlier in the verse.

and buckets. lit. 'and (vessels for) bringing up.'

15-22. Joash lapses from his former religious devotion after Jehoiada's death. These verses are without parallel in Kings.

16. *among the kings*. Contrast what is related of Joash in verse 25. Jehoiada was the son-in-law of king Jehoram (xxii. 11).

17. *the king hearkened unto them*. The nature of their request may be inferred from the next verse.

18. *forsook the house of the* LORD. A

the house of the LORD, the God of their fathers, and served the Asherim and the idols; and wrath came upon Judah and Jerusalem for this their guiltiness. 19. Yet He sent prophets to them, to bring them back unto the LORD; and they admonished them, but they would not give ear.

20. And the spirit of God clothed Zechariah the son of Jehoiada the priest; and he stood above the people, and said unto them: 'Thus saith God: Why transgress ye the commandments of the LORD, that ye cannot prosper? because ye have forsaken the LORD, He hath also forsaken you.' 21. And they conspired against him, and stoned him with stones at the commandment of the king in the court of the house of the LORD. 22. Thus Joash the king remembered not the kindness which Jehoiada his father had done to him, but slew his son. And when he died, he said: 'The LORD look upon it, and require it.'

בֵּית יְהוָה אֱלֹהֵי אֲבוֹתֵיהֶם
וַיַּעַבְדוּ אֶת־הָאֲשֵׁרִים וְאֶת־
הָעֲצַבִּים וַיְהִי־קֶצֶף עַל־
יְהוּדָה וִירוּשָׁלִַם בְּאַשְׁמָתָם
19 זֹאת׃ וַיִּשְׁלַח בָּהֶם נְבִאִים
לַהֲשִׁיבָם אֶל־יְהוָה וַיָּעִידוּ
בָם וְלֹא הֶאֱזִינוּ׃
20 וְרוּחַ אֱלֹהִים לָבְשָׁה אֶת־
זְכַרְיָה בֶּן־יְהוֹיָדָע הַכֹּהֵן
וַיַּעֲמֹד מֵעַל לָעָם וַיֹּאמֶר לָהֶם
כֹּה ׀ אָמַר הָאֱלֹהִים לָמָה
אַתֶּם עֹבְרִים אֶת־מִצְוֺת יְהוָה
וְלֹא תַצְלִיחוּ כִּי־עֲזַבְתֶּם
אֶת־יְהוָה וַיַּעֲזֹב אֶתְכֶם׃
21 וַיִּקְשְׁרוּ עָלָיו וַיִּרְגְּמֻהוּ אֶבֶן
בְּמִצְוַת הַמֶּלֶךְ בַּחֲצַר בֵּית
22 יְהוָה׃ וְלֹא־זָכַר יוֹאָשׁ הַמֶּלֶךְ
הַחֶסֶד אֲשֶׁר עָשָׂה יְהוֹיָדָע
אָבִיו עִמּוֹ וַיַּהֲרֹג אֶת־בְּנוֹ
וּכְמוֹתוֹ אָמַר יֵרֶא יְהוָה
וְיִדְרֹשׁ׃

circumlocution for 'they abandoned the worship of God' (cf. xxix. 6).

the Asherim. See on xiv. 2.

wrath came. The punishment was invasion by the Arameans (verses 23ff.).

19. *prophets to them.* Better, 'among them.'

20. *the son of Jehoiada.* The king's former tutor.

stood above the people. He addressed them from the inner court of the Temple (cf. verse 21) which was on a higher level than the outer court where the people congregated.

21. *in the court of the house of the LORD.* They were guilty of murder and desecration of the Temple.

22. *require it.* Cf. the use of the verb in Gen. ix. 5.

23. And it came to pass, when the year was come about, that the army of the Arameans came up against him; and they came to Judah and Jerusalem, and destroyed all the princes of the people from among the people, and sent all the spoil of them unto the king of Damascus. 24. For the army of the Arameans came with a small company of men; and the LORD delivered a very great host into their hand, because they had forsaken the LORD, the God of their fathers. So they executed judgment upon Joash. 25. And when they were departed from him —for they left him in great diseases —his own servants conspired against him for the blood of the sons of Jehoiada the priest, and slew him on his bed, and he died; and they

23 וַיְהִי ׀ לִתְקוּפַת הַשָּׁנָה עָלָה
עָלָיו חֵיל אֲרָם וַיָּבֹאוּ אֶל־
יְהוּדָה וִירוּשָׁלַם וַיַּשְׁחִיתוּ
אֶת־כָּל־שָׂרֵי הָעָם מֵעָם
וְכָל־שְׁלָלָם שִׁלְּחוּ לְמֶלֶךְ
24 דַּרְמָשֶׂק׃ כִּי בְמִצְעַר אֲנָשִׁים
בָּאוּ חֵיל אֲרָם וַיהוָה נָתַן
בְּיָדָם חַיִל לָרֹב מְאֹד כִּי עָזְבוּ
אֶת־יְהוָה אֱלֹהֵי אֲבוֹתֵיהֶם
וְאֶת־יוֹאָשׁ עָשׂוּ שְׁפָטִים׃
25 וּבְלֶכְתָּם מִמֶּנּוּ כִּי־עָזְבוּ אֹתוֹ
בְּמַחֲלֻיִים רַבִּים הִתְקַשְּׁרוּ
עָלָיו עֲבָדָיו בִּדְמֵי בְּנֵי יְהוֹיָדָע
הַכֹּהֵן וַיַּהַרְגֻהוּ עַל־מִטָּתוֹ

23f. (cf. 2 Kings xii. 18f.). Syrian invasion of Judah. The Chronicler's account supplements that in Kings. The latter deals with the threat of invasion by Hazael king of Aram which was averted by a gift of some of the Temple treasures by Joash. The Chronicler describes an actual attack which may have taken place subsequently, representing it as a judgment of God. There are other details in which the two accounts are complementary.

23. *when the year was come about.* At the same time in the following year.

princes of the people. Who were the prime movers in the people's apostasy (verses 17f.).

the king of Damascus. viz. Hazael (cf. 2 Kings xii. 18).

24. *a small company of men.* This fact was evidence that what happened was by God's will.

they had forsaken. The subject is the people of Judah.

they executed. The pronoun refers to the Aramean army.

25-27 (cf. 2 Kings xii. 20-22). The assassination of Joash.

25. The Chronicler gives fuller details than does 2 Kings xii. 21 which merely narrates that the assassination took place at Beth-millo on the way to Silla, but does not mention the motive of the murder or that Joash was *left* by the Arameans *in great diseases.*

they were departed. After the departure of the Aramean force.

great diseases. lit. 'many diseases'; wounds and consequent complications which weakened Joash and exposed him to the mercy of the conspirators.

the sons of Jehoiada. In verses 20ff. only one son, Zechariah, is named; but this

buried him in the city of David, but they buried him not in the sepulchres of the kings. 26. And these are they that conspired against him: Zabad the son of Shimeath the Ammonitess, and Jehozabad the son of Shimrith the Moabitess. 27. Now concerning his sons, and the multitude of the burdens against him, and the rebuilding of the house of God, behold, they are written in the commentary of the book of the kings. And Amaziah his son reigned in his stead.

וַיָּמֹת וַֽיִּקְבְּרֻהוּ בְּעִיר דָּוִיד
וְלֹא קְבָרֻהוּ בְּקִבְרוֹת
26 הַמְּלָכִֽים׃ וְאֵלֶּה הַמִּֽתְקַשְּׁרִים
עָלָיו זָבָד בֶּן־שִׁמְעָת
הָֽעַמּוֹנִית וִיהוֹזָבָד בֶּן־
27 שִׁמְרִית הַמּוֹאָבִֽית׃ וּבָנָיו וְרֹב
הַמַּשָּׂא עָלָיו וִיסוֹד בֵּית
הָאֱלֹהִים הִנָּם כְּתוּבִים עַל־
מִדְרַשׁ סֵפֶר הַמְּלָכִים וַיִּמְלֹךְ
אֲמַצְיָהוּ בְנוֹ תַּחְתָּֽיו׃

25 CHAPTER XXV כה

1. Amaziah was twenty and five years old when he began to reign; and he reigned twenty and nine years in Jerusalem; and his mother's name was Jehoaddan of Jerusalem. 2. And he did that which was right in the eyes of the LORD, but not with a whole heart. 3. Now it came to

1 בֶּן־עֶשְׂרִים וְחָמֵשׁ שָׁנָה מָלַךְ
אֲמַצְיָהוּ וְעֶשְׂרִים וָתֵשַׁע שָׁנָה
מָלַךְ בִּירוּשָׁלִָם וְשֵׁם אִמּוֹ
2 יְהוֹעַדָּן מִירוּשָׁלִָֽם׃ וַיַּעַשׂ
הַיָּשָׁר בְּעֵינֵי יְהוָה רַק לֹא
3 בְּלֵבָב שָׁלֵֽם׃ וַיְהִי כַּאֲשֶׁר

ירב ק׳ v. 27.

does not preclude the possibility that other sons of Jehoiada were also killed on the king's orders.

they buried . . . kings. This is an addition to 2 Kings xii. 22.

26. The nationality of the mothers of the conspirators is omitted in Kings and the names of the conspirators or of their mothers have a slightly different form.

27. *the burdens.* The phrase may signify the warnings of the prophets (cf. verse 19).

rebuilding. lit. 'foundation,' i.e. the measures he adopted to repair the Temple.

commentary. See on xiii. 22.

CHAPTER XXV

THE REIGN OF AMAZIAH

1-4 (corresponding, with some variations, to 2 Kings xiv. 2-6). Duration and character of Amaziah's reign (798-790 B.C.E.).

2. *but not with a whole heart.* 2 Kings xiv. 3f. has instead: *yet not like David his father . . . the high places were not taken*

pass, when the kingdom was established unto him, that he slew his servants who had killed the king his father. 4. But he put not their children to death, but did according to that which is written in the law in the book of Moses, as the LORD commanded, saying: 'The fathers shall not die for the children, neither shall the children die for the fathers; but every man shall die for his own sin.'

5. Moreover Amaziah gathered Judah together, and ordered them according to their fathers' houses, under captains of thousands and captains of hundreds, even all Judah and Benjamin; and he numbered them from twenty years old and upward, and found them three hundred thousand chosen men, able to go forth to war, that could handle spear and shield. 6. He hired also a hundred thousand mighty men of valour out of Israel for a hundred talents of silver. 7. But there came a man of God to him, saying: 'O king, let not the army of Israel go

חָזְקָה הַמַּמְלָכָה עָלָיו וַיַּהֲרֹג
אֶת־עֲבָדָיו הַמַּכִּים אֶת־
4 הַמֶּלֶךְ אָבִיו׃ וְאֶת־בְּנֵיהֶם
לֹא הֵמִית כִּי כַכָּתוּב בַּתּוֹרָה
בְּסֵפֶר מֹשֶׁה אֲשֶׁר־צִוָּה יְהוָה
לֵאמֹר לֹא־יָמוּתוּ אָבוֹת עַל־
בָּנִים וּבָנִים לֹא־יָמוּתוּ עַל־
אָבוֹת כִּי אִישׁ בְּחֶטְאוֹ יָמוּתוּ׃
5 וַיִּקְבֹּץ אֲמַצְיָהוּ אֶת־יְהוּדָה
וַיַּעֲמִידֵם לְבֵית־אָבוֹת לְשָׂרֵי
הָאֲלָפִים וּלְשָׂרֵי הַמֵּאוֹת
לְכָל־יְהוּדָה וּבִנְיָמִן
וַיִּפְקְדֵם לְמִבֶּן עֶשְׂרִים שָׁנָה
וָמַעְלָה וַיִּמְצָאֵם שְׁלֹשׁ־מֵאוֹת
אֶלֶף בָּחוּר יוֹצֵא צָבָא אֹחֵז
6 רֹמַח וְצִנָּה׃ וַיִּשְׂכֹּר מִיִּשְׂרָאֵל
מֵאָה אֶלֶף גִּבּוֹר חָיִל בְּמֵאָה
7 כִכַּר־כָּסֶף׃ וְאִישׁ הָאֱלֹהִים
בָּא אֵלָיו לֵאמֹר הַמֶּלֶךְ אַל־

v. 6. קמץ בטפחא

away; the people still sacrificed and offered in the high places. Cf. verses 14ff. below.

3. *was established unto him.* In 2 Kings xiv. 5: *established in his hand.* The literal meaning here is 'was strong upon him.'

who had killed the king his father. Cf. xxiv. 25.

4. *but did.* The verb is implied.

in the book of Moses. In Deut. xxiv. 16.

5-10 (not in Kings). Amaziah's military preparations.

5. *and ordered them.* lit. 'and made them stand.'

under captains. lit. 'for captains.'

three hundred thousand . . . spear and shield. King Asa recruited a similar number of spearmen from Judah (xiv. 7), but in addition 280,000 armed men from Banjamin. Jehoshaphat had an army of 1,160,000 (xvii. 14ff.). The smaller number of Amaziah's army was the cause of his hiring 100,000 troops from Israel. These mercenaries became a source of trouble to him (verses 10, 13).

with thee; for the LORD is not with Israel, even with all the children of Ephraim. 8. But if thou wilt go, and do engage never so valiantly in battle, God will cast thee down before the enemy; for God hath power to help, and to cast down.' 9. And Amaziah said to the man of God: 'But what shall we do for the hundred talents which I have given to the army of Israel?' And the man of God answered: 'The LORD is able to give thee much more than this.' 10. Then Amaziah separated them, to wit, the army that was come to him out of Ephraim, to go back home; wherefore their anger was greatly kindled against Judah, and they returned home in fierce anger.

11. And Amaziah took courage, and led forth his people, and went to the Valley of Salt, and smote of the

יָבוֹא עִמְּךָ צְבָא יִשְׂרָאֵל כִּי
אֵין יְהוָה עִם־יִשְׂרָאֵל כֹּל בְּנֵי
8 אֶפְרָיִם׃ כִּי אִם־בֹּא אַתָּה
עֲשֵׂה חֲזַק לַמִּלְחָמָה יַכְשִׁילְךָ
הָאֱלֹהִים לִפְנֵי אוֹיֵב כִּי יֶשׁ־
כֹּחַ בֵּאלֹהִים לַעְזוֹר
9 וּלְהַכְשִׁיל׃ וַיֹּאמֶר אֲמַצְיָהוּ
לְאִישׁ הָאֱלֹהִים וּמַה־לַּעֲשׂוֹת
לִמְאַת הַכִּכָּר אֲשֶׁר נָתַתִּי
לִגְדוּד יִשְׂרָאֵל וַיֹּאמֶר אִישׁ
הָאֱלֹהִים יֵשׁ לַיהוָה לָתֶת לְךָ
10 הַרְבֵּה מִזֶּה׃ וַיַּבְדִּילֵם
אֲמַצְיָהוּ לְהַגְּדוּד אֲשֶׁר־בָּא
אֵלָיו מֵאֶפְרַיִם לָלֶכֶת
לִמְקוֹמָם וַיִּחַר אַפָּם מְאֹד
בִּיהוּדָה וַיָּשׁוּבוּ לִמְקוֹמָם
בָּחֳרִי־אָף׃
11 וַאֲמַצְיָהוּ הִתְחַזַּק וַיִּנְהַג אֶת־
עַמּוֹ וַיֵּלֶךְ גֵּיא הַמֶּלַח וַיַּךְ

7. *Israel . . . all the children of Ephraim.* Both are synonyms for the Northern Kingdom.

8. *wilt go.* Together with the soldiers from Israel.

and do engage never so valiantly. lit. 'do, be strong for war.' Another rendering is: 'do it (valiantly), be strong for the battle.' The words are spoken ironically.

God will cast thee down. For relying upon the mercenaries from the kingdom of Israel which had not the favour of God.

9. *shall we do.* lit. 'to do'; the meaning is, 'Am I to lose my money?'

the LORD is able, etc. One is never the loser by obeying the will of God.

10. *in fierce anger.* Because they were deprived of the opportunity of gaining spoils from the battle.

11-13 (cf. 2 Kings xiv. 7). Edom's defeat. The mercenaries' revenge on the cities of Judah.

11. *took courage.* lit. 'strengthened himself.'

children of Seir ten thousand. 12. And other ten thousand did the children of Judah carry away alive, and brought them unto the top of the Rock, and cast them down from the top of the Rock, that they all were broken in pieces. 13. But the men of the army whom Amaziah sent back, that they should not go with him to battle, fell upon the cities of Judah, from Samaria even unto Beth-horon, and smote of them three thousand, and took much spoil.

14. Now it came to pass, after that Amaziah was come from the slaughter of the Edomites, that he brought the gods of the children of Seir, and set them up to be his gods, and prostrated himself before them, and offered unto them. 15. Wherefore the anger of the LORD was kindled against Amaziah, and He sent unto him a prophet, who said

אֶת־בְּנֵי־שֵׂעִיר עֲשֶׂרֶת
12 אֲלָפִים׃ וַעֲשֶׂרֶת אֲלָפִים
חַיִּים שָׁבוּ בְּנֵי יְהוּדָה וַיְבִיאוּם
לְרֹאשׁ הַסָּלַע וַיַּשְׁלִיכוּם
מֵרֹאשׁ הַסֶּלַע וְכֻלָּם נִבְקָעוּ׃
13 וּבְנֵי הַגְּדוּד אֲשֶׁר הֵשִׁיב
אֲמַצְיָהוּ מִלֶּכֶת עִמּוֹ
לַמִּלְחָמָה וַיִּפְשְׁטוּ בְּעָרֵי
יְהוּדָה מִשֹּׁמְרוֹן וְעַד־בֵּית
חוֹרוֹן וַיַּכּוּ מֵהֶם שְׁלֹשֶׁת
אֲלָפִים וַיָּבֹזּוּ בִּזָּה רַבָּה׃
14 וַיְהִי אַחֲרֵי בוֹא אֲמַצְיָהוּ
מֵהַכּוֹת אֶת־אֲדוֹמִים וַיָּבֵא
אֶת־אֱלֹהֵי בְּנֵי שֵׂעִיר
וַיַּעֲמִידֵם לוֹ לֵאלֹהִים
וְלִפְנֵיהֶם יִשְׁתַּחֲוֶה וְלָהֶם
15 יְקַטֵּר׃ וַיִּחַר־אַף יְהוָה
בַּאֲמַצְיָהוּ וַיִּשְׁלַח אֵלָיו נָבִיא

the Valley of Salt. See on I Chron. xviii. 12.

the children of Seir. The Edomites, whose land included mount Seir (cf. Deut. ii. 5).

12. *other ten thousand.* The first word is understood.

the Rock. Identified by some with Petra ('the rock city'), the capital of Edom.

13. *the men of the army.* lit. 'the sons of the troop.'

fell upon. lit. 'spread out in.'

from Samaria. The city was in the Northern Kingdom and the raid on Judah may have started from there. *Samaria* may possibly denote here the Northern Kingdom and not the city of that name.

unto Beth-horon. See on I Chron. vi. 53. There the raid came to an end.

14-16 (not in Kings). Amaziah's apostasy followed by a Divine warning. This section is an introduction to, and provides the reason for, the disaster which befell Amaziah in his war with Joash, king of Israel (verses 17-24).

14. *prostrated . . . offered.* Better, 'used to prostrate . . . offer.'

unto him: 'Why hast thou sought after the gods of the people, which have not delivered their own people out of thy hand?' 16. And it came to pass, as he talked with him, that [the king] said unto him: 'Have we made thee of the king's counsel? forbear; why shouldest thou be smitten?' Then the prophet forbore, and said: 'I know that God hath determined to destroy thee, because thou hast done this, and hast not hearkened unto my counsel.'

17. Then Amaziah king of Judah took advice, and sent to Joash, the son of Jehoahaz the son of Jehu, king of Israel, saying: 'Come, let us look one another in the face.' 18. And Joash king of Israel sent to Amaziah king of Judah, saying: 'The thistle that was in Lebanon sent to the cedar that was in Lebanon, saying: Give thy daughter to my son to wife; and there passed

וַיֹּאמֶר אֵלָיו לָמָּה דָרַשְׁתָּ אֶת־
אֱלֹהֵי הָעָם אֲשֶׁר לֹא־הִצִּילוּ
16 אֶת־עַמָּם מִיָּדֶךָ׃ וַיְהִי ׀
בְּדַבְּרוֹ אֵלָיו וַיֹּאמֶר לוֹ
הַלְיוֹעֵץ לַמֶּלֶךְ נְתַנּוּךָ חֲדַל־
לְךָ לָמָּה יַכּוּךָ וַיֶּחְדַּל הַנָּבִיא
וַיֹּאמֶר יָדַעְתִּי כִּי־יָעַץ
אֱלֹהִים לְהַשְׁחִיתֶךָ כִּי־עָשִׂיתָ
זֹּאת וְלֹא שָׁמַעְתָּ לַעֲצָתִי׃
17 וַיִּוָּעַץ אֲמַצְיָהוּ מֶלֶךְ יְהוּדָה
וַיִּשְׁלַח אֶל־יוֹאָשׁ בֶּן־יְהוֹאָחָז
בֶּן־יֵהוּא מֶלֶךְ יִשְׂרָאֵל לֵאמֹר
18 לְךָ נִתְרָאֶה פָנִים׃ וַיִּשְׁלַח
יוֹאָשׁ מֶלֶךְ־יִשְׂרָאֵל אֶל־
אֲמַצְיָהוּ מֶלֶךְ־יְהוּדָה לֵאמֹר
הַחוֹחַ אֲשֶׁר בַּלְּבָנוֹן שָׁלַח
אֶל־הָאֶרֶז אֲשֶׁר בַּלְּבָנוֹן
לֵאמֹר תְּנָה אֶת־בִּתְּךָ לִבְנִי

15. *which have not delivered*, etc. A proof that they were powerless; yet Amaziah worshipped them and forsook God Who gave him victory over Edom.

16. *of the king's counsel.* Or, 'counsellor to the king.'

thou hast done this. Worshipped idols (verse 14).

17-24 (corresponding to 2 Kings xiv. 8-14). Amaziah's disastrous war with Joash.

17. *took advice.* Or, 'was advised,' on the question of seeking satisfaction from the king of Israel for the raid of his soldiers on the cities of Judah.

let us look one another in the face. i.e. 'let us test our strength in battle.' Filled with confidence after his defeat of Edom, Amaziah sends a challenge to Joash.

18. *thistle . . . cedar.* Joash replies with a parable (cf. Judg. ix. 8ff.) in which he compares Amaziah to the former, a thorny reed, and himself to the latter, the most majestic of trees.

give thy daughter, etc. The point of the parable is the dangerous folly of over-estimating oneself. The thistle, imagining itself to be the equal of the cedar, presumptuously suggests a marriage alliance between them; but the difference in their status was made apparent when

by the wild beasts that were in
Lebanon, and trod down the thistle.
19. Thou sayest—lo, thou hast
smitten Edom; will thy heart therefore lift thee up to glory therein?
abide now at home; why shouldest
thou meddle with evil, that thou
shouldest fall, even thou, and Judah
with thee?' 20. But Amaziah would
not hear; for it was of God, that He
might deliver them into the hand
[of their enemies], because they had
sought after the gods of Edom.
21. So Joash king of Israel went up;
and he and Amaziah king of Judah
looked one another in the face at
Beth-shemesh, which belongeth to
Judah. 22. And Judah was put to
the worse before Israel; and they
fled every man to his tent. 23. And
Joash king of Israel took Amaziah
king of Judah, the son of Joash, the

לָאִשָּׁה וַתַּעֲבֹר חַיַּת הַשָּׂדֶה
אֲשֶׁר בַּלְּבָנוֹן וַתִּרְמֹס אֶת־
19 הַחוֹחַ׃ אָמַרְתָּ הִנֵּה הִכִּיתָ
אֶת־אֱדוֹם וּנְשָׂאֲךָ לִבְּךָ
לְהַכְבִּיד עַתָּה שְׁבָה בְּבֵיתֶךָ
לָמָּה תִתְגָּרֶה בְּרָעָה וְנָפַלְתָּ
20 אַתָּה וִיהוּדָה עִמָּךְ׃ וְלֹא־
שָׁמַע אֲמַצְיָהוּ כִּי מֵהָאֱלֹהִים
הִיא לְמַעַן תִּתָּם בְּיָד כִּי דָרְשׁוּ
21 אֵת אֱלֹהֵי אֱדוֹם׃ וַיַּעַל יוֹאָשׁ
מֶלֶךְ־יִשְׂרָאֵל וַיִּתְרָאוּ פָנִים
הוּא וַאֲמַצְיָהוּ מֶלֶךְ־יְהוּדָה
בְּבֵית שֶׁמֶשׁ אֲשֶׁר לִיהוּדָה׃
22 וַיִּנָּגֶף יְהוּדָה לִפְנֵי יִשְׂרָאֵל
23 וַיָּנֻסוּ אִישׁ לְאֹהָלָיו׃ וְאֵת
אֲמַצְיָהוּ מֶלֶךְ־יְהוּדָה בֶּן־

a wild beast passed and trod the thistle under foot while it was powerless to injure the tall cedar. Let not Amaziah think too highly of himself lest he come to harm.

the wild beasts. Better, 'a wild beast'; lit. 'the (or, a) beast of the field.'

19. *thou sayest.* In thy heart; thinkest.

lift thee up to glory therein? In 2 Kings xiv. 10: *will thy heart lift thee up? glory therein and remain at home.* Will this victory give him a false sense of power and make him feel capable of over-coming the army of any other country?

meddle with evil. Better, 'provoke cala-mity,' look for trouble.

20. This is an addition to the account in Kings, pointing the moral of the incident.

for it. Amaziah's obstinacy.

deliver them. The king of Judah and his people.

they had sought after the gods of Edom. Cf. verse 14.

21. *went up.* Into Judah. So confident was Joash of his supremacy that he launched the attack against Amaziah on the latter's own territory.

looked one another in the face. This is an ironical repetition of the wording of the challenge which Amaziah had made to Joash (verse 17).

Beth-shemesh. See on 1 Chron. vi. 44.

22. *was put to the worse.* lit. 'was smitten,' defeated.

23. *took Amaziah.* As a prisoner of war.

son of Jehoahaz, at Beth-shemesh, and brought him to Jerusalem, and broke down the wall of Jerusalem from the gate of Ephraim unto the corner gate, four hundred cubits. 24. And [he took] all the gold and silver, and all the vessels that were found in the house of God with Obed-edom, and the treasures of the king's house, the hostages also, and returned to Samaria.

25. And Amaziah the son of Joash king of Judah lived after the death of Joash son of Jehoahaz king of Israel fifteen years. 26. Now the rest of the acts of Amaziah, first and last, behold, are they not written in

יוֹאָשׁ בֶּן־יְהוֹאָחָז תָּפַשׂ יוֹאָשׁ
מֶלֶךְ־יִשְׂרָאֵל בְּבֵית שָׁמֶשׁ
וַיְבִיאֵהוּ יְרוּשָׁלַםִ וַיִּפְרֹץ
בְּחוֹמַת יְרוּשָׁלַםִ מִשַּׁעַר
אֶפְרַיִם עַד־שַׁעַר הַפּוֹנֶה
אַרְבַּע מֵאוֹת אַמָּה׃ וְכָל־ 24
הַזָּהָב וְהַכֶּסֶף וְאֵת כָּל־
הַכֵּלִים הַנִּמְצְאִים בְּבֵית־
הָאֱלֹהִים עִם־עֹבֵד אֱדוֹם
וְאֶת־אֹצְרוֹת בֵּית הַמֶּלֶךְ וְאֵת
בְּנֵי הַתַּעֲרֻבוֹת וַיָּשָׁב שֹׁמְרוֹן׃
וַיְחִי אֲמַצְיָהוּ בֶן־יוֹאָשׁ מֶלֶךְ 25
יְהוּדָה אַחֲרֵי מוֹת יוֹאָשׁ בֶּן־
יְהוֹאָחָז מֶלֶךְ יִשְׂרָאֵל חֲמֵשׁ
עֶשְׂרֵה שָׁנָה׃ וְיֶתֶר דִּבְרֵי 26
אֲמַצְיָהוּ הָרִאשֹׁנִים
וְהָאַחֲרוֹנִים הֲלֹא הִנָּם

Jehoahaz. Another form of Ahaziah's name (see on xxi. 17).

broke down the wall. Better, 'made a breach in the wall.'

the gate of Ephraim. Now known as 'the Damascus gate,' on the north side of the city in the direction leading to Ephraim, a name for the Northern Kingdom.

the corner gate. Located in the north-west angle of the city wall.

four hundred cubits. This demolition created a gap through which Jerusalem was exposed to easy attack from the north.

24. *with Obed-edom.* Who, with his family, acted as doorkeepers in the Temple (1 Chron. xxvi. 4-8, 15). This is not found in 2 Kings xiv. 14.

hostages. lit. 'sons of pledges,' held as a guarantee of loyal behaviour on the part of the conquered towards their victors.

25-28 (corresponding to 2 Kings xiv. 17-20). The assassination of Amaziah.

25. *fifteen years.* Amaziah's reign lasted twenty-nine years (verse 1) and it began in the second year of the reign of Joash king of Israel (2 Kings xiv. 1). As Joash reigned sixteen years (2 Kings xiii. 10), Amaziah was in the fourteenth year of his reign when Joash died and, therefore, must have lived another fifteen years after him, as stated here.

the book of the kings of Judah and Israel? 27. Now from the time that Amaziah did turn away from following the LORD they made a conspiracy against him in Jerusalem; and he fled to Lachish; but they sent after him to Lachish, and slew him there. 28. And they brought him upon horses, and buried him with his fathers in the city of Judah.

כְּתוּבִים עַל־סֵפֶר מַלְכֵי־
27 יְהוּדָה וְיִשְׂרָאֵל׃ וּמֵעֵת
אֲשֶׁר־סָר אֲמַצְיָהוּ מֵאַחֲרֵי
יְהוָה וַיִּקְשְׁרוּ עָלָיו קֶשֶׁר
בִּירוּשָׁלַםִ וַיָּנָס לָכִישָׁה
וַיִּשְׁלְחוּ אַחֲרָיו לָכִישָׁה
28 וַיְמִיתֻהוּ שָׁם׃ וַיִּשָּׂאֻהוּ עַל־
הַסּוּסִים וַיִּקְבְּרוּ אֹתוֹ עִם־
אֲבֹתָיו בְּעִיר יְהוּדָה׃

26 CHAPTER XXVI כו

1. And all the people of Judah took Uzziah, who was sixteen years old, and made him king in the room of

1 וַיִּקְחוּ כָּל־עַם יְהוּדָה אֶת־
עֻזִּיָּהוּ וְהוּא בֶּן־שֵׁשׁ עֶשְׂרֵה
שָׁנָה וַיַּמְלִיכוּ אֹתוֹ תַּחַת אָבִיו

26. *first and last.* Not in 2 Kings xiv. 18. See on 1 Chron. xxix. 29.

book of the kings of Judah and Israel. In Kings: *kings of Judah* only with the addition *of chronicles* after *book.*

27. *now from the time . . . the LORD.* This cause of the conspiracy is an addition of the Chronicler to the bare statement in 2 Kings xiv. 19f.

in Jerusalem. Though he was captured at Beth-shemesh by Joash (verse 23), he was subsequently released and allowed to return to his capital.

Lachish. See on xi. 9.

28. *upon horses.* The Hebrew is literally 'the horses,' perhaps those of the pursuers. It has been suggested that the noun in the plural denotes a conveyance drawn by horses, and no indignity was intended to the dead king.

the city of Judah. In 2 Kings xiv. 20: *the city of David.* Both refer to the same place. Inscriptions of Assarhaddon likewise describe Manasseh as 'king of the city of Judah.'

CHAPTER XXVI

THE REIGN OF UZZIAH

1-5 (corresponding to 2 Kings xiv. 21f., xv. 2f.). Uzziah's accession to the throne; his piety. The years of his reign were 790-739 B.C.E.

1. *all the people.* The unanimous approval of Amaziah's successor is mentioned because of the conspiracy which led to the violent death of the former king. The hostility to Amaziah was personal and did not extend to his house.

Uzziah. He is called *Azariah* in 1 Chron. iii. 12 and elsewhere. The names are not very dissimilar in Hebrew and the meanings are much the same,

his father Amaziah. 2. He built Eloth, and restored it to Judah, after that the king slept with his fathers. 3. Sixteen years old was Uzziah when he began to reign; and he reigned fifty and two years in Jerusalem; and his mother's name was Jecoliah of Jerusalem. 4. And he did that which was right in the eyes of the LORD, according to all that his father Amaziah had done. 5. And he set himself to seek God in the days of Zechariah, who had understanding in the vision of God; and as long as he sought the LORD, God made him to prosper.

6. And he went forth and warred against the Philistines, and broke down the wall of Gath, and the wall of Jabneh, and the wall of Ashdod;

2 אֲמַצְיָהוּ׃ הוּא בָּנָה אֶת־
אֵילוֹת וַיְשִׁבֶהָ לִיהוּדָה אַחֲרֵי
שְׁכַב־הַמֶּלֶךְ עִם־אֲבֹתָיו׃
3 בֶּן־שֵׁשׁ עֶשְׂרֵה שָׁנָה עֻזִּיָּהוּ
בְמָלְכוֹ וַחֲמִשִּׁים וּשְׁתַּיִם שָׁנָה
מָלַךְ בִּירוּשָׁלִָם וְשֵׁם אִמּוֹ
4 יְכָילְיָה מִן־יְרוּשָׁלִָם׃ וַיַּעַשׂ
הַיָּשָׁר בְּעֵינֵי יְהוָה כְּכֹל אֲשֶׁר־
5 עָשָׂה אֲמַצְיָהוּ אָבִיו׃ וַיְהִי
לִדְרֹשׁ אֱלֹהִים בִּימֵי זְכַרְיָהוּ
הַמֵּבִין בִּרְאֹת הָאֱלֹהִים
וּבִימֵי דָּרְשׁוֹ אֶת־יְהוָה
הִצְלִיחוֹ הָאֱלֹהִים׃
6 וַיֵּצֵא וַיִּלָּחֶם בַּפְּלִשְׁתִּים
וַיִּפְרֹץ אֶת־חוֹמַת גַּת וְאֵת
חוֹמַת יַבְנֵה וְאֵת חוֹמַת אַשְׁדּוֹד

v. 3. יתיר י׳

viz. 'Jah is my strength' and 'Jah hath helped.'

2. *he built . . . and restored.* The meaning is, 'he built (fortified) Eloth after he had restored' it to Judah.

Eloth. See on viii. 17.

the king. viz. Uzziah's father, Amaziah, during whose lifetime he began to rule but not as a crowned king (see on the next verse).

3. *sixteen years old.* A repetition of the king's age from verse 1, resuming the narrative interrupted by verse 2.

he reigned fifty and two years. There is a tradition that he reigned the first fifteen years during the life of his father.

4. *according to all that his father Amaziah had done.* Referring to his father's piety during his early years (xxv. 2) and not his evil deeds in the latter part of his life.

5. *and he set himself.* lit. 'and he was.'

Zechariah. All that is known of him is stated here and, although Uzziah is mentioned in the Book of Zechariah xiv. 5, the identity of name is only a coincidence.

6-10 (not in Kings). Uzziah's military successes, defence measures and prosperity.

6. *Gath.* See on 1 Chron. xviii. 1.

Jabneh. The *Jabneel* of Josh. xv. 11. Its post-Biblical name was Jamnia (1 Macc. iv. 15) and its location between Joppa and Ashdod, ten to twelve miles

and he built cities in [the country of]
Ashdod, and among the Philistines.
7. And God helped him against the
Philistines, and against the Arabians
that dwelt in Gur-baal, and the
Meunim. 8. And the Ammonites
gave gifts to Uzziah; and his name
spread abroad even to the entrance
of Egypt; for he waxed exceeding
strong. 9. Moreover Uzziah built
towers in Jerusalem at the corner
gate, and at the valley gate, and at
the Turning, and fortified them.
10. And he built towers in the
wilderness, and hewed out many
cisterns, for he had much cattle;
in the Lowland also, and in the
table-land; and he had husbandmen
and vinedressers in the mountains
and in the fruitful fields; for he
loved husbandry.

וַיִּבְנֶה עָרִים בְּאַשְׁדּוֹד
7 וּבַפְּלִשְׁתִּים׃ וַיַּעְזְרֵהוּ
הָאֱלֹהִים עַל־פְּלִשְׁתִּים
וְעַל־הָעַרְבִיִּים הַיּוֹשְׁבִים
8 בְּגוּר־בָּעַל וְהַמְּעוּנִים׃ וַיִּתְּנוּ
הָעַמּוֹנִים מִנְחָה לְעֻזִּיָּהוּ וַיֵּלֶךְ
שְׁמוֹ עַד־לְבוֹא מִצְרַיִם כִּי
9 הֶחֱזִיק עַד־לְמָעְלָה׃ וַיִּבֶן
עֻזִּיָּהוּ מִגְדָּלִים בִּירוּשָׁלַם
עַל־שַׁעַר הַפִּנָּה וְעַל־שַׁעַר
הַגַּיְא וְעַל־הַמִּקְצוֹעַ וַיְחַזְּקֵם׃
10 וַיִּבֶן מִגְדָּלִים בַּמִּדְבָּר וַיַּחְצֹב
בֹּרוֹת רַבִּים כִּי מִקְנֶה־רַב
הָיָה לוֹ וּבַשְּׁפֵלָה וּבַמִּישׁוֹר
אִכָּרִים וְכֹרְמִים בֶּהָרִים
וּבַכַּרְמֶל כִּי־אֹהֵב אֲדָמָה
הָיָה׃

v. 7. יתיר י׳

south of the former. It was the seat of the Great Sanhedrin and the religious and national centre of the Jews for a long time after the destruction of Jerusalem in 70 C.E.

Ashdod. One of the five principal Philistine cities, about midway between Joppa and Gaza, the modern Esdud.

7. *Gur-baal.* The place has not been identified.

Meunim. See on I Chron. iv. 41.

8. *gifts.* See on I Chron. xviii. 2. In the Hebrew the noun is singular used in a collective sense.

he waxed exceeding strong. lit. 'he strengthened (his kingdom) to a great height.'

9. *the corner gate.* See on xxv. 23.

the valley gate. Mentioned again in Neh. ii. 13, iii. 13, in the vicinity of the south-west corner of the wall, the modern Jaffa gate.

the Turning. Or, 'the angle' of the wall, a point of strategical importance; mentioned also in Neh. iii. 19, 24f.

10. *the wilderness.* Large tracts of pasture land in southern Judea. The *towers* served the purpose of defence against raids by the Bedouin.

cisterns. For the storage of rain.

11. Moreover Uzziah had an army of fighting men, that went out to war by bands, according to the number of their reckoning made by Jeiel the scribe and Maaseiah the officer, under the hand of Hananiah, one of the king's captains. 12. The whole number of the heads of fathers' houses, even the mighty men of valour, was two thousand and six hundred. 13. And under their hand was a trained army, three hundred thousand and seven thousand and five hundred, that made war with mighty power, to help the king against the enemy. 14. And Uzziah prepared for them, even for all the host, shields, and spears, and helmets, and coats of mail, and bows, and stones for slinging. 15. And he made in Jerusalem engines, invented by skilful men, to be on the towers and upon the corners, wherewith to shoot arrows and great stones. And his name spread far abroad; for he was marvellously helped, till he was strong.

11 וַיְהִי לְעֻזִּיָּהוּ חַיִל עֹשֵׂה
מִלְחָמָה יוֹצְאֵי צָבָא לִגְדוּד
בְּמִסְפַּר פְּקֻדָּתָם בְּיַד יְעוּאֵל
הַסּוֹפֵר וּמַעֲשֵׂיָהוּ הַשּׁוֹטֵר עַל
12 יַד־חֲנַנְיָהוּ מִשָּׂרֵי הַמֶּלֶךְ׃ כֹּל
מִסְפַּר רָאשֵׁי הָאָבוֹת לְגִבּוֹרֵי
חָיִל אַלְפַּיִם וְשֵׁשׁ מֵאוֹת׃
13 וְעַל־יָדָם חֵיל צָבָא שְׁלֹשׁ
מֵאוֹת אֶלֶף וְשִׁבְעַת אֲלָפִים
וַחֲמֵשׁ מֵאוֹת עוֹשֵׂה מִלְחָמָה
בְּכֹחַ חָיִל לַעְזֹר לַמֶּלֶךְ עַל־
14 הָאוֹיֵב׃ וַיָּכֶן לָהֶם עֻזִּיָּהוּ
לְכָל־הַצָּבָא מָגִנִּים וּרְמָחִים
וְכוֹבָעִים וְשִׁרְיֹנוֹת וּקְשָׁתוֹת
15 וּלְאַבְנֵי קְלָעִים׃ וַיַּעַשׂ ׀
בִּירוּשָׁלִַם חִשְּׁבֹנוֹת מַחֲשֶׁבֶת
חוֹשֵׁב לִהְיוֹת עַל־הַמִּגְדָּלִים
וְעַל־הַפִּנּוֹת לִירוֹא בַּחִצִּים
וּבָאֲבָנִים גְּדֹלוֹת וַיֵּצֵא שְׁמוֹ
עַד־לְמֵרָחוֹק כִּי־הִפְלִיא
לְהֵעָזֵר עַד כִּי־חָזָק׃

v. 11. יעיאל ק׳ v. 12. קמץ בז״ק v. 15. הש׳ בדגש

the table-land. The high plateau east of the Jordan and south of Heshbon.

11-15 (not in Kings). Uzziah's army and its equipment.

11. *fighting men.* lit. 'doing battle.'

by bands. Or, 'by detachments.' This was apparently an auxiliary army used for minor operations, freeing the main army for more serious engagements (cf. verse 13).

12. *the mighty men of valour.* They were probably members of the wealthier families (cf. 2 Kings xv. 20).

14. *stones for slinging.* These had to be selected for smoothness to be suitable for the purpose (cf. 1 Sam. xvii. 40).

15. *engines.* A kind of catapult.

16. But when he was strong, his heart was lifted up so that he did corruptly, and he trespassed against the LORD his God; for he went into the temple of the LORD to burn incense upon the altar of incense. 17. And Azariah the priest went in after him, and with him fourscore priests of the LORD, that were valiant men; 18. and they withstood Uzziah the king, and said unto him: 'It pertaineth not unto thee, Uzziah, to burn incense unto the LORD, but to the priests the sons of Aaron that are consecrated it pertaineth to burn incense; go out of the sanctuary; for thou hast trespassed; neither shall it be for thy honour from the LORD God.' 19. Then Uzziah was wroth; and he had a censer in his hand to burn incense; and while he was wroth with the priests, the leprosy broke forth in his forehead before the priests in the house of the LORD, beside the altar of incense. 20. And Azariah the chief priest, and all the priests, looked upon him, and, behold, he was leprous in his

16 וּכְחֶזְקָתוֹ גָּבַהּ לִבּוֹ עַד־
לְהַשְׁחִית וַיִּמְעַל בַּיהוָה
אֱלֹהָיו וַיָּבֹא אֶל־הֵיכַל יְהוָה
לְהַקְטִיר עַל־מִזְבַּח
17 הַקְּטֹרֶת׃ וַיָּבֹא אַחֲרָיו
עֲזַרְיָהוּ הַכֹּהֵן וְעִמּוֹ כֹּהֲנִים ׀
לַיהוָה שְׁמוֹנִים בְּנֵי־חָיִל׃
18 וַיַּעַמְדוּ עַל־עֻזִּיָּהוּ הַמֶּלֶךְ
וַיֹּאמְרוּ לוֹ לֹא־לְךָ עֻזִּיָּהוּ
לְהַקְטִיר לַיהוָה כִּי לַכֹּהֲנִים
בְּנֵי־אַהֲרֹן הַמְקֻדָּשִׁים
לְהַקְטִיר צֵא מִן־הַמִּקְדָּשׁ כִּי
מָעַלְתָּ וְלֹא־לְךָ לְכָבוֹד
19 מֵיְהוָה אֱלֹהִים׃ וַיִּזְעַף עֻזִּיָּהוּ
וּבְיָדוֹ מִקְטֶרֶת לְהַקְטִיר
וּבְזַעְפּוֹ עִם־הַכֹּהֲנִים
וְהַצָּרַעַת זָרְחָה בְמִצְחוֹ לִפְנֵי
הַכֹּהֲנִים בְּבֵית יְהוָה מֵעַל
20 לְמִזְבַּח הַקְּטֹרֶת׃ וַיִּפֶן אֵלָיו
עֲזַרְיָהוּ כֹּהֵן הָרֹאשׁ וְכָל־
הַכֹּהֲנִים וְהִנֵּה־הוּא מְצֹרָע

marvellously helped. By God (cf. verse 7).

16-20 (not in Kings). Uzziah's arrogance and act of sacrilege, punished by leprosy.

16. *so that he did corruptly.* lit. 'until to destroy (him).'

he went into the temple, etc. Although a lay-Israelite, he presumed to function as a priest.

17. *Azariah the priest.* He was in fact High Priest (verse 20 and see on I Chron. v. 36).

18. *neither shall it be for thy honour.* A euphemism for 'thou shalt be disgraced, or, punished.'

19. *beside the altar.* lit. 'from above the altar.' As he stood by the altar, part of his body was above it.

forehead, and they thrust him out quickly from thence; yea, himself made haste also to go out, because the LORD had smitten him. 21. And Uzziah the king was a leper unto the day of his death, and dwelt in a house set apart, being a leper; for he was cut off from the house of the LORD; and Jotham his son was over the king's house, judging the people of the land. 22. Now the rest of the acts of Uzziah, first and last, did Isaiah the prophet, the son of Amoz, write. 23. So Uzziah slept with his fathers; and they buried him with his fathers in the field of burial which belonged to the kings; for they said: 'He is a leper'; and Jotham his son reigned in his stead.

בְּמִצְחוֹ וַיַּבְהִלוּהוּ מִשָּׁם וְגַם־
הוּא נִדְחַף לָצֵאת כִּי נִגְּעוֹ
21 יְהוָה׃ וַיְהִי עֻזִּיָּהוּ הַמֶּלֶךְ
מְצֹרָע ׀ עַד־יוֹם מוֹתוֹ וַיֵּשֶׁב
בֵּית הַחָפְשׁוּת מְצֹרָע כִּי נִגְזַר
מִבֵּית יְהוָה וְיוֹתָם בְּנוֹ עַל־
בֵּית הַמֶּלֶךְ שׁוֹפֵט אֶת־עַם
22 הָאָרֶץ׃ וְיֶתֶר דִּבְרֵי עֻזִּיָּהוּ
הָרִאשֹׁנִים וְהָאַחֲרֹנִים כָּתַב
יְשַׁעְיָהוּ בֶן־אָמוֹץ הַנָּבִיא׃
23 וַיִּשְׁכַּב עֻזִּיָּהוּ עִם־אֲבֹתָיו
וַיִּקְבְּרוּ אֹתוֹ עִם־אֲבֹתָיו
בִּשְׂדֵה הַקְּבוּרָה אֲשֶׁר
לַמְּלָכִים כִּי אָמְרוּ מְצוֹרָע
הוּא וַיִּמְלֹךְ יוֹתָם בְּנוֹ תַּחְתָּיו׃

v. 21. החפשית ק׳

20. *thrust him out quickly.* lit. 'hurried him,' leprosy being regarded as a defilement.

21-23 (corresponding, with variations, to 2 Kings xv. 5-7). The last days of Uzziah.

21. *a house set apart.* The meaning of the phrase is uncertain. Some scholars interpret it: 'in (his) house in freedom,' i.e. he was not compelled to live in isolation outside the community like an ordinary leper.

was over the king's house. On account of his leprosy, the king had to withdraw from the conduct of public affairs and his duties were undertaken by his son.

22. *first and last.* See on 1 Chron. xxix. 29.

did Isaiah . . . write. In 2 Kings xv. 6: *written in the book of the kings of Judah.* The only reference to Uzziah in the Book of Isaiah is vi. 1. The present verse suggests that the prophet wrote a history of the reign which has not been preserved.

23. *in the field of burial.* Not in the royal tombs, but in neighbouring ground. 2 Kings xv. 7 relates that *they buried him with his fathers in the city of David.*

he is a leper. Consequently, unfit to be interred in the tombs of the kings.

27 CHAPTER XXVII כז

1. Jotham was twenty and five years
old when he began to reign; and he
reigned sixteen years in Jerusalem;
and his mother's name was Jerushah
the daughter of Zadok. 2. And he
did that which was right in the eyes
of the LORD, according to all that his
father Uzziah had done; howbeit he
entered not into the temple of the
LORD. And the people did yet
corruptly. 3. He built the upper
gate of the house of the LORD, and
on the wall of Ophel he built much.
4. Moreover he built cities in the
hill-country of Judah, and in the
forests he built castles and towers.
5. He fought also with the king of
the children of Ammon, and prevailed against them. And the child-

1 בֶּן־עֶשְׂרִים וְחָמֵשׁ שָׁנָה יוֹתָם
בְּמָלְכוֹ וְשֵׁשׁ עֶשְׂרֵה שָׁנָה מָלַךְ
בִּירוּשָׁלִָם וְשֵׁם אִמּוֹ יְרוּשָׁה
2 בַּת־צָדוֹק׃ וַיַּעַשׂ הַיָּשָׁר
בְּעֵינֵי יְהוָה כְּכֹל אֲשֶׁר־עָשָׂה
עֻזִּיָּהוּ אָבִיו רַק לֹא־בָא אֶל־
הֵיכַל יְהוָה וְעוֹד הָעָם
3 מַשְׁחִיתִים׃ הוּא בָּנָה אֶת־
שַׁעַר בֵּית־יְהוָה הָעֶלְיוֹן
וּבְחוֹמַת הָעֹפֶל בָּנָה לָרֹב׃
4 וְעָרִים בָּנָה בְּהַר־יְהוּדָה
וּבֶחֳרָשִׁים בָּנָה בִּירָנִיּוֹת
5 וּמִגְדָּלִים׃ וְהוּא נִלְחַם עִם־
מֶלֶךְ בְּנֵי־עַמּוֹן וַיֶּחֱזַק עֲלֵיהֶם

CHAPTER XXVII

THE REIGN OF JOTHAM

THIS chapter corresponds, with variations and amplifications, to 2 Kings xv. 32-38.

1f. Jotham's character and reign (739-735 B.C.E.).

1. *he reigned sixteen years.* These years evidently include those of his regency in the lifetime of Uzziah (xxvi. 21). His independent rule lasted about five years.

2. *according to all that . . . Uzziah had done.* i.e. Uzziah's good deeds.

howbeit he entered not into the temple. To burn incense on the altar as Uzziah had done (xxvi. 16ff.). In 2 Kings xvi. 35 *howbeit* is followed by *the high places were not taken away.*

and the people did yet corruptly. In Kings: *the people still sacrificed and offered in the high places.*

3f. His building operations.

3. *he built the upper gate.* By *built* is meant work of restoration. For *the upper gate*, see on xxiii. 20.

on the wall of Ophel he built much. This adds to the information given in Kings. *Ophel* means 'swelling' and is the name applied to a spur on the southern side of the Temple mount.

4. This verse also gives additional information to the brief account of the reign in Kings.

5f. Jotham's military successes and power.

ren of Ammon gave him the same year a hundred talents of silver, and ten thousand measures of wheat, and ten thousand of barley. So much did the children of Ammon render unto him, in the second year also, and in the third. 6. So Jotham became mighty, because he ordered his ways before the LORD his God. 7. Now the rest of the acts of Jotham, and all his wars, and his ways, behold, they are written in the book of the kings of Israel and Judah. 8. He was five and twenty years old when he began to reign, and reigned sixteen years in Jerusalem. 9. And Jotham slept with his fathers, and they buried him in the city of David; and Ahaz his son reigned in his stead.

וַיִּתְּנוּ־לוֹ בְנֵי־עַמּוֹן בַּשָּׁנָה
הַהִיא מֵאָה כִּכַּר־כֶּסֶף
וַעֲשֶׂרֶת אֲלָפִים כֹּרִים חִטִּים
וּשְׂעוֹרִים עֲשֶׂרֶת אֲלָפִים זֹאת
הֵשִׁיבוּ לוֹ בְּנֵי עַמּוֹן וּבַשָּׁנָה
6 הַשֵּׁנִית וְהַשְּׁלִישִׁת׃ וַיִּתְחַזֵּק
יוֹתָם כִּי הֵכִין דְּרָכָיו לִפְנֵי
7 יְהוָה אֱלֹהָיו׃ וְיֶתֶר דִּבְרֵי
יוֹתָם וְכָל־מִלְחֲמֹתָיו וּדְרָכָיו
הִנָּם כְּתוּבִים עַל־סֵפֶר מַלְכֵי
8 יִשְׂרָאֵל וִיהוּדָה׃ בֶּן־עֶשְׂרִים
וְחָמֵשׁ שָׁנָה הָיָה בְמָלְכוֹ וְשֵׁשׁ־
עֶשְׂרֵה שָׁנָה מָלַךְ בִּירוּשָׁלִָם׃
9 וַיִּשְׁכַּב יוֹתָם עִם־אֲבֹתָיו
וַיִּקְבְּרוּ אֹתוֹ בְּעִיר דָּוִיד
וַיִּמְלֹךְ אָחָז בְּנוֹ תַּחְתָּיו׃

28 CHAPTER XXVIII כח

1. Ahaz was twenty years old when he began to reign; and he reigned sixteen years in Jerusalem; and he

1 בֶּן־עֶשְׂרִים שָׁנָה אָחָז בְמָלְכוֹ
וְשֵׁשׁ־עֶשְׂרֵה שָׁנָה מָלַךְ

5. *measures.* See on ii. 9.

6. *he ordered.* lit. 'he prepared.'

7-9 (corresponding to 2 Kings xv. 36, 38). Summary of the reign.

7. *his wars.* With the Ammonites (verse 5) and Aram and Israel (2 Kings xv. 37).

the kings of Israel and Judah. As usual Kings omits *Israel and.*

CHAPTER XXVIII

THE REIGN OF AHAZ

1-4 (corresponding to 2 Kings xvi. 2-4). Character of the reign which extended from 735 to 720 B.C.E.

1. *Ahaz.* In an inscription of Tiglath-pileser III the name is given as *Ja-u-ha-zi* which corresponds to the fuller Hebrew form *Jehoahaz.*

did not that which was right in the eyes of the LORD, like David his father; 2. but he walked in the ways of the kings of Israel, and made also molten images for the Baalim. 3. Moreover he offered in the valley of the son of Hinnom, and burnt his children in the fire, according to the abominations of the heathen, whom the LORD cast out before the children of Israel. 4. And he sacrificed and offered in the high places, and on the hills, and under every leafy tree. 5. Wherefore the LORD his God delivered him into the hand of the king of Aram; and they smote him, and carried away of his a great multitude of captives, and brought them to Damascus. And he was also delivered into the hand of the king of Israel, who smote him with a great slaughter. 6. For Pekah the son of Remaliah slew in Judah a

בִּירוּשָׁלִָם וְלֹא־עָשָׂה הַיָּשָׁר
בְּעֵינֵי יְהוָה כְּדָוִיד אָבִיו׃
2 וַיֵּלֶךְ בְּדַרְכֵי מַלְכֵי יִשְׂרָאֵל
וְגַם מַסֵּכוֹת עָשָׂה לַבְּעָלִים׃
3 וְהוּא הִקְטִיר בְּגֵיא בֶן־הִנֹּם
וַיַּבְעֵר אֶת־בָּנָיו בָּאֵשׁ
כְּתֹעֲבוֹת הַגּוֹיִם אֲשֶׁר הֹרִישׁ
4 יְהוָה מִפְּנֵי בְּנֵי יִשְׂרָאֵל׃ וַיְזַבֵּחַ
וַיְקַטֵּר בַּבָּמוֹת וְעַל־הַגְּבָעוֹת
5 וְתַחַת כָּל־עֵץ רַעֲנָן׃ וַיִּתְּנֵהוּ
יְהוָה אֱלֹהָיו בְּיַד מֶלֶךְ אֲרָם
וַיַּכּוּ־בוֹ וַיִּשְׁבּוּ מִמֶּנּוּ שִׁבְיָה
גְדוֹלָה וַיָּבִיאוּ דַּרְמָשֶׂק וְגַם
בְּיַד־מֶלֶךְ יִשְׂרָאֵל נִתָּן וַיַּךְ־
6 בּוֹ מַכָּה גְדוֹלָה׃ וַיַּהֲרֹג פֶּקַח
בֶּן־רְמַלְיָהוּ בִּיהוּדָה מֵאָה

קמץ בז״ק v. 5.

3. *the valley of the son of Hinnom.* The Hebrew *Ge-ben-hinnom* was later shortened to *Ge-hinnom* from which 'Gehenna' (the place of punishment of the wicked in the Hereafter) is derived. The valley (and the name) gained odium from the abominable religious rites associated with human sacrifices which were practised there. It lies to the south-west of Jerusalem.

burnt his children in the fire. This amplifies 2 Kings xvi. 3 which states that he *made his son to pass through the fire.* Since his son Hezekiah lived to succeed him, a Talmudical legend (Sanh. 63b) relates that Hezekiah's mother smeared his body with the blood of the salamander, and the fire did not consume him.

4. *and he sacrificed.* He not only allowed his people to indulge in idol-worship, as some of his predecessors had done, but he was guilty of it personally.

5-7 (cf. 2 Kings xvi. 5-9; Isa. vii. 1-9). Invasion of Judah by Aram and Israel. The present account supplements that of Kings which deals with an earlier stage in the campaign, when the kings of Aram and Israel made a joint attack on Jerusalem but failed to take it.

5. Ahaz is delivered into the hands of the two kings who inflict upon him severe punishment. This was probably the second phase of the campaign.

the king of Aram. viz. Rezin who is named in 2 Kings xvi. 5f.

the king of Israel. viz. Pekah who is also named in 2 Kings xvi. 5.

hundred and twenty thousand in one day, all of them valiant men; because they had forsaken the LORD, the God of their fathers. 7. And Zichri, a mighty man of Ephraim, slew Maaseiah the king's son, and Azrikam the ruler of the house, and Elkanah that was next to the king. 8. And the children of Israel carried away captive of their brethren two hundred thousand women, sons, and daughters, and took also away much spoil from them, and brought the spoil to Samaria.

9. But a prophet of the LORD was there, whose name was Oded; and he went out to meet the host that came to Samaria, and said unto them: 'Behold, because the LORD, the God of your fathers, was wroth with Judah, He hath delivered them into your hand, and ye have slain them in a rage which hath reached up unto heaven. 10. And now ye purpose to bring the children of

וְעֶשְׂרִים אֶלֶף בְּיוֹם אֶחָד הַכֹּל
בְּנֵי־חָיִל בְּעָזְבָם אֶת־יְהוָה
7 אֱלֹהֵי אֲבוֹתָם׃ וַיַּהֲרֹג זִכְרִי ׀
גִּבּוֹר אֶפְרַיִם אֶת־מַעֲשֵׂיָהוּ
בֶּן־הַמֶּלֶךְ וְאֶת־עַזְרִיקָם נְגִיד
הַבָּיִת וְאֶת־אֶלְקָנָה מִשְׁנֵה
8 הַמֶּלֶךְ׃ וַיִּשְׁבּוּ בְנֵי־יִשְׂרָאֵל
מֵאֲחֵיהֶם מָאתַיִם אֶלֶף נָשִׁים
בָּנִים וּבָנוֹת וְגַם־שָׁלָל רָב
בָּזְזוּ מֵהֶם וַיָּבִיאוּ אֶת־הַשָּׁלָל
לְשֹׁמְרוֹן׃
9 וְשָׁם הָיָה ׀ נָבִיא לַיהוָה עֹדֵד
שְׁמוֹ וַיֵּצֵא לִפְנֵי הַצָּבָא הַבָּא
לְשֹׁמְרוֹן וַיֹּאמֶר לָהֶם הִנֵּה
בַּחֲמַת יְהוָה אֱלֹהֵי־אֲבוֹתֵיכֶם
עַל־יְהוּדָה נְתָנָם בְּיֶדְכֶם
וַתַּהַרְגוּ־בָם בְּזַעַף עַד
10 לַשָּׁמַיִם הִגִּיעַ׃ וְעַתָּה בְּנֵי־

7. *ruler of the house.* The overseer of the royal household.

8-15 (no parallel in Kings). The capture and subsequent return of 200,000 of the population of Judah. A similar act of consideration to captives is recorded in 2 Kings vi. 21ff.

8. *women, sons, and daughters.* The men had been slain (verse 9).

9. *Oded.* All that is known of him is the account in this passage. He is, of course, not identical with *Oded* mentioned in xv. 8.

because the LORD . . . wroth with Judah. Better, 'on account of the wrath of the LORD, the God of your fathers against Judah.' Divine anger at the apostasy of Judah, not the power or merit of Israel, was the reason that the Israelite force had been victorious.

unto heaven. A hyperbole, expressing the vehemence of the rage. Others regard *heaven* as a reverential substitute for God Whose name must not be taken in vain, a circumlocution which is common in later Jewish literature.

10. *ye purpose.* lit. 'ye say.'

Judah and Jerusalem into subjection for bondmen and bondwomen unto you; but are there not even with you acts of guilt of your own against the LORD your God? 11. Now hear me therefore, and send back the captives, that ye have taken captive of your brethren; for the fierce wrath of the LORD is upon you.' 12. Then certain of the heads of the children of Ephraim, Azariah the son of Jehohanan, Berechiah the son of Meshillemoth, and Jehizkiah the son of Shallum, and Amasa the son of Hadlai, stood up against them that came from the war, 13. and said unto them: 'Ye shall not bring in the captives hither; for ye purpose that which will bring upon us guilt against the LORD, to add unto our sins and to our guilt; for our guilt is great, and there is fierce wrath against Israel.' 14. So the armed men left the captives and the spoil before the princes and all the congregation. 15. And the men that have been mentioned by name rose

יְהוּדָה וִירוּשָׁלִַם אַתֶּם אֹמְרִים
לִכְבֹּשׁ לַעֲבָדִים וְלִשְׁפָחוֹת
לָכֶם הֲלֹא רַק־אַתֶּם עִמָּכֶם
אֲשָׁמוֹת לַיהוָה אֱלֹהֵיכֶם׃
וְעַתָּה שְׁמָעוּנִי וְהָשִׁיבוּ הַשִּׁבְיָה 11
אֲשֶׁר שְׁבִיתֶם מֵאֲחֵיכֶם כִּי
חֲרוֹן אַף־יְהוָה עֲלֵיכֶם׃
וַיָּקֻמוּ אֲנָשִׁים מֵרָאשֵׁי בְנֵי־ 12
אֶפְרַיִם עֲזַרְיָהוּ בֶן־יְהוֹחָנָן
בֶּרֶכְיָהוּ בֶן־מְשִׁלֵּמוֹת
וִיחִזְקִיָּהוּ בֶּן־שַׁלֻּם וַעֲמָשָׂא
בֶּן־חַדְלָי עַל־הַבָּאִים מִן־
הַצָּבָא׃ וַיֹּאמְרוּ לָהֶם לֹא־ 13
תָבִיאוּ אֶת־הַשִּׁבְיָה הֵנָּה כִּי
לְאַשְׁמַת יְהוָה עָלֵינוּ אַתֶּם
אֹמְרִים לְהֹסִיף עַל־חַטֹּאתֵנוּ
וְעַל־אַשְׁמָתֵנוּ כִּי־רַבָּה
אַשְׁמָה לָנוּ וַחֲרוֹן אָף עַל־
יִשְׂרָאֵל׃ וַיַּעֲזֹב הֶחָלוּץ אֶת־ 14
הַשִּׁבְיָה וְאֶת־הַבִּזָּה לִפְנֵי
הַשָּׂרִים וְכָל־הַקָּהָל׃ וַיָּקֻמוּ 15
הָאֲנָשִׁים אֲשֶׁר־נִקְּבוּ בְשֵׁמוֹת

v. 13. קמץ בטפחא

even with you. The *you* is strongly emphasized in the text. The men of Israel are guilty of sins which make them also liable to God's punishment; the retention of the Judean captives will add to their iniquities and bring down upon them dire punishment.

12. *certain.* lit. 'men.'

stood up against. To oppose the suggestion to keep the captives.

13. *ye purpose . . . the LORD.* lit. 'for guilt against the Lord upon us ye speak.'

15. *the men that have been mentioned.* In verse 12.

up, and took the captives, and with the spoil clothed all that were naked among them, and arrayed them, and shod them, and gave them to eat and to drink, and anointed them, and carried all the feeble of them upon asses, and brought them to Jericho, the city of palm-trees, unto their brethren; then they returned to Samaria.

16. At that time did king Ahaz send unto the kings of Assyria to help him. 17. For again the Edomites had come and smitten Judah, and carried away captives. 18. The Philistines also had invaded the cities of the Lowland, and of the South of Judah, and had taken Beth-shemesh, and Aijalon, and Gederoth,

וַיַּחֲזִיקוּ בַשִּׁבְיָה וְכָל־
מַעֲרֻמֵּיהֶם הִלְבִּישׁוּ מִן־
הַשָּׁלָל וַיַּלְבִּשׁוּם וַיַּנְעִלוּם
וַיַּאֲכִלוּם וַיַּשְׁקוּם וַיְסֻכוּם
וַיְנַהֲלוּם בַּחֲמֹרִים לְכָל־
כּוֹשֵׁל וַיְבִיאוּם יְרֵחוֹ עִיר־
הַתְּמָרִים אֵצֶל אֲחֵיהֶם וַיָּשׁוּבוּ
שֹׁמְרוֹן׃
16 בָּעֵת הַהִיא שָׁלַח הַמֶּלֶךְ אָחָז
עַל־מַלְכֵי אַשּׁוּר לַעְזֹר לוֹ׃
17 וְעוֹד אֲדוֹמִים בָּאוּ וַיַּכּוּ
בִיהוּדָה וַיִּשְׁבּוּ־שֶׁבִי׃
18 וּפְלִשְׁתִּים פָּשְׁטוּ בְּעָרֵי
הַשְּׁפֵלָה וְהַנֶּגֶב לִיהוּדָה
וַיִּלְכְּדוּ אֶת־בֵּית־שֶׁמֶשׁ וְאֶת־
אַיָּלוֹן וְאֶת־הַגְּדֵרוֹת וְאֶת־

took the captives. Under their protection.

that were naked among them. lit. 'their nakedness.'

anointed them. With perfumed oil, used in the East as a protection to the skin from the heat of the sun.

Jericho. Near the frontier of the two kingdoms.

the city of palm-trees. Jericho is so described in Deut. xxxiv. 3; Judg. i. 16, iii. 13.

unto their brethren. lit. 'near' their brethren in the Southern Kingdom.

16-21 (corresponding, with amplifications, to 2 Kings xvi. 7-9). Ahaz appeals to Assyria for help.

16. *at that time.* When attacked by Aram and Israel.

the kings of Assyria. In 2 Kings xvi. 7 Tiglath-pileser (III) is named.

17f. Additional to the account in Kings.

17. *again the Edomites had come.* For the first occasion, cf. xxi. 8ff. Others render the Hebrew for *again* as 'besides,' i.e. in addition to the enemies mentioned in verses 5ff. the Edomites made an attack.

18. *invaded.* Better, 'raided.'

Beth-shemesh. See on 1 Chron. vi. 44.

Aijalon. See on xi. 10.

Gederoth. South-west of Jabneh (see on xxvi. 6), the modern Ghedera.

and Soco with the towns thereof, and Timnah with the towns thereof, Gimzo also and the towns thereof; and they dwelt there. 19. For the LORD brought Judah low because of Ahaz king of Israel; for he had cast away restraint in Judah, and acted treacherously against the LORD. 20. And Tillegath-pilneser king of Assyria came unto him, and distressed him, but strengthened him not. 21. For Ahaz stripped the house of the LORD, and the house of the king and the princes, and gave thereof unto the king of Assyria; but it helped him not.

22. And in the time of his distress did he act even more treacherously against the LORD, this same king Ahaz. 23. For he sacrificed unto the gods of Damascus, which smote

שׂוֹכוֹ וּבְנוֹתֶיהָ וְאֶת־תִּמְנָה
וְאֶת־בְּנוֹתֶיהָ וְאֶת־גִּמְזוֹ וְאֶת־
בְּנוֹתֶיהָ וַיֵּשְׁבוּ שָׁם׃ כִּי־ 19
הִכְנִיעַ יְהוָה אֶת־יְהוּדָה
בַּעֲבוּר אָחָז מֶלֶךְ־יִשְׂרָאֵל
כִּי הִפְרִיעַ בִּיהוּדָה וּמָעוֹל
מַעַל בַּיהוָה׃ וַיָּבֹא עָלָיו 20
תִּלְּגַת פִּלְנְאֶסֶר מֶלֶךְ אַשּׁוּר
וַיָּצַר לוֹ וְלֹא חֲזָקוֹ׃ כִּי־חָלַק 21
אָחָז אֶת־בֵּית יְהוָה וְאֶת־בֵּית
הַמֶּלֶךְ וְהַשָּׂרִים וַיִּתֵּן לְמֶלֶךְ
אַשּׁוּר וְלֹא לְעֶזְרָה לוֹ׃
וּבְעֵת הָצֵר לוֹ וַיּוֹסֶף לִמְעוֹל 22
בַּיהוָה הוּא הַמֶּלֶךְ אָחָז׃
וַיִּזְבַּח לֵאלֹהֵי דַּרְמֶשֶׂק 23

Soco. See on xi. 7.

Timnah. The modern Tilneh or Tibneh, fifteen miles south-west of Jerusalem.

Gimzo. Now called Jimzu, three miles south-east of Lydda.

19. *king of Israel.* A synonym here of Judah.

cast away restraint. In idolatrous worship.

20. *Tillegath-pilneser.* In 1 Chron. v. 6 the form of the name is *Tillegath-pilneser*, in Kings it is *Tiglath-pileser*.

came unto him. lit. 'upon him,' i.e. with hostile intent.

but strengthened him not. The Assyrian king, invited by Ahaz, came ostensibly to help Judah, but in fact helped himself. According to the Assyrian monuments, he captured and depopulated Galilee in 733 B.C.E., entered Damascus in the following year and in 722 also subdued Samaria.

21. *but it helped him not.* lit. 'but not for help to him.' Although the capture of Damascus and the execution of the Syrian king (2 Kings xvi. 9) reduced the pressure and removed the danger from Ahaz and his country, the Assyrian expedition was of no real help to him.

22-25 (cf. 2 Kings xvi. 10-18). Apostasy of Ahaz and the spread of idolatry in his kingdom.

22. *his distress.* lit. 'distressing to him' (cf. verses 20, 23).

23. *he sacrificed unto the gods of Damascus.* In 2 Kings xvi. 10f. it is stated that an altar was made on the instruction of Ahaz after the pattern of one which he

him; and he said: 'Because the gods
of the kings of Aram helped them,
therefore will I sacrifice to them,
that they may help me.' But they
were the ruin of him, and of all
Israel. 24. And Ahaz gathered
together the vessels of the house of
God, and cut in pieces the vessels of
the house of God, and shut up the
doors of the house of the LORD; and
he made him altars in every corner
of Jerusalem. 25. And in every
city of Judah he made high places to
offer unto other gods, and provoked
the LORD, the God of his fathers.
26. Now the rest of his acts, and all
his ways, first and last, behold, they
are written in the book of the kings
of Judah and Israel. 27. And Ahaz
slept with his fathers, and they
buried him in the city, even in

הַמַּכִּים בּוֹ וַיֹּאמֶר כִּי אֱלֹהֵי
מַלְכֵי־אֲרָם הֵם מַעְזְרִים
אוֹתָם לָהֶם אֲזַבֵּחַ וְיַעְזְרוּנִי
וְהֵם הָיוּ־לוֹ לְהַכְשִׁילוֹ
24 וּלְכָל־יִשְׂרָאֵל׃ וַיֶּאֱסֹף אָחָז
אֶת־כְּלֵי בֵית־הָאֱלֹהִים
וַיְקַצֵּץ אֶת־כְּלֵי בֵית־
הָאֱלֹהִים וַיִּסְגֹּר אֶת־דַּלְתוֹת
בֵּית־יְהוָה וַיַּעַשׂ לוֹ מִזְבְּחוֹת
בְּכָל־פִּנָּה בִּירוּשָׁלִָם׃
25 וּבְכָל־עִיר וָעִיר לִיהוּדָה
עָשָׂה בָמוֹת לְקַטֵּר לֵאלֹהִים
אֲחֵרִים וַיַּכְעֵס אֶת־יְהוָה
26 אֱלֹהֵי אֲבֹתָיו׃ וְיֶתֶר דְּבָרָיו
וְכָל־דְּרָכָיו הָרִאשֹׁנִים
וְהָאַחֲרוֹנִים הִנָּם כְּתוּבִים
עַל־סֵפֶר מַלְכֵי יְהוּדָה
27 וְיִשְׂרָאֵל׃ וַיִּשְׁכַּב אָחָז עִם־
אֲבֹתָיו וַיִּקְבְּרֻהוּ בָעִיר

had seen in Damascus and he offered sacrifices upon it.

the gods of the kings of Aram. By *Aram* Assyria must be intended, since at that time (732 B.C.E.) Aram was conquered by Tiglath-pileser (cf. 2 Kings xvi. 9).

24. *cut in pieces.* The same Hebrew verb is translated *cut off* in 2 Kings xvi. 17 and is followed by *the borders of the bases* instead of *the vessels of the house of God.* Additional details in Kings are that he *removed the laver . . . took down the sea from off the brazen oxen and put it upon a pavement of stone.*

shut up the doors, etc. He stopped the ritual of the Temple by closing the doors, which were reopened by his son xxix. 3). He suppressed the worship of God in favour of the Assyrian cult, not only in the Temple, but throughout Jerusalem.

26f. (corresponding, with variations, to 2 Kings xvi. 19f.). The end of the reign of Ahaz and Hezekiah's succession.

26. *first and last.* See on 1 Chron. xxix. 29.

Jerusalem; for they brought him not into the sepulchres of the kings of Israel; and Hezekiah his son reigned in his stead.

בִּירוּשָׁלַ͏ִם כִּי לֹא הֱבִיאֻהוּ
לְקִבְרֵי מַלְכֵי יִשְׂרָאֵל וַיִּמְלֹךְ
יְחִזְקִיָּהוּ בְּנוֹ תַּחְתָּיו׃

29 CHAPTER XXIX כט

1. Hezekiah began to reign when he was five and twenty years old; and he reigned nine and twenty years in Jerusalem; and his mother's name was Abijah the daughter of Zechariah. 2. And he did that which was right in the eyes of the LORD, according to all that David his father had done. 3. He in the first year of his reign, in the first month, opened the doors of the house of the LORD, and repaired them. 4. And he brought in the priests and the Levites, and gathered them together into the broad place

1 יְחִזְקִיָּהוּ מָלַךְ בֶּן־עֶשְׂרִים
וְחָמֵשׁ שָׁנָה וְעֶשְׂרִים וָתֵשַׁע
שָׁנָה מָלַךְ בִּירוּשָׁלָ͏ִם וְשֵׁם אִמּוֹ
2 אֲבִיָּה בַּת־זְכַרְיָהוּ׃ וַיַּעַשׂ
הַיָּשָׁר בְּעֵינֵי יְהוָה כְּכֹל אֲשֶׁר־
3 עָשָׂה דָּוִיד אָבִיו׃ הוּא בַשָּׁנָה
הָרִאשׁוֹנָה לְמָלְכוֹ בַּחֹדֶשׁ
הָרִאשׁוֹן פָּתַח אֶת־דַּלְתוֹת
4 בֵּית־יְהוָה וַיְחַזְּקֵם׃ וַיָּבֵא
אֶת־הַכֹּהֲנִים וְאֶת־הַלְוִיִּם
וַיַּאַסְפֵם לִרְחוֹב הַמִּזְרָח׃

27. *they brought him not . . . kings of Israel.* The statement in 2 Kings xvi. 20 that he *was buried with his fathers* must mean 'in the same city' and not in the same sepulchre.

the kings of Israel. Not 'of Judah' because David and Solomon had reigned over the whole land.

CHAPTERS XXIX-XXXII

THE REIGN OF HEZEKIAH

CHAPTER XXIX

1f. (corresponding to 2 Kings xviii. 1-3). Hezekiah's accession to the throne and his piety. The years of his reign were 720-692 B.C.E.

1. *Hezekiah.* In Chron. the Hebrew form of the name is *Yechizkiyyahu*, in Kings *Chizkiyyah.*

Abijah. In 2 Kings xviii. 2: *Abi.*

3-11 (not in Kings). Hezekiah reopens the Temple and instructs the priests and Levites.

3. *the first month.* Of the year following his enthronement, Nisan.

opened the doors. Which his father had shut (xxviii. 24).

4. *the priests and the Levites.* The latter were entrusted with the greater part of the work, the former being employed on cleansing *the inner part of the house* (verse 16) and offering the sacrifices (verses 22ff.).

the broad place of the east. The open

on the east; 5. and said unto them: 'Hear me, ye Levites: now sanctify yourselves, and sanctify the house of the LORD, the God of your fathers, and carry forth the filthiness out of the holy place. 6. For our fathers have acted treacherously, and done that which was evil in the sight of the LORD our God, and have forsaken Him, and have turned away their faces from the habitation of the LORD, and turned their backs. 7. Also they have shut up the doors of the porch, and put out the lamps, and have not burned incense nor offered burnt-offerings in the holy place unto the God of Israel. 8. Wherefore the wrath of the LORD was upon Judah and Jerusalem, and He hath delivered them to be a horror, an astonishment, and a hissing, as ye see with your eyes. 9. For, lo, our fathers have fallen by the sword, and our sons and our daughters and our wives are in captivity for this. 10. Now it is in my heart to make a covenant with the LORD, the God of Israel, that His fierce anger may turn away from us.

5 וַיֹּאמֶר לָהֶם שְׁמָעוּנִי הַלְוִיִּם
עַתָּה הִתְקַדְּשׁוּ וְקַדְּשׁוּ אֶת־
בֵּית יְהוָה אֱלֹהֵי אֲבוֹתֵיכֶם
וְהוֹצִיאוּ אֶת־הַנִּדָּה מִן־
6 הַקֹּדֶשׁ: כִּי־מָעֲלוּ אֲבֹתֵינוּ
וְעָשׂוּ הָרַע בְּעֵינֵי יְהוָה־
אֱלֹהֵינוּ וַיַּעַזְבֻהוּ וַיַּסֵּבּוּ פְנֵיהֶם
7 מִמִּשְׁכַּן יְהוָה וַיִּתְּנוּ־עֹרֶף: גַּם
סָגְרוּ דַּלְתוֹת הָאוּלָם וַיְכַבּוּ
אֶת־הַנֵּרוֹת וּקְטֹרֶת לֹא
הִקְטִירוּ וְעֹלָה לֹא־הֶעֱלוּ
8 בַקֹּדֶשׁ לֵאלֹהֵי יִשְׂרָאֵל: וַיְהִי
קֶצֶף יְהוָה עַל־יְהוּדָה
וִירוּשָׁלִָם וַיִּתְּנֵם לְזַעֲוָה לְשַׁמָּה
וְלִשְׁרֵקָה כַּאֲשֶׁר אַתֶּם רֹאִים
9 בְּעֵינֵיכֶם: וְהִנֵּה נָפְלוּ
אֲבוֹתֵינוּ בֶּחָרֶב וּבָנֵינוּ
וּבְנוֹתֵינוּ וְנָשֵׁינוּ בַּשְּׁבִי עַל־
10 זֹאת: עַתָּה עִם־לְבָבִי
לִכְרוֹת בְּרִית לַיהוָה אֱלֹהֵי
יִשְׂרָאֵל וְיָשֹׁב מִמֶּנּוּ חֲרוֹן אַפּוֹ:

v. 8. לזועה ק׳

space on the eastern side of the Temple area.

5. *the filthiness.* The dirt which had accumulated in the unused Temple. Some commentators understand the noun as figurative of idolatrous images.

6. *our fathers.* The generation of Ahaz.

turned their backs. lit. 'gave neck,' an expression for apostasy.

7. *the doors of the porch.* The outer doors of the Temple.

the lamps, etc. Cf. xiii. 11.

8. *wrath . . . horror.* An allusion to the disasters which overwhelmed the people in the reign of Ahaz.

10. *a covenant.* Such as was entered into during the reign of Asa (xv. 12).

11. My sons, be not now negligent;
for the LORD hath chosen you to
stand before Him, to minister unto
Him, and that ye should be His
ministers, and offer unto Him.'

12. Then the Levites arose,
Mahath the son of Amasai, and Joel
the son of Azariah, of the sons of
the Kohathites; and of the sons of
Merari, Kish the son of Abdi, and
Azariah the son of Jehallelel; and of
the Gershonites, Joah the son of
Zimmah, and Eden the son of Joah;
13. and of the sons of Elizaphan,
Shimri and Jeiel; and of the sons of
Asaph, Zechariah and Mattaniah;
14. and of the sons of Heman, Jehiel
and Shimei; and of the sons of
Jeduthun, Shemaiah and Uzziel.
15. And they gathered their brethren, and sanctified themselves, and
went in, according to the commandment of the king by the words of
the LORD, to cleanse the house of
the LORD. 16. And the priests went
in unto the inner part of the house
of the LORD, to cleanse it, and
brought out all the uncleanness that
they found in the temple of the
LORD into the court of the house of
the LORD. And the Levites took it,
to carry it out abroad to the brook

בָּנַי עַתָּה אַל־תִּשָּׁלוּ כִּי־בָכֶם 11
בָּחַר יְהֹוָה לַעֲמֹד לְפָנָיו
לְשָׁרְתוֹ וְלִהְיוֹת לוֹ מְשָׁרְתִים
וּמַקְטִרִים׃
וַיָּקֻמוּ הַלְוִיִּם מַחַת בֶּן־עֲמָשַׂי 12
וְיוֹאֵל בֶּן־עֲזַרְיָהוּ מִן־בְּנֵי
הַקְּהָתִי וּמִן־בְּנֵי מְרָרִי קִישׁ
בֶּן־עַבְדִּי וַעֲזַרְיָהוּ בֶּן־
יְהַלֶּלְאֵל וּמִן־הַגֵּרְשֻׁנִּי יוֹאָח
בֶּן־זִמָּה וְעֵדֶן בֶּן־יוֹאָח׃ וּמִן־ 13
בְּנֵי אֱלִיצָפָן שִׁמְרִי וִיעוּאֵל
וּמִן־בְּנֵי אָסָף זְכַרְיָהוּ
וּמַתַּנְיָהוּ׃ וּמִן־בְּנֵי הֵימָן 14
יְחוּאֵל וְשִׁמְעִי וּמִן־בְּנֵי יְדוּתוּן
שְׁמַעְיָה וְעֻזִּיאֵל׃ וַיַּאַסְפוּ 15
אֶת־אֲחֵיהֶם וַיִּתְקַדְּשׁוּ וַיָּבֹאוּ
כְמִצְוַת־הַמֶּלֶךְ בְּדִבְרֵי יְהֹוָה
לְטַהֵר בֵּית יְהֹוָה׃ וַיָּבֹאוּ 16
הַכֹּהֲנִים לִפְנִימָה בֵית־יְהֹוָה
לְטַהֵר וַיּוֹצִיאוּ אֵת כָּל־
הַטֻּמְאָה אֲשֶׁר מָצְאוּ בְּהֵיכַל
יְהֹוָה לַחֲצַר בֵּית יְהֹוָה וַיְקַבְּלוּ
הַלְוִיִּם לְהוֹצִיא לְנַחַל־

v. 11. מלרע v. 13. ויעיאל ק׳ v. 14. יחיאל ק׳

11. *to stand before Him.* As stated in Deut. x. 8.

12-19 (not in Kings). The cleansing of the Temple.

15. *went in.* Into the Temple.

by the words of the LORD. The king's directions were in accord with the command of God.

Kidron. 17. Now they began on the first day of the first month to sanctify, and on the eighth day of the month came they to the porch of the LORD; and they sanctified the house of the LORD in eight days; and on the sixteenth day of the first month they made an end. 18. Then they went in to Hezekiah the king within [the palace], and said: 'We have cleansed all the house of the LORD, even the altar of burnt-offering, with all the vessels thereof, and the table of showbread, with all the vessels thereof. 19. Moreover all the vessels, which king Ahaz in his reign did cast away when he acted treacherously, have we prepared and sanctified; and, behold, they are before the altar of the LORD.'

20. Then Hezekiah the king arose early, and gathered the princes of the city, and went up to the house of the LORD. 21. And they brought seven bullocks, and seven rams, and seven lambs, and seven he-goats, for a sin-offering for the kingdom and for the

17 קִדְרוֹן חוּצָה׃ וַיָּחֵלּוּ בְּאֶחָד
לַחֹדֶשׁ הָרִאשׁוֹן לְקַדֵּשׁ וּבְיוֹם
שְׁמוֹנָה לַחֹדֶשׁ בָּאוּ לְאוּלָם
יְהוָה וַיְקַדְּשׁוּ אֶת־בֵּית־יְהוָה
לְיָמִים שְׁמוֹנָה וּבְיוֹם שִׁשָּׁה
עָשָׂר לַחֹדֶשׁ הָרִאשׁוֹן כִּלּוּ׃
18 וַיָּבוֹאוּ פְנִימָה אֶל־חִזְקִיָּהוּ
הַמֶּלֶךְ וַיֹּאמְרוּ טִהַרְנוּ אֶת־
כָּל־בֵּית יְהוָה וְאֶת־מִזְבַּח
הָעוֹלָה וְאֶת־כָּל־כֵּלָיו וְאֶת־
שֻׁלְחַן הַמַּעֲרֶכֶת וְאֶת־כָּל־
19 כֵּלָיו׃ וְאֵת כָּל־הַכֵּלִים אֲשֶׁר
הִזְנִיחַ הַמֶּלֶךְ אָחָז בְּמַלְכוּתוֹ
בְּמַעֲלוֹ הֵכַנּוּ וְהִקְדָּשְׁנוּ וְהִנָּם
לִפְנֵי מִזְבַּח יְהוָה׃
20 וַיַּשְׁכֵּם יְחִזְקִיָּהוּ הַמֶּלֶךְ וַיֶּאֱסֹף
אֵת שָׂרֵי הָעִיר וַיַּעַל בֵּית
21 יְהוָה׃ וַיָּבִיאוּ פָרִים־שִׁבְעָה
וְאֵילִים שִׁבְעָה וּכְבָשִׂים
שִׁבְעָה וּצְפִירֵי עִזִּים שִׁבְעָה
לְחַטָּאת עַל־הַמַּמְלָכָה וְעַל־

16. *the brook Kidron.* See on xv. 16.

17. Clearing out the defilement occupied eight days, and a similar period was spent in cleansing the Temple, the work being completed on the sixteenth day of the month.

20-30 (not in Kings). Rededication of the Temple with sacrifices, music and song.

20-24. The burnt- and sin-offerings.

21. *they brought seven bullocks,* etc. The bullocks, rams and lambs were sacrificed as burnt-offerings, the goats as sin-offerings.

the kingdom. The royal household.

the sanctuary. The Temple and its ministers.

sanctuary and for Judah. And he
commanded the priests the sons of
Aaron to offer them on the altar of
the LORD. 22. So they killed the
bullocks, and the priests received
the blood, and dashed it against the
altar; and they killed the rams, and
dashed the blood against the altar;
they killed also the lambs, and
dashed the blood against the altar.
23. And they brought near the he-
goats for the sin-offering before the
king and the congregation, and they
laid their hands upon them; 24. and
the priests killed them, and they
made a sin-offering with their blood
upon the altar, to make atonement
for all Israel; for the king commanded that the burnt-offering and
the sin-offering should be made for
all Israel.

25. And he set the Levites in the
house of the LORD with cymbals,
with psalteries, and with harps,
according to the commandment of
David, and of Gad the king's seer,
and Nathan the prophet; for the
commandment was of the LORD by
His prophets. 26. And the Levites

הַמִּקְדָּשׁ וְעַל־יְהוּדָה וַיֹּאמֶר
לִבְנֵי אַהֲרֹן הַכֹּהֲנִים לְהַעֲלוֹת
22 עַל־מִזְבַּח יְהוָה׃ וַיִּשְׁחֲטוּ
הַבָּקָר וַיְקַבְּלוּ הַכֹּהֲנִים אֶת־
הַדָּם וַיִּזְרְקוּ הַמִּזְבֵּחָה וַיִּשְׁחֲטוּ
הָאֵלִים וַיִּזְרְקוּ הַדָּם הַמִּזְבֵּחָה
וַיִּשְׁחֲטוּ הַכְּבָשִׂים וַיִּזְרְקוּ הַדָּם
23 הַמִּזְבֵּחָה׃ וַיַּגִּישׁוּ אֶת־שְׂעִירֵי
הַחַטָּאת לִפְנֵי הַמֶּלֶךְ וְהַקָּהָל
וַיִּסְמְכוּ יְדֵיהֶם עֲלֵיהֶם׃
24 וַיִּשְׁחָטוּם הַכֹּהֲנִים וַיְחַטְּאוּ
אֶת־דָּמָם הַמִּזְבֵּחָה לְכַפֵּר
עַל־כָּל־יִשְׂרָאֵל כִּי לְכָל־
יִשְׂרָאֵל אָמַר הַמֶּלֶךְ הָעוֹלָה
וְהַחַטָּאת׃
25 וַיַּעֲמֵד אֶת־הַלְוִיִּם בֵּית יְהוָה
בִּמְצִלְתַּיִם בִּנְבָלִים וּבְכִנֹּרוֹת
בְּמִצְוַת דָּוִיד וְגָד חֹזֵה־הַמֶּלֶךְ
וְנָתָן הַנָּבִיא כִּי בְיַד־יְהוָה
26 הַמִּצְוָה בְּיַד־נְבִיאָיו׃ וַיַּעַמְדוּ

Judah. The rest of the people.

22. *received the blood.* In basins; the ritual of the burnt-offering is described in Lev. i. 11ff.

23. *laid their hands upon them.* Cf. Lev. iv. 15.

24. *should be made.* Not in the text.

25-30. Instrumental and vocal music accompanies the service of rededication.

25. *commandment of David.* Cf. 1 Chron. xv. 16 which states that David made the musical arrangements for the Temple, and it may be assumed that he consulted the two contemporary prophets on the matter.

was of the LORD. lit. 'by the hand of the Lord,' i.e. the commandment given by the prophets with regard to the music was Divinely inspired.

stood with the instruments of David,
and the priests with the trumpets.
27. And Hezekiah commanded to
offer the burnt-offering upon the
altar. And when the burnt-offering
began, the song of the LORD began
also, and the trumpets, together with
the instruments of David king of
Israel. 28. And all the congregation
prostrated themselves, and the
singers sang, and the trumpeters
sounded; all this continued until the
burnt-offering was finished. 29. And
when they had made an end of
offering, the king and all that were
present with him bowed themselves
and prostrated themselves.
30. Moreover Hezekiah the king and
the princes commanded the Levites
to sing praises unto the LORD with
the words of David, and of Asaph
the seer. And they sang praises
with gladness, and they bowed their
heads and prostrated themselves.

31. Then Hezekiah answered and
said: 'Now ye have consecrated
yourselves unto the LORD, come
near and bring sacrifices and thank-
offerings into the house of the LORD.'

הַלְוִיִּם בִּכְלֵי דָוִיד וְהַכֹּהֲנִים
27 בַּחֲצֹצְרוֹת׃ וַיֹּאמֶר חִזְקִיָּהוּ
לְהַעֲלוֹת הָעֹלָה לְהַמִּזְבֵּחַ
וּבְעֵת הֵחֵל הָעוֹלָה הֵחֵל
שִׁיר־יְהוָה וְהַחֲצֹצְרוֹת וְעַל־
יְדֵי כְּלֵי דָוִיד מֶלֶךְ יִשְׂרָאֵל׃
28 וְכָל־הַקָּהָל מִשְׁתַּחֲוִים וְהַשִּׁיר
מְשׁוֹרֵר וְהַחֲצֹצְרוֹת
מַחְצְצְרִים הַכֹּל עַד לִכְלוֹת
29 הָעֹלָה׃ וּכְכַלּוֹת לְהַעֲלוֹת
כָּרְעוּ הַמֶּלֶךְ וְכָל־הַנִּמְצְאִים
30 אִתּוֹ וַיִּשְׁתַּחֲווּ׃ וַיֹּאמֶר
יְחִזְקִיָּהוּ הַמֶּלֶךְ וְהַשָּׂרִים
לַלְוִיִּם לְהַלֵּל לַיהוָה בְּדִבְרֵי
דָוִיד וְאָסָף הַחֹזֶה וַיְהַלְלוּ
עַד־לְשִׂמְחָה וַיִּקְּדוּ וַיִּשְׁתַּחֲווּ׃
31 וַיַּעַן יְחִזְקִיָּהוּ וַיֹּאמֶר עַתָּה
מִלֵּאתֶם יֶדְכֶם לַיהוָה גֹּשׁוּ
וְהָבִיאוּ זְבָחִים וְתוֹדוֹת לְבֵית

v. 28. יתיר צ׳

26. *the instruments of David.* Cf. I Chron. xxiii. 5.

the priests with the trumpets. The priests sounded trumpets when Solomon dedicated the Temple (v. 12).

27. *together with the instruments.* Or, 'according to the guidance of the instruments,' lit. 'by the hand of the instruments,' i.e. led or accompanied by them.

28. *the singers sang.* lit. 'the song sings.'

this continued. Not in the text.

29. *bowed . . . prostrated.* Fell on their knees and then made a complete prostration.

30. *to sing praises,* etc. Or, 'to sing psalms' composed by David and by Asaph.

31-36 (not in Kings). The people's offerings.

31. *Hezekiah answered.* He reacted to the demands of the occasion.

And the congregation brought in sacrifices and thank-offerings; and as many as were of a willing heart brought burnt-offerings. 32. And the number of the burnt-offerings, which the congregation brought, was threescore and ten bullocks, a hundred rams, and two hundred lambs; all these were for a burnt-offering to the LORD. 33. And the consecrated things were six hundred oxen and three thousand sheep. 34. But the priests were too few, so that they could not flay all the burnt-offerings; wherefore their brethren the Levites did help them, till the work was ended, and until the priests had sanctified themselves; for the Levites were more upright in heart to sanctify themselves than the priests. 35. And also the burnt-offerings were in abundance, with the fat of the peace-offerings, and with the drink-offerings for every burnt-offering. So the service of the house of the LORD was firmly established. 36. And Hezekiah rejoiced, and all the people, because of that which God had prepared for

יְהוָה וַיָּבִיאוּ הַקָּהָל זְבָחִים
וְתוֹדוֹת וְכָל־נְדִיב לֵב עֹלוֹת׃
32 וַיְהִי מִסְפַּר הָעֹלָה אֲשֶׁר־
הֵבִיאוּ הַקָּהָל בָּקָר שִׁבְעִים
אֵילִים מֵאָה כְּבָשִׂים מָאתָיִם
לְעֹלָה לַיהוָה כָּל־אֵלֶּה׃
33 וְהַקֳּדָשִׁים בָּקָר שֵׁשׁ מֵאוֹת
34 וְצֹאן שְׁלֹשֶׁת אֲלָפִים׃ רַק
הַכֹּהֲנִים הָיוּ לִמְעָט וְלֹא יָכְלוּ
לְהַפְשִׁיט אֶת־כָּל־הָעֹלוֹת
וַיְחַזְּקוּם אֲחֵיהֶם הַלְוִיִּם עַד־
כְּלוֹת הַמְּלָאכָה וְעַד־
יִתְקַדְּשׁוּ הַכֹּהֲנִים כִּי הַלְוִיִּם
יִשְׁרֵי לֵבָב לְהִתְקַדֵּשׁ
35 מֵהַכֹּהֲנִים׃ וְגַם־עֹלָה לָרֹב
בְּחֶלְבֵי הַשְּׁלָמִים וּבַנְּסָכִים
לָעֹלָה וַתִּכּוֹן עֲבוֹדַת בֵּית־
36 יְהוָה׃ וַיִּשְׂמַח יְחִזְקִיָּהוּ וְכָל־
הָעָם עַל הַהֵכִין הָאֱלֹהִים

v. 34. קמץ בז״ק

as were of a willing heart brought burnt-offerings. Since these offerings were wholly burnt on the altar and no portion was eaten by the offerer, only generous donors brought this class of sacrifice.

33. *the consecrated things.* The peace-offerings and thank-offerings.

34. *the Levites were more upright*, etc. They apparently responded to Hezekiah's call with more zeal than did the priests and hastened to make themselves ritually clean while the latter were dilatory. The priests were more closely associated with the Court and therefore more prone to follow the example set by the king. 2 Kings xvi. 16 records, e.g., that Urijah the priest offered sacrifices at the bidding of Ahaz upon an altar other than that normally used in the Temple.

35. *and also*, etc. An additional reason why the Levites were needed to assist the priests.

firmly established. i.e. restored to its former state, before it was discontinued by Ahaz.

36. *which God had prepared.* viz. the

the people; for the thing was done suddenly.

לָעָם כִּי בְּפִתְאֹם הָיָה הַדָּבָר׃

30 CHAPTER XXX ל

1. And Hezekiah sent to all Israel and Judah, and wrote letters also to Ephraim and Manasseh, that they should come to the house of the LORD at Jerusalem, to keep the passover unto the LORD, the God of Israel. **2.** For the king had taken counsel, and his princes, and all the congregation in Jerusalem, to keep the passover in the second month. **3.** For they could not keep it at that time, because the priests had not sanctified themselves in sufficient number, neither had the people gathered themselves together to Jerusalem. **4.** And the thing was right in the eyes of the king and of

1 וַיִּשְׁלַח יְחִזְקִיָּהוּ עַל־כָּל־
יִשְׂרָאֵל וִיהוּדָה וְגַם־אִגְּרוֹת
כָּתַב עַל־אֶפְרַיִם וּמְנַשֶּׁה
לָבוֹא לְבֵית־יְהוָה בִּירוּשָׁלָםִ
לַעֲשׂוֹת פֶּסַח לַיהוָה אֱלֹהֵי
2 יִשְׂרָאֵל׃ וַיִּוָּעַץ הַמֶּלֶךְ וְשָׂרָיו
וְכָל־הַקָּהָל בִּירוּשָׁלָםִ
לַעֲשׂוֹת הַפֶּסַח בַּחֹדֶשׁ הַשֵּׁנִי׃
3 כִּי לֹא יָכְלוּ לַעֲשֹׂתוֹ בָּעֵת
הַהִיא כִּי הַכֹּהֲנִים לֹא־
הִתְקַדְּשׁוּ לְמַדַּי וְהָעָם לֹא־
4 נֶאֶסְפוּ לִירוּשָׁלָםִ׃ וַיִּישַׁר
הַדָּבָר בְּעֵינֵי הַמֶּלֶךְ וּבְעֵינֵי

rapid transition from idolatry to the service as ordained by God.

the thing was done suddenly. The reformation took place in the first year of Hezekiah's reign (verse 3).

CHAPTER XXX

OBSERVANCE OF THE PASSOVER

THIS chapter has no parallel in Kings.

1-5. The king and his advisers decide on the date of the celebration of the Passover.

1. *to all Israel.* The remnants of the tribes of the Northern Kingdom which had been overrun by Assyria two years before Hezekiah came to the throne.

Ephraim and Manasseh. Though included in *all Israel*, they are specifically mentioned on account of their importance.

2. *in the second month.* Though the observance is commanded to take place in the first month (Exod. xxxiv. 18), persons who for certain specified reasons were unable to keep it in that month were to celebrate it in the second (Num. ix. 10f.).

3. *at that time.* In the first month.

4. *the thing.* The celebration of the Passover in the second month.

all the congregation. 5. So they established a decree to make proclamation throughout all Israel, from Beer-sheba even to Dan, that they should come to keep the passover unto the LORD, the God of Israel, at Jerusalem; for they had not kept it in great numbers according as it is written.

6. So the posts went with the letters from the king and his princes throughout all Israel and Judah, and according to the commandment of the king, saying: 'Ye children of Israel, turn back unto the LORD, the God of Abraham, Isaac, and Israel, that He may return to the remnant that are escaped of you out of the hand of the kings of Assyria. 7. And be not ye like your fathers, and like your brethren, who acted treacherously against the LORD, the God of their fathers, so that He delivered them to be an astonishment, as ye see. 8. Now be ye not stiffnecked, as your fathers were; but yield yourselves unto the LORD, and enter into His sanctuary, which He hath sanctified for ever, and serve the LORD your God, that His

5 כָּל־הַקָּהָל׃ וַיַּעֲמִידוּ דָבָר
לְהַעֲבִיר קוֹל בְּכָל־יִשְׂרָאֵל
מִבְּאֵר־שֶׁבַע וְעַד־דָּן לָבוֹא
לַעֲשׂוֹת פֶּסַח לַיהוָה אֱלֹהֵי־
יִשְׂרָאֵל בִּירוּשָׁלִָם כִּי לֹא לָרֹב
עָשׂוּ כַּכָּתוּב׃
6 וַיֵּלְכוּ הָרָצִים בָּאִגְּרוֹת מִיַּד
הַמֶּלֶךְ וְשָׂרָיו בְּכָל־יִשְׂרָאֵל
וִיהוּדָה וּכְמִצְוַת הַמֶּלֶךְ
לֵאמֹר בְּנֵי יִשְׂרָאֵל שׁוּבוּ אֶל־
יְהוָה אֱלֹהֵי אַבְרָהָם יִצְחָק
וְיִשְׂרָאֵל וְיָשֹׁב אֶל־הַפְּלֵיטָה
הַנִּשְׁאֶרֶת לָכֶם מִכַּף מַלְכֵי
7 אַשּׁוּר׃ וְאַל־תִּהְיוּ כַּאֲבוֹתֵיכֶם
וְכַאֲחֵיכֶם אֲשֶׁר מָעֲלוּ בַּיהוָה
אֱלֹהֵי אֲבוֹתֵיהֶם וַיִּתְּנֵם לְשַׁמָּה
8 כַּאֲשֶׁר אַתֶּם רֹאִים׃ עַתָּה
אַל־תַּקְשׁוּ עָרְפְּכֶם
כַּאֲבוֹתֵיכֶם תְּנוּ־יָד לַיהוָה
וּבֹאוּ לְמִקְדָּשׁוֹ אֲשֶׁר הִקְדִּישׁ
לְעוֹלָם וְעִבְדוּ אֶת־יְהוָה

5. *from Beer-sheba even to Dan.* See on 1 Chron. xxi. 2.

they had not kept it in great numbers. Only the pious minority had been keeping it. Another rendering is: 'they had not kept it for a long time'; hence the need for the proclamation.

6-9. Hezekiah's letters of exhortation to all Israel to revert to the worship of God.

6. *the posts.* lit. 'the runners.'

the remnant that are escaped. Or, 'the escaped remnant which is left.'

the kings of Assyria. viz. Tiglath-pileser (1 Chron. v. 26) and Shalmaneser (2 Kings xvii. 6).

8. *yield yourselves.* lit. 'give a hand.'

fierce anger may turn away from you. 9. For if ye turn back unto the LORD, your brethren and your children shall find compassion before them that led them captive, and shall come back into this land; for the LORD your God is gracious and merciful, and will not turn away His face from you, if ye return unto Him.'

10. So the posts passed from city to city through the country of Ephraim and Manasseh, even unto Zebulun; but they laughed them to scorn, and mocked them. 11. Nevertheless divers of Asher and Manasseh and of Zebulun humbled themselves, and came to Jerusalem. 12. Also in Judah was the hand of God to give them one heart, to do the commandment of the king and of the princes by the word of the LORD.

13. And there assembled at Jerusalem much people to keep the feast of unleavened bread in the

אֱלֹהֵיכֶם וְיָשֹׁב מִכֶּם חֲרוֹן
9 אַפּוֹ׃ כִּי בְשׁוּבְכֶם עַל־יְהוָה
אֲחֵיכֶם וּבְנֵיכֶם לְרַחֲמִים
לִפְנֵי שׁוֹבֵיהֶם וְלָשׁוּב לָאָרֶץ
הַזֹּאת כִּי־חַנּוּן וְרַחוּם יְהוָה
אֱלֹהֵיכֶם וְלֹא־יָסִיר פָּנִים
מִכֶּם אִם־תָּשׁוּבוּ אֵלָיו׃
10 וַיִּהְיוּ הָרָצִים עֹבְרִים מֵעִיר ׀
לָעִיר בְּאֶרֶץ־אֶפְרַיִם וּמְנַשֶּׁה
וְעַד־זְבֻלוּן וַיִּהְיוּ מַשְׂחִקִים
11 עֲלֵיהֶם וּמַלְעִגִים בָּם׃ אַךְ
אֲנָשִׁים מֵאָשֵׁר וּמְנַשֶּׁה וּמִזְּבֻלוּן
12 נִכְנְעוּ וַיָּבֹאוּ לִירוּשָׁלִָם׃ גַּם
בִּיהוּדָה הָיְתָה יַד הָאֱלֹהִים
לָתֵת לָהֶם לֵב אֶחָד לַעֲשׂוֹת
מִצְוַת הַמֶּלֶךְ וְהַשָּׂרִים בִּדְבַר
יְהוָה׃
13 וַיֵּאָסְפוּ יְרוּשָׁלִַם עַם־רָב
לַעֲשׂוֹת אֶת־חַג הַמַּצּוֹת

9. *shall find compassion.* lit. '(shall be) for compassion.'

His face. The pronoun is implied.

10-12. Only Judah and four of the northern tribes respond to the call.

10. *the posts passed.* lit. 'the runners were passing.'

even unto Zebulun. They did not apparently go farther north where the country was in ruins and its former inhabitants deported by Assyria.

11. *divers.* lit. '(some) men.'

humbled themselves. Before God.

came to Jerusalem. To worship again in the Temple.

12. *one heart.* Unanimity.

the commandment of the king . . . by the word of the LORD. i.e. the commandment given by the king was in accord with the will of God.

13-22. The Passover celebration.

13. *the feast of unleavened bread.* An

second month, a very great congregation. 14. And they arose and took away the altars that were in Jerusalem, and all the altars for incense took they away, and cast them into the brook Kidron. 15. Then they killed the passover lamb on the fourteenth day of the second month; and the priests and the Levites were ashamed, and sanctified themselves, and brought burnt-offerings into the house of the LORD. 16. And they stood in their place after their order, according to the law of Moses the man of God; the priests dashed the blood, which they received of the hand of the Levites. 17. For there were many in the congregation that had not sanctified themselves; therefore the Levites had the charge of killing the passover lambs for every one that was not clean, to sanctify them unto the LORD. 18. For a multitude of the people, even many of Ephraim and Manasseh, Issachar and Zebulun, had not cleansed themselves,

בַּחֹדֶשׁ הַשֵּׁנִי קָהָל לָרֹב מְאֹד׃
14 וַיָּקֻמוּ וַיָּסִירוּ אֶת־הַמִּזְבְּחוֹת
אֲשֶׁר בִּירוּשָׁלִָם וְאֵת כָּל־
הַמְקַטְּרוֹת הֵסִירוּ וַיַּשְׁלִיכוּ
15 לְנַחַל קִדְרוֹן׃ וַיִּשְׁחֲטוּ הַפֶּסַח
בְּאַרְבָּעָה עָשָׂר לַחֹדֶשׁ הַשֵּׁנִי
וְהַכֹּהֲנִים וְהַלְוִיִּם נִכְלְמוּ
וַיִּתְקַדְּשׁוּ וַיָּבִיאוּ עֹלוֹת בֵּית
16 יְהוָה׃ וַיַּעַמְדוּ עַל־עָמְדָם
כְּמִשְׁפָּטָם כְּתוֹרַת מֹשֶׁה אִישׁ־
הָאֱלֹהִים הַכֹּהֲנִים זֹרְקִים
17 אֶת־הַדָּם מִיַּד הַלְוִיִּם׃ כִּי־
רַבַּת בַּקָּהָל אֲשֶׁר לֹא־
הִתְקַדָּשׁוּ וְהַלְוִיִּם עַל־שְׁחִיטַת
הַפְּסָחִים לְכֹל לֹא טָהוֹר
18 לְהַקְדִּישׁ לַיהוָה׃ כִּי מַרְבִּית
הָעָם רַבַּת מֵאֶפְרַיִם וּמְנַשֶּׁה
יִשָּׂשכָר וּזְבֻלוּן לֹא הִטֶּהָרוּ

alternative designation of the Passover (cf. Exod. xii. 17).

in the second month. See on verse 2.

14. *the altars for incense.* Or, 'the vessels for incense.'

the brook Kidron. See on xv. 16.

15. *were ashamed.* Of their dilatoriness in preparing themselves for the Temple services which was the cause of the deferment of the celebration to the second month.

brought burnt-offerings. To atone for the delay in sanctifying themselves.

16. *they stood in their place.* The subject refers to the Levites who were not allowed to carry the blood to the altar, that being the function of the priests.

according to the law of Moses. Which assigns to the priests the duty of receiving the blood and splashing it against the side of the altar (cf. Lev. i. 11).

which they received. Not in the text.

17. *had not sanctified themselves.* And could not slay their Paschal lamb.

had the charge of killing. lit. '(were) upon the killing.'

to sanctify them. viz. the Paschal lambs

yet did they eat the passover otherwise than it is written. For Hezekiah had prayed for them, saying: 'The good LORD pardon 19. every one that setteth his heart to seek God, the LORD, the God of his fathers, though [he be] not [cleansed] according to the purification that pertaineth to holy things.' 20. And the LORD hearkened to Hezekiah, and healed the people. 21. And the children of Israel that were present at Jerusalem kept the feast of unleavened bread seven days with great gladness; and the Levites and the priests praised the LORD day by day, singing with loud instruments unto the LORD. 22. And Hezekiah spoke encouragingly unto all the Levites that were well skilled in the service of the LORD. So they did eat throughout the feast for the seven days, offering sacrifices of peace-offerings, and giving thanks to the LORD, the God of their fathers.

23. And the whole congregation took counsel to keep other seven

כִּֽי־אָכְלוּ אֶת־הַפֶּסַח בְּלֹא
כַכָּתוּב כִּי הִתְפַּלֵּל יְחִזְקִיָּהוּ
עֲלֵיהֶם לֵאמֹר יְהוָה הַטּוֹב
19 יְכַפֵּר בְּעַד׃ כָּל־לְבָבוֹ הֵכִין
לִדְרוֹשׁ הָאֱלֹהִים ׀ יְהוָה
אֱלֹהֵי אֲבוֹתָיו וְלֹא כְּטָהֳרַת
20 הַקֹּדֶשׁ׃ וַיִּשְׁמַע יְהוָה אֶל־
יְחִזְקִיָּהוּ וַיִּרְפָּא אֶת־הָעָם׃
21 וַיַּעֲשׂוּ בְנֵֽי־יִשְׂרָאֵל הַנִּמְצְאִים
בִּירוּשָׁלִַם אֶת־חַג הַמַּצּוֹת
שִׁבְעַת יָמִים בְּשִׂמְחָה גְדוֹלָה
וּמְהַלְלִים לַיהוָה יוֹם ׀ בְּיוֹם
הַלְוִיִּם וְהַכֹּהֲנִים בִּכְלֵי עֹז
22 לַיהוָה׃ וַיְדַבֵּר יְחִזְקִיָּהוּ עַל־
לֵב כָּל־הַלְוִיִּם הַמַּשְׂכִּילִים
שֵׂכֶל־טוֹב לַיהוָה וַיֹּאכְלוּ
אֶת־הַמּוֹעֵד שִׁבְעַת הַיָּמִים
מְזַבְּחִים זִבְחֵי שְׁלָמִים
וּמִתְוַדִּים לַיהוָה אֱלֹהֵי
אֲבוֹתֵיהֶם׃
23 וַיִּוָּעֲצוּ כָּל־הַקָּהָל לַעֲשׂוֹת

which the laymen, on account of their defilement, could not do.

18. *otherwise than it is written.* Cf. Num. ix. 6.

20. *healed the people.* Forgave their sin in response to Hezekiah's prayer.

21. *singing.* Not in the text.

loud instruments. lit. 'instruments of strength.'

22. *spoke encouragingly.* lit. 'spoke upon the heart,' words of commendation.

giving thanks. Or, 'making confession' (R.V.). The Jewish commentators render as A.J.

23-27. An additional festival of seven days' duration.

23. *other seven days.* After the Passover was ended, to continue their thanks-

days; and they kept other seven days with gladness. 24. For Hezekiah king of Judah did give to the congregation for offerings a thousand bullocks and seven thousand sheep; and the princes gave to the congregation a thousand bullocks and ten thousand sheep; and priests sanctified themselves in great numbers. 25. And all the congregation of Judah, with the priests and the Levites, and all the congregation that came out of Israel, and the strangers that came out of the land of Israel, and that dwelt in Judah, rejoiced. 26. So there was great joy in Jerusalem; for since the time of Solomon the son of David king of Israel there was not the like in Jerusalem. 27. Then the priests the Levites arose and blessed the people; and their voice was heard

שִׁבְעַת יָמִים אֲחֵרִים וַיַּעֲשׂוּ
שִׁבְעַת יָמִים שִׂמְחָה׃ כִּי 24
חִזְקִיָּהוּ מֶלֶךְ־יְהוּדָה הֵרִים
לַקָּהָל אֶלֶף פָּרִים וְשִׁבְעַת
אֲלָפִים צֹאן וְהַשָּׂרִים הֵרִימוּ
לַקָּהָל פָּרִים אֶלֶף וְצֹאן
עֲשֶׂרֶת אֲלָפִים וַיִּתְקַדְּשׁוּ
כֹהֲנִים לָרֹב׃ וַיִּשְׂמְחוּ ׀ כָּל־ 25
קְהַל יְהוּדָה וְהַכֹּהֲנִים וְהַלְוִיִּם
וְכָל־הַקָּהָל הַבָּאִים מִיִּשְׂרָאֵל
וְהַגֵּרִים הַבָּאִים מֵאֶרֶץ
יִשְׂרָאֵל וְהַיּוֹשְׁבִים בִּיהוּדָה׃
וַתְּהִי שִׂמְחָה גְדוֹלָה בִּירוּשָׁלִָם 26
כִּי מִימֵי שְׁלֹמֹה בֶן־דָּוִיד מֶלֶךְ
יִשְׂרָאֵל לֹא כָזֹאת בִּירוּשָׁלִָם׃
וַיָּקֻמוּ הַכֹּהֲנִים הַלְוִיִּם וַיְבָרֲכוּ 27
אֶת־הָעָם וַיִּשָּׁמַע בְּקוֹלָם

giving to God. A similar addition to the Feast of Tabernacles was observed by Solomon on the completion of the Temple (cf. vii. 9), but it preceded the Feast.

kept other seven days with gladness. The words *other* and *with* are implied.

24. *for Hezekiah,* etc. The king's generosity enabled the people to prolong the celebration.

priests sanctified themselves in great numbers. That sufficient should be available to deal with the unusually large number of offerings.

25. *all the congregation that came out of Israel.* From the tribes of the Northern Kingdom.

the strangers. The LXX has 'proselytes' which agrees with the Jewish traditional interpretation. The Torah made provision for *strangers* to join in the Passover (cf. Exod. xii. 48).

26. *since the time of Solomon.* The celebration in Hezekiah's reign was only comparable with the rejoicings at the dedication of the Temple (v. 3ff.).

27. *the priests the Levites.* The priests belonged to the tribe of Levi.

and their voice was heard [*of the LORD*]. lit. 'and it (the priests' petition) was heard (by God through) their voice.

[of the LORD], and their prayer came up to His holy habitation, even unto heaven.

וַתָּב֧וֹא תְפִלָּתָ֛ם לִמְע֥וֹן קָדְשׁ֖וֹ
לַשָּׁמָֽיִם׃

31 CHAPTER XXXI לא

1. Now when all this was finished, all Israel that were present went out to the cities of Judah, and broke in pieces the pillars, and hewed down the Asherim, and broke down the high places and the altars out of all Judah and Benjamin, in Ephraim also and Manasseh, until they had destroyed them all. Then all the children of Israel returned, every man to his possession, into their own cities.

2. And Hezekiah appointed the courses of the priests and the Levites after their courses, every man according to his service, both the priests and the Levites, for burnt-offerings and for peace-offerings, to minister, and to give thanks, and to praise in the gates of the camp of the LORD. 3. He ap-

1 וּכְכַלּ֣וֹת כָּל־זֹ֗את יָצְא֨וּ כָּל־
יִשְׂרָאֵ֜ל הַנִּמְצְאִ֣ים לְעָרֵ֣י
יְהוּדָ֡ה וַיְשַׁבְּר֣וּ הַמַּצֵּב֣וֹת
וַיְגַדְּע֣וּ הָאֲשֵׁרִ֣ים וַיְנַתְּצ֣וּ אֶת־
הַבָּמ֣וֹת וְאֶת־הַֽמִּזְבְּחֹ֡ת
מִכָּל־יְהוּדָ֨ה וּבִנְיָמִ֜ן
וּבְאֶפְרַ֧יִם וּמְנַשֶּׁ֛ה עַד־לְכַלֵּ֑ה
וַיָּשׁ֜וּבוּ כָּל־בְּנֵ֤י יִשְׂרָאֵל֙ אִ֣ישׁ
בַּאֲחֻזָּת֖וֹ לְעָרֵיהֶֽם׃
2 וַיַּעֲמֵ֣ד יְחִזְקִיָּ֡הוּ אֶת־
מַחְלְק֣וֹת הַכֹּהֲנִ֣ים וְ֠הַלְוִיִּם
עַל־מַחְלְקוֹתָ֞ם אִ֣ישׁ ׀ כְּפִ֣י
עֲבֹדָת֗וֹ לַכֹּהֲנִים֙ וְלַלְוִיִּ֔ם
לְעֹלָ֖ה וְלִשְׁלָמִ֑ים לְשָׁרֵ֤ת
וּלְהֹדוֹת֙ וּלְהַלֵּ֔ל בְּשַׁעֲרֵ֖י
3 מַחֲנ֥וֹת יְהוָֽה׃ וּמְנָ֨ת הַמֶּ֜לֶךְ

CHAPTER XXXI

HEZEKIAH'S REORGANIZATION OF RELIGIOUS WORSHIP

1. Destruction of all traces of idolatry in the Northern and Southern Kingdoms. In the parallel passage, 2 Kings xviii. 4, the northern tribes are not included, but in the Chronicler's account Hezekiah's jurisdiction also extended to them (cf. xxx. 6ff.).

pillars . . . Asherim. See on xiv. 2.

2-10. Reorganization of the courses of the priests and Levites and provision for their maintenance. Cf. the scheme planned by David (1 Chron. xxiii-xxvi).

2. *the courses.* i.e. the groupings described in 1 Chron. xxiv. 1ff.

after their courses. According to the system of courses which operated in the Temple before the introduction of idolatry in the previous reign.

the camp. lit. 'camps,' the various parts of the Temple (cf. 1 Chron. ix. 18f.).

pointed also the king's portion of his substance for the burnt-offerings, to wit, for the morning and evening burnt-offerings, and the burnt-offerings for the sabbaths, and for the new moons, and for the appointed seasons, as it is written in the Law of the LORD. 4. Moreover he commanded the people that dwelt in Jerusalem to give the portion of the priests and the Levites, that they might give themselves to the law of the LORD. 5. And as soon as the commandment came abroad, the children of Israel gave in abundance the first-fruits of corn, wine, and oil, and honey, and of all the increase of the field; and the tithe of all things brought they in abundantly. 6. And the children of Israel and Judah, that dwelt in the cities of Judah, they also brought in the tithe of oxen and sheep, and the tithe of hallowed things which were hallowed unto the LORD their God, and laid them by heaps. 7. In the third month

מִן־רְכוּשׁוֹ לָעֹלוֹת
הַבֹּקֶר וְהָעֶרֶב וְהָעֹלוֹת
לַשַּׁבָּתוֹת וְלֶחֳדָשִׁים
וְלַמֹּעֲדִים כַּכָּתוּב בְּתוֹרַת
4 יְהוָה: וַיֹּאמֶר לָעָם לְיוֹשְׁבֵי
יְרוּשָׁלַםִ לָתֵת מְנָת הַכֹּהֲנִים
וְהַלְוִיִּם לְמַעַן יֶחֶזְקוּ בְּתוֹרַת
5 יְהוָה: וְכִפְרֹץ הַדָּבָר הִרְבּוּ
בְנֵי־יִשְׂרָאֵל רֵאשִׁית דָּגָן
תִּירוֹשׁ וְיִצְהָר וּדְבַשׁ וְכֹל
תְּבוּאַת שָׂדֶה וּמַעְשַׂר הַכֹּל
6 לָרֹב הֵבִיאוּ: וּבְנֵי יִשְׂרָאֵל
וִיהוּדָה הַיּוֹשְׁבִים בְּעָרֵי
יְהוּדָה גַּם־הֵם מַעְשַׂר בָּקָר
וָצֹאן וּמַעְשַׂר קֳדָשִׁים
הַמְקֻדָּשִׁים לַיהוָה אֱלֹהֵיהֶם
הֵבִיאוּ וַיִּתְּנוּ עֲרֵמוֹת עֲרֵמוֹת:
7 בַּחֹדֶשׁ הַשְּׁלִשִׁי הֵחֵלּוּ

3. *he appointed.* Not in the text.

the king's portion. Hezekiah's personal contribution to the provision of the sacrifices.

as it is written in the Law. In Num. xxviii f.

4. *the portion of the priests and the Levites.* The first-fruits and tithes.

that they might give themselves. Or, 'that they might hold firmly' (cf. Neh. xiii. 10ff.).

5. *the first-fruits of corn.* These dues to the priests were termed *terumah* (Num. xviii. 8, 11f.) and *bikkurim* (Num. xviii. 13).

honey. Obtained from dates. The Torah does not include honey among the produce to which the law of the first-fruits applied.

increase of the field. Such as grapes, figs and pomegranates which were subject to this law.

6. *the children of Israel.* Cf. xi. 16.

the tithe of oxen and sheep. Cf. Lev. xxvii. 32f.

the tithe of hallowed things. Although these were legally exempt from the tithe.

7. *the third month.* On the sixth day of that month is the Feast of Weeks or

they began to lay the foundation of the heaps, and finished them in the seventh month. 8. And when Hezekiah and the princes came and saw the heaps, they blessed the LORD, and His people Israel. 9. Then Hezekiah questioned the priests and the Levites concerning the heaps. 10. And Azariah the chief priest, of the house of Zadok, answered him and said: 'Since the people began to bring the offerings into the house of the LORD, we have eaten and had enough, and have left plenty; for the LORD hath blessed His people; and that which is left is this great store.'

11. Then Hezekiah commanded to prepare chambers in the house of the LORD; and they prepared them. 12. And they brought in the offerings and the tithes and the hallowed things faithfully; and over them Conaniah the Levite was ruler, and Shimei his brother was second.

הָעֲרֵמוֹת לִיסּוֹד וּבַחֹדֶשׁ
8 הַשְּׁבִיעִי כִּלּוּ׃ וַיָּבֹאוּ יְחִזְקִיָּהוּ
וְהַשָּׂרִים וַיִּרְאוּ אֶת־הָעֲרֵמוֹת
וַיְבָרְכוּ אֶת־יְהוָה וְאֵת עַמּוֹ
9 יִשְׂרָאֵל׃ וַיִּדְרֹשׁ יְחִזְקִיָּהוּ
עַל־הַכֹּהֲנִים וְהַלְוִיִּם עַל־
10 הָעֲרֵמוֹת׃ וַיֹּאמֶר אֵלָיו
עֲזַרְיָהוּ הַכֹּהֵן הָרֹאשׁ לְבֵית
צָדוֹק וַיֹּאמֶר מֵהָחֵל הַתְּרוּמָה
לָבִיא בֵית־יְהוָה אָכוֹל
וְשָׂבוֹעַ וְהוֹתֵר עַד־לָרוֹב כִּי
יְהוָה בֵּרַךְ אֶת־עַמּוֹ וְהַנּוֹתָר
11 אֶת־הֶהָמוֹן הַזֶּה׃ וַיֹּאמֶר
יְחִזְקִיָּהוּ לְהָכִין לְשָׁכוֹת בְּבֵית
12 יְהוָה וַיָּכִינוּ׃ וַיָּבִיאוּ אֶת־
הַתְּרוּמָה וְהַמַּעֲשֵׂר וְהַקֳּדָשִׁים
בֶּאֱמוּנָה וַעֲלֵיהֶם נָגִיד כּוֹנַנְיָהוּ
הַלֵּוִי וְשִׁמְעִי אָחִיהוּ מִשְׁנֶה׃

v. 7. הס׳ בדגש v. 12. יתיר ו׳

Pentecost when the grain harvest is finished.

the seventh month. On the fifteenth begins the Feast of Tabernacles, the harvest festival.

8. *they blessed the LORD.* For inspiring the people to set aside the tithes with zeal.

9. *Hezekiah questioned,* etc. The heaps were so large that the king inquired whether the priests and Levites had refrained from taking their portion.

10. *Azariah.* He may have been the same man as the chief priest in the reign of Uzziah (xxvi. 17).

the house of Zadok. One of the leading priestly families (1 Chron. xxiv. 3).

the people. Not in the text.

the LORD hath blessed, etc. Azariah explains that although the priests were taking all they needed from the heaps, the people were so generous with their offerings that even that which was left was a *great store.*

11-19. Construction of new store-chambers and arrangements for their

13. And Jehiel, and Azaziah, and Nahath, and Asahel, and Jerimoth, and Jozabad, and Eliel, and Ismachiah, and Mahath, and Benaiah, were overseers under the hand of Conaniah and Shimei his brother, by the appointment of Hezekiah the king, and Azariah the ruler of the house of God. 14. And Kore the son of Imnah the Levite, the porter at the east gate, was over the freewill-offerings of God, to distribute the offerings of the LORD, and the most holy things. 15. And under him were Eden, and Miniamin, and Jeshua, and Shemaiah, Amariah, and Shecaniah, in the cities of the priests, in their office of trust, to give to their brethren by courses, as well to the great as to the small; 16. beside them that were reckoned by genealogy of males, from three years old and upward, even every one that entered into the house of the LORD, for his daily portion, for their service in their charges according to their

13 וִיחִיאֵל וַעֲזַזְיָהוּ וְנַחַת
וַעֲשָׂהאֵל וִירִימוֹת וְיוֹזָבָד
וֶאֱלִיאֵל וְיִסְמַכְיָהוּ וּמַחַת
וּבְנָיָהוּ פְּקִידִים מִיַּד כָּונַנְיָהוּ
וְשִׁמְעִי אָחִיו בְּמִפְקַד יְחִזְקִיָּהוּ
הַמֶּלֶךְ וַעֲזַרְיָהוּ נְגִיד בֵּית־
14 הָאֱלֹהִים׃ וְקוֹרֵא בֶן־יִמְנָה
הַלֵּוִי הַשּׁוֹעֵר לַמִּזְרָחָה עַל
נִדְבוֹת הָאֱלֹהִים לָתֵת תְּרוּמַת
15 יְהוָה וְקָדְשֵׁי הַקֳּדָשִׁים׃ וְעַל־
יָדוֹ עֵדֶן וּמִנְיָמִן וְיֵשׁוּעַ
וּשְׁמַעְיָהוּ אֲמַרְיָהוּ וּשְׁכַנְיָהוּ
בְּעָרֵי הַכֹּהֲנִים בֶּאֱמוּנָה לָתֵת
לַאֲחֵיהֶם בְּמַחְלְקוֹת כַּגָּדוֹל
16 כַּקָּטָן׃ מִלְּבַד הִתְיַחְשָׂם
לִזְכָרִים מִבֶּן שָׁלוֹשׁ שָׁנִים
וּלְמַעְלָה לְכָל־־הַבָּא
לְבֵית־־יְהוָה לִדְבַר־יוֹם
בְּיוֹמוֹ לַעֲבוֹדָתָם בְּמִשְׁמְרוֹתָם

v. 13. יתיר ו׳

supervision and distribution of the offerings.

11. *chambers.* See on 1 Chron. ix. 26b.

13. *the ruler of the house of God.* See on 1 Chron. ix. 11.

14. *the porter at the east gate.* lit. 'the porter towards the east.'

the most holy things. E.g. the showbread, the meal-offerings, sin-offerings and trespass-offerings which were eaten by the priests within the precincts of the Temple.

15. *the cities of the priests.* Enumerated in Josh. xxi. 10ff. and 1 Chron. vi. 39ff. The officials mentioned in verses 12-14 resided in Jerusalem.

in their office of trust. lit. 'in faithfulness.'

as well to the great as to the small. i.e. both old and young.

16f. These verses are parenthetical.

16. *his daily portion.* Or, 'as the duty of every day required' (R.V.).

17. *and them that were reckoned,* etc.

courses; 17. and them that were reckoned by genealogy of the priests by their fathers' houses, and the Levites from twenty years old and upward, in their charges by their courses; 18. even to give to them that were reckoned by genealogy of all their little ones, their wives, and their sons, and their daughters, through all the congregation; for in their office of trust they administered the sacred gifts; 19. also for the sons of Aaron the priests, that were in the fields of the open land about their cities, in every city, there were men that were mentioned by name, to give portions to all the males among the priests, and to all that were reckoned by genealogy among the Levites.

20. And thus did Hezekiah throughout all Judah; and he wrought that which was good and right and faithful before the LORD his God. 21. And in every work that he began in the service of the house of God, and in the law, and in the commandments, to seek his God, he did it with all his heart, and prospered.

17 בְּמַחְלְקוֹתֵיהֶם׃ וְאֵת הִתְיַחֵשׂ
הַכֹּהֲנִים לְבֵית אֲבוֹתֵיהֶם
וְהַלְוִיִּם מִבֶּן עֶשְׂרִים שָׁנָה
וּלְמָעְלָה בְּמִשְׁמְרוֹתֵיהֶם
18 בְּמַחְלְקוֹתֵיהֶם׃ וּלְהִתְיַחֵשׂ
בְּכָל־טַפָּם נְשֵׁיהֶם וּבְנֵיהֶם
וּבְנוֹתֵיהֶם לְכָל־קָהָל כִּי
בֶאֱמוּנָתָם יִתְקַדְּשׁוּ־קֹדֶשׁ׃
19 וְלִבְנֵי אַהֲרֹן הַכֹּהֲנִים בִּשְׂדֵי
מִגְרַשׁ עָרֵיהֶם בְּכָל־עִיר
וָעִיר אֲנָשִׁים אֲשֶׁר נִקְּבוּ
בְּשֵׁמוֹת לָתֵת מָנוֹת לְכָל־זָכָר
בַּכֹּהֲנִים וּלְכָל־הִתְיַחֵשׂ
בַּלְוִיִּם׃
20 וַיַּעַשׂ כָּזֹאת יְחִזְקִיָּהוּ בְּכָל־
יְהוּדָה וַיַּעַשׂ הַטּוֹב וְהַיָּשָׁר
וְהָאֱמֶת לִפְנֵי יְהוָה אֱלֹהָיו׃
21 וּבְכָל־מַעֲשֶׂה אֲשֶׁר־הֵחֵל ׀
בַּעֲבוֹדַת בֵּית־הָאֱלֹהִים
וּבַתּוֹרָה וּבַמִּצְוָה לִדְרֹשׁ
לֵאלֹהָיו בְּכָל־לְבָבוֹ עָשָׂה
וְהִצְלִיחַ׃

They received their portion of the priestly dues.

and the Levites, etc. These received their allocation of the tithes.

18. *even to give to them.* Not in the text.

in their office of trust. See on verse 15.

they administered the sacred gifts. lit. 'they sanctified themselves (in) holiness.'

19. *that were in the fields.* Who resided outside Jerusalem.

20f. A summary of Hezekiah's activity.

20. *faithful.* lit. 'the truth.'

21. *he did it.* Each one of the undertakings described above.

32 CHAPTER XXXII לב

1. After these things, and this
faithfulness, Sennacherib king of
Assyria came, and entered into
Judah, and encamped against the
fortified cities, and thought to make
a breach therein for himself. 2. And
when Hezekiah saw that Sennacherib was come, and that he was
purposed to fight against Jerusalem,
3. he took counsel with his princes
and his mighty men to stop the
waters of the fountains which were
without the city; and they helped
him. 4. So there was gathered
much people together, and they
stopped all the fountains, and the
brook that flowed through the midst
of the land, saying: 'Why should the

1 אַחֲרֵי הַדְּבָרִים וְהָאֱמֶת
הָאֵלֶּה בָּא סַנְחֵרִיב מֶלֶךְ־
אַשּׁוּר וַיָּבֹא בִיהוּדָה וַיִּחַן עַל־
הֶעָרִים הַבְּצֻרוֹת וַיֹּאמֶר
2 לְבִקְעָם אֵלָיו׃ וַיַּרְא יְחִזְקִיָּהוּ
כִּי־בָא סַנְחֵרִיב וּפָנָיו
לַמִּלְחָמָה עַל־יְרוּשָׁלִָם׃
3 וַיִּוָּעַץ עִם־שָׂרָיו וְגִבֹּרָיו
לִסְתּוֹם אֶת־מֵימֵי הָעֲיָנוֹת
אֲשֶׁר מִחוּץ לָעִיר וַיַּעְזְרוּהוּ׃
4 וַיִּקָּבְצוּ עַם־רָב וַיִּסְתְּמוּ אֶת־
כָּל־הַמַּעְיָנוֹת וְאֶת־הַנַּחַל
הַשּׁוֹטֵף בְּתוֹךְ־הָאָרֶץ לֵאמֹר

CHAPTER XXXII

1 (cf. 2 Kings xviii. 13). Sennacherib's invasion of Judah. The story of the invasion is preceded in 2 Kings xviii. 7 by the account of Hezekiah's rebellion against the king of Assyria which the Chronicler omits.

these things, and this faithfulness. i.e. these faithful things: the reforms described in the preceding chapters.

Sennacherib. He was the son of Sargon (Isa. xx. 1) and reigned over Assyria 705-682 B.C.E. Under this dynasty Assyria reached the zenith of its power.

and thought to make a breach. He finally captured them (2 Kings xviii. 13). Their number, according to an Assyrian inscription, was forty-six.

2-8. Hezekiah's defensive measures and encouragement of the people. In 2 Kings xviii. 14-16, the account of the invasion is followed by that of Hezekiah's surrender.

2. *and that he was purposed to fight.* lit. 'and his face (was) for war.'

3. *to stop the waters*, etc. Hezekiah had made *the pool, and the conduit, and brought water into the city* (2 Kings xx. 20). This conduit is now assumed to be the tunnel east of Jerusalem, 586 yards long, cut in the rock and leading to the Lower Pool of Siloam, which may then have been within the walls of the city. A record in ancient Hebrew characters of the construction of the tunnel was discovered near its entrance in 1880.

4. *the brook that flowed.* Probably the Gihon, which is now known as the Virgin Spring.

kings of Assyria come, and find
much water?' 5. And he took
courage, and built up all the wall
that was broken down, and raised it
up to the towers, and another wall
without, and strengthened Millo in
the city of David, and made weapons
and shields in abundance. 6. And
he set captains of war over the
people, and gathered them together
to him in the broad place at the gate
of the city, and spoke encouragingly
to them, saying: 7. 'Be strong and
of good courage, be not afraid nor
dismayed for the king of Assyria,
nor for all the multitude that is with
him; for there is a Greater with us
than with him: 8. with him is an arm
of flesh; but with us is the LORD our
God to help us, and to fight our
battles.' And the people rested
themselves upon the words of
Hezekiah king of Judah.

9. After this did Sennacherib king
of Assyria send his servants to
Jerusalem — now he was before

לָמָּה יָבוֹאוּ מַלְכֵי אַשּׁוּר
5 וּמָצְאוּ מַיִם רַבִּים׃ וַיִּתְחַזַּק
וַיִּבֶן אֶת־כָּל־הַחוֹמָה
הַפְּרוּצָה וַיַּעַל עַל־הַמִּגְדָּלוֹת
וְלַחוּצָה הַחוֹמָה אַחֶרֶת וַיְחַזֵּק
אֶת־הַמִּלּוֹא עִיר דָּוִיד וַיַּעַשׂ
6 שֶׁלַח לָרֹב וּמָגִנִּים׃ וַיִּתֵּן שָׂרֵי
מִלְחָמוֹת עַל־הָעָם וַיִּקְבְּצֵם
אֵלָיו אֶל־רְחוֹב שַׁעַר הָעִיר
וַיְדַבֵּר עַל־לְבָבָם לֵאמֹר׃
7 חִזְקוּ וְאִמְצוּ אַל־תִּירְאוּ
וְאַל־תֵּחַתּוּ מִפְּנֵי מֶלֶךְ אַשּׁוּר
וּמִלִּפְנֵי כָּל־הֶהָמוֹן אֲשֶׁר־
8 עִמּוֹ כִּי־עִמָּנוּ רַב מֵעִמּוֹ׃ עִמּוֹ
זְרוֹעַ בָּשָׂר וְעִמָּנוּ יְהוָה אֱלֹהֵינוּ
לְעָזְרֵנוּ וּלְהִלָּחֵם מִלְחֲמֹתֵנוּ
וַיִּסָּמְכוּ הָעָם עַל־דִּבְרֵי
יְחִזְקִיָּהוּ מֶלֶךְ־יְהוּדָה׃
9 אַחַר זֶה שָׁלַח סַנְחֵרִיב מֶלֶךְ־
אַשּׁוּר עֲבָדָיו יְרוּשָׁלַיְמָה וְהוּא

5. *raised it up to the towers.* Or, 'repaired the towers,' lit. 'and he brought up (fortifications) upon the towers.'

and another wall without. The second outer wall was built in the lower city and is presumed to be that which enclosed the Pool of Siloam. Parts of this wall have been discovered in recent years.

Millo. See on 1 Chron. xi. 8.

weapons. Better, 'missiles'; the root-meaning is 'to send.'

6. *the broad place at the gate.* In xxix. 4, there is mention of *the broad place on the east*, and Neh. viii. 16 speaks of *the broad place of the water gate* and *the broad place of the gate of Ephraim.* It is uncertain which of these gates is intended here.

8. *an arm of flesh.* Cf. Jer. xvii. 5.

9-19 (cf. 2 Kings xviii. 17-36). Sennacherib's message of abuse and threats.

9. *send his servants.* They were Tartan

Lachish, and all his power with him —unto Hezekiah king of Judah, and unto all Judah that were at Jerusalem, saying: 10. 'Thus saith Sennacherib king of Assyria: Whereon do ye trust, that ye abide the siege in Jerusalem? 11. Doth not Hezekiah persuade you, to give you over to die by famine and by thirst, saying: The LORD our God will deliver us out of the hand of the king of Assyria? 12. Hath not the same Hezekiah taken away His high places and His altars, and commanded Judah and Jerusalem, saying: Ye shall worship before one altar, and upon it shall ye offer? 13. Know ye not what I and my fathers have done unto all the peoples of the lands? Were the gods of the nations of the lands in any wise able to deliver their land out of my hand? 14. Who was there among all the gods of those nations

עַל־לָכִ֔ישׁ וְכָל־מֶֽמְשַׁלְתּ֖וֹ
עִמּ֑וֹ עַל־יְחִזְקִיָּ֙הוּ֙ מֶ֣לֶךְ
יְהוּדָ֔ה וְעַל־כָּל־יְהוּדָ֛ה אֲשֶׁ֥ר
10 בִּירוּשָׁלַ֖ם לֵאמֹֽר׃ כֹּ֚ה אָמַ֔ר
סַנְחֵרִ֖יב מֶ֣לֶךְ אַשּׁ֑וּר עַל־מָה֙
אַתֶּ֣ם בֹּֽטְחִ֔ים וְיֹשְׁבִ֥ים בְּמָצ֖וֹר
11 בִּירוּשָׁלִָֽם׃ הֲלֹ֤א יְחִזְקִיָּ֙הוּ֙
מַסִּ֣ית אֶתְכֶ֔ם לָתֵ֥ת אֶתְכֶ֛ם
לָמ֖וּת בְּרָעָ֣ב וּבְצָמָ֑א לֵאמֹ֕ר
יְהוָ֣ה אֱלֹהֵ֔ינוּ יַצִּילֵ֕נוּ מִכַּ֖ף
12 מֶ֥לֶךְ אַשּֽׁוּר׃ הֲלֹא־ה֣וּא
יְחִזְקִיָּ֔הוּ הֵסִ֥יר אֶת־בָּמֹתָ֖יו
וְאֶת־מִזְבְּחֹתָ֑יו וַיֹּ֩אמֶר֩
לִֽיהוּדָ֨ה וְלִירֽוּשָׁלִַ֜ם לֵאמֹ֗ר
לִפְנֵ֨י מִזְבֵּ֧חַ אֶחָ֛ד תִּֽשְׁתַּחֲו֖וּ
13 וְעָלָ֥יו תַּקְטִֽירוּ׃ הֲלֹ֣א תֵֽדְע֗וּ
מֶ֤ה עָשִׂ֙יתִי֙ אֲנִ֣י וַאֲבוֹתַ֔י לְכֹ֖ל
עַמֵּ֣י הָאֲרָצ֑וֹת הֲיָכ֣וֹל יָֽכְל֗וּ
אֱלֹהֵי֙ גּוֹיֵ֣ הָאֲרָצ֔וֹת לְהַצִּ֥יל
14 אֶת־אַרְצָ֖ם מִיָּדִֽי׃ מִ֠י בְּכָל־
אֱלֹהֵ֞י הַגּוֹיִ֤ם הָאֵ֙לֶּה֙ אֲשֶׁ֣ר

(commander-in-chief), Rab-saris (chief of the eunuchs) and Rab-shakeh (chief cupbearer) (2 Kings xviii. 17).

Lachish. See on xi. 9.

11. *persuade.* lit. 'entice.'

12. *taken away His high places,* etc. The argument runs thus: How can you expect help from your God in the face of Hezekiah's abolition of all His local places of worship in favour of a single altar in Jerusalem? The Assyrian mind could not comprehend that the one altar in the central Sanctuary was more acceptable to God than the multitude of altars spread all over the country.

13. *all the peoples of the lands.* A list of them is given in 2 Kings xviii. 34.

which my fathers utterly destroyed, that could deliver his people out of my hand, that your God should be able to deliver you out of my hand? 15. Now therefore let not Hezekiah beguile you, nor persuade you after this manner, neither believe ye him; for no god of any nation or kingdom was able to deliver his people out of my hand, and out of the hand of my fathers; how much less shall your God deliver you out of my hand?'

16. And his servants spoke yet more against the LORD God, and against His servant Hezekiah. 17. He wrote also a letter, to taunt the LORD, the God of Israel, and to speak against Him, saying: 'As the gods of the nations of the lands, which have not delivered their people out of my hand, so shall not the God of Hezekiah deliver His people out of my hand.' 18. And they cried with a loud voice in the Jews' language unto the people of Jerusalem that were on the wall, to terrify them, and to affright them; that they might take the city. 19. And they spoke of the God of Jerusalem, as of the gods of the

הֶחֱרִ֣ימוּ אֲבוֹתַ֔י אֲשֶׁ֣ר יָכ֔וֹל
לְהַצִּ֥יל אֶת־עַמּ֖וֹ מִיָּדִ֑י כִּ֤י
יוּכַל֙ אֱלֹ֣הֵיכֶ֔ם לְהַצִּ֥יל אֶתְכֶ֖ם
15 מִיָּדִֽי׃ וְעַתָּ֡ה אַל־יַשִּׁיא֩
אֶתְכֶ֨ם חִזְקִיָּ֜הוּ וְאַל־יַסִּ֨ית
אֶתְכֶ֤ם כָּזֹאת֙ וְאַל־תַּאֲמִ֣ינוּ
ל֔וֹ כִּֽי־לֹ֣א יוּכַ֗ל כָּל־אֱל֙וֹהַּ֙
כָּל־גּ֣וֹי וּמַמְלָכָ֔ה לְהַצִּ֥יל עַמּ֛וֹ
מִיָּדִ֖י וּמִיַּ֣ד אֲבוֹתָ֑י אַ֣ף כִּ֔י
אֱלֹ֣הֵיכֶ֔ם לֹֽא־יַצִּ֥ילוּ אֶתְכֶ֖ם
מִיָּדִֽי׃
16 וְעוֹד֙ דִּבְּר֣וּ עֲבָדָ֔יו עַל־יְהוָ֖ה
הָֽאֱלֹהִ֑ים וְעַ֖ל יְחִזְקִיָּ֥הוּ עַבְדּֽוֹ׃
17 וּסְפָרִ֣ים כָּתַ֔ב לְחָרֵ֕ף לַיהוָ֖ה
אֱלֹהֵ֣י יִשְׂרָאֵ֑ל וְלֵאמֹ֨ר עָלָ֜יו
לֵאמֹ֗ר כֵּֽאלֹהֵ֞י גּוֹיֵ֣ הָאֲרָצ֗וֹת
אֲשֶׁ֨ר לֹא־הִצִּ֤ילוּ עַמָּם֙ מִיָּדִ֔י
כֵּ֠ן לֹֽא־יַצִּ֞יל אֱלֹהֵ֧י יְחִזְקִיָּ֛הוּ
18 עַמּ֖וֹ מִיָּדִֽי׃ וַיִּקְרְא֨וּ בְקוֹל־
גָּד֤וֹל יְהוּדִית֙ עַל־עַ֣ם
יְרוּשָׁלִַ֔ם אֲשֶׁ֣ר עַל־הַחוֹמָ֔ה
לְיָֽרְאָ֖ם וּֽלְבַהֲלָ֑ם לְמַ֖עַן
19 יִלְכְּד֥וּ אֶת־הָעִֽיר׃ וַֽיְדַבְּר֔וּ
אֶל־אֱלֹהֵ֖י יְרוּשָׁלִָ֑ם כְּעַ֗ל

18. *they cried,* etc. To incite them to revolt against Hezekiah.

the Jews' language. viz. Hebrew (cf. Neh. xiii. 24).

peoples of the earth, which are the work of men's hands.

20. And Hezekiah the king, and Isaiah the prophet the son of Amoz, prayed because of this, and cried to heaven. 21. And the LORD sent an angel, who cut off all the mighty men of valour, and the leaders and captains, in the camp of the king of Assyria. So he returned with shame of face to his own land. And when he was come into the house of his god, they that came forth of his own bowels slew him there with the sword. 22. Thus the LORD saved Hezekiah and the inhabitants of Jerusalem from the hand of Sennacherib the king of Assyria, and from the hand of all, and guided them on every side. 23. And many brought gifts unto the LORD to

אֱלֹהֵי עַמֵּי הָאָרֶץ מַעֲשֵׂה יְדֵי
הָאָדָם׃
20 וַיִּתְפַּלֵּל יְחִזְקִיָּהוּ הַמֶּלֶךְ
וִישַׁעְיָהוּ בֶן־אָמוֹץ הַנָּבִיא
עַל־זֹאת וַיִּזְעֲקוּ הַשָּׁמָיִם׃
21 וַיִּשְׁלַח יְהוָה מַלְאָךְ וַיַּכְחֵד
כָּל־גִּבּוֹר חַיִל וְנָגִיד וְשָׂר
בְּמַחֲנֵה מֶלֶךְ אַשּׁוּר וַיָּשָׁב
בְּבֹשֶׁת פָּנִים לְאַרְצוֹ וַיָּבֹא
בֵּית אֱלֹהָיו וּמִיצִיאֵו מֵעָיו
22 שָׁם הִפִּילֻהוּ בֶחָרֶב׃ וַיּוֹשַׁע
יְהוָה אֶת־יְחִזְקִיָּהוּ וְאֵת ׀ יֹשְׁבֵי
יְרוּשָׁלַםִ מִיַּד סַנְחֵרִיב מֶלֶךְ־
אַשּׁוּר וּמִיַּד־כֹּל וַיְנַהֲלֵם
23 מִסָּבִיב׃ וְרַבִּים מְבִיאִים

v. 21. ומיציאי ק׳

20-23. The prayer of Hezekiah and Isaiah is answered. Fuller details are found in 2 Kings xix.

20. *to heaven.* See on xxviii. 9.

21. *cut off all the mighty men*, etc. Their number was 185,000 (2 Kings xix. 35). The sudden annihilation of the entire Assyrian army occurred, according to tradition, during the first night of the Passover before the walls of Jerusalem. Herodotus records an Egyptian tradition that another calamity befell Sennacherib when a plague of field-mice broke out in his camp at Pelusium in Egypt. In one night the mice gnawed the thongs of the soldiers' shields and their bows and, by depriving them of their main weapons, exposed them helplessly to their enemies.

they that came forth of his own bowels. viz. his sons Adrammelech and Sarezer (2 Kings xix. 37). There is a record in the Babylonian chronicle that Sennacherib was killed on the twentieth of Tebeth, in an insurrection, by one son whose name is given by ancient historians as Adrammelech. If Sarezer was not guilty of the actual murder, he may have been an accomplice to whom, as well as to his brother, the murder is attributed.

slew him. lit. 'felled him.' The murder took place some time after the flight, although it is not known exactly how long.

22. *from the hand of all.* i.e. all their other enemies.

and guided them. With care and gentleness as a shepherd guides his flock. The same Hebrew verb occurs in *He leadeth me beside the still waters* (Ps. xxiii. 2).

Jerusalem, and precious things to Hezekiah king of Judah; so that he was exalted in the sight of all nations from thenceforth.

24. In those days Hezekiah was sick even unto death; and he prayed unto the LORD; and He spoke unto him, and gave him a sign. 25. But Hezekiah rendered not according to the benefit done unto him; for his heart was lifted up; therefore there was wrath upon him, and upon Judah and Jerusalem. 26. Notwithstanding Hezekiah humbled himself for the pride of his heart, both he and the inhabitants of Jerusalem, so that the wrath of the LORD came not upon them in the days of Hezekiah.

27. And Hezekiah had exceeding much riches and honour; and he provided him treasuries for silver, and for gold, and for precious stones, and for spices, and for shields, and for all manner of goodly vessels;

מִנְחָה לַיהוָה לִירוּשָׁלִַם
וּמִגְדָּנוֹת לִיחִזְקִיָּהוּ מֶלֶךְ
יְהוּדָה וַיִּנַּשֵּׂא לְעֵינֵי כָל־
הַגּוֹיִם מֵאַחֲרֵי־כֵן׃
24 בַּיָּמִים הָהֵם חָלָה יְחִזְקִיָּהוּ
עַד־לָמוּת וַיִּתְפַּלֵּל אֶל־
יְהוָה וַיֹּאמֶר לוֹ וּמוֹפֵת נָתַן
25 לוֹ׃ וְלֹא־כִגְמֻל עָלָיו הֵשִׁיב
יְחִזְקִיָּהוּ כִּי גָבַהּ לִבּוֹ וַיְהִי
עָלָיו קֶצֶף וְעַל־יְהוּדָה
26 וִירוּשָׁלִָם׃ וַיִּכָּנַע יְחִזְקִיָּהוּ
בְּגֹבַהּ לִבּוֹ הוּא וְיוֹשְׁבֵי
יְרוּשָׁלִָם וְלֹא־בָא עֲלֵיהֶם
קֶצֶף יְהוָה בִּימֵי יְחִזְקִיָּהוּ׃
27 וַיְהִי לִיחִזְקִיָּהוּ עֹשֶׁר וְכָבוֹד
הַרְבֵּה מְאֹד וְאוֹצָרוֹת עָשָׂה־
לוֹ לְכֶסֶף וּלְזָהָב וּלְאֶבֶן יְקָרָה
וְלִבְשָׂמִים וּלְמָגִנִּים וּלְכֹל כְּלֵי

24-26. Hezekiah's sickness and humbled pride. A fuller account is found in 2 Kings xx. 1-11 and Isa. xxxviii.

24. *in those days.* Before the catastrophe which had overtaken the Assyrian armies. According to tradition, Hezekiah's illness occurred three days before Sennacherib's defeat. On the third day Hezekiah went to the Temple to offer his prayer; and on the same evening, which was the beginning of the Passover, the Assyrians were miraculously destroyed.

He spoke . . . gave him a sign. The promise which God gave him through the prophet Isaiah and the sign are detailed in 2 Kings xx. 5f., 8-11.

25. *his heart was lifted up.* Evidenced by the display of his wealth to the Babylonian embassy (2 Kings xx. 12f.).

there was wrath upon him, etc. This was revealed in Isaiah's prediction of the Babylonian captivity (2 Kings xx. 17f.).

26. *Hezekiah humbled himself.* He exclaimed, *Good is the word of the LORD which thou* (Isaiah) *hast spoken* (2 Kings xx. 19).

came not upon them in the days of Hezekiah. The Babylonian conquest came more than a century later.

27-31. Hezekiah's wealth and successful enterprise.

28. store-houses also for the increase of corn, and wine, and oil; and stalls for all manner of beasts, and flocks in folds. 29. Moreover he provided him cities, and possessions of flocks and herds in abundance; for God had given him very much substance. 30. This same Hezekiah also stopped the upper spring of the waters of Gihon, and brought them straight down on the west side of the city of David. And Hezekiah prospered in all his works. 31. Howbeit in the business of the ambassadors of the princes of Babylon, who sent unto him to inquire of the wonder that was done in the land, God left him, to try him, that He might know all that was in his heart.

32. Now the rest of the acts of Hezekiah, and his good deeds, behold, they are written in the vision of Isaiah the prophet the son of Amoz, and in the book of the

28 חֶמְדָּה׃ וּמִסְכְּנוֹת לִתְבוּאַת
דָּגָן וְתִירוֹשׁ וְיִצְהָר וְאֻרָוֹת
לְכָל־בְּהֵמָה וּבְהֵמָה וַעֲדָרִים
29 לָאֲוֵרוֹת׃ וְעָרִים עָשָׂה לוֹ
וּמִקְנֵה־צֹאן וּבָקָר לָרֹב כִּי
נָתַן־לוֹ אֱלֹהִים רְכוּשׁ רַב
30 מְאֹד׃ וְהוּא יְחִזְקִיָּהוּ סָתַם
אֶת־מוֹצָא מֵימֵי גִיחוֹן הָעֶלְיוֹן
וַיַּישְּׁרֵם לְמַטָּה־מַּעְרָבָה
לְעִיר דָּוִיד וַיַּצְלַח יְחִזְקִיָּהוּ
31 בְּכָל־מַעֲשֵׂהוּ׃ וְכֵן בִּמְלִיצֵי ׀
שָׂרֵי בָּבֶל הַמְשַׁלְּחִים עָלָיו
לִדְרֹשׁ הַמּוֹפֵת אֲשֶׁר הָיָה
בָאָרֶץ עֲזָבוֹ הָאֱלֹהִים לְנַסּוֹתוֹ
לָדַעַת כָּל־בִּלְבָבוֹ׃
32 וְיֶתֶר דִּבְרֵי יְחִזְקִיָּהוּ וַחֲסָדָיו
הִנָּם כְּתוּבִים בַּחֲזוֹן יְשַׁעְיָהוּ
בֶן־אָמוֹץ הַנָּבִיא עַל־סֵפֶר

v. 30. יתיר י׳ והש׳ דגושה

27. ***shields.*** These were weapons in general or a type of costly shield made of precious metal.

29. ***he provided him cities.*** The context implies that they were places of security for his flocks in times of war or raids.

30. *the upper spring of the waters of Gihon.* See on verse 3f.

31. *the business.* Not in the text.

ambassadors. lit. 'interpreters.'

princes of Babylon. viz. Merodach-baladan and his advisers.

the wonder. Hezekiah's miraculous recovery and the supernatural sign (see on verse 24).

32f. (cf. 2 Kings xx. 20f.). Hezekiah's record and death.

32. *and in the book.* The first two words represent the Hebrew preposition *al*, 'upon.' The translation of *al* as 'in' with the omission of *and* (so R.V.) would imply that *the vision of Isaiah* was included in *the book of the kings.* The most probable interpretation of *al* in this context is 'besides,' 'in addition to.' The

kings of Judah and Israel. 33. And
Hezekiah slept with his fathers, and
they buried him in the ascent of the
sepulchres of the sons of David;
and all Judah and the inhabitants of
Jerusalem did him honour at his
death. And Manasseh his son
reigned in his stead.

מַלְכֵי־יְהוּדָה וְיִשְׂרָאֵל׃
33 וַיִּשְׁכַּב יְחִזְקִיָּהוּ עִם־אֲבֹתָיו
וַיִּקְבְּרֻהוּ בְּמַעֲלֵה קִבְרֵי בְנֵי־
דָוִיד וְכָבוֹד עָשׂוּ־לוֹ בְמוֹתוֹ
כָּל־יְהוּדָה וְיֹשְׁבֵי יְרוּשָׁלִָם
וַיִּמְלֹךְ מְנַשֶּׁה בְנוֹ תַּחְתָּיו׃

33 CHAPTER XXXIII לג

1. Manasseh was twelve years old
when he began to reign; and he
reigned fifty and five years in
Jerusalem. 2. And he did that
which was evil in the sight of the
LORD, after the abominations of the
nations, whom the LORD cast out
before the children of Israel. 3. For
he built again the high places which
Hezekiah his father had broken
down; and he reared up altars for
the Baalim, and made Asheroth,
and worshipped all the host of
heaven, and served them. 4. And

1 בֶּן־שְׁתֵּים עֶשְׂרֵה שָׁנָה מְנַשֶּׁה
בְמָלְכוֹ וַחֲמִשִּׁים וְחָמֵשׁ שָׁנָה
2 מָלַךְ בִּירוּשָׁלִָם׃ וַיַּעַשׂ הָרַע
בְּעֵינֵי יְהוָה כְּתוֹעֲבוֹת הַגּוֹיִם
אֲשֶׁר הוֹרִישׁ יְהוָה מִפְּנֵי בְּנֵי
3 יִשְׂרָאֵל׃ וַיָּשָׁב וַיִּבֶן אֶת־
הַבָּמוֹת אֲשֶׁר נִתַּץ יְחִזְקִיָּהוּ
אָבִיו וַיָּקֶם מִזְבְּחוֹת לַבְּעָלִים
וַיַּעַשׂ אֲשֵׁרוֹת וַיִּשְׁתַּחוּ לְכָל־
צְבָא הַשָּׁמַיִם וַיַּעֲבֹד אֹתָם׃

rendering would then be, 'in addition to the book of the kings,' i.e. Hezekiah's acts are recorded not only in *the book of the kings* but also in *the vision* (prophecies) *of Isaiah* (xxxvi-xxxix).

33. *the ascent of the sepulchres.* The higher ground of the area set aside for the royal sepulchres. The Talmudical explanation is 'the best of the sepulchres' (B.K. 16b).

did him honour. i.e. perfumed the bier with spices (cf. xvi. 14).

CHAPTER XXXIII

REIGN OF MANASSEH AND AMON

1-9 (corresponding to 2 Kings xxi. 1-9). Duration of Manasseh's reign and his apostasy.

1. *fifty and five years.* Manasseh's was the longest reign of any king of Judah or Israel (692-638 B.C.E.). Kings adds that his mother's name was *Hephzi-bah.*

2. *the abominations.* These are enumerated in the following verses.

3. *his father had broken down.* Cf. xxxi. 1.

made Asheroth. See on xiv. 2. The reading in 2 Kings xxi. 3 is: *made an Asherah, as did Ahab king of Israel.*

the host of heaven. The heavenly luminaries, not, as in xviii. 18, the angelic beings.

he built altars in the house of the
LORD, whereof the LORD said: 'In
Jerusalem shall My name be for
ever.' 5. And he built altars for all
the host of heaven in the two courts
of the house of the LORD. 6. He
also made his children to pass
through the fire in the valley of the
son of Hinnom; and he practised
soothsaying, and used enchantments,
and practised sorcery, and appointed
them that divined by a ghost or a
familiar spirit; he wrought much
evil in the sight of the LORD, to
provoke Him. 7. And he set the
graven image of the idol, which he
had made, in the house of God, of
which God said to David and
Solomon his son: 'In this house, and
in Jerusalem, which I have chosen
out of all the tribes of Israel, will I
put My name for ever; 8. neither
will I any more remove the foot of
Israel from off the land which
I have appointed for your fathers;
if only they will observe to do all
that I have commanded them, even
all the law and the statutes and the

4 וּבָנָה מִזְבְּחוֹת בְּבֵית יְהוָה
אֲשֶׁר אָמַר יְהוָה בִּירוּשָׁלַם
5 יִהְיֶה־שְּׁמִי לְעוֹלָם׃ וַיִּבֶן
מִזְבְּחוֹת לְכָל־צְבָא הַשָּׁמָיִם
בִּשְׁתֵּי חַצְרוֹת בֵּית־יְהוָה׃
6 וְהוּא הֶעֱבִיר אֶת־בָּנָיו בָּאֵשׁ
בְּגֵי בֶן־הִנֹּם וְעוֹנֵן וְנִחֵשׁ וְכִשֵּׁף
וְעָשָׂה אוֹב וְיִדְּעוֹנִי הִרְבָּה
לַעֲשׂוֹת הָרַע בְּעֵינֵי יְהוָה
7 לְהַכְעִיסוֹ׃ וַיָּשֶׂם אֶת־פֶּסֶל
הַסֶּמֶל אֲשֶׁר עָשָׂה בְּבֵית
הָאֱלֹהִים אֲשֶׁר אָמַר אֱלֹהִים
אֶל־דָּוִיד וְאֶל־שְׁלֹמֹה בְנוֹ
בַּבַּיִת הַזֶּה וּבִירוּשָׁלַם אֲשֶׁר
בָּחַרְתִּי מִכֹּל שִׁבְטֵי יִשְׂרָאֵל
אָשִׂים אֶת־שְׁמִי לְעֵילוֹם׃
8 וְלֹא אוֹסִיף לְהָסִיר אֶת־רֶגֶל
יִשְׂרָאֵל מֵעַל הָאֲדָמָה אֲשֶׁר
הֶעֱמַדְתִּי לַאֲבוֹתֵיכֶם רַק ׀
אִם־יִשְׁמְרוּ לַעֲשׂוֹת אֵת כָּל־
אֲשֶׁר צִוִּיתִים לְכָל־הַתּוֹרָה

4. *he built altars.* For *the host of heaven,* as explained in the next verse.

in Jerusalem . . . for ever. By the building of the Temple (cf. vii. 16).

5. *the two courts.* The court of the priests and the court of the Israelites.

6. *his children.* In 2 Kings xxi. 6: *his son.*

to pass through the fire. A rite of Molech worship.

the valley of the son of Hinnom. See on xxviii. 3.

soothsaying, etc. All these superstitious practices are forbidden in the Torah (cf. Deut. xviii. 10f.).

7. *the graven image of the idol.* In

ordinances by the hand of Moses.'
9. And Manasseh made Judah and
the inhabitants of Jerusalem to err,
so that they did evil more than did
the nations, whom the LORD destroyed before the children of Israel.
10. And the LORD spoke to
Manasseh, and to his people; but
they gave no heed. 11. Wherefore
the LORD brought upon them the
captains of the host of the king of
Assyria, who took Manasseh with
hooks, and bound him with fetters,
and carried him to Babylon. 12. And
when he was in distress, he besought
the LORD his God, and humbled
himself greatly before the God of
his fathers. 13. And he prayed
unto Him; and He was entreated of
him, and heard his supplication, and
brought him back to Jerusalem into
his kingdom. Then Manasseh knew
that the LORD He was God.

וְהַחֻקִּים וְהַמִּשְׁפָּטִים בְּיַד־
9 מֹשֶׁה׃ וַיֶּתַע מְנַשֶּׁה אֶת־
יְהוּדָה וְיֹשְׁבֵי יְרוּשָׁלִָם לַעֲשׂוֹת
רָע מִן־הַגּוֹיִם אֲשֶׁר הִשְׁמִיד
יְהוָה מִפְּנֵי בְּנֵי יִשְׂרָאֵל׃
10 וַיְדַבֵּר יְהוָה אֶל־מְנַשֶּׁה וְאֶל־
11 עַמּוֹ וְלֹא הִקְשִׁיבוּ׃ וַיָּבֵא יְהוָה
עֲלֵיהֶם אֶת־שָׂרֵי הַצָּבָא אֲשֶׁר
לְמֶלֶךְ אַשּׁוּר וַיִּלְכְּדוּ אֶת־
מְנַשֶּׁה בַּחֹחִים וַיַּאַסְרֻהוּ
בַּנְחֻשְׁתַּיִם וַיּוֹלִיכֻהוּ בָּבֶלָה׃
12 וּכְהָצֵר לוֹ חִלָּה אֶת־פְּנֵי יְהוָה
אֱלֹהָיו וַיִּכָּנַע מְאֹד מִלִּפְנֵי
13 אֱלֹהֵי אֲבֹתָיו׃ וַיִּתְפַּלֵּל אֵלָיו
וַיֵּעָתֶר לוֹ וַיִּשְׁמַע תְּחִנָּתוֹ
וַיְשִׁיבֵהוּ יְרוּשָׁלִַם לְמַלְכוּתוֹ
וַיֵּדַע מְנַשֶּׁה כִּי יְהוָה הוּא
הָאֱלֹהִים׃

2 Kings xxi. 7: *the graven image of Asherah.*

9. *more than did the nations.* As the effect of the evil influence of Manasseh, his subjects became more heathen than the heathens.

10. God's warning unheeded. The Divine message is recorded at length in 2 Kings xxi. 11-15.

the LORD spoke. 2 Kings xxi. 10 adds: *by His servants the prophets* and omits *to Manasseh, and to his people.*

11-13 (not in Kings). Manasseh's punishment, repentance and restoration.

11. *the king of Assyria.* He was either Esarhaddon or Asurbanipal. In the inscriptions relating to the reign of both of them Manasseh's name appears in a list of tributary kings.

with hooks. The cruelty of leading prisoners with hooks in their nostrils was widely practised in ancient times, and is illustrated on Assyrian reliefs preserved in the British Museum (cf. 2 Kings xix. 28).

to Babylon. Where the king had a residence although his capital was Nineveh.

14. Now after this he built an outer wall to the city of David, on the west side of Gihon, in the valley, even to the entrance at the fish gate; and he compassed about Ophel, and raised it up a very great height; and he put captains of the army in all the fortified cities of Judah. 15. And he took away the strange gods, and the idol out of the house of the LORD, and all the altars that he had built in the mount of the house of the LORD, and in Jerusalem, and cast them out of the city. 16. And he built up the altar of the LORD, and offered thereon sacrifices of peace-offerings and of thanksgiving, and commanded Judah to serve the LORD, the God of Israel. 17. Nevertheless the people did sacrifice still in the high places, but only unto the LORD their God.

18. Now the rest of the acts of Manasseh, and his prayer unto his God, and the words of the seers that

14 וְאַחֲרֵי־כֵן בָּנָה חוֹמָה חִיצוֹנָה
לְעִיר־דָּוִיד מַעְרָבָה לְגִיחוֹן
בַּנַּחַל וְלָבוֹא בְשַׁעַר הַדָּגִים
וְסָבַב לָעֹפֶל וַיַּגְבִּיהֶהָ מְאֹד
וַיָּשֶׂם שָׂרֵי־חַיִל בְּכָל־הֶעָרִים
15 הַבְּצֻרוֹת בִּיהוּדָה׃ וַיָּסַר
אֶת־אֱלֹהֵי הַנֵּכָר וְאֶת־הַסֶּמֶל
מִבֵּית יְהוָה וְכָל־הַמִּזְבְּחוֹת
אֲשֶׁר בָּנָה בְּהַר בֵּית־יְהוָה
וּבִירוּשָׁלִָם וַיַּשְׁלֵךְ חוּצָה
16 לָעִיר׃ וַיִּכֶן* אֶת־מִזְבַּח יְהוָה
וַיִּזְבַּח עָלָיו זִבְחֵי שְׁלָמִים
וְתוֹדָה וַיֹּאמֶר לִיהוּדָה
לַעֲבוֹד אֶת־יְהוָה אֱלֹהֵי
17 יִשְׂרָאֵל׃ אֲבָל עוֹד הָעָם
זֹבְחִים בַּבָּמוֹת רַק לַיהוָה
אֱלֹהֵיהֶם׃
18 וְיֶתֶר דִּבְרֵי מְנַשֶּׁה וּתְפִלָּתוֹ
אֶל־אֱלֹהָיו וְדִבְרֵי הַחֹזִים

v. 16. ויבן ק׳

14-17 (not in Kings). Manasseh's new fortifications and abolition of idolatry.

14. *Gihon.* See on xxxii. 4.

the fish gate. In the north wall, possibly the modern Damascus gate. Nearby was a fish market from which it derived its name.

he compassed. With the wall he built.

Ophel. See on xxvii. 3.

15. *he took away . . . the idol.* Which he had placed in the house of God (verse 7).

all the altars that he had built, etc. Cf. verses 4f.

16. *he built up.* Or, 'rebuilt, repaired.'

17. It proved beyond Manasseh's power entirely to abolish the high places, but he insisted that the offerings brought there should be in the service of God and not of Baal.

18-20 (cf. 2 Kings xxi. 17f.). Summary of the reign.

18. *his prayer.* Cf. verses 12f. A 'Prayer of Manasseh' is included in the

spoke to him in the name of the LORD, the God of Israel, behold, they are written among the acts of the kings of Israel. 19. His prayer also, and how [God] was entreated of him, and all his sin and his transgression, and the places wherein he built high places, and set up the Asherim and the graven images, before he humbled himself; behold, they are written in the history of the seers. 20. So Manasseh slept with his fathers, and they buried him in his own house; and Amon his son reigned in his stead.

21. Amon was twenty and two years old when he began to reign; and he reigned two years in Jerusalem. 22. And he did that which was evil in the sight of the LORD, as did Manasseh his father; and Amon sacrificed unto all the graven images which Manasseh his father had made, and served them. 23. And he humbled not himself before the LORD, as Manasseh his father had humbled himself; but this same Amon became guilty more and more.

הַֽמְדַבְּרִים אֵלָיו בְּשֵׁם יְהוָה
אֱלֹהֵי יִשְׂרָאֵל הִנָּם עַל־דִּבְרֵי
19 מַלְכֵי יִשְׂרָאֵל׃ וּתְפִלָּתוֹ
וְהֵֽעָתֶר־לוֹ וְכָל־חַטָּאתוֹ
וּמַעְלוֹ וְהַמְּקֹמוֹת אֲשֶׁר בָּנָה
בָהֶם בָּמוֹת וְהֶעֱמִיד הָאֲשֵׁרִים
וְהַפְּסִלִים לִפְנֵי הִכָּנְעוֹ הִנָּם
כְּתוּבִים עַל דִּבְרֵי חוֹזָי׃
20 וַיִּשְׁכַּב מְנַשֶּׁה עִם־אֲבֹתָיו
וַֽיִּקְבְּרֻהוּ בֵּיתוֹ וַיִּמְלֹךְ אָמוֹן
בְּנוֹ תַּחְתָּיו׃
21 בֶּן־עֶשְׂרִים וּשְׁתַּיִם שָׁנָה אָמוֹן
בְּמָלְכוֹ וּשְׁתַּיִם שָׁנִים מָלַךְ
22 בִּירוּשָׁלִָם׃ וַיַּעַשׂ הָרַע בְּעֵינֵי
יְהוָה כַּאֲשֶׁר עָשָׂה מְנַשֶּׁה אָבִיו
וּֽלְכָל־הַפְּסִילִים אֲשֶׁר עָשָׂה
מְנַשֶּׁה אָבִיו זִבַּח אָמוֹן
23 וַיַּֽעַבְדֵם׃ וְלֹא נִכְנַע מִלִּפְנֵי
יְהוָה כְּהִכָּנַע מְנַשֶּׁה אָבִיו כִּֽי
הוּא אָמוֹן הִרְבָּה אַשְׁמָה׃

Apocrypha, but its authenticity is not accepted.

the words of the seers. See on verse 10.

19. *the history of the seers.* This translation agrees with the LXX and is adopted in A.V., but R.V. transliterates the Hebrew word: 'the history of Hozai.' If a prophet or historian of that name existed he is otherwise unknown.

20. *in his own house.* 2 Kings xxi. 18 reads: *in the garden of his own house, in the garden of Uzza.*

21-25 (corresponding to 2 Kings xxi. 19-26). The reign of Amon (638-637 B.C.E.).

21. The name of his mother is added in Kings.

23. This verse has no parallel in Kings.

24. And his servants conspired against him, and put him to death in his own house. 25. But the people of the land slew all them that had conspired against king Amon; and the people of the land made Josiah his son king in his stead.

24 וַיִּקְשְׁרוּ עָלָיו עֲבָדָיו וַיְמִיתֻהוּ
25 בְּבֵיתוֹ׃ וַיַּכּוּ עַם־הָאָרֶץ אֵת
כָּל־הַקֹּשְׁרִים עַל־הַמֶּלֶךְ
אָמוֹן וַיַּמְלִיכוּ עַם־הָאָרֶץ
אֶת־יֹאשִׁיָּהוּ בְנוֹ תַּחְתָּיו׃

34 CHAPTER XXXIV לד

1. Josiah was eight years old when he began to reign; and he reigned thirty and one years in Jerusalem. 2. And he did that which was right in the eyes of the LORD, and walked in the ways of David his father, and turned not aside to the right hand or to the left. 3. For in the eighth year of his reign, while he was yet young, he began to seek after the God of David his father; and in the twelfth year he began to purge Judah and Jerusalem from the high places, and the Asherim, and the

1 בֶּן־שְׁמוֹנֶה שָׁנִים יֹאשִׁיָּהוּ
בְמָלְכוֹ וּשְׁלֹשִׁים וְאַחַת שָׁנָה
2 מָלַךְ בִּירוּשָׁלִָם׃ וַיַּעַשׂ הַיָּשָׁר
בְּעֵינֵי יְהוָה וַיֵּלֶךְ בְּדַרְכֵי דָּוִיד
אָבִיו וְלֹא־סָר יָמִין וּשְׂמֹאול׃
3 וּבִשְׁמוֹנֶה שָׁנִים לְמָלְכוֹ וְהוּא
עוֹדֶנּוּ נַעַר הֵחֵל לִדְרוֹשׁ
לֵאלֹהֵי דָּוִיד אָבִיו וּבִשְׁתֵּים ׀
עֶשְׂרֵה שָׁנָה הֵחֵל לְטַהֵר אֶת־
יְהוּדָה וִירוּשָׁלִַם מִן־הַבָּמוֹת
וְהָאֲשֵׁרִים וְהַפְּסִלִים

24. *his servants.* His courtiers; the conspiracy was planned inside the palace.

25. *the people of the land.* See on xxiii. 20.

CHAPTERS XXXIV-XXXV

REIGN OF JOSIAH

CHAPTER XXXIV

1f. (corresponding to 2 Kings xxii. 1f.). Introduction to Josiah's reign (637-608 B.C.E.).

1. *eight years old when he began to reign.* Under the guardianship of the priests and elders. His mother's name, recorded in Kings, was *Jedidah, the daughter of Adaiah of Bozkath.*

2. *father.* As often, the word denotes 'ancestor.'

3-7 (cf. 2 Kings xxiii. 4-20). Josiah's removal of all traces of idolatry.

3. *in the eighth year,* etc. The religious training he received from his instructors between the ages of eight and sixteen created within him zeal to restore his people to the worship of God, and he set about purging the land of idolatry upon which task he spent six years (verse 8).

graven images, and the molten images. 4. And they broke down the altars of the Baalim in his presence; and the sun-images, that were on high above them, he hewed down; and the Asherim, and the graven images, and the molten images, he broke in pieces, and made dust of them, and strewed it upon the graves of them that had sacrificed unto them. 5. And he burnt the bones of the priests upon their altars, and purged Judah and Jerusalem. 6. And so did he in the cities of Manasseh and Ephraim and Simeon, even unto Naphtali, with their axes round about. 7. And he broke down the altars, and beat the Asherim and the graven images into powder, and hewed down all the sun-images throughout all the land of Israel, and returned to Jerusalem.

8. Now in the eighteenth year of his reign, when he had purged the land, and the house, he sent Shaphan

4 וְהַמַּסֵּכוֹת׃ וַיְנַתְּצוּ לְפָנָיו אֵת
מִזְבְּחוֹת הַבְּעָלִים וְהַֽחַמָּנִים
אֲשֶׁר־לְמַעְלָה מֵעֲלֵיהֶם גִּדֵּעַ
וְהָאֲשֵׁרִים וְהַפְּסִלִים
וְהַמַּסֵּכוֹת שִׁבַּר וְהֵדַק וַיִּזְרֹק
עַל־פְּנֵי הַקְּבָרִים הַזֹּבְחִים
5 לָהֶם׃ וְעַצְמוֹת כֹּהֲנִים שָׂרַף
עַל־מִזְבְּחוֹתָים* וַיְטַהֵר אֶת־
6 יְהוּדָה וְאֶת־יְרוּשָׁלִָם׃ וּבְעָרֵי
מְנַשֶּׁה וְאֶפְרַיִם וְשִׁמְעוֹן וְעַד־
נַפְתָּלִי בְּחַר* בָּתֵּיהֶם סָבִיב׃
7 וַיְנַתֵּץ אֶת־הַמִּזְבְּחוֹת וְאֶת־
הָאֲשֵׁרִים וְהַפְּסִלִים כִּתַּת
לְהֵדַק וְכָל־הַחַמָּנִים גִּדַּע
בְּכָל־אֶרֶץ יִשְׂרָאֵל וַיָּשָׁב
לִירוּשָׁלִָם׃
8 וּבִשְׁנַת שְׁמוֹנֶה עֶשְׂרֵה לְמָלְכוֹ
לְטַהֵר אֶת־הָאָרֶץ וְהַבָּיִת
שָׁלַח אֶת־שָׁפָן בֶּן־אֲצַלְיָהוּ

v. 5. יתיר י׳ v. 6. בחרבתיהם ק׳

the Asherim. See on xiv. 2.

4. *in his presence.* Under his personal supervision.

the sun-images. See on xiv. 4.

5. *he burnt the bones of the priests.* More fully in 2 Kings xxiii. 16: *he took the bones out of the sepulchres, and burned them upon the altar, and defiled it.*

6. *so did he.* Not in the text.

in the cities . . . unto Naphtali. As with Hezekiah (cf. xxx. 1), Josiah's jurisdiction extended to the northern region.

with their axes. Or, 'in their ruins' (R.V.), which the Assyrian invasion had caused.

8-13 (corresponding to 2 Kings xxii. 3-7). The repair and restoration of the Temple. Cf. the similar undertaking in the reign of Joash (xxiv. 4ff.).

8. *Shaphan.* 2 Kings xxii. 3 describes him as *the scribe.*

the son of Azaliah, and Maaseiah the governor of the city, and Joah the son of Joahaz the recorder, to repair the house of the LORD his God. 9. And they came to Hilkiah the high priest and delivered the money that was brought into the house of God, which the Levites, the keepers of the door, had gathered of the hand of Manasseh and Ephraim, and of all the remnant of Israel, and of all Judah and Benjamin, and they returned to Jerusalem. 10. And they delivered it into the hand of the workmen that had the oversight of the house of the LORD; and the workmen that wrought in the house of the LORD gave it to mend and repair the house; 11. even to the carpenters and to the builders gave they it, to buy hewn stone, and timber for couplings, and to make beams for the houses which the kings of Judah had destroyed. 12. And the men did the work faithfully; and the overseers of them were Jahath and Obadiah, the Levites, of the sons of Merari; and

וְאֶת־מַעֲשֵׂיָהוּ שַׂר־הָעִיר
וְאֵת יוֹאָח בֶּן־יוֹאָחָז הַמַּזְכִּיר
לְחַזֵּק אֶת־בֵּית יְהוָה אֱלֹהָיו׃
9 וַיָּבֹאוּ אֶל־חִלְקִיָּהוּ ׀ הַכֹּהֵן
הַגָּדוֹל וַיִּתְּנוּ אֶת־הַכֶּסֶף
הַמּוּבָא בֵית־אֱלֹהִים אֲשֶׁר
אָסְפוּ־הַלְוִיִּם שֹׁמְרֵי הַסַּף
מִיַּד מְנַשֶּׁה וְאֶפְרַיִם וּמִכֹּל
שְׁאֵרִית יִשְׂרָאֵל וּמִכָּל־יְהוּדָה
10 וּבִנְיָמִן וַיָּשֻׁבֵי* יְרוּשָׁלִָם׃ וַיִּתְּנוּ
עַל־יַד עֹשֵׂה הַמְּלָאכָה
הַמֻּפְקָדִים בְּבֵית יְהוָה וַיִּתְּנוּ
אֹתוֹ עוֹשֵׂי הַמְּלָאכָה אֲשֶׁר
עֹשִׂים בְּבֵית יְהוָה לִבְדּוֹק
11 וּלְחַזֵּק הַבָּיִת׃ וַיִּתְּנוּ לֶחָרָשִׁים
וְלַבֹּנִים לִקְנוֹת אַבְנֵי מַחְצֵב
וְעֵצִים לַמְחַבְּרוֹת וּלְקָרוֹת
אֶת־הַבָּתִּים אֲשֶׁר הִשְׁחִיתוּ
12 מַלְכֵי יְהוּדָה׃ וְהָאֲנָשִׁים
עֹשִׂים בֶּאֱמוּנָה בַּמְּלָאכָה
וַעֲלֵיהֶם ׀ מֻפְקָדִים יַחַת
וְעֹבַדְיָהוּ הַלְוִיִּם מִן־בְּנֵי

v. 9. וישבו ק׳

Maaseiah . . . Joah. They are not mentioned in Kings.

the recorder. See on 1 Chron. xviii. 15.

9. *they came to Hilkiah*, etc. According to 2 Kings xxii. 4, Hilkiah did not receive the money but only checked the total.

10. *the workmen.* These were the overseers, the artisans being referred to in the next verse.

11. *the houses.* See on 1 Chron. xxviii. 11.

12. *overseers.* From these words to the end of verse 13 is without a parallel in Kings.

Zechariah and Meshullam, of the sons of the Kohathites, to preside over it; and other of the Levites, all that had skill with instruments of music. 13. Also they were over the bearers of burdens, and presided over all that did the work in every manner of service; and of the Levites there were scribes, and officers, and porters.

14. And when they brought out the money that was brought into the house of the LORD, Hilkiah the priest found the book of the Law of the LORD given by Moses. 15. And Hilkiah answered and said to Shaphan the scribe: 'I have found the book of the Law in the house of the LORD.' And Hilkiah delivered the book to Shaphan. 16. And Shaphan carried the book to the king, and moreover brought back word unto the king, saying: 'All that was committed to thy servants, they do

מְרָרִי וּזְכַרְיָה וּמְשֻׁלָּם מִן־
בְּנֵי הַקְּהָתִים לְנַצֵּחַ וְהַלְוִיִּם
כָּל־מֵבִין בִּכְלֵי־שִׁיר׃ וְעַל 13
הַסַּבָּלִים וּמְנַצְּחִים לְכֹל עֹשֵׂה
מְלָאכָה לַעֲבוֹדָה וַעֲבוֹדָה
וּמֵהַלְוִיִּם סוֹפְרִים וְשֹׁטְרִים
וְשׁוֹעֲרִים׃
וּבְהוֹצִיאָם אֶת־הַכֶּסֶף 14
הַמּוּבָא בֵּית יְהוָה מָצָא
חִלְקִיָּהוּ הַכֹּהֵן אֶת־סֵפֶר
תּוֹרַת־יְהוָה בְּיַד־מֹשֶׁה׃ וַיַּעַן 15
חִלְקִיָּהוּ וַיֹּאמֶר אֶל־שָׁפָן
הַסּוֹפֵר סֵפֶר הַתּוֹרָה מָצָאתִי
בְּבֵית יְהוָה וַיִּתֵּן חִלְקִיָּהוּ אֶת־
הַסֵּפֶר אֶל־שָׁפָן׃ וַיָּבֵא שָׁפָן 16
אֶת־הַסֵּפֶר אֶל־הַמֶּלֶךְ וַיָּשֶׁב
עוֹד אֶת־הַמֶּלֶךְ דָּבָר לֵאמֹר
כֹּל אֲשֶׁר־נִתַּן בְּיַד־עֲבָדֶיךָ

14-21 (corresponding to 2 Kings xxii. 8-13). The discovery of the book of the Law. It had been lost and forgotten for almost seventy years during the reigns of Manasseh (fifty-five years), his son Amon (two years) and the ten years which elapsed between Josiah's accession at the age of eight and his attainment of the age of eighteen when the discovery was made. During that long period king and people were steeped in idolatry, the Temple services were neglected, and copies of the book of the Law must have been destroyed, so that the finding of a copy in the Temple, probably preserved by one of the faithful priests, was in fact a startling event.

14. This verse is an addition to Kings.

the book of the Law. i.e. Deuteronomy or, according to a modern view, chapters v-xxviii, or only xii-xxvi of the Book. The version in Chronicles suggests that the copy lay concealed at the bottom of the chest which contained the coins deposited in the treasury.

15. *the book of the Law.* The use of the definite article implies that Hilkiah was aware that such a book was once in existence.

it. 17. And they have poured out
the money that was found in the
house of the LORD, and have
delivered it into the hand of the
overseers, and into the hand of the
workmen.' 18. And Shaphan the
scribe told the king, saying: 'Hilkiah
the priest hath delivered me a book.'
And Shaphan read therein before the
king. 19. And it came to pass,
when the king had heard the words
of the Law, that he rent his clothes.
20. And the king commanded
Hilkiah, and Ahikam the son of
Shaphan, and Abdon the son of
Micah, and Shaphan the scribe, and
Asaiah the king's servant, saying:
21. 'Go ye, inquire of the LORD for
me, and for them that are left in
Israel and in Judah, concerning the
words of the book that is found; for
great is the wrath of the LORD that
is poured out upon us, because our

17 הֵם עֹשִׂים׃ וַיַּתִּיכוּ אֶת־
הַכֶּסֶף הַנִּמְצָא בְּבֵית־יְהוָה
וַיִּתְּנוּהוּ עַל־יַד הַמֻּפְקָדִים
וְעַל־יַד עוֹשֵׂי הַמְּלָאכָה׃
18 וַיַּגֵּד שָׁפָן הַסּוֹפֵר לַמֶּלֶךְ
לֵאמֹר סֵפֶר נָתַן לִי חִלְקִיָּהוּ
הַכֹּהֵן וַיִּקְרָא־בוֹ שָׁפָן לִפְנֵי
19 הַמֶּלֶךְ׃ וַיְהִי כִּשְׁמֹעַ הַמֶּלֶךְ
אֵת דִּבְרֵי הַתּוֹרָה וַיִּקְרַע אֶת־
20 בְּגָדָיו׃ וַיְצַו הַמֶּלֶךְ אֶת־
חִלְקִיָּהוּ וְאֶת־אֲחִיקָם בֶּן־
שָׁפָן וְאֶת־עַבְדּוֹן בֶּן־מִיכָה
וְאֵת ׀ שָׁפָן הַסּוֹפֵר וְאֵת עֲשָׂיָה
21 עֶבֶד־הַמֶּלֶךְ לֵאמֹר׃ לְכוּ
דִרְשׁוּ אֶת־יְהוָה בַּעֲדִי וּבְעַד
הַנִּשְׁאָר בְּיִשְׂרָאֵל וּבִיהוּדָה
עַל־דִּבְרֵי הַסֵּפֶר אֲשֶׁר נִמְצָא
כִּי־גדוֹלָה חֲמַת־יְהוָה אֲשֶׁר
נִתְּכָה בָנוּ עַל אֲשֶׁר לֹא־

17. *they have poured out the money.* Shaphan first reports on the mission which had been entrusted to him by the king (cf. 2 Kings xxii. 3ff.).

poured out the money. Emptied the chest.

18. *a book.* Shaphan uses the indefinite article in speaking to the king who was in ignorance of the existence of the book of the Law.

read therein. i.e. portions of it.

19. *he rent his clothes.* To express his grief on hearing the dire punishment which would follow on the neglect of God's commandments as foretold in the discovered book.

20. *the king's servant.* This was probably the title of an important officer who was in close attendance on the king. The inscription, 'To Obadiah the servant of the king,' has been found on an ancient Hebrew seal.

21. *inquire of the LORD.* Through a prophet.

M

fathers have not kept the word of the LORD, to do according unto all that is written in this book.'

22. So Hilkiah, and they whom the king [had commanded], went to Huldah the prophetess, the wife of Shallum the son of Tokhath, the son of Hasrah, keeper of the wardrobe—now she dwelt in Jerusalem in the second quarter—and they spoke to her to that effect. 23. And she said unto them: 'Thus saith the LORD, the God of Israel: Tell ye the man that sent you unto me: 24. Thus saith the LORD: Behold, I will bring evil upon this place, and upon the inhabitants thereof, even all the

שָׁמְרוּ אֲבוֹתֵינוּ אֶת־דְּבַר
יְהוָה לַעֲשׂוֹת כְּכָל־הַכָּתוּב
עַל־הַסֵּפֶר הַזֶּה׃
22 וַיֵּלֶךְ חִלְקִיָּהוּ וַאֲשֶׁר הַמֶּלֶךְ
אֶל־חֻלְדָּה הַנְּבִיאָה אֵשֶׁת ׀
שַׁלֻּם בֶּן־תָּוְקְהַת בֶּן־חַסְרָה
שׁוֹמֵר הַבְּגָדִים וְהִיא יוֹשֶׁבֶת
בִּירוּשָׁלַםִ בַּמִּשְׁנֶה וַיְדַבְּרוּ
23 אֵלֶיהָ כְּזֹאת׃ וַתֹּאמֶר לָהֶם
כֹּה־אָמַר יְהוָה אֱלֹהֵי יִשְׂרָאֵל
אִמְרוּ לָאִישׁ אֲשֶׁר־שָׁלַח
24 אֶתְכֶם אֵלָי׃ כֹּה אָמַר יְהוָה
הִנְנִי מֵבִיא רָעָה עַל־הַמָּקוֹם
הַזֶּה וְעַל־יוֹשְׁבָיו אֵת כָּל־

v. 22. יתיר ו׳

22-28 (corresponding to 2 Kings xxii. 14-20). Huldah's oracle in reply to the king's inquiry.

22. *they whom the king* [*had commanded*]. In 2 Kings xxii. 14 their names are given: Hilkiah the priest, Ahikam, Achbor, Shaphan and Asaiah.

went to Huldah. The Talmud (Meg. 14b) explains that they did not go to her contemporary, Jeremiah, because a woman was more tender-hearted and would pray on behalf of the people who had sinned in ignorance. Modern authorities suggest that Jeremiah had only begun his prophetic career about five years before the discovery and had not attained widespread recognition by that time. Another hypothesis is that the choice fell upon her because she was the wife of a Temple official who was probably a priest.

the prophetess. The title is also given to Miriam (Exod. xv. 20), Deborah (Judg. iv. 4), Isaiah's wife (Isa. viii. 3) and Noadiah (Neh. vi. 14).

Tokhath . . . Hasrah. In 2 Kings xxii. 14: *Tikvah . . . Harhas.*

keeper of the wardrobe. i.e. of the priestly vestments; others explain, of the royal robes.

the second quarter (mishneh). One of the two geographical sections into which Jerusalem was divided (cf. Neh. iii. 9, 12). It is mentioned again in Zeph. i. 10 and was possibly a later addition to the old city. The translation of A.V., 'the college,' follows the Targum which explains *mishneh* in its later sense of 'study.'

23. *tell ye the man.* In the sight of God in Whose name the prophetess speaks, the king is no more than *the man.*

curses that are written in the book which they have read before the king of Judah; 25. because they have forsaken Me, and have offered unto other gods, that they might provoke Me with all the works of their hands; therefore is My wrath poured out upon this place, and it shall not be quenched. 26. But unto the king of Judah, who sent you to inquire of the LORD, thus shall ye say to him: Thus saith the LORD, the God of Israel: As touching the words which thou hast heard, 27. because thy heart was tender, and thou didst humble thyself before God, when thou heardest His words against this place, and against the inhabitants thereof, and hast humbled thyself before Me, and hast rent thy clothes, and wept before Me; I also have heard thee, saith the LORD. 28. Behold, I will gather thee to thy fathers, and thou shalt be gathered to thy grave in peace, neither shall

הָֽאָלוֹת הַכְּתוּבוֹת עַל־הַסֵּפֶר
אֲשֶׁר קָֽרְאוּ לִפְנֵי מֶלֶךְ
25 יְהוּדָֽה׃ תַּחַת ׀ אֲשֶׁר עֲזָבוּנִי
וַֽיְקַטִּירוּ לֵֽאלֹהִים אֲחֵרִים
לְמַעַן הַכְעִיסֵנִי בְּכֹל מַעֲשֵׂי
יְדֵיהֶם וְתִתַּךְ חֲמָתִי בַּמָּקוֹם
26 הַזֶּה וְלֹא תִכְבֶּֽה׃ וְאֶל־מֶלֶךְ
יְהוּדָה הַשֹּׁלֵחַ אֶתְכֶם לִדְרוֹשׁ
בַּֽיהוָה כֹּה תֹאמְרוּ אֵלָיו כֹּֽה־
אָמַר יְהוָה אֱלֹהֵי יִשְׂרָאֵל
27 הַדְּבָרִים אֲשֶׁר שָׁמָֽעְתָּ׃ יַֽעַן
רַךְ־לְבָבְךָ וַתִּכָּנַע ׀ מִלִּפְנֵי
אֱלֹהִים בְּשָׁמְעֲךָ אֶת־דְּבָרָיו
עַל־הַמָּקוֹם הַזֶּה וְעַל־יֹשְׁבָיו
וַתִּכָּנַע לְפָנַי וַתִּקְרַע אֶת־
בְּגָדֶיךָ וַתֵּבְךְּ לְפָנָי וְגַם־אֲנִי
28 שָׁמַעְתִּי נְאֻם־יְהוָה׃ הִנְנִי
אֹסִפְךָ אֶל־אֲבֹתֶיךָ וְנֶאֱסַפְתָּ
אֶל־קִבְרוֹתֶיךָ בְּשָׁלוֹם וְלֹא־

v. 25. יתיר י׳

24. *all the curses.* Cf. Deut. xxvii. 15ff., xxviii. 15ff.

25. *therefore is My wrath poured out.* In 2 Kings xxii. 17: *therefore My wrath shall be kindled.*

26. *as touching.* Not in the Hebrew. Another way of construing the verse is to regard verse 27 as in parenthesis and attach the last clause of verse 26 to verse 28: 'the words which thou hast heard (i.e. because thou hast paid heed to them) . . . behold, I will gather thee,' etc.

the words. Of the book of the Law.

27. *tender.* Not hard but receptive of the message of the Torah.

28. *thy grave.* The Hebrew has the plural, probably referring to a mausoleum which contained several graves.

in peace. This is an assurance that the Temple and State would not be destroyed in his lifetime; or that, despite *all the evil* destined to come upon the land, he would have peace. There is no allusion here to a peaceful ending to his life, which was in fact violent (cf. xxxv. 23f.).

thine eyes see all the evil that I will bring upon this place, and upon the inhabitants thereof.' And they brought back word unto the king.

29. Then the king sent and gathered together all the elders of Judah and Jerusalem. 30. And the king went up to the house of the LORD, and all the men of Judah and the inhabitants of Jerusalem, and the priests, and the Levites, and all the people, both great and small; and he read in their ears all the words of the book of the covenant that was found in the house of the LORD. 31. And the king stood in his place, and made a covenant before the LORD, to walk after the LORD, and to keep His commandments, and His testimonies, and His statutes, with all his heart, and with all his soul, to perform the words of the covenant that were written in this book. 32. And he caused all that were found in Jerusalem and Benjamin to stand to it. And the inhabitants of Jerusalem did accord-

תִרְאֶינָה עֵינֶיךָ בְּכֹל הָרָעָה
אֲשֶׁר אֲנִי מֵבִיא עַל־הַמָּקוֹם
הַזֶּה וְעַל־יֹשְׁבָיו וַיָּשִׁיבוּ אֶת־
הַמֶּלֶךְ דָּבָר׃
29 וַיִּשְׁלַח הַמֶּלֶךְ וַיֶּאֱסֹף אֶת־
כָּל־זִקְנֵי יְהוּדָה וִירוּשָׁלִָם׃
30 וַיַּעַל הַמֶּלֶךְ בֵּית־יְהוָה וְכָל־
אִישׁ יְהוּדָה וְיֹשְׁבֵי יְרוּשָׁלִַם
וְהַכֹּהֲנִים וְהַלְוִיִּם וְכָל־הָעָם
מִגָּדוֹל וְעַד־קָטָן וַיִּקְרָא
בְאָזְנֵיהֶם אֶת־כָּל־דִּבְרֵי
סֵפֶר הַבְּרִית הַנִּמְצָא בֵּית
31 יְהוָה׃ וַיַּעֲמֹד הַמֶּלֶךְ עַל־
עָמְדוֹ וַיִּכְרֹת אֶת־הַבְּרִית
לִפְנֵי יְהוָה לָלֶכֶת אַחֲרֵי יְהוָה
וְלִשְׁמוֹר אֶת־מִצְוֹתָיו וְעֵדְוֹתָיו
וְחֻקָּיו בְּכָל־לְבָבוֹ וּבְכָל־
נַפְשׁוֹ לַעֲשׂוֹת אֶת־דִּבְרֵי
הַבְּרִית הַכְּתוּבִים עַל־הַסֵּפֶר
32 הַזֶּה׃ וַיַּעֲמֵד אֵת כָּל־הַנִּמְצָא
בִּירוּשָׁלִַם וּבִנְיָמִן וַיַּעֲשׂוּ יֹשְׁבֵי

29-33 (corresponding, with some variations, to 2 Kings xxiii. 1-3). A national covenant is made to observe the laws of God.

30. *the Levites.* In 2 Kings xxiii. 2: *the prophets.* There, too, some Hebrew MSS. have the reading 'the Levites.'

both great and small. lit. 'from great to small,' i.e. old and young, or rich and poor.

31. *in his place.* In Kings: *on the platform.*

32. *he caused . . . to stand to it.* In 2 Kings xxiii. 3: *all the people stood to the covenant,* i.e. they accepted the covenant without reserve.

ing to the covenant of God, the God of their fathers. 33. And Josiah took away all the abominations out of all the countries that pertained to the children of Israel, and made all that were found in Israel to serve, even to serve the LORD their God. All his days they departed not from following the LORD, the God of their fathers.

יְרוּשָׁלִָם כִּבְרִית אֱלֹהִים
33 אֱלֹהֵי אֲבוֹתֵיהֶם׃ וַיָּסַר
יֹאשִׁיָּהוּ אֶת־כָּל־הַתּוֹעֵבוֹת
מִכָּל־הָאֲרָצוֹת אֲשֶׁר לִבְנֵי
יִשְׂרָאֵל וַיַּעֲבֵד אֵת כָּל־
הַנִּמְצָא בְּיִשְׂרָאֵל לַעֲבוֹד אֶת־
יְהוָה אֱלֹהֵיהֶם כָּל־יָמָיו לֹא
סָרוּ מֵאַחֲרֵי יְהוָה אֱלֹהֵי
אֲבוֹתֵיהֶם׃

35 CHAPTER XXXV לה

1. And Josiah kept a passover unto the LORD in Jerusalem; and they killed the passover lamb on the fourteenth day of the first month. 2. And he set the priests in their charges, and encouraged them to the service of the house of the LORD. 3. And he said unto the Levites that taught all Israel, that were holy unto the LORD: 'Put the holy ark in the

1 וַיַּעַשׂ יֹאשִׁיָּהוּ בִירוּשָׁלִַם פֶּסַח
לַיהוָה וַיִּשְׁחֲטוּ הַפֶּסַח
בְּאַרְבָּעָה עָשָׂר לַחֹדֶשׁ
2 הָרִאשׁוֹן׃ וַיַּעֲמֵד הַכֹּהֲנִים
עַל־מִשְׁמְרוֹתָם וַיְחַזְּקֵם
3 לַעֲבוֹדַת בֵּית יְהוָה׃ וַיֹּאמֶר
לַלְוִיִּם הַמְּבוֹנִים לְכָל־
יִשְׂרָאֵל הַקְּדוֹשִׁים לַיהוָה תְּנוּ

v. 3. המבינים ק׳

33. *Josiah took away.* Cf. verses 3-7.

all the countries. The northern and southern portions of the land.

all his days, etc. But after his death, in the reign of his son Jehoiakim, there was a lapse into idolatry (cf. xxxvi. 5).

CHAPTER XXXV

1-19 (cf. 2 Kings xxiii. 21-23). Josiah's celebration of the Passover.

1-6. His preparations for the festival.

1. *fourteenth day of the first month.* He observed it on the prescribed date (cf. Exod. xii. 6), unlike Hezekiah who had to defer it for a month (xxx. 13).

2. *set the priests in their charges.* Assigned to them their respective duties.

encouraged them. As Hezekiah had done (cf. xxix. 5ff., xxx. 22).

3. *put the holy ark,* etc. It must have been removed from its place in the Holy of Holies during the period of apostasy in one of the preceding reigns, and

house which Solomon the son of David king of Israel did build; there shall no more be a burden upon your shoulders; now serve the LORD your God, and His people Israel. 4. And prepare ye after your fathers' houses by your courses, according to the writing of David king of Israel, and according to the writing of Solomon his son. 5. And stand in the holy place according to the divisions of the fathers' houses of your brethren the children of the people, and [let there be for each] a portion of a fathers' house of the Levites. 6. And kill the passover lamb, and sanctify yourselves, and prepare for your brethren, to do according to the word of the LORD by the hand of Moses.'

7. And Josiah gave to the children of the people, of the flock, lambs and kids, all of them for the passover-offerings, unto all that were present,

אֶת־אֲרוֹן־הַקֹּדֶשׁ בַּבַּיִת
אֲשֶׁר בָּנָה שְׁלֹמֹה בֶן־דָּוִיד
מֶלֶךְ יִשְׂרָאֵל אֵין־לָכֶם מַשָּׂא
בַּכָּתֵף עַתָּה עִבְדוּ אֶת־יְהוָה
אֱלֹהֵיכֶם וְאֵת עַמּוֹ יִשְׂרָאֵל׃
4 וְהָכוֹנוּ לְבֵית־אֲבוֹתֵיכֶם
כְּמַחְלְקוֹתֵיכֶם בִּכְתָב דָּוִיד
מֶלֶךְ יִשְׂרָאֵל וּבְמִכְתַּב שְׁלֹמֹה
5 בְנוֹ׃ וְעִמְדוּ בַקֹּדֶשׁ לִפְלֻגּוֹת
בֵּית הָאָבוֹת לַאֲחֵיכֶם בְּנֵי
הָעָם וַחֲלֻקַּת בֵּית־אָב
6 לַלְוִיִּם׃ וְשַׁחֲטוּ הַפָּסַח
וְהִתְקַדְּשׁוּ וְהָכִינוּ לַאֲחֵיכֶם
לַעֲשׂוֹת כִּדְבַר־יְהוָה בְּיַד־
מֹשֶׁה׃
7 וַיָּרֶם יֹאשִׁיָּהוּ לִבְנֵי הָעָם צֹאן
כְּבָשִׂים וּבְנֵי־עִזִּים הַכֹּל
לַפְּסָחִים לְכָל־הַנִּמְצָא

v. 4. והכינו ק'

Josiah now ordered it to be restored. A Rabbinical explanation is that he commanded it to be hidden in a secret place so that it would escape capture by an invading army.

there shall no more be a burden upon your shoulders. lit. 'you have no burden upon the shoulder.' After carrying it to its appointed place, they would not have to do it again.

4. *according to the writing of David.* Cf. 1 Chron. xxiii. 27, xxviii. 19ff.

the writing of Solomon. Who carried out the plans of David (cf. viii. 14).

5. *the holy place.* lit. 'holiness.'

the children of the people. The lay Israelites.

a portion of . . . the Levites. Each of the divisions of the Levites is to attend on one of the divisions of the Israelites.

7-9. Gifts of cattle by the king and princes to the people.

7. *Josiah gave.* lit. 'lifted up,' set aside. Similarly lavish gifts for the Passover offerings were made by Hezekiah (xxx. 24).

the children of the people. See on verse 5.

to the number of thirty thousand, and three thousand bullocks; these were of the king's substance. 8. And his princes gave willingly unto the people, to the priests, and to the Levites. Hilkiah and Zechariah and Jehiel, the rulers of the house of God, gave unto the priests for the passover-offerings two thousand and six hundred [small cattle], and three hundred oxen. 9. Conaniah also, and Shemaiah and Nethanel, his brethren, and Hashabiah and Jeiel and Jozabad, the chiefs of the Levites, gave unto the Levites for the passover-offerings five thousand [small cattle], and five hundred oxen.

10. So the service was prepared, and the priests stood in their place, and the Levites by their courses, according to the king's commandment. 11. And they killed the passover lamb, and the priests dashed [the blood, which they received] of their hand, and the Levites flayed them. 12. And they removed the portions that were to be burnt, that they might give them to the divisions of the fathers' houses of the children of the people, to present unto the LORD, as it is

לְמִסְפַּר שְׁלֹשִׁים אֶלֶף וּבָקָר
שְׁלֹשֶׁת אֲלָפִים אֵלֶּה מֵרְכוּשׁ
8 הַמֶּלֶךְ׃ וְשָׂרָיו לִנְדָבָה לָעָם
לַכֹּהֲנִים וְלַלְוִיִּם הֵרִימוּ
חִלְקִיָּה וּזְכַרְיָהוּ וִיחִיאֵל נְגִידֵי
בֵּית הָאֱלֹהִים לַכֹּהֲנִים נָתְנוּ
לַפְּסָחִים אַלְפַּיִם וְשֵׁשׁ מֵאוֹת
9 וּבָקָר שְׁלֹשׁ מֵאוֹת׃ וְכָונַנְיָהוּ
וּשְׁמַעְיָהוּ וּנְתַנְאֵל אֶחָיו
וַחֲשַׁבְיָהוּ וִיעִיאֵל וְיוֹזָבָד שָׂרֵי
הַלְוִיִּם הֵרִימוּ לַלְוִיִּם
לַפְּסָחִים חֲמֵשֶׁת אֲלָפִים
וּבָקָר חֲמֵשׁ מֵאוֹת׃
10 וַתִּכּוֹן הָעֲבוֹדָה וַיַּעַמְדוּ
הַכֹּהֲנִים עַל־עָמְדָם וְהַלְוִיִּם
עַל־מַחְלְקוֹתָם כְּמִצְוַת
11 הַמֶּלֶךְ׃ וַיִּשְׁחֲטוּ הַפָּסַח
וַיִּזְרְקוּ הַכֹּהֲנִים מִיָּדָם וְהַלְוִיִּם
12 מַפְשִׁיטִים׃ וַיָּסִירוּ הָעֹלָה
לְתִתָּם לְמִפְלַגּוֹת לְבֵית־
אָבוֹת לִבְנֵי הָעָם לְהַקְרִיב

v. 9. יתיר ו׳

bullocks. For festival peace-offerings which were eaten as part of the Paschal meal whenever the Paschal lamb did not suffice for all the members of a party.

8. *gave willingly.* lit. 'lifted up for a freewill-offering.'

the rulers of the house of God. See on 1 Chron. ix. 11.

oxen. For the same purpose as the bullocks in verse 7.

10-15. The offerings of the lambs and bullocks.

12. *they removed.* From the Paschal lambs.

the portions that were to be burnt. E.g. the fat (cf. Lev. iii. 9).

they might give them. The Paschal lambs.

to present. The portions which were to be burnt.

written in the book of Moses. And so did they with the oxen. 13. And they roasted the passover with fire according to the ordinance; and the holy offerings sod they in pots, and in caldrons, and in pans, and carried them quickly to all the children of the people. 14. And afterward they prepared for themselves, and for the priests; because the priests the sons of Aaron were busied in offering the portions that were to be burnt and the fat until night; therefore the Levites prepared for themselves, and for the priests the sons of Aaron. 15. And the singers the sons of Asaph were in their place, according to the commandment of David, and Asaph, and Heman, and Jeduthun the king's seer; and the porters were at every gate; they needed not to depart from their service, for their brethren the Levites prepared for them.

16. So all the service of the LORD was prepared the same day, to keep the passover, and to offer burnt-offerings upon the altar of the LORD, according to the commandment of

לַיהוָה כַּכָּתוּב בְּסֵפֶר מֹשֶׁה
13 וְכֵן לַבָּקָר׃ וַיְבַשְּׁלוּ הַפֶּסַח
בָּאֵשׁ כַּמִּשְׁפָּט וְהַקֳּדָשִׁים
בִּשְּׁלוּ בַּסִּירוֹת וּבַדְּוָדִים
וּבַצֵּלָחוֹת וַיָּרִיצוּ לְכָל־בְּנֵי
14 הָעָם׃ וְאַחַר הֵכִינוּ לָהֶם
וְלַכֹּהֲנִים כִּי הַכֹּהֲנִים בְּנֵי
אַהֲרֹן בְּהַעֲלוֹת הָעוֹלָה
וְהַחֲלָבִים עַד־לָיְלָה וְהַלְוִיִּם
הֵכִינוּ לָהֶם וְלַכֹּהֲנִים בְּנֵי
15 אַהֲרֹן׃ וְהַמְשֹׁרְרִים בְּנֵי־אָסָף
עַל־מַעֲמָדָם כְּמִצְוַת דָּוִיד
וְאָסָף וְהֵימָן וִידְתוּן חוֹזֵה
הַמֶּלֶךְ וְהַשֹּׁעֲרִים לְשַׁעַר
וָשָׁעַר אֵין לָהֶם לָסוּר מֵעַל
עֲבֹדָתָם כִּי־אֲחֵיהֶם הַלְוִיִּם
הֵכִינוּ לָהֶם׃
16 וַתִּכּוֹן כָּל־עֲבוֹדַת יְהוָה בַּיּוֹם
הַהוּא לַעֲשׂוֹת הַפֶּסַח וְהַעֲלוֹת
עֹלוֹת עַל מִזְבַּח יְהוָה כְּמִצְוַת

as it is written in the book of Moses. This ritual is not found in the laws of the Passover, but in connection with the peace-offering (Lev. iii. 6ff.).

13. ***they roasted.*** The usual meaning of the verb is 'to cook,' but the Paschal lamb was roasted and not cooked, *according to the ordinance* in Exod. xii. 8f.

the holy offerings. The bullocks or oxen which were brought as peace-offerings (see on verse 7).

sod they. The same verb as *roasted.*

14. ***they prepared.*** The subject is the Levites.

were busied. Not in the text.

15. ***in their place.*** lit. 'upon their stand,' where they sang the Hallel Psalms (Pss. cxiii-cxviii) while the lambs were being offered.

16-19. The great celebration.

16. ***the same day.*** lit. 'on that day,' the fourteenth of Nisan.

king Josiah. 17. And the children
of Israel that were present kept the
passover at that time, and the feast
of unleavened bread seven days.
18. And there was no passover like
to that kept in Israel from the days
of Samuel the prophet; neither did
any of the kings of Israel keep such
a passover as Josiah kept, and the
priests, and the Levites, and all
Judah and Israel that were present,
and the inhabitants of Jerusalem.
19. In the eighteenth year of the
reign of Josiah was this passover
kept.

20. After all this, when Josiah had
prepared the temple, Neco king of
Egypt went up to fight against
Carchemish by the Euphrates; and

הַמֶּלֶךְ יֹאשִׁיָּהוּ׃ וַיַּעֲשׂוּ בְנֵי־ 17
יִשְׂרָאֵל הַנִּמְצְאִים אֶת־הַפֶּסַח
בָּעֵת הַהִיא וְאֶת־חַג הַמַּצּוֹת
שִׁבְעַת יָמִים׃ וְלֹא־נַעֲשָׂה 18
פֶסַח כָּמֹהוּ בְּיִשְׂרָאֵל מִימֵי
שְׁמוּאֵל הַנָּבִיא וְכָל־מַלְכֵי
יִשְׂרָאֵל ׀ לֹא־עָשׂוּ כַּפֶּסַח
אֲשֶׁר־עָשָׂה יֹאשִׁיָּהוּ וְהַכֹּהֲנִים
וְהַלְוִיִּם וְכָל־יְהוּדָה וְיִשְׂרָאֵל
הַנִּמְצָא וְיוֹשְׁבֵי יְרוּשָׁלִָם׃
בִּשְׁמוֹנֶה עֶשְׂרֵה שָׁנָה לְמַלְכוּת 19
יֹאשִׁיָּהוּ נַעֲשָׂה הַפֶּסַח הַזֶּה׃
אַחֲרֵי כָל־זֹאת אֲשֶׁר הֵכִין 20
יֹאשִׁיָּהוּ אֶת־הַבַּיִת עָלָה נְכוֹ
מֶלֶךְ־מִצְרַיִם לְהִלָּחֵם
בְּכַרְכְּמִישׁ עַל־פְּרָת וַיֵּצֵא

18. *from the days of Samuel.* Who was the last of the judges. In 2 Kings xxiii. 22: *from the days of the judges.*

neither did any of the kings, etc. Hezekiah (xxx. 21) had observed a memorable Passover, but the present celebration exceeded it in the number of sacrifices offered.

19. *in the eighteenth year.* The year in which the book of the Law was discovered (cf. xxxiv. 8ff.).

20-24 (a fuller account than in 2 Kings xxiii. 29f.). Josiah's encounter with Neco and his death.

20. *after all this*, etc. Rashi comments that a pious king like Josiah did not deserve the tragic fate that befell him, and was not saved by a miracle as was Hezekiah when attacked by Sennacherib (xxxii. 21f.).

Neco king of Egypt. He is identified with Neco II, son of Psammetichus. He was the second king of the twenty-sixth dynasty and reigned over Egypt from 609 to 594 B.C.E.

against Carchemish. In 2 Kings xxiii. 29: *against the king of Assyria* whose power was at that time weakened by his war with Babylon. Neco advanced to the Euphrates with the object of re-imposing Egyptian rule over Syria. Carchemish is the modern Jerabis on the west bank of the Euphrates. A noted fortress and trading centre, the ancient northern capital of the Hittite empire, it was also the gateway from Syria to Mesopotamia.

Josiah went out against him. 21. But
he sent ambassadors to him, saying:
'What have I to do with thee, thou
king of Judah? I come not against
thee this day, but against the house
wherewith I have war; and God hath
given command to speed me;
forbear thee from meddling with
God, who is with me, that He
destroy thee not.' 22. Nevertheless
Josiah would not turn his face from
him, but disguised himself, that he
might fight with him, and hearkened
not unto the words of Neco, from
the mouth of God, and came to fight
in the valley of Megiddo. 23. And
the archers shot at king Josiah; and
the king said to his servants: 'Have
me away; for I am sore wounded.'
24. So his servants took him out of
the chariot, and put him in the

21 לִקְרָאתוֹ יֹאשִׁיָּהוּ׃ וַיִּשְׁלַח
אֵלָיו מַלְאָכִים ׀ לֵאמֹר ׀ מַה־
לִּי וָלָךְ מֶלֶךְ יְהוּדָה לֹא־
עָלֶיךָ אַתָּה הַיּוֹם כִּי אֶל־בֵּית
מִלְחַמְתִּי וֵאלֹהִים אָמַר
לְבַהֲלֵנִי חֲדַל־לְךָ מֵאֱלֹהִים
אֲשֶׁר־עִמִּי וְאַל־יַשְׁחִיתֶךָ׃
22 וְלֹא־הֵסֵב יֹאשִׁיָּהוּ פָּנָיו מִמֶּנּוּ
כִּי לְהִלָּחֶם־בּוֹ הִתְחַפֵּשׂ וְלֹא
שָׁמַע אֶל־דִּבְרֵי נְכוֹ מִפִּי
אֱלֹהִים וַיָּבֹא לְהִלָּחֵם
23 בְּבִקְעַת מְגִדּוֹ׃ וַיֹּרוּ הַיֹּרִים
לַמֶּלֶךְ יֹאשִׁיָּהוּ וַיֹּאמֶר הַמֶּלֶךְ
לַעֲבָדָיו הַעֲבִירוּנִי כִּי
24 הָחֳלֵיתִי מְאֹד׃ וַיַּעֲבִירֻהוּ
עֲבָדָיו מִן־הַמֶּרְכָּבָה

Josiah went out against him. His intention was to deny Neco passage through his territory.

21. *but he.* The subject is Neco.

what have I to do with thee? An idiomatic expression, lit. 'what to me and to thee?'

I come. Not in the text.

the house wherewith I have war. lit. 'my house of war,' viz. Assyria.

God hath given command, etc. Neco claims that he is acting under God's orders in attacking Assyria, and Josiah should not hinder him. The Chronicler evidently regarded the claim as genuine (cf. verse 22).

22. *would not turn his face from him.* i.e. he persisted in opposing Neco's advance.

but disguised himself. As Ahab did in the battle of Ramoth-gilead (xviii. 29) after he had been warned by a prophet of God. The disguise was intended to be a protection to the king against the danger of being singled out for attack.

Megiddo. The modern Tel el-Mutesellino in the plain of Esdraelon. It was an ancient fortress on the military and trade route between Egypt and the Euphrates. The battle took place in 608 B.C.E.

23. *the archers shot at king Josiah.* Ahab also met his death by a shot from an archer despite his disguise (xviii. 33).

have me away. lit. 'cause me to pass.'

I am sore wounded. lit. 'I have become ill.' The same cry was uttered by Ahab when he was shot by the archer.

second chariot that he had, and brought him to Jerusalem; and he died, and was buried in the sepulchres of his fathers. And all Judah and Jerusalem mourned for Josiah. 25. And Jeremiah lamented for Josiah; and all the singing men and singing women spoke of Josiah in their lamentations, unto this day; and they made them an ordinance in Israel; and, behold, they are written in the lamentations. 26. Now the rest of the acts of Josiah, and his good deeds, according to that which is written in the Law of the LORD, 27. and his acts, first and last, behold, they are written in the book of the kings of Israel and Judah.

וַיַּרְכִּיבֻהוּ עַל רֶכֶב הַמִּשְׁנֶה
אֲשֶׁר־לוֹ וַיּוֹלִיכֻהוּ יְרוּשָׁלַ͏ִם
וַיָּמָת וַיִּקָּבֵר בְּקִבְרוֹת אֲבֹתָיו
וְכָל־יְהוּדָה וִירוּשָׁלַ͏ִם
מִתְאַבְּלִים עַל־יֹאשִׁיָּהוּ׃
25 וַיְקוֹנֵן יִרְמְיָהוּ עַל־יֹאשִׁיָּהוּ
וַיֹּאמְרוּ כָל־הַשָּׁרִים ׀
וְהַשָּׁרוֹת בְּקִינוֹתֵיהֶם עַל־
יֹאשִׁיָּהוּ עַד־הַיּוֹם וַיִּתְּנוּם
לְחֹק עַל־יִשְׂרָאֵל וְהִנָּם
26 כְּתוּבִים עַל־הַקִּינוֹת׃ וְיֶתֶר
דִּבְרֵי יֹאשִׁיָּהוּ וַחֲסָדָיו כַּכָּתוּב
27 בְּתוֹרַת יְהוָה׃ וּדְבָרָיו
הָרִאשֹׁנִים וְהָאַחֲרֹנִים הִנָּם
כְּתוּבִים עַל־סֵפֶר מַלְכֵי־
יִשְׂרָאֵל וִיהוּדָה׃

24. *the second chariot.* The war-chariot was small and only had room for standing. A larger conveyance was required to accommodate a wounded man.

to Jerusalem; and he died. In 2 Kings xxiii. 30: *carried him in a chariot dead from Megiddo.*

in the sepulchres of his fathers. In Kings: *in his own sepulchre.* He may have prepared a tomb for himself among the sepulchres of his ancestors.

25 (supplementary to the account in Kings). Lamentations for the dead king.

Jeremiah lamented. He composed a dirge or elegy. A reference to it is probably to be found in the denunciation of Shallum the son Josiah (Jer. xxii. 10) and, according to the Targum on Zech. xii. 11, in that verse.

unto this day. When *Chronicles* was written.

they made them an ordinance. To recite the elegy at a stated period, possibly on the anniversary of Josiah's death.

the lamentations. A collection of elegies which has not been preserved. The Biblical Book of Lamentations contains no explicit reference to Josiah, but Jewish tradition applies Lam. iv. 1, 20 to the fallen king.

26f. (cf. 2 Kings xxiii. 28). An epilogue to Josiah's reign.

26. *his good deeds,* etc. Cf. the tribute paid to him in 2 Kings xxiii. 25.

27. *first and last.* See on 1 Chron. xxix. 29.

36 CHAPTER XXXVI לו

1. Then the people of the land took
Jehoahaz the son of Josiah, and made
him king in his father's stead in
Jerusalem. 2. Joahaz was twenty
and three years old when he began
to reign; and he reigned three
months in Jerusalem. 3. And the
king of Egypt deposed him at
Jerusalem, and fined the land a
hundred talents of silver and a talent
of gold. 4. And the king of Egypt
made Eliakim his brother king over
Judah and Jerusalem, and changed
his name to Jehoiakim. And Neco
took Joahaz his brother, and carried
him to Egypt.

1 וַיִּקְחוּ עַם־הָאָרֶץ אֶת־
יְהוֹאָחָז בֶּן־יֹאשִׁיָּהוּ וַיַּמְלִיכֻהוּ
2 תַחַת־אָבִיו בִּירוּשָׁלָם׃ בֶּן־
שָׁלוֹשׁ וְעֶשְׂרִים שָׁנָה יוֹאָחָז
בְּמָלְכוֹ וּשְׁלֹשָׁה חֳדָשִׁים מָלַךְ
3 בִּירוּשָׁלָם׃ וַיְסִירֵהוּ מֶלֶךְ־
מִצְרַיִם בִּירוּשָׁלָם וַיַּעֲנֹשׁ אֶת־
הָאָרֶץ מֵאָה כִכַּר־כֶּסֶף
4 וְכִכַּר זָהָב׃ וַיַּמְלֵךְ מֶלֶךְ־
מִצְרַיִם אֶת־אֶלְיָקִים אָחִיו
עַל־יְהוּדָה וִירוּשָׁלַם וַיַּסֵּב
אֶת־שְׁמוֹ יְהוֹיָקִים וְאֶת־
יוֹאָחָז אָחִיו לָקַח נְכוֹ וַיְבִיאֵהוּ
מִצְרָיְמָה׃

CHAPTER XXXVI

FATE OF THE KINGDOM OF JUDAH

1-4 (corresponding to 2 Kings xxiii. 30b-34). The reign of Jehoahaz (607 B.C.E.).

1. *the people of the land.* See on xxiii. 20.

Jehoahaz. In 1 Chron. iii. 15 and Jer. xxii. 11 he is called *Shallum.* He was about two years younger than his brother Jehoiakim (cf. verses 2, 5), but apparently he was more acceptable on account of his sympathy with the pro-Assyrian and anti-Egyptian policy of his father.

and made him king. 2 Kings xxiii. 30 inserts *and anointed him* before these words. The ceremony of anointing confirmed his title to the throne which could have been contested by his elder brother.

2. *Joahaz.* A contraction of Jehoahaz.

he reigned . . . in Jerusalem. 2 Kings xxiii. 31f. adds that his mother's name was *Hamutal the daughter of Jeremiah of Libnah* and that he *did that which was evil in the sight of the LORD.*

3. *the king of Egypt deposed him at Jerusalem.* This is amplified in 2 Kings xxiii. 33: *Pharaoh-necoh put him in bands at Riblah in the land of Hamath, that he might not reign in Jerusalem.* The difference in Hebrew between *and he deposed him* and *and he put him in bands* is only the change of one letter and one transposition.

fined the land. For supporting the anti-Egyptian activity of the population.

4. *changed his name to Jehoiakim.* The change was in the first part of the name,

5. Jehoiakim was twenty and five
years old when he began to reign;
and he reigned eleven years in
Jerusalem; and he did that which
was evil in the sight of the LORD his
God. 6. Against him came up
Nebuchadnezzar king of Babylon,
and bound him in fetters, to carry
him to Babylon. 7. Nebuchadnezzar also carried of the vessels of
the house of the LORD to Babylon,
and put them in his temple at
Babylon. 8. Now the rest of the
acts of Jehoiakim, and his abominations which he did, and that which
was found in him, behold, they are
written in the book of the kings of
Israel and Judah; and Jehoiachin his
son reigned in his stead.

5 בֶּן־עֶשְׂרִים וְחָמֵשׁ שָׁנָה
יְהוֹיָקִים בְּמָלְכוֹ וְאַחַת עֶשְׂרֵה
שָׁנָה מָלַךְ בִּירוּשָׁלִָם וַיַּעַשׂ
הָרַע בְּעֵינֵי יְהוָה אֱלֹהָיו׃
6 עָלָיו עָלָה נְבוּכַדְנֶאצַּר מֶלֶךְ
בָּבֶל וַיַּאַסְרֵהוּ בַּנְחֻשְׁתַּיִם
7 לְהֹלִיכוֹ בָּבֶלָה׃ וּמִכְּלֵי בֵּית
יְהוָה הֵבִיא נְבוּכַדְנֶאצַּר
לְבָבֶל וַיִּתְּנֵם בְּהֵיכָלוֹ בְּבָבֶל׃
8 וְיֶתֶר דִּבְרֵי יְהוֹיָקִים
וְתוֹעֲבוֹתָיו אֲשֶׁר־עָשָׂה
וְהַנִּמְצָא עָלָיו הִנָּם כְּתוּבִים
עַל־סֵפֶר מַלְכֵי יִשְׂרָאֵל
וִיהוּדָה וַיִּמְלֹךְ יְהוֹיָכִין בְּנוֹ
תַּחְתָּיו׃

from *El* (God) to *Jeho* (the Lord), the remainder in Hebrew being the same in both names and meaning 'will establish' or 'establishes.' A change of name was a mark of promotion (cf. Gen. xli. 45; Dan. i. 7).

carried him to Egypt. Where he died (2 Kings xxiii. 34).

5-8 (a fuller account in 2 Kings xxiii. 35-xxiv. 7). The reign of Jehoiakim (607-597 B.C.E.).

5. *in Jerusalem.* 2 Kings xxiii. 35f. adds the name of his mother, *Zebudah*, and the manner in which Jehoiakim raised from the people the fine imposed by the Egyptian king.

6. *Nebuchadnezzar.* In the Books of Jeremiah and Ezekiel the form of the name is *Nebuchadrezzar* which conforms more closely to the Babylonian name.

to carry him to Babylon. This intention was not fulfilled. In Kings there is no mention of Jehoiakim's deportation to Babylon, but it is stated that he rebelled after submitting to Nebuchadnezzar for three years. Irregular marauding bands of Babylonians and others began to raid and harass the country as God's punishment for the sins of the king and people (2 Kings xxiv. 1ff.).

7. *also carried of the vessels.* There is no record of this in Kings during the reign of Jehoiakim.

8. *that which was found in him.* i.e. the idolatrous acts which he committed in secret and were later discovered. Additional information about his reign is found in Jer. xxxvi.

behold, they are written, etc. 2 Kings xxiv. 6 adds that Jehoiakim *slept with his*

9. Jehoiachin was eight years old when he began to reign; and he reigned three months and ten days in Jerusalem; and he did that which was evil in the sight of the LORD.
10. And at the return of the year king Nebuchadnezzar sent, and brought him to Babylon, with the goodly vessels of the house of the LORD, and made Zedekiah his brother king over Judah and Jerusalem.

11. Zedekiah was twenty and one

9 בֶּן־שְׁמוֹנֶה שָׁנִים יְהוֹיָכִין
בְּמָלְכוֹ וּשְׁלֹשָׁה חֳדָשִׁים
וַעֲשֶׂרֶת יָמִים מָלַךְ בִּירוּשָׁלִָם
וַיַּעַשׂ הָרַע בְּעֵינֵי יְהוָה׃
10 וְלִתְשׁוּבַת הַשָּׁנָה שָׁלַח הַמֶּלֶךְ
נְבוּכַדְנֶאצַּר וַיְבִאֵהוּ בָבֶלָה
עִם־כְּלֵי חֶמְדַּת בֵּית־יְהוָה
וַיַּמְלֵךְ אֶת־צִדְקִיָּהוּ אָחִיו
עַל־יְהוּדָה וִירוּשָׁלִָם׃
11 בֶּן־עֶשְׂרִים וְאַחַת שָׁנָה

fathers, but neither here nor there is any mention made of his burial. Jer. xxii. 18f. predicted an ignominious end for him: *They shall not lament for him . . . he shall be buried with the burial of an ass, drawn and cast forth beyond the gates of Jerusalem.*

9f. (2 Kings xxiv. 8-17 has a fuller account). The reign of Jehoiachin (597 B.C.E.).

9. *Jehoiachin.* In 1 Chron. iii. 6 he is named *Jeconiah.*

eight years old when he began to reign. It has been suggested that by *began to reign* at this tender age is meant nomination by his father as successor to the throne. His actual reign began at the age of eighteen as recorded in 2 Kings xxiv. 8.

and ten days. Omitted in Kings.

in Jerusalem. This is followed in Kings by the name of his mother, *Nehushta*, who was taken captive with Jehoiachin to Babylon (2 Kings xxiv. 12, 15).

10. *at the return of the year.* See on 1 Chron. xx. 1.

king Nebuchadnezzar sent, etc. According to 2 Kings xxiv. 11f., this was preceded by a siege of Jerusalem and the surrender of Jehoiachin, his mother, his servants, princes and officers.

brought him to Babylon. Together with those mentioned in the preceding note, the men of valour, the chief men of the land, the craftsmen and smiths (2 Kings xxiv. 14ff.).

with the goodly vessels. Including the treasures of the Temple and palace (2 Kings xxiv. 13).

Zedekiah. This is the name given to *Mattaniah* by the king of Babylon (2 Kings xxiv. 17). The alteration of name was to mark his promotion to the throne of Judah or to stamp him as the vassal of Nebuchadnezzar. *Mattaniah* means 'gift of the Lord' and *Zedekiah* signifies 'righteousness, or, justice, of the Lord.' The latter is interpreted by the Rabbis as a warning by Nebuchadnezzar that Divine justice would overtake him should he break his oath of allegiance and prove disloyal.

his brother. In fact he was the brother of Jehoiachin's father, Jehoiakim (cf. 2 Kings xxiv. 17; 1 Chron. iii. 15), but the word for *brother* may denote a relative.

11-21 (cf. 2 Kings xxiv. 18-xxv. 21). The reign of Zedekiah (597-586 B.C.E.).

years old when he began to reign; and he reigned eleven years in Jerusalem; 12. and he did that which was evil in the sight of the LORD his God; he humbled not himself before Jeremiah the prophet speaking from the mouth of the LORD. 13. And he also rebelled against king Nebuchadnezzar, who had made him swear by God; but he stiffened his neck, and hardened his heart from turning unto the LORD, the God of Israel. 14. Moreover all the chiefs of the priests, and the people, transgressed very greatly after all the abominations of the nations; and they polluted the house of the LORD which He had hallowed in Jerusalem. 15. And the LORD, the God of their fathers, sent to them by His messengers, sending betimes and often; because He had

צִדְקִיָּ֣הוּ בְמָלְכ֑וֹ וְאַחַ֤ת עֶשְׂרֵה֙
שָׁנָ֔ה מָלַ֖ךְ בִּירוּשָׁלִָֽם׃ וַיַּ֣עַשׂ 12
הָרַ֔ע בְּעֵינֵ֖י יְהוָ֣ה אֱלֹהָ֑יו לֹ֣א
נִכְנַ֗ע מִלִּפְנֵ֛י יִרְמְיָ֥הוּ הַנָּבִ֖יא
מִפִּ֥י יְהוָֽה׃ וְ֠גַם בַּמֶּ֤לֶךְ 13
נְבוּכַדְנֶאצַּר֙ מָרָ֔ד אֲשֶׁ֥ר
הִשְׁבִּיע֖וֹ בֵּֽאלֹהִ֑ים וַיֶּ֣קֶשׁ אֶת־
עָרְפּ֗וֹ וַיְאַמֵּץ֙ אֶת־לְבָב֔וֹ
מִשּׁ֕וּב אֶל־יְהוָ֖ה אֱלֹהֵ֥י
יִשְׂרָאֵֽל׃ גַּ֠ם כָּל־שָׂרֵ֨י 14
הַכֹּהֲנִ֤ים וְהָעָם֙ הִרְבּ֣וּ
לִמְעָול־מַ֔עַל כְּכֹ֖ל תֹּעֲב֣וֹת
הַגּוֹיִ֑ם וַֽיְטַמְּאוּ֙ אֶת־בֵּ֣ית יְהוָ֔ה
אֲשֶׁ֥ר הִקְדִּ֖ישׁ בִּירוּשָׁלִָֽם׃
וַיִּשְׁלַח֩ יְהוָ֨ה אֱלֹהֵ֧י אֲבוֹתֵיהֶ֛ם 15
עֲלֵיהֶ֖ם בְּיַ֣ד מַלְאָכָ֑יו הַשְׁכֵּ֣ם
וְשָׁל֔וֹחַ כִּֽי־חָמַ֥ל עַל־עַמּ֖וֹ

v. 13. קמץ בז״ק v. 14. יתיר ו׳

11-16. Zedekiah's apostasy and neglect of prophetic warnings.

11. The name of the queen-mother occurs in 2 Kings xxiv. 18 as *Hamutal the daughter of Jeremiah of Libnah*, who was also the mother of Jehoahaz (cf. 2 Kings xxiii. 31). Zedekiah was therefore a full brother of Jehoahaz but not of Jehoiakim who was born of a different mother (see on verse 5).

12. *humbled not himself before Jeremiah.* Either because of his fear of the nobles who opposed Jeremiah or in the vain hope of being able to resist the might of Babylon, Zedekiah rejected the prophet's repeated advice to submit to Nebuchadnezzar (cf. Jer. xxi. 1ff., xxxvii. 3ff., xxxviii. 17ff.).

13. *who had made him swear by God.* To be his loyal vassal. Zedekiah violated his oath of fealty and thereby transgressed the law of God (cf. Ezek. xvii. 11ff.).

from turning. Or, 'from returning.'

unto the LORD, the God of Israel. Who commanded, *Ye shall not swear by My name falsely* (Lev. xix. 12).

14. *they polluted the house of the LORD.* By their pagan rites (cf. Ezek. viii. 5ff.).

15. *sending betimes and often.* An idiom-

compassion on His people, and on
His dwelling-place; 16. but they
mocked the messengers of God, and
despised His words, and scoffed at
His prophets, until the wrath of the
LORD arose against His people, till
there was no remedy.

17. Therefore He brought upon
them the king of the Chaldeans, who
slew their young men with the sword
in the house of their sanctuary, and
had no compassion upon young man
or maiden, old man or hoary-headed;
He gave them all into his hand.
18. And all the vessels of the house
of God, great and small, and the
treasures of the house of the LORD,
and the treasures of the king, and of
his princes; all these he brought to
Babylon. 19. And they burnt the
house of God, and broke down the
wall of Jerusalem, and burnt all the

16 וְעַל־מְעוֹנוֹ׃ וַיִּהְיוּ מַלְעִבִים
בְּמַלְאֲכֵי הָאֱלֹהִים וּבוֹזִים
דְּבָרָיו וּמִתַּעְתְּעִים בִּנְבִאָיו
עַד עֲלוֹת חֲמַת־יְהוָה בְּעַמּוֹ
עַד־לְאֵין מַרְפֵּא׃
17 וַיַּעַל עֲלֵיהֶם אֶת־מֶלֶךְ
כַּשְׂדִּיִּים וַיַּהֲרֹג בַּחוּרֵיהֶם
בַּחֶרֶב בְּבֵית מִקְדָּשָׁם וְלֹא
חָמַל עַל־בָּחוּר וּבְתוּלָה זָקֵן
18 וְיָשֵׁשׁ הַכֹּל נָתַן בְּיָדוֹ׃ וְכֹל
כְּלֵי בֵּית הָאֱלֹהִים הַגְּדֹלִים
וְהַקְּטַנִּים וְאֹצְרוֹת בֵּית יְהוָה
וְאוֹצְרוֹת הַמֶּלֶךְ וְשָׂרָיו הַכֹּל
19 הֵבִיא בָבֶל׃ וַיִּשְׂרְפוּ אֶת־
בֵּית הָאֱלֹהִים וַיְנַתְּצוּ אֵת
חוֹמַת יְרוּשָׁלִָם וְכָל־

v. 17. יתיר י׳

atic expression frequently found in *Jeremiah*, lit. 'to rise early and to send.'

because He had compassion. God afforded them an opportunity to repent which would have averted the disastrous consequences of their sins.

16. *they mocked the messengers of God.* Cf. Jer. xxvi. 20ff., xxxii. 2ff., xxxvii. 15f., xxxviii. 6.

till there was no remedy. The Divine mercy could no longer be exercised because of the nation's persistence in evil.

17-21 (supplementary to 2 Kings xxv. 1-21). Destruction of Jerusalem, massacre of the people, burning of the Temple and captivity.

17. *Chaldeans.* This people originally lived on the sea-coast south-east of Babylon; but when their king, Nabopolassar the father of Nebuchadnezzar, conquered Babylon, he established a Chaldeo-Babylonian empire with a new dynasty, and then Chaldea and Babylonia became synonymous.

in the house of their sanctuary. Ezek. ix. 1ff. graphically describes a vision of the massacre.

18. *all the vessels.* Which remained after the previous plunder (cf. verse 10).

palaces thereof with fire, and destroyed all the goodly vessels thereof. 20. And them that had escaped from the sword carried he away to Babylon; and they were servants to him and his sons until the reign of the kingdom of Persia; 21. to fulfil the word of the LORD by the mouth of Jeremiah, until the land had been paid her sabbaths; for as long as she lay desolate she kept sabbath, to fulfil threescore and ten years.

22. Now in the first year of Cyrus king of Persia, that the word of the LORD by the mouth of Jeremiah might be accomplished, the LORD stirred up the spirit of Cyrus king of Persia, that he made a proclamation throughout all his kingdom, and put

אַרְמְנוֹתֶיהָ שָׂרְפוּ בָאֵשׁ וְכָל־
20 כְּלֵי מַחֲמַדֶּיהָ לְהַשְׁחִית׃ וַיֶּגֶל
הַשְּׁאֵרִית מִן־הַחֶרֶב אֶל־
בָּבֶל וַיִּהְיוּ־לוֹ וּלְבָנָיו
לַעֲבָדִים עַד־מְלֹךְ מַלְכוּת
21 פָּרָס׃ לְמַלֹּאות דְּבַר־יְהוָה
בְּפִי יִרְמְיָהוּ עַד־רָצְתָה
הָאָרֶץ אֶת־שַׁבְּתוֹתֶיהָ כָּל־
יְמֵי הָשַּׁמָּה שָׁבָתָה לְמַלֹּאות
שִׁבְעִים שָׁנָה׃
22 וּבִשְׁנַת אַחַת לְכוֹרֶשׁ מֶלֶךְ
פָּרַס לִכְלוֹת דְּבַר־יְהוָה בְּפִי
יִרְמְיָהוּ הֵעִיר יְהוָה אֶת־רוּחַ
כּוֹרֶשׁ מֶלֶךְ־פָּרַס וַיַּעֲבֶר־
קוֹל בְּכָל־מַלְכוּתוֹ וְגַם־

20. *them that had escaped.* lit. 'the remnant.'

to him and his sons. By *sons* Nebuchadnezzar's successors are meant, viz. Evil-merodach and the two succeeding usurpers, Neriglissar and Nabonidus.

the kingdom of Persia. Under Cyrus, when the Babylonian dynasty came to an end.

21. *by the mouth of Jeremiah.* Cf. Jer. xxv. 11, xxix. 10.

the land had been paid her sabbaths. i.e. the land was compensated by years of desolation for the period in which the sabbatical years (Lev. xxv. 2ff.) had not been observed.

threescore and ten years. This is probably to be understood as a round figure. Seventy times seven (the sabbatical year occurring once in seven years) give a total of 490 years which go back to the origin of the monarchy. The Chronicler is evidently of the opinion that the law of the sabbatical year had long been neglected.

22f. (identical with Ezra i. 1-3a). The proclamation of Cyrus.

22. *in the first year of Cyrus.* Not of his reign (he became king of Elam in 558) but of his rule over Babylon which began in 539. The date of the proclamation is 538.

the word of the LORD by the mouth of Jeremiah. Foretelling the restoration after seventy years of exile (cf. Jer. xxix. 10).

the spirit. The king's favourable disposition towards the Judean captives. This was predicted by Isaiah (cf. Isa. xli. 25, xliv. 28, xlv. 1-7, 13).

it also in writing, saying: 23. 'Thus saith Cyrus king of Persia: All the kingdoms of the earth hath the LORD, the God of heaven, given me; and He hath charged me to build Him a house in Jerusalem, which is in Judah. Whosoever there is among you of all His people—the LORD his God be with him—let him go up.'

23 בְּמִכְתָּ֖ב לֵאמֹֽר׃ כֹּֽה־אָמַ֞ר
כּ֣וֹרֶשׁ ׀ מֶ֣לֶךְ פָּרַ֗ס כָּל־
מַמְלְכ֤וֹת הָאָ֙רֶץ֙ נָ֣תַן לִ֗י יְהֹוָה֙
אֱלֹהֵ֣י הַשָּׁמַ֔יִם וְהֽוּא־פָקַ֤ד
עָלַי֙ לִבְנוֹת־ל֣וֹ בַ֔יִת
בִּירֽוּשָׁלִַ֖ם אֲשֶׁ֣ר בִּֽיהוּדָ֑ה מִֽי־
בָכֶ֣ם מִכָּל־עַמּ֗וֹ יְהֹוָ֧ה אֱלֹהָ֛יו
עִמּ֖וֹ וְיָֽעַל׃

חזק ונתחזק

23. *all the kingdoms of the earth.* The title of 'king of the four quarters of the world' was taken over by Cyrus from the kings of Babylon.

hath the LORD . . . given me. He attributes his victory to God's will and help.

a house. The Temple.

let him go up. To the land of his fathers.

The last two verses are the introduction to the Book of Ezra. They were appended to the tragic account of national disaster which is narrated in this chapter in order to end *Chronicles* on a hopeful note. The Chronicler had the task of relating the eclipse of Israel's nationhood, but the edict of Cyrus heralded the termination of captivity and gave promise of a renewal of the glories of the past.

AUTHORITIES QUOTED

TERMS AND ABBREVIATIONS

AUTHORITIES QUOTED OR CONSULTED

Aboth—*Pirkë Aboth, Sayings of the Fathers:* Mishnaic tractate.

Barnes, W. E. (Christian Hebraist), *Chronicles* (Cambridge Bible).

Bennett, W. H. (Christian Hebraist), *Chronicles* (Expositor's Bible).

Benzinger, I. (Christian Hebraist), *Die Bücher der Chronik; Hebräische Archäologie.*

Bertheau, E. (Christian Hebraist), *Die Bücher der Chronik.*

Be'ur—*Commentary on Chronicles* (in Hebrew) by disciples of Moses Mendelssohn (18th century).

Buhl, F. (Christian Bible Scholar), *Geographie des alten Palästina.*

Dictionary of the Bible, ed. J. Hastings.

Driver, S. R. (Christian Hebraist), *Introduction to the Literature of the Old Testament.*

Eisenstein, J. D. (American Jewish Scholar), *Otsar Yisrael* (Hebrew Encyclopedia).

Elmslie, W. A. L. (Christian Hebraist), *Chronicles* (Cambridge Bible, revised ed.).

Encyclopedia Biblica, ed. T. K. Cheyne and J. Sutherland Black.

Ewald, H. (Bible Historian), *The History of Israel.*

Harvey-Jellie, W. R. (Christian Hebraist), *Chronicles* (Century Bible).

Herodotus (Greek Historian, 5th century B.C.E.).

Hilprecht, H. V. (Archaeologist), *Explorations in Bible Lands.*

Jerome (Christian Translator of the Bible and Commentator, 346-420 C.E.).

Josephus, Flavius (Jewish Historian, 1st century C.E.).

Keil, C. F. (Christian Hebraist), *Die Bücher der Chronik.*

Kimchi, David (1160-1235, Jewish Commentator).

Kittel, R. (Christian Hebraist), *Die Bücher der Chronik.*

Metsudath David ('Tower of David'), *Commentary on Chronicles* by David Altschul (17th century).

Midrash—Rabbinic homilies on the Pentateuch, etc.

Mishnah—Codification of Jewish Law (*c.* 200 C.E.).

Oettli, S. (Christian Hebraist), *Die Bücher der Chronik.*

Peshitta—Syriac Translation of the Bible (2nd century C.E.).

Ralbag (Rabbi Levi ben Gershon, 1288-1344, Jewish Commentator and Philosopher).

Rashi (Rabbi Solomon ben Isaac, 1040-1105, Jewish Commentator).

Seder Olam—Early Jewish Chronicle.

Septuagint—Greek Translation of the Bible, begun in the third century B.C.E.

Smith, G. A. (Christian Hebraist), *Historical Geography of the Holy Land; Jerusalem.*

Talmud—Corpus of Jewish Law and Thought (compiled at the end of the fifth century C.E.).

Targum—Aramaic Translation of the Bible (1st and 2nd centuries C.E.).

Vulgate—Latin Translation of the Bible (4th century C.E.).

TERMS AND ABBREVIATIONS

ad loc. At that place.

A.J. American-Jewish Translation of the Scriptures.

A.J.S.L.L. American Journal of Semitic Languages and Literature.

A.V. Authorized Version.

B.C.E. Before the Christian era.

B.K. *Baba Kamma,* Talmudic tractate.

c. About.

C.E. Common era.

cf. Compare, refer to.

ed. Edition, or edited by.

e.g. For example.

etc. And so forth.

f. Following verse or chapter (plural ff.).

i.e. That is.

kerë. The Hebrew as it is read according to the Masoretes.

kethib. The Hebrew as it is written according to tradition.

lit. Literally.

loc. cit. At the place quoted.

LXX. Septuagint (see Authorities Quoted or Consulted).

Macc. Apocryphal Book of Maccabees.

Meg. *Megillah,* Talmudic tractate.

MS. Manuscript (plural MSS.).

M.T. Masoretic text.

R.V. Revised Version.

Sanh. *Sanhedrin,* Talmudic tractate.

viz. namely.

Zeb. *Zebachim,* Talmudic tractate.

INDEX

INDEX

I. Names and Subjects

A

B

H

I

INDEX

S

T

U

V

II. Hebrew Words